100 YEARS OF
BASEBALL

DAVID NEMEC

SAUL WISNIA

Publications International, Ltd.

David Nemec is a baseball historian, author of *The Beer and Whisky League* and *Great Baseball Feats, Facts & Firsts*, and co-author of *The Ultimate Baseball Book* and *20th Century Baseball Chronicle*. He has written numerous baseball history, quiz, and memorabilia books as well as the franchise histories for major-league team yearbooks. His consulting work includes the book *Greatest Baseball Players of All Time*.

Saul Wisnia is a former sportswriter for the *Washington Post* whose work has appeared in *Sports Illustrated*, *The Boston Globe*, and *Boston Magazine*. He authored *Baseball's Prime-Time Stars*, coauthored *Babe Ruth* and *Wit & Wisdom of Baseball*, and was a contributing writer to *Best of Baseball* and *Treasury of Baseball*. He has also served as archivist for the Sports Museum of New England and cohosted a weekly Boston sports radio talk show.

Editorial Assistance:
Michael Bradley
Bruce Herman
Michael Sandrolini
Stuart Shea
Mary Ullmer

Louis Weber, CEO
Publications International, Ltd.
7373 North Cicero Avenue
Lincolnwood, Illinois 60712

Permission is never granted for commercial purposes.

Manufactured in China.

8 7 6 5 4 3 2 1

ISBN: 0-7853-7567-8

Library of Congress Control Number: 2002104419

Picture credits:

Front cover: **Underwood & Underwood/Corbis.**

Back cover: **National Baseball Library & Archive, Cooperstown, NY:** top; **PhotoFile:** center; **Brian Spurlock/SportsChrome:** bottom.

Greg Abramowitz Photography: 461L; Tom DiPace: 455BR, 460B, 465B; Mitchell Layton: 454, 455BL, 458TL&BR, 462TL, 495TR&BL, 496, 499RC; **Allsport USA:** 475TC, 479TL; Brian Bahr: 503LC; Al Bello: 490, 502; Jim Commentucci: 407RC; Jonathan Daniel: 451, 468, 471BR, 488, 491TR& LC, 503TC; Tim Defrisco: 480; Stephen Dunn: 476, 491TC, 492; Steve Green: 405BR; Otto Greule: 409BL, 466, 467BL, 469, 471BL, 474, 475TL&TR, 481, 482, 483TC,TR&BL, 491TL, 493, 450, 479TR, 503TL, 505; Jim Gund: 475B, 483BR; Will Hart: 432; Jed Jacobsohn: 504, 519; Ken Levine: 477; Lonnie Major: 471TL; Greg Newkirk: 471TR; Joe Patronite: 410TL; Mike Powell: 453; Janice Rettaliata: 472; Earl Richardson: 353B; George Rose: 405R; Kirk Schlea: 410TR; Bruce L. Schwartzman: 404BR; Don Smith: 398-399; Jamie Squire: 503TR; Rick Stewart: 470,478, 486; **AP/Wide World Photos:** 120, 175TL, 178, 191B, 194B, 220, 282, 298BR, 346B, 349BR, 352TL, 354BL, 367TR, 377, 383TR, 387B, 391B, 402B, 409BR, 412, 413T&BL, 418, 429BL, 436, 437TL&TC, 444, 508, 510, 511, 513TL,LC&RC, 516, 517, 518; **Archive Photos/Reuters:** Mike Blake: 457R; Jeff Christensen: 455T; John Kuntz: 460T; **Dennis Bancroft/Florida Marlins:** 494; **J. Brooks:** 239BC; **M. Brown Collection:** 11T, 18BC&BR, 47BL&BR, 84TL, 117B, 136BR, 139BL, 193BR, 244BL, 246BR, 248TL, 267BL, 293BR, 294B, 300BL, 303BL&BR, 351B, 352BL, 397; **Thomas Carwile:** 78T; **Chicago Historical Society:** 68, 76B, 125T; **Cleveland Press:** 238; **Corbis:** 115, 116, 143BL, 165, 169, 187T, 188BL, 196, 197B, 251BL, 355, 357B, 369, 370, 373, 374, 390, 394, 395TL, 401B, 404TL, 407TL, 417B, 425T, 429TL, 433TL, 440; **Steve Crandall/New York Yankees:** 498; Tom DiPace: 506, 508, 509, 512, 513TR, 514, 515; **Kenneth A. Felden:** 19B, 20B, 21B, 46T, 69T, 78BR, 86BL, 131BR, 190TR; **Focus on Sports:** 467TR&BR, 473, 483TL&BC, 487, 489; Michael Ponzini: 485; **FPG International:** 93B, 117TL, 137BR, 158, 281; Lee Balterman: 408B; Richard Mackson: 400B, 417TR, 421TL, 423, 447, 448, 449BL; Mike Malyszko: 439; Hy Peskin: 215; J. Zimmerman: 342; **Barry Halper:** 134TR; **Dick Johnson:** 48R, 195BL, 239BR, 245T, 248TC, 354BR, 402TL, 404BL, 406, 409TL; **Ace Marchant:** 16BR, 297B, 356TL; **National Archives:** 121TR; **National Baseball Library & Archive, Cooperstown, NY:** Table of contents TL, 6, 8-9, 10, 11, 12, 13TL&B, 14TL&BL, 15, 16TR, 17T, 18T, 19T, 20T, 21T&LC, 22, 23, 24, 26, 27T&B, 28, 29T&B, 30, 31B, 32, 33, 34, 35, 36, 37, 38, 39, 40, 42L, 43T, 44TR&B, 45, 46B, 47T, 48L, 49TL,TR,BL&BR, 50, 51C, 52, 53B, 54, 55, 56, 57, 58, 59, 60, 61, 62, 63, 65, 66, 69B, 70, 71, 72, 73T, 74-75, 76T, 77, 79TR,BL&BR, 80, 81T&B, 82, 83T&C, 84B, 85T, 86T, 87TL&TC, 88, 89, 90, 91, 92, 93T, 94, 95, 96, 97, 99, 100, 101TL,TR&BL, 103, 104, 105, 106, 109, 110, 112, 113TL&BL, 114, 117TC&TR, 118, 119, 121TL,BL&BR, 124, 125BL, 127, 128-129, 131TL&TR, 132, 133B, 134TL&B, 135, 136TL&TR, 137T,BL&BC, 138BL&BR, 139T, 140B, 141BR, 142, 143TL&B, 145, 146, 147TL&B, 148, 150, 150, 151BL,BR&B, 152, 154, 155T, 159TR&BR, 162, 163, 164, 166, 167TC&TR, 168, 171, 174, 175TR&BR, 176, 179, 181, 184, 185, 186L, 188T&BR, 189B&BL, 190TC&BL, 191T, 192BL, 193TR, 194T, 195TL, 197TL&TR, 198, 200, 201BL&B, 202, 204, 205, 206, 207, 208, 209, 211, 212, 213TL&BL, 214, 216, 217TL&TR, 218, 219, 221, 222, 223, 224, 225TR,BL&BR, 226, 227, 228, 229TR&B, 230, 232, 233TL&BL, 235, 236-237, 239TR, 240, 241T&LC, 243T&BC, 244TL,TR&BR, 245B, 246T, 247, 248TR&B,

249TL&BL, 250, 251BR, 253, 255, 258, 259TL&B, 262, 263T&B, 267TR, 269, 270, 271TC&TR, 272, 274, 276, 278, 279TL&BR, 283TL&BR, 284, 286, 288, 292, 293TL&BL, 295, 296TR&BR, 298T&BL, 299BR, 300T, 301T, 302, 304, 305TL&BL, 307, 309T&BR, 311, 312, 314, 315, 316, 317TL, 320, 321TC&TR, 325TL, 328, 331, 332, 333TL&TC, 334, 336, 337TR&BR, 338, 339, 340, 341TL, 343, 344-345, 346T, 347TL,TR&B, 349TL, 350TL,BL&BR, 351TL&TR, 352BR, 354TR, 356TR, 357T, 358, 366, 367TL, 368, 371TL&TR, 372, 375TL,TC&B, 378, 379TL, 385, 386, 387TC, 396, 408T, 414, 416, 422, 424, 429TR&BR; **PhotoFile:** Table of contents TR,C&BL, 84TR, 87TR, 113BR, 130B, 140T, 141T, 147TC, 149, 155BR, 156, 159BL, 160, 167TL&B, 172, 177, 180, 182-183, 186BR, 189TL, 192TL, 193TL, 195TR, 197TC, 199, 201T, 203, 213B, 217BL&BR, 225TL, 229TL&TC, 231, 233TR&BR, 234, 236, 238T, 239TL, 242B, 243BR, 246BL, 249TR&BR, 251TL&TR, 252, 254, 256, 257, 259TC&TR, 260, 261, 263RC, 264, 265, 267T&BR, 268, 271TL&B, 273, 275, 277, 279TR&BL, 280, 283TC&BC, 285, 287TL,TC,TR&BL, 290-291, 293TR, 294TL&BL, 296TL&TC, 297TL&TR, 299TL,TR&BL, 301B, 303TL,TC&TR, 305TR&BR, 306, 308, 309BL, 310, 313, 317TR,BL&BR, 318, 319, 321TL&B, 322, 323, 324, 325TR,BL&BR, 329TL,TR&BL, 330, 333TR&B, 335, 337TL&BL, 341TC,TR,BL&BR, 344, 347TC, 348T&TR, 352TR, 353T, 354TL&TC, 356B, 359, 360, 361, 363TL,TC&TR, 364, 367TC&BC, 371BL&BR, 375TR, 376, 379TR&BL, 380, 382, 383TL&TC, 384, 387TL, 388, 389, 391C,TL&TR, 392, 395BL&BR, 400T, 401TC&TR, 403TL&BL, 405L, 407TR&LC, 409TC&TR, 410B, 411, 417TL, 419, 420, 421TR,BL&BR, 425BL&BR, 427, 430, 431, 433TR,BL&BR, 434, 435, 437TR&B, 438, 441, 442, 445, 446, 449TL,TR&BR; **Patrick Quinn:** 16TL, 87B; **SportsChrome:** 461C, 462B; Jeff Carlick: 457L; Scott Cunningham: 499B; Brian Spurlock: Table of content BR, 452-453; Rob Tringali Jr.: 459, 464, 465T, 499T&LC, 500; Michael Zito: 463T, 495TC; **Sports Illustrated:** David Liam Kyle: 479BL; John Iacono: 506-507; V.J. Lovero: 477BR, 482; Bill Smith: 465TL; **Sports Photo Masters:** Jonathan Kirn: 458BL; Craig Melvin: 462TR, 463C; Mitchell B. Reibel: 456, 458TR, 461R; Chuck Rydlewski: 501; Don Smith: 495TL, 497; **Transcendental Graphics:** 7, 13TR, 14BR, 16BL, 17B, 18BL, 21RC, 25, 31T, 40-41, 42R&BR, 43C&B, 44TL, 49TC, 51TL,TC&TR, 53T&C, 64, 67, 73B, 78BL&BC, 79TL, 81LC&RC, 83B, 86BR, 98, 101BR, 107, 108, 111, 113TR, 123, 125BC&BR, 130T, 131BL, 133TL&BL, 136BL, 138TL, 141BL, 144, 151T, 153, 155BL, 157, 159TL, 161, 173, 175BL, 187B, 190TL&BR, 192B, 193BL&BC, 195BR, 201BR, 210, 239BL, 241B, 242TL&TR, 243BL, 263LC, 266, 287BR, 289, 296BL, 300BR, 326, 327, 329BR, 348BR, 349TR, 350TR, 362, 363B, 365, 379BR, 381, 383B, 387TR, 393, 395TR, 401TL, 404TR, 413BR, 426, 443.

Decade Icons: Allsport USA: Jeff Carlick, Jonathan Daniel, Otto Greule; **AP/Wide World Photos; Corbis; Tom DiPace; Mitchell Layton/Greg Abramowitz Photography; Library of Congress; National Baseball Library & Archive, Cooperstown, NY; PhotoFile; Transcendental Graphics.**

KEY
Numbers indicate pages.

T—Top	R—Right	LC—Left Center
C—Center	TL—Top Left	RC—Right Center
B—Bottom	TC—Top Center	BL—Bottom Left
L—Left	TR—Top Right	BC—Bottom Center
		BR—Bottom Right

CONTENTS

AMERICA'S GAME TAKES SHAPE IN 1800s

No, Abner Doubleday did not invent baseball. A 1907 historical report on "America's National Game," delivered by a commission hand-picked by major-league executives, gave the famed Civil War general credit for the feat, based on the testimony of one man (Abner Graves) who claimed to have seen the event firsthand. According to Graves, who had only a rotting ball as evidence, his childhood chum Doubleday mapped out the first baseball diamond and rules in the sleepy New York hamlet of Cooperstown back in 1839.

The commission took this story as the gospel, even though the facts showed that Doubleday—already deceased by this time—was a West Point cadet in 1839 who never mentioned anything about inventing baseball in his many letters and diaries. Facts or no facts, the National Baseball Hall of Fame opened during 1939 in legendary Cooperstown itself, with the "Doubleday ball" as a featured attraction.

In fact, baseball grew out of various ball-and-stick games played throughout the United States during the first half of the 19th century. It was played in small towns and big cities, by everyone from common laborers to bank presidents and doc-

Surviving photos of Alexander Joy Cartwright (standing, center) *often show him in formal attire.*

tors. It was a favorite pastime of both Yankee and Rebel soldiers during lulls in Civil War fighting—as well as by slave children on Southern plantations.

For Americans, baseball was their game, a sport that had links to British games such as cricket and rounders but had been adapted by colonists into their own. The most popular early version was called "town ball." There were no foul lines or fixed positions, and fielders aimed to hit baserunners with the ball—then a method of getting men out. Understandably, things could get ugly, and some colleges even banned baseball as a sport not befitting young gentlemen.

In Manhattan, however, the game grew so popular that a group of local men led by shipping clerk Alexander Cartwright formed the New York Knickerbocker Base Ball Club in 1845. It was Cartwright's group that actually devised the first diamond and foul lines and formalized rules such as three strikes to a batter. On June 19 of the following year, the Knickerbockers played in the first known organized baseball game—a 23-1 loss to the New York Base Ball Club on Elysian Fields in Hoboken, New Jersey. Interest spread, and within a decade there were approximately 50 teams in the area.

When the *New York Mercury* first identified baseball as "the national pastime" in 1856, it seemed an accurate description. The earliest clubs were comprised mostly of young, well-educated men, but the game's appeal soon spread to the working class—which formed teams of its own. Even when the Civil War came along, play continued to go on everywhere from prison camps to the fields behind Abe Lincoln's White House. Young poet Walt Whitman wrote of baseball in this period: "It is our game—the American game. It will take our people out-of-doors, fill them with oxygen, give them a larger physical stoicism." Now more properly organized, the game was accepted on collegiate campuses

Elysian Fields in Hoboken, New Jersey, was the site of the first formal interclub match on June 19, 1846.

as a sport for men and women. And, like all things American, it didn't take long for someone to get the idea of making a profit from it. In 1869, a group of Ohio businessmen financed the development of the first professional team—the Cincinnati Red Stockings.

The Red Stockings made just a $1.39 profit their first season, playing 65 games versus amateur clubs (star shortstop George Wright's outrageous salary of $1,400 was a major expense). But the excitement generated was so high that in 1871 the National Association of Professional Base Ball Players was formed. Nine teams were assembled in cities from Boston to Cleveland, but after five years several folded due to a tight economy and powerful Cincinnati's ability to buy up the best players.

In 1876, a group of scrupulous businessmen put together another new league, which did in the National Association altogether and proved far more stable. Owners in the National League didn't allow their players to drink, forbade gambling at games, and set ticket prices at 50 cents. They also paid far lower wages, and they devised a "reserve clause" that kept the top five players on each team from jumping to another club without permission.

The National League's leading figure in its formative years was Chicago White Stockings owner A.G. Spalding, a former ace pitcher. He shrewdly marketed the league by producing its annual guide and opening a sporting goods business that produced "official" balls, uniforms, and equipment for the NL. Led by star player-manager Cap Anson, Chicago captured championships in four of the league's first seven seasons as other cities built up their teams.

Rivals to the National League sprang up briefly—including a "Players' League" comprised of players upset with the reserve clause—but the NL squashed them all. Outstanding clubs such as the great Boston Beaneaters of the 1890s helped a rabidly loyal fan base grow. By 1900, there was enough of a following so that the leaders of another successful alliance—the minor Western League—felt confident enough to rename their circuit the "American League" and emerge as a direct rival to the National League for players and patrons in the spring of 1901.

The era of modern baseball was about to begin.

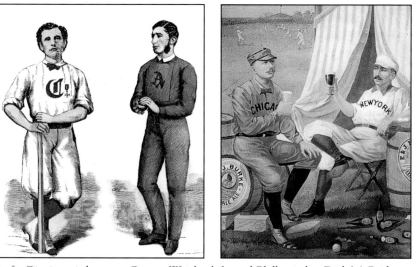

Left: *Cincinnati shortstop George Wright, left, and Philly pitcher Dick McBride.*
Right: *Chicago's Cap Anson, left, and New York's Buck Ewing propose a toast.*

THE 1900s

The 1900s saw the emergence of Ban Johnson's American League. Though runs were down in both the NL and AL, interest in baseball was up, as fans delighted in the newly created World Series.

The first decade of the 20th century saw the last of the major "Monopoly Wars" and a new period of unprecedented peace and prosperity in baseball. After 1903—when the National League and the American League laid down arms and agreed to live together in a two-league format and to play the first modern World Series—there were no major interleague wars until 1913 and no more franchise shifts until 1953. With the nation's economy recovered from the war-related depression of the late 1890s, attendance skyrocketed.

Major-league bats were peaceful, too. The versatile and exciting "run-and-gun" offensive style of the 1890s, which produced a generation of terrorized pitchers and hundreds of batting records that still stand, came to an abrupt halt with the adoption of the foul-strike rule by the NL in 1901 and the AL in 1903. Batting averages and ERAs plummeted. The 1900s were the heyday of dead ball, a plodding, one-run-at-a-time style of play. To our great-grandparents, these were the "good old days" of singles-hitting, basestealing, and dominant pitching that were swept away forever by Babe Ruth in 1920.

In a larger sense, the American League arose from the very same circumstances that produced the American Association, the Union Association, and the Players' League: the dissatisfaction of major-league caliber cities, owners, and players who were denied entry into the National League or oppressed by its collusive and authoritarian practices. But the more immediate inspiration was Ban Johnson—a shrewd former sportswriter and president of the minor Western League—who had been carefully gathering economic backing and making plans for the most successful assault yet on National League supremacy. After the 1899 season he was ready and announced that the Western League was changing its name to the American League, which would operate as a major league beginning in 1901. For the 1900 season, the AL operated franchises in Chicago, Detroit, Cleveland, Milwaukee, Indianapolis, Kansas City, Minneapolis, and Buffalo.

Johnson had timed his move well; in 1900 the National League was at an historic weak point. Attendance was down because of the economy and because the one-league, 12-team structure was simply

Winner of 297 games in the 1890s, Kid Nichols (top left) retired in 1906 with 361 wins. Roger Bresnahan (top right) invented the padded catcher's mask and shin-guards. A scorecard from the 1903 World Series (bottom).

boring. The National League ownership was deeply divided between a faction led by Chicago's Jim Hart that included Brooklyn's Charles Ebbets, Philadelphia's John Rogers, and Pittsburgh's Barney Dreyfuss, and a faction led by New York Giants owner Andrew Freedman that included Arthur Soden of Boston, Frank and Stanley Robison of St. Louis, and John Brush of Cincinnati. Freedman had drawn up a desperate scheme to turn the National League into one giant syndicate that would pool all players and franchises into a commonly owned entity. According to Freedman, his plan would eliminate the problem of weak or noncompetitive clubs and guarantee each owner an annual profit. It would also make the "National League" a single corporate establishment.

The conflict between these two factions came to a head over the election of the National League president in 1901. Freedman supported incumbent Nick Young; the opposition nominated Al Spalding.

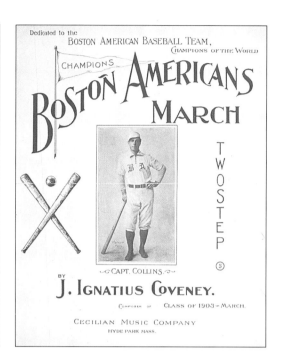

Third baseman Jimmy Collins (top) managed AL Boston to its World Series victory over Pittsburgh in 1903. The triumph earned Boston its own march, composed by J. Ignatius Coveney. Boston, down 3-1, came back to win the best-of-nine Series. The Series was the first of the 20th century, and Boston's improbable win helped send a signal that the AL was here to stay. Boston fans climb over the outfield wall and storm onto the playing field in this photo from the early 1900s (bottom).

Naturally, the vote was 4-4 and it remained deadlocked through 25 ballots. Finally, when Freedman and his friends walked out, Spalding was named president. Freedman's response was to go to the New York Supreme Court, where a judge granted a permanent injunction against Spalding.

Because of this infighting, the National League was left essentially leaderless for the most critical year in its history. With the expiration of the "National Agreement" in 1901, the AL began to raid NL rosters, grabbing such stars as Nap Lajoie from the Philadelphia Phillies and signing him to the AL's

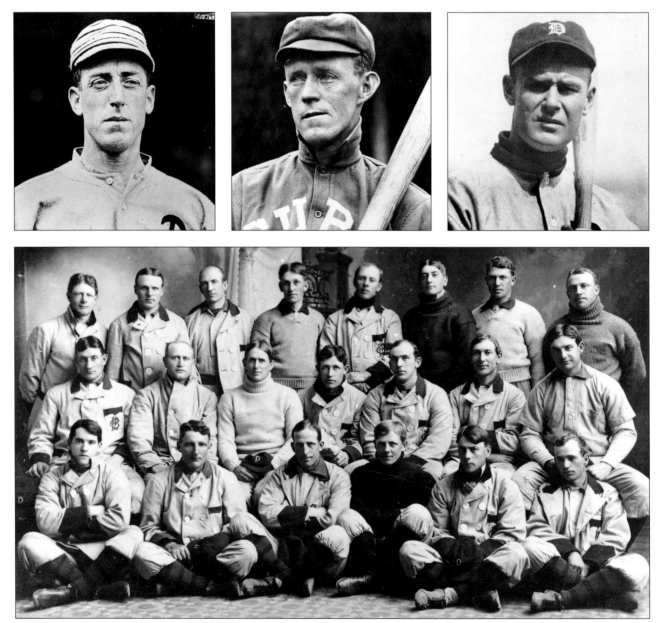

Eddie Plank (top left) was 25 years old when he broke into the majors with AL Philadelphia in 1901. *Second baseman Johnny Evers (top middle)* helped form the Cubs' famous infield when he joined Joe Tinker and Frank Chance full-time in 1903. *Sam Crawford (top right)* jumped to Detroit in 1903 and led the American League in triples with 25. *The 1903 Pittsburgh club (bottom)* could not hold on to its early Series lead.

Philadelphia Athletics. The National League fought the Lajoie signing in Pennsylvania state courts and won, but Johnson merely transferred him to Cleveland and kept him out of the state of Pennsylvania. A series of related lawsuits backfired on the NL, as judges repeatedly overturned contracts based on the reserve clause, for the same reasons that they had done so in the 1880s and 1890s.

By 1902, all the old National League tricks, such as trying to bribe defecting players back into the fold and offering the stronger AL clubs entry into the NL, had failed. The American League was holding the line and—after dropping its weaker teams in Indianapolis, Kansas City, Minneapolis, and Buffalo and replacing them with Philadelphia, Boston, Baltimore, and Washington—was making its owners happy with large profits. After Spalding resigned and Freedman gave up and left baseball, the NL's new president, Harry Pulliam, reconciled for peace. Before the 1903 season, the two leagues agreed to respect each other's contracts and operate under a single three-man commission that would include the two league presidents and Garry Herrmann of Cincinnati. A close friend of Herrmann, Ban Johnson immediately became the real power behind the National Commission and remained so until 1919.

New York Giants owner John T. Brush (top left) fought the AL's attempts to put another team in New York and made several enemies in baseball. He and manager John McGraw refused to let his Giants play the 1904 World Series. Rube Foster, pictured in 1905 with the Royal Ponciana Base Ball Club (top right), *later formed the Negro National League. Wee Willie Keeler (bottom)* continued his run of .300-plus seasons when he jumped to New York of the AL in 1903.

The spitball helped Jack Chesbro (top) win 41 games in 1904. When his spitter sailed over the catcher's head and the winning run scored on the last day of the season, however, AL New York lost the pennant. Ban Johnson (bottom) was the driving force behind the AL's success.

Philadelphia's Shibe Park in 1909, which seated 30,000-plus fans in three decks. Later that season, 25,000-seat Forbes Field opened in Pittsburgh and wooden League Park in Cleveland and Sportsman's Park in St. Louis were renovated in steel and concrete. Another reason for baseball's marked increase in popularity was the tough, AL-inspired crackdown on both player and fan unruliness; baseball hadn't been so genteel since the 1850s.

For the players, the new era brought a return to the reserve clause and business as usual. But the new National Commission was too smart, at least at first, to polarize the players by anything so inflammatory as a salary cap. Players of the 1900s were paid fairly well compared to the 1890s and were treated with the kind of mostly benevolent paternalism that has characterized the more peaceful chapters in 20th-century baseball labor relations. Through judicious

5,000 was unusually large in the 1890s, teams of the 1900s averaged more than that. The biggest drawing card of the era, John McGraw's New York Giants, drew almost one million fans in 1908, or over 10,000 per game. The World Series was also a big hit. The eight-game 1903 Series drew over 100,000 fans; the seven-game 1909 Series drew one and a half times that. This prosperity enabled clubs of the 1900s to build the first really permanent ballparks—steel and concrete affairs that one-by-one replaced the old wooden parks. The first example was

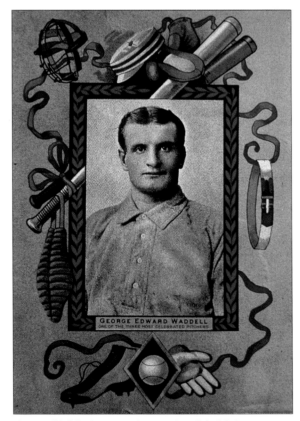

Rube Waddell had 349 strikeouts for Philadelphia in 1904, an AL record that stood for more than 70 years. In 1905, he led the AL with 26 wins, eight relief wins, 46 appearances, 287 strikeouts, and a 1.48 ERA.

Sol White, Rube Foster, and Charlie Grant, shown top row center to far right in this 1906 photo (top), led the Philadelphia Giants to the "Colored Championship of the World." The Chicago Cubs' infield of 1906 (bottom, left to right): 3B Harry Steinfeldt, SS Joe Tinker, 2B Johnny Evers, and 1B Frank Chance. The players, minus Steinfeldt, were immortalized in Franklin P. Adams's verse, "Baseball's Sad Lexicon," better known as, "Tinker to Evers to Chance." The celebrated trio actually did not turn many double plays. They did, however, implement the first known version of the rotation play.

co-opting of the leadership of the weak players' union, the Players' Protective Association, Johnson and the owners were able to avoid significant labor trouble for a decade.

The 20th century opened with a drastic rule change. For the first time, in 1901 in the NL and in 1903 in both leagues, a foul ball was counted as a strike. This caused the single greatest change in the way baseball was played until Babe Ruth and the home run era. ERAs dropped all the way below the levels of 1880s baseball; a British journalist once described baseball as a game in which "the odds against (the batter) are so great that our English love of fair play is offended." From 1893 to 1899, the National League ERA had been above 4.00 every year except for 1898 and 1899, when it fell to 3.60 and 3.85. However, 1904 was the first of six consecutive years that neither league's ERA rose above 2.99. The 1900s produced a generation of individual pitchers at least as dominant as the pitchers of the 1960s, another historic low point in hitting. The Gibsons, Koufaxes, and Marichals of the 1900s were: Christy

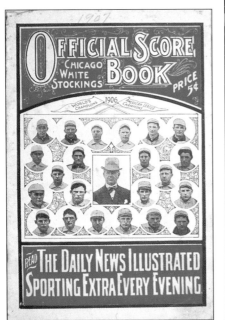

An official 1907 Chicago scorebook (top left) pictured the 1906 world champion White Stockings on its cover. At center is owner Charlie Comiskey. Jim McGuire, Dusty Rhoads, Ben Hopkins, and Addie Joss of Cleveland (top right, left to right). Cleveland almost won the pennant with the brilliant pitching of Joss and was particularly heartbroken in 1908, when it lost the pennant to Detroit by .004 points. Honus Wagner (bottom left) is pictured on a cigar label from 1910. Wagner won seven batting titles in the 1900s. Cleveland second baseman Nap Lajoie is featured in this 1910 advertisement for Coca-Cola (bottom right), which promoted itself as "The Great National Drink at the Great National Game."

Mathewson, who averaged a 29-14 record and a 1.97 ERA per year for the decade; Cy Young, who averaged a 27-15 record and a 2.12 ERA per year; and Three Finger Brown, who averaged a 29-13 record and a 1.63 ERA. These pitchers and their contemporaries rewrote the all-time record book permanently. Virtually all of the majors' all-time leaders in career earned run average played during the 1900s, including Ed Walsh (1.82), Addie Joss (1.88), Rube Waddell (2.16), Ed Reulbach (2.28), and Eddie Plank (2.34). Five of the top 10 in career shutouts played during the 1900s, as well as five 300-game winners.

Defense—aided by bigger gloves, better-maintained fields, advances in catchers' equipment such as shin-guards—also improved. While defensive improvement has been a constant throughout baseball history, the 1900s were a time of particularly rapid advances in fielding. From 1893, when the modern pitching distance was established, to 1899, the overall National League fielding average climbed 11 points, from .931 to .942. But from 1900 to 1908, the NL fielding average climbed 19 points, from .942 to .961. The difference between the best- and worst-fielding teams narrowed, indicating that fielding techniques and equipment were becoming more standardized. In 1894, for example, Baltimore led the NL in fielding average at .944, 36 points better than Washington's .908—an unheard-of margin today. Only 10 years later, in 1904, the difference between NL-leading New York (.956) and last-place Philadelphia (.937) was down to 19 points.

The 1900s' decline in offense was across-the-board and affected every hitting category, even home runs. Not that home runs had ever been a very important part of offense in the 1890s; in 1894 the average National League club hit only 52 homers and in 1895 only 40. But these would have been high figures in the dead-ball era; National League clubs averaged 22 home runs in 1904 and 23 in 1905.

Batting averages and slugging averages fell even more. In 1893, National League batting champion Billy Hamilton hit .380 and top slugger Ed Delahanty slugged .583. From 1894 to 1899, the National League leaders compiled batting averages of .438, .409, .410, .424, .385, and .410; leading slugging averages in those years were .679, .654, .631, .569, .494, and .582. Honus Wagner, the dominant

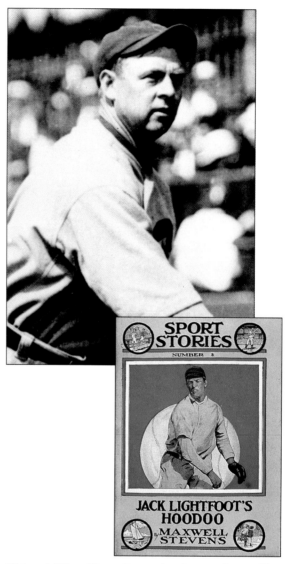

Chicago's Three Finger Brown (top), so nicknamed because of a boyhood accident with his father's haycutter, led the NL with a 1.04 ERA in 1906. Giants great Christy Mathewson appeared on the cover of Jack Lightfoot's Hoodoo, a 1906 pulp novel (bottom).

hitter of the 1900s, led the league in batting average in 1903 at .355, in 1904 at .349, in 1906 at .339, in 1907 at .350, in 1908 at .354, and in 1909 at .339. Outside of 1908, none of these performances would have been good enough to make the top five a decade earlier. League-leading slugging performances of the 1900s declined even more than batting averages—50 to 100 points lower than the 1890s.

Individual decade leaders in the major offensive categories followed the same pattern. The top hitter for average in the 1890s was Wee Willie Keeler, who

batted .387 for the decade; his 1900s counterpart was Wagner, who hit .352. The biggest RBI total for the 1890s was Hugh Duffy's 1,085; the highest one-year total was Sam Thompson's 165. The bests in the 1900s were Wagner's 956 for the decade and 126 in 1901. No hitter in the 1900s approached Buck Freeman's single-season home run record of 25 or Hugh Duffy's 80 for the 1890s.

The unfortunate batters of the 1900s were left with few ways to score runs beyond the hit-and-run, the bunt, and the stolen base. These strategies had all been developed in the slugging 1890s, but in the more conservative 1900s they were applied very differently. Instead of using the hit-and-run to aggressively exploit the weaknesses in opposing defenses as managers Frank Selee and Ned Hanlon had done, it became primarily a way to play for one run and to stay out of the double play. Instead of a means of getting on base, the bunt was used more and more exclusively as a sacrifice.

The dominant offensive weapon of the 1900s was the stolen base; this decade is remembered today as a period of running offenses and such great basestealers as Ty Cobb and Honus Wagner. Compared to later decades, there was a lot of basestealing in the 1900s, but even this element of offense declined as compared to the

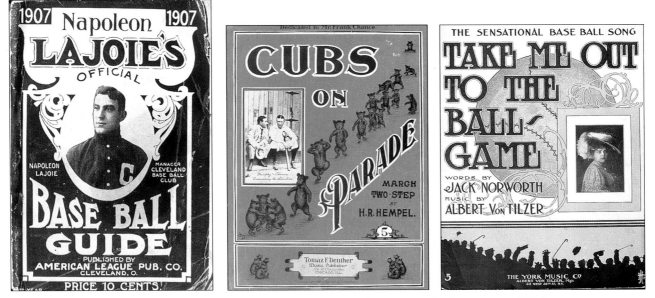

A meeting at home plate before the 1907 World Series included (top) Chicago's Frank Chance, arms folded, Detroit manager Hughie Jennings, with bat, and Ty Cobb, facing Jennings. Nap Lajoie's Base Ball Guide in 1907 (bottom left). After winning the 1907 Series, the Cubs got their own march (bottom middle). "Take Me Out to the Ballgame" (bottom right) was written by Jack Norworth in 1908.

1890s. In 1906, Henry Chadwick called for some league action to restore the stolen base to its former preeminence. Next to a column of stolen-base statistics for 1905, Chadwick wrote: "The table in question will astonish the magnates of the leading clubs when they see by the figures what a comparatively poor record their crack players had in baserunning last season to that of four years ago." Throughout the decade, team stolen base totals stayed well below the levels of the 1890s. NL teams averaged 195 stolen bases in 1903, 197 in 1904, and 200 in 1905; they averaged 229 in 1893, 259 in 1894, and 241 in 1895. While the scoring rules governing the definition of the stolen base had changed, making a precise comparison impossible, the best single-season mark of the 1900s (Cobb's 76 in 1909) doesn't even compare to Billy Hamilton's top season of the 1890s, 111.

As if pitchers of the 1900s didn't have enough of an advantage over hitters, managers in this decade began to rely less and less on a single pitching ace and more and more on efficient three- or

Despite an impressive pitching staff (Harry Howell and Rube Waddell each had 1.89 ERAs), the 1908 St. Louis Browns (top) could finish no higher than fourth in the American League. Johnny Evers and Tris Speaker were featured on a 1909 box of Darby Chocolates. Speaker, who often played a shallow center field to take away hits, was elected in 1937 to the Hall of Fame, where his plaque calls him "the greatest center fielder of his day."

four-man rotations. This was a gradual process, but pitchers' workloads in the 1900s were much more evenly distributed within the pitching staff than in previous decades, contributing to the trend toward pitching dominance. In the 1890s, for example, personal seasonal leaders in games pitched typically were in the low to mid-50s, with a high of 75 games pitched by Wild Bill Hutchinson in 1892. Only once (in 1897) did a pitcher lead the league with fewer than 50 games. But in the 1900s it happened five times. The typical leader in games pitched was in the high 40s, with the single-season highs being claimed by Ed Walsh's 66 in 1909 for the AL and Christy Mathewson's 56 in 1908 for the NL. The gradual decrease in workload is even more apparent in innings-pitched totals. The average league leader in this category in the 1890s threw 421 innings; a decade later this fell to 381. While in the 1890s and earlier it was not unusual to have one or two pitchers pitch the majority of a team's games, by the 1900s this was the rare exception.

While this 1909 photo (top) might lead one to believe otherwise, Ty Cobb, left, and Honus Wagner hardly were friendly. When Cobb informed the "krauthead" of his intention to steal second during that year's World Series, Wagner delivered a message with a tag to Cobb's mouth. Bottom: Wagner's NL pennant-winning Pittsburgh club of 1909.

Adding to hitters' woes was the development of the spitball, which—along with related trick pitches such as the shine ball, emery ball, and mud ball— was perfectly legal until 1920.

It's no wonder that in 1904 Honus Wagner called for help for his beleaguered fellow major-league hitters. The answer, Wagner said, was to eliminate the foul-strike rule, move pitchers three feet farther back from the plate so that "the spitball wouldn't break so well," and reduce the number of balls required for a walk to three. Boston infielder Bob Unglaub had an even more eccentric solution: draw an arc through the outfield 80 yards from home plate and require that all fielders remain on the in-field side of the line until the ball was hit, thus adding a touch of excitement to long fly balls.

Forbes Field (top), shown in 1909, was home to the Pittsburgh Pirates from that year until 1970. Philadelphia's Shibe Park (middle left), which opened April 12, 1909, was the first concrete-and-steel ballpark. Shibe was the site of the first night game in the American League on May 16, 1939. John Cullen Murphy's illustration (middle right) complements the "Tinker to Evers to Chance" poem by Franklin P. Adams. New York Giants manager John McGraw plugged Tuxedo pipe tobacco on a trolley poster in 1910 (bottom).

UPSTART AL RAIDS BROOKLYN'S ROSTER

Seeking his third consecutive pennant with Brooklyn in 1901, manager Ned Hanlon instead was overwhelmed by a Pittsburgh team that had not been similarly decimated by AL raiders. Hanlon, before 1901, suffered the defection of Fielder Jones, Lave Cross, and Joe McGinnity. Unable to replace the three stars, Brooklyn sank to third place while the Phillies advanced a notch to the second spot. Neither club, though, could pose much of a challenge to the Pirates, who would soon emerge as the first dynasty in the new century.

In 1901, Pittsburgh lost only one player of consequence to the upstart AL—third baseman Jimmy

Clark Griffith coaxed NL players into jumping to the AL, with Griffith himself going from the Cubs to the White Sox in 1901.

Williams—and pilot Fred Clarke more than replaced him with Tommy Leach. Rookie Kitty Bransfield seized the first base job, and another newcomer, Lefty Davis, took over in right field alongside Ginger Beaumont in center and Clarke in left. This combination proved lethal, giving the Pirates an outfield with a combined average above .300. Honus Wagner, meanwhile, found a new niche at shortstop after incumbent Bones Ely was permitted to take his .208 batting average to the AL. With Deacon Phillippe winning 22 games, Jack Chesbro 21, and Jesse Tannehill chipping in with 18 victories and a league-leading 2.18 ERA, the Pirates hardly missed fractious Rube Waddell, the 1900 ERA champion, who was sold to the Chicago Cubs in May. Attaining first place on June 16, Pittsburgh remained there the rest of the way but had to subdue a late threat from Philadelphia before claiming the first NL pennant in the city's history.

The AL, in its fledgling season as a major league, also had a tight race into September. Led by 33-game winner Cy Young, slugging first sacker Buck Freeman, and third baseman-manager Jimmy Collins, its three prize thefts from the NL, Boston had the inside track on the first AL major-league pennant. But a late slump by pitchers Ted Lewis and George Winter opened the door for the Chicago White Sox to cop the honor under Clark Griffith, who had been swiped prior to the season from the crosstown Cubs by Sox owner Charlie Comiskey. Comiskey had also managed the Sox to the AL flag in 1900 when the loop was still a minor league. He later opted to give up the reins to focus on the front office because he believed the dual role would be too burdensome with the AL now endeavoring to achieve major-league status.

With the two leagues at loggerheads, a postseason clash to settle bragging rights for the 1901 season was still a pipe dream.

1901

NAP LAJOIE

A's second sacker tears up the new league

The American League opened for business as a second major league in 1901 and raided National League rosters for established "name" players. It was a young star, however, that did the most to validate the credibility of the new league.

Napoleon "Nap" Lajoie was a slick-fielding, 26-year-old second baseman who had batted .326, .361, .324, .378, and .337 in his first five seasons for the Philadelphia Phillies (very good but not unthinkable batting averages for the high-scoring late 1890s). His career, however, had given little hint of what was to come. Playing for the Athletics in 1901, the Phillies' crosstown AL competitors, Lajoie put on a one-man slugging exhibition and won the century's first Triple Crown. He led the AL in hit-

ting at .422, in home runs with 14, and in RBI with 125. (This Triple Crown is retrospective, since the concept did not exist in 1901.) Nap dominated many offensive categories in his league, including runs (145), hits (229), doubles (48), on-base average (.451), and slugging percentage (.635). His .422 batting average is the highest mark of this century. Lajoie could not single-handedly win the pennant; the A's pitching let them down, and they finished fourth.

While some say that Lajoie's 1901 numbers were inflated because AL competition was still a cut below NL standards and because foul balls were not counted as strikes in 1901, it must be remembered that all of this was no less true for Lajoie than for all of the men he outhit.

SEASON'S BEST

Jesse Burkett

- The first AL game is played on April 24—Chicago 8, Cleveland 2.

- St. Louis's Jesse Burkett leads the NL in batting (.382), runs (139), and hits (228).

- Philly's Nap Lajoie leads the AL in BA (.422), homers (14), RBI (125), hits (229), doubles (48), total bases (345), runs (145), SA (.635), and OBP (.451).

- Boston's Cy Young leads both major leagues with 33 wins and a 1.62 ERA.

- Connie Mack manages the fledgling Philadelphia A's and will be their only manager until 1951.

- Pirate Honus Wagner leads the NL in steals (49) and RBI (126).

- The modern infield-fly rule is adopted.

MACKMEN, PIRATES EACH RAISE A FLAG

One who did not agree with White Sox owner Charlie Comiskey's philosophy on running a team was Connie Mack, who opted to function as manager and part-owner of the Philadelphia Athletics at the club's inception and continued to give dual service for over half a century. In 1901, Mack appeared to have taken on more than he could handle. That season his A's started so poorly they were out of the race, for all practical purposes, by July. In the final two months of the season, however, the Mackmen played the best ball in the new league, stirring hope for the next season. The A's first had to counter the loss of three former Philadelphia Phillies—Nap Lajoie, pitcher Bill Bernhard, and outfielder Elmer Flick—when the Phils sued for their return.

All three stars were transferred to Cleveland to circumvent the courts and keep them out of the NL's clutches. To replace them, Mack pilfered Topsy Hartsel from the Cubs and Danny Murphy from the New York Giants and then purchased Rube Waddell from Los Angeles, where he had wandered after his erratic behavior exasperated three previous ML teams. Mack had the right tonic for Waddell, offering patience and a paternal hand, and Rube churned out 24 wins. When Mack got 20 victories from second-year southpaw Eddie Plank, the A's had little difficulty suppressing a surprise challenge from the St. Louis Browns.

In 1902, Pittsburgh's only challenge en route to its second straight flag was the ML record for wins, then at 102. By the final day of the season the Pirates were so far in front that Cincinnati Reds owner Garry Herrmann, fielding a squad decimated by injuries and defections to the AL, begged to cancel the game. But Pittsburgh owner Barney Dreyfuss, perched at 102 wins and seeing a new record within his grasp, turned down Herrmann's plea. In a pique, Reds manager Joe Kelley proceeded to make a joke

Ginger Beaumont helped lead the Pirates to a 103-36 record and the NL pennant in 1902, hitting a league-best .357. Pittsburgh repeated in 1903, with Beaumont, a blazing leadoff hitter, scoring an NL-high 137 runs. He scored 100 runs or more in four straight seasons.

of the game, sending pitcher Rube Vickers behind the plate and encouraging several of his players, including himself, to smoke cigarettes while they were in the field. Vickers committed a record six passed balls in his only game as a catcher, and the Pirates breezed to an easy, if controversial, 103rd win to set a new ML record. Once again, the war between the two leagues held at bay any chance of a postseason championship series.

CY YOUNG

Tried-and-true pitcher racks up 32 more victories

Denton True Young pitched long enough to see baseball change from a game where "box-men" threw from a flattened square to bare-handed catchers 50 feet away to one where hurlers toed a rubber and aimed toward gloved and masked receivers 60 feet, six inches down the line. Whatever the rules, however, the right-hander managed just fine. He managed, in fact, to win 511 games over his 22-year career—more than any major leaguer before or since.

Born just after the Civil War in Gilmore, Ohio, Young (the Cy was short for Cyclone, which his pitches often appeared to emerge from) joined the Cleveland Spiders in 1890. Cy had already won 286 National League games when he jumped to the Boston Pil-

grims of the brand-new American League in 1901. Coming off his worst season (19-19), Cy would lead the AL in victories each of the next three years—including a 32-11 mark in 1902. His 43 starts, 41 complete games, and 384⅔ innings that year also topped the AL. His 2.15 ERA and 160 strikeouts ranked in the top five.

A 20-game winner 15 times (a major-league record), Young was 19-15 at age 42 before finally hanging up his fastball in 1911. The charter Hall of Fame member still ranks among baseball's best with 906 games pitched, 7,356 innings, and 76 shutouts (his 313 losses top all comers). Since his death at age 88 in 1955, baseball has singled out its best pitchers with a most appropriate honor—the Cy Young Award.

SEASON'S BEST

- Milwaukee moves to St. Louis—the AL's first franchise shift.

- Pittsburgh's Honus Wagner leads the NL in runs (105), RBI (91), doubles (33), SA (.467), and steals (42).

- Pittsburgh's Jack Chesbro leads the NL in wins (28) and winning percentage (.824) and pitches 41 consecutive scoreless innings.

- John McGraw jumps the AL in midseason to manage the Giants.

- Washington's Ed Delahanty wins the AL batting title (.376).

- Pirate Ginger Beaumont leads the NL in batting (.357) and hits (194).

- Boston's Cy Young leads the AL in wins (32) and CGs (41).

- Nig Clarke of Corsicana in the Texas League hits eight homers in a game.

Ed Delahanty

PILGRIMS WIN THE FIRST WORLD SERIES

John McGraw profited more than any other baseball figure of his time by the arrival of peace between the two major leagues. On the threshold of being squeezed out of the AL in 1902 because of his "rowdyism" as player-manager of the Baltimore Orioles, McGraw fled to the New York Giants, then the worst team in the majors. McGraw promptly lured Joe McGinnity back to the NL and engineered a number of other player deals that took advantage of the tumultuous climate. When peace was declared a few months later, he had already assembled many of the components of a team that would push the powerful Pittsburgh Pirates nearly to the wire in 1903 before falling 6½ games short.

Missing Jack Chesbro and Jesse Tannehill, two late defections to the AL just before peace reigned, Pittsburgh skipper Fred Clarke elevated Deacon Phillippe and Sam Leever to his top two hill spots and was rewarded with 49 wins against only 14 losses from the pair. Their mark was nearly matched in the AL by the Boston Pilgrims' mound duo of Cy Young and Long Tom Hughes, who were a combined 48-16, but Boston manager Jimmy Collins also had Bill Dinneen on tap. When Dinneen went 21-13, the Pilgrims now had the best three-man rotation in the majors. This helped them to atone for their failures in both 1901 and 1902 when they had been a popular preseason choice to win the pennant. In 1903, it was the A's turn to disappoint as they finished 14½ games in arrears of Boston and thereby frustrated their faithful who had hoped that the first interleague postseason battle since 1890 would have an all-Pennsylvania flavor.

Instead, an overflow throng of 16,242 assembled at Boston's Huntington Grounds on October 1 to witness the first modern "World Series" game. To their chagrin Phillippe triumphed 7-3 over Young. Phillippe also won two of the next three frays in the best-of-nine affair before overwork caught up to him—an injury to Leever in a trapshooting competition and Ed Doheny's mental breakdown forced Clarke to use Phillippe in five of the Series' eight games. After racing to a 3-1 lead, the Pirates then dropped the next four contests, two to Young and two to Dinneen. Also a 3-0 victor in Game 2 of the Series, Dinneen emerged as the fall affair's first hero, posting three wins in four tries to go with a 2.06 ERA.

A photograph of Huntington Grounds, home park of the 1903 AL Boston Pilgrims and site of the first modern World Series game. The eight-game Series lasted nearly two weeks.

JOE MCGINNITY

Giants' Iron Man carries the load, wins 31 games

When Joe McGinnity joined the Brooklyn Superbas in 1900, sportswriters asked about his off-season work occupation. The 29-year-old McGinnity said simply, "I'm an iron man. I work in my father-in-law's iron factory." The barrel-chested 5'11", 206-pounder from Rock Island, Illinois, couldn't have been more accurate; for in an era when pitchers routinely finished what they started, he proved the greatest "iron man" of them all.

Beginning with an 1899 rookie season, when he led the National League with 28 wins and 380 innings pitched, the right-hander with the quick underhand delivery would go on to pace the senior circuit in victories and innings five times each over an eight-year span. He averaged a 27-15 record and 370 innings a year during the stretch, but the 1903 season marked perhaps his greatest achievement. Topping the majors with 31 wins, 55 games pitched, 44 complete games, and an astounding 434 innings, McGinnity threw both ends of a doubleheader three times in the heat of the pennant race—and won all six decisions. Teaming with fire-balling, 30-game winner Christy Mathewson, McGinnity helped the Giants to 84 victories and a second-place finish just a year after they had gone 48-88 for the worst record in the majors. Joe's 1904 encore was just as remarkable (with a league-best 35-8 posting, 1.61 ERA, and 408 innings), and he compiled a 0.00 ERA over 17 innings when New York won the 1905 World Series. His major-league career lasted just 10 seasons, but his durability and 247-144 record over that span earned him a spot in the Hall of Fame.

SEASON'S BEST

- The AL's Baltimore team moves to New York, the last franchise move until 1953.

- Foul balls are counted as strikes by both leagues for the first time.

- Cleveland's Nap Lajoie leads the AL in BA (.355) and SA (.533).

- Pirate Ginger Beaumont leads the NL in hits (209), runs (137), and total bases (272).

- Washington star Ed Delahanty falls from a railway trestle to his death.

- Boston's Buck Freeman leads the AL in homers (13), total bases (281), and RBI (104).

- When part of the Phillies' park—the Baker Bowl—collapses, 12 fans are killed.

- Giant Christy Mathewson tops the NL in strikeouts (267) and wins 30 games. Teammate Joe McGinnity pitches 434 innings and wins 31 games.

Nap Lajoie

GIANTS WIN PENNANT, BLOW OFF SERIES

Seeking to become the first team since the 1885 to 1888 St. Louis Browns to sweep four straight ML pennants, Pittsburgh's dynasty ended with a thud. In 1904, John McGraw's New York Giants devoured the rest of the NL and set a new ML record with 106 victories.

But if McGraw and Giants owner John "Tooth" Brush expected their triumph would captivate New York, they were wrong. The pair faced stiff competition for the hearts of Gothamites from the upstart New York Highlanders, who had joined the AL the previous year. Ironically, McGraw and Brush had paved the way for a rival team in New York when they conspired to kill the Baltimore AL franchise, thinking it would sink the junior circuit. AL president Ban Johnson, however, thwarted their scheme by moving the Maryland team to the Big Apple and outbidding Charlie Comiskey to furnish it with his crafty pitcher-manager, Clark Griffith.

After finishing fourth in 1903, Griffith bagged Jack Powell in a trade to team with his mound ace, Jack Chesbro. The dynamic hill duo posted an AL-record 64 wins by pitching teammates—41 of them by Chesbro. For a time it seemed that the pair would catapult the Highlanders to the pennant and force an all-New York World Series. By the final Friday morning of the season, however, the Boston Pilgrims held a slim half-game lead. In a schedulemaker's dream, the Pilgrims faced the Highlanders that afternoon in the opener of a season-ending five-game series in the Big Apple. New York won on Friday to go a half-game up, but Boston shot back in front by sweeping a doubleheader the following afternoon. The season came down to a Sunday twinbill, with the Highlanders needing both games to win the flag.

In the opener, New York staked Chesbro to a 2-0 lead, but Boston tied the game in the seventh. It remained 2-2 in the ninth when Lou Criger singled and moved around to third on a sacrifice and a ground out. Chesbro then uncorked the most famous wild pitch in history as Criger scampered home with the pennant-clinching run. But Boston's thrilling victory proved somewhat empty. Fearing the Highlanders would win the pennant, McGraw and Brush had earlier refused to meet the AL victor in a championship match. Both claimed they still refused to recognize the AL, but many believed the real truth was they didn't want to risk their supremacy against another New York club.

New York Giants manager John McGraw, whose team won the 1904 NL pennant with a major-league record 106 wins but refused to play a championship series against the AL pennant winner.

JACK CHESBRO

Hurler's 41 wins tarnished by one wild pitch

Jack Chesbro had already been a 20-game winner three consecutive years for the Highlanders preceeding 1904, but in that season he went a little beyond this usual benchmark of pitching greatness. Throwing 130 more innings (for a grand total of 454⅔) than he ever had before, the 30-year-old right-hander from North Adams, Massachusetts, nearly pitched a mediocre New York club to the American League pennant with the incredible total of 41 victories—the most by a major-league pitcher in one season since the turn of the century.

Fashioning a nifty 1.82 ERA to go along with his 41-12 record, Chesbro completed 48 of 51 starts and went 3-0 in four relief appearances to account for nearly 45 percent of his team's 92 victories. Un-

fortunately, his heroic efforts were overshadowed by what happened in New York the final day of the season. On that day, his team needed a doubleheader sweep of the Boston Pilgrims in order to win the American League pennant. Pitching the first game, Chesbro was in the ninth inning of a 2-2 battle when his spitball sailed over catcher Red Kleinow's head and allowed the winning run to score, giving Boston the title. Perhaps unnerved by the experience, Chesbro went just 67-66 the rest of his career—only once winning more than 20 games. He never pitched in the World Series, and after he died in 1931, the Hall of Famer's widow spent the rest of her life trying to get the fatal 1904 ruling changed from wild pitch to passed ball.

SEASON'S BEST

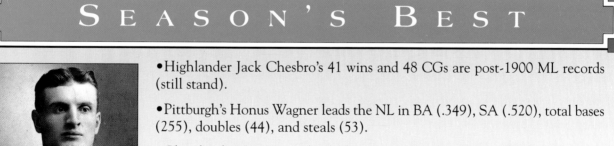

Rube Waddell

- Highlander Jack Chesbro's 41 wins and 48 CGs are post-1900 ML records (still stand).

- Pittsburgh's Honus Wagner leads the NL in BA (.349), SA (.520), total bases (255), doubles (44), and steals (53).

- Cleveland's Nap Lajoie leads the AL in BA (.381), SA (.554), hits (211), total bases (307), RBI (102), and doubles (50).

- Giant Joe McGinnity leads the NL in wins (35), winning percentage (.814), ERA (1.61), shutouts (nine), innings (408), and saves (five).

- Rube Waddell of the A's fans 349, setting an all-time ML record for a 154-game season.

- The Pilgrims' Cy Young pitches the first perfect game of the 20th century on May 5.

- Giant Christy Mathewson wins 33 and leads the NL in Ks (212).

GIANTS RIP THROUGH THE HELPLESS A'S

In 1895, the Philadelphia Phillies scored 1,068 runs in 133 games but still finished third. A decade later, the game's balance had tilted so heavily in favor of pitchers that Connie Mack's Philadelphia A's won the 1905 AL pennant despite scoring a mere 623 runs in 152 games. Just two lengths back at the wire were the Chicago White Sox with four regulars who posted BAs of .201 or less.

Mack's crew was led in hitting by first baseman Harry Davis at .284. Davis also topped the AL in homers and RBI with the paltry totals of eight and

In the best-pitched World Series ever, in which the winning New York Giants had an ERA of 0.00 and the losing Philadelphia A's posted a 1.47 ERA, New York's Turkey Mike Donlin managed to get six hits.

83, respectively, as only two regulars in the AL batted as high as .300. Indeed, the AL's four first division teams had only three players—Sam Crawford of the Tigers and Chicago's Jiggs Donahue and Frank Isbell—who broke .285.

In the NL, the dead-ball era had not yet taken so pervasive a grip on the game. John McGraw's Giants led the majors with a .273 BA, thanks largely to Turkey Mike Donlin's .356 mark. Since the Giants also enjoyed a quintet of hurlers who won 15 games or more, they repeated routinely as champs, taking the lead on April 23 and holding it the rest of the summer against Pittsburgh and the refurbished Chicago Cubs.

Responding to harsh criticism, McGraw and Giants owner John Brush acquiesced to the public demand to meet the A's in the postseason. The second 20th century World Series was made a best-of-seven clash, a format that would continue until 1919, and shaped up as a duel between Giants pitching great Christy Mathewson and A's 26-game winner Rube Waddell. When Waddell injured his arm on the eve of the Series in a scuffle with teammate Andy Coakley, Mack had no one to match Mathewson. Even a healthy Waddell would have been unlikely to turn the tide, however, as Mathewson notched three shutouts in a six-day period to hand the Giants the NL's first modern postseason triumph. Joe McGinnity recorded a fourth shutout for the New Yorkers, beating Eddie Plank 1-0 in Game 4, and the A's hurlers likewise did their part to establish that when the championship was on the line, the dead-ball style of play prevailed.

In five World Series games, the A's managed to cross the plate just three times, and not one of their runs was earned, enabling the Giants to post a perfect 0.00 Series ERA. The Giants were only slightly more productive, hitting .203 as a team and tallying just seven earned runs.

CHRISTY MATHEWSON

Matty wins 31, tosses three Series shutouts

One of the first college-educated men to play professional baseball, Christy Mathewson was a handsome, blond, former Bucknell class president. While he was gentle in disposition, he was overpowering on the mound. Strong and seemingly larger than his 6'1½", 195-pound frame (leading to his nickname, "Big Six"), the Factoryville, Pennsylvania, son of a gentleman farmer joined the Giants late in the 1900 season at age 19 and was a 20-game winner the following year. In 1903, he went 30-13 as New York improved from a last-place finish to second, and the following year he went 33-12, helping the Giants to win the pennant.

Denied a chance to pitch in the 1904 World Series when New York manager John McGraw refused to play the Boston Pilgrims of the "lesser" American League, Mathewson set about earning the Giants a return trip in 1905 in case the skipper changed his mind. McGraw did, and after leading the league in wins (with a 31-8 mark), ERA (1.27), strikeouts (206), and shutouts (eight), Christy shined even brighter in the World Series against Connie Mack's mighty Philadelphia Athletics. Pitching four-hit shutouts in the first and third games, he came back on one day's rest in the fifth contest and beat Chief Bender on a 2-0 six-hitter for the win and the championship. Christy's scoreless 27-inning performance has never been matched in Series play. The charter Hall of Famer went on to pitch in three more Series battles for New York over a 17-year career that included 373 victories and 80 shutouts—both third on the all-time lists—and a 2.13 ERA that ranks fifth.

SEASON'S BEST

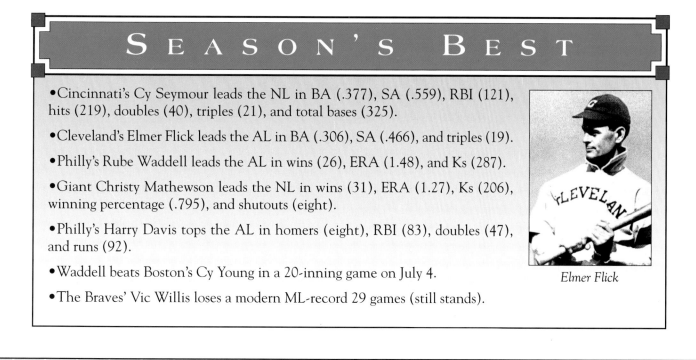

- Cincinnati's Cy Seymour leads the NL in BA (.377), SA (.559), RBI (121), hits (219), doubles (40), triples (21), and total bases (325).

- Cleveland's Elmer Flick leads the AL in BA (.306), SA (.466), and triples (19).

- Philly's Rube Waddell leads the AL in wins (26), ERA (1.48), and Ks (287).

- Giant Christy Mathewson leads the NL in wins (31), ERA (1.27), Ks (206), winning percentage (.795), and shutouts (eight).

- Philly's Harry Davis tops the AL in homers (eight), RBI (83), doubles (47), and runs (92).

- Waddell beats Boston's Cy Young in a 20-inning game on July 4.

- The Braves' Vic Willis loses a modern ML-record 29 games (still stands).

Elmer Flick

CUBS GO 116-36, THEN LOSE TO SOX

When a team paces its league in batting, fielding, and ERA, it is awarded the team "triple crown" and generally wins the pennant. Conversely, a team that finishes last in its loop in batting usually also brings up the rear in the standings.

The 1906 season, though, was unique. For the only time in modern major-league history, a team triple crown winner failed to take the pennant, and a team that was last in batting won. In the 1906 AL race, Cleveland—with four .300-hitting regulars, three 20-game winners, and the best double-play combo in the majors—came in third. Meanwhile, the Chicago White Sox finished first without a single regular who was able to hit over the .280 mark.

The Sox' improbable triumph caused them to be dubbed "The Hitless Wonders." It stemmed in part from a 19-game winning streak that helped fend off Cleveland and the tenacious New York Highlanders but more from the leadership of center fielder-manager Fielder Jones, the prototypical dead-ball star. A steady .300 hitter earlier in his career, Jones batted just .230 in 1906 but ranked second in the AL in walks and was also a leader in sacrifice hits.

A photograph of West Side Park, home of the Cubs, during the third game of the 1906 World Series against the crosstown rival Sox.

Still, the White Sox attack resembled being pecked to death by chickadees, and the team was given no chance against its crosstown rival, the Chicago Cubs, in the 1906 World Series. That summer the Cubs had streaked to an all-time record 116 wins under player-manager Frank Chance. With Chance at first, Johnny Evers at second, Joe Tinker at shortstop, and Harry Steinfeldt, the RBI leader, at third base, the Cubs boasted the best infield in the game. Pitching, though, was their real forte. The Cub hurlers were so potent that Carl Lundgren, who won 17 games during the regular season, wasn't used at all in the World Series because his 2.21 ERA was nearly half a run higher than the team's 1.76 mark.

When the Hitless Wonders triumphed 2-1 in the Series opener, it was viewed as a freak event—especially after the Cubs took the second and fourth clashes to knot the battle at 2-all. In the final two games, the Sox uncorked 26 hits, more than they usually saw in a week. The uncharacteristic offensive barrage produced eight runs in each contest and doomed the Cubs to being on the wrong end of the biggest upset in sports history to that point.

MORDECAI BROWN

Three Finger yields one run every nine innings

Mordecai Brown was seven years old when he caught his right hand in a corn grinder on his uncle's Indiana farm and had almost his entire forefinger chopped off. His middle finger was left mangled and crooked and his pinky partially stubbed, but he still found work as a coal miner and eventually played baseball. An infielder in the minors, he switched to pitching when he learned he could add spin and extra dip to the ball by throwing it off his stub — and by 1903 Mordecai was in the majors with the Cardinals.

Traded to the Cubs the following winter after going 9-13, he began a string of eight straight winning seasons. His first of six consecutive 20-win campaigns came in 1906, when he went 26-6 with a 20th-century record-low ERA of 1.04, 27 complete games, and a National League-high 10 shutouts as the Cubs won a major-league record 116 games and a World Series matchup with their crosstown rival White Sox. Brown allowed just six hits combined in Games 1 (a 2-1 loss) and 4 (a 1-0 win). When he sought his third complete game in five days, however, he was shelled for seven runs in less than two innings of the sixth and final contest.

Brown got the Cubs back to the Series three more times, and a fitness regime helped him remain an outstanding starter and reliever until his 1916 retirement. He posted a 239-129 lifetime record with 48 saves and a 2.06 ERA (third all-time), and one year after his 1948 death, Brown was elected to the Hall of Fame.

SEASON'S BEST

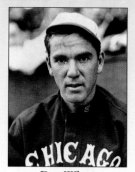

Doc White

- White Sox win 19 straight games, an all-time AL record.

- St. Louis's George Stone leads the AL in BA (.358), SA (.501), and total bases (291).

- Pittsburgh's Honus Wagner tops the NL in BA (.339), doubles (38), and total bases (237).

- New York's Al Orth leads the AL in wins (27) and CGs (36).

- Cubs set modern ML records for wins (116) and fewest runs allowed (381).

- Cub Three Finger Brown leads the NL with a 1.04 ERA and 10 shutouts.

- Cardinal Jack Taylor's streak of 118 consecutive complete games ends.

- On September 1, Joe Harris of Boston and Jack Coombs of the A's duel 24 innings; A's win 4-1.

- Doc White of the White Sox leads the league with a 1.52 ERA, walking only 38 in 219 innings.

TIGERS RUN OUT OF LUCK IN WS

The Detroit Tigers attributed their first AL pennant to Ty Cobb's emergence as a star in 1907, plus the continued excellence of center fielder Sam Crawford and a quartet of pitchers who produced 88 of the team's 92 wins. Connie Mack attributed the Tigers' flag to a moment of highway robbery.

On September 27, the AL race was in a virtual dead heat as manager Hughie Jennings's Detroit squad squared off against Mack's A's at Philadelphia. When the Tigers won, it lured a near record crowd to Columbia Park the next afternoon to watch the two combatants play a doubleheader that would probably decide the pennant. The opener went into overtime but then seemed to be settled when the A's Harry Davis socked a ball into the overflow crowd. Umpire Silk O'Loughlin, however, earned Mack's everlasting enmity at this moment when he claimed that someone in the mob had interfered with Crawford's chance to make the catch and ruled Davis out. The game ended as a 17-inning draw called by darkness, and since the custom of the time did not require teams to make up tied or postponed games, even if they had direct bearing on a pennant race, the Tigers left Philadelphia in first place and the A's did not have another opportunity to catch them.

In the NL, no one ever had an opportunity at any point in the 1907 season to catch the Cubs. Winning by a 17-game margin over Pittsburgh, Frank Chance's club was again made a prohibitive favorite in the World Series. Carl Lundgren was once again not used in the fray, even though he had lifted his win total to 18 and shaved his ERA to 1.17. Lundgren simply was not needed. Detroit's only bright moment in the Series was erased during the ninth inning of the opener when a passed ball by Tigers catcher Boss Schmidt allowed the Cubs to tie the game at 3-all. Three innings later darkness forced the contest to be called a draw, but unlike the regular season, drawn games in the World Series were replayed—to the Tigers' chagrin. The following afternoon Detroit tallied a run in the top of the second, but it was the last time a Jennings' team led in the Series. Three days later Three Finger Brown capped a Cubs' sweep when he blanked Cobb, Crawford, and company, 2-0.

The 1907 world champion Chicago Cubs. Some of the more notable players include Three Finger Brown; double-play combo Tinkers, Evers, and Chance; and Carl Lundgren.

HONUS WAGNER

The Dutchman does it in the field, at the plate

Honus Wagner's .381 season in 1900 had proven only a prelude to an outstanding career. Moved from the outfield to shortstop the following season where his speed, huge hands, and rifle arm made him an immediate success, he won seven more batting crowns in the next 11 years while hitting .350 or better on five occasions. The 1907 campaign was one such season, as Wagner led the National League and tied arch-rival Ty Cobb for major-league leadership with a .350 mark while besting runner-up Cobb and everyone else with 61 stolen bases (a career high) and a .513 slugging average. Wagner's 38 doubles and 264 total bases also topped the senior circuit, and he drove in 82 runs—one of 15 consecutive seasons he topped 70 RBI despite hitting 10 homers twice in the dead-ball era.

Homers aside, Wagner could produce as well as anyone. All told, there were five stolen base titles, four RBI crowns, and 10 occasions on which the funny-looking Dutchman with the hook nose paced the league in either doubles or triples. He was the NL slugging leader six times from 1900 to 1910. His proficiency at the plate was matched only by his peerless play at short, where his long arms enabled him to get to almost anything hit his way. Humble and extremely popular with fans, he finished with a .327 career batting average, 3,418 hits, 722 steals, and 1,732 RBI over 21 seasons. Returning to Pittsburgh and coaching from 1933 until his retirement at age 77 in 1951, Honus was made a charter member of the Hall of Fame in 1936.

SEASON'S BEST

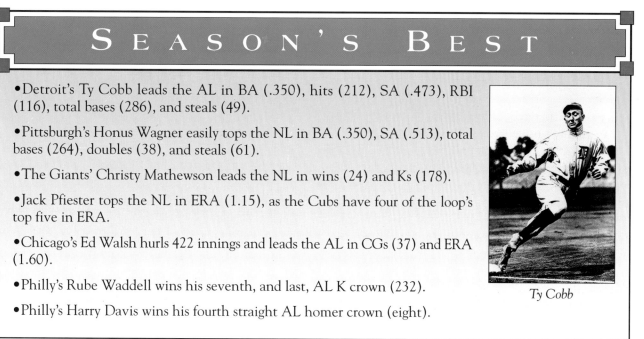

- Detroit's Ty Cobb leads the AL in BA (.350), hits (212), SA (.473), RBI (116), total bases (286), and steals (49).

- Pittsburgh's Honus Wagner easily tops the NL in BA (.350), SA (.513), total bases (264), doubles (38), and steals (61).

- The Giants' Christy Mathewson leads the NL in wins (24) and Ks (178).

- Jack Pfiester tops the NL in ERA (1.15), as the Cubs have four of the loop's top five in ERA.

- Chicago's Ed Walsh hurls 422 innings and leads the AL in CGs (37) and ERA (1.60).

- Philly's Rube Waddell wins his seventh, and last, AL K crown (232).

- Philly's Harry Davis wins his fourth straight AL homer crown (eight).

Ty Cobb

CUBS CAPITALIZE ON MERKLE'S ERROR

As the final day of the 1908 season dawned, historians had to harken back to 1889 for the last time the pennant races in two major leagues had both come down to the last game. In the AL, for the second year in a row, Detroit stood to profit from a postponement. If the Tigers could beat White Sox lefty Doc White, they would be victorious over Cleveland by a meager half game (or .004 percentage points). Chicago, which had sustained two postponed games, meanwhile would bag the pennant by .002 percentage points over Cleveland with a White Sox victory.

Detroit won to climax what ought to have been an unbearably exciting finish to the AL season, but few noticed. All eyes were on the NL where the Cubs, Pirates, and Giants were locked in an excruciatingly tight three-way race. Only the Giants did not control their own destiny. Indeed, if the Pirates beat the Cubs in their final game of the season, they would clinch the pennant and eliminate any need for the Cubs and Giants to make up a tie game of September 23.

When the Cubs won, the tie game loomed all important. First, however, the Giants had to beat Boston three straight games to force the replay. Once that happened, New York and Chicago ended the regular season with identical 98-55 records, and 19-year-old Fred Merkle could only pray that his life would not forever after be marred by his mistake two weeks earlier. On September 23, in the bottom of the ninth of a 1-1 tie against the Cubs at the Polo Grounds, Merkle had neglected to touch second base after an apparent game-winning hit. During the ensuing melee, Cubs second sacker Johnny Evers persuaded umpire Hank O'Day to abide by the letter of the rules and call Merkle out. Since the crowd had overrun the field in the confusion making further play impossible, O'Day's decision caused the game to end with a 1-1 score.

A baserunning gaffe by New York's Fred Merkle late in the 1908 season may have cost the Giants the National League pennant.

In the replay on October 8 at the Polo Grounds, the Cubs silenced a record 35,000 spectators when ace Three Finger Brown, working in relief, topped Christy Mathewson, 4-2. On the heels of so much season-ending tension, the World Series was anticlimactic. Again the Cubs tamed the Tigers, winning in five games. When Orval Overall stifled the Bengals 2-0 in the finale, it gave the Bruins their second straight world championship. No one could have known then that Overall would be the last Cubs pitcher to end a postseason series with a win.

ED WALSH

Big Ed wins 40 games, leads league in saves

Ed Walsh had labored in a Plains, Pennsylvania, coal mine driving a mule team before turning to baseball. Perhaps it was stubbornness gained from his former coworkers that helped him put together one of baseball's most extraordinary pitching performances. Walsh broke in with the White Sox in 1904 and mastered the then-legal spitball. He became one of baseball's best hurlers by 1907, going 24-18 with a league-leading 1.60 ERA in an incredible 422⅓ innings pitched. It was only a prelude of what was to come.

Going to the mound virtually every other day for the White Sox in 1908, the confident, swaggering Walsh started 49 games, relieved in 17 others, and proceeded to pitch a major league-record 464 innings—twice what's expected from reliable starters today. He accounted for 45½ percent of Chicago's 88 victories with his 40-15 record—the highest such percentage in AL history—and for the second straight year led the league in games, starts, complete games (42), and saves (six). He was also tops in wins, strikeouts (269), and shutouts (11), and his 1.42 ERA ranked third. How dominating was he? No other American Leaguer recorded more than 24 wins or 325 innings.

The load took its toll on Walsh, and while he remained effective for four more seasons, he was virtually through at age 32. Later a White Sox coach when his son Ed (also a pitcher) broke in with the team, his early success and scintillating 1.82 career ERA (best for the dead-ball era) were enough to win him Hall of Fame selection in 1946.

SEASON'S BEST

Christy Mathewson

- White Sox Ed Walsh leads the AL in wins (40), winning percentage (.727), Ks (269), CGs (42), shutouts (11), and innings (464—a 20th-century record).

- Detroit's Ty Cobb wins the AL bat crown (.324) and also leads in SA (.475), total bases (276), RBI (108), hits (188), doubles (36), and triples (20).

- Pirate Honus Wagner tops the NL in BA (.354), hits (201), steals (53), RBI (109), doubles (39), triples (19), SA (.542), and total bases (308).

- Giant Christy Mathewson leads the NL in wins (37), ERA (1.43), Ks (259), shutouts (12), CGs (34), innings (391), and saves (five).

- Cleveland's Addie Joss pitches a perfect game over Chicago on Oct. 2. Joss leads the AL in ERA (1.16).

- Washington's Walter Johnson pitches three shutouts in four days vs. New York.

PITTSBURGH FROSH TAMES THE TIGERS

On April 12, 1909, the Philadelphia A's celebrated the opening of Shibe Park, the first all-concrete-and-steel stadium, by beating Boston, 8-1. Some two and one-half months later, the Cubs spoiled the Pirates' debut at Forbes Field, the second modern stadium, by taking a 3-2 squeaker. Yet, the Pirates proceeded to end the Cubs' three-year reign as NL champs by winning a club-record 110 games while the A's proved unable to stop the Tigers' Hughie Jennings from becoming the first manager ever to win pennants in each of his initial three seasons as a helmsman.

The Cubs had the consolation of winning 104 games, a record for an also-ran. The A's, however, knew only of despair. They led the AL for most of August, only to succumb to the Bengals' George Mullin and Ed Willett, two of the AL's top three winningest pitchers in 1909.

As the Tigers also had the loop's top two run producers in Ty Cobb and Sam Crawford, their triumph was hardly a shock. The Pirates, in contrast, seemed built around one outstanding player, Honus Wagner, and a collection of aging and uneven pitchers. Some felt the Series could only be won by Pittsburgh if Wagner forgot his 35-year-old legs and played to his zenith.

Pirates player-manager Fred Clarke, himself past 36, had a surprise for the Tigers up his sleeve. While the Bengals were looking for 25-game winner Howie Camnitz in the Series opener, Detroit instead drew 27-year-old rookie Babe Adams. When the young hurler from Michigan bested Mullin, it started the Tigers off on the wrong foot for the third postseason affair in a row.

This time, however, Detroit rallied, albeit with little support from Cobb, who hit just .231 in his final Series experience. After six games, the Series was tied at 3-all. For the crucial final contest, Clarke gave the ball for the third time to Adams. This left Jennings to choose either Mullin, working on just one day's rest, or Wild Bill Donovan. The latter had been idle since winning the second contest a full week earlier. Jennings picked Donovan for the start and then switched to Mullin when the Pirates sprang to a 4-0 lead. It did not matter. Adams was invincible, shutting down Detroit 8-0 to become the only rookie ever to win three games in a Series. As for Wagner, he too had a good Series, outstripping Cobb in the lone meeting between the dead-ball era's two greatest stars.

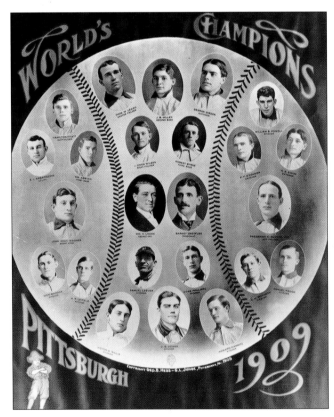

Honus Wagner, middle row left, made the 1909 Pirates go, but it was rookie pitcher Babe Adams, bottom row center, who tamed the Tigers with three victories in the World Series.

TY COBB

Fiery flyhawk leads in batting, homers, steals

Arguments over who was the greatest ballplayer of all time will never be decided, but when the topic comes around to the player most despised in his day, the responses are usually unanimous. Ty Cobb was the most accomplished batsman of the dead-ball era and baseball's all-time hit leader for nearly 60 years, but it was the intensity and anger this complex man brought to each game that trademarked his career—and earned him a league full of admirers and enemies.

There was some history to his inner demons. He was born in Narrows, Georgia, to an educated and demanding father who saw no point in his son's love for baseball. Tyrus, then just 18 years old, was just beginning to prove himself to the old man as a minor-league standout. As fate would have it, his mother Amanda accidentally killed William Cobb with a shotgun when he returned home unexpectedly one night from a business trip. Ty had little time to mourn—the Detroit Tigers called him up just three weeks later—and he would spend the next 23 seasons taking his feelings out on every ball and person that got in his way. After winning batting and RBI championships in 1907 and 1908, he had his first truly spectacular season in 1909—hitting a then-career high .377 for his third straight title while also leading the American League in homers (nine) and RBI (107) in his only Triple Crown campaign. The pacesetter in hits (216), runs (116), slugging (.517), total bases (296), and steals (76) as well, he led Detroit to its third straight pennant while establishing himself as baseball's leading star.

SEASON'S BEST

Honus Wagner

- Pittsburgh's Honus Wagner leads the NL in BA (.339), SA (.489), total bases (242), doubles (39), and RBI (100).

- Detroit's Ty Cobb wins his only AL Triple Crown (.377, nine, 107). Cobb also leads in SA (.517), total bases (296), hits (216), runs (116), and steals (76).

- Detroit's George Mullin leads the AL in wins (29) and winning percentage (.784).

- Philly's Harry Krause leads the AL in ERA (1.39).

- Forbes Field and Shibe Park open—the first all-concrete-and-steel stadiums.

- On July 19, Cleveland shortstop Neal Ball performs the majors' first unassisted triple play.

- Chicago's Three Finger Brown leads the NL in wins (27), CGs (32), and saves (seven).

- Giant Christy Mathewson goes 25-6 and posts an ML-leading 1.14 ERA.

THE 1910s

Baseball faced serious challenges in the 1910s: dead-ball games, the rival Federal League, the Great War, and the shameful Black Sox scandal of 1919. Impressively, the grand game survived each and every crisis.

The end of the dead-ball era coincides exactly with the end of the 1910s. After the 1919 season, baseball instituted changes that diminished the impact of the foul-strike rule in the early 1900s, the lively ball experiment of 1911, or any other event in 20th-century baseball history. For the 1920 season, all pitchers (except for spitball pitchers who were "grandfathered" and allowed to use the pitch until they retired) were forbidden to throw the spitball, emery ball, shine ball, and other artificial breaking pitches or "trick" deliveries. Furthermore, a series of related new on-the-field procedures meant that a constant supply of fresh, unmarked baseballs was kept in play. This change was the main, though not the only, cause for the emergence of the home run era and the 1920s phenomenon of Babe Ruth, the archetype of the modern power hitter.

Baseball in the 1910s was virtually the same as in the pitching-dominated 1900s. Gavvy Cravath hit 24 home runs in 1915 and Wildfire Schulte hit 21 in 1911, the offensive peak year of the era. But for the most part in the 1910s, players led the league in home runs with totals around 10. The best individual home run total for the decade was 29 by Babe Ruth in 1919, a performance that astounded contemporaries and the significance of which would not become apparent until the next decade. League home run totals ranged from a low of 98 in the American League in 1918 to a high of 316 in the NL in 1911; the average year hovered around 200 to 250 in the National League and 150 to 200 in the American League. This represents only a slight increase over the first decade of the dead-ball era, the 1900s.

The greatest individual hitters of the 1910s are found not in the columns of home run leaders, but

President William Howard Taft threw out the first ball in Washington on Opening Day in 1910 (left), beginning a sacred tradition. Honus Wagner didn't want his picture on a baseball card because it was sponsored by a tobacco company (they produced it anyway), but gladly loaned his mug for an ice cream pin (top right). Baseball was a game not to be missed, as the sheet music to "I Can't Miss That Ball Game" showed (bottom right).

were under 3.00 six times between 1910 and 1919; American League ERAs were comparable, rising above 3.00 only in 1911, 1912, and 1919. The 1910s brought a new generation of great individual pitchers as well. Replacing Christy Mathewson, Cy Young, and Three Finger Brown were Walter Johnson, who averaged a 29-15 record with a 1.59 ERA for the decade; Grover Cleveland Alexander, who averaged a 28-13 record with a 2.07 ERA; and a young left-hander named Babe Ruth, who had an 89-46 record from 1914 to 1919 and went 3-0 for Boston in two World Series, compiling the third-best World Series ERA in history.

As in the 1900s, the stolen base was considered one of the premier offensive weapons. The home run was not a part of the game at this time. Yearly league stolen base totals ranged from 1,000 to 2,000, as they do today. Like today, players who led the league in swipes had totals ranging from 50 to 90. The list of the all-time greatest individual basestealing seasons consists entirely of players before 1920 and after 1960. There is not one player from the intervening four decades in the top 50. Below the Rickey Hendersons, Vince Colemans, and Maury Willses appear Ty Cobb's 96 stolen bases in 1915, Clyde Milan's 88 in 1912, Eddie Collins's 81 in 1910, and Fritz Maisel's 74 in 1914.

Smoky Joe Wood (top) was one of the premier pitchers of the early 1910s, with a 34-5 record and 10 shutouts in 1912. Another dominant pitcher of the decade, Walter Johnson (bottom).

among the leaders in batting averages, slugging averages, and triples. Ty Cobb hit .387 for the decade, with nine batting titles and eight slugging averages above .500; he also hit 160 triples. Cobb had only 48 home runs during the decade and never led the league. Joe Jackson hit .354 for the 1910s, slugged over .500 for the decade, and led the league in triples twice, with 26 in 1912 and 21 in 1916. He averaged slightly over four home runs per year and never led the league.

In spite of outstanding individual performances by such hitters, the 1910s (like the previous decade) was dominated by pitchers. National League ERAs

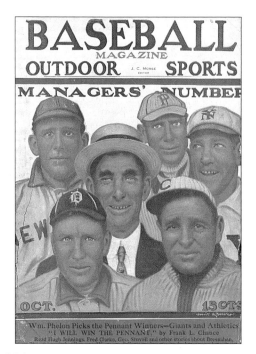

Philadelphia's Connie Mack (center) was among the managers featured in Baseball Magazine *in 1910.*

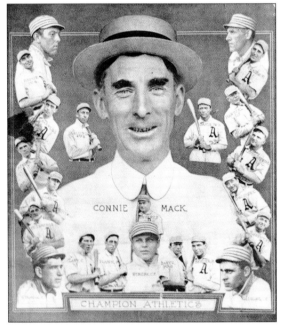

Workhorse spitballer Ed Walsh (top left) won 27 games in 1911 and 1912, but his arm was finished by 1916. Chalmers started the tradition of giving a car to the league MVP, and Detroit's Ty Cobb was the recipient in 1911 (top right). Connie Mack's A's (bottom) dominated early in the decade, winning consecutive World Series titles in 1910 and 1911.

There was one big difference between the base-stealers of the dead-ball era and those of today's basestealing renaissance—baserunning in the 1900s and 1910s was too reckless. As a rule, statisticians agree that a basestealing success ratio of about 67 percent is the break-even point; in other words, below that a player is making so many outs by being caught stealing that he is negating the benefit of advancing the extra bases when he succeeds. Max Carey, who played for Pittsburgh from 1910 to 1926 and then Brooklyn until 1929, had an excellent career success ratio of 79 percent, but figures like Carey's are more the exception than the rule for the dead-ball years. Although records are rather sketchy from this time period, it is estimated that the great Cobb and Collins stole successfully only 65 percent of the time, and other famous baserunners of the day were far worse. Honus Wagner made it safely 60 percent of the time, Tris Speaker 57 percent, and Joe Jackson an atrocious 54 percent.

So that was baseball in the 1910s: lots of singles, few home runs, and fearsome pitching. There was little the offense could do to create excitement beyond stealing bases. For the most part, the stolen base had little effect on run production—whatever the great players of the 1910s may have said later, when as old men, they shook their heads in disapproval at the home run happy 1920s and 1930s—and the fans were bored. Total major-league attendance in the 1910s never reached the 1900s record of over seven million, which was set in 1909. For the entire decade, attendance was a little over 50 million, or just about what it had been in the previous decade, but it showed a disturbing downward trend in the late 1910s, even dropping below five million in some years.

Nevertheless, in some trends of the 1910s there were subtle signs that things were beginning to change. One sign was the adoption of the lively, cork-center baseball in 1911. After trying it out in the 1910 World Series, both leagues made the new ball official beginning with the 1911 regular season. A mini-explosion of offense resulted; ERAs rose from 3.02 in 1910 to 3.39 in the NL and from 2.53 to 3.34 in the AL. Homers in 1911 also rose by 102 in the NL and by 54 in the AL. There were also a number of individual achievements, like Wildfire Schulte's 21 homers for the Cubs, Cobb's .420 average, and Jackson's .408 BA (along with Cobb's .410 the next year, the only averages over .400 in the decade).

Giants pitcher Rube Marquard (top left) won 19 straight in 1912, but might be more famous for giving "Home Run" Baker his nickname. White Sox pitchers from left: Jim Scott, Ed Walsh, and Ed Cicotte pictured in 1914 (top right). The A's "$100,000 infield" (bottom): Stuffy McInnis at first, Frank Baker at third, Jack Barry at short, and Eddie Collins at second.

Stars of the early 1910s were featured on a 1912 board game.

In 1912, both leagues experienced a slight drop-off in home runs (from 316 to 287 in the NL and 199 to 154 in the AL), but ERAs held steady at 3.40 and 3.34. Then, even though the lively ball was kept in use, pitchers gradually regained their control of the game. The National League ERA declined to 3.20 in 1913 and in following years to 2.78, 2.75, and 2.61; AL ERAs went from 2.93 in 1913 to 2.73, 2.94, 2.81, and finally 2.66 in 1917. In 1913 there were no National League pitchers under a 2.00 ERA for the season, but in 1914 there were three. History has always shown that increased offense stimulates fan interest; it was probably not coincidental that the low-scoring 1913 and 1914 seasons were the nadir of attendance in the 1910s, or that baseball's response to the crisis in fan confidence after the Black Sox scandal was to increase offense by handicapping pitchers.

Another development that later contributed to the birth of the home run offense was the building of enclosed urban concrete-and-steel ballparks, a process that began in 1909 with the construction of Philadelphia's Shibe Park. Between Shibe and Yankee Stadium in 1923, 14 teams built concrete-and-steel parks. The old wooden parks had been located on the outskirts of cities and were either not enclosed or had extremely deep fences, with fans sitting in the stands surrounding the infield or standing along the baselines. On exceptional occasions, huge crowds would be accommodated by stringing ropes

in the outfield behind the fielders and putting fans there; sometimes balls hit over these temporary barriers would be ruled home runs. But all of the new parks were intended to be permanent and some even monumental. They were situated as close to the centers of the cities as possible. As a result, not only were all the new parks enclosed, but they were limited in size by city lots and streets. Gradually, baseball had more and more parks with home run fences that could be reached consistently by batted balls.

Some of the parks built in the 1910s included: Comiskey Park, which originally had outfield distances of approximately 360 feet down the foul lines, 382 in the alley, and 420 in center; Fenway Park, which had a slope called "Duffy's Cliff" about 320 feet away in left, a 315-foot foul line in right, and an irregular center field configuration similar to today's Fenway but much deeper; Tiger Stadium, 350 feet in left, 375 in right, and 470 in center; and Wrigley Field, 330 feet in left, 440 in center, and 320 in right. These distances are approximate because they were subject to many adjustments during the decade.

Another phenomenon of the 1910s that played an indirect part in the home run era was growing gambling-related corruption. This culminated in the Black Sox scandal of 1919. In the minds of fans,

American League umpire Billy Evans (right) was considered a diplomat, but once got into a scrape under the grandstand after being challenged by Detroit's Ty Cobb.

The 1912 Lincoln Giants of the Negro League (top).
Detroit's George Moriarity wrote a song (bottom left) while
the Giants' Rube Marquard starred in a vaudeville act
(bottom right) in 1912.

baseball corruption became linked with the entire
dead-ball style of play; owners promoted Babe Ruth
and home run hitting as a way to sweep away the
past and recapture the imagination of the public.

Baseball in the 1910s was still the nation's only
major sport and (aside from horse-racing) the primary object of betting interest, as it had been since
the mid-19th century. And even though the major
leagues had periodically cracked down on game-fixing and other abuses since the 1880s, these problems
had never entirely disappeared. The game-throwing
escapades of Hal Chase and his fellow Giant Heinie
Zimmerman were far from isolated events. The
1900s and 1910s were marked by uncountable accusations and rumors of corruption. In 1908, White
Sox owner Charles Comiskey reassured the public
that the close pennant races had not been fixed; in
1903 fan suspicion over the outcome of the Cubs-
White Sox city series caused Cubs shortstop Joe Tinker to say in an interview, "Soreheads howl fake as a
rule after postseason games, but if they would only
stop to think they could see that it is out of the question. To fake a ball game, everyone must be in on
the deal. This makes it impossible to fix matters." In
1919, eight of his fellow Chicagoans would prove
Tinker tragically wrong.

The Black Sox scandal didn't break until the fall
of 1920, but expert observers of the 1919 World Series, in which a relatively weak Cincinnati team defeated the powerful White Sox of Joe Jackson and
Eddie Collins, smelled a rat. Led by Hugh Fullerton,
journalists cited the poor performances of Lefty
Williams, who went 0-3 with a 6.61 ERA after having a 23-11 record with a 2.64 ERA during the regular season; Swede Risberg, who hit .080 and

committed four errors at short; and a number of very suspiciously timed misplays by pitcher Eddie Cicotte and others. In hindsight, a few other clues to the fix are apparent, including a last-minute shift in the World Series odds from 3-1 Sox to 8-5 Reds and a fascinating team photograph taken just before the Series that shows manager Kid Gleason stationed off to one side of the team and as far away as he could get from the eight conspirators, who are grouped in a circle around the ringleader, first baseman Chick Gandil.

When the truth came out in the form of confessions by Cicotte and third baseman Buck Weaver, the baseball world was shocked to learn that eight White Sox had agreed to throw the Series for promised bribes ranging as high as $20,000 for Jackson and $35,000 for Gandil. The scheme was bankrolled by reputed New York City underworld figure Arnold Rothstein through a complicated set of arrangements involving other gamblers and intermediaries such as Hal Chase. With a little help from the crooked Chicago criminal justice system, and possibly Comiskey, the eight players (like the gamblers) avoided any legal punishment for their crimes. But the players could not escape new com-

missioner Kenesaw Mountain Landis, who banned them for life.

The Black Sox case is a perfect illustration of a pattern that nearly all game-fixing scandals in the history of professional team sports have followed. Typically, there are three preconditions necessary before athletes are willing to throw a game (or manipulate a point spread) for money. First, there must be large amounts of money bet on a small number of games (as in the World Series or other championship games) so that the return for the gamblers justifies a large bribe; second, the players must be underpaid by their team—otherwise, the risk of losing a career's worth of income by being caught is too great; and third, there must be an atmosphere of exploitation and corruption among the players. All of these conditions existed for the 1919 White Sox. They resented Comiskey, and were notoriously poorly paid by him, as he ran one of the most profitable franchises in baseball. The baseball establishment before Landis had demonstrated a great reluctance to investigate corruption. It whitewashed scandals whenever it could, as in fact Comiskey tried to do with the Black Sox scandal. Accordingly, it never occurred to the players who knew of or sus-

Ban Johnson, standing right, was on hand for the 1912 World Series (left). Giants pitcher Christy Mathewson made the front page of the Police Gazette *in 1913 (right). That year, he won 25 games and had a string of 68 consecutive innings without giving up a walk. Mathewson was the Giants' lone bright spot in the Series, with two complete games and a win.*

Pittsburgh's Max Carey (top left) led the NL with 61 stolen bases in 1913. Cleveland's Nap Lajoie (top center) collected his 3,000th hit in 1914. Top right: Braves manager George Stallings sits between his two top pitchers of 1914, 26-game winner Bill James, left, and 27-game winner Dick Rudolph. The Federal League's 1914 Buffalo team (bottom left). Legendary athlete Jim Thorpe (bottom right) had six uneventful seasons in the majors.

pected the scandal beforehand to report it. As Buck Weaver asked—after being lumped with the rest by Landis for "guilty knowledge"—whom was he supposed to tell?

The dead-ball period in general was characterized by exploitation of the players and low salaries. In 1912, Walter Johnson wrote a magazine article in which he lamented, "We are free-born Americans with a Constitution [but] our business philosophy is that of a wolf pack." As time went on, baseball's labor relations grew worse, leading to two minor strikes (the first in baseball history) in 1912 and 1918. In the fall of 1912, the players made an attempt, their first since the Brotherhood of the 1890s, to form a union, the Fraternity of Professional Baseball Players of America. Its leader was Dave Fultz, an outfielder who would later become (like Monte Ward) a lawyer. Fultz's organization was timid compared to the old Brotherhood and it concentrated on side issues like conditions for minor leaguers and small increases in salary for the lower-paid players. In 1914 the Fraternity enjoyed some successes, such as convincing teams to pay for play-

ers' uniforms and to provide written reasons for player suspensions, but these concessions were made with the threat of another "Monopoly War" hanging over the owners.

The Federal League arose out of the same causes that precipitated the Monopoly Wars of 1882 to 1903 and was backed by an impressive group of millionaires, including Robert Ward of the Ward Baking empire and oil baron Albert Sinclair. The Feds, though, never posed the same threat to the baseball monopoly as past would-be major leagues. Since there were already two established major leagues totaling 16 teams in 1914, the Federal League attempted to carve out an entirely new market for major-league baseball in such non-major league cities as Indianapolis, Baltimore, Buffalo, and Kansas City, as well as in big-league towns Chicago, Brooklyn, Pittsburgh, and St. Louis. But like the Union Association in 1884, the Feds discovered that the country would not support three major leagues; Fed-

The Federal League landed a few prominent players in its second year of existence, including Joe Tinker, who went from the Cubs to the Chi-Feds in 1914 (top). The St. Louis Feds (bottom), who went 61-89 in 1914, signed Philadelphia pitcher Eddie Plank, who went 21-11 in 1915 and helped the team to a second-place finish with an 87-67 record.

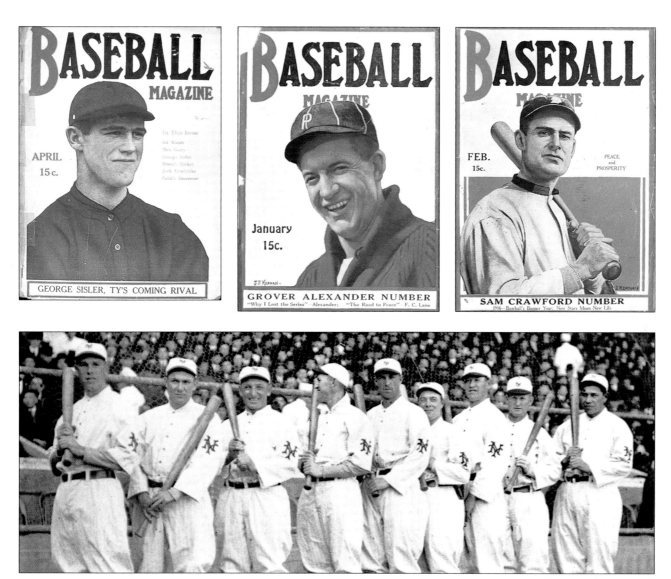

Baseball magazine covers featured St. Louis hitting wizard George Sisler in 1915 (top left), Philadelphia pitcher Grover Cleveland Alexander in 1916 (top center), and Detroit slugger Sam Crawford (top right), also in 1916. The New York Giants Opening Day lineup (bottom) in 1915 included Olympian Jim Thorpe, considered the world's greatest athlete.

eral League attendance lagged behind the break-even point for most of its franchises. In Baltimore, the Feds were even outdrawn by the minor-league Orioles.

After a dry run as a minor league in 1913, the Federal League declared major-league status and quickly took advantage of the low major-league salary structure by luring away almost 50 National League and American League players, including Hal Chase, who got a $3,000 raise to play in Buffalo, and Three Finger Brown, who received $10,000 to become pitcher-manager of the St. Louis Federals. Numerous other players were traded due to Federal

League offers to gain large raises, causing some owners to despair. Connie Mack sold three-quarters of his "$100,000 Infield" to the highest bidder, condemning the Athletics to seven straight seasons in the AL cellar.

But by the end of the 1915 season, the most important Federal League backer, Robert Ward, was dead, and the others were ready to give up after suffering tremendous losses. In a surprisingly generous settlement, the NL and AL allowed Sinclair and Chicago Whales owner Charles Weeghman to buy the Chicago Cubs and St. Louis owner Phil Ball to buy the Browns; two other Federal League owners

A trio of greats (top left): Ty Cobb, left, Joe Jackson, center, and Sam Crawford. Tris Speaker (top right), revived in Cleveland, beat Cobb for the 1916 AL batting title with a .386 average. Boston players Rabbit Maranville of the Braves, left, and Ernie Shore of the Red Sox posed in 1914 (bottom).

were paid amounts in the hundreds of thousands of dollars for their interests, and some of the smaller Federal owners were paid for their players' contracts. The total cost to the two major leagues for the Federal League was about $5 million.

A footnote to the Federal League war is that the Feds initiated several antitrust lawsuits against baseball as part of their original strategy. Most of these were dropped after the settlement, but one wandered through the courts until it reached the Supreme Court in 1922, where Oliver Wendell Holmes wrote a famous decision exempting baseball from antitrust laws on the grounds that it is not interstate commerce. Ever since then, baseball has existed in a kind of legal limbo—with periodic threats of new lawsuits and legislative actions hanging over major-league baseball's head to subject it to the laws that govern other businesses.

On the field in the 1910s, two teams, in particular, dominated. These two teams, in turn, had two strong personalities who dominated. One was manager John McGraw who created his second New York Giants dynasty from 1911 to 1913, when the Giants won three NL pennants in a row. McGraw had a solid infield with second baseman Larry Doyle, who hit .310, .330, and .280 with 77, 90, and 73 RBI between 1911 and 1913; shortstop Art Fletcher, who hit .282 in 1912 and .297 in 1913; and third baseman Buck Herzog, who stole 108 bases over the three pennant-winning years. Catching was Chief Meyers, who hit .332, .358, and .312. But the true strength of the Giants was the pitching of veteran Christy Mathewson—who won 74 games and lost 36 from 1911 to '13 and twice led the league in ERA: 1.99 in 1911 and 2.06 in 1913—and young Rube Marquard, who went 73-28. The Giants played smart, aggressive baseball in the Ned Hanlon-McGraw tradition and had arrogance and pride, summed up by Doyle's famous exclamation: "Oh, it's great to be young and a Giant."

McGraw's American League counterpart, and in many ways his opposite, was Connie Mack, a dignified ex-catcher who managed the Philadelphia Athletics for the astoundingly long span of 53 years. Mack's restrained style was emphasized by his dress; unlike McGraw and nearly all other managers, Mack wore a suit and tie with a stiff, celluloid collar and never ventured out of the dugout or raised his voice. The story goes that Mack would invite the umpire over to the dugout steps, question him politely about a call, and then thank him for coming.

But Mack, nicknamed "The Tall Tactician," was a sharp baseball mind who kept the first charts on pitchers and batters and had a great eye for talent.

"Commy," *a book on Charles Comiskey* (top), *appeared the year of the Black Sox scandal. A home run song was dedicated to home run king Babe Ruth in 1919* (bottom).

Between 1910 and '14, the A's won four AL pennants and three World Series, two of them against the New York Giants. They were built on the greatest infield in baseball: Stuffy McInnis at first, a .308 lifetime hitter who hit .327 in 1912 and .326 in 1913; second baseman Eddie Collins, one of the first Hall of Famers, who hit .333 in 25 major-league seasons and stole 743 bases; third baseman Home Run Baker, who hit .307 lifetime and led the AL in home runs from 1911 to 1914 and drove in 259 runs in 1912 and 1913 combined; and shortstop Jack Barry. The Mackmen were deep in starting pitching, with Jack Coombs (31-9, 1.30 ERA in 1910); Eddie Plank, who won 97 games and lost 41 between 1910 and 1914; and Chief Bender, who led the AL in winning percentage in 1910, 1911, and 1914.

Together, John McGraw and Connie Mack won eight of the 20 pennants in the 1910s.

Pop Lloyd, a shortstop in the Negro League, played 12 seasons in Cuba, where he once outhit Ty Cobb (.369) by batting .500 in a 12-game series against the Detroit Tigers.

COOMBS'S A'S BREEZE TO WORLD TITLE

A manager who assembles a pitching staff that registers an ERA below 2.00 naturally expects to win the pennant. When the A's did not cop the AL flag in 1909 despite a 1.92 ERA, Connie Mack, knowing that it was unlikely he could develop better hitting in the dead-ball era, decided that his pitching still could bear improvement. Right-hander Jack Coombs made Mack's strategy pay off, winning 31 games in 1910 and clocking a 1.30 ERA that contributed mightily to the A's AL-record 1.79 ERA. When the White Elephants also paced the AL in hitting and fielding to nab the "team triple crown," Mack's third pennant followed with almost ludicrous

With Jack Coombs leading the way, the 1910 A's posted an AL-record 1.79 team ERA. Coombs won 31 games with a 1.30 ERA.

ease. Practically the only stumbling block in the A's march to the flag came on Opening Day when they fell victim to Walter Johnson's 1-0 one-hitter at Washington as William H. Taft inaugurated the tradition of the reigning president throwing out the first ball to launch each new season. By July 1, the A's were already so far in front that Mack could begin spotting his regulars like 36-year-old Harry Davis and trying out such novices as 19-year-old first sacker Stuffy McInnis. Many actually think Mack's 1910 club was among the five best teams in history.

The Chicago Cubs were determined to disprove that belief in the World Series that fall. With Joe Tinker, Johnny Evers, Frank Chance, and Harry Steinfeldt playing their final season together as the era's top infield unit and Three Finger Brown joined on the mound by King Cole, whose dazzling 20-4 record set a new rookie winning percentage mark, the Cubs won as easily in the NL as the A's had in the AL. So one-sided had the two pennant races been that the Series, for the first time, was looked upon not only as the end-all but as the be-all for the season.

In the opener, on October 17 at Philadelphia, Mack sat down Coombs in favor of Chief Bender, almost always his first choice in money games. The guileful Bender, whose mother reportedly was a full-blooded Chippewa, responded by spinning a three-hitter to outduel Orval Overall, 4-1. The next day it was Coombs's turn to drub Brown, 9-3. Carting a 2-0 Series lead to Chicago, the A's took two out of the next three contests to land their first world championship. Even though he did not start the first game and the Series went just five, Coombs nevertheless collected three victories, including the finale. He and Bender hurled every inning for the A's as Mack kept Hall of Famer Eddie Plank and 18-game winner Cy Morgan on the bench for the entire Octoberfest.

NAP LAJOIE

Cleveland star rides off with the first Chalmers

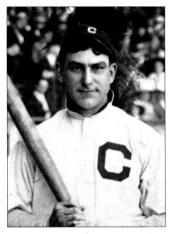

Although never quite reaching his Triple Crown heights (.422, 14, 125) of 1901 again, Nap Lajoie had added two more batting and slugging titles while continuing his expert play at second base following a controversial 1902 sale to Cleveland. He had been so popular as a player and manager in Ohio that the team was briefly named after him. He appeared to be slowing down toward the end of the decade (batting .302 from 1907 to 1909), but in 1910 had a resurgence at just the right time.

The Chalmers automobile company had decided to award each year's batting champion with a new car, and Lajoie battled three-time defending champ Ty Cobb all summer for the prize. Cobb had a comfortable lead entering the final day, and with the Detroit star sidelined by injury, Lajoie knew he needed a perfect performance in a doubleheader with St. Louis to come back. Out of baseball's universal hatred for Cobb he nearly got it—the Browns allowed him to bunt for six straight singles while letting a fly ball drop for another hit—but Ty still won .38415 to .38411.

Chalmers decided to award cars to both players, a move that seemed prophetic when later research showed Lajoie should actually have won the title because one of Cobb's games was counted twice. Lajoie did manage to pace the circuit in hits (227), doubles (51), and total bases (304) that year, and retired in 1916 with a .338 batting average, 3,244 hits, and 658 doubles—all high on the all-time lists. Always popular with fans, players, and sportswriters, the graceful second sacker was elected to the Hall of Fame in 1937.

SEASON'S BEST

- Phillie Sherry Magee tops the NL in BA (.331), SA (.507), RBI (123), runs (110), and total bases (263).

- Philly's Jack Coombs leads the AL with 31 wins and 13 shutouts (an all-time AL record).

- William Taft is the first president to throw out a first ball.

- Comiskey Park, home of the White Sox, opens for play.

- Washington's Walter Johnson leads the AL in Ks (313), CGs (38), and innings (373).

Sherry Magee

- Cleveland's Nap Lajoie leads the AL in hits (227), doubles (51), and total bases (304).

- Cleveland's Cy Young wins No. 500 on July 19.

- Detroit's Sam Crawford tops the AL in triples (19), RBI (120), and runs produced (198).

BAKER'S HOMERS POWER THE ATHLETICS

Injuries held Frank Chance to just 31 games in 1911, and Johnny Evers was hampered all season by a nerve ailment. The amount of action they missed negated right fielder Wildfire Schulte's new 20th-century record of 21 homers and caused the Cubs to tumble from the NL's top rung. Replacing them were John McGraw's New York Giants, who first had an obstacle of their own to conquer. On April 14, the Giants' Polo Grounds home went up in smoke, and while the fire damage was being repaired, McGraw's men had to share the digs of the hated New York Highlanders.

Lefty Rube Marquard, the venerable Christy Mathewson, and relief ace Doc Crandall nevertheless kept the Giants close on the Cubs' tail as among them they collected 65 victories and just 25 defeats. On August 24, the New Yorkers seized first place and then wrapped up the "rag" by winning 20 of their last 24 games. The closing surge buoyed the younger team members, but the veteran Giants, knowing the task ahead of them in the World Series, were less optimistic.

For the second year in a row, Connie Mack's A's had romped in the AL. As good as his 1910 team had been, Mack had an additional weapon in 1911. Stuffy McInnis joined Eddie Collins, Jack Barry, and Frank Baker on a full-time basis to give the A's a young but immensely talented inner perimeter that sportswriters quickly dubbed "The $100,000 Infield."

Until early August, Detroit held strong against the Mackmen, and Cleveland with its two phenomenal rookies—Shoeless Joe Jackson (.408) and Vean Gregg (23-7)—also made a mild run at the A's. However, it was the A's superior pitching that took command of the race, and by closing day, Philadelphia sat 13½ games ahead of the field.

The World Series opened in New York with Mathewson edging Chief Bender, 2-1, giving the Giants a momentary lead. The A's came back to win the next three games, two of them on late four-baggers by Baker. Baker's slugging heroics were so unprecedented in Series play that he was instantly tagged "Home Run."

On the brink of clinching, the A's kicked away Game 5 in 10 innings when Larry Doyle of the Giants tallied the winning run on a sacrifice fly even though he missed touching home plate. The A's failure to protest Doyle's omission might have become one of the game's most notorious gaffes but instead became a footnote. In Game 6, Bender cruised to a 13-2 win, again showing why he was the pitcher Mack wanted when the chips were down.

Philadelphia's Frank Baker got his nickname by hitting two game-winning home runs off Giant aces Rube Marquard and Christy Mathewson in the 1911 Series.

TY COBB

Terrible Tyrus raps .420 in his best year ever

The respected but despised Ty Cobb had followed up his spectacular Triple Crown season of 1909 with another batting title the following year—his fourth straight—but the honor had been tainted somewhat by an attempt by the Browns to hand the championship to Cleveland's Nap Lajoie on the final afternoon. Just to make sure there would be no chance for such a close finish in 1911, Cobb responded by putting together the greatest year of his career.

Setting an American League record (later broken by George Sisler) by hitting in 40 consecutive games, Ty batted a career-high .420 to top Joe Jackson of Cleveland. Jackson's .408 average, by the way, made him the highest-hitting runner-up in this century. A great admirer of Cobb, Jackson still had a chance to catch the leader

when the Tigers came to Cleveland for six late-season games. Jackson approached his hero with a smile and open hand, but when Ty responded with a cold shoulder, the flustered youngster wound up having a poor series that locked up the title for Cobb. Such behavior was typical for Terrible Tyrus, who cursed and spiked his way to a league-leading 248 hits, 47 doubles, 24 triples, 147 runs, 144 RBI, and a .621 slugging percentage—all career highs. He added a major-league record 83 stolen bases for good measure, and only the prodigious slugging of Philadelphia's Frank "Home Run" Baker, with 11 homers, denied him a second Triple Crown. For his efforts, Cobb was named the AL's first-ever "Most Valuable Player" in voting by sportswriters, no easy feat for a man of his reputation.

SEASON'S BEST

Joe Jackson

- Cub Wildfire Schulte wins the first Chalmers Award (MVP) in the NL. Schulte tops the NL in homers (21), SA (.534), RBI (121), and total bases (308).

- Ty Cobb receives the first AL Chalmers Award. Cobb leads the AL in BA (.420), RBI (144), steals (83), SA (.621), hits (248), runs (147), doubles (47), triples (24), and total bases (367). He also hits in 40 straight games, a new AL record.

- Cleveland rookie Vean Gregg wins 23 games and tops the AL in ERA (1.81).

- Phillie Pete Alexander wins 28 games—a 20th-century ML rookie record.

- The Polo Grounds—the Giants' home—is ravaged by fire and has to be rebuilt.

- Cleveland's Joe Jackson hits .408 to set an ML rookie record.

- Giant Christy Mathewson posts 26 wins and leads the NL in ERA at 1.99.

BoSox Nip Giants in WS Thriller

ew seasons have been as turbulent as 1912. Along with the Detroit player strike, Fenway Park and Tiger Stadium, currently the majors' two oldest facilities, both opened for business. For the first time in history, a Washington team challenged for a pennant. Huge personnel turnover also occured, further evidence that it was a transitional season. The New York Highlanders used a record 44 players, and even the A's needed 17 pitchers in a vain attempt to defend their championship.

The A's sag enabled Boston to claim its first AL flag since 1904. In the interim the team had adopted a new nickname—the Red Sox—and unearthed in Tris Speaker and Smoky Joe Wood the best defensive outfielder and the best young pitcher in the game. When Wood went an astounding 34-5 and Speaker hit .383, the Crimson Hose rose from fourth place in 1911 to first, drilling 105 victories to set a new AL mark.

In the NL, however, the more things changed the more they remained the same. Though many new faces dotted the loop, the pennant race still belonged exclusively to the Giants, the Pirates, and the Cubs while the other five clubs scrapped for the remaining spot in the first division. In 1912, the Cincinnati Reds earned the privilege of finishing a remote fourth to John McGraw's Giants, and even Pittsburgh, in second, staggered home 10 games back. The best offensive team in the majors with a .286 BA and 823 runs, the Giants also flaunted the

deepest pitching staff after rookie spitballer Jeff Tesreau was added and banged out 17 wins and a loop-leading 1.96 ERA.

Favored in the Series because of their depth and experience, the Giants fell behind Boston, 3-1. Backed against the wall, Rube Marquard and Tesreau then won on successive days to knot the Series at 3-all and set up the first-ever winner-take-all postseason game. McGraw summoned Christy Mathewson and Boston skipper Jake Stahl called on Hugh Bedient. The two had dueled four days earlier to a 2-1 Boston win. It seemed Mathewson's destiny to triumph 2-1 when the Giants pushed home a run in the top of the 12th, but he then was victimized by two egregious defensive lapses in the bottom of the frame. The first, Fred Snodgrass's muffed fly ball, was more highly publicized, but it was really the foul pop that Speaker hit that went uncaught later in the inning that ultimately permitted Boston to plate two unearned runs and gain a 3-2 victory in one of baseball's greatest postseason games.

The 1912 Boston Red Sox, with a new home and a new nickname, won the AL pennant and the World Series thanks to outfielder Tris Speaker and fireballer Smoky Joe Wood.

JOE WOOD

Foes can't touch Smoky Joe's heat; Wood goes 34-5

Of all the many "what if" stories in baseball history, few are as compelling as the tale of Joe Wood. Arm miseries kept the fireballing righty from achieving the greatness that appeared his for the taking, but for one season he was as dominating as any pitcher before or since.

Wood joined the Red Sox in 1908 at age 18, and within three years he was a 23-game winner. Boston began the 1912 season in brand-new Fenway Park. With Wood leading the way, the BoSox dominated the AL all summer. Joe was 16-4 after a July 4 setback at Philly, but he would not lose again until September 20—winning 16 straight to tie an AL record set the same season by Senators great Walter Johnson. Included in the streak was a 1-0 victory over Johnson before a packed Fenway

crowd September 6. After this, Johnson said, "No man alive throws faster than Smoky Joe Wood."

All told, Wood led the league in wins (going 34-5), complete games (35), and shutouts (10). For good measure, he added three more victories in a World Series triumph over the Giants. Joe finished second to Johnson with 258 Ks and a 1.91 ERA, but pitched 366 innings including the Series. The following spring, he felt the first twinges of the arm woes that would deny him from ever winning more than 15 again. The Red Sox gave up on him after 1916, but he battled back as an outfielder with Cleveland and eventually played on the 1920 world champs. Two years later, he hit .297 with 92 RBI before calling it quits.

SEASON'S BEST

- Giant second baseman Larry Doyle wins the NL Chalmers Award.

- Boston's Tris Speaker sets an AL record for doubles (53) and wins the Chalmers.

- Giant Rube Marquard wins 19 straight games.

- Cub Heinie Zimmerman tops the NL in BA (.372), SA (.571), total bases (318), hits (207), RBI (103), homers (14), and doubles (41).

- Detroit's Ty Cobb leads the AL in BA (.410), SA (.586), and hits (227).

- White Sox Joe Jackson hits .395 with 26 triples (a new AL record).

- Boston's Joe Wood tops the AL in wins (34), winning percentage (.872), shutouts (10), and CGs (35).

- Chief Wilson of the Pirates cracks an all-time ML-record 36 triples.

- Washington's Walter Johnson wins 32 and tops the AL in Ks (303) and ERA (1.39).

Heinie Zimmerman

MACK'S A'S SLAY McGRAW'S GIANTS

Washington's first ML pennant seemed a realistic possibility when the 1913 season began, especially when rookie pitcher Joe Boehling was unbeatable in the early going. Boehling continued to be effective, winning 17 games and, when his efforts were combined with Walter Johnson's 36-7 season, the Senators owned a hill duo that won 53 games and lost just 14. Unfortunately, the rest of Washington's hurlers went 37-50, dropping the Senators 6½ games behind the resurgent A's by the season's end. Were it not for a tinge of complacency the previous year, Philadelphia's triumph would have resulted in its fourth straight pennant. In any case, the A's had the field entirely to themselves. Joe Wood's hand and arm injuries cost the Red Sox any chance to defend their championship, Detroit had no pitching, Chicago had no hitting, Washington had two pitchers and little else, Cleveland for some reason could

never quite click as a team for a full season, and St. Louis and New York were hopelessly outclassed.

John McGraw's Giants likewise were without competition for the moment in the NL. Events in the senior loop went according to form in almost every respect but one. The Philadelphia Phillies, bolstered by knuckleballer Tom Seaton's 27 wins and another 22 from Pete Alexander, achieved second place, their highwater mark since 1901. Even that heady finish left the Phils over a dozen games back of the Giants.

Luckless in the past two fall frays, McGraw made a bold move in the Series opener. He pitted Rube Marquard against Chief Bender, preferring not to risk his ace, Christy Mathewson, against the A's money hurler. Bender won the lidlifter as expected, but McGraw's strategy nonetheless seemed a success initially as Mathewson blanked the A's 3-0 in Game 2 to even the count at 1-all. The next three days, though, belonged to the A's. Complete game wins by Bullet Joe Bush, Bender, and Eddie Plank made Mack the first pilot in the 20th century to snare three world championships. The 3-1 finale marked Mathewson's last fall appearance and saddled him with his fifth loss in six Series outings since he'd won the opener in 1911. Bender, on the other hand, was 6-3 at that point in Series action and topped all pitchers in 20th-century postseason wins.

Connie Mack's Philadelphia A's again were king of the hill in 1913, capturing their third World Series in four seasons. The A's beat the Giants in five games.

1913

WALTER JOHNSON

Big Train goes 36-7, wins "pitching triple crown"

Walter Johnson has been called the greatest right-hander who ever lived. "The Big Train" threw his whiplike sidearm fastball (and not much else) for two decades. Spotted out West by a traveling cigar salesman, who sent awed descriptions of the 19-year-old bush leaguer's mighty fastball ("He knows where it's going, otherwise there'd be dead bodies all over Idaho") to the Senators, Johnson arrived in the big leagues in 1907 as green as could be. After conquering early wildness—he threw 21 wild pitches in 1910—he hit his stride in 1912, going 33-12 with 303 strikeouts.

The following year, Johnson topped this with the best performance of his career and one of the greatest pitching seasons in history, when he went 36-7 and led the 1913 AL in wins,

ERA (1.09), and strikeouts (243) to become one of only six American League pitchers ever to win the "pitching triple crown." His 1.09 ERA, the third-lowest of all time, combined with his league-best 11 shutouts and 55⅔ consecutive scoreless innings (an ML record that stood until 1968) demonstrate Johnson's utter dominance of AL hitters.

His greatest season more or less told the story of the rest of Johnson's career, which lasted until 1927. Though he won 20 or more games for the next six years, Washington settled back into the second division. It wasn't until 1924 that the Senators won the pennant. They then beat the Giants in the World Series 4-3, with Johnson winning Game 7 in relief.

SEASON'S BEST

- Brooklyn's Jake Daubert tops the NL in BA (.350) and wins the Chalmers Award.

- Washington's Walter Johnson takes the Chalmers Award in the AL. He tops the loop in wins (36), ERA (1.09), Ks (243), winning percentage (.837), CGs (29), and shutouts (11). Johnson hurls 55⅔ consecutive scoreless innings, an all-time AL record.

- Philly's Gavvy Cravath tops the NL in hits (179), homers (19), total bases (298), SA (.568), and RBI (128).

- Detroit's Ty Cobb again tops the AL in BA with a .390 mark.

- Tom Seaton of the Phils tops the NL with 27 wins and 168 Ks.

- White Sox Joe Jackson leads the AL in SA (.551), hits (197), and doubles (39).

- Philly's Home Run Baker leads the AL in homers (12) and RBI (126).

Gavvy Cravath

WHAT A STUNNER! BRAVES WIN IT ALL

While the specter of World War I loomed over the Western World, baseball had a war of its own in 1914 as a new alliance bid to become a third major league. The previous autumn, the Federal League, an independent minor circuit, had announced plans to achieve major-league status by raiding NL and AL teams for players. The Chicago Cubs swiftly lost Joe Tinker and Three Finger Brown to the Feds and further compounded the damage by swapping Johnny Evers, whom they judged to be washed up, to the Boston Braves for Bill Sweeney.

Trading Evers may have been the worst transaction the Cubs made to this point. It certainly qualified as the Braves' best move since the late 1890s. After lagging deep in the second division for a decade, the Braves stirred a smidgen of interest in 1913 by finishing fifth under George Stallings. The jury was still out as to whether Stallings was a tactical genius or a tangle of superstitious beliefs.

Though the Braves languished in last place as late as July 18, Stallings continued to evoke his lucky talismans. He knew that the Fed raiders had helped to create a unique parity in the NL and that he had the pitching and defense to prevail if he could just pull his team into contention. By July 21, the Braves were in fourth place, and three weeks later they reached second with only the Giants above them.

On September 2, Stallings's men wrested the lead away from the Giants for the first time and six days later took first for keeps. The smart money was still on John McGraw to whip his team to the front again down the homestretch, but instead the Giants slumped and the Braves copped 34 of their last 44 games to win going away.

The AL race once again lacked drama as the A's won routinely for the fourth time in five seasons. Those bettors who had lost big on McGraw's Giants felt sure to recoup when the Braves met the A's in the World Series. A four-game sweep seemed probable, and many bet for just that to happen. All but a prescient handful bet on the wrong team to sweep. The Braves stunned Chief Bender 7-1 in the Series opener at Philadelphia, won again the following day, 1-0, and then came home so Bostonians could watch in giddy disbelief as their Braves dismantled the A's twice more in succession to cap one of the greatest comeback stories in sports annals.

In a dismal Series for Philadelphia, the A's Eddie Murphy is tagged out at third by Boston's Charlie Deal. The Braves, in last place in July, swept the 1914 World Series, stunning the A's and most fans.

TRIS SPEAKER

Red Sox outfielder shines in all facets of the game

Bought by Boston from Houston of the Texas League in 1907 for $750, Tris Speaker proved quite a bargain over 22 seasons by becoming arguably the game's all-time greatest center fielder. He spent his first two seasons as a bench player, making constant adjustments at the plate and practicing his fielding with Red Sox pitching great Cy Young. Given a starting center field shot in 1909, Speaker's hard work began paying off immediately.

Hitting .309 that season, Tris played the shallowest center in baseball and registered a major league-record 35 outfield assists. Often sneaking in to take a pickoff throw from the catcher and retire startled runners at second, he still managed to track down the deepest flies. Named the American League Most Valuable Player after hitting .383 for the world champion 1912 Red Sox, he hit .338 in 1914 while topping the majors with 46 doubles, 193 hits, and 287 total bases. He was also among the leaders with 18 triples, 101 runs, and 42 stolen bases.

Sent to the Indians in 1916 in a controversial move after helping Boston to another World Series title, Tris hit .388 in 1920 while managing Cleveland to the championship. Speaker's .345 career batting average, 3,514 hits, 1,882 runs, 223 triples, and 792 doubles (most in ML history) rank him among the game's elite offensive players. Perhaps the opening line of his Hall of Fame plaque sums him up best: "Greatest center fielder of his day."

SEASON'S BEST

- The Federal League debuts as a third major league.

- The Braves' Johnny Evers wins the NL Chalmers Award.

- Philly's Eddie Collins (loop-high 122 runs) is the easy Chalmers winner in the AL.

- Washington's Walter Johnson leads the majors in wins (28), shutouts (nine), CGs (33), and Ks (225).

- Phillie Pete Alexander leads the NL in CGs (32), innings (355), strikeouts (214), and wins (27).

- Honus Wagner and Nap Lajoie each collect their 3,000th hit.

- Red Sox Babe Ruth makes his major-league debut on July 11.

- Red Sox Dutch Leonard posts a 20th-century record-low 1.01 ERA.

- Phillie Sherry Magee leads the NL in hits (171), RBI (103), doubles (39), SA (.509), and total bases (277).

Eddie Collins

- Detroit's Ty Cobb leads the ML in BA (.368) and SA (.513).

BoSox Ink the Babe, Oust the Phillies

Over the winter of 1914, Connie Mack was demoralized by the A's shocking loss in that year's World Series and angry at his stars for trying to extort pay raises by threatening to jump to the Federal League. He reacted by jettisoning most of them and claimed he could replace them with players just as good.

Mack was either a knave or a fool. His A's dropped 56 games in the standings in 1915 and were even worse the following year. However, while Philadelphia suffered, the Boston Red Sox thrived. In 1914, the Red Sox purchased a young pitcher named Babe Ruth from Baltimore of the International League after Mack and John McGraw had both passed up an opportunity to land him. A year later, Bostonians hoped for an all-Beantown World Series as Ruth was conceivably on course to lead all AL pitchers in winning percentage and all Red Sox hitters in home runs.

The Red Sox withstood a late charge from Detroit to capture the AL flag, but the Phillies punctured Boston's dream by holding off the Braves and capturing their first pennant. With the races tight for a change in both the NL and the AL, the closest flag chase in ML history was somewhat obscured. In 1915, only .004 percentage points separated the top three teams in the renegade Federal League when the curtain descended.

The FL champions, the Chicago Whales, clamored to make the World Series a three-way affair, but the two established major circuits were not about to let their uninvited guest in for a slice of the pie. In the first postseason game ever hosted by the Phils, 31-game winner Pete Alexander hurled the home boys to a 3-1 win. The Red Sox then bagged the next three games by identical 2-1 counts as Boston manager Bill Carrigan kept Ruth, his rookie whiz, on the bench and relied on veteran pitchers Rube Foster, Dutch Leonard, and Ernie Shore.

In Game 5, back in Philadelphia, Phils owner William Baker put 400 extra seats in right field, and Red Sox outfielder Harry Hooper made him pay for it by bouncing two balls into the temporary seats—hits that now would be ground-rule doubles but then counted as homers. Baker's team, in a sense, was a victim of his greed as Hooper's second crowd-shortened homer came in the ninth inning, giving the Red Sox their fourth straight one-run victory.

The 1915 Red Sox featured Babe Ruth, standing in the top row, sixth from left.

TY COBB

Detroit's speed demon pilfers 96, scores 144

A competitive ferocity that bordered on paranoia prompted Ty Cobb to fight his own teammates, carry a handgun except while in uniform, and go after heckling fans in the stands—but he was always in control on the field. By the spring of 1915, he had already won eight consecutive batting titles, hit over .400 twice, and paced the American League at one time or another in every major offensive cat-

egory except walks. His legendary split-handed batting grip assured he would seldom miss contact; he struck out just 357 times in 11,429 at bats, for an average of less than 15 Ks a year. Ty was routinely bunting his way on, going from first to third on grounders, or breaking up plays with spike-first slides. In the outfield, his aggressiveness helped compensate for a mediocre arm, as he recklessly (and usually successfully) charged every ball hit near him.

One area of the game Cobb especially enjoyed was stealing bases. He did so at will—regardless of the situation—and was never fazed by being thrown out. Injuries had dropped his steal totals the two previous seasons, but there was no stopping him in 1915 as he pilfered 96 to set a major-league record. This mark would stand nearly 50 years until Maury Wills surpassed it in 1962, swiping 104. Cobb's thievery helped him lead the majors in hits (208) and runs (144) while winning his ninth straight batting crown with a .369 mark—not bad for a 28-year-old who had only been in the majors for 11 seasons.

SEASON'S BEST

- Detroit's Ty Cobb leads the AL in BA (.369), total bases (274), runs (144), hits (208), and steals (an ML-record 96).

- Washington's Walter Johnson tops the AL in wins (27), CGs (35), and Ks (203).

- Phillie Pete Alexander tops the NL in wins (31), ERA (1.22), CGs (36), strikeouts (241), and shutouts (12).

- The Phils' Gavvy Cravath hits an ML-record 24 homers. He leads the NL in RBI (115), SA (.510), total bases (266), runs (89), and walks (86).

- New York's Larry Doyle tops the NL in BA (.320), doubles (40), and hits (189).

- Eddie Plank becomes the first southpaw to win 300 games.

- The Federal League folds after the season.

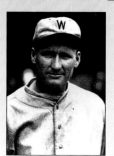

Walter Johnson

BOSTON'S PITCHING STYMIES BROOKLYN

nyone who had been out of the country during the summer of 1915 would have thought, upon returning in October, that newspapers had mistakenly printed the final major-league standings upside down. But it was no mistake. Both Connie Mack's A's and John McGraw's Giants truly finished last in 1915.

The Federal League peace settlement rewarded the Giants with Benny Kauff, the Feds' top star, giving McGraw confidence that he could reclaim the NL throne. Despite two record winning streaks, his Giants were reduced by late September to the spoiler's role. When the Giants played lackadaisically in a critical series with Brooklyn, McGraw was accused by the Phillies and the Braves, both of whom were also in hot contention, of lying down so that his old crony Wilbert Robinson could pilot Brooklyn to its first flag since 1900.

A different accusation confronted Connie Mack after his A's took it on the chin a record 117 times in 1916. Locals called him a charlatan for charging major-league prices to watch a shoestring operation. Mack's eighth-place A's finished a record 40 games behind seventh-place Washington. The Senators, however, trailed the pennant-winning Red Sox by just 14½ games. Now the AL, with the exception of the A's, suddenly achieved the parity that the NL had had, which resulted in three successive former have-nots winning NL flags. Nevertheless, the Red Sox still triumphed by a narrow two-game margin, surviving a season-long holdout by Joe Wood and Tris Speaker's sale to Cleveland when he too demanded a salary hike. Babe Ruth, though just 21, was now considered a veteran hurler, and Sox manager Bill Carrigan slated him to make his first fall classic start in the second game of the World Series.

The Sox took the opener at Fenway Park, 6-5, after quelling a furious four-run ninth-inning rally by Brooklyn. In Game 2, Ruth ceded Brooklyn a run in the first, and the Sox reached Brooklyn lefty Sherry Smith for a single tally in the third. After that, the game settled into the greatest postseason southpaw duel in history. Inning after inning, Ruth and Smith chalked up zeros. When the Sox finally broke the scoreless skein with a run in the 14th, the Series was, for all intents and purposes, over. Brooklyn would go on to win just one game against Boston's superior pitching.

Boston's Babe Ruth went 23-12 with a 1.75 ERA in 1916, just his second full season. He also won a Series game for the champion BoSox.

PETE ALEXANDER

Philly phenom tosses an all-time record 16 shutouts

An alcoholic and epileptic who died broke and alone in a small rented room, Grover Cleveland "Pete" Alexander was his own worst enemy—except on the pitching mound. Out there, the only people in trouble were those crouching at the plate. For 20 years, Alexander made them pay with the same lack of mercy he showed toward himself.

It is ironic that such a troubled man made his living as an expert of control, but it was his pinpoint accuracy (he walked just 953 in 5,189⅔ career innings) that enabled Alexander to rack up a National League-record 90 shutouts. Bursting on the baseball scene for the Phillies in 1911 with a major-league-best 28 victories, he began a stretch of five straight 20-win campaigns two years later—including 30 each year from 1915 through '17. His highwater mark came in 1916 when he led the National

League in wins (going 33-12), ERA (1.55), innings (389), complete games (38), and strikeouts (167) and set a major-league record of 16 shutouts that still stands. Using a live fastball and sharp-breaking curve, he walked just 50 batters all season.

After winning one-third (190) of Philadelphia's games between 1911 and '17, Alexander was traded to the Cubs where his hard lifestyle and epilepsy gradually took their toll. Sent to the Cardinals in 1926 in time to help them beat the Yankees in the World Series with a dramatic bases-loaded strikeout of Tony Lazzeri, the Hall of Famer eventually won 373 games (tied with Christy Mathewson for the NL record). Unfortunately, Alexander squandered his baseball earnings and spent later years recounting his exploits for carnival-goers.

SEASON'S BEST

Tris Speaker

- Cleveland's Tris Speaker leads the AL in BA (.386), SA (.502), hits (211), and doubles (41).

- Cincinnati's Hal Chase leads the NL in BA (.339) and hits (184).

- Phillie Pete Alexander tops the NL in CGs (38), ERA (1.55), wins (33), Ks (167), and shutouts (16—an all-time ML record).

- Washington's Walter Johnson leads the AL in wins (25), CGs (36), and Ks (228).

- Red Sox Babe Ruth wins 23 games and tops the AL in ERA (1.75) and shutouts (9).

- Detroit's Sam Crawford collects his ML-record 312th and last triple.

- On August 13, Ruth beats Johnson, 1-0 in 13 innings.

CHISOX OUTCLASS BUMBLING GIANTS

Very quietly, the Chicago White Sox rebuilt during the mid-1910s. Taking advantage of the troubled financial times during World War I, Sox owner Charlie Comiskey bought and traded for many of the game's top performers until he pieced together one of the dead-ball era's finest teams. In 1917, Comiskey's White Sox became the last team during the 1910s to win 100 games and left defending champion Boston nine lengths in arrears.

John McGraw's Giants, winners by a slightly wider margin of 10 games in the NL, got most of the ink in 1917 and embarked on their fifth World Series since 1905 as solid favorites. It was during the second week in October 1917 that the rest of the nation awoke to Chicago's secret. The White Sox not only had pitching and defense as was their custom, but now they also could hit and score. Moreover, they were smarter and better trained in fundamentals than the Giants.

All of that began to come clear in Game 5 at Chicago. The two teams had previously traded pairs of victories, each winning twice in its home park, and in the fifth contest the Giants looked ready to take command when they bolted to a 5-2 lead heading into the bottom of the seventh. Then the roof fell in on New York. The White Sox belted Slim Sallee for three runs and continued the onslaught into the next inning against Pol Perritt, finally winning 8-5. Red Faber, working in relief after starting Games 2 and 4, was the chief beneficiary of Chicago's 14-hit at-tack. The Sox had also collected 14 safeties in Game 2, making them only the second team to achieve so high a figure twice in a Series.

Two days later, in New York, Faber got his third start against Rube Benton, who had blanked Chicago 2-0 in Game 3. Benton continued his mastery against the Sox—he concluded the Series with a perfect 0.00 ERA—but was undone by his teammates' inability to execute basic plays. In the third inning, Eddie Collins reached on a bad throw and Joe Jackson on a dropped fly. Happy Felsch then got aboard on a fielder's choice as Giants third baseman Heinie Zimmerman chased Collins across the plate in a botched rundown that earned Zimmerman goat's horns, though the fault was not really his. When all three runners—Collins, Jackson, and Felsch—eventually scored, the AL had its seventh fall classic triumph in the past eight seasons.

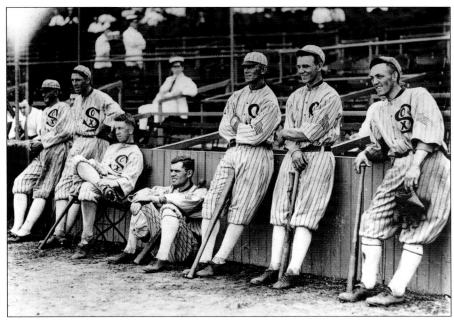

The White Sox were a powerhouse by 1917, comfortably winning the pennant and the World Series.

TY COBB

Revitalized Cobb wins back his batting crown

Despite a .371 average that topped his two previous seasons, Ty Cobb's record string of nine consecutive batting championships was stopped in 1916 by Cleveland's Tris Speaker. When Cobb warmed up for the following campaign by spiking Buck Herzog of the Giants in an exhibition game—then beating him up in a hotel room brawl that followed—it was obvious Ty was hungry to get his title back.

Get it back he did—batting .383 to far outdistance AL runner-up George Sisler (.353) and all other major leaguers. His power totals, which had been declining, were also back up; his 44 doubles, 23 triples, .571 slugging average, and 336 total bases topped the league. His 55 stolen bases earned Ty his sixth title in that department. The revitalized Cobb won batting crowns the next two seasons as well (giving him a record 12 career titles),

but in 1920, his reign as the game's greatest star would end. A fellow named Ruth slugged the ridiculous total of 54 home runs that year—42 more than Cobb ever hit. Fans were drawn to the power game and away from the aggressive base-to-base style Ty had mastered.

Embittered by the changing strategy he felt was ruining baseball, Cobb played in Detroit through 1926 (also managing his last six seasons) and spent two seasons with Connie Mack's Athletics before retiring with a record 4,191 hits, 2,245 runs, 892 stolen bases, and .367 lifetime batting average. The charter Hall of Famer died rich from shrewd investments with his biggest records intact. While hit-leader Pete Rose and steal-king Lou Brock later surpassed two of those high marks, Ty's .367 batting average appears safe.

SEASON'S BEST

•Detroit's Ty Cobb leads the AL in BA (.383), SA (.571), hits (225), total bases (336), doubles (44), triples (23), and steals (55).

•Edd Roush of Cincinnati takes his first NL bat crown (.341).

Eddie Cicotte

•Cardinal Rogers Hornsby tops the NL in total bases (253), triples (17), and SA (.484).

•Phillie Pete Alexander leads the NL in wins (30), Ks (201), CGs (35), shutouts (eight), and innings (388).

•White Sox Eddie Cicotte tops the AL in wins (28) and ERA (1.53).

•Cincinnati's Fred Toney and Chicago's Hippo Vaughn toss no-hitters against each other on May 2, though Vaughn loses his in the 10th.

•Red Sox Ernie Shore pitches a controversial perfect game on June 23.

RED SOX PREVAIL IN WAR-TORN SEASON

When America plunged full force into World War I, baseball was immediately affected. The loss of many players either to the draft or enlistment caused all but one minor league to shut down by the middle of the 1918 season, and Provost Marshall General Crowder's "work or fight" order necessitated an end to the major-league season on Labor Day.

In the NL, where the Chicago Cubs held a prohibitive 10½-game lead, the curtailed schedule had little impact on the standings, but that was not the case in the AL. The Cleveland Indians, who were mounting their first pennant bid since 1908, were just 2½ games short of the Boston Red Sox after the

Already a star on the mound, Babe Ruth was emerging as a power hitter with a league-leading 11 homers in 1918.

season-ending action on Labor Day. Moreover, the abbreviated schedule had created tremendous inequities, depriving Cleveland of a fair shot. As the Indians had been scheduled to play at home most of September, they had participated in many more road games than home games at this juncture. Boston, in contrast, had been scheduled to finish on the road and thus played the majority of its games at its Fenway Park home.

Still, the Indians had a chance until player-manager Tris Speaker was suspended for the balance of the season after he assaulted umpire Tom Connolly during a disputed play at home plate in a game at Philadelphia on August 28. In the remaining week of the season the Red Sox gradually pulled away.

Secretary of War Newton Baker had to grant baseball a special dispensation before the World Series could be played. With so many stars in the armed services and the ball again deadened, never was pitching more dominant than in the 1918 fall match. In six games, the Red Sox tallied just nine runs but nevertheless managed to win 4-2 as the Cubs could post only 10 markers. Career minor leaguer George Whiteman, given a belated ML chance because of service call-ups, was Boston's offensive star though he hit just .250. The overall Series star was Babe Ruth, who ran his postseason scoreless string to a record 29⅔ innings before the Cubs finally broke through for two runs off him in the eighth inning of Game 4.

With better luck, Cubs lefty Hippo Vaughn might have been the star. Loser of the famous double no-hit game the previous year, Vaughn also found himself on the losing side in two of three Series starts despite surrendering just 17 hits and three runs in 27 innings. Incredibly, the entire Cubs pitching staff registered a 1.04 ERA, but it only served in a losing cause.

1918

WALTER JOHNSON

Hurler's a half-run better than everyone else

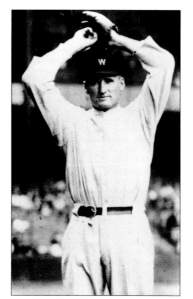

After four years at the top of the American League charts in wins, Walter Johnson failed to lead the league in the category during 1917. His strikeout total was under 200 for the first time in eight seasons, his ERA had crept up to 2.30 (the first year it had been over 1.89 since 1909), and critics may have suspected the 30-year-old was losing his stuff. Despite the fact that the Senators were a sub-.500 team for the second straight season, the Big Train himself feared his hardest-throwing days were behind him.

Further decline loomed on the horizon when Johnson began 1918 with three straight losses. However, he rebounded to post one of his finest seasons in helping Washington improve to a third-place finish, just four games behind the world champion Boston Red Sox. Leading the league in wins (with a 23-13 mark), shutouts (eight), and strike-outs (162, his big-number days indeed gone), he fashioned an ERA of just 1.27, nearly 0.50 below that of any other major leaguer and lower than any AL hurler has posted since. He finished every game he pitched—29 starts and 10 relief appearances—and even batted .267 including five hits in 20 pinch-hitting appearances.

World War I prompted an early finish to the season, but Johnson would have nine more seasons and 140 victories left in his Hall of Fame career—reaching his highest glory with a 23-7 mark to lead the Senators to their only world championship in 1924. His 416 victories rank second to Cy Young, and his record of 110 shutouts appears to be one of baseball's untouchables.

SEASON'S BEST

- Owing to World War I, the season is ended on Labor Day, September 2.

- The majority of the minor leagues shut down in midseason due to the war.

- Detroit's Ty Cobb leads the AL in BA (.382) and triples (14).

- Washington's Walter Johnson tops the majors in wins (23), Ks (162), ERA (1.27), and shutouts (eight).

- On August 1 vs. the Pirates, Brave Art Nehf pitches 20 scoreless innings before finally losing 2-0 in 21 innings.

- Brooklyn's Zach Wheat wins the NL bat crown (.335).

- Chicago's Hippo Vaughn tops the NL in wins (22), ERA (1.74), and Ks (148).

- Red Sox Babe Ruth (13-7, 2.22 ERA) also leads the AL in SA (.555) and homers (11).

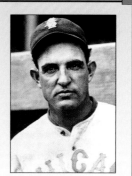

Hippo Vaughn

SAY IT AIN'T SO!
CHISOX DUMP WS

We can only wonder now what would have occurred if Tris Speaker had not picked 1919 to have his worst season. Had Speaker hit anywhere near his career mark of .345 rather than his full-season low of .296, Cleveland might well have won the AL flag. The World Series in 1919 would almost certainly have been played on the square, and there might never have been a push to juice up the ball and tailor the game to the talents of one Babe Ruth in order to wipe away the aftertaste of baseball's most horrendous scandal.

Of course, it is possible that Cleveland on its own merits could not have finished just 3½ games back of the Chicago White Sox in 1919. Many think Charlie Comiskey's crew began dumping games long before the World Series that year. In the permissive climate of the times, as later events would show, the ChiSox were probably not alone.

In terms of talent, though, the White Sox appeared to stand alone. After the 1919 Series was proven to have been fixed, Edd Roush contended that his Cincinnati Reds would have won even if the Series had not fallen prey to suspicious play, but hardly anyone listened to him. Then again, maybe someone should have listened. In 1919, the Reds posted a superior record to the White Sox by seven games and had in Slim Sallee, Hod Eller,

and Dutch Ruether three starters who were a combined 60-22. The trio joined with Ray Fisher, Jimmy Ring, and Dolf Luque in the Series to limit the Sox to just 20 runs and a .224 BA. Ironically, the only two Sox players the Reds did not suppress were Joe Jackson and Buck Weaver, two accused fixers, who hit .375 and .324, respectively, while the impeccably honest Eddie Collins batted just .226 and another Soxer whose hose remained lily-white, Nemo Leibold, stroked an anemic .056.

The 1919 season was truly the end of an era, yet it was also the beginning of one. Four teams in the AL, including the New York entry, still had never tasted postseason action. That would soon change, but the Black Sox scandal was not the only reason the balance of power shifted in the AL, nor even the biggest reason. In the winter of 1919-20, Red Sox owner Harry Frazee, strapped for cash to finance his theater endeavors, sold Babe Ruth to New York for $125,000, thereupon setting off a chain of events that would alter baseball for the next half century.

Sox star Eddie Collins (front row, far left) never forgave his mates for tanking the Series.

EDDIE CICOTTE

White Sox hurler goes 29-7 before throwing the Series

Eddie Cicotte's spectacular 1919 season should be mentioned as a highlight on his Hall of Fame plaque, but instead it is remembered for one of the darkest incidents in baseball history—the Black Sox scandal. Cicotte was among the ringleaders of the Chicago player contingent that conspired with gamblers to throw the 1919 World Series. The incident cost the righty his career and likely induction in Cooperstown.

A thinking-man's hurler who used a repertoire of distinctive pitches rather than overpowering stuff, Cicotte was a solid starter for Boston before changing his Sox to White in 1912 and becoming the ace on an increasingly competitive Chicago team. He led the league in wins and ERA (1.53) with a 28-12 mark for the 1917 world champs. Two years later he was tops in the ML in wins and winning percentage with a 29-7 record. He also had an AL-best 30 complete games and had tossed 306⅔ innings. Chicago won another pennant but was then upset by the underdog Reds in a best-of-nine World Series. The usually sure-fielding Cicotte made two crucial errors in one loss and went 1-2 for the Series. After a 21-10 season in 1920, he was banished for life by Commissioner Landis as one of the eight players who had thrown the Series. Out of baseball at age 36, his 208-149 record and 2.37 ERA would forever be overshadowed by his part in the scandal.

SEASON'S BEST

- The season is abbreviated to 140 games because of the war.

- Red Sox Babe Ruth hits an ML-record 29 homers and tops the AL in runs (103), RBI (114), SA (.657), OBP (.456), and total bases (284).

- Cincinnati's Edd Roush wins his second NL bat crown (.321).

- Detroit's Ty Cobb wins his final AL bat crown (.384).

- White Sox Eddie Cicotte tops the ML in wins (29) and winning percentage (.806).

- Washington's Walter Johnson leads the AL in ERA (1.49), Ks (147), and shutouts (seven).

- Brooklyn's Hy Myers tops the NL in RBI (73), SA (.436), and total bases (223).

- On September 28, the Giants beat the Phils 6-1 in an ML-record 51 minutes.

- Joe Wilhoit of Wichita (Western League) hits in 69 consecutive games.

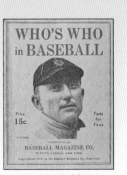

WHO'S WHO in BASEBALL

Ty Cobb

THE 1920s

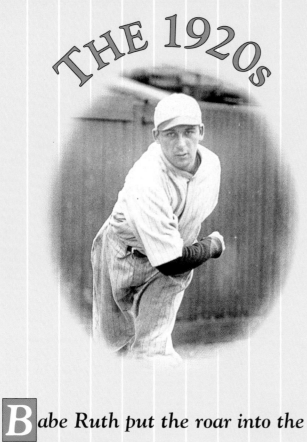

Babe Ruth put the roar into the Roaring '20s with his majestic home runs and crowd-stirring charisma. Scoring was up all over and fans couldn't wait to get to the ballpark.

THE 1920S

By 1920, postwar America was abandoning its sleepy, rural origins and becoming a dynamic, exuberant, urban-based society. Baseball emerged from the war years faced with new competition for the public's time and attention. Motion pictures and radio were to become national rages during the coming decade, and the rise of the automobile would give people added mobility and entertainment options. Baseball's stolid image needed a facelift in order to keep pace with the tempo of the "Roaring '20s." Following the example provided by a burly ex-pitcher, the game's architects tinkered with the rules and ushered in a new era, one featuring revved up offenses and a near obsessive emphasis on home runs and the sluggers blasting them. The 1920s produced an avalanche of hitting and, not coincidentally, attendance records. And, fortunately for the national pastime, the public flocked to watch Babe Ruth redefine the dimensions of the game. Ruth's unique ability to hit baseballs a long distance and his magnetic personality captured the public's attention as no player ever had. He may have saved baseball from dying of a cancer that was eating away at its core.

For 1920 was not just the year Babe Ruth signed on with the Yankees. It also brought forth in September the revelation that players and gamblers had conspired to fix the 1919 World Series for personal profit. Rumors had circulated throughout the winter and summer of 1920 that team members of the Chicago White Sox purposely lost the Series. Then, with two weeks to play in the 1920 season, outfielder Joe Jackson and pitcher Eddie Cicotte confessed their roles in the fix to a Chicago grand jury. A total of eight players were lost to baseball because of their

One of the first acts of baseball's first commissioner, Judge Kenesaw Mountain Landis (top), was to suspend eight Chicago players for fixing the 1919 World Series. Members of the Black Sox and their attorneys (bottom) are shown in this 1920 photograph. The players were found innocent, but were nonetheless banned from baseball for life.

The Negro National League's 1920 Detroit Stars (top left). Cleveland's Ray Chapman, left, readies to throw (top right). Chapman died as a direct result of being hit by a pitch on August 16, 1920. Cleveland's Bill Wambsganss tags Otto Miller for an unassisted triple play in Game 5 of the 1920 World Series (bottom left). Jake Ruppert (bottom right), who brought Babe Ruth to the Yankees.

alleged roles in the scandal. The eight—Jackson, Cicotte, Chick Gandil, Swede Risberg, Buck Weaver, pitcher Lefty Williams, Happy Felsch, and Fred Mc-Mullin—were dubbed the "Black Sox."

The news of their complicity struck like a thunderbolt. So seriously did this episode undermine the public's confidence in the integrity of the game that

sportswriter John Lardner wrote in 1938: "It nearly wrecked baseball for all eternity.... The public came within a whisker's breadth of never seeing another box score, never heckling another umpire, never warming another hot stove. It was close—too close for comfort."

Lardner's account was not pure hyperbole. The unfolding Black Sox scandal triggered a flood of reports—accurate and otherwise—of other fixes by other players, including some of the game's brightest stars. There was talk of suspending the World Series and canceling the 1921 season. As it became obvious that this was not an isolated affair, the lords of baseball belatedly realized that they had to take quick and decisive action to save the game. As a re-

sult, in November 1920 they turned over effective control of the game to an autocratic federal court judge named Kenesaw Mountain Landis by appointing him as the sport's first commissioner.

Judge Landis, who had presided over the 1915 Federal League antitrust suit, was able to restore the public's faith in the national pastime, and he did it by ruthlessly purging the game of its crooked elements. His first action was to place a lifetime ban on the eight Black Sox, even though they were acquitted in their 1921 conspiracy trial for lack of evi-

dence. Landis knew what he was doing. Though several reports of attempts to influence the outcome of games surfaced through much of the 1920s, the rampant game-rigging of the preceding decade was eliminated. By one count, Landis banned, suspended, or blacklisted 20 players from organized ball because of their ties, or suspected connections, with gambling on the outcomes of baseball games. He also outlawed the once common practice of contending teams "rewarding" noncontenders for defeating their opponents. The owners eventually came to regret the power they ceded to the vitriolic Landis, but his puritan imprint on the game, coupled with Ruth's heroics, were greatly needed salves for baseball's festering wound.

The game, of course, survived the scandals and subsequently flourished. The 1920s became known as the "Golden Age of Sports," largely because of baseball's grip on the national consciousness. Many of the greatest players in the game's history dis-

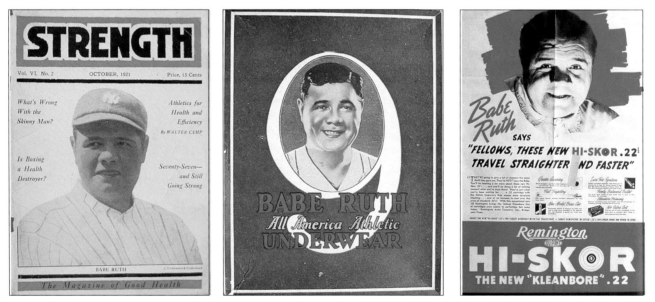

New York's Babe Ruth revised the notion of a hitter in the 1920s, and by the end of the decade, power hitters became the norm. The Bambino was everywhere in those days: as the subject of board games (top), to the cover of Strength *magazine (bottom left),* to ads for All-America Athletic underwear (bottom middle) and Hi-Skor ammunition (bottom right).*

Chicago's Eddie Collins on the cover of Baseball Magazine *in 1923* (top left), *when he hit .360. The Giants again bested Babe Ruth's Yankees* (top right) *in the '22 World Series. Washington's Walter Johnson* (bottom left) *won his first Series game in 1924, as a Game 7 reliever. Rube Foster* (bottom right), *Negro League president.*

played their skills during the decade, including such holdovers from the dead-ball era as Ty Cobb, Rogers Hornsby, Tris Speaker, and George Sisler. Longtime pitchers Walter Johnson, Grover Cleveland Alexander, and the last spitballer, Burleigh Grimes, also performed in this decade. The 1920s also spawned a flock of new heroes headed by Lou Gehrig, Al Simmons, Jimmie Foxx, Paul Waner, and Mel Ott. Indeed, a full 35 percent of the immortals residing in Cooperstown played during the 1920s.

Yet Ruth clearly outshined the others. Not only did he create a new style of play in 1920, he almost single-handedly prevented a widespread repudiation of the game at the turnstiles in 1921 following the Black Sox scandal. As attendance tumbled in both leagues, Ruth retained the public's interest by fashioning perhaps the greatest single season in baseball history. In 1921, the Bambino blasted 59 home runs, batted .378, knocked home a record 171 runs, and scored 177 times, the highest total in the century. En route to slugging .846 that year he also collected 204 hits, of which 44 were doubles and 16 were triples, giving him an all-time-high 457 total bases. That got the fannies back in the seats, to paraphrase a latter-day promoter.

The story of Ruth's arrival in New York is well known. A brilliant pitcher early in his career, Ruth was moved to the outfield full-time in 1919, after leading the league in home runs the year before as a part-time player. He proceeded to swat a record 29 home runs in 1919, an impressive feat considering that only nine blows were struck at his home field, Fenway Park, and the schedule had been shortened to 140 games. Red Sox owner Harry Frazee abruptly sold his new drawing card to the Yankees for $125,000 prior to the 1920 season, after Frazee took a bath financing his first love, namely Broadway shows. His quest for more money, however, led him to make a deal that stands as the worst decision in Red Sox (or baseball) history. Stripped of the game's greatest talent, the Sox fell into a well of mediocrity from which they did not emerge until 1946.

Outfielder Goose Goslin led the league with 129 RBI in 1924, then led the Washington Senators to the World Series championship with a .344 Series average, three home runs, and seven RBI.

season. The Babe repaid this generosity by doubling Yankee attendance at the Polo Grounds and nearly doubling his home run output. His 54 home runs that year must be regarded as a turning point in the game's history. While several players have since exceeded the total, at the time it was regarded as a staggering achievement. Ruth—who personally exceeded the home run totals of every other major-league club that year—was the prime factor in a 40-percent jump in American League attendance, took a good deal of the sting out of the Black Sox scandal, and rewrote game strategy all in a year's work. Brash and bawdy, he emerged as the perfect hero for the Roaring '20s. The Babe spent close to 15 years commanding the attention of the American public as has no other athlete in sports history, and he is still considered the greatest player to ever take the field.

The newly crowned "Sultan of Swat" made an immediate and enduring impression on the game. In the wake of his monumental 1920 season, home run production soared in both leagues. In the years preceding Ruth's full-time move to the outfield, the American League record for home runs in a season was 16, set by Socks Seybold in 1902. Gavvy Cra-

vath, playing in Philadelphia's tiny Baker Bowl, won six National League home run crowns in the 1910s without hitting more than 24 balls out in a season. Before Ruth, seven home run titles in the 18-year history of the American League were won with fewer than 10 blows.

The game's changing emphasis is further revealed by the fact that in 1919 the American League hit a record 241 home runs. The league average in the 1920s was almost twice that. National League batters fared even better. After hitting a meager 207 home runs in 1919, the senior circuit sluggers went on to average 521 four-base blows a year in the 1920s, including a high of 754 home runs in 1929. As balls started sailing out of major-league parks with increasing frequency, stolen bases and sacri-

Top: *Lou Gehrig, left, and Babe Ruth.*
Bottom: *Branch Rickey is credited with developing the farm system.*

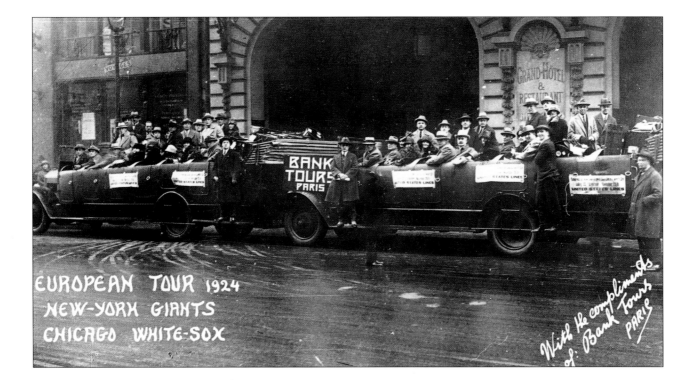

fices—two staples of the dead-ball era—fell dramatically, and did not again become significant offensive weapons until the 1960s.

Nineteen-twenty has been christened the dawn of the so-called "lively ball" era. But what actually caused the increase in offense is a matter of considerable debate. Some historians argue that the baseball was never purposefully "juiced up" to create more offense. Instead, they argue that hitters were greatly aided by the absence of spitballs and other trick pitches, which except for Burleigh Grimes and a handful of others (under a grandfather clause) were banned in 1920. Also, umpires began using more fresh balls in games. In baseball's leaner days, balls were kept in play indefinitely and got rubbed up, softened, darkened, and otherwise "deadened" by extensive use. The simple use of more new balls made it easier for batters to hit the ball hard and far. Furthermore, batters emulating Ruth's uppercut hitting style began swinging for the fences of the enclosed parks built in the 1910s and early 1920s, where the ball carried farther. Whatever the factors, players who batted in both eras were emphatic that the ball "had a rabbit in it" after 1920.

Actually, the increase in offensive output in the 1920s over the 1910s goes well beyond home runs and is unmatched in the game's modern history. All through the 1910s, the major-league batting average

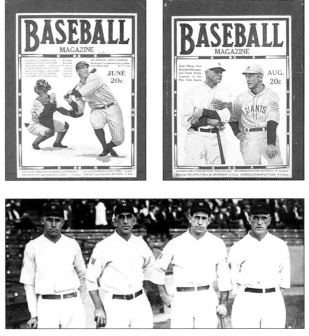

The New York Giants and Chicago White Sox toured Europe in '24 (top). Lou Gehrig graced the cover of Baseball *magazine in 1924, a year before becoming a full-time player (middle left). Brooklyn manager Zach Wheat and New York Giants captain Frankie Frisch squared off on a 1925* Baseball *cover (middle right). The 1925 Senators infield (bottom, left to right): Ossie Bluege, Roger Peckingpaugh, Bucky Harris, and Joe Judge. Peckingpaugh, the AL's MVP that season, had a disastrous World Series with eight errors.*

hovered around .250 and pitchers allowed fewer than three runs a game. In 1919, the American League batting mark jumped to .268 then rose above .280 through the entire 1920s. The league earned run average dipped below four runs a game in only two seasons. A similar pattern prevailed in the National League. In the 1920s, outfielders began to play deeper and farther apart, thus widening the alleys in which line drive hitters belted the ball.

A quick study of the record books confirms the extent to which baseball worshipped at the altar of offense in the decade. Baseball's top average hitters—Rogers Hornsby, Ty Cobb, George Sisler, and Harry Heilmann—exceeded the sacred .400 barrier seven times in the decade. Fourteen of the top 25 batting averages of this century, and 34 of the top 70, were recorded in the 1920s. Six of the top 10 slugging averages in history were posted in the

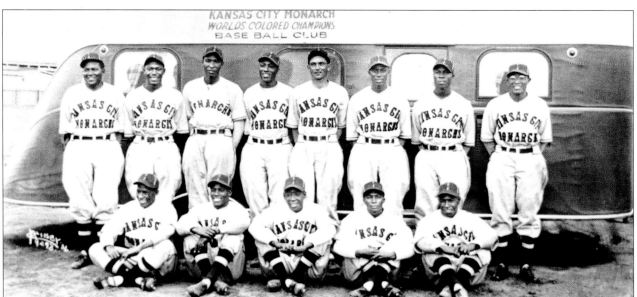

Action from the 1925 World Series (top left), in which the Pittsburgh Pirates defeated Walter Johnson and the Washington Senators in seven games. New York Yankee Wally Pipp (top right) is most famous for the headache he suffered in 1925, which led to Lou Gehrig's streak of 2,130 consecutive games played. The 1925 Kansas City Monarchs (bottom) of the Negro National League.

decade, including five tallied by the incomparable Ruth. Six of the top 10 runs scored totals of the century, including four by the Babe, were established in the period. Existing 20th century single-season records for batting average, slugging average, total bases, hits, runs, and walks were all posted in the Golden Age. Whatever they did or didn't do to the ball, the game changed suddenly, dramatically, and irrevocably in the 1920s.

Equipment innovations followed in short order. As players saw Ruth profit from hitting home runs, they quickly switched to thick-barreled bats with thin handles that increased bat speed and generated more force. Fielders soon realized that their existing mitts were inadequate for the faster-paced game, and the 1920s saw the introduction of a new generation of fielding gloves that were larger and better padded than their predecessors. Better gloves and more sharply hit balls led to more exciting fielding plays, as is reflected by a rise in double plays after 1920. Owners contributed to the home run frenzy in the decade by altering the dimensions of their fields as an aid to their sluggers.

All the new-found action on the field created a lot of commotion at the gate. Major-league attendance topped nine million in 1920, up from 6.5 million in the 1919 season, and averaged 9.3 million a year through the 1920s. The previous decade saw

St. Louis's Grover Cleveland Alexander (top) *was 39 years old when he beat the Yanks in the '26 World Series's final game. Washington's Sam Rice* (bottom) *made a famous diving catch in the stands in the '25 Series.*

only 5.6 million fans a year pass through the turnstiles. Prior to the 1920s, the National League attendance peak came in 1908, and slipped as low as 1.4 million in 1918. AL totals fared better in the 1910s, but still showed an enormous jump from 1920 on. Baseball owners saw an immediate link between the churned up offense and rising attendance totals, and they did nothing to discourage the growing imbalance between batters and pitchers.

Ironically, the frenzy on the field lent stability to the business in the 1920s, once Judge Landis succeeded in restoring the game's integrity. No competing leagues arose to challenge the primacy of the majors as had the Federal League and even the American League in preceding decades. The same 16 franchises remained in operation in the same lo-

Judge Landis on the cover of Sportlife *in 1925. The magazine article focused on Landis's decision to get into baseball.*

cations, and, with the exception of the Yankees, in the same parks. The players remained fairly docile in their relationships with the owners, and many players prospered. As salary levels rose, more players signed out of high school and worked their way up through the minors, so the clubs fielded less collegians as the decade progressed.

Teams continued to be constructed mainly by the purchasing of players from minor-league clubs and other big-league teams. As a result, the wealthiest teams tended to fare the best. The Yankees, under the strong ownership of brewery magnate Jacob Ruppert, spent lavishly to acquire talent while winning six pennants in the decade. They were rewarded by averaging more than one million fans a year, the highest in the majors. The Giants, Cubs, and Tigers, while lacking the Yankees' success in the standings, also flourished at the gate.

Several other franchises, however, struggled to survive. The Red Sox' Harry Frazee sold many of the best players, in addition to Ruth, thus condemning the once powerful club to seven last-place finishes in 10 years. Similarly, the crosstown Braves, drawing a meager 250,000 fans a year, finished last or next-to-last eight times in the decade. It became increasingly apparent that some cities were not capable of supporting two teams, even though overhead costs for

A scandal brought Ty Cobb to Philadelphia in 1927, but the A's and manager Connie Mack (top left) were no match for the Yankees. Negro League star Cool Papa Bell (top right) was so fast he could turn out the light and be in bed before the room got dark, according to teammate Satchel Paige. The most famous team of all-time, the 1927 New York Yankees (bottom), who went 110-44 and won the AL pennant by 19 games.

running a club were minuscule by current standards. In Philadelphia, Connie Mack's woeful A's ended a seven-year stay in the American League cellar in 1922, and gradually rose to the top by decade's end, but like the Phillies, had a rough time turning a profit.

St. Louis was the smallest of the two-team cities and this fact was reflected in the clubs' payrolls. The Browns' entire player outlay in 1925, including the salary of its star player, George Sisler, was barely $100,000, roughly one-quarter of what Ruppert paid his players. To cope with St. Louis's limited revenue potential in the days before radio and television income, Cardinal manager-president Branch Rickey developed a minor-league "farm system" to funnel low-cost talent to his club.

Rickey joined the Cardinals as manager in 1919 and became club president as well a year later. He was the leading innovator of his time and was considered a great judge of talent. His farm system was established by purchasing several "independent" minor-league teams and signing "working agreements" with others, which enabled him to sign players cheaply and control them at a young age. Using

Babe Ruth is greeted at home after one of his record three homers in Game 4 of the '28 Series (top). George Sisler, left, was reunited with Rogers Hornsby in Boston in 1928 (bottom). In his only year with the Braves, Hornsby won the batting title with a .387 average.

this system, Rickey developed such players as Jim Bottomley, Pepper Martin, and Dizzy Dean. The Cardinals won five pennants between 1926 and

1934. Rickey's system was so successful that after buying pitcher Jesse Haines in 1919, the club did not purchase another established player for another 25 years.

The Cardinals' methods, however, drew sharp criticism from Commissioner Landis and minor-league operators, who said that a loss of independence would kill the minor leagues. At the time, selling young talent to the big leagues was a major source of revenue for the clubs. But Rickey and his system prevailed, and the practice became widespread in the 1930s and 1940s. By then, Rickey had unwittingly helped save the minors from bankruptcy; without the support of the big leagues, minor leagues may not have survived the Depression, World War II, and later the rise of other entertainment options (especially television). Yet in the 1920s, baseball's booming popularity provided profits for club owners across the spectrum of the professional ranks.

While the largess was not evenly distributed, the 1920s were a lucrative time for baseball people. Major-league attendance topped 9.5 million in 1929, and gate receipts reached $17 million. Ruth pulled down $70,000 in 1929, and the average salary

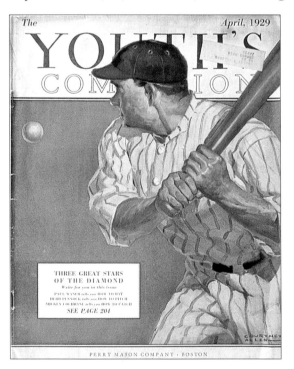

Ty Cobb retired in 1928 with five major-league records in hand, including one that still stands: batting average (.367). His records for hits (4,191), runs (2,245), stolen bases (892), and RBI (1,961) have since been broken. Top: Giants player Travis Jackson is standing by as Cobb, in street clothes, shakes hands with Giants manager John McGraw. The "finest glove in baseball" belonged to Rogers Hornsby (bottom left). New York's Babe Ruth was seen from a different perspective on the cover of Youth's Companion *in 1929 (bottom right).*

for big leaguers was roughly $7,000. Though that may sound paltry by today's standards, it's not a bad sum considering that the major-league average in the mid-1960s was only $14,000.

As the decade drew to a close, baseball had never had it so good. Then on October 29, 1929, the bottom fell out. The stock market crash not only cost many players and owners a great deal of money, it also set off the Depression, which wiped out the prosperity and good will built up throughout the country in the 1920s. Baseball, like everything else, was hit hard by the Depression, and it set off an economic retrenchment that took the game nearly 10 years from which to emerge.

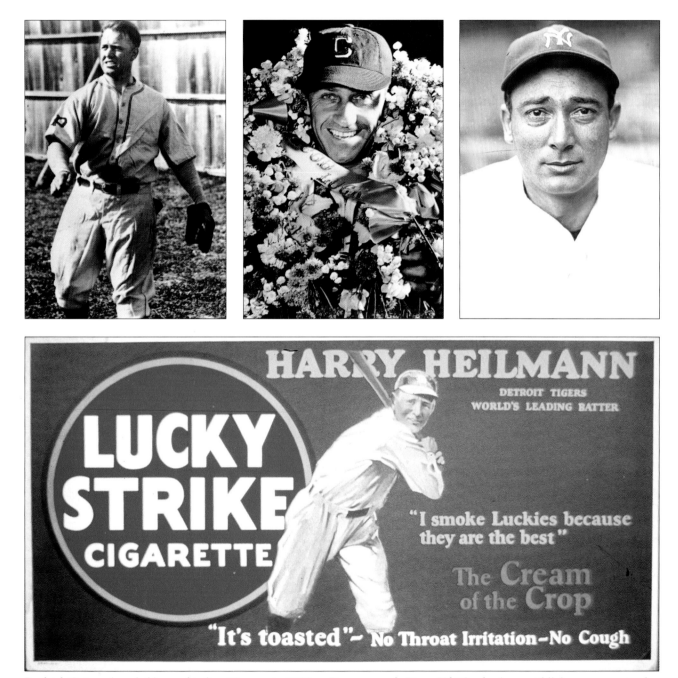

Burleigh Grimes (top left) won his first 10 starts in 1929, a Pirates record. Pirate Kiki Cuyler (top middle) was mysteriously benched in the 1927 World Series, then traded to the Cubs. Tony Lazzeri (top right), part of the '27 Yankees' "Murderer's Row." Detroit's Harry Heilmann (bottom) revealed letters that led to "resignations" by Ty Cobb and Tris Speaker and the ousting of Ban Johnson.

INDIANS OVERCOME CHAPMAN TRAGEDY

Babe Ruth's presence, coupled with the stench over the Chicago White Sox clubhouse after the 1919 World Series, appeared to put New York in the AL driver's seat as the century's third decade began. In recent years the heretofore ragtag team had revised its nickname to the Yankees, adopted pinstripe uniforms, and gotten a financial injection from new owners Colonel Jake Ruppert and Captain Tillinghast L'Hommedieu Huston. Miller Huggins was Ruppert's managerial choice in 1918. Huston had wanted Brooklyn manager Wilbert Robinson at the time and blamed Huggins for the fact that a pennant had not as yet followed. His dissatisfaction with Huggins only grew when Robinson spirited Brooklyn to the NL forefront in the early months of the 1920 season while the Yankees, even with Ruth bombing home runs at an astronomical rate, could not pull away from the dissension-riddled Chicago White Sox and the pesky Cleveland Indians.

In mid-August, Cleveland came to the Polo Grounds, which the Yankees then shared with the New York Giants, for a crucial series. Solid at every position, Cleveland was especially strong at shortstop where Ray Chapman, not yet 30, was just reaching his prime. Then, on August 16, tragedy struck the Indians. On a dank, overcast day, Chapman was hit in the temple by a fastball delivered by Yankee sidearmer Carl Mays. The ball came at Chapman out of the misty backdrop of white shirts in the center field bleachers, and there is some question as to whether he ever saw it.

Chapman took a couple of steps out of the batter's box after he was struck and then dropped to the ground. He was carried to the clubhouse unconscious and later taken to a New York hospital, where he died early the following morning. With his passing seemed to go all chance that Cleveland, already regarded as star-crossed, could hoist its first pennant. Their morale at zero, the Indians returned to Cleveland in a daze, but

Harry Coveleski, left, and his brother, Stan, pictured in 1920. Stan helped lead the Indians to the World Series title despite the tragic death of shortstop Ray Chapman.

Few believed Cleveland would succeed after the death of shortstop Ray Chapman (top). Behind the pitching of Grover Cleveland Alexander (bottom), St. Louis captured the 1926 Series.

player-manager Tris Speaker rallied them magnificently.

Needing a replacement for Chapman, Speaker coaxed owner Jim Dunn to summon former University of Alabama star Joe Sewell north from Cleveland's New Orleans farm team. Later in the season, Speaker (badly lacking a fourth starter to go with Jim Bagby, Stan Coveleski, and Ray Caldwell) persuaded Dunn to buy pitcher Duster Mails from Sacramento of the Pacific Coast League. Mails more than filled the bill, going 7-0 in the stretch, while Sewell hit .329 as Chapman's replacement.

With Bagby, Caldwell, and Coveleski on pace to win 75 games among them, the pennant seemed to belong to Cleveland. The White Sox and Yankees, however, were hanging tough. Then, on September 28, following a Grand Jury investigation, indict-

ments were returned against eight members of the White Sox who were accused of rigging the 1919 World Series. Except for Chick Gandil, who had quit prior to the 1920 season, all were suspended.

On the day the indictments came, Cleveland was in first by half a game. The Indians went on to win the flag by two games over the White Sox and three over the Yankees. "Our Tribe would have won the pennant even had the crummy Chicago thieves been allowed to finish the season," crowed one Cleveland paper, and it was probably correct. Bagby, in the closing days, was nearly invincible. He won his 31st game on the next-to-last day of the season. Bagby could then rest until the second game of the World Series, as Speaker preferred to lead with Coveleski when he learned the Dodgers would start Rube Marquard rather than their 23-game winner, Burleigh Grimes.

Coveleski won the opener at Ebbets Field, but Grimes trimmed Bagby 3-0 the next day. Sherry Smith sent the Tribe back to Cleveland a game down with a tense 2-1 win on October 7. After Coveleski evened the Series on October 9, a capacity crowd of 26,684 came out to Cleveland's Dunn Field the next day to witness a second duel between Bagby and Grimes. What they saw in the first inning was a grand-slam homer by Cleveland's Elmer Smith, the first such in Series play. In the fourth, they saw Bagby hit the first Series homer by a pitcher, a three-

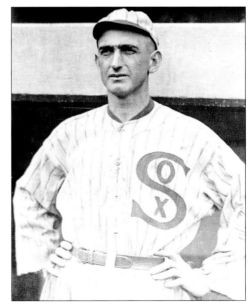

"Shoeless" Joe Jackson proclaimed his innocence after the Black Sox scandal, but was nevertheless banned from baseball.

run blow that seemingly put the game out of Brooklyn's reach. Brooklyn, though, started the fifth with singles from Pete Kilduff and Otto Miller. Pitcher Clarence Mitchell, who had relieved Grimes, was then permitted to bat for himself. (It seems that Mitchell was such a good hitter that he had led Brooklyn that year in pinch hits.)

The crowd got its last indelible visual treat when Mitchell hit a line shot at second baseman Bill Wambsganss, who speedily converted it into the only unassisted triple play in Series action. Bagby then breezed to an 8-1 win. Two days later, after Mails and Coveleski posted successive shutouts, Cleveland was atop the baseball world.

SEASON'S BEST

•In January, the Red Sox sell Babe Ruth to the Yankees for $125,000. Ruth responds by setting ML records for homers (54), runs (158), and slugging (.847).

•Late in the season, eight members of the White Sox are suspended for allegedly dumping the 1919 World Series. Eventually, these players are found innocent of rigging the Series by a Chicago jury. Nevertheless, Judge Kenesaw Mountain Landis permanently bars the eight players from organized baseball. Joe Jackson, Ed Cicotte, and Lefty Williams are among the eight men out.

•Washington's Walter Johnson wins his 300th game.

•Rube Foster organizes the Negro National League.

•Cleveland shortstop Ray Chapman is beaned by New York pitcher Carl Mays on August 16 and dies the next day.

•St. Louis's George Sisler wins the AL bat title with a .407 average. He sets an ML record with 257 hits.

•St. Louis's Rogers Hornsby cops his first NL bat title (.370). He tops the league in hits (218), doubles (44), total bases (329), and SA (.559) and ties for the RBI crown (94).

•Jim Bagby of Cleveland is the last AL right-hander until 1968 to win 30 games in a season.

George Sisler

•The spitball and all other similar pitches are abolished.

•On October 2, Pittsburgh and Cincinnati play the last ML tripleheader.

•Cleveland's Tris Speaker sets a new ML record with 11 consecutive base hits.

•On May 1, Leon Cadore of Brooklyn and Joe Oeschger of Boston both pitch all 26 innings of a 1-1 tie.

•Chicago's Pete Alexander heads the NL in wins (27), ERA (1.91), CGs (33), innings (363), and strikeouts (173).

•In Game 5 of the World Series, Cleveland second baseman Bill Wambsganss makes an unassisted triple play.

BABE RUTH

Yankees' new investment yields enormous dividend

He was, quite simply, the most popular figure in American sports history. A brash, undisciplined kid from the streets of Baltimore, he cavorted with presidents, poets, and paupers. He was the single-most talked about and beloved American icon to emerge from the Roaring '20s, a decade filled with larger-than-life heroes. He was George Herman Ruth—the Babe—and he forever changed the way baseball was viewed and played.

He learned the game at St. Mary's Industrial School for Boys, where he had been sent after being classified as "incorrigible." Then in 1913, the 18-year-old Ruth was signed by the minor-league Baltimore Orioles. One year later, he was pitching in Fenway Park for the Red Sox. By 1916, the 6'2", barrel-chested youngster was the best left-hander in baseball with a 23-12 mark and AL-best 1.75 ERA. He helped the Red Sox to world championships in three of four seasons through 1918. He tossed a World Series-record (since broken) 29⅔ consecutive scoreless innings during this period, but after manager Ed Barrow noticed he could also hit, Ruth began taking a regular turn in the outfield in 1919. He slugged a major league-record 29 home runs—more than 10 major-league *teams* hit that season. Runs in the early 20th century most often came from singles, steals, and sacrifices (the "inside" baseball that had made Ty Cobb famous), and Ruth's critics pointed to Boston's fall to sixth place in '19 as proof the new style was nothing more than a meaningless aberration.

Red Sox owner Harry Frazee's real love was the theatre. As he found himself needing money to produce more shows, he developed a habit of sending star ballplayers to the Yankees for cold cash and warm, talentless bodies. Ruth was a hotter commodity than ever in the winter of 1920. By taking a record offer he couldn't refuse from New York owner Jake Ruppert—$125,000 plus a $300,000 loan on Fenway Park's mortgage—Frazee succeeded in making the worst transaction in baseball history. Babe Ruth had eclipsed his 1919 home run record by July 19, and wound up with an unheard-of 54 homers. That was better than 14 of the 16 big-league clubs. No mere slugger, he hit .376 (fourth in the league) and led the AL with 158 runs and 137 RBI while adding 36 doubles, nine triples, and 14 steals. His .847 slugging average that year is still a major-league record, and his feats drew 1,289,422 fans to the Polo Grounds—a figure which topped the previous big-league attendance record by over 380,000.

GIANTS WIN THE BIG APPLE BATTLE

Just about every baseball figure agreed that the game needed an overseer after the Black Sox scandal, and most secretly felt that for the game to regain its popularity the flamboyant and eternally boyish Babe Ruth had to replace the aging and intransigent Ty Cobb as a public icon. In 1921, both needs were filled when Kenesaw Mountain Landis began his tenure as the game's first commissioner, and the Ruth-led Yankees won their first pennant.

Cleveland tried its best to prevent the latter occurrence, only to fade in the backstretch after Tris Speaker and catcher Steve O'Neill were injured. Between the Indians and the third-place St. Louis Browns was a crevasse of 13 games, but it still represented the Browns' highest finish since their inaugural season in 1902.

The St. Louis NL entry also finished third, marking the first time Mound City enthusiasts could boast that both their clubs had made it into the first division. The senior race, however, really belonged to the Pirates and Giants. The two old rivals vied all season for the lead before New York thought it had settled the issue by sweeping a five-game series between the two in late August. Pittsburgh came back, though, to retake the lead but then sagged in late September as manager George Gibson's pitching collapsed. When the Giants clinched in the final fortnight, it provided the game with a further bonanza in 1921: the first-ever Subway Series with the entire best-of-nine match to be played at the Polo Grounds. This stadium still functioned as home to both the Giants and the Yankees.

Action from the opening game of the 1921 World Series at the Polo Grounds shows Yankee submariner Carl Mays on the mound. The Yankees won the first two games of the Subway Series, but went on to lose the World Series. An injury kept Babe Ruth out of Games 7 and 8; the Giants took advantage with 2-1 and 1-0 victories.

The two teams alternated being the home team, with the Yankees accorded the honor in the first game. Miller Huggins designated his ace, 27-game winner Carl Mays, to oppose John McGraw's pick, Shuffling Phil Douglas. Less than a year later Douglas would be banned from the game for trying to solicit a bribe offer from Cardinals outfielder Les Mann, but in 1921 he was McGraw's most frequent choice when the game was important.

Douglas had no chance in the opener, however, as Mays blanked the Giants on five hits. The following day Waite Hoyt cut the Giants' fare to just two hits in carving the Yankees' second straight shutout. Down 2-0 and still scoreless in the Series, McGraw nearly lost hope when the Yankees racked up four runs in the top of the third inning in Game 3. His disposition changed when the Giants echoed with four runs in the bottom of the frame and then rolled to a 13-5 win on a record 20 hits.

Two days later, Douglas evened matters by topping Mays, 4-2, and the fans only now became fully interested in the outcome, especially when Ruth uncorked his first fall homer, albeit a ninth-inning solo shot in a losing cause. When Hoyt came back to win Game 5, prevented only by an unearned run from posting his second Series shutout, the tide again seemed to turn in the Yankees' favor. But in Game 6, the Giants blasted southpaw Harry Harper, making his next-to-last ML appearance after being idled most of the season by a broken finger.

By throwing Harper to the wolves, Huggins bought an extra day of rest for Mays and Hoyt. Since the two had allowed the Giants only five runs in their four previous outings and Ruth had yet to cut loose with his bat, the Yankees manager saw the Series only going two more games. He was right about everything except that Ruth was about to unload.

In the final two games Mays and Hoyt limited the Giants to just three runs (only one of them earned), but the Yankees came out on the short end of both encounters as Douglas and Art Nehf held the Bombers to a single tally and none in the final 16 innings. An error by Yankees shortstop Roger Peckinpaugh in the first frame of Game 8 accounted for the contest's only run. While this made Hoyt a 1-0 loser in the Series coda, he did tie Christy Mathewson's 1905 fall record by registering a perfect 0.00 ERA in 27 innings.

Huggins readily forgave Hoyt for the loss but arranged for Peckinpaugh to be traded to Boston.

Cleveland outfielder Tris Speaker (top) hit .362 and banged out 52 doubles in 1921, while second baseman Rogers Hornsby (bottom) won his second NL batting title with a .397 average for the Cardinals.

The Yankees skipper also soured mysteriously on Mays. Though he never blamed his ace for the Ray Chapman incident the season before, he was quick to fault him for the two Series defeats to the Giants, hinting that Mays—even while surrendering just five earned runs in 26 innings—might not have given an altogether honest effort. It was that allegation, more than his pitch that killed Chapman, which probably has kept Mays from ever receiving serious Hall of Fame consideration.

SEASON'S BEST

•Yankee Babe Ruth goes on a tear. The Babe clubs 59 homers to shatter his own year-old record, and, in the process, hits his 137th career homer, breaking Roger Connor's mark of 136. Ruth also sets a new ML RBI record with 171. In addition to producing an all-time ML-record 457 total bases, he scores 177 runs, a post-1900 record that still stands.

•Rogers Hornsby, now installed at second for the Cards, cops his second NL bat crown at .397. He tops the NL in hits (235), RBI (126), runs (131), doubles (44), and total bases (378). He also leads in runs produced (236), OBP (.458), and SA (.639) and ties in triples (18).

•Yank Carl Mays leads the AL in winning percentage (.750), innings (337), and games (49) and ties for the lead in wins (27) and saves (seven).

•Detroit's Harry Heilmann hits .394 to win his first AL bat title. He also leads in hits (237).

•The introduction of a livelier ball results in the Tigers hitting .316 as a team, an AL record. The AL as a whole hits a league-record .292.

•Red Faber's AL-leading 2.48 ERA is the only ERA figure below 3.00 in that circuit. Faber and teammate Dickie Kerr account for 44 of the White Sox's 62 victories.

•On August 5, Harold Arlin of radio station KDKA in Pittsburgh does the first broadcast of a baseball game.

Harry Heilmann

•Chewing gum magnate William Wrigley buys the Cubs.

•On April 28, Cleveland pitcher George Uhle collects six RBI in a game.

•The game's moguls rule that 17 pitchers can continue to use the spitball for the rest of their careers.

•Specs Toporcer of the Cards is the first infielder in ML history to wear glasses.

•Red Sox Stuffy McInnis's .999 fielding average is a new ML record for first basemen.

•Detroit's Ty Cobb collects his 3,000th hit at age 34.

•The Browns' Jack Tobin, George Sisler, and Baby Doll Jacobson all collect more than 200 hits.

•Brooklyn's Burleigh Grimes leads the NL in CGs (30) and Ks (136), and he ties for the lead in wins (22).

BABE RUTH

Bambino enjoys his greatest year: .378 BA, 59 HRs

Babe Ruth's natural ability would have made him a star in any generation, but part of what set his career apart was timing. Leaving puritan Boston and setting up shop in Manhattan just as the country was beginning its most frivolous and free-spirited decade, Ruth came to personify all the wild and wonderful hopes of Americans with his strength and vitality on and off the field. He hit hard, lived hard, even struck out hard—and he did it all with a smile on his face and a stylish flair for the dramatic.

There seemed nothing he could do for an encore after his spectacular 1920 season—a year so fantastic few thought it would ever be duplicated—but the Babe, of course, found a way. He had five homers in April, no less than 10 for any other month of the season, and 59 by year's end to top his own year-old record by five. He raised his average slightly to .378, had 119 extra-base hits (including 16 triples

and 44 doubles), and again led the league in both runs (177) and RBI (171). His league-leading slugging average was down a point to .846, but he posted a career-high 17 steals and amassed 457 total bases—setting another record that has successfully stood the test of time. By amassing 204 hits and 144 walks, he was reaching base more than half the time

he came to bat. When he hit his 138th career homer on July 15, he became the greatest home run hitter in major-league history at the tender age of 26. He even found time to pitch two games—winning both—all while leading the Yankees to their first pennant ever.

The Yanks beat the crosstown Giants in the first two games of the World Series, but Ruth scraped up his elbow stealing third base in Game 3 and developed an infection that hampered him the rest of the Series. He wound up hitting .313 with just one homer as the Yankees lost the best-of-nine affair in eight games. Ruth drew criticism from *New York Sun* columnist Joe Vila for his overly dramatic style of limping through the remaining contests in bandages. Publicity over the incident displayed the Babe's ability to draw attention no matter what he was doing and helped his legend take on greater shape. His big appetite for food and life, together with his other adventures, were front-page news; people everywhere were drawn in by his magnetism. Teams throughout baseball were now looking for power hitters and abandoning the "inside" game. Even as they would find them and averages and home run totals soared, Ruth maintained his exalted spot high atop the game.

GIANTS WHIP YANKS IN NY REMATCH

Fans in St. Louis prayed in 1922 for a repeat of the 1921 campaign: a World Series between two teams representing the same city. They got their wish—a one-city Series—but unfortunately the combatants were also repeat performers. When October rolled in, it was once again the Yankees and Giants playing for all the glory at the Polo Grounds rather than the Cardinals and the Browns going for the gold at Sportsman's Park.

The threadbare Cardinals had only begun sharing Sportsman's the previous season after forsaking Robison Field, the last wooden facility in the ma-

jors. Improvement in the standings had followed rapidly, owing to manager Branch Rickey's commitment to grooming players on minor-league farm teams and the continued development of budding young stars such as Rogers Hornsby and Austin McHenry. In 1922, Hornsby set a galaxy of NL records as he crushed 42 homers and totaled 152 RBI and 250 hits while batting .401, but the Cards would drop a notch from third to fourth when McHenry went home to Ohio in midseason after being diagnosed with a brain tumor. He died that November.

In a rematch of the 1921 Subway Series, the Giants again topped the Yankees in the 1922 World Series, played at the Polo Grounds. The Giants hit .309 as a team; Bob Meusel was the only Yankee to hit .300. Babe Ruth managed just one RBI.

Irish Meusel, right, of the Giants, brother of Yankees' Bob Meusel, left, knocked in 132 runs in 1922. The brothers faced each other in three consecutive World Series, from 1921 to 1923.

The other St. Louis entry shot to its best performance ever, winning 93 games, as the Browns produced in George Sisler the one player in 1922 capable of exceeding even Hornsby. Though hampered in the late going by an arm injury, Sisler hit .420 and led the AL with 134 runs. Accompanying him were left fielder Ken Williams, who wrested both the home run and RBI crowns away from Babe Ruth; center fielder Baby Doll Jacobson; and right fielder Jack Tobin. The following year the three would become the only trio of outfield teammates to hit .300 as a unit four years in a row. It was in 1922 that Jacobson and Williams joined with Sisler and second baseman Marty McManus to make the Browns the first team with four 100-RBI men.

But even all that firepower was still not enough to put the Browns over the top. After battling the Yankees dead even all season, the Browns came up one game short. The reason for their narrow miss, rather surprisingly, was not inadequate pitching—the Browns actually led the AL in ERA. What the Yankees had more of than the Browns (and indeed any other AL team) were skilled glovemen, particu-

larly in the infield. Wally Pipp led AL first basemen in total chances, Aaron Ward topped second sackers in assists, Everett Scott did the same for shortstops, and Joe Dugan replaced fading Frank Baker at third late in the season. The four helped compensate for a subpar year from Ruth, who missed the first month of the season while serving a suspension for engaging in an illegal barnstorming tour the previous fall.

The Giants followed the same formula to their second straight pennant—an exceptionally talented infield crew, steady if seldom spectacular pitching, and a long-ball hitting left fielder. Their infield consisted of three Hall of Famers—George Kelly at first, Frankie Frisch at second, and Dave Bancroft at short—plus a third sacker in Heinie Groh who had the best glove of the lot and still holds the NL season record for the highest fielding average at his position. On the mound, manager John McGraw had no 20-game winners and lacked a reliable fourth starter after Phil Douglas was banished in midsummer. Despite this fact, he was still enjoying the best relief pitching in the loop. McGraw's counterpart to Ruth was Irish Meusel, brother of Yankees right fielder Bob Meusel.

The siblings both had a good Series in 1922, Bob hitting .300 and Irish leading all participants in RBI, but Ruth again fell flat in postseason competition. In five contests, he produced just three total bases and one RBI while hitting .118. With the Se-

Ken Williams (left) did it all for the Browns in 1922, leading the AL in homers (39) and RBI (155) while hitting .337. Alas, the Browns fell short of the AL pennant. Lefty Eppa Rixey (right) led second-place Cincinnati with a league-leading 25 wins in 1922.

ries restored to a best-of-seven format, only a 3-3 tie in the second encounter—the game was called due to darkness after 10 innings—kept the Yankees from going down to defeat in four straight games.

Minutes after the final game ended, Til Huston smashed a glass and vowed, "Miller Huggins has managed his last game for the Yankees." Instead it developed that Huston had watched his last game as

Yankees co-owner, for Ed Barrow, serving in his first season as general manager, threatened to quit unless Huston stopped meddling with the operation of the team. The following May, Jake Ruppert bought out Huston's share for $1.5 million. With Huston no longer around to snipe at him, Huggins for the first time began to feel secure enough in his job to do it his way.

SEASON'S BEST

• Suspended part of the season for an illegal barnstorming tour the previous fall, the Yankees' Babe Ruth drops to 35 homers.

• The AL gives out a league MVP Award for the first time; George Sisler of the Browns wins handily. Sisler leads the AL with a .420 BA, a record for first basemen in this century. He also hits in 41 straight games, a new AL record.

• Ken Williams of the Browns becomes the new AL homer king (39). Williams also leads in RBI (155), total bases (367), and runs produced (244). On April 22, he becomes the first player since 1897 to hit three homers in a game.

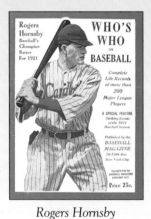

Rogers Hornsby

• St. Louis's Rogers Hornsby sets post-1900 NL records with 42 homers, 152 RBI, and a .722 slugging average. His .401 BA makes him the first NLer this century to top the .400 mark. Hornsby hits in 33 straight games.

• Eddie Rommel of the seventh-place A's leads the AL with 27 wins.

• Ray Grimes of the Cubs drives in at least one run in an ML-record 17 straight games.

• White Sox owner Charlie Comiskey forks over $125,000 to San Francisco of the Pacific Coast League for Willie Kamm.

• Detroit's Harry Heilmann hits 21 homers; 10 of them come in Shibe Park against the A's.

• On August 25, the Cubs beat the Phils, 26-23, in the highest-scoring game in ML history.

• The Supreme Court rules baseball is a sport, not a business, and thus not subject to anti-trust laws.

• Pittsburgh's Max Carey sets a stolen-base percentage record of .962 when he's successful in 51 of 53 attempts. Carey steals a record (since broken) 31 consecutive bases.

• On April 30, White Sox Charlie Robertson tosses a perfect game vs. Detroit—baseball's last until 1956.

• Chicago's Red Faber tops the AL in ERA (2.80), CGs (31), and innings (353).

GEORGE SISLER

Brownie hits a sizzling .420 en route to MVP Award

Babe Ruth's record-smashing 54 homers in 1920 had been the most staggering example of an overall shift toward greater power and more offense in general throughout the major leagues. Suddenly pitching and defense no longer dominated the game, and the reaction of fans to Ruth's exploits prompted major-league officials to take efforts to keep game-day balls in better shape. The whiter, lighter balls seemed to explode off bats. While no one excelled at this new style better than the Babe, for several years—including one glorious 1922 season—George Sisler of the St. Louis Browns came close.

An Ohio native who had starred for the Browns at first base since 1915 after a brief trial with the club as a pitcher (including two victories over Walter Johnson), Sisler reached a new level by playing every inning of all 154 games in 1920 en route to a major league-record 257 hits. His .407 batting average that year also topped the majors, and his 19 homers were second only to Ruth. Adding in 49 doubles, 18 triples, and 42 stolen bases, it was what almost anybody would consider a career year—but for this stern, silent perfectionist it was only a warm-up for what would come two years later.

After hitting .371 in '21, Sisler took advantage of a series of suspensions and illnesses that beset Ruth in 1922, and managed to grab the spotlight and the American League Most Valuable Player Award. Playing his usual flawless first base, George put together a then-AL record 41-game hitting streak en route to a .420 batting average—tops in the majors and third in big-league history behind crosstown-rival Rogers Hornsby's .424 posting with the Cardinals in 1924 and Nap Lajoie's .422 mark with the Philadelphia A's in 1901. Always capable of beating out an infield hit or bunt, the left-handed Sisler still preferred to choke up on a 42-ounce hickory bat and pull the ball with the best power hitters. Years later, he would claim proudly that he never bunted once during his 41-game streak—the last several games of which he played despite a severe shoulder injury that eventually forced him to swing one-handed.

Slight (at just 5'10", 170 pounds) but very resourceful, Sisler knocked in 105 runs in '22 despite falling off to just eight home runs. He added an AL-best 18 triples and 51 steals in carrying the Brownies through a summer-long pennant battle with the Yankees that fell one game short. Eye trouble that plagued him late in his career and the fact he never played on a pennant winner probably cost Sisler even greater fame, but his .340 lifetime batting average, 375 steals, and 2,812 hits assured him a spot in Cooperstown. A Sisler finally made it into the World Series when his son, Dick, hit a home run on the final day of the 1950 season to put the Phillies into the fall classic against the Yankees. Unfortunately, like his father before him, Dick and his team were defeated by the Bronx Bombers.

YANKS KO GIANTS IN ROUND THREE

In 1923, Yankees manager Miller Huggins made his special project the reformation of Babe Ruth, who disdained training rules and abhorred the notion of accepting discipline from a man he labeled not altogether affectionately "The Runt." Eventually, a sort of uneasy truce was struck between the two with Ruth according his manager a measure of respect, if never quite admiration. Huggins was willing to settle for that, especially when Ruth nearly fashioned a Triple Crown season in 1923.

With his second reclamation project, Huggins was less successful. Still disgruntled over pitcher Carl Mays's failure to bring the Yankees a world championship, Huggins punished Mays by pitching him so

rarely in 1923 that other AL teams assumed his arm was shot and allowed him to pass through waivers to the NL, where he had several more fine seasons in Cincinnati. Mays's departure was little felt in 1923, though, as Huggins possessed no fewer than five pitchers who won between 16 and 21 games. Led by Sad Sam Jones (21-8), the quintet drove the Yankees to their third straight flag by a whopping 16-game margin over second-place Detroit.

For the third straight time, Huggins's men were confronted in their quest for their first world championship by John McGraw's New York Giants. Though the Giants had no slugger on the order of Ruth, their starting lineup continued to be graced by a dazzling array of future Hall of Famers and was backed by a solid corps of subs led by veteran outfielder Casey Stengel and rookie shortstop Travis Jackson. If the Giants had a weakness, it was the absence of a take-charge pitcher as, for the second year in a row, McGraw lacked a 20-game winner. Pushed hard all season by a revived Cincinnati team that featured not one, but *three* 20-game winners, the Giants finally asserted their superior offensive punch to win by 4½ games.

Although the World Series for the third consecutive season was the exclusive property of

The Yankees, now in their own ballpark, again met New York's other team in the '23 World Series. This time, the Yankees prevailed, winning the first of their record 22 championships.

Cincinnati's Dolf Luque (top left) had a career year in 1923 with 27 wins and a 1.93 ERA. The "House That Ruth Built" (top right) opened in 1923. Frankie Frisch (bottom left) led the Giants to their third straight pennant with a .348 average. Detroit's Harry Heilmann (bottom right) led the AL with a .403 average.

Giants put together a 5-4 victory when Stengel hit a line drive in the ninth inning between left fielder Bob Meusel and center fielder Whitey Witt. Stengel legged it out for a game-winning inside-the-park homer. This dinger was the first of a multitude of postseason four-baggers in "The House That Ruth Built." Two days later in Game 3, Stengel clubbed the second homer in Yankee Stadium postseason history when he lifted a drive over the right field wall. His blast on this occasion represented the lone run in a 1-0 duel between Art Nehf and Sam Jones.

After producing just five four-baggers during the regular season, Stengel seemed poised to become perhaps the most improbable Series hero since 1906 when substitute third baseman George Rohe propelled the White Sox to their astonishing upset of the Cubs. The other four days of fall action in 1923 belonged to the Yankees, however, as Ruth finally came out of his Series slumber with a vengeance.

In Game 2 at the Polo Grounds, the Babe launched a solo shot over the roof in right to break a 1-1 tie in the fourth. Just one inning later, the Babe homered again to end the scoring in a 4-2 Yankees win. After the Yankees won Games 4 and 5 to grab a 3-1 lead, Ruth opened the scoring in Game 6 with a first-inning homer off Art Nehf to put the Yankees up 1-0. By the eighth inning, the Giants had pulled ahead 4-1. Nehf, however, suddenly lost his effectiveness, and the Yankees scored five times to go in front 6-4.

New York, there was a significant innovation in 1923. For the first time since the mid-1910s, the two New York rivals occupied separate homes. On April 18, 1923, Yankee Stadium opened for business directly across the river from the Polo Grounds. So much ballyhoo accompanied its debut that the Giants immediately felt compelled to embellish and expand their own home, increasing its capacity to 54,000.

Yankee Stadium was host to the Series opener on October 10. With a record 55,307 on hand, the

When the Giants went down quietly in the bottom of the eighth and again in the ninth against Sam Jones, the Bronx Bombers rang up the first of their record 22 world championships. Though Ruth was ostensibly the Series MVP with eight runs, eight walks, and a .368 BA, the Yankees' fielding was just as large a factor in their triumph. While getting five gift runs in the Series on Giant errors, the Yankees made McGraw's men earn every one of their 17 tallies.

His judgment vindicated now that Huggins had finally manufactured a world champion, owner Jake Ruppert waited for, and fully expected, an encore performance in 1924.

SEASON'S BEST

•New York's Babe Ruth is selected the AL's MVP. Ruth regains the AL homer crown by belting 41. Among his other notable achievements for the the year, he reaches base an all-time record 379 times and collects a record 170 walks. Ruth is the AL runner-up in batting with a .393 BA, his personal best. His .545 OBP sets an ML record that will stand until 1941.

•Rogers Hornsby of St. Louis takes his fourth consecutive NL bat crown (.384).

•Detroit's Harry Heilmann begins his odd knack for copping the AL bat crown every other year as he hits .403.

•The Phils' Cy Williams hits 41 homers to top the NL.

•Cleveland's Tris Speaker sets a new modern record for doubles with 59.

•Yankee Stadium opens on April 18; New York wins 4-1 over Boston on a three-run homer by Ruth.

•Radio station WEAF in New York becomes the first station to broadcast a World Series.

•The Yankees collect an AL-record 30 hits vs. Boston on September 28.

•On July 7 vs. Boston, Cleveland scores 13 runs in the sixth and wins 27-3.

Tris Speaker

•New York Giants pitcher Jack Bentley hits .427 in 89 at bats.

•On August 24, Yankee Carl Mays beats the A's for an AL-record 23rd consecutive time.

•George Burns, Red Sox first baseman, performs an unassisted triple play on September 14. Ernie Padgett, Braves shortstop, performs an unassisted triple play on October 6.

•Yankee Everett Scott leads AL shortstops in fielding average for the eighth consecutive year.

•Detroit's Ty Cobb scores his 1,736th run, moving him ahead of Honus Wagner on the all-time list.

•Paul Strand of Salt Lake City in the PCL collects an organized baseball-record 325 hits in a season.

•Pete Schneider of Vernon in the PCL hits five homers and a double in one game.

•Giant Frankie Frisch leads the NL in hits (223), total bases (311), and runs produced (215).

BABE RUTH

The Babe lops off the fat, belts out the homers

Babe Ruth's injured elbow felt better after the 1921 World Series, and so he had prepared for an off-season barnstorming tour throughout Pennsylvania, upstate New York, and Oklahoma with a team he called "The Babe Ruth All-Stars." World Series players were not supposed to engage in such activities, but Ruth had matched his yearly salary on similar trips the previous two years and wanted the money. He went on tour despite the sharp warnings of Commissioner Kenesaw Mountain Landis, and when it was through he and teammate Bob Muesel were each fined their World Series loser's share of $3,362 and suspended for the first six weeks of the 1922 season.

Not seeing action until May 20, Ruth had gone 0-for-4 to loud booing in his first game and struggled much of the season. Fighting with umpire Bill Dinneen cost him another five-game suspension in June, and in the end he batted just .315 in 110 games with 35 home runs—all dramatic drop-offs from the previous two seasons. The Yankees lost in the World Series again to the Giants, and an out-of-shape Ruth hit a woeful .118 with no homers. The crowning touch on the dismal year came when future New York City mayor Jimmy Walker blasted Ruth at a postseason dinner for letting down the "dirty-faced kids" who looked up to him. Tearful and hurt, Ruth vowed to work out all winter on his Sudbury, Massachusetts, farm (where he occasionally visited his wife Helen between escapades) and return stronger than ever in 1923—when the team would be moving out of the Polo Grounds and into the brand-new Yankee Stadium.

The Bambino lived up to his word, shedding 20 pounds on the farm and christening Yankee Stadium (which would come to be known as "The House That Ruth Built" with an Opening Day home run to beat the Red Sox before a record crowd of 74,217. Leading the Yankees to their third straight pennant in a runaway, the Babe batted a career-high .393 (second in the AL to Harry Heilmann's .403) and led the circuit in homers (41), RBI (131), runs (151), slugging (.764), and total bases (399) while stealing 17 bases and walking a major league-record 170 times—nearly half of them coming intentionally. Ruth's annual salary of $52,000 (the average major-league wage was well under $10,000 at the time) had fueled frustrated fans the year before, but now nobody seemed to mind—especially when he topped off the year with three homers and a .368 mark in postseason play as the Yankees finally defeated the Giants in the World Series.

SENATORS PREVAIL IN WS CLASSIC

In the spring of 1924, oddsmakers favored a fourth straight all-New York World Series. Certainly it was inconceivable that any AL team could unseat the Yankees. The Tigers and the Indians, second and third respectively in 1923, did not have enough pitching, and Washington, which had snuck into fourth, finally had hitters to go with Walter Johnson. The problem was that Johnson was now 36 years old and on the downside of a lustrous, though painfully frustrating, career. After nearly spurring the Senators to a pennant in 1913, the Big Train had endured a string of mediocre teams, and his 1924 club promised to be yet one more.

In what would be seen as primarily a box-office ploy, Washington owner Clark Griffith replaced manager Donie Bush after the 1923 season with second sacker Bucky Harris. Though just 27 years of age, Harris accomplished something innumerable older and more experienced men had been unable to do ever since the first Washington major-league team surfaced in 1871. With a revitalized Johnson as his mound bellwether and

outfielders Sam Rice and Goose Goslin as his offensive beacons, Harris prodded Washington to its first ML pennant after an exhausting fight with the Yankees and the hard-hitting Tigers. When the three teams crossed the tape, the Senators were just two games ahead of the Yankees and six up on Detroit.

The National League chase was even closer, making the 1924 campaign the most exciting season since 1908 to fans of both loops. McGraw's Giants led the majors with 857 runs and a .300 batting average. For the third consecutive year, however, they lacked a clear-cut staff leader. Pitchers Jack Bentley and Virgil Barnes tied for the club lead with 16 wins each, while Art Nehf and Hugh McQuillan contributed 14 apiece. The quartet's combined total of 60 victories exceeded by only 10 the triumphs achieved by Brooklyn's star duo of Dazzy Vance and Burleigh Grimes (50 total).

The NL leader in wins, Ks, and ERA, Vance had Brooklyn on the threshold of ending the Giants' three-year reign as the season entered the final weekend. While

Frankie Frisch, left, and the Giants were back in the World Series in 1924, but against a new opponent. Bucky Harris, right, just 27 years old, managed Washington to its first pennant and Series win.

that it go forward. On October 4, Washington's Griffith Stadium became the first park outside New York City to house a postseason game since 1920. Johnson was, of course, Harris's choice to open, and McGraw countered with Nehf.

Though both hurlers were on the ropes almost from the outset, each went the distance for the 12-inning 4-3 marathon, eventually won by the Giants. This set the tone for the most bitterly fought Series to that point. The teams traded victories through Game 6 with neither able to gain an edge.

In the seventh game, Harris crossed up McGraw by starting right-hander Curly Ogden to induce the Giants to field a left-handed hitting lineup. Then Harris brought in lefty George Mogridge after Ogden faced just two batters. But neither Mogridge nor Giants starter Barnes were around at the finish. If ever a Series went full circle, it was the 1924 classic. As had the opener, the final went 12 innings, and in at the finish for Washington was Johnson, working his fourth inning in relief. After Johnson put down the Giants in the top of the frame, Bentley took the rubber for New York with ancient Hank Gowdy behind the plate. A series hero 10 years earlier with the Miracle Braves, Gowdy got the inning

Dazzy Vance (top) *of Brooklyn led the majors with 28 wins and 262 strikeouts in 1924. Manager John McGraw* (bottom) *led his Giants to a record fourth consecutive NL pennant.*

Brooklyn faced last-place Boston, the Giants finished with the seventh-place Phillies. Before one of the last games, substitute outfielder Jimmy O'Connell of the Giants approached Phils shortstop Heinie Sand and offered him $500 to go easy on the Giants that day. Sand reported the offer, and Commissioner Kenesaw Mountain Landis was swiftly involved. Even though O'Connell claimed he was put up to the bribe attempt by several Giants teammates, he and coach Cozy Dolan were the only two held culpable by Landis, who socked them with a lifetime banishment.

AL president Ban Johnson, feeling that the guilt reached much deeper, demanded that the World Series be canceled after the Giants held on to win the NL flag by 1½ games over Brooklyn. To the relief of those fans in the nation's capital, Landis insisted

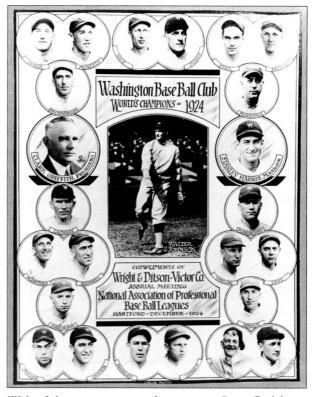

Walter Johnson, center, was the winner in Game 7 of the '24 World Series, pitching four scoreless innings in relief.

off to a bad start when he was tangled up in his mask trying to snare a pop foul hit by Muddy Ruel. Ruel then delivered a hit to raise his Series BA to .095. But, perhaps because of the O'Connell incident, fate was not done punishing McGraw and his Giants.

With 18-year-old rookie Fred Lindstrom at third in place of injured Heinie Groh, Earl McNeely topped a grounder that struck a pebble and popped over the helpless Lindstrom's head, allowing the Series-winning run to trot home.

SEASON'S BEST

- Giants manager John McGraw wins his NL-record 10th and last pennant.

- Washington's Walter Johnson wins the AL MVP Award. Johnson's 23 wins and 158 strikeouts pace the AL. He also leads in ERA (2.72), winning percentage (.767), and shutouts (six). Johnson's AL strikeout crown is his record 12th.

- The NL joins the AL in giving a league MVP Award; the first NL winner is Brooklyn's Dazzy Vance. Vance leads the majors in wins with 28, Ks with 262, and ERA at 2.16.

- St. Louis's Rogers Hornsby leads the NL with a .424 BA, a post-1900 ML record. He tops the NL in hits (227), doubles (43), walks (89), total bases (373), and SA (.696) and ties in runs (121).

- New York's Babe Ruth tops the AL in homers (46) and BA (.378). Although he tops the majors in runs (143), walks (142), OBP (.513), SA (.739), and total bases (391), Ruth fails to win the Triple Crown when he finishes second in RBI to Washington's Goose Goslin, 129 to 121.

- Washington's Firpo Marberry (15 saves) becomes the first relief specialist in ML history.

- Jim Bottomley of the Cards collects an ML-record 12 RBI in a September 16 game vs. Brooklyn.

- Giant Heinie Groh's .983 fielding average sets an ML record for third basemen.

- The Giants' Jimmy O'Connell is banned from baseball for offering an oral bribe to a Phils player on the last weekend of the season.

Jim Bottomley

- Pittsburgh's Max Carey leads NL outfielders in chances accepted a loop-record ninth time.

- On August 2, Joe Hauser of the A's sets a new AL record with 14 total bases in a game.

- Sam Rice of Washington hits in 31 consecutive games.

- Freddy Lindstrom of the Giants, age 18, becomes the youngest World Series participant.

- Lyman Lamb of Tulsa in the Western League hits an organized baseball-record 100 doubles.

- WMAQ in Chicago broadcasts the home games of both the Cubs and the White Sox.

- Pittsburgh rookie shortstop Glenn Wright knocks in 111 runs and tops NL shortstops in assists and double plays.

ROGERS HORNSBY

The Rajah bats .424—highest mark this century

Nicknamed "Rajah" for his handsome hazel-eyed appearance and regal production at the plate, Rogers Hornsby was actually a rather dour and aloof man who generally preferred his own company over that of anybody else. Put a bat in his hands, however, and the greatest right-handed hitter in big-league history was as loud a conversationalist as they came—especially in 1924. It was during that season that he compiled the highest batting average (.424) by a major leaguer this century.

The performance was not entirely out of character—Hornsby had hit in 33 consecutive games and won the Triple Crown just two years before with a .401 batting average, 42 homers, and 152 RBI. His efforts in 1924 did, however, mark a new height in a career that had begun with little fanfare when the right-hander first came up with St. Louis as a 140-pound shortstop in 1915. Hitting for little power (27 homers his first five sea-

sons combined) and barely breaking .300 while playing every infield position, Hornsby eventually filled out into a 5'11", 200-pound regular at second base who began crushing National League pitching at a record clip in 1920. The Cardinals remained a second division team throughout the first half of the '20s, but Hornsby's steady excellence made the sweltering summer days at Sportsman's Park more bearable for Redbird fans.

From 1920 through '25, he won six straight batting titles, becoming the only right-handed batter to hit .400 three times along the way. For good measure, Rogers led the NL in slugging each of those seasons as well. His success came at the same time that graceful first baseman George Sisler was performing a similar brand of heroics for the crosstown Browns. St. Louis fans always loved comparing the two, despite the fact that Hornsby thought it was no contest. Never a smoker or drinker, the Rajah was fanatical about keeping his batting eyes sharp for on-the-field challenges. He kept away from books and the movies.

Consistency was his benchmark. His glorious MVP season of 1924 included just 22 games in which he was hitless. He collected one hit in 46 contests, two hits in 47, three hits in 25, and four hits in three. His 227 total safeties led the majors, and his 121 runs, 43 doubles, 89 walks, .696 slugging average, and 373 total bases topped all National Leaguers. His 25 home runs were second in the senior circuit to Brooklyn's Jack Fournier, and he led his nearest rival for the league batting crown—Dodger Zach Wheat—by an incredible margin of .049. One historian later calculated that the Rajah's .424 batting average would have come out to .506 if walks counted for hits as in the 19th century. However you slice it, this was a season for the ages.

PITTSBURGH WINS IT IN THE RAIN

Washington's championship win in 1924 was seen as an aberration by the baseball community—a refreshing one, to be sure, but not something that was likely to occur again anytime soon. The Yankees were everyone's choice to regain the AL flag. Waiting to take their place in the Bombers' lineup were two highly touted rookies, a young first sacker named Lou Gehrig and center fielder Earle Combs, who had been injured most of the previous year. The best news of all for New Yorkers was that Babe Ruth had just turned 30 and was coming off one of his finest seasons.

On April 8, however, as the Yankees were nearing the end of spring training, Ruth keeled over with what was reported as an enormous "bellyache." He had surgery, reportedly for an intestinal abscess, and was shelved until June. Even after Ruth returned to active duty he performed at only about half of his customary efficiency. His season came to an abrupt end in September when manager Miller Huggins suspended him and slapped him with a record $5,000 fine for insubordination.

Huggins was backed by general manager Ed Barrow, but it was nonetheless a lost year for the Yankees. They sank all the way to seventh place, leaving the retooled Philadelphia A's as Washington's only serious challenger. The A's were still a young team, whereas the Senators were the oldest and most experienced club in the majors. With Walter Johnson winning 20 for one last time at age 37, Stan Coveleski also producing a final 20-win campaign at 36, and 31-year-old Dutch Ruether winning 18 games after being picked up on waivers from the NL, Bucky Harris had little trouble steering Washington to a repeat Series engagement.

For the first time since 1920, though, the New York Giants were not awaiting the AL titlists. Still reeling from the Jimmy O'Connell scandal, John McGraw and his team mounted only token resistance when a young Pittsburgh Pirates team rocketed out of the starting gate. Brooklyn,

The Pittsburgh Pirates' infield in 1925 included third baseman Pie Traynor, second from left, who that year began a run of six consecutive .300-plus seasons.

also expected to contend, tumbled to sixth. The Dodgers were 27 games behind the first-place Bucs as Burleigh Grimes, 22-13 in 1924, skidded to 12-19 with a 5.04 ERA and left Dazzy Vance to carry on alone. Still the best pitcher in the NL, Vance went 22-9 for a team that was otherwise 46-76.

Pittsburgh had no one close to Vance's caliber, but manager Bill McKechnie was able to call on five solid starters, all of whom won between 15 and 19 games. Among them were bespectacled Lee Meadows, Ray Kremer, Jughandle Johnny Morrison, so nicknamed because of his sweeping curveball, and Emil Yde, one of the best hitting hurlers of his day. Backing the quintet was the best offense in the majors that showcased seven .300-hitting regulars, led by Kiki Cuyler at .357 with 144 runs and 26 triples, and an eighth regular, second baseman Eddie Moore, who batted .298 and tallied 106 runs.

In the World Series, the Bucs got off to a rocky start, losing the opener 4-1 to Johnson at Pittsburgh. The following afternoon, Pirate Vic Aldridge edged Coveleski 3-2. After an off day while the teams traveled to Washington, the Senators won the next two games and took a seemingly insurmountable 3-1 lead. Never before had a team rallied from so large a deficit in fall play, and the Pirates seemed only to stave off the inevitable when Aldridge took the finale in Washington, sending the teams back to Pittsburgh.

Goose Goslin's homer gave Washington an early lead in Game 6, but Kremer blanked the Nats from the third inning on. A little help from Moore—namely a solo homer in the fifth—gave him the run

Pittsburgh's Kiki Cuyler (top left) had 26 triples and 144 runs to lead the majors. Cleveland's Tris Speaker (top center) *hit .389 in '25. Roger Peckingpaugh (top right)* was the AL MVP, but his play in the field cost the Senators the Series. Philadelphia's Al Simmons (bottom) *led the majors with 253 hits.*

he needed for a 3-2 win, creating a seventh game matchup between Johnson and Aldridge.

Both hurlers were 2-0 thus far in the Series, and a low-scoring game was expected. On this day, however, Aldridge was wild. He gave up three walks and two wild pitches and was charged with four runs before McKechnie lifted him after he retired just one batter in the top of the first. Staked to a 4-0 lead, Johnson seemed a lock to win. He got through the first two innings unscathed, but by the third inning Forbes Field was inundated by a steady drizzle. Nicked for three runs, Johnson continued to labor

on in the gray, grisly mist. Harris could have turned at any point to Firpo Marberry, his rested relief ace, but elected literally to sink or swim with Johnson. Though he surrendered 15 hits, Johnson had seven runs to work with and would probably have won with better defensive help. Shortstop Roger Peckin-paugh, who made a record eight errors in the Series, dropped a pop fly in the seventh and followed with a wild throw an inning later. Unfortunately for the Washington team, this led to four unearned runs and a 9-7 Pittsburgh triumph that capped the most remarkable Series comeback yet.

SEASON'S BEST

•Babe Ruth's famous "bellyache" idles him for much of the season, holds him to a .290 BA and 25 homers.

•St. Louis's Rogers Hornsby is selected the NL MVP. Hornsby wins his sixth straight NL bat crown (.403). He wins his second Triple Crown, leading in homers (39) and RBI (143). He also leads the majors in SA (.756), runs produced (237), and OBP (.489). Hornsby's .756 SA sets an all-time NL record.

•Washington shortstop Roger Peckinpaugh wins the AL MVP Award, even though he commits eight errors in the World Series.

•Bob Meusel, Ruth's New York teammate, leads the AL in homers (33) and RBI (138).

•Detroit's Harry Heilmann continues his penchant for taking the AL bat crown every other year, as he hits .393.

•Brooklyn's Dazzy Vance leads the majors with 22 wins and 221 Ks.

Bob Meusel

•Joe Sewell of Cleveland fans just four times in 608 at bats.

•George Burns of the Reds steals home for the 27th time, setting an NL career record.

•Washington's Sam Rice collects an AL-record 182 singles.

•The Senators' Walter Johnson hits .433, a season record for pitchers with 75-plus at bats.

•Tony Lazzeri of Salt Lake City in the PCL hits 60 homers, a new organized baseball record.

•The Browns' George Sisler hits in 34 straight games to begin the season.

•Eddie Collins of the White Sox and Cleveland's Tris Speaker each collect their 3,000th hit.

•Pittsburgh's Max Carey tops the NL in steals for a record 10th time.

•Philly's Al Simmons collects 253 hits, an AL record for outfielders.

•On May 5 in St. Louis, Detroit's Ty Cobb goes six-for-six with three homers and 16 total bases.

•Yankee Everett Scott's streak of 1,307 consecutive games played ends. Lou Gehrig starts a skein of 2,130 consecutive games.

•Pittsburgh's Glenn Wright performs an unassisted triple play on May 7.

ROGERS HORNSBY

Player-manager hits .403, wins Triple Crown

After hitting a major league-record .424 in 1924, Rogers Hornsby found himself saddled with an unwanted addition to his responsibilities the following spring. Cardinals owner Sam Breadon and manager Branch Rickey had both tired of second-division finishes and each other. When Rickey left the clubhouse and went to work in the front office, Breadon turned to the 29-year-old Hornsby on Mother's Day, 1925, and asked his second baseman to take on the ballclub's managerial duties as well. Throwing out Rickey's clubhouse blackboard with the declaration "If you don't know how to make the plays by now, you're not going to stay," the harsh but motivated Hornsby set about the task of turning the Redbirds into winners.

Perhaps figuring he could be his own best example, the Rajah turned in another incredible season as St. Louis improved 12½ games to 77-76 for a fourth-place finish. He amassed major league-leading totals of 39 homers and 143 RBI in winning his second Triple Crown (accomplishing a feat matched only by Ted Williams). His .403 average earned him his sixth straight batting title while making him one of a select few major leaguers to ever top the coveted .400 mark two years in succession. In fact, Hornsby's stupendous season (which also included 203 hits, 41 doubles, 133 runs, and a major league-leading .756 slugging mark) upped his overall bat-

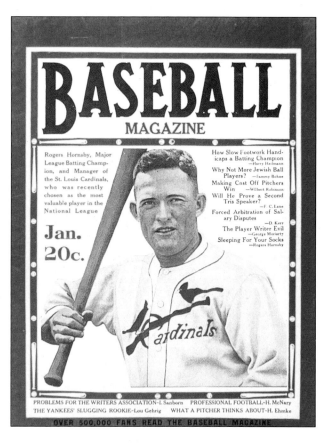

ting average over a five-year span to .402—the greatest stretch of sustained hitting in major-league history.

Despite his exploits, the fans of St. Louis entered 1926 having been denied a championship team since the American Association Browns of 1888. Led by Hornsby (.317 with 93 RBI) and a solid supporting cast, the Cards outlasted the Reds in a thrilling pennant race before beating the mighty Yankees in the World Series of '26. The Rajah led all Series batters with four RBI, and made the key managerial move of the classic by putting in hung-over, 39-year-old Grover Cleveland Alexander to pitch to Tony Lazerri with the bases loaded in the fourth inning of the seventh game. Lazerri struck out, Alexander finished the game, and Hornsby was cited as a cunning genius.

Whether he was a genius or not, Hornsby was a hard man to get along with—and after a winter of disputes with owner Breadon he was traded to the Giants for Frankie Frisch before the 1927 season. Thus began an odyssey that eventually brought the Rajah to Boston, Chicago, and back to St. Louis for player and managerial stints. He never piloted another pennant winner, but his seven batting titles, .358 lifetime BA (second only to Ty Cobb), .577 slugging percentage, and 2,930 hits made him a Hall of Fame lock despite his hard-edged reputation.

CARDS STUN YANKS, THROW A PARADE

While the NL had no team as ill-fated as Cleveland, the St. Louis Cardinals were close. By the spring of 1926, it had been 38 years since a Mound City entry had last won an ML pennant, and even the most optimistic St. Louis fans could not foresee a breakthrough on the horizon. Despite the presence of Rogers Hornsby, the closest thing in the NL to a one-man gang, the Cardinals had finished a poor fourth in 1925, 18 games out of the hunt. No one would have predicted the 1926 season would bring the Cardinals' first pennant. It seemed especially surprising with the knowledge that Hornsby, in his first full season as the Cards' player-manager, would find the dual load so onerous that his BA dropped 86 points from .403 to a merely mortal .317.

It was not that one of the other Redbirds suddenly emerged to take up the slack, either. First baseman Jim Bottomley's .367 BA in 1925 sagged to .299 in '26; left fielder Ray Blades tumbled from .342 to .305; and Chick Hafey, who hit .302 in his first full season, was incapacitated much of the 1926 campaign and held to just 225 at bats and a .271 BA. Offensive production, however, was down everywhere in 1926, making it only the second season since 1919 that no team hit .300. The Cardinals, even with so many of their individual averages declining, still paced the National League in runs and homers. With young shortstop Tommy Thevenow anchoring the infield and Pete Alexander posting nine late-season wins after being picked up from the Cubs on waivers, Hornsby's club was just good enough to squeak home two games ahead of Cincinnati. In a down year, the Cards set a new NL record for the lowest winning percentage by a flag winner with a .578 (89-65) mark.

In 1926, the Yankees debuted the first player in history to hit 60 home runs in a season. His name was Tony Lazzeri, and the previous year he had clubbed 60 dingers on the nose for Salt Lake City of the Pacific Coast League to break Babe Ruth's old

St. Louis celebrated the Cardinals' first World Series championship as a crowd estimated at more than a million packed the streets.

professional record of 59. A second baseman, Lazzeri teamed with Mark Koenig, another keystoner in his first full ML season, to shore up the Yankees' middle infield, their biggest weakness the previous year. Helped by Lazzeri's 18 homers, a new rookie record, and the switch-hitting Koenig's 93 runs, Miller Huggins's Bombers had a 10-game lead in mid-August.

Just when the Yankees were ready to put their lead car in cruise control, though, Cleveland, the Philadelphia A's, and Washington all caught fire. Bucky Harris's Senators, recouping after a slow start, looked for a time as if they might claim a third straight AL flag. It was not to be, though, as age caught up to Walter Johnson and their other hurlers, leaving Cleveland and Philadelphia to carry on the challenge.

The Indians, sparked by first sacker George Burns's record 64 doubles and .358 BA, pulled to within four games of the top by Labor Day, but the Yankees stiffened. Though the Tribe remained close all of September, they had no one of Ruth's ilk to propel them over the top. While Ruth hit 47 homers all by himself, Cleveland notched just 27 as a team, creating a run differential of 109 that spelled a three-game gap between the two clubs at the finish.

In the World Series, Ruth swatted four dingers to set a new fall mark, but three of them came in Game 4, a 10-5 New York blowout, and all but one of the four was a solo shot. Led by ancient Pete Alexander, the Cards' hurlers otherwise held the Bambino in check, limiting him to just two singles. Alexander breezed to a complete-game win in Game 2 and again in Game 6 to knot the Series at 3-all

Pittsburgh's Paul Waner (top left) *led the NL in triples (22). Grover Cleveland Alexander* (top right) *keyed the Cardinals' Series win. Cleveland's George Uhle* (bottom left) *topped the majors in wins (27). New York's Lou Gehrig* (bottom right) *drove in 107 runs.*

and set up a tense Game 7 fray for the third year in a row.

Huggins gave the ball to Waite Hoyt in the deciding clash at Yankee Stadium and sent Herb Pennock to the bullpen. Between them, the pair had a perfect 3-0 mark in the Series thus far. Jesse Haines, a shutout winner in Game 3, was Hornsby's choice. The Yankees nicked Haines for a run in the third but then surrendered three unearned runs the next inning and trailed the Cards 3-2 in the bottom of the seventh. A furious New York rally loaded the bases with two out and rookie star Lazzeri at the plate.

In desperation, Hornsby summoned Alexander, who had gone a full nine innings just the day before. Alexander promptly got a pitch too far inside, and Lazzeri yanked it down the left field line. At the last

instant, the ball curved deep into the seats in foul territory, depriving the rookie of a heroic grand slam.

Mustering all his savvy, the 39-year-old Alexander fanned Lazzeri. Two frames later, with two down in the bottom of the ninth, Ruth singled off Alexan- der. Representing the tying run, he tried to catch the Cards napping. With Bob Meusel at bat, Ruth set sail for second base, but the Cards were ready. St. Louis catcher Bob O'Farrell gunned the ball to Hornsby, who put the tag on the Babe to make the longshot Cardinals the 1926 world champs.

SEASON'S BEST

• Cards catcher Bob O'Farrell wins the NL MVP Award.

• George Burns of Cleveland takes the AL MVP prize. Burns sets a new ML record with 64 doubles and hits .358.

• Yankee Babe Ruth tops the AL in homers with 47, 26 more than anyone else. He also leads in runs (139), total bases (365), SA (.737), OBP (.516), RBI (145), walks (144), and runs produced (237).

Heinie Manush

• Cincinnati's Bubbles Hargrave breaks Rogers Hornsby's stranglehold on the NL bat title, winning with a .353 average.

• Cleveland's George Uhle leads the majors with 27 wins.

• Philly's Lefty Grove wins his first AL ERA crown (2.51) and again tops the loop in Ks (194).

• Firpo Marberry has 22 saves for Washington, a new ML record.

• Detroit's Heinie Manush takes the AL bat crown (.378).

• Hack Wilson of the Cubs wins his first NL home run crown (21).

• St. Louis's Jim Bottomley tops the NL in RBI (120), doubles (40), and total bases (305).

• In his first full season as the Cards' player-manager, Hornsby slumps to .317. On December 20, the Cards deal Hornsby to the Giants for Frankie Frisch and Jimmy Ring.

• The Red Sox finish last in the AL and lose a club-record 107 games.

• On September 26, the Browns and Yankees play the shortest game in AL history—55 minutes. That same day, the two teams play the shortest doubleheader in ML history—two hours and seven minutes.

• Giant Mel Ott, age 17, becomes the youngest player to get a pinch hit in NL history.

• On August 28, Dutch Levsen of Cleveland becomes the last pitcher to win two complete games in one day.

• On August 15, Babe Herman doubles into a double play as three Dodgers wind up on third base.

• Ruth hits a World Series single-game record three homers in Game 4 and a record four homers overall.

BABE RUTH

The Babe bounces back with 47 HRs, 145 RBI

Babe Ruth had followed up his spectacular 1923 season with a similar campaign in 1924 (winning his only batting title with a .378 average while adding a league-best 46 homers and 143 runs), but in 1925, trouble once again came the Babe's way. He was fat, his marriage was disintegrating, and his eating, boozing, and womanizing grew to such huge proportions during spring training that on April 9 he collapsed with stomach pain and was rushed to New York's St. Vincent's Hospital for an intestinal abscess. He returned to action June 1, but was later suspended nine days and fined a then-record $5,000 by Yankee manager Miller Huggins for arriving late to an August 29 game. His .290 batting average, 25 homers, and 66 RBI were by far the worst figures in his career to that point, and the Yankees finished in seventh place just two years after a World Series win.

Just as in 1923, Ruth vowed to reform himself and win back the respect of his fans and teammates.

He no longer had the farm to retreat to (he and Helen sold it as their separation became official), so he spent the winter working out in Artie McGovern's New York gymnasium. He reported to spring training weighing 212 pounds and in the best shape since his early years with the Red Sox. He hit 47 homers (his best since the record 59 in 1921 and 26 more than major-league runner-up Hack Wilson) and also topped the majors with 145 RBI, 139 runs, a .737 slugging percentage, and 365 total bases. The Yankees won back the pennant, and Ruth hit a record four homers in a seven-game World Series loss to the Cardinals—including three in the fourth contest alone.

His reformation complete, Ruth's up-and-down career settled into one of steady excellence. Joined in the New York lineup by a cast of heavy hitters including Lou Gehrig and Tony Lazerri, he outshone them all and topped his own record with 60 homers in 1927 (a mark which would stand 34 years). He

also led the league each season while averaging 51 home runs from 1927 through '31. The Yankees won two more world championships in '28 and '32, but when age finally caught up with Ruth he was unceremoniously released following the 1934 season. After two dismal months with the Boston Braves (highlighted only by his last three career homers, which came in one game) he retired for good, and when he died of throat cancer in 1948, tens of thousands of mourners filed by his coffin inside Yankee Stadium. His "unbreakable" records of 714 homers and 2,211 RBI have since been passed by Henry Aaron, but the Babe's legend as the game's greatest icon will remain forever.

MURDERER'S ROW BLOWS OUT FOES

Rare is the season when the manager of an also-ran cannot claim that with just a break or two along the way his club would have won the pennant. In 1927, however, about all that seven of the eight AL managers could say was that they were thankful that the season had only lasted 154 games.

As for the eighth manager—Miller Huggins—he could boast that his Yankees had led the AL from wire to wire and won 110 games to set a new loop record. Huggins had little inclination to boast, though, as the wealth of talent he had at his disposal in 1927 might almost have made him sheepish to talk about his club. Babe Ruth alone hit more home runs that any other AL team, and Lou Gehrig's 47 dingers were more than the two most prolific sluggers combined on any of the other 15 teams in the majors. Offense was only one chapter in the team's saga, though, as Huggins's pitching staff also fash-

ioned the top ERA in the AL. The Yankees' stinginess on defense so well complemented their attack that they outscored their opponents by an average of 2½ runs a game.

It was Jake Ruppert's dream come true. An ideal game to the Yankees owner was one that his team won 12-0; and when told that most spectators preferred a slightly more competitive contest, he decried the notion. Ruppert perhaps remembered an afternoon in 1921 when he had watched the last few pitches of a close late-season game with his hands covering his eyes and his mouth exhorting over and over, "Oh, win this game for me. Please win this game for me, boys. If you win it, I'll give you anything. I'll give you the brewery."

The boys never got the Ruppert Brewery, nor even a single vat in it, but by the end of the 1927 season they were known everywhere as "Murderer's

Babe Ruth clubbed three homers in Game 4 of the '26 Series, then led the Yankees' "Murderer's Row" with 60 in 1927.

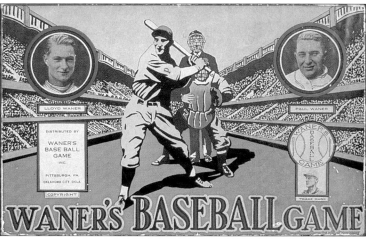

After leading the Cards to the World Series title, Rogers Hornsby (top left) was dealt to the Giants for Frankie Frisch (top center) and Jimmy Ring. Yankee Wilcy Moore (top right) had 19 wins and 13 saves. The Waner brothers of Pittsburgh, Lloyd and Paul (bottom), combined for 460 hits.

Row" and acclaimed the best team in history. If the Yankees had a weakness, it was the absence of a first-rate catcher. There was really no way for anyone to capitalize on this situation, however. In 1927, the backstop job was to be shared by three journeymen—Pat Collins, Johnny Grabowski, and Ben Bengough. Although Bengough had the longest stint with the team, putting in eight seasons in pinstripes, Collins got most of the work in big games.

There was only one problem with this plan; there were no big games for the Yankees in 1927. Consequently, all three catchers appeared equally in the World Series against Pittsburgh. In contrast to the Yankees' 19-game romp over their closest pur-suer, the Philadelphia A's, the Pirates did not clinch the NL flag until the final day of the season. After leading most of the early going, Pittsburgh was caught in August by the Chicago Cubs. A cellar dweller for the first time in their history just two years earlier, the Bruins had been completely re-vamped by manager Joe McCarthy after he took the reins in 1926 but still lacked enough pitching to hold together for a full season. On September 1, the Cubs gave way again to the Pirates, who stayed in front the rest of the way though never by more than a game or two.

On the final Sunday evening of the season, the Corsairs stood just a game and a half up on the defending champion Cardinals and two games ahead of the New York Giants. Pittsburgh was carried by the Waner brothers. Center fielder Paul, the older of the two and a second-year vet, hammered .380, and right fielder Lloyd set a bevy of rookie records when he stroked .342 on 223 hits and tallied 133 runs. The scintillating siblings also combined for just about every season record in the book for brothers who were teammates.

The Waners' performance overshadowed the trouble in left field, where Kiki Cuyler was benched in midseason after a scrape with manager Donie Bush. So deep was the friction between the two that Bush kept Cuyler in purgatory all during the Series, denying him even a single at bat. It is doubtful that Cuyler would have changed the outcome if he had played. According to legend, Huggins, knowing the Pirates were lurking in the stands to see for them-

selves if the Murderer's Row was as good as their press, instructed Waite Hoyt just to "lay it in there" for the Yankees' batting practice at Forbes Field before the Series opener. Huggins then sent Ruth, Gehrig, and Bob Meusel up to the plate and could barely suppress his mirth when the trio smashed consecutive blasts into the bleachers. Pirates play-

ers, the legend continues, crept out of the stands so intimidated they were beaten in four straight.

In actuality, however, Pittsburgh put up a sturdy fight before succumbing, and though the Corsairs indeed were swept, it was Yankees shortstop Mark Koenig (rather than Ruth, Gehrig, or Meusel) who led all Series hitters with a .500 BA.

SEASON'S BEST

•Yankee Lou Gehrig is selected the AL MVP. Gehrig's 175 RBI set a new ML record (since broken). Gehrig hits 47 homers, giving him and Babe Ruth a teammate-record 107 that will stand until 1961.

•Ruth slugs an ML-record 60 home runs (since broken). Ruth himself hits more homers than every other team in the AL except his own. He leads the majors in runs (158), walks (138), SA (.772), and OBP (.487).

•Pirates rookie Lloyd Waner hits 198 singles. Lloyd collects an ML rookie-record 223 hits. Paul Waner, brother of Lloyd, is the NL MVP. He leads the NL in batting (.380), hits (237), triples (17), total bases (338), and RBI (131). The Waner brothers hit a combined .367 with 460 hits—both are ML season sibling records.

•Cub Charlie Root tops the majors in wins with 26.

•Wilcy Moore wins 19 games for the Yankees and ties for the AL lead in saves (13). Moore leads the majors in ERA (2.28).

•For the fourth odd year in succession, Detroit's Harry Heilmann takes the AL bat title (.398).

•The Yankees score an ML-record 975 runs (since broken).

•Ty Cobb signs with the A's prior to the season after 22 years with Detroit. Cobb gets his 4,000th hit on July 19, off Detroit's Sam Gibson.

•Walter Johnson retires with an ML-record 3,508 Ks (since broken). Johnson's 110 shutouts are an all-time ML record.

Charlie Root

•On May 17, the Braves' Bob Smith pitches a 22-inning complete game, losing 4-3 to the Cubs.

•On May 3, Jesse and Virgil Barnes become the first brothers in ML history to oppose each other as starting pitchers.

•The A's have a record seven future Hall of Famers on their active roster in 1927.

•On May 30, Cubs shortstop Jimmy Cooney makes an unassisted triple play. The following day, Tigers first baseman Johnny Neun makes an unassisted triple play.

•Giant Rogers Hornsby tops the NL in walks (86) and OBP (.448), and he ties in runs (133).

LOU GEHRIG

With 175 RBI, Yankees slugger outdoes Ruth

He was the "two" in the greatest one-two punch in big-league history, and the finest second banana ever to play the game. Quiet, steady Lou Gehrig followed flamboyant, unpredictable Babe Ruth in the Yankee batting order for nearly a decade. It is a testimony to his unwavering excellence on the field and his gentle leadership off it that Gehrig emerged as a star in his own right who won four American League Most Valuable Player Awards—including one during the Babe's heralded 60-homer campaign of 1927.

Lou's German immigrant mother, Christina, worked as a cook and housekeeper at Columbia University. After a prep career that concluded with his hitting a grand slam completely out of Chicago's Wrigley Field, the New York native wound up attending Columbia himself. Leaving school and signing with the Yankees for a $1,500 bonus, he toiled in the minors at Hartford and made the majors for brief trials in 1923 and '24. It wasn't until 1925, however, that Gehrig got his big shot. First baseman Wally Pipp (a lifetime .281 hitter and former home run champ in his own right) reported to Yankee manager Miller Huggins with a severe headache on June 1, and Huggins suggested he take the day off. Gehrig (who had pinch-hit the day before) took his place. Some 14 years later he was still

there, setting a record for consecutive games played (2,130). He would be stopped only by the disease that killed him.

After hitting .295 with 20 homers in 126 contests that season, Gehrig exploded in 1926 (batting .313 with 16 homers, 107 RBI, and a league-leading 20 triples) as he and Ruth led the Yankees to the first of eight pennants they would win in Lou's time with the team. New York was stopped in the World Series by the Cardinals that fall, but there would be no denying Gehrig or the club that came to be known as "Murderer's Row" the following year. Ruth topped his own record with a fabulous 60-homer season that captivated the nation, but Gehrig quietly put together an even greater all-around year. Finishing runner-up in the home run derby with 47, Gehrig bested Ruth and all other American Leaguers with 175 RBI, 52 doubles, and 447 total bases. Lou was second in hits with 218 and third in batting at .373, had 149 runs and a .765 slugging mark to trail only Ruth, and then added a .308 batting average as the Yankees swept Pittsburgh in the World Series. The Babe's 60 homers would remain baseball's most revered record for over a generation, but it was Lou who walked away as MVP after rules of the time prohibited the previous year's winner Ruth from qualifying for the award.

YANKS EDGE A'S, SWEEP THE CARDS

The New York Yankees began the 1928 season as if they would once again make mincemeat of their opposition. Heading into July, it looked certain to be another Bronx runaway. But then Connie Mack's Philadelphia Athletics, a distant bridesmaid the year before, got hot, winning 25 of 33 games in the season's fourth month. The Yankees' seemingly insurmountable lead continued to melt like snow in summer throughout August as the A's kept up their torrid pace.

On Friday, September 7, the A's caught the Yankees. The following day, they performed the truly unbelievable, seizing first place away from New York with a win. The next afternoon, September 9, the two combatants met at Yankee Stadium in a Sunday doubleheader. An unprecedented crowd of 85,265 filed through the turnstiles and sat gleeful for five hours as the Yankees swept the twinbill, 5-0 and 7-3, to recapture the AL lead. Still hopeful, Mack turned to his veteran players down the stretch. Among the vets were the likes of Ty Cobb, Tris Speaker, and Eddie Collins. All past 40, the three greats had their best days too far behind them to spur the A's. There was a beacon of hope in the form of another veteran who, at age 45, was older than any of them. His name was Jack Quinn, and he continued to craft win after win. Quinn finished the season at 18-7. He paired with Lefty Grove (24-8) to give Mack a 42-15 hill twosome, but it was not enough to match the Yankees threesome of George Pipgras, Waite Hoyt, and Herb Pennock, who combined for 64 wins plus 14 saves. Though the A's stayed in contention until the next-to-last day of the season, they never again saw first place.

The New York Giants matched the A's fabulous July performance, winning 25 games in September. For John McGraw, who wanted one last pennant to eradicate the smirch on his 1924 NL championship squad before he retired, it was sadly too little too late. Now under Bill McKechnie, the St. Louis Cardinals had begun the season's final month just far enough in front to weather the Giants' charge.

On September 29, the day after the Yankees clinched in the AL, the Cards wrapped up their second flag in three

Lou Gehrig hit .374 with 142 RBI in 1928, then set a World Series record with a 1.727 slugging average.

Philadelphia catcher Mickey Cochrane (top) was the 1928 AL MVP, winning the honor by just two votes over St. Louis outfielder Heinie Manush (bottom).

not finished in the first division since 1917, and the Boston Braves had experienced just one first-division glimpse since 1916. In 1928, though, the Braves did have their first 20th-century batting champ as Rogers Hornsby, playing with his third club in three seasons, hit .387 to set a modern franchise record. The Phils set only a new franchise record for losses, bowing 109 times, but nevertheless gave some small hope to their supporters in the form of three promising rookies: first sacker Don Hurst, third baseman Pinky Whitney, and right fielder Chuck Klein, who clanged 91 hits and 11 homers in little more than a third of the season.

Though the Cardinals—with 21-game winner Bill Sherdel, 20-game winner Jesse Haines, and the redoubtable Pete Alexander still good for 16 wins at age 41—looked to have enough pitching to give the Yankees a tussle in the World Series, the 1928 affair was perhaps the most one-sided postseason match ever. After being thoroughly outclassed in the first two games, the Cards took a brief 2-0 lead during

With Yankees owner Jake Ruppert at his side, Babe Ruth signed a new contract with the Yankees (top). Freddie Lindstrom (bottom) had 231 hits for the Giants in '28, setting a National League record for third basemen.

seasons by a two-game margin. The Chicago Cubs were four games back, and Pittsburgh, hampered when last year's 19-game winner Lee Meadows was kayoed by a sore arm, finished nine games in arrears for fourth place. It was the third successive season that the same four clubs had comprised the NL's first division, and the quartet would continue to dominate the senior loop deep into the next decade while the other four NL clubs—Cincinnati, Brooklyn, Boston, and Philadelphia—would make an occasional foray into the upper regions for a single season, only to sink back into the depths again almost immediately.

The AL, despite having to tolerate the Yankees, actually had much better balance. Only the Boston Red Sox, demoralized by Babe Ruth's sale in 1919 to the Yankees and a spate of further one-sided deals between the two clubs that made Boston seem like a New York chattel, could not boast of a .500 finish thus far in the 1920s. Indeed, every other AL team had made at least one serious pennant bid during the decade. The Philadelphia Phillies, in contrast, had

Game 3 at St. Louis. Gehrig put an end to that by clubbing two homers and allowing the Yankees to win routinely, 7-3. The following afternoon the Bronx Bombers put on the most awesome power display in fall play to that point.

Facing Sherdel and Alexander, Ruth crushed three homers, Gehrig blasted his fourth dinger of the Series, and Ced Durst—playing in place of injured Earle Combs—contributed a fifth Yankee four-bagger. Virtually the only moment of controversy, or doubt, in the entire Series occurred when Sherdel fanned Ruth in the finale while the Cardinals still held a slim 2-1 lead, only to have plate umpire Cy Pfirmin rule the K had come on a "quick pitch." Given a reprieve, Ruth promptly parked one, and the Cardinals were cooked.

SEASON'S BEST

- Jim Bottomley of the Cards is named NL MVP.

- Philly catcher Mickey Cochrane wins the AL MVP by two votes over St. Louis's Heinie Manush.

- Rogers Hornsby, playing now for the Braves, tops the NL in batting (.387).

Hack Wilson

- Washington's Goose Goslin wins the AL bat crown (.379) by one point over St Louis's Heinie Manush.

- Yankee Babe Ruth tops the majors in homers (54), runs (163), walks (135), and SA (.709). Ruth and teammate Lou Gehrig tie for the ML lead in RBI with 142.

- Manush tops the AL in hits (241) and ties in doubles (47).

- Cub Hack Wilson again ties for the NL homer crown (31), this time with Bottomley.

- Dodger Dazzy Vance's 2.09 ERA is the best in the majors. Vance wins 22 games, ties for the NL lead in shutouts (four), and leads the majors in Ks (200).

- Giant Larry Benton ties for most wins in ML (25) and leads the NL in winning percentage (.735).

- Ty Cobb retires with ML record for BA (.367) (record still stands). In addition, he retires with ML records in hits (4,191), runs (2,245), stolen bases (892), and RBI (1,961) (all since broken).

- Tris Speaker retires as the all-time ML leader in doubles (792) and assists by an outfielder (448).

- Eddie Collins plays the last of his career-record 2,650 games at second base.

- Giant Freddy Lindstrom's 231 hits set an NL record for third basemen and top the senior loop.

- The last-place Phils have a 5.52 staff ERA, a new ML high.

- Taylor Douthit of the Cards handles 566 chances, an all-time ML record for an outfielder.

- Ruth hits .625 in the World Series to set a Series BA record. Gehrig hits .545 and has a 1.727 SA, an all-time World Series record. Between them, Ruth and Gehrig hit seven homers and knock in 13 runs.

JIM BOTTOMLEY

Sunny Jim named MVP, leads Cards to NL flag

When Branch Rickey took over as president and field manager of the Cardinals in 1919, the team's biggest claims to glory since 1892 had been a pair of third-place finishes. They were a cash-poor club in danger of going under, but Rickey had an uncommonly good eye for spotting young talent and a unique way of harvesting it. Major-league teams had previously been assembled primarily by purchasing individual players from minor-league outfits, but with the blessing of Sam Breadon, then owner of the St. Louis Cardinals, Rickey began to buy entire minor-league *teams* on which he could develop future prospects. The "farm-bred" Cardinals were world champs by 1926, and one of the first players to rise out of the system and star for the club was the 1928 Most Valuable Player— Jim Bottomley.

Born in Oglesby, Illinois, Bottomley arrived with the parent club from the minor-league chain in 1922 and hit .325 in 37 games. He batted a lusty .371 with 94 RBI in '23 after taking over at first base (where he would remain for the next decade), had a major league-record 12 RBI in one game in 1924, and was the National League RBI king in '26 with 120 for Rickey's first championship Cardinal team. Bottomley then compiled a .345 batting average in the World Series triumph over the Yankees.

Known as much for his perpetual grin and habit of wearing his cap tilted over his left eye as for his slugging prowess, Sunny Jim's best overall year came in 1928 as the Cards took another pennant and again battled the Yanks in the Series. Batting a solid .325, Bottomley was the league leader in triples (20) and runs batted in (136) while tying for the home run crown with Hack Wilson (31). Jim's career-best .628 slugging percentage placed second in the NL, his 362 total bases first, and he belted a home run and a triple in a lost cause as New York swept St. Louis in the Series. His recognition as MVP that year made him the first player so honored to have risen from within a team's own farm system, the first of many that Rickey would harvest from this pool.

Bottomley turned in another outstanding season in '29 (batting .314 with 29 homers and 137 RBI) but never knocked in 100 runs after that year. He spent his last seasons as a productive but unspectacular batsman with the Reds and Browns, briefly managing as well. His career is largely forgotten today in the wake of more glamorous stars of his era, but Sunny Jim made enough of an impression with his .310 lifetime batting average, 1,422 RBI (in just 1,991 games), and .500 slugging percentage to eventually earn Hall of Fame recognition 15 years after his 1959 death.

A'S EMERGE AS THE NEW AL POWER

After his club made the St. Louis Cardinals its second straight sweep victim in the 1928 World Series, rival owners seriously questioned whether New York Yankees owner Jake Ruppert ought to break up his team to restore competitive balance. Yankees manager Miller Huggins cautioned that this fear was premature, for he knew that his team had an enemy within that could cause its demise. The enemy was complacency.

When the Yanks got off to a slow start in 1929, Huggins was able to hide his anxiety at first. By August, however, his team was still far behind Connie Mack's Philadelphia A's. This caused Huggins to call a team meeting. When he was asked by Ruppert how it had gone, Huggins answered by saying, "They're through, Colonel. Start getting ready for next year." Huggins then revealed how he'd tried all of his managerial tricks, but none had made the slightest impact. "I couldn't then make them mad. I couldn't even make them laugh. When I realized that I might as well have been talking to that wall over there, I quit."

Sadly, for Huggins, there was no next year. Exhausted by his failure to motivate the club, he entered a hospital a few weeks later after an ugly blemish under his right eye refused to go away. Five days later he was dead at 50 of erysipelas. The Athletics by then had extended their lead to double digits; it would reach 18 games when the season ended.

Built around left fielder Al Simmons, first baseman Jimmie Foxx, catcher Mickey Cochrane, and Lefty Grove, arguably the game's all-time best southpaw hurler, the A's had the most potent team in the AL in 1929. Mack's real catalyst, though, was second baseman Max Bishop. In 1929, with the game in the throes of an era when few teams hit below .280, Bishop batted .232 and collected just 110 hits but nevertheless posted 102 runs. He was a rare player who collected tons of walks even though he

Max Bishop scores ahead of A's teammate Mule Haas, whose two-run homer in the bottom of the ninth tied Game 7 of the '29 Series at 2-2. Philly went on to beat the Cubs 3-2.

The Cubs won the '29 pennant (top) as Rogers Hornsby (bottom left) *came to Chicago. Philly's Lefty O'Doul (bottom center)* set an NL record for hits (254). Miller Huggins (bottom right), *who helped build the Yankees, died of erysipelas in 1929.*

seemingly posed little threat at bat. Nicknamed "Camera Eye" for his skill at coaxing free passes, Bishop had company in Cochrane. Contact was Cochrane's middle name. He struck out less than any catcher in history and walked nearly as often as Bishop. The two were ideal table-setters for Foxx and Simmons.

In 1929, Mack's first flag-winner since 1914 found itself facing in the Chicago Cubs a team that had just set a new 20th-century record with 982 runs. The Cubs' main men were center fielder Hack Wilson, who broke his own year-old team record by crushing 39 homers, and second baseman Rogers Hornsby, who likewise banged 39 dingers in 1929 to grab a share of the Cubs' team mark.

It was pitching, though, that decided the Series. The A's, with a deep staff that included six hurlers who won 11 or more games, were expected to start Grove in the opener or give the nod to 24-game winner George Earnshaw. Mack, however, surprised

everyone by opening with 35-year-old Howard Ehmke, who had worked only 55 innings all season. Once a fine pitcher, Ehmke by this point had lost his fastball—but that was exactly what Mack liked about him. By changing speeds cleverly, Ehmke fanned a record 13 Cubs and won Game 1, beating Charlie Root 3-1 in front of a disbelieving Chicago crowd at Wrigley Field.

The A's also won Game 2 in the Windy City and took a commanding 2-0 lead home to Philadelphia. But Guy Bush outdueled Earnshaw 3-1 in Game 3, bringing the Cubs within one of tying. After routing Jack Quinn in Game 4, Chicago, behind Root, was sitting on a seemingly secure 8-0 lead going into the bottom of the seventh. Then lightning struck. The A's piled up run upon run, aided by two fly balls that Wilson lost in the late-afternoon autumn sun. Cubs skipper Joe McCarthy sent Root to the showers and brought in Art Nehf. Then he tried Sheriff Blake. Finally he resorted to Pat Mal-

one, scheduled to be his next day's starter. Nothing helped. The A's scored 10 runs and captured the game 10-8, setting a Series single-game record for the greatest comeback.

Expected to wilt, the Cubs instead bolted to a 2-0 lead in Game 5, and Malone held it into the bottom of the ninth. Then Bishop singled with one out and Mule Haas drilled a homer to knot the count. Malone managed to get a second out but then surrendered a double to Simmons. Moments later, Bing Miller cracked a two-bagger to drive Simmons across with the Series-winning run.

SEASON'S BEST

•Rogers Hornsby of the Cubs wins the NL MVP (the AL discontinued the award after the 1928 season). Hornsby's .380 BA sets a Cubs team record—the fourth such record he has set in the decade.

•Lefty O'Doul of the Phils, the NL bat champ with a .398 mark, is the MVP runner-up. O'Doul's 254 hits tie the all-time NL record. He also reaches base an NL-record 334 times.

•Chuck Klein of the Phils wins the NL homer crown (43) in his first full season.

Charlie Gehringer

•Yankee Babe Ruth tops the majors with 46 homers and a .697 SA.

•George Earnshaw of the A's leads the majors with 24 wins.

•Cub Hack Wilson's 159 RBI are the most in the majors.

•Lefty Grove of the A's posts a 2.81 ERA, the only one in the majors below 3.00.

•Yankees manager Miller Huggins dies near the end of the season.

•Giant Mel Ott, age 20, becomes the youngest player ever to hit 40 homers in a season; he hits 42.

•Braves owner Emil "Judge" Fuchs manages his own team for the full season—the last owner to do so.

•Ike Boone of the Mission Reds in the PCL collects 553 total bases.

•Johnny Frederick of Brooklyn sets an ML rookie record with 52 doubles.

•The 1929 Phils are the only team in NL history to have four 200-hit men.

•Dale Alexander of Detroit collects 215 hits, setting an AL rookie record for a 154-game season.

•Philly's Al Simmons leads the AL in total bases (373), RBI (157), and runs produced (237).

•Detroit's Charlie Gehringer tops the AL in runs (131), triples (19), and steals (28), and he ties in hits (215).

•The Indians and Yankees become the first teams to put numbers on their uniforms and keep them on.

•On July 5, the Giants become the first ML team to use a public address system.

•New York's Bill Walker leads the NL in ERA at 3.08, the highest NL-leading mark in this century.

AL SIMMONS

Outfielder knocks in 157, pushes A's over the top

Owner-manager Connie Mack's Philadelphia Athletics had won four pennants and three world championships between 1910 and 1914 when he decided to dismantle the club and start rebuilding another winner. It would, however, take 15 years of fruitless labor before Mr. Mack would get the formula right again. When he finally achieved success in 1929, the player at center stage for the start of the next Athletics dynasty was slugging center fielder and AL MVP Al Simmons.

Confident to the point of cockiness, Simmons had a swagger and style that gained him a reputation as a player who seldom erred or looked awkward afield. Even an unorthodox batting stance in which the right-hander lifted his striding left foot high in the air while his right stayed stiff as if immersed in a bucket seemed to look smooth, although Simmons never appreciated the Bucketfoot Al appellation it earned him. Bought from minor-league Shreveport by Mack for an amount somewhere between $40,000 and $70,000, he was a .308 hitter his rookie season of 1924 and a star the next year when he exploded for a .384 batting average, 129 RBI, and a major league-best 253 hits—a total topped only three times in big-league history—for second-place Philadelphia.

Simmons followed with three more outstanding campaigns (hitting a combined .359 with over 100 RBI each season), but it wasn't until 1929 that the A's got over the hump. Sluggers Jimmie Foxx, Mickey Cochrane, and Mule Haas all came together, George Earnshaw and Lefty Grove each won 20 games, but Simmons was responsible for putting Philadelphia over the top. Batting .365 with 34 homers (figures that ranked second and third, respectively, in the AL), Simmons led the junior circuit with 157 runs batted in as the A's went 104-46 and outdistanced the two-time defending world champion Yankees by 18 games for the pennant. Among his 212 hits were 41 doubles and nine triples (good for a .642 slugging average), and his 373 total bases topped the league. Always a great postseason player, he then added two homers and a .300 mark as Philadelphia topped the Cubs in a five-game World Series.

The A's repeated as AL champs the following two seasons, with Simmons adding a pair of batting titles and four more Series homers to his growing list of laurels. He continued as a major threat for one more year in Philly and another two with the White Sox, and Simmons later hit .327 with 112 RBI for the '36 Tigers. His final years were spent in pursuit of his late-established goal of 3,000 hits (he fell 73 short), but his lifetime batting average of .334 and 1,827 career RBI were more than enough to get Bucketfoot Al into the Hall of Fame in 1953.

THE 1930s

Baseball couldn't escape the throes of the Great Depression. Attendance sagged and troubled clubs had to sell away their stars. Wealthy teams, especially the New York Yankees, dominated the game.

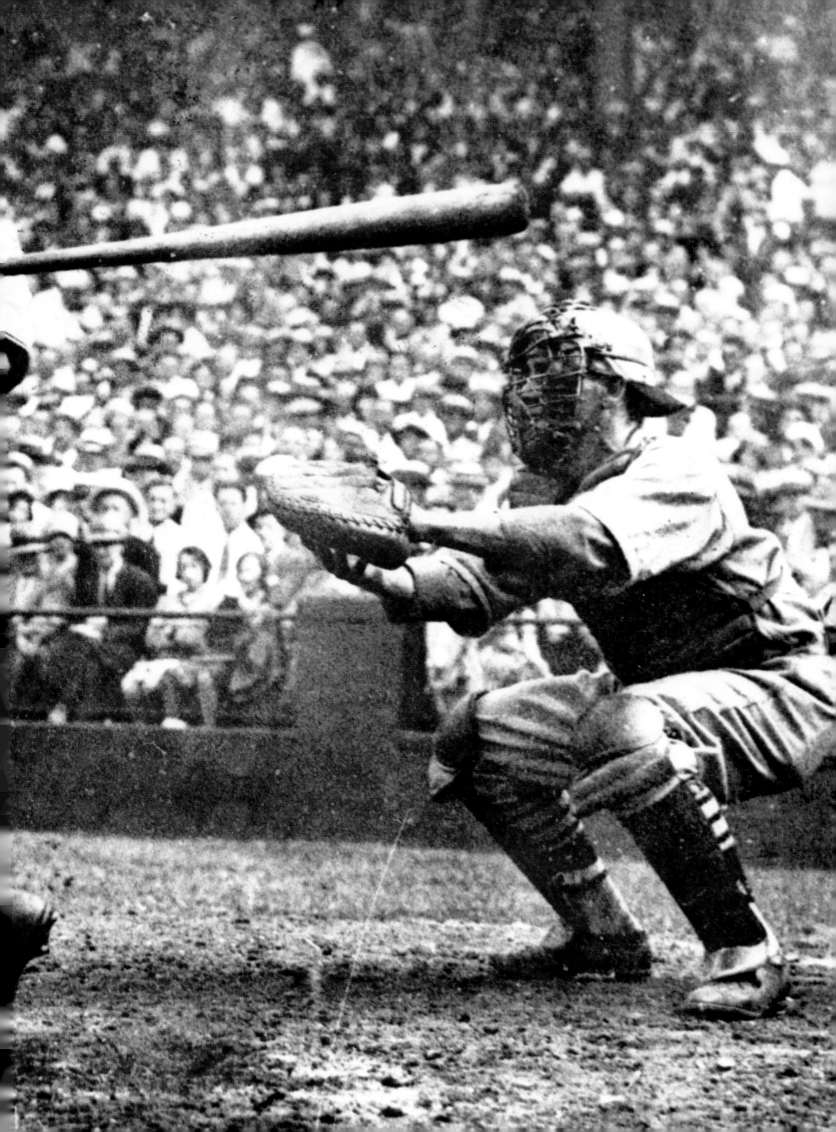

Whhen the Depression altered American life in the 1930s, baseball wasn't immune from its debilitating effects. In 1930, the Depression had not yet fully taken hold, but baseball owners, anticipating a decline in attendance, allegedly had the ball juiced up to infuse more offense and action into the sport. It worked. Hits and run totals were the highest in years, particularly in the National League, where open season was declared on pitchers. The league batting average that season was .303, as five of the century's 10 highest team batting averages and five of the top 20 team run totals were tallied. Home runs flew out at a record pace and fans flocked into the parks at an unprecedented rate. Major-league attendance topped the 10-million mark in 1930, a level that was unequaled until the end of World War II.

The good times were short-lived, however. After 1930, attendance dropped for four straight years as all but two major-league teams posted attendance declines. As unemployment climbed to 13 million in 1932, gate receipts for the 16 major-league teams plummeted to $10.8 million from $17 million in 1929. At the same time, average player salaries sank to $4,500 from the pre-Depression high of $7,500.

By 1934, close to 40 percent of the nonfarm workforce was unemployed and baseball teams suffered at the turnstiles. After peaking at 10.1 million in 1930, major-league attendance sank to under six million in 1934, the lowest since the war-shortened 1918 season. It would be 1936 before the game's vital signs began improving, and by 1939—buoyed by new stars such as Joe DiMaggio, Ted Williams, and Bob Feller and a strengthening economy—gate receipts would reach new highs.

The Depression also had a direct bearing on what happened on the field. Success in the standings became directly linked to prosperity at the gate, and so naturally, the wealthier clubs enjoyed the most success in the decade. The Yankees and Tigers won seven pennants between them in the American League, while the Cubs, Giants, and the farm system-fed Cardinals won three flags each in the NL.

With the economy in a shambles, baseball's competitive balance was knocked askew. Connie Mack had built the Philadelphia A's into a dynasty

After hitting a career-high 42 homers in 1929, Mel Ott (top) won or shared five home run titles in the 1930s. Catcher Al Lopez (bottom) wasn't much of a hitter, but his defense was key for the Dodgers and Braves in the '30s.

Jimmie Foxx helped the A's capture the 1930 World Series (top left), then was sold off to Boston in 1936. Burleigh Grimes (top right) went 17-9 in 1931. Here he says hello to Commissioner Kenesaw Mountain Landis. Babe Ruth's days as a pitcher were pretty much over by 1930, but he still managed to pitch his own fan club (bottom left). A's hurler Lefty Grove (bottom right) smoked 'em for a career-high 31 wins in 1931.

from 1929 to 1931 with young stars like Mickey Cochrane, Al Simmons, Jimmie Foxx, and Lefty Grove. But in 1932, the A's drew only 400,000 fans to Shibe Park, the club's third consecutive year of declining attendance. Claiming imminent fiscal ruin, Mack began raising revenue by selling the club's most viable assets, its star players. In 1933, he sold Simmons, a two-time batting champion, to the White Sox, and the A's fell from second to third. In 1934, Mack divested himself of catcher Cochrane and pitching ace Grove, selling them to the Tigers and the Red Sox, respectively. Philadelphia sank to fifth place. After falling into the cellar in 1935, the A's shipped Foxx, the game's top right-handed slug-

ger, to Boston. In less than five years, Mack had completely dismantled his championship club, committing his team to years of dismal showings. From 1936 until his death in 1956, Mack's A's finished no higher than fourth in the AL and came in last 11 times.

Mack was not alone in making moves based on financial hardships. Clark Griffith made several shrewd trades in the winter of 1932 that helped his Washington Senators win the pennant in 1933. But the major factor in guiding Washington to the flag was player-manager Joe Cronin, who batted .309 and drove home 118 runs. Yet their success on the field didn't prevent the Senators from losing money

that year, so Griffith sold former batting champ Goose Goslin to the Tigers. Then, the Senators tumbled all the way to seventh in 1934, and Griffith took an even larger loss. This time, he sold his most valuable property, Cronin, to the Red Sox for $225,000. Cronin also happened to be Griffith's son-in-law.

St. Louis's clubs may have had it toughest of all. In 1934, the Cardinals defeated the Giants by two games in a bitterly contested pennant race, and Dizzy Dean, the last National Leaguer to win 30 games, was the ringleader of the "Gashouse Gang," one of the most popular and colorful groups of players ever assembled. Yet the Redbirds drew only

335,000 fans to Sportsman's Park in 1934. The next year, the St. Louis Browns attracted a measly 81,000 fans. The Browns pulled in less than 1.2 million paying spectators for the entire decade, effectively crippling the franchise both competitively and financially. Except for a brief moment of glory during World War II, the club finished no higher than sixth place from 1935 until it was sold and moved to Baltimore in 1954.

Into this have and have-not environment stepped Tom Yawkey, a Bostonian who inherited $7 million

Philadelphia A's manager Connie Mack stands between two of his stars, catcher Mickey Cochrane, left, and pitcher Lefty Grove at the 1931 World Series (top). Mack later broke up his dynasty by selling off his star players. The 1932 Pittsburgh Crawfords (bottom) of the Negro League included the "Black Babe Ruth," Josh Gibson, third from left.

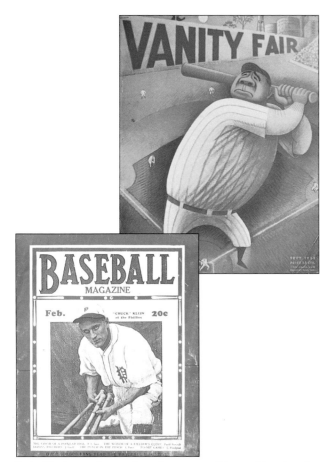

Babe Ruth was featured on this cover of Vanity Fair *(top) in 1933, a year in which he hit "only" 34 home runs. Phillie Chuck Klein made* Baseball *magazine's cover (bottom) in 1932, the year he was NL MVP. He won the Triple Crown the next season.*

on his 30th birthday in 1933. Three days later he bought the moribund Red Sox, a club that had brought up the rear in the American League in seven of the previous eight years. Yawkey committed all his energy and resources into turning the club around. He bought respectability in the ensuing years, as he paid top dollar for the likes of Lefty Grove, Wes Ferrell, Joe Cronin, and Jimmie Foxx, but a pennant (as well as a profit) continued to elude the feckless Sox until 1946.

Detroit owner Frank Navin apparently invested more shrewdly in the 1930s. In 1934, he purchased Mickey Cochrane and Goose Goslin to team with stars Charlie Gehringer and Hank Greenberg, and the Tigers won pennants in 1934 and '35. The payoff came when attendance in Detroit tripled to a league-high 919,000 in 1934, equivalent to one-third of the eight-team league's draw. The following

year, the Tigers became one of the very few clubs to spin the turnstiles one million times in a season during the 1930s.

The Yankees also managed that feat, and ended as the sport's top draw of the decade by attracting over nine million fans. Owner Jacob Ruppert saw the correlation between success in the standings and fiscal strength, and he poured money into his club to keep it stocked with talent. To that end, the Yankees followed the Cardinals' lead by purchasing a minor-league team, the Newark Bears, in 1931 as a cost-effective means of developing players. Ruppert was also lucky. He took what was considered a gamble in late 1934 by plunking down $35,000 and five ballplayers to acquire a young outfielder from the San Francisco Seals named Joe DiMaggio. Joe D. had been the most closely scrutinized minor leaguer in years, and it was estimated that the purchase price for him would have reached $125,000 if he hadn't suffered a knee injury in 1934. After he was hurt, other teams backed away from DiMaggio, but Ruppert was willing to risk his investment. Subsequently, DiMaggio became the major contributor in the four Yankee pennant teams of the late 1930s.

Economic factors colored most of the major developments of the period. Minor-league teams had to be particularly innovative to stay afloat, and, with that in mind, 11 minor-league clubs installed lights

When Pie Traynor, left, replaced George Gibson as manager in 1934, he led the Pirates back to respectability. But the closest his team came to a pennant was a second-place finish in 1938.

and began playing night baseball in 1930. The concept proved immediately popular in the lower leagues and may have saved many clubs from bankruptcy. However, night ball was resisted in the big leagues until 1935, when Larry MacPhail had his Cincinnati Reds play seven games under the lights that year. The practice was harshly criticized by baseball's conservative wing. *The Sporting News*, considered the weekly "Bible of Baseball," argued against the implementation of night baseball on the grounds that it would be "bad for digestion, sleep, and morale." It turned out to be good for the Reds' balance sheet, and when MacPhail left to run the Dodgers in 1938, he immediately installed lights and had "Dem Bums" playing in prime time. By 1940, six of the eight NL clubs played a portion of their schedules after dark.

Baseball also discovered that radio was an important revenue source in the 1930s. In use since the 1921 World Series, the clubs had never directly received income from the new broadcast medium, and originally they saw it as a threat to the gate. In 1933, a radio company paid for exclusive rights to air the World Series, and by '36 those rights cost $100,000. The lowly Boston Braves were the first team to command a fee for local rights to broadcast their games, and in '33 the club received $5,000. By decade's end,

The Sewell brothers (top left), Joe, left, and Luke, were teammates in Cleveland until Joe's release after the 1930 season. Babe Ruth was featured on a 1934 cover from a baseball tour of Japan (top right). Ruth took some time during the tour to visit with blind children (bottom).

both the Yankees and the Giants took in over $100,000 a year in local broadcast rights fees.

Another lasting baseball innovation born of the Depression is the All-Star Game. Conceived by the *Chicago Tribune* as a promotional gimmick, the first game was played July 6, 1933, at Comiskey Park be-

A scene from Navin Field during the 12-inning Game 2 of the 1934 World Series between the Tigers and Cardinals (top). The Tigers and Schoolboy Rowe won the game 3-2, but the Cards won the Series in seven games. The Indianapolis ABC's (bottom left), part of the Negro League of the 1930s. Bill Terry (bottom right) is the last NL player to hit .400, accomplishing the feat with a .401 mark in 1930. In 1932, he took over as manager of the Giants for an ailing John McGraw. In 1933, the club won the World Series.

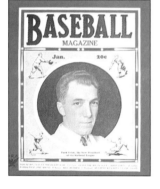

Boston's Lefty Grove and St. Louis's Dizzy Dean share a laugh (top left). Pepper Martin, front, and the Cards' "Gashouse Gang" clown around (top right). A Baseball Magazine cover featuring NL President Ford Frick (bottom left). Boston's Jimmie Foxx (bottom right) slammed 50 homers and drove in 175 runs in 1938.

fore 49,000 fans. The spectacle of the National League stars playing against the American League elite was an immediate hit. Fittingly enough, the game-winning blow in the first game was struck by the biggest star of them all, as 38-year-old Babe Ruth blasted a two-run homer to propel the American League to a 4-2 win.

Another large group of players, some of superstar ability, were toiling under relative obscurity during the 1930s. These players were members of the Negro Leagues that played in organized ball's shadow from 1920 until the color barrier fell in 1946.

The Negro Leagues were an outgrowth of the invisible but unbreakable barrier that slammed down on African-American athletes in the late 19th century to keep them out of organized baseball. As a result, African-American ballplayers wrote a separate history of the game in the first half of the 20th century. All-African-American professional teams, including the Homestead Grays, were formed in the 1910s and made money by going on barnstorming tours, taking on challengers for a percentage of the gate. The first successful organized league of these clubs was started in 1920 by Rube Foster, the owner of the Chicago American Giants and one of the great African-American players of the early part of the century. His Negro National League consisted of eight teams from Midwestern cities that went through numerous franchise shifts and financial instability before folding in 1931.

The embryonic league did spawn some outstanding ballplayers, however, including a fleet-footed outfielder for the St. Louis Stars named Cool Papa Bell. Bell joined the Stars in 1922 and played in the Negro Leagues through the 1946 season, and has often been described as the fastest man to ever play baseball. He once scored from first on a sacrifice bunt in a game against major-league All-Stars.

Bell was clocked rounding the bases in less than 13 seconds and is said to have had a career batting average in the high .300s.

A teammate once said that Bell was "so fast he could turn off the lights and be under the covers before the room got dark." The speaker was Satchel Paige, African-American baseball's most famous player. Paige started pitching professionally in 1926 and was still getting paid to pitch 40 years later. Dizzy Dean said that Paige was the best pitcher he ever saw, a sentiment shared by many others. In his prime, Paige possessed one of the game's great fastballs. He called it his be ball "because it be where I want it to be." There is little hard data available which can summarize Paige's career, but he once estimated that he won 2,000 games in his life, pitched about 100 no-hitters, and played for 250 teams, mostly on a hired one-game basis. His popularity may have exceeded that of any player since Babe Ruth, and after he joined the Cleveland Indians as a 42-year-old rookie in

1948, more than 200,000 people turned out to watch him in his first three starts.

Paige, like many African-American players between the wars, was a baseball nomad. If the money was there, so was he. Satchel said he pitched year-round, summer in the United States and winter in Latin America, for 30 years, and he frequently jumped contracts if a better offer arose.

The 1937 Giants (top) celebrated the NL pennant, but lost the Series. Roy Campanella called Josh Gibson (bottom left) "the greatest ballplayer I ever saw." Yankee Bill Dickey (bottom center) hit .332 with 29 HRs and 133 RBI in 1937. Two of the greatest of their time, Lou Gehrig, left, and Detroit's Hank Greenberg chat before a game (bottom right).

Negro and major-league baseball, as "the greatest ballplayer I ever saw." But like Paige and the others, virtually no records of Gibson's exist. He was credited with hitting 75 home runs for the Homestead Grays when he was 19 years old, but it's not known how many games this encompasses.

After the first Negro Major League died in 1931, another was formed by Pittsburgh Crawfords owner Gus Greenlee in 1933. Greenlee was a wealthy numbers king in Pittsburgh and had constructed the Crawfords beginning in 1931. He counted Bell, Paige, and Gibson among his players. Greenlee pulled six teams together for the inaugural season. The ride was bumpy, but the league survived until 1948. In the latter half of the 1930s and through the war years, the league was fairly prosperous, and in 1937 a Negro American League was formed as a counterpart major league. The two held championship contests for several years in the early 1940s.

Throughout the life of all-African-American baseball, the major revenue source came from barn-

Carl Hubbell (top) fanned a league-high 159 batters in 1937, and his Series win helped the Giants avert a Yankee sweep. Red Barber (bottom) was New York City's first baseball radio broadcaster and claimed to "broadcast with a Brooklyn heart." He later became the first to telecast a big-league baseball game.

One of Paige's teammates among his many clubs was Josh Gibson, the greatest slugger in Negro League annals. Beginning in 1930, Gibson hammered balls for 17 years before he died of a stroke in early 1947. He was called the "black Babe Ruth," and his power was legendary. An eyewitness claims he saw Gibson hit a ball out of Yankee Stadium in a 1934 game, a feat no major leaguer has accomplished. A hulking 6'2", 215-pound catcher, Gibson was described by Roy Campanella, a veteran of both

When Bill McKechnie managed Cincinnati to the 1939 NL pennant, he became the only manager to have won pennants in three different cities. The others were Pittsburgh and St. Louis.

Top: *Ten of the original 17 players inducted into the Hall of Fame in 1939. Front, left to right: Eddie Collins, Babe Ruth, Connie Mack, and Cy Young. Back, left to right: Honus Wagner, Pete Alexander, Tris Speaker, Nap Lajoie, George Sisler, and Walter Johnson. Missing is Ty Cobb; the other six were deceased. Cubs player-manager Gabby Hartnett was featured in a 1939 Wheaties ad (bottom left). Joe Cronin (bottom right) flourished at Fenway, leading the AL with 51 doubles in 1938.*

storming. This created an Achilles' heel for the Negro Major Leagues: a lack of strong central authority. Without a stabilizing force, club owners looked out for themselves first, and if that meant canceling a league contest because of a better barnstorming offer, so be it. The leagues' lax attitude towards the playing schedule gave the pennant contests little legitimacy in the eyes of players and fans, and the result was little fan interest in the pennant races.

One annual event that was taken seriously was the East-West All-Star Game. The first All-Star

With Lou Gehrig retired, Joe DiMaggio (top) picked up the slack for the Yankees, winning MVP honors in 1939 after leading the majors with a .381 batting average. The majors' first night game was played May 24, 1935, at Crosley Field (bottom).

Game was staged in 1933—the same year of the inaugural major-league All-Star Game—and was held in Comiskey Park. The early games were comprised of stars from league teams and barnstorming clubs. Each annual contest was called the most important African-American sporting event of the year and was always a good draw. Attendance the first year was 20,000 and reached a peak of 52,000 in 1943.

Eventually, however, the Negro Leagues went the same way as other Jim Crow institutions like segregated schools. Jackie Robinson's arrival in Brooklyn sharply deflected attention from the Negro Leagues, and by 1948, one year after Robinson broke the majors' color barrier, the Negro National League folded from lack of support. The Negro American League hung on until 1960, but its franchises were shifted out of major-league cities. The league eventually became a feeder system where such players as Willie Mays, Hank Aaron, and Ernie Banks were developed for the majors.

By 1965, the only all-African-American pro team in existence was the Indianapolis Clowns, a sports entertainment act similar in concept to the Harlem Globetrotters. In 1971, the Hall of Fame finally chose to recognize the contributions of pre-integration African-American players to the history of the game and voted to induct Satchel Paige. In the ensuing six years, eight of Paige's peers, including Cool Papa Bell and Josh Gibson, joined him in Cooperstown.

The Hall of Fame itself is a product of the Depression. In the midst of the nation's economic gloom, organized baseball decided to celebrate itself by constructing a monument to the game and its stars. The Hall of

Fame was born in 1936, and its charter members were the biggest stars of the first 35 years of the modern major leagues. The first player chosen was Ty Cobb, and he was joined by Honus Wagner, Christy Mathewson, Walter Johnson, and the man considered by many as the greatest player ever, Babe Ruth. In recognition of his enormous impact on the game's style of play, and his role in injecting the sport with a new-found excitement and popularity, the Bambino was selected for the Hall barely one year after playing his last game. The following year nine more players, managers, and administrators were enshrined. By the time the National Baseball Hall of Fame and Museum at Cooperstown was opened in June 1939, 22 men whose achievements spanned the game's first 100 years had been elevated to immortality.

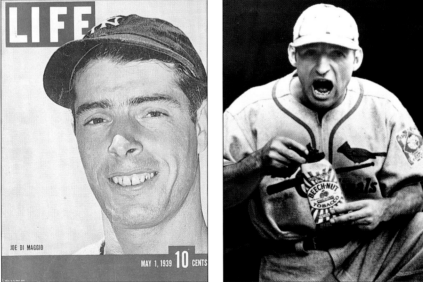

Lou Gehrig, second from left, and Joe DiMaggio, fourth from left, watch the action from the bench as the Yankees bat in the late 1930s (top). "Joltin' Joe" was larger than Life on this magazine cover from 1939 (bottom left), the year he was named AL MVP and the Yankees swept the World Series. St. Louis "Gashouse Gang" member Pepper Martin (bottom right) did everything with zeal, including chewing tobacco.

SCORES SOAR; A'S FOLD THE CARDS

In 1930, Philadelphia A's second baseman Max Bishop hiked his BA from .232 to .252, a mark that in most eras is about the norm for a middle infielder. That year, however, Bishop's figure of .252 was among the lowest in the AL for players with at least 400 at bats. The 1930 season saw the greatest offensive deluge since the mid-1890s after baseball moguls, anticipating that the economic depression would severely cut attendance, juiced up the ball in the hope that high scoring totals would keep the turnstiles clicking.

For batters, it was the biggest boon since the spitball and all other deliveries that defaced or soiled the ball were banned in 1920. For most pitchers, however, it was an affront to their pride and a threat to their livelihood. In 1930, the last-place Philadelphia Phillies had only one regular hurler—Phil Collins (4.78)—who had an ERA below 5.70. As a consequence, the Phils lost 102 games despite hitting .315 as a team and scoring an average of 6.13 runs per game.

The Phils were only one of six teams in the NL to hit .300. Though the third-place New York Giants led the loop with a .319 mark, the St. Louis Cardinals had a more evenly balanced attack. In 1930, every one of the Cards' eight regulars hit at least .303, leading to an NL-record 1,004 runs and St. Louis's third pennant since 1926.

Two games back of the Cards when the curtain descended were the reigning NL champs, the

Mickey Cochrane makes a gem of a defensive play, diving to tag out a runner at the plate in 1930. Cochrane hit .357 and helped power Connie Mack's mighty Philadelphia Athletics to their second consecutive World Series title.

St. Louis's Chick Hafey (top) hit .336 in 1930, then held out for $15,000. Lou Gehrig (bottom) hit 41 home runs and drove in 174 runs, but it wasn't enough to overcome the Athletics.

Chicago Cubs. The Cubs' failure to repeat despite a .309 BA and 998 runs could be attributed, amazingly, to an inability to generate even more offense after star second baseman Rogers Hornsby was shelved by a foot injury. Minus Hornsby's big bat, the Cubs were forced to employ Footsie Blair (.278) at second base and Clyde Beck (.213) at short.

Eclipsed by the cornucopia of high batting and slugging averages was Dazzy Vance's NL-leading 2.61 ERA (1.15 runs lower than that of runner-up Carl Hubbell). In a season loaded with oddities, Vance's performance was the most bizarre of all. Toiling for fourth-place Brooklyn, which finished at 86-68, Vance ought to have won around 30 games with his glittering ERA. Instead he posted a very undazzling record of 17-15.

AL ERA champ Lefty Grove parlayed his 2.54 mark into a 28-5 record. That effort pushed the Philadelphia A's to their second straight pennant by a cozy 8 games over second-place Washington. The Senators had the dual distinction of being the only club in the majors to steal at least 100 bases and notch a staff ERA under 4.00. Moreover, Washington actually outhit the A's .302 to .294 but had no guns to match the likes of Jimmie Foxx and Al Simmons. The A's twin cannons hammered 73 homers and knocked home 321 runs between them. Owing to their production, Bishop, notwithstanding his low BA, once again tallied well over 100 runs.

As overwhelming as Foxx's and Simmons's stats were, Babe Ruth and Lou Gehrig were still the offensive kingpins in the AL. In 1930, the two New York Yankees' bammers combined for 327 RBI and 90 homers. The Yanks nevertheless finished 16 games off the A's pace when Bob Shawkey, Miller Huggins's replacement at the Bombers' helm, could do no better than his predecessor at motivating his charges. "The trouble with this club," Waite Hoyt said one day after glancing around the clubhouse, "is there are too many guys on it who aren't Yankees." A few days later Hoyt himself was no longer a Yankee after he and shortstop Mark Koenig were traded to the Tigers. By Opening Day in 1931, only Ruth, Gehrig, Tony Lazzeri, Earle Combs, Herb Pennock, and George Pipgras remained from the team that had seemed invincible just four years earlier.

As so often happens when the championship is at stake, pitchers reasserted themselves in the 1930 World Series. In the opener at Philadelphia's Shibe Park, Lefty Grove granted the high-scoring Cardinals just two runs in a 5-2 triumph. The following day, George Earnshaw was even stingier, allowing St. Louis just one marker as he won 6-1.

The Phillies' Chuck Klein, at left, posted a .386 batting average with 40 homers and 170 RBI in 1930, while the Giants' Bill Terry hit .401, the last National Leaguer to eclipse the .400 mark.

After a travel day, the Series resumed in St. Louis on October 4 with Bill Hallahan, the Cards' ace southpaw, topping Rube Walberg, the A's second-best lefty, by a 5-0 count. The next afternoon the Cards evened the Series when third sacker Jimmy Dykes undermined Grove with a fourth-inning throwing error that handed St. Louis two unearned runs. A mere 24 hours later, however, Grove came on when Earnshaw was removed in the eighth for a pinch hitter and turned in two scoreless relief innings to get a 2-0 whitewash that sent the Series back to Philly with the Mackmen up 3-2.

On October 8, Cards manager Gabby Street again sent Hallahan to the hill, but this time the A's got to the southpaw fireballer early and often. The beneficiary of a 5-0 lead after just four frames, Earnshaw sailed to a 7-1 verdict that brought the A's their second straight ML crown.

SEASON'S BEST

- The Cubs' Hack Wilson is named NL MVP after driving in an ML-record 190 runs. Wilson also sets an NL record with 56 home runs.

- Dodger Dazzy Vance's 2.61 ERA is 1.15 runs better than the next-lowest ERA in the NL.

- The Phillies' Lefty Grove leads the majors in wins (28), winning percentage (.848), Ks (209), and, amazingly, saves (nine). Grove's 2.54 ERA is .77 runs better than the next-lowest ERA in the AL.

- Al Simmons of the A's tops the AL in batting (.381), runs (152), and runs produced (281).

Al Simmons

- Giant Bill Terry leads the NL with a .401 BA, the last .400 average in the league.

- After a long holdout, Babe Ruth signs for $80,000—an ML-record salary at this juncture. While Ruth leads the AL with 49 homers, he also becomes the first documented player to fan 1,000 times in his career.

- Philly's Chuck Klein scores 158 runs, a 20th-century NL record (still stands). Klein also tops the NL in doubles (59) and runs produced (288). The latter is an all-time NL record.

- Cub Gabby Hartnett's .630 SA sets an ML record for catchers.

- Cincy's Harry Heilmann becomes the first player to homer in every major-league park in use during his career.

- On May 6, Gene Rye of Waco in the Texas League hits three home runs in one inning.

- At age 46, Jack Quinn of the A's becomes the oldest player to homer in an ML game.

- Cardinal George Watkins sets an ML rookie record when he hits .373.

- Brave Wally Berger sets NL rookie records with 38 homers and 119 RBI.

- Senator Sam Rice's 207 hits, 121 runs, and 271 total bases all set records for a player over age 40.

HACK WILSON

Cubs outfielder bats in 190—an all-time ML record

Although the home run era may have begun in 1920, its effects continued throughout the Roaring '20s, as the number of runs scored shot up year after year until 1930. The baseball was deadened the next season, ensuring that 1930 would go down in history—20th-century history, at least—as the absolute peak of the batting outburst.

It was fun while it lasted. The American League batted .288; the National, .303; AL pitchers compiled an ERA of 4.65; the NL hurlers, an ugly 4.97. The St. Louis Cardinals finished first with an ERA of 4.40 and 1,004 runs scored. Incredibly, last-place Philadelphia outhit them .315 to .314. The lopsided Phillies had two .380 hitters in their lineup (Chuck Klein and Lefty O'Doul), but their pitchers allowed 1,199 runs and had an ERA of 6.71.

If Ty Cobb was the symbol of the dead-ball era and Babe Ruth the hero of 1920, the personification of 1930 was the wild Lewis "Hack" Wilson. The free-swinging, home run bashing, and utterly eccentric Chicago Cubs center fielder put together one of the few National League seasons that can be compared with the best of Ruth and Lou Gehrig. A legendary drinker and carouser who was once even reprimanded by Commissioner Kenesaw Mountain Landis reputedly for socializing with Al Capone, the 5'6", 190-pound, spindly-legged, barrel-chested slugger, after failing to impress the New York Giants, came to Chicago in 1926. There he blossomed, batting over .300 and upping his home run totals each year until 1930.

Wilson had an overwhelming year in 1930. He drove in a major league-record 190 RBI, clobbered a National League-record 56 home runs, drew 105 walks, and scored 146 runs. He batted .356 and slugged .723. If not the National League's best hitter that year—an argument could be made for Chuck Klein—he was at least the most flamboyant. Chicago fans reveled in the sight of the comically stubby Wilson wildly flailing at the ball with his favored 40-ounce tree trunk of a bat. In the spirit of the times in which he lived, Hack swung away with abandon.

Only a year later, Wilson's glory was over. His hitting fell off even more drastically than the rest of the league's, to only 13 home runs and a .261 batting average. By 1934, he was out of baseball at age 34; 14 years later, he was dead.

CARDINAL HITTERS PEPPER THE A'S

Still serving as both the Philadelphia A's manager and co-owner after 30 years, Connie Mack was only now reaching his apex. In 1931, he embarked on a quest for an unprecedented prize. Since the introduction in 1884 of postseason competition between two rival major leagues, no team had ever won three consecutive World Series.

Mack's A's seemed a solid bet to be the first to achieve this height when they cakewalked to their third successive AL flag by 13½ games over the revitalized New York Yankees in their first season under Joe McCarthy. With the ball dejuiced somewhat in 1931, offensive marks slipped back toward the norm everywhere but in Yankee Stadium. Babe Ruth and Lou Gehrig incredibly broke their own year-old AL teammates record when they compiled 347 RBI, helping the Yankees to score a 20th century-high 1,067 runs. Any realistic ambitions the Yankees had, though, of terminating the A's run were scorched by a 17-game Philadelphia winning streak in May and then reduced to ashes when the A's went on another 13-win tear in July. The two skeins embraced an individual AL-record 16-game winning streak by Lefty Grove. Nearly unbeatable in 1931, Grove lost his bid for a 17th-straight win when left fielder Jim Moore, subbing for Al Simmons, misplayed a ball that saddled the A's star with a 1-0 defeat. After the game, Grove's infamous temper was directed not just at Moore, but also Simmons, who had taken the day off.

For the rest of the season, though, Grove directed his anger at the other seven AL teams as he became the only 20th-century hurler to win 30 while working less than 300 innings. His closest counterparts in the NL included Heinie Meine of Pittsburgh and a southpaw from St. Louis, Redbird Bill Hallahan, who tied for the senior loop lead with a mere 19 wins apiece. It marked the first time that a loop hill leader had fewer than 20 wins. The totals slugging leader Chuck Klein accumulated were equally as

Pepper Martin powered the Cardinals in the 1931 World Series, batting .500 with five stolen bases. Thanks to Martin's bat, the Cards topped the A's in seven games.

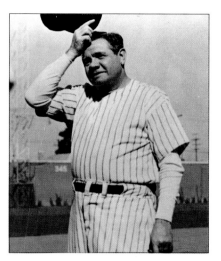

unimposing. Klein's NL-best 31 homers and 121 RBI in 1931 would not even have ranked him in the top five in either department a year earlier.

When the Cardinals won their second straight NL flag with ease, romping home 13½ games ahead of the New York Giants, it would have made for a dull year throughout the senior loop except for the tightest three-way batting race in history. By just a fraction of a percentage point St. Louis's Chick Hafey (.34889) edged New York's Bill Terry (.34861) for hitting honors, and Hafey's teammate, Jim Bottomley, finished less than a point back at .34817.

Al Simmons of the A's, meanwhile, led the majors with a .390 BA, and with Jimmie Foxx, Max Bishop, and Mickey Cochrane again complementing Simmons, observers gauged Mack's 1931 club to be the best he had ever fielded. Still, Mack had learned in 1914 what overconfidence could do to a team in the World Series. Taking no chances, he started Grove in the first game and rejoiced when his ace reeled in an easy 6-2 win.

The following day, though, it was Gabby Street's turn to glow. Fearing Grove, the Cards manager had thrown Paul Derringer against him, preferring to save Hallahan for the second clash. Street's strategy paid a huge dividend when Hallahan shut the A's down cold, 2-0.

A rain interruption allowed Mack to start Grove again three days later when the Series resumed in Philadelphia, but suddenly a minor irritation that had surfaced in Game 2 erupted into a thorn that would haunt the A's for the rest of the Series. The

Lou Gehrig (top left) *had an AL-record 184 RBI and tied Babe Ruth* (top right) *with 46 homers, Ruth's last title. The Giants' Bill Terry* (top center) *lost the batting title by .0003. Al Simmons's homer* (bottom) *spoiled Burleigh Grimes's Series shutout.*

thorn was Cardinals center fielder Pepper Martin, who had found a chink in the A's armor. Since the stolen base was by then a rarely used weapon, Cochrane's arm had seldom been tested, but Martin discovered that he could steal almost at will on the A's star catcher.

After Martin's baserunning produced a 5-2 St. Louis win in Game 3, Grove begged Mack to replace Cochrane with backup catcher Joe Palmisano. Mack demurred when Earnshaw tossed a two-hit 3-0 shutout in Game 4, but it did not escape his notice that Martin collected the Cards' only two safeties.

In Game 5, Martin nailed three hits and drove home four runs in a 5-1 St. Louis win. Back in St.

Louis two days later, Grove put a momentary lid on Martin and was able to triumph 8-1 and even the Series at 3-all.

Mack again called on Earnshaw in the deciding seventh game but had Grove in the bullpen if needed. Burleigh Grimes, the winner of Game 3, was Street's selection, but, like Mack, Street sent his ace, Hallahan, to the bullpen. Holding a 4-0 lead in the ninth, the Cards seemingly had the game iced. All at once the A's exploded for two runs and had two on with two out. Street hurriedly summoned Hallahan to face left-handed hitter Max Bishop and was rewarded when Bishop laced a liner right at Martin, giving St. Louis the championship.

SEASON'S BEST

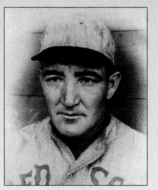

Earl Webb

• The Baseball Writers Association of America appoints two committees, one in each league, to elect the MVPs.

• Lefty Grove is selected as the first BBWAA winner in the AL. Grove tops the majors in wins (31), Ks (175), winning percentage (.886), and ERA (2.06), and he ties in CGs (27). He wins 16 straight games during the season, tying an AL record.

• Frankie Frisch of the Cards wins the MVP Award in the NL.

• Phillie Chuck Klein tops the NL in homers with 31 and RBI with 121.

• Cardinal Chick Hafey wins the batting title at .349, slightly better than Giant Bill Terry who also hits .349.

• No NL pitcher wins 20 games—the first time that's happened in ML history. The AL's Grove, in contrast, becomes the last southpaw to win 30 games in a season.

• Yankee Lou Gehrig has an ML-record 301 runs produced. Gehrig tallies an all-time AL-record 184 RBI. He also tops the AL in hits (211), runs (163), and total bases (410).

• Babe Ruth wins his last home run crown by tying with teammate Gehrig for the title (46).

• Bill Walker of the Giants wins his second NL ERA title (2.26).

• The Yankees have six men who score 100 or more runs. The team scores an all-time ML-record 1,067 runs.

• Joe McCarthy, fired the previous year by the Cubs, becomes manager of the Yankees.

• Cleveland's Wes Ferrell hits a season-record nine home runs while serving as a pitcher.

• The AL rules that all teams must have numbers on their uniforms.

• The sacrifice fly rule is abolished. Balls bouncing over or going through a fence, heretofore considered home runs, are now ruled doubles.

• Earl Webb of the Red Sox hits an all-time ML-record 67 doubles.

• Brooklyn's Babe Herman becomes the first MLer to hit for the cycle twice in a season.

• Terry tops the NL in runs (121), runs produced (224), and triples (20).

LEFTY GROVE

Philly lefty finds the groove, wins 31 of 35

Robert Moses Grove had compiled a 25-1 record by late August 1931, but when he lost his bid for a major league-record 17th consecutive victory in a 1-0 defeat to St. Louis, the visitor's locker room at Sportsman's Park was not the place for the faint of heart. Angered that the only run of the game had scored on a dropped fly ball by rookie left fielder Jimmy Moore—playing in place of Al Simmons, who had taken the day off—Grove let loose with a verbal diatribe against Simmons, Moore, and anybody else he could think of as he ripped apart wooden locker doors and stomped upon his uniform. Grove followed up this postgame tirade by not talking to his teammates for several days, then went about the business of winning his next five starts and finishing up a 31-4 MVP season for the American League champions.

An intense and irritable competitor as anyone who has ever played the game, Lefty's success on the mound more than made up for his tirades and sulking. Despite the fact he did not reach the majors until age 25, the wiry, 6'3" sourpuss compiled a lifetime 300-141 record, including a dazzling 128-33 slate from 1928 through '32 that coincided with three straight pennants for the A's. The AL leader in walks and strikeouts as a rookie in '26, he soon gained control of his dazzling fastball and was strikeout king for the next six seasons while gradually cutting down on his free passes. By 1927 Grove was a 20-game winner, and his great stretch of success began in the following season.

It was a period of domination no pitcher would approach again until Sandy Koufax some 30 years later. From 1928 through '33, Grove led the AL in victories, ERA, strikeouts, and winning percentage four times each; complete games three times; shutouts twice; and even once in saves. His 1931 campaign was the topper. In addition to his career-best record of 31-4 (the most wins and best percentage in the majors), Grove was the league leader in ERA (2.06), strikeouts (175), shutouts (four), and complete games (27). He even pitched 11 games in relief — saving five of them — walking just 62 batters in 288⅔ innings. He added two complete game wins and a 2.42 ERA in the World Series, but Philadelphia lost in seven games to the Cardinals.

Forsaking blazers for brains and developing assorted pitches to offset his declining fastball, Grove had just one more 20-win season but four more ERA titles (earning a record nine) after his 1934 sale to the Red Sox. His .680 winning percentage is the highest ever for a 300-game winner. Grove made the Hall of Fame in 1947, undoubtedly saving sportswriters from another tirade.

YANKS WIN; RUTH CALLS HIS SHOT

Thwarted on the final lap in his bid to become the first pilot ever to garner three consecutive world championships, Philadelphia manager Connie Mack set his sights on a new goal in 1932. He began the season determined his A's would become the first AL team to cop four straight pennants. In Mack's path, however, were Joe McCarthy's New York Yankees. McCarthy had a goal of his own. The former Cubs skipper wanted to be the first manager in the 20th century to win a flag in two major leagues.

Along with his twin stalwarts, Babe Ruth and Lou Gehrig, McCarthy still had such championship holdovers as Tony Lazzeri, Earle Combs, and George Pipgras. In recent years, however, they had been joined by a new crop of stars like Bill Dickey, Lyn Lary, Lefty Gomez, and Ben Chapman, plus the accrual via trades of Red Ruffing and Joe Sewell. McCarthy received an additional boost in 1932 when two more rookies arrived, ready for full duty. One of the newcomers, shortstop Frankie Crosetti, immediately stole Lary's job, and the second, pitcher Johnny Allen, topped the league in winning percentage with a dazzling 17-4 season.

Along with Gomez, Ruffing, and Pipgras, Allen completed a four-man rotation that bagged 75 wins while bowing just 27 times. Combined with what McCarthy brought to the team, the Yankees were blowout winners in 1932, rolling home 13 games up on the A's. An adroit psychologist as well as a master tactician, McCarthy ordered new Yankees uniforms a half size too large and had his players square off their caps to make them appear even bigger. He also proved himself to be a stern disciplinarian while at the same time dodging the stormy clashes with Ruth that had exhausted Miller Huggins. Two autumns after he took command of the Yankees he had them back in the World Series against his former employers, the Chicago Cubs.

While the Yanks' road to the confrontation was serene, the Cubs' trek was difficult. On August 7,

Cubs players insist Babe Ruth was pointing toward pitcher Charlie Root; Yankees players claim he was "calling his shot" in Wrigley Field's center field bleachers.

McCarthy's replacement at the Chicago helm, Rogers Hornsby, was bounced even though he had the Cubs close to first place. Hornsby's crime was that he had disagreed once too often with team president William Veeck, the father of promotional genius Bill Veeck. The elder Veeck finally prevailed on club owner William Wrigley to axe Hornsby and install first sacker Charlie Grimm. Many worried that the fun-loving Grimm, who was nicknamed Jolly Cholly, would be unable to control his former teammates, but their fears proved to be unfounded. The Cubs responded jubilantly to Grimm's relaxed leadership and fended off a season-long challenge from the Pittsburgh Pirates to reach the wire four games in front.

Pittsburgh's unexpected pennant bid would probably have earned George Gibson the Manager of the Year Award if it had been in existence. Back for his second tour at the Pirates' helm, Gibson somehow guided his men home 18 games over .500 even though they led the NL in no major batting, pitching, or fielding departments and were outscored by their opponents 711 to 701. The New York Giants, in contrast, finished sixth, 10 games below .500, despite outscoring their opposition 755 to 706. The Giants' worst finish since 1915 was blamed on the internal turmoil that resulted when John McGraw, in failing health, resigned in June after 30 years at the helm and chose as his successor Bill Terry rather than the more popular Fred Lindstrom.

Philly's Chuck Klein was the NL MVP, tying Mel Ott in homers (38) and leading the league in stolen bases (20).

Chicago's Lon Warneke (top) led the NL in wins (22) and ERA (2.37). Pittsburgh's Paul Waner (bottom left) set a then-National League record with 62 doubles. Washington's Al Crowder (bottom right), who won 26 games in 1932, pitched 327 innings without hitting a batter or throwing a wild pitch.

Though Grimm had the Cubs upbeat when they began the World Series, their optimism was short-lived. The Yankees swept the affair in four quick games. More than that, the 1932 fall clash engendered ill will between the two combatants that lasted for a number of years. Most of it stemmed from the Cubs' failure to vote former Yankees shortstop Mark Koenig a full Series share. The Cubs had logic on their side because Koenig had not joined the team until August, but the Yankees felt that his contribution—a .353 BA in 33 games as a replacement for injured Billy Jurges—outweighed his short sojourn.

The bitter feelings stemming from the Koenig vote were at their peak when the only real moment of drama in the Series occurred. In the fifth inning of Game 3 at Chicago's Wrigley Field, Babe Ruth stepped to the plate with the contest tied 4-4. Reacting to fierce needling from the Cubs bench, Ruth

pointed somewhere after he took two strikes from Charlie Root. Cubs players afterward insisted he pointed toward Root on the mound as if to signal that he still had a strike left, whereas Yankees players contended he gestured toward the center field bleachers as if to "call his shot." In any case, Ruth launched his last postseason home run on the very next pitch, creating one of the most indelible moments in Series history. New York went on to sweep the Series in four easy games.

SEASON'S BEST

•Philly's Jimmie Foxx is selected AL MVP. Foxx leads the AL in homers (58), RBI (169), SA (.749), runs (151), and total bases (438). His 58 homers are the most at this juncture by anyone other than Babe Ruth.

•Philly's Chuck Klein is the NL MVP. Klein ties for the homer crown (38), and he leads the NL in runs produced (251).

•Al Crowder of Washington tops the majors with 26 wins.

•John McGraw steps down as Giants manager after 40 games and turns the reins over to player Bill Terry.

•The Red Sox again tumble into the cellar and set a new club record for losses with 111.

•St. Louis rookie Dizzy Dean tops the NL with 191 Ks.

•Lon Warneke of the Cubs is the NL's top winner with 22.

•Brooklyn's Lefty O'Doul wins his second NL bat crown in four years (.368).

•Pittsburgh's Paul Waner sets an NL record (since broken) with 62 doubles.

Mel Ott

•New York's Mel Ott wins his first NL homer crown (38, tied with Klein).

•After the 1932 season, the A's sell Al Simmons, Jimmy Dykes, and Mule Haas to the White Sox for $100,000.

•Brooklyn's Johnny Frederick hits an ML-record six pinch-hit home runs during the season.

•On June 3, Yankee Lou Gehrig becomes the first player in the 20th century to hit four home runs in a game.

•Philly's Don Hurst tops the NL in RBI with 143, a record for NL first basemen.

•On July 10, Ed Rommel of the A's gives up a record 29 hits and 14 runs in relief. Rommel also pitches an AL relief-record 17 innings in the game.

•On July 10, Johnny Burnett of Cleveland bangs out an ML-record nine hits.

•Four-year vet Wes Ferrell of Cleveland wins 20-plus games for the fourth straight year.

•Gehrig leads all World Series hitters with a .529 BA, three homers, and eight RBI.

JIMMIE FOXX

"The right-handed Ruth" blasts 58 round-trippers

His home run totals have slowly been passed over the years by players whose longer careers offered them far more at bats, but in his day Jimmie Foxx was considered the greatest slugger in the American League—and a man whose 534 homers ranked second only to Babe Ruth when he retired. He was, in fact, often called "the right-handed Ruth." In his AL MVP year of 1932, he challenged the Babe's most revered record—60 home runs in a season—before finishing just two short.

Growing up big and strong on a farm just as fellow Marylander Ruth was leaving to find fame and fortune in Boston, Foxx was powerful enough as a high school player to attract the attention of former A's star Frank "Home Run" Baker. Baker saw fit to recommend the strapping youngster to his old boss, Connie Mack. Originally a catcher, Foxx made the big leagues as a 17-year-old and sat on the Philly bench behind Hall of Famer Mickey Cochrane for two years before Mack converted him to first base. A regular starter in 1928, he registered a .327 batting average and totaled 100 home runs and 393 RBI for Philadelphia's three consecutive pennant winners from 1929 through '31 (hitting at a .344 clip in World Series play) before 1932 saw him explode with his greatest all-around season.

A menacing figure at the plate who flexed his huge arms visibly just before hitting the ball, the

ever-grinning Foxx led the AL in homers, RBI (169), runs (151), slugging (.749), walks (169), and total bases (438) in 1932 while placing second in batting at .364—finishing just .003 behind Dale Alexander in his bid for a Triple Crown. Foxx got hotter as the year progressed in his pursuit of Ruth's record, and his eventual failure to catch the Babe has been the subject of speculation ever since. Legendary sportswriter Fred Leib claimed a right field screen erected at Sportsman's Park in St. Louis since Ruth's assault five years earlier cost Foxx five homers, while other reports suggested Jimmie hit at least three more balls against a brand-new screen in front of the left field bleachers at Cleveland's League Park.

Despite such obstacles, his homer output remains the highest by any player other than Ruth, Roger Maris, Mark McGwire, Sammy Sosa, and Barry Bonds (Hank Greenberg also hit 58 in 1938). It also ended the Babe's hold on the AL home run leadership after six consecutive seasons and established Double-X as the premier slugger in the league. Foxx even managed to lead the league with a .994 fielding percentage—but none of it was enough to keep the three-time champion A's from dropping to third place. The dynasty had come to a close, and it wouldn't be long before Mack would break up the championship squad and sell off its brightest stars—Foxx included.

GIANTS TAG OUT CRONIN'S NATS

Joe McCarthy, it seemed, was no more immune to complacency than Miller Huggins. In 1933, his Yankees staggered out of the gate and never really got on track as another Joe—Cronin, the shortstop and player-manager for the Washington Senators—provided the year's top story. Buoyed by a series of shrewd off-season trades that supplied him with pitchers Earl Whitehill, Lefty Stewart, and Jack Russell, catcher Luke Sewell, and outfielders Goose Goslin and Fred Schulte, Cronin got the Senators home seven games ahead of the Yankees with a club-record 99 wins.

In third place, slipping yet another notch in 1933, were Connie Mack's Philadelphia A's. Pleading financial hardship as he had when he broke up his 1910 to '14 championship dynasty, Mack bartered away his pennant chances for cash by ped-

dling Al Simmons, Mule Haas, and Jimmy Dykes to the Chicago White Sox. The three helped the Pale Hose to an 18½-game improvement over a disastrous 102-loss season in 1932.

Another team that appeared to begin the long return trip to respectability was Bill McKechnie's Boston Braves, whose fourth-place finish landed them in the first division for the first time since 1921. What's more, McKechnie actually had the Braves involved in the NL pennant race as late as September before they ultimately wound up nine games off the pace.

Back on top in the National League, for the first time since 1924, were the New York Giants in Bill Terry's first full year at their wheel. Terry provided much of his own offensive punch with a .322 BA, and Mel Ott, who had 23 homers and 103 RBI, furnished most of the remainder. The Giants also relied on their pitching staff. They counted on leader Carl Hubbell and 22-year-old Hal Schumacher, a 19-game winner in his second major-league season. Pittsburgh had no one to match Hubbell, and Heinie Meine, the Pirates' second-best pitcher, faded in the late-summer heat. Nevertheless, manager George Gibson once again did a commendable job by guiding the Cor-

The '33 Senators won the last pennant by a Washington-based major-league team. Alas, the Series wasn't as close as this pickoff play at first; the Giants won in five.

sairs into the runner-up spot, just four games out. Charlie Grimm, in contrast, drew sharp criticism when his favored Cubs limped home third despite the addition of Babe Herman, who led the club in both RBI and homers. In his defense, Grimm could cite injuries to Kiki Cuyler and several other key performers for Chicago, but an even bigger factor was the Bruins' inability to beat last-place Cincinnati. A tie in their season series with the Reds doomed the Cubs to third, a mere three games ahead of the Braves.

Also a disappointment in 1933 were the Philadelphia Phillies. After posting their lone first-division finish between 1917 and 1948 in 1932, the Phils took a huge backward step to seventh when Don Hurst, who set an NL record for first basemen with 143 RBI in 1932, could knock home barely half that many and Phil Collins, for several years the team's best hurler, sagged to just eight wins. The Phils' lowly finish almost certainly prevented Triple Crown winner Chuck Klein from garnering his second straight MVP Award.

If Phillie fans were distressed with their team's 1933 seventh-place showing, Boston Red Sox rooters were delighted to see their club in the seventh slot when the season ended. Better yet, in their first season under their energetic new owner Tom Yawkey the Crimson Hose won 63 games, their highest total since 1924.

On July 6, 1933, John McGraw came out of retirement for one day to pilot the NL in the first All-Star Game at Chicago's Comiskey Park, and Connie Mack filled the same role for the AL squad. Conceived as a one-shot method to raise funds for the National Association of Professional Baseball Play-

The AL team (top) won the first All-Star Game as Babe Ruth, standing fourth from left, hit the first All-Star HR. AL MVP Jimmie Foxx (bottom left) won the Triple Crown. NL MVP Carl Hubbell (bottom right) had two complete games and no earned runs in the Series.

ers, the game was so successful that moguls immediately and unanimously agreed that it should be made an annual event. There were precious few other promotional devices the game's leaders tried in the middle of the Depression that proved nearly as popular, and that included the World Series.

In the opener of the 1933 fall classic, 46,672 were in the audience at the Polo Grounds to watch Hubbell top Lefty Stewart by a 4-2 score, but the crowds in each of the remaining four games were disappointing. Game 2 in New York saw a drop of over 11,000, and the financial picture was even more bleak when the two teams journeyed to the nation's capital.

155

In 1925, the three Series games in Washington had pulled an average of 37,000. The three contests in 1933 averaged about 10,000 less. Washington owner Clark Griffith was not alone in being concerned more by the empty seats than by his team's imminent departure in just five games. Even before reliever Dolf Luque threw the last pitch to seal the 4-3 win in 10 innings on October 7 that gave the Giants the Series, Griffith had mentally conceded defeat—and not just on the field of play.

SEASON'S BEST

•Giant pitcher Carl Hubbell wins the NL MVP vote. Hubbell's 1.66 ERA is the lowest ever by an NL lefty for over 300 innings.

•Jimmie Foxx of the A's wins the AL MVP to become the first player ever to cop consecutive awards. Foxx takes the Triple Crown in the AL, batting .356 with 48 homers and 163 RBI. He also leads in SA (.703) and total bases (403).

•Philly's Chuck Klein wins the Triple Crown in the NL, batting .368 with 28 homers and 120 RBI. Klein also leads the NL in hits (223), doubles (44), total bases (365), and runs produced (193). Klein sets a 20th-century NL record when he collects 200 hits for the fifth consecutive year. In November, the financially strapped Phillies send Klein to the Cubs for three second-line players and $65,000.

Lefty Grove

•This is the only time both leagues have a Triple Crown winner the same season.

•Lefty Grove of the A's and Washington's Al Crowder tie for the ML lead in wins with 24.

•In the first All-Star Game, the AL beats the NL 4-2 at Comiskey Park. Babe Ruth hits the first homer in All-Star competition—a two-run shot.

•NL pitchers have a collective ERA nearly a full run below the AL's (3.34-4.28).

•Yankee Lou Gehrig surpasses Everett Scott's record streak of 1,307 consecutive games played.

•Nick Altrock, age 57, pinch-hits in a game for Washington.

•On July 19, Dizzy Dean fans 17 Cubs, a modern ML record (since broken). Dean again tops the NL in Ks (199).

•Washington's Heinie Manush has a 33-game hitting streak.

•On July 19, Wes and Rick Ferrell become the first pair of brothers on opposing teams to homer in the same game.

•Tom Yawkey buys the moribund Red Sox. The bank takes over the bankrupt Reds—Powell Crosley eventually buys the club.

•Cardinal Pepper Martin tops the NL in runs (122) and steals (26).

•Ruth leads the AL for the last time in a major offensive department—walks with 114.

•Cincinnati's Red Lucas paces the majors in fewest walks per game—an incredible .74.

JOE CRONIN

"The Boy Manager" gets things done in Washington

The first big leaguer to rise from player to the presidency of his league, Joe Cronin made sure he'd have plenty of time to make his mark in the game. He reached the majors while still in his teens, and after just seven years, he stepped into the role of player-manager of the 1933 American League champions at the ripe old age of 26.

He was known throughout baseball as the "The Boy Manager" when he led the Washington Senators into the '33 World Series. Due to the strength of his leadership and peerless play at shortstop (where he batted .309 with 118 RBI and an AL-best 45 doubles), Cronin's story was as much an example of persistence as excellence. Playing semi-pro ball while working as a bank clerk, the native San Franciscan was signed by the Pirates in 1925 but got into just 50 games over two seasons while batting just .257.

He was sent to the minors and hitting .245—seemingly at the end of the line—when an injury to shortstop Bobby Reeves prompted desperate Washington to pick him up in 1928.

Leaping at the chance to play every day, Cronin was among the American League leaders with a .346 mark and 126 RBI by 1930, earning MVP honors. He developed into one of the game's great RBI men, driving in 100 or more runs from 1930 to '34 and eight times overall despite hitting 20 homers only once. Cronin relied on steady play rather than flash at short, all the while earning a reputation as a field general. This prompted Washington owner Clark Griffith to name him player-manager for 1933. While it probably did not hurt that Cronin had by this time married Griffith's daughter Mildred, Joe responded to the honor by leading the Senators to the pennant. Although he hit just five home runs, his 118 RBI placed fourth in the AL as he won a spot on the AL squad for the first-ever All-Star Game at Comiskey Park. Washington beat out the Yankees for the pennant by seven games with a 99-53 record, then lost a five-game World Series to the Giants despite a .318 batting average from Joe.

Cronin had a mixed year in '34; he hit .284 with 101 RBI, but the Senators dropped to seventh. Proving money can be thicker than family, Griffith sold his son-in-law to the Red Sox when Boston owner Tom Yawkey offered up $250,000, at that time a record sum paid for a single ballplayer. Maintaining his player-manager role, Joe was a hit in cozy Fenway Park, staying a solid 90-100 RBI man for seven more years and then becoming the game's best pinch hitter. He quit as a player in '45, but stayed on as manager and led the Red Sox to the 1946 pennant. From there it was up to the front office, where Cronin served as Red Sox general manager (1948 to '58) and American League President (1959 to '73). His story—along with 1,424 career RBI and a 1,236-1,055 managerial record—made him an easy pick for the Hall of Fame in 1956.

DEANS, CARDINALS CAGE THE TIGERS

Asked in the 1934 preseason to assess the chances of his seven NL rivals, New York Giants manager Bill Terry paused when he came to the Brooklyn Dodgers and then said, "Brooklyn? Is Brooklyn still in the league?" Sixth in 1933, the Dodgers repeated their lowly finish the following year under freshman pilot Casey Stengel, but by the close of the season Terry wished they were out of the league.

In first place for 127 days of the 1934 campaign, the Giants commenced the final Saturday on the schedule tied with the St. Louis Cardinals at 93-58. They were slated to play the Dodgers a single game that afternoon at the Polo Grounds and another single contest the following day. The Cards, meanwhile, were opposing the last-place Cincinnati Reds.

By Sunday evening Terry was ready to throttle the reporter who had printed his preseason forecast, for the Dodgers knocked off his favored Giants in both clashes on the final weekend while the Cards put away the Reds to win the NL flag by two lengths.

St. Louis's return to the top after a three-year absence was spurred by player-manager Frankie Frisch, who had replaced Gabby Street as pilot midway through the previous season, and General Manager Branch Rickey's flair for dipping into the Cards' vast farm system to uncover replacements for worn parts. From the 1931 championship team, only Frisch, Pepper Martin, and Bill Hallahan were still significant contributors. Trades had brought shortstop Leo Durocher, pitcher Bill Walker, and catcher Spud Davis, and the Cards' farm teams had supplied Ripper

Collins, Joe Medwick, and, above all, the brothers Dean—Jay Hanna and Paul, who were more familiarly known as Dizzy and Daffy.

In the spring of 1934, Dizzy, a 20-game winner for the first time the previous year, predicted that he and his rookie sibling would win 40 games between them. It seemed a bit of youthful braggadocio—

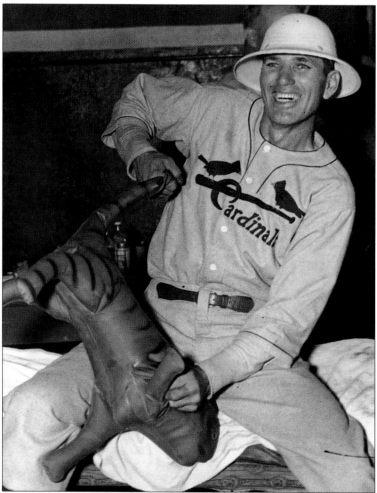

Dizzy Dean and the "Gashouse Gang" took the Tigers by the tail in the World Series, winning in seven games. Dean had two wins, including a shutout.

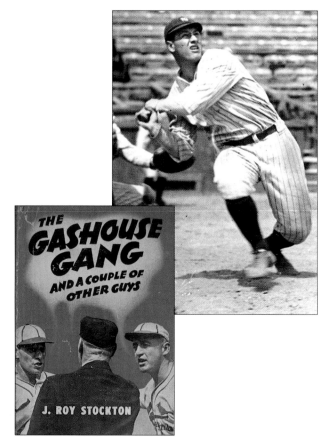

Yankee Lou Gehrig (top) won the Triple Crown in '34, but not the AL MVP Award. Bottom: St. Louis manager Frankie Frisch, right, was pictured on the book jacket of The Gashouse Gang.

Daffy was barely 20 and Dizzy just turned 23. But by September 30, the day the Cards clinched the flag, Dizzy's prediction had proved to be far too conservative. Between them, the Deans gave the other seven NL teams a "Double D" headache all summer by winning a sibling teammates-record 49 games.

In the AL, it was a season for G-men. New York Yankees southpaw Lefty Gomez led the loop in wins, Ks, and ERA; Yankees first sacker Lou Gehrig won the Triple Crown; and Goose Goslin, Charlie Gehringer, Hank Greenberg, and Gee Walker lifted the Detroit Tigers over Joe McCarthy's favored New Yorkers for the Bengals' first pennant since 1909. On this occasion, however, it was not complacency but injuries and age that stymied McCarthy's club. Babe Ruth, nearing 40, hit just .288 in 1934 and seldom played a full nine innings, while center fielder Earle Combs, pitcher Johnny Allen, and catcher Bill Dickey were all shelved during the stretch run by serious injuries.

Also suffering from their share of injuries were Joe Cronin's Washington Senators. However, their collapse to seventh place—one of the biggest tumbles ever by a defending flag winner—was more the fault of their pitching staff. Cronin's two aces, Earl Whitehill and General Crowder, a combined 46-23 in 1933, went 18-21. Even though he had recently become owner Clark Griffith's son-in-law, Cronin found himself sold to the Boston Red Sox. He went for $250,000 during the off-season when the Senators' sharp drop in the AL standings caused attendance in Washington to dwindle even further, hitting Griffith hard in the wallet.

The World Series afforded major-league baseball a much needed financial shot in the arm when it evolved into one of the most hotly contested post-season matchups ever. Detroit could do little against the Dean brothers but obliterated almost all of the other Cardinals pitchers to seize a 3-2 lead after the fifth game in St. Louis.

With the Series slated to finish at Navin Field (now Tiger Stadium), Detroit looked certain to bag its first 20th-century championship. In Game 6, however, Daffy Dean edged Schoolboy Rowe, 4-3, setting up a seventh game between Daffy's brother and submarine-baller Eldon Auker. After two scoreless frames, the Cards broke the game open with a seven-run third. The Tigers still trailed 7-0 in the top of the sixth when Medwick slugged a triple and slid hard into Tigers third sacker Marv Owen, provoking a near-riot. Medwick's aggressive play would later help earn his team the nickname of "The Gashouse Gang." At that moment, however, Detroit

Charlie Gehringer (left) was second in the AL (.351), while Paul Waner (right) won the NL batting title (.362).

fans found it so objectionable that they pelted him with garbage and verbal abuse when he tried to take his position in left field. Commissioner Kenesaw Mountain Landis was finally forced to remove Med- wick from the game for his own protection. It was the only victory the sullen crowd had that day as St. Louis won, 11-0, for its third world title in nine years.

SEASON'S BEST

•The Cardinals' Dizzy Dean is selected the NL MVP. Dean leads the NL in winning percentage (.811), shutouts (seven), and Ks (195). He becomes the last NL hurler to win 30 games, winning 30 exactly.

•Detroit player-manager Mickey Cochrane is the AL MVP.

•New York's Lou Gehrig wins the Triple Crown in the AL, batting .363 with 49 homers and 165 RBI. He also leads in SA (.706) and total bases (409). Gehrig ties an AL record by leading the loop in RBI for a fifth time.

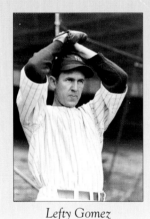

Lefty Gomez

•Paul Waner of Pittsburgh tops the NL in batting at .362. Waner also leads the NL in runs (122) and hits (217).

•Yankee Lefty Gomez leads the AL in wins (26), winning percentage (.839), Ks (158), CGs (25), and ERA (2.33), and he ties in shutouts (six).

•Giant Carl Hubbell's 2.30 ERA is the best in the majors.

•In the All-Star Game, Hubbell fans Babe Ruth, Gehrig, Jimmie Foxx, Al Simmons, and Joe Cronin consecutively. The AL wins the All-Star Game 9-7.

•The Yankees' Ruth hits his 700th career homer.

•The Yankees obtain prospect Joe DiMaggio from the PCL San Francisco Seals for $25,000 and five players.

•Senators owner Clark Griffith sends his son-in-law, Joe Cronin, to the Red Sox for Lyn Lary and $250,000.

•Hal Trosky of Cleveland collects 374 total bases, setting an ML rookie record.

•A few members of the Reds fly to a game in Chicago—the first ML teammates to travel together by air.

•On May 1, the Yankees' Burleigh Grimes wins the last game in ML history by a pitcher legally allowed to throw a spitball.

•Detroit's Schoolboy Rowe ties an AL record with 16 straight wins.

•Detroit's Goose Goslin has a 30-game hitting streak.

•New York's Mel Ott leads the NL in homers (35), RBI (135), and runs produced (219).

•Cardinal Ripper Collins tops the NL in total bases (369) and SA (.615) and ties in homers (35).

•Tiger Charlie Gehringer leads the AL in hits (214), runs (134), and runs produced (250).

DIZZY DEAN

Flaky hurler makes fans laugh, hitters cry

In his first two seasons pitching for the St. Louis Cardinals, 1931 and 1932, Jay Hanna "Dizzy" Dean won 38 games. With his younger brother Paul (also known as "Daffy") joining the team in 1934, the colorful Dizzy boldly predicted that "Me and Paul will probably win 40 games." As it turned out, Dizzy was a better pitcher than prognosticator. The brother act won almost 50 games. Diz became the premier pitcher in baseball, leading the Cardinals to the National League pennant with 30 victories—no NL pitcher since has won that many games in a season—and Paul produced 19 wins.

Dean featured an explosive fastball, a tight breaking curve, and excellent command of both pitches. He was just as aggressive on the mound as he was fun-loving off it, and he would intimidate hitters by throwing his fastball high and inside. Sometimes he would tell hitters that the heater was coming and still throw it by them.

In '34, Dean's superb pitching kept the Cardinals on the heels of the New York Giants, who led the league for most of the year. Dizzy then sparked a 21-4 September spurt that enabled the Cards to pull even with the Giants on the 28th. While the Brooklyn Dodgers were beating the Giants, the Cardinals won their last three games—two on shutouts by Dean—to take the pennant. Dizzy was named the Most Valuable Player with his 30 victories, against only seven losses, for an .811 winning percentage. Dizzy also led the league in complete games (24), shutouts (seven), and strikeouts (195). Dean placed second in earned run average (2.66) and games pitched (50). He even contributed seven saves out of the bullpen, tying him for second in the NL. Opponents had a .241 batting average and a .286 on-base percentage against Dean, third-best in the league.

Shortly before the World Series against the Detroit Tigers, Dizzy said, "Me 'n' Paul will win two games each." Although Detroit managed to beat Dizzy 3-1 in Game 5, his wins in Games 1 and 7 and Paul's victories in Games 3 and 6 gave St. Louis its second championship in four years. To those who chided his boastful statement, Dizzy pitched one of his immortal lines: "If you say you're going to do it, and you go out and do it, it ain't bragging."

Dean went out and did it for two more seasons—28 wins in 1935 and 24 in 1936—until a line drive broke his toe in the 1937 All-Star Game. The foot injury forced him to alter his pitching delivery, which subsequently caused a sore arm. Dizzy was never again the same pitcher.

DETROITERS MOTOR TO WORLD TITLE

Baseball historians customarily pass lightly over cellar dwellers in detailing the highlights of a particular season, but the 1935 campaign was an exception as the two tailenders, the Boston Braves and the Philadelphia A's, each brought up the rear in their respective leagues in a storybook manner.

After two consecutive fourth-place finishes in the NL, Braves skipper Bill McKechnie firmly believed he was only a key player away from mounting a genuine pennant bid. McKechnie and team owner Judge Fuchs differed, though, on what constituted a key player. Interested more in a box-office attraction than a budding talent, Fuchs signed 40-year-old Babe Ruth after the Bambino was released in the off-season by the Yankees, and the result was one of the sorriest chapters in the game's history.

Ruth joined the Braves thinking he was being groomed to manage the club. Miserably out of shape, he could play just 28 games before he mercifully decided to retire when he realized Fuchs had no intention of giving him McKechnie's job. In his next-to-last game, Ruth became the first slugger ever to nail three home runs at Pittsburgh's Forbes Field. As it turned out, this was to be the Braves' only salutary moment all season as they lost 115 games and posted a 20th-century NL record-low winning percentage of .248.

In the AL, the A's finished in the basement only three years after Connie Mack had bid unsuccessfully for a record fourth straight pennant. Mack cited the usual culprit in the team's demise: financial woes. It was the sole reason, he claimed, that he had

While many clubs were strapped for fans and finances, Detroit was rich with stars and captured the Series in six games.

Even home run hitters Babe Ruth, left, and Wally Berger couldn't keep the Braves from losing 115 games in '35.

sold or traded every one of his stars except Jimmie Foxx in the three intervening seasons since the A's last pennant win.

Foxx, too, was destined to go after the 1935 campaign. He was sold off to the Boston Red Sox for yet another bundle of cash, but Mack continued to cry poverty as he fielded a long string of deplorable teams. Some analysts think there was another reason the A's were perennial doormats in the last two decades of Mack's tenure. It had to do with his odd psychological makeup. If Mack was not exactly a masochist, he certainly did not find losing too bitter a pill to swallow.

Mickey Cochrane, dealt to Detroit two years earlier by Mack so he could become the Tigers' player-manager, was sympathetic to his old mentor in 1935. Cochrane, nevertheless, had no qualms about beating up on the A's. The Tigers needed every win they could get against the AL's weaker members, for Joe McCarthy's New York Yankees sat right on their tail all season before finishing three games back. As in 1934, the difference was the injury factor. After missing half of the previous season

with a fractured skull, Earle Combs went down with a broken collarbone. This forced McCarthy to move Ben Chapman to center field and put Jesse Hill in left. When Hill collected only 33 RBI in 107 games and Bill Dickey had an off year, McCarthy for once was lauded, rather than condemned, for the job he did in bringing the Bombers home second.

There were two 36-year-old player-managers in the NL—Frankie Frisch and Bill Terry—who were castigated by writers in their respective cities of St. Louis and New York for losing the pennant in the final weeks to a third 36-year-old player-manager, the Cubs' Charlie Grimm. Ceding his first-base post to Phil Cavarretta, a rookie half his age, Grimm appeared in just two games in 1935. He sat on the bench all of September as his team rattled off 21 straight wins, the longest skein in the majors since the Giants' record 26-game streak in 1916. The final three victories came in St. Louis. The 20th win in that streak clinched the flag as Bill Lee topped Dizzy Dean, 6-2, in the first game of a twinbill on September 26.

Still fueled by the heat from their winning streak, the Cubs bagged the World Series opener at Detroit, 3-0, behind 20-game winner Lon Warneke. The Tigers won the next three games, though, before bowing again to Warneke, 3-1, in Game 5 at Chicago.

Hoping history would repeat, the Cubs then returned to Detroit, where the Cardinals had snatched the 1934 Series by winning the last two games. It seemed a reasonable possibility, especially with slug-

Cubs catcher Gabby Hartnett (left) hit .344 and led NL catchers in assists, double plays, and fielding average to cop the NL MVP Award. Pittsburgh's Arky Vaughan (right) set a team record with a .385 average, but was third in the MVP voting.

163

ger Hank Greenberg out with the broken wrist he sustained in Game 2. Greenberg's replacement at first base, Marv Owen, managed only one hit in 20 at bats in the Series, and Flea Clifton, subbing at third for Owen, went 0-for-16. But the Tigers got 12 hits from their other cast members in Game 6, including a ninth-inning single by Goose Goslin that plated Cochrane with the run that gave Tommy Bridges a 4-3 win and the Motor City its first world title since 1887.

SEASON'S BEST

Wes Ferrell

• Cubs catcher Gabby Hartnett is NL MVP.

• Hank Greenberg wins the AL MVP Award. Greenberg's 170 RBI top the majors by 40 and the AL by 51. He also leads in total bases (389) and runs produced (255).

• Boston pitcher Wes Ferrell rebounds from a sore arm to top the AL in wins with 25.

• The Cardinals' Dizzy Dean again paces the NL in wins (28).

• Pittsburgh's Arky Vaughan tops the NL in hitting at .385.

• Washington's Buddy Myer wins the AL batting title by a single point over Cleveland's Joe Vosmik (.349-.348).

• Released by the Yankees, Babe Ruth signs a three-year contract with the Braves. On May 25, Ruth hits three homers vs. Pittsburgh at Forbes Field, then retires a few days later.

• Ruth retires with a .690 career SA (still an ML record). Ruth also sets ML career records in homers (714), RBI (2,211), walks (2,056), OBP (.474), and extra-base hits (1,356) (all since broken).

• On May 24, the Reds beat the Phils 2-1 at Crosley Field in the first ML night game. On July 10, Cub Babe Herman hits the first homer in a night game.

• The Cubs win 21 straight games, setting an ML record for most consecutive wins without a tie.

• William Wrigley of the Cubs is the first owner to allow all of his team's games to be broadcast.

• Philly's Jimmie Foxx leads in SA (.636) and ties Greenberg for the AL homer crown (36). After the season, the A's sell Foxx and Johnny Marcum to the Red Sox for $150,000.

• Wally Berger of the cellar-dwelling Braves leads the NL in homers (34) and RBI (130).

• Ducky Medwick of St. Louis leads the NL in total bases (365) and runs produced (235).

• Chicago's Augie Galan tops the NL in runs (133) and steals (22).

• New York's Lou Gehrig paces the AL in runs (125) and walks (132).

• Vosmik leads the AL in hits (216), doubles (47), and triples (20).

• Cub Phil Cavarretta, age 19, compiles 82 RBI and plays in the World Series.

HANK GREENBERG

Hammerin' Hank powers Tigers, knocks in 170

He lost nearly five seasons to war and another to injury, but in between Hank Greenberg was arguably the greatest run producer in baseball history. His standard of driving in .92 runs per game ties him with Lou Gehrig and Sam Thompson for the highest such ratio ever, and he did it while fighting off the insults, inside pitches, and spikes that came his way as one of the game's finest Jewish players. Known as one of the most intelligent and good-natured gentlemen in the majors, the slugger who eventually would challenge Babe Ruth's mark of 60 homers had his first of two MVP seasons in 1935. He also led the Tigers to the world championship with a major league-best 36 homers and 170 runs batted in.

Such proficiency for production had not come easily. Tall (6'3½") and gangly as a teenager growing up in New York City, Greenberg struggled before eventually becoming a semi-pro star and signing with Detroit in 1929. Coming up briefly with the Tigers a year later, he was a regular at first base within four seasons. In '34, he hit .339 with 26 homers, 139 RBI, and an incredible 63 doubles (the fourth-highest total in major-league history) as the Tigers took the American League pennant. He hit .321 with seven more RBI in the World Series, but Detroit lost to the Cardinals in seven games.

Hank's '35 season was his finest yet. In addition to his ML-best homer, RBI, and total base (389) marks, he was among the AL's top five in runs (121), hits (203), doubles (46), triples (16), and slugging (.628). He hit .328 and led Detroit back into the World Series—this time they faced the Cubs. Hank had his left wrist broken by an inside pitch during Game 2 (the Tigers managed to win the Series without him), then rebroke it 12 games into the following year. With Greenberg finished for the season, Detroit fell to second.

Greenberg came back stronger than ever with 183 RBI (the third-most ever) in '37, then challenged Ruth the following year with his 58-homer campaign—which tied him with Jimmie Foxx for the most hit by a right-handed batter. He added a second MVP Award in 1940 in leading Detroit to another pennant. After four-and-one-half years in the Army, he returned in '45 just in time to hit a pennant-winning grand slam on the final day of the season. Eventually a farm director and general manager with the Indians and part-owner of the White Sox, Greenberg's .605 slugging mark (fifth best in history), 331 homers, and 1,276 RBI in just 1,394 games hint at what he could have done with more time. For what he did do and the class he did it with, Hank made the Hall of Fame in 1956.

BRONX BOMBERS BOMB THE GIANTS

As might be expected, the strongest second-division team in the first half of the 20th century was fielded by the Cleveland Indians. Always adorned with statistical leaders and future Hall of Famers even when they finished far out of the money, the 1936 Indians were no exception. That season they had Earl Averill, the AL hit leader and batting title runner-up; RBI king Hal Trosky; 20-game winner Johnny Allen; and a 17-year-old rookie named Bob Feller who fanned 15 St. Louis Browns in his ML debut, yet finished fifth albeit only three games behind the second-place Detroit Tigers.

The Tigers' also-ran status in 1936 was pretty well cemented when they fell prey to disabling injuries and illnesses even more drastically than had the New York Yankees in the two previous campaigns. Hank Greenberg was the first Bengals star to go down for the count. His season was ended just 12 games into the campaign when he suffered his second wrist fracture in six months in a collision at first base with New York Yankees outfielder Jake Powell. The Tigers accused Powell of running into Greenberg deliberately but had only their own uninspired play to blame for player-manager Mickey Cochrane's nervous breakdown soon thereafter. After only 53 games, Cochrane had to flee to a Wyoming hospital to recover.

Even a completely healthy Greenberg and Cochrane might have made little difference in the 1936 AL race as the Yankees tallied 1,065 runs (just two short of their modern record) and boasted a record five players who amassed 100 RBI. Four were veterans Lou Gehrig, Twinkletoes Selkirk, Tony Lazzeri, and Bill Dickey, while the fifth was a rookie whose arrival in 1936 generated even more ballyhoo than Feller's.

The hoopla began on the Opening Day of spring training when Lazzeri and Frankie Crosetti drove up

The Giants had their chances in the first inning of Game 6, with the bases loaded and Mel Ott at the plate. They scored two runs, but the Yankees scored seven in the top of the ninth to wrap up the first Subway Series since 1923.

to the team's Grapefruit League spring training camp in St. Petersburg with a fellow San Francisco Italian in the backseat. No sooner had the door opened and their passenger emerged, when pitcher Red Ruffing, eyeing him skeptically, said, "So you're the great DiMaggio." Other team members were also dubious of the heralded rookie's credentials—but not for long. Joe DiMaggio followed three successive banner years in the Pacific Coast League by clicking for 206 hits, 125 RBI, 132 runs, and a .323 BA in his first ML season. Even before the most one-sided pennant race thus far in the decade had concluded with the Yankees 19½ games in front, several AL club owners had already begun to fear that the Bronx Bombers had a new dynasty in the making.

At the very least, the game once again had a Subway Series as Bill Terry's New York Giants put on a late march to the NL flag. Five games back of the Giants in a second-place tie were the St. Louis Cardinals and Chicago Cubs, who took turns leading the loop in the early going. The Cards ruled the roost until June when the Cubs went on a roll and won 15 straight games. In late July, the Giants put together a 15-game streak of their own and surged ahead. When Terry's club took three out of four from the Cubs in a late-August series, the spotlight then fell on Carl Hubbell, the Giants southpaw star who ended the season unbeaten in his last 16 decisions.

Hubbell continued to have a charmed left arm in the World Series opener at the Polo Grounds. By keeping the ball low and making the Yankees beat it into the ground, he posted a 7-1 triumph that was all the more remarkable in that none of his out-

Top, left to right: *Earl Averill (232 hits), Hal Trosky (162 RBI), and Joe Medwick (64 doubles). NL MVP Carl Hubbell (bottom).*

fielders had a single chance. Game 2 was also remarkable, but only from the Yankees' standpoint. After sending Giants starter Hal Schumacher to the showers with a seven-run assault in the third inning, Joe McCarthy's crew continued the slaughter against four relievers and finished the day's action with a Series-record 18 runs on 17 hits.

The following day, Freddie Fitzsimmons held the Bombers to just four safeties. He still took a 2-1 loss, however, when one of the hits was a solo homer by Gehrig and another was Crosetti's game-winning single in the eighth. In Game 4, Gehrig homered again in the third inning to help send Hubbell to a 5-2 loss, his first defeat in months.

In Game 5 at Yankee Stadium, Schumacher survived a 10-hit barrage and staggered to a 5-4 win

that gave Giants fans a flicker of hope, but the Yankees ended matters the following day. In front of 38,427 unhappy onlookers at the Polo Grounds, the Bombers pounded out 17 hits for the second time in the Series. They led only 6-5, though, going into the top of the ninth. The Yankees pieced together five singles and four walks to tally seven runs and put the game and the Series out of the Giants' reach.

SEASON'S BEST

- The Yankees' Lou Gehrig is AL MVP. Gehrig leads the majors in homers (49), runs (167), OBP (.478), SA (.696), walks (130), and runs produced (270). He also hits 14 homers vs. Cleveland, setting an ML record versus one opponent in a season.

- The Giants' Carl Hubbell wins his second NL MVP Award. He also wins an all-time ML-record 24 straight games over a two-year period. His 26 wins top the majors.

- Chicago's Luke Appling wins the AL bat crown with a .388 BA, highest in this century by an ML shortstop.

- Pittsburgh's Paul Waner wins his last NL bat crown (.373).

- The Hall of Fame is created; in the first vote for enshrinement, the leading vote-getter is Ty Cobb. Babe Ruth, Honus Wagner, Christy Mathewson, and Walter Johnson join Cobb as the first Hall electees.

- Ducky Medwick cracks an all-time NL-record 64 doubles. Medwick paces the NL in total bases (367), RBI (138), hits (223), and runs produced (235).

Luke Appling

- Cleveland's Hal Trosky leads ML in total bases (405) and RBI (162).

- On August 23, 17-year-old Indian Bob Feller sets a new AL record (since broken) when he Ks 17 batters in a game.

- Pirate Woody Jensen's 696 at bats are the most by anyone on a 154-game schedule.

- The Yankees' Joe DiMaggio scores 132 runs, setting an AL rookie record.

- Chuck Klein, back with the Phils, hits four homers in a 10-inning game on July 10.

- The NL wins the All-Star Game for the first time, 4-3 at Braves Field.

- The Yankees collect an ML-record 2,703 total bases. The team produces an ML-record 997 RBI.

- On May 24, Yankee Tony Lazzeri becomes the first MLer to hit two grand slams in a game. He drives in an AL-record 11 runs.

- Cardinal Dizzy Dean is the last ML pitcher to lead his league in CGs (28) and saves (11) in the same season.

- Detroit's Tommy Bridges tops the AL with 23 wins and 175 Ks.

- Boston's Lefty Grove leads the AL in shutouts (six) and ERA (2.81).

LOU GEHRIG

Iron Horse belts 49 homers, stars in Series

On June 1, 1925, Yankee first baseman Wally Pipp complained to manager Miller Huggins of a headache and was granted the day off. The youngster who took his place at first that day was Henry Louis Gehrig. Some 11 years and over 1,650 consecutive games later he was still there, providing New York fans with unsurpassed consistency and an MVP season as leader of the most successful team in major-league history.

The fact that many more fans were beginning to acknowledge Gehrig's achievements by '36 was not surprising. For the first decade of his career, Lou had usually performed in the shadow of his teammate and fellow slugger Babe Ruth, whose majestic home runs and dramatic exploits on and off the field consistently made headlines. This was nothing special—every player in the majors had to line up behind the larger-than-life Babe when it came to popularity and production— but Gehrig was particularly intriguing because the quiet style with which he excelled so contrasted the brash, unpredictable way Ruth approached baseball and life. Lou had accepted his role and flourished in it, hitting 32 or more homers and driving in 126 or more runs all but one year from 1926 to '34. When the Yankees released Ruth following the '34 season, it appeared Gehrig was finally ready to emerge as baseball's greatest slugger.

Ironically, after one season as the team's leading star in 1935 (compiling a .329 batting average with 30 homers and 119 RBI), Gehrig was sharing the Yankee spotlight once again in '36 when the club brought up a rookie by the name of Joe DiMaggio. Joltin' Joe hit .323 with 29 homers and 125 RBI, but Lou proved up to the challenge by turning in one of his most productive campaigns. Playing in all 155 contests to keep his consecutive-game streak alive, the Iron Horse led the majors with 49 homers, 167 runs, and a .696 slugging percentage while placing fourth in the AL in batting (.354) and second in RBI (152) and total bases (403). He also paced the majors with 130 walks (one of three straight seasons following Ruth's departure he would do so), and struck out just 46 times in leading the Yankees back to the World Series after a four-year hiatus. There DiMaggio hit .346 in a six-game victory over the Giants, but Gehrig had seven runs batted in and two homers—including a shot off Carl Hubbell in the fourth contest that resulted in Hubbell's first loss in months and gave the Yanks a commanding 3-1 Series edge.

Lou was still just 33, and it looked like his heroics could continue indefinitely. Nobody could yet imagine just how little time there was left in his career and his life.

DOMINANT YANKS BREEZE TO TITLE

Mickey Cochrane's return was just about the only good news in the seven cities housing AL also-rans in 1937 as the New York Yankees won 102 games and finished 13 lengths ahead of the competition for the second year in a row.

Once again the Yankees' closest pursuer was Detroit, and once again the Bengals were beset by injuries. On May 25, just 29 games after Cochrane's return to action from a nervous breakdown that had idled him most of the previous season, the player-manager suffered a fractured skull when he was struck by a high fastball hurled by New York right-hander Bump Hadley. It was nearly the second on-field fatality perpetrated by a Yankees pitcher as Cochrane hovered near death for several days before he was judged out of danger. Though Mickey recovered near the end of the season and resumed dugout control of the Tigers, he never again played. Cochrane's most prized hurler the past two seasons, Schoolboy Rowe, also missed most of the season, plagued by a sore arm.

The Yankees were not without several casualties of their own, mainly Twinkletoes Selkirk, Jake Powell, and rookie outfielder Tommy Henrich. Manager Joe McCarthy's squad was so deep in reserve talent, however, that none of the injured was missed.

Yet, even though the AL race was essentially over by Labor Day, action in one junior circuit city still solicited nationwide attention on the closing day of the season. In Detroit, over 22,000 bought tickets to an otherwise meaningless game in order to watch Cleveland's Johnny Allen shoot for a perfect 16-0 season. Already the holder of an AL record with 17 straight wins over two seasons, Allen had battled back from a mid-summer appendectomy to resume his place in the Cleveland rotation and surpass Tom Zachary's 1929 mark for the most wins in a season without a loss when he clocked his 13th triumph on September 21. On October 3, he risked his perfect season, which had extended to 15-0, against a fellow North Carolina native, Jake Wade.

Joe DiMaggio, "The Yankee Clipper," crossed the plate an AL-leading 151 times and drove in 167 as New York sailed through 1937.

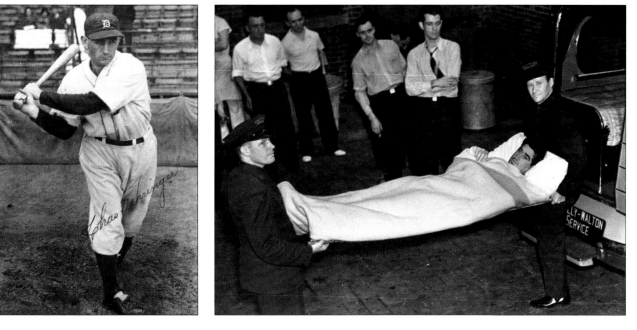

Charlie Gehringer (top left) *hit a career-high .371. Mickey Cochrane* (top right) *never played again after fracturing his skull when hit by a pitch. Mel Ott* (bottom) *led the NL in walks (102).*

Detroit got on the board in the bottom of the first when Pete Fox doubled and Hank Greenberg rifled a shot past Cleveland third sacker Bad News Hale to bring Fox home. Unluckily for Allen, that one run stood up as Wade chose that day to hurl the finest game of his career and hold Cleveland to just one hit. In the Indians locker room after the game, Allen, never known for taking defeat calmly, had to be restrained from attacking Hale in the belief that the third sacker should have come up with Greenberg's first-inning single.

The NL had no single game that contained anywhere near the sort of drama that surrounded Allen's

unsuccessful bid for perfection, but it did have some excitement of its own. The St. Louis Cardinals bred the Player of the Year in hitting machine Joe Medwick and the Boston Braves, who had the weakest hitting attack in the loop, nevertheless unveiled two older rookies who were each 20-game winners—Lou Fette and Jim Turner.

Cliff Melton of the Giants was the third NL rookie 20-game winner in 1937. The gangly left-hander teamed with Carl Hubbell to give manager Bill Terry one of the best southpaw duos in history as Hubbell fashioned a loop-best 22-8 mark. Hubbell also extended his regular-season winning streak (which stood at 16 at the end of the 1936 campaign) to an all-time record 24 games before finally meeting defeat at the hands of the Brooklyn Dodgers at the Polo Grounds in the first game of a Memorial Day doubleheader.

Without a hill pair to match Hubbell and Melton, the Chicago Cubs had to be content with second place, 3 games back of the Giants. The Yankees, however, were another matter. Able to showcase two 20-game winners of their own—Lefty Gomez (21-11) and Red Ruffing (20-7)—the Bombers launched the 1937 World Series by winning each of the first three games by a one-sided score. Hubbell prevented a four-game sweep by besting Bump Hadley, 7-3, on October 9 at the Polo Grounds, but the following afternoon the denizens of Coogans Bluff, for the second year in a row, were

made to watch in anguish as the Yankees rang up yet another championship on enemy turf. The victory went to Gomez and was his fifth fall triumph thus far in his career without a loss. Author of the im-

mortal line, "I'd rather be lucky than good," Gomez would complete his fall action, all spent with the Yankees, the owner of a record six Series wins without a defeat.

SEASON'S BEST

•The Cardinals' Ducky Medwick is named NL MVP. In the All-Star Game, he is the first player to collect four hits. Medwick wins the last Triple Crown in the NL, batting .374 with 31 homers and 154 RBI. He also leads the NL in runs (111), hits (237), doubles (56), SA (.641), runs produced (234), and total bases (406).

•The Tigers' Charlie Gehringer is AL MVP. He also wins the AL bat title at .371.

•The Giants' Carl Hubbell again leads the majors in wins with 22. Hubbell tops the NL in winning percentage (.733) and Ks (159).

•New York's Lou Gehrig is runner-up for the AL bat crown (.351), hitting .300 for the last time.

•Pirate Gus Suhr's NL-record streak of 822 consecutive games ends (record since broken).

•Detroit's Rudy York sets ML records with 18 homers and 49 RBI in a month (August).

•On May 25, Detroit's Mickey Cochrane is beaned by Yankee Bump Hadley, ending Cochrane's playing career.

Lefty Gomez

•The Braves have two rookie 20-game winners, Lou Fette and Jim Turner; both are over age 30. Turner leads the NL in ERA (2.38) and ties for the lead in shutouts (five).

•Cleveland's Johnny Allen tops the AL with a loop-record .938 winning percentage. Allen wins his first 15 starts of the season, then loses on the season's closing day.

•Pirate pitcher Red Lucas leads the NL in pinch hits for the fourth time.

•New York's Mel Ott ties Medwick for the NL homer crown (31) and leads in walks (102).

•The Yankees' Joe DiMaggio tops the AL in runs (151) and total bases (418).

•Detroit's Hank Greenberg tops the AL in runs produced (280).

•Beau Bell of the Browns leads the AL in hits (218) and doubles (51).

•New York's Lefty Gomez tops the AL in wins (21), shutouts (six), Ks (194), and ERA (2.33).

•Cleveland's Bob Feller, in his first full season, Ks 150 batters in 149 innings.

•The Yankees have three men with 130-plus RBI—DiMaggio (167), Gehrig (159), and Bill Dickey (133).

JOE MEDWICK

Funny-running Ducky grabs the Triple Crown

The Cardinals of the 1930s were a colorful bunch of roughhousing rabble-rousers known as "The Gashouse Gang," always talking a big game and usually backing it up on the field. Joe Medwick fit right in as the left fielder for this wild crew, attacking the ball, the basepaths, and anyone who stood in his way with a cocky aggressiveness and consistent success. Joe was dubbed with the moniker Ducky for his peculiar gait when running. Throughout his career, however (and especially in '37, his Triple Crown season), there was nothing funny about the way he went about his work.

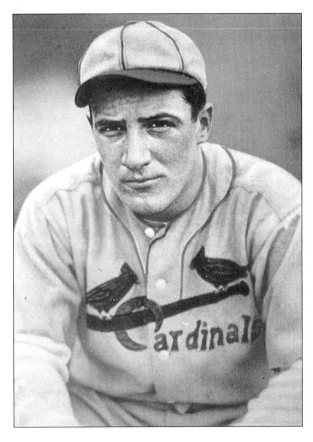

Medwick, a hot-tempered, 5'10" chatterbox, had grown up in New Jersey dreaming of having a football career at Notre Dame. However, after hitting .419 with 22 homers in his first minor-league season at Scottsdale, Joe realized his true calling and quickly traveled through Branch Rickey's burgeoning Cardinals farm system. Reaching the parent club late in 1932, he immediately took over in left field and began his pursuit of the two things he thought most important in life, "base hits and buckerinos." He was soon getting plenty of both. After hitting .319 with 106 RBI in his second full season, he picked up a World Series winner's share with 11 hits and a .379 mark in a seven-game triumph over the Tigers. Despite his success, it was his hard slide into Detroit third baseman Marv Owen late in an 11-0 St. Louis blowout during the Series finale that folks most remembered. Peppered with bottles, food, and garbage upon returning to left field the following inning, he was ordered removed for his own safety by Commissioner Kenesaw Mountain Landis.

Two more exceptional years followed, including an RBI crown in '36, when he also led the league in hits (223) and doubles (an NL-record 64), but it was Ducky's incredible MVP season of '37 that most stands out. Taking the NL's last Triple Crown with a .374 batting mark, 31 homers (tied with Mel Ott), and 154 RBI, he also led the league in runs (111), hits (237), doubles (56), total bases (406), and slugging (.641). One of the league's best defensive outfielders with a .988 fielding mark, the notorious bad-ball hitter struck out just 50 times in 633 at bats. Only a failure to lead the league in triples—he finished sixth with 10—kept Medwick from a clean sweep of every NL offensive department for the fourth-place Cards that season.

Medwick would lead the league in RBI and doubles a third straight year in '38 and continue to be productive for another decade, but he never approached his 1937 performance again. He always figured it was his unpopularity with sportswriters that delayed his Hall of Fame induction—but his .324 batting average and .505 slugging mark eventually got him to Cooperstown in 1968.

CUBS HOIST FLAG, THEN BOW TO YANKS

In 1938, as in the two previous seasons, the AL pennant race centered on how early in September the New York Yankees would wrap up the honor. However, the campaign's most dramatic moment, for the second year in a row, boiled down to a Cleveland Indians versus Detroit Tigers clash on the closing day. Just as in 1937, neither team had anything at stake—the Indians had already clinched third and the Tigers fourth—but a significant individual record was under siege. The mark was no less than Babe Ruth's 60 home runs in 1927. Threatened by

Bill Dickey topped his regular season, in which he hit .313 with 27 HRs and 115 RBI, with a .400 batting average in the Series.

Jimmie Foxx in 1932, it had since seemed unassailable, but on farewell day in 1938, Detroit first sacker Hank Greenberg had 58 homers and a two-for-one chance to shatter the barrier as the Tigers and Indians were scheduled for a doubleheader. Greenberg had two small stumbling blocks on this quest: the games were slated for Cleveland's cavernous Municipal Stadium, and in the first contest, Bob Feller hurled for the Tribe.

Feller chose that afternoon to set a new modern strikeout record when he fanned 18 Tigers, including Greenberg twice, and there were no home runs for Hammerin' Hank.

Ohio's other major-league representative, the Cincinnati Reds, also figured prominently in an action sequence that grabbed the nation but had no bearing on a pennant race. On June 11, Reds portsider Johnny Vander Meer hurled a 3-0 no-hitter against the Boston Braves. Vander Meer's no-no was only the second in the NL during the 1930s. Four nights later, in the first game ever to be played under the lights at Brooklyn's Ebbets Field, Vander Meer blanked the Dodgers without a safety, 6-0, and became the only hurler ever to post back-to-back no-hitters.

Vander Meer's feat was instrumental in Cincinnati's climb to fourth place, marking its best finish in over a decade. It was also Cincy's first season under Bill McKechnie, who had been enticed away from the Boston Braves by Reds general manager Larry MacPhail. The two could not have been more different. A teetotaler who was called "Deacon Bill" because of his religious upbringing, McKechnie was a member for 25 years of the Wilkinsburg Methodist Church choir. MacPhail, one of the game's great drinking men, would have been among the last to have gone to hear his manager sing. Shortly after the World War I armistice, MacPhail and seven other members of a U.S. artillery battalion had tried to

Cubs pitcher Bill Lee (top left) *led the NL with 22 wins in 1938, but received little support in the Series. Reds catcher Ernie Lombardi* (top right) *was the only catcher to win an undisputed batting title (.342). Pittsburgh's Arky Vaughan* (bottom right) *hit .322 in '38. Two of the best at first: Detroit's Hank Greenberg and New York's Lou Gehrig* (bottom left).

kidnap the Kaiser from a Dutch castle where he had sought sanctuary. The plan failed, but MacPhail somehow wound up with the German monarch's ashtray, which he kept in plain view on his desk at Crosley Field.

In 1935, MacPhail had introduced night baseball to the majors when he put lights in Crosley, but the innovation was still considered a novelty. The Dodgers were only the second ML team to illumi-nate their park, and it would be another 50 years yet before the Chicago Cubs would make night ball unanimous by installing lights in Wrigley Field.

The lack of illumination in Wrigley played a key part in the season's most important game. On September 27, the Pittsburgh Pirates met the Cubs at Wrigley for the first game of an all-critical three-game set. After holding a huge lead in the NL race for most of the season, the Pirates had watched their advantage steadily evaporate in the two months since catcher Gabby Hartnett had replaced Charlie Grimm at the Bruins helm. Finally, they stood at only a game and a half advantage. When a sore-armed Dizzy Dean, for whom the Cubs had paid the St. Louis Cardinals $200,000 prior to the season, won 2-1 on the 27th, the Cubs stood only half a game out. The next day Hartnett broke the Pirates' backs with two out in the ninth inning of a 5-5 game. The umpires were debating whether to call the game as soon as Hartnett hit because it was already so dark batters could hardly see the ball. A tie would have meant the game had to be replayed, but Hartnett took the decision out of the umpires' hands by sending a pitch by Pirates reliever Mace Brown over the left field wall.

Hartnett's "Homer in the Gloaming" effectively knocked the Pirates out of the race and enabled the Cubs to continue their odd pattern of appearing in a

World Series every third season. Beginning in 1929, the 1938 season marked the Cubs' fourth try in 10 years at the major-league crown—and for the fourth time, they missed their target. As had happened in 1932 when they last met the Yankees, the Cubs were swept by New York in four games. The otherwise dull rout had one intriguing note. The Cubs, amazingly, had the three top fall hitters—outfielder Joe Marty (.500), third baseman Stan Hack (.471), and outfielder Phil Cavarretta (.462). Chicago's other six regulars hit a combined .130, however, and the Cubs managed to tally just nine runs in the fray.

SEASON'S BEST

•Boston's Jimmie Foxx is AL MVP. Foxx wins the AL bat crown (.349) and also leads in RBI (175), SA (.704), runs produced (264), and total bases (398).

•Cincinnati's Ernie Lombardi is NL MVP. Lombardi is the first catcher to win a consensus bat title. (Bubbles Hargrave in 1926 had fewer than 400 at bats.)

•Detroit's Hank Greenberg hits 58 homers to lead the AL. Greenberg hits a record 39 homers at home. He also leads the AL in runs (144) and ties for the lead in walks (119).

•The Yankees' Lou Gehrig has 100 or more RBI for the 13th consecutive season, setting an ML record. Gehrig hits the last of his all-time ML-record 23 grand slams.

•Cincinnati's Johnny Vander Meer no-hits Boston on June 11. Vander Meer becomes the only pitcher in ML history to throw back-to-back no-hitters, as he blanks the Dodgers on June 15.

•On October 2, Bob Feller fans an ML-record 18 batters (since broken). Feller's 240 Ks top the majors; NL K leader Clay Bryant of Chicago has just 135.

•Cub Bill Lee leads the majors with 22 wins. Lee tops the majors in shutouts (nine) and ERA (2.66).

•Cardinal Frenchy Bordagaray sets an NL record with a .465 BA as a pinch hitter and gets 20 pinch hits.

Johnny Vander Meer

•The Phils move to Shibe Park on July 4 after 51 years in the Baker Bowl.

•Red Sox Pinky Higgins sets an ML record with 12 hits in 12 consecutive at bats.

•The Giants, Dodgers, and Yankees allow their home games to be broadcast on a regular basis.

•New York's Red Ruffing tops the AL in wins (21) and winning percentage (.750).

•Pitcher Red Lucas retires with 114 career pinch hits, an ML record to this juncture.

•New York's Mel Ott tops the NL in homers (36) and runs (116).

•St. Louis's Ducky Medwick paces the NL in doubles (47), RBI (122), and runs produced (201).

•Cardinal Johnny Mize leads the NL in slugging (.614), triples (16), and total bases (326).

JIMMIE FOXX

Double-X amasses 35 homers and 104 RBI—at home

Denied a Triple Crown by the slimmest of margins in 1932 when his batting average of .364 fell just short of league leader Dale Alexander's .367, Jimmie Foxx made sure things weren't so close the following year. Outdistancing second-place batter Heinie Manush by 20 points with a .356 mark, Double-X also led American Leaguers with 48 homers and 163 RBI en route to his second consecutive MVP Award. Foxx had two more outstanding years for the A's in 1934 and '35, but could not keep the former three-time AL champs from dropping to last place. Just as he had a generation before, owner-manager Connie Mack was breaking down his championship club and rebuilding. When Foxx himself was sold to the Red Sox a year later, it would add another rich chapter to his career and lead to a third MVP season in 1938.

Already a veteran of 11 major-league campaigns, Foxx was still just 28 when he came to Boston for the princely sum of $150,000. Red Sox owner Tom Yawkey was spending lavishly to put together a winner, and Jimmie joined Joe Cronin and former A's teammates Lefty Grove and Doc Cramer as part of the master plan. Popular with his new club and its fans from the start, Foxx hit 77 homers and drove in 270 runs his first two seasons in Boston, but when his batting average slipped over 50 points to .285 in '37, there was some speculation his best days were behind him.

Foxx quieted such thoughts quickly, leading the majors in '38 by hitting .349 while also paving the way in slugging (.704), total bases (398), and RBI (175)—the most runs he had ever knocked in during his long career. His 50 home runs (still a club record) would normally have been enough to win him a second Triple Crown. Hank Greenberg, however, happened to hit 58 that year to tie Foxx's right-handed record and deny Double-X a second trifecta sweep. Admittedly aided by Fenway Park's friendly 315-foot left field wall—he hit .405 at home with 35 home runs and 104 RBI in 74 games—Foxx was also among the AL's top five in hits (197) and runs (139) to help Boston rise from fifth to second place.

Jimmie was joined by rookie Ted Williams in 1939. While Williams took away his RBI title, Foxx was tops in the AL with 35 homers and second with a .360 batting mark. Two more solid years followed, and Foxx learned to place hits as age sapped some of his great power. By the time he finished up in 1945, his 534 homers ranked second only to Ruth. Now, over 50 years later, the Hall of Famer ranks 11th in the category, but his .609 slugging mark remains the fourth-best ever.

NEW YORK MAKES IT FOUR IN A ROW

A strong case can be made that Miller Huggins's 1927 Murderer's Row crew was not the greatest team ever, nor even the New York Yankees' greatest team. Many analysts cast their vote for the 1939 Yankees, who won 106 of 151 games and finished 17 lengths ahead of the second-place Boston Red Sox, 41½ lengths ahead of the sixth-place Washington Senators, and a colossal 64½ lengths in front of the last-place St. Louis Browns. Incredibly, the Yankees won more games in 1939 on the road alone (54) than both leagues' last-place teams, the Browns and Phillies, won all season.

By 1939, Yankees skipper Joe McCarthy had heard mutterings for several years that he was no more than a push-button manager. Who couldn't win with all the talent he had? An outfield comprised of Joe DiMaggio, Twinkletoes Selkirk, Tommy Henrich, and Charlie "King Kong" Keller; an infield with Red Rolfe at third, Joe Gordon up from the Yankees minor-league powerhouse in Newark to replace Tony Lazzeri at second, Frankie Crosetti at short, and behind the plate, the perennial All-Star Bill Dickey. The powerful Yankee arsenal was rounded out by a mound staff led by Red Ruffing and Lefty Gomez, plus five other hurlers who won 10 or more games in 1939 and Johnny Murphy, one of the first pitchers to carve a successful career as a bullpen operative. With so many household names, even the tragic loss in 1939 of Lou Gehrig was absorbed with scarcely a beat missed.

McCarthy never bothered to defend himself against the push-button accusations. He allowed his spokesmen to be the close observers of the era who were well aware that many of his players were household names solely because they were Yankees. If most of them had been in the employ of other teams, they would probably have labored their entire careers in obscurity. Ruffing, for one, was a chronic loser with the Red Sox; Henrich was buried for years in the Indians' farm system; Crosetti was a virtuoso in the field but so anemic a hitter that he was im-

The Yankees celebrated their fourth straight World Series championship.

Top, left to right: *NL President Ford Frick, Commissioner Judge Landis, AL President William Harridge, and National Association President William Bramham open the Hall of Fame. Joe DiMaggio* (bottom) *was the AL MVP.*

mediately displaced when Phil Rizzuto completed his minor-league apprenticeship; and most of the other Yankees regulars, though all good, were no better than many other players in their time who never played on a pennant winner, let alone made an All-Star squad.

Yet, for all that, seven members of the 1939 Yankees, including McCarthy and General Manager Ed Barrow, are in the Hall of Fame, and an eighth, Joe Gordon, probably should be. In sharp contrast were the Cincinnati Reds, the NL flag winners in 1939 and '40. For years the Reds shared with the 1889 and '90 Brooklyn Bridegrooms the unwanted distinction of being the only two teams to win consecutive ML pennants without any Hall of Fame players on their rosters. The Reds' Hall of Fame drought finally ended in 1986 when catcher Ernie Lombardi, long overdue for induction, was at last selected.

In 1938, Lombardi had become the first and only catcher in ML history to win a batting title with enough plate appearances to qualify under present-day rules. Though he slumped to .287 in 1939,

he continued to provide the Reds' mound staff with solid leadership and one of the strongest arms in the game. Working with Lombardi were Bucky Walters and Paul Derringer. These two hurlers, who had been 20-game losers earlier in the decade, blossomed into the NL's best hill tandem. In 1939, Walters posted a loop-leading 27 wins; when added to Derringer's 25, the Reds had the NL's last pitching duo to win over 50 games.

Down the stretch, it was Derringer's hot hand and the bat of first baseman Frank McCormick that kept the Reds ahead of a late rush by the St. Louis Cardinals. On September 29, Derringer finally turned the key on the Cardinals with a 5-3 win, and the Reds added to their lead in the final days of the season to win by 4½ games. Sixth in 1938, the Cards were likewise carried to unexpected heights by a first sacker—Johnny Mize, winner of two legs of the Triple Crown with a .349 BA and 28 home runs.

Led by Keller and Dickey, who clipped five home runs and 11 RBI between them, the Yankees scored their fifth world championship and third Series sweep in the 1930s. Even though the Reds departed in four games, they did not go quietly. Only in the second and third contests did the Yankees exert complete control, and the Reds let a 4-2 lead

A Red Sox rookie named Ted Williams (left) *broke into the majors with a .327 batting average and league-leading 145 RBI. Reds pitcher Bucky Walters* (right) *won 27 games and claimed NL MVP honors.*

in Game 4 escape when New York scored two runs in the top of the ninth, one unearned. In the first extra frame, Keller crashed into Lombardi in a play at the plate and jarred the ball loose, allowing three runs to score while the dazed Reds catcher "snoozed" with the ball lying unattended beside him. When Murphy held the Reds scoreless in the bottom half of the 10th, McCarthy had the unprecedented honor of being the winning manager in four straight postseason championships.

SEASON'S BEST

- The Yankees' Joe DiMaggio is AL MVP. DiMaggio leads the majors with a .381 BA. He is the last righty to top .380 in a season.

- Cincinnati's Bucky Walters is NL MVP. Walters leads the majors with 27 wins; teammate Paul Derringer wins 25. Walters tops ML in innings (319) and ERA (2.29).

- Lou Gehrig's string of 2,130 consecutive games played ends on May 2. Gehrig gives his famous farewell address at Yankee Stadium after he learns he has amyotrophic lateral sclerosis. He is the first MLer to have his uniform number retired.

- On August 26, the first major-league game is televised—Reds vs. Dodgers at Ebbets Field.

- The Hall of Fame is officially dedicated and opens on June 12. Gehrig is voted into the Hall in 1939 by a special ballot.

- On May 16, the first AL night game is played—Indians versus A's at Shibe Park.

- Lefty Grove of the Red Sox wins the last of his ML-record nine ERA crowns (2.54).

- Boston rookie Ted Williams leads the majors in RBI with 145—most ever by an ML rookie. Williams tops the majors in runs produced with 245.

- The sacrifice fly rule is reinstated.

- In August, the Yankees' Red Rolfe scores at least one run in 18 consecutive games. Rolfe tops the AL in runs (139), hits (213), and doubles (46).

- Red Sox Jim Tabor hits two grand slams in a game on July 4.

- Eighteen years after his ML debut, Brave Johnny Cooney hits his first ML homer on September 24; he hits another the next day.

- Boston's Jimmie Foxx leads the AL in homers (35) and slugging (.694).

Bob Feller

- The Cardinals' Johnny Mize leads the NL in homers (28), BA (.349), SA (.626), and total bases (353).

- Cleveland's Bob Feller leads the AL in wins (24), innings (297), and Ks (246).

- Red Frank McCormick again leads the NL in hits (209). He also leads in RBI (128) and runs produced (209).

- Cincinnati manager Bill McKechnie becomes the first ML skipper to win pennants with three different teams.

1939

LOU GEHRIG

Yankees' mountain of strength crippled by disease

Lou Gehrig wore many nicknames during his 15-year career with the New York Yankees between 1925 and 1939, but none fit him better than "The Iron Horse."

From the day he became the Yankees starting first baseman on June 2, 1925, until he removed himself from the lineup on May 2, 1939, Gehrig played in every game, despite illness or injury. He once played the day after being hit so hard on the head with a pitch, it was thought his skull was fractured. On those few occasions during road trips when Gehrig felt he couldn't play, manager Joe McCarthy would put him first in the lineup as the shortstop, then replace him in the bottom of the first with Frank Crosetti.

During his 15 years of nonstop playing, Gehrig was a superstar of the era. He won the Most Valuable Player Award as a member of the fabled "Murderer's Row" in 1927; won a batting title and Triple Crown in 1934; took the American League home run titles in 1931, '34, and '36; and drove in over 150 runs seven times, still a major-league record. He had an AL-record 184 RBI in 1931. Gehrig helped lead the Yankees to six world championships and ranks in the top 10 in 10 World Series hitting departments. Only Babe Ruth had totaled more home runs than Gehrig by the late 1930s.

It was during the 1938 Series, when he batted just .286, that Gehrig's skills showed signs of eroding. In spring training the following year, the 36-year-old Yankee captain's hitting reflexes seemed slow and he didn't move around first base with his usual grace. On May 1, Gehrig was batting under .150. The day before he had left five men on base. He told McCarthy to scratch him from the lineup for the team's May 2 game in Detroit. When the Yankees were announced without Gehrig's name and Tigers fans were told Lou had voluntarily removed himself from the lineup, Detroit fans gave Gehrig a standing ovation. His incredible, almost superhuman streak of 2,130 consecutive games played was over. "Lou just told me he felt it would be best for the club if he took himself out," McCarthy told the press that day. "It's tough to see your mates on base," Gehrig explained, "have a chance to win a game and not be able to do anything about it."

A few weeks later the world discovered why Gehrig couldn't do anything about it. He had contracted the rare muscle disease amyotrophic lateral sclerosis, a fatal illness now called "Lou Gehrig's Disease." Two years later, Gehrig died just two weeks short of his 38th birthday.

THE 1940s

Night games, televised games, and World War II changed the way the game was played during the 1940s. Nothing, however, could match the dramatics of Jackie Robinson, who shattered the color barrier in 1947.

By 1940, America had emerged from the Depression, which had kept many fans away from ballparks during the 1930s. The country was back at full employment and fans were flocking to ball games all over the land. Baseball was truly the national pastime, because, in addition to the two major leagues' 16 teams, there were almost 500 minor-league clubs who would attract more than 35 million spectators in 1940.

So baseball entered the new decade with high hopes—and no idea of the monumental changes that the game would undergo in the ensuing 10 years. Night games, televised games, World War II, and the breaking of the color barrier (African-Americans would finally be permitted to play in the major leagues in 1947) would precipitate more changes in the game than in any decade since the 1880s.

Larry MacPhail, general manager of the Cincinnati Reds, was the first man to have lights installed in his ballpark, in 1935. The first night game was played at Crosley Field. MacPhail figured that since most people worked days, night games would draw more weekday spectators. He was right, as Cincinnati's night games outdrew the club's weekday crowds.

The other major-league ballclubs did not follow suit. Baseball was run by traditionalists who maintained the game should be played in daylight. The second major-league club to install lights was the Brooklyn Dodgers, who did so in 1939, because MacPhail had by then become the team's general manager. But by 1948, every team in the major leagues had a lighted ballpark and was playing night games, except for the Chicago Cubs, who did not light Wrigley Field until 1988.

Philadelphia's Shibe Park, site of the first night game in the American League. Night games became popular with fans who worked during the day, and especially with President Franklin Roosevelt. Roosevelt requested in 1942 that the number of night games be doubled so workers in defense plants wouldn't take afternoons off to attend ball games.

Although the leagues under baseball commissioner Judge Kenesaw Mountain Landis set the teams' allotment of night games at a miserly seven, in 1941 the season's 77 night games drew more than 1.5 million fans, an average of almost 20,000 per game. With the United States at war during the 1942 season, President Franklin Roosevelt wrote to Judge Landis and asked that the number of night games be doubled so that employees in defense plants would not take off afternoons to attend ball games. It actually took a war and a presidential request to extend night baseball.

Meanwhile, attendance in the major leagues, which fell during the war, afterwards grew steadily, reaching a record high of 10.8 million in 1945, then leaping to 18.5 million in 1946 when most of the servicemen had returned from battle.

If night baseball spurred attendance, television sent it soaring—and then drastically cut into the

Top left: *The Yankees were in peak form in 1941, thanks to rookie Phil Rizzuto, left, and Joltin' Joe DiMaggio. A baseball team from Havana, Cuba, featured Martin Dihigo, center, the first Cuban player elected to the Hall of Fame* (top right). Bottom left: *The Walker brothers, Dixie, left, and Harry. Dixie won the NL batting title (.357) in 1944 with the Dodgers, while his sibling, Harry, accomplished the same feat for the Phillies and Cardinals in 1947, hitting .363. Umpire Bill Klem (bottom right) worked the last of his 18 World Series in 1940. Klem, regarded as the greatest umpire in the game, brought dignity and respect to his profession.*

that in 1948, major-league attendance reached a record high of 21 million.

The Boston Braves won the National League pennant in '48 and drew 1.46 million fans. Figuring the televising of home games had fueled interest in the team, the Braves sold the television rights to all of their home games for the next two years and the coverage of most of their home games through the 1952 season, all for the sum of $40,000. By the time the contract had run out, the Braves' home attendance had fallen 81 percent. Their fans had decided they preferred to watch the games on television rather than go to the ballpark. And in 1953, when baseball's attendance shrunk to 14 million paying customers, the Braves moved to Milwaukee and refused all offers to televise home games.

That contrasts markedly with baseball's current relationship with television. In 1988, the major

Brooklyn Bleacher Bums lined up outside the stadium before Game 3 of the 1941 Series, the first Subway Series to include the borough of Brooklyn. Alas, the Yanks ousted the Dodgers in five games.

gate receipts of many ballclubs. The first ball games to be televised were played at Ebbets Field in 1939, a doubleheader between the Dodgers and the Reds. Incidentally, the Cincinnati starter in the first game was Johnny Vander Meer, who had pitched a no-hitter in his previous outing. He promptly threw a no-hitter at the Dodgers and became the only man in history to hold the opposition hitless in back-to-back starts. But few people saw the televised game simply because there were few sets to receive it.

By 1947, however, television sets (most with five- and seven-inch screens) were selling almost as fast as they could be produced. That was the year NBC began televising major-league games and attracting a whole new audience to ballparks. People who had only casually followed baseball began going to games and enjoying themselves. The result was

Yankees catcher Bill Dickey, left, poses with actor Gary Cooper in 1942's Pride of the Yankees (top). Ray Dandridge (bottom) hit .343 in nine Mexican League seasons, and averaged .355 in the Negro National League.

BOBBY DOERR, Red Sox

The South Bend Blue Sox (top) *were part of the four-team All-American Girls Professional Baseball League, which debuted in 1943. Red Sox second baseman Bobby Doerr* (bottom) *drove in at least 100 runs five times during the decade.*

leagues signed a four-year contract with CBS that would pay each team almost $10 million a year. A separate deal with cable TV would bring each team an additional $4 million. Each team also cuts its own deal with local TV. Yankees owner George Steinbrenner signed with a cable network that would pay the team $41 million annually for 12 years. Radio broadcast rights bring in additional monies.

Yet in 1941 neither the Yankees nor the New York Giants could sell their radio rights for the $75,000 that the Dodgers earned from radio. Apparently Larry MacPhail could convince companies to sponsor the broadcasts of Dodger games announced by the old redhead, Red Barber.

By the 1942 season, no ballclub was much concerned about broadcast rights, because the U.S. was at war and every general manager was worried about which player he would lose next to the military. In '42, a total of 31 National League and 40 American League players who had appeared in at least one major-league game were called into the armed forces. In '43, 119 AL players and 100 from the NL were drafted. In '44, the NL lost more players to the service, 174 to 168 from the AL. In '45, there were 180 AL players and 204 NL players called up by Uncle Sam.

Those who were drafted last received their discharges within a year and were back on the ballfield

the following season. Bob Feller, Hank Greenberg, and a few others were not so fortunate, as they were among the early call-ups in 1941 and had to serve almost four years before being discharged. Feller was the best pitcher in the American League and Greenberg the AL home run champion. Both players were sorely missed by their ballclubs, Feller by the Cleveland Indians and Greenberg by the Detroit Tigers. In 1944, the Tigers would have certainly won the pennant with Greenberg in the lineup, as they finished only 1 game behind the first-place St. Louis Browns. The Tigers of '44 didn't have a player who hit more than 18 home runs. In his last full season, 1940, Greenberg had hit 41 home runs, driven in 150 runs, and led the Tigers to victory in the pennant race.

May 7, 1941, was the last day Greenberg played before reporting to duty at Camp Custer, Michigan. In that game he powered home runs off Ernie Bonham and Atley Donald as the Tigers beat the Yankees, 7-4. Greenberg was the highest-paid player in the majors that year. He entered the Army as a poorly paid buck private, but he didn't complain. "I'm not crying about being dropped from $55,000 a year to $21 a month," Greenberg said. "I'm just going to do my duty to this country like every other ballplayer who's drafted into the Army. Winning the war against Hitler is more important to me than playing baseball."

Some owners, notably Ed Barrow of the Yankees—who was never known for his generosity with player contracts—tried to take advantage of the war to hold down salaries. Joe DiMaggio, the best center

Negro League great Cool Papa Bell, sliding into third (top), never got a shot in the majors. The Reds' Joe Nuxhall (bottom left) was 15 years, 10 months, and 11 days old when he pitched in his first major-league game, mop-up duty against the Cards. Despite the death of their father prior to Game 2, Walker, left, and Mort Cooper (bottom right) went on to play in the 1943 World Series.

Joltin' Joe was finally drafted in 1943, along with a dozen of his teammates, but the Yankees still won the pennant. The teams that lost the most players to the military, the Philadelphia Athletics (36) in the AL and the Philadelphia Phillies (35) in the NL, usually finished last anyway. A's owner and manager Connie Mack had grown used to his teams holding the last position after his earlier seasons of success.

By 1944, baseball had been stripped of most of its stars as rosters were filled by men who were 4-F, very young, or very old. Retired players like Paul and Lloyd Waner, Debs Garms, and Pepper Martin returned to the majors. The Reds played two men in the infield who suffered from epilepsy and even used a 15-year-old pitcher, Joe Nuxhall, in one game. By the following season the talent in the major leagues was even worse. The St. Louis Browns used a one-armed outfielder, Pete Gray. In fact, approximately only one-third of the men who were regulars in 1945 played at least 100 games in '46.

Despite the wartime interruption, the 1940s proved to be the most exciting decade ever for pennant races. Eight races were decided by 2 games or less, another by 2½ games.

In the American League in 1940, the Tigers finished 1 game ahead of the Indians and 2 games ahead of the Yankees. In 1944, the St. Louis Browns finished 1 game ahead of the Tigers. In 1945, the

Cleveland's Bob Feller (top) threw the only Opening Day no-hitter when he blanked the White Sox in 1940. Former Tiger great Mickey Cochrane (bottom) *coached the Great Lakes Naval Base team during World War II. His 1944 squad finished 48-2.*

fielder in the game, asked Barrow for a raise in the spring of '41. Barrow said he couldn't see increasing DiMaggio's salary when he might lose him to the military before season's end. Actually, DiMaggio had a marriage exemption that kept him out of the service until 1943.

In the spring of 1942 there was talk of an impending wage freeze to aid the war effort. Barrow tried to use this to withhold raises to DiMaggio and six other Yankee stars. They finally got a little more money out of Barrow. DiMaggio needed the salary increase as he had to help out his Italian-born father who, having never applied for U.S. citizenship, was no longer allowed on his fishing boat in San Francisco harbor for so-called "security reasons."

Bill Veeck bought the Indians in 1946; Cleveland's attendance doubled in 1947.

Tigers finished 1½ games ahead of the Washington Senators. In 1948, the Indians and Red Sox finished the season tied for first place, then met in a one-game playoff which Cleveland won. In 1949, the Yankees broke a first-place tie with the Red Sox by beating the Crimson Hose in the final game of the season.

In the National League in 1941, the Dodgers finished 2½ games ahead of the Cardinals. In 1942, the Cardinals finished 2 games ahead of the Dodgers. In 1946, the Cardinals and Dodgers finished in a tie for first place, then met in the league's

Manager Mel Ott led the Giants to fourth place in 1947, but still made the cover of Time *(top left). Among the contributions of baseball executive Larry MacPhail (top center) were the introduction of night baseball and plastic batting helmets. Johnny Mize, who belted 51 homers in 1947, was a perfect fit for a Louisville Slugger ad (top right). Bottom left: Persistence by Dodgers general manager Branch Rickey, right, helped Jackie Robinson break the color barrier in baseball. Robinson signed with Montreal of the minor leagues and was brought up to the Dodgers in '47. Cardinals great Stan Musial (bottom right) hawked cigarettes in a 1940s Chesterfield ad.*

first playoff series. St. Louis won the first two games of the three-game set to capture the pennant. In 1949, the Dodgers finished 1 game up on the Cards.

The Dodger-Cardinal games were wars throughout the decade. Pitchers on both sides threw at hitters, baserunners slid with their spikes high and unkind thoughts in their minds, and there were fisticuffs on the field.

In 1940, the Dodgers bought veteran slugger Joe Medwick from the Cardinals for $125,000 and four players. Medwick had been in Brooklyn only six days when the Cardinals came in for a series. He stayed in the same hotel with Dodger player-manager Leo Durocher, and they happened to be joined in the elevator by the Cards pitcher who would start that day, Bob Bowman. Durocher made a nasty remark and Bowman said, "There's at least one automatic out in your lineup—you." Medwick snarled, "You'll be out of there before you get to Leo."

That afternoon Bowman's first pitch to Medwick cracked him in the temple and knocked him unconscious. There were fights all over the field, and after Medwick was carried off on a stretcher, Larry MacPhail—the toughest general manager in

the game—ran in front of the Cardinal dugout and challenged the entire team. One good thing came out of the affair: The next year, MacPhail introduced plastic batting helmets to baseball.

The 1941 season was noteworthy for another reason as it was the year in which two baseball standards were set that may never be matched. Joe

Dodgers shortstop Pee Wee Reese, Yankees shortstop Phil Rizzuto, and Dodgers pitcher Hugh Casey (left to right) study the Navy's bluejacket's manual in 1943. Each spent the 1943-45 seasons in the Navy.

Happy Chandler (top), *elected commissioner in 1945, supported Jackie Robinson's entry into the major leagues. Radio broadcaster Russ Hodges* (bottom) *was with five other teams before he became the voice of the Giants for two decades.*

DiMaggio hit in 56 consecutive games, and Ted Williams of the Red Sox batted over .400 for the season. DiMaggio's streak would have gone well beyond 56 games if Cleveland third baseman Ken Keltner hadn't made two exceptional plays on shots off Joe's bat on July 17. After going hitless in that game, DiMaggio proceeded to hit in another 16 consecutive games.

Ted Williams, age 22 in '41, would later say, "Joe DiMaggio was by far the best right-handed hitter I ever saw." But many feel that Ted Williams was the finest all-around hitter in baseball history. With a .401 average in 1930, Bill Terry had been the last man to bat over .400 in the majors. Williams went into the final doubleheader of the season with his

average at .399955, which rounded off to .400. In the first game he went 4-for-5, and in the second he went 2-for-3, pushing his final average to .406. Williams also hit 37 homers in '41, becoming the only American League player ever to hit over .400 with more than 20 home runs in the same season.

For all of the dramatics of the 1940s—all of the tight pennant races and all of the changes that were introduced to the game by night baseball and television—no single event matched in significance the day in 1947 when Jackie Robinson of the Dodgers broke the color barrier and opened the doors for African-American players to begin entering the major leagues.

Branch Rickey, the Dodgers general manager, was the man who signed Robinson and assigned him to the organization's top farm team (Montreal) in 1946. Robinson had a great year and seemed certain to make the big club the next season. But 15 of the major-league clubs voted that Robinson not be allowed in the major leagues, with Rickey casting the only affirmative vote. But the new baseball commissioner, Happy Chandler, had the final say in the matter. "I told Mr. Rickey," Chandler said when he was inducted into the Hall of Fame in 1982, "that someday I was going to have to meet my maker, and

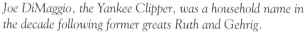

Joe DiMaggio, the Yankee Clipper, was a household name in the decade following former greats Ruth and Gehrig.

Ted Williams (top left) went 6-for-8 in a doubleheader on the last day of '41, boosting his average to .406. Player-manager Lou Boudreau (top right) is all smiles after the Indians won the '48 World Series. Bob Feller (bottom left) led the AL in wins (20), strikeouts (196), and shutouts (five) in 1947. Ralph Kiner (bottom center) won four straight HR crowns in the '40s. This record album by Yogi Berra (bottom right) was part of a series of instructional records by major-league stars.

if He asked me why I didn't let that boy play and I said it was because he was black, that might not be a satisfactory answer. So I said, 'You bring him in and I'll approve the transfer of his contract from Montreal to Brooklyn.' I was just doing what justice and mercy required me to do under the circumstances."

Chandler was a person with an open mind. At this time, African Americans were still segregated from whites in the South. Hotels, restaurants, theaters, rest rooms, even drinking fountains that African Americans could use were clearly marked as "Colored." Some of the Dodger players at first were not pleased by the prospect of playing ball with an African American. Dodgers manager Leo Durocher heard about the dissenting feelings and called a team meeting in spring training. "If this fellow Robinson is good enough to play on this ballclub—and from what I've seen and heard he is—he's going to play for me," Durocher said. "I'm the manager of this club and I'm interested in one thing: winning. I'll play an elephant if he can do the job, and to make room for him, I'll send my own brother home."

Outfielder Dixie Walker had the most intolerant attitude on the Dodgers, and he requested that Rickey trade him. A deal couldn't be worked out until the following year, when Walker was sent to Pittsburgh.

Jackie Robinson was a unique individual, a graduate of UCLA, where he had been an All-America football player, and a man of great courage and patience. When he was playing his way to the NL's Rookie of the Year Award in 1947, he was subjected to many vile racial epithets. Insults were hurled at the young star, and Jackie heard slurs from spectators and opposing players alike.

Although he had never played first base (second was his natural position), Robinson was assigned there and excelled, quickly adapting to the artful footwork that was required around the bag. A number of players tried to land their spikes in Robinson's left Achilles tendon as he stretched for throws. But Robinson proved too quick for them.

Oscar Charleston, center, was one of the greatest players in Negro League history. He later became a manager for Branch Rickey's Brooklyn Brown Dodgers and the Indianapolis Clowns (top). April 27, 1947, was Babe Ruth Day at Yankee Stadium. The Bambino, sick with cancer, died a year later.

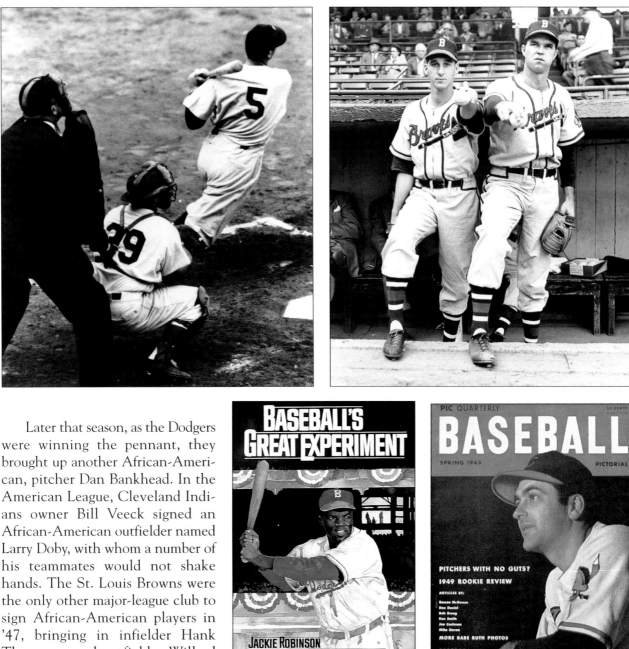

Later that season, as the Dodgers were winning the pennant, they brought up another African-American, pitcher Dan Bankhead. In the American League, Cleveland Indians owner Bill Veeck signed an African-American outfielder named Larry Doby, with whom a number of his teammates would not shake hands. The St. Louis Browns were the only other major-league club to sign African-American players in '47, bringing in infielder Hank Thompson and outfielder Willard Brown. The Boston Red Sox waited the longest to hire an African-American player, Pumpsie Green in 1959.

Baseball has never been the same since that breakthrough season of 1947. African-American players have gone on to dominate the game in the many seasons since then, as would have many great African-American players from Negro Leagues in earlier years. Negro League All-Stars such as Satchel Paige, Josh Gibson, Buck Leonard, Cool Papa Bell, Judy Johnson, Oscar Charleston, Martin Dihigo, and John Henry Lloyd certainly would have been All-

Joe DiMaggio flopped in the '49 Series (top left). Warren Spahn, left, and Johnny Sain gave Boston a remarkable lefty-righty combination (top right). Jackie Robinson made the Great Experiment *(bottom left) a success. Cleveland shortstop Lou Boudreau (bottom right) hit over .350 with more than 100 RBI in '48.*

Stars in the major leagues had they been given a chance. A special committee on the Negro Leagues has since inducted all of them into the Baseball Hall of Fame in Cooperstown, where they justly belong.

CINCY SUBS SINK TIGERS IN SEVEN

On April 16, 1940, Bob Feller of the Cleveland Indians hurled the first Opening Day no-hitter in ML history. Two months later, the Indians' players initiated the "Crybaby Rebellion" aimed at convincing owner Alva Bradley to oust manager Ossie Vitt, who had shouted at the mound, where Feller was being cuffed around, "Look at him! He's supposed to be my ace! I'm supposed to win a pennant with that kind of pitching!" Three months later, with the AL pennant on the line, Feller found himself facing a Detroit Tigers pitcher who was so obscure that he did not even make the team picture that year.

It was the last Friday afternoon of the season, Ladies Day, with over 45,000 in the stands at Cleveland's Municipal Stadium. Pitching for the Tigers was one Floyd Giebell. Giebell was nearly 31 years old when he received a call-up from the minors in September. He had been designated as the sacrificial lamb by Del Baker, the Tigers manager. It was a foregone conclusion that Feller, already a 27-game winner, would triumph. Baker chose to save his regular starters, knowing that even after

Feller won Detroit would still hold a one-game lead with two to play.

Two hours after Baker had given him the ball, Giebell was carried off the field by his jubilant teammates, a 2-0 victor in the game that brought Detroit its third pennant in seven seasons and denied Cleveland its first since the madcap 1920 campaign. Giebell would never win another game in the majors, and, after the season ended two days later, Vitt would never manage another game in the majors.

Almost unnoticed in the closing days of the 1940 AL season were Joe McCarthy's New York Yankees. Bidding for their fifth straight pennant, the Yankees staged a furious finishing kick and narrowly

Cincinnati's Bill Werber scores the first run in Game 6, in which the Reds tied the Series.

Hank Greenberg (top left) *earned MVP honors, Joe DiMaggio* (top center) *won his second straight batting title, and Ted Williams* (top right) *scored an AL-leading 134 runs.* Bottom: *Mike McCormick, left, and Frank McCormick powered the Reds.*

missed overtaking Detroit before landing two games short. The spark for the closing dash was provided by Tiny Bonham, who went 9-3 after he was recalled in early August from the Yankees' Kansas City farm club. Summoning Bonham was an anathema to McCarthy because it was tantamount to a public admission that his once-invincible pitching staff was in disrepair. Yet if McCarthy had swallowed his pride and recalled Bonham earlier in the season, even just a few weeks earlier, the probability is that the Yankees would not only have won their fifth pennant in

a row but, as events turned out, eight straight pennants between 1936 and 1943.

In 1940, for the first time in their history, the Cincinnati Reds were bent on winning a second consecutive flag. Their final victory margin of 12 games reflected none of the tragedy that, for a time, threatened to ruin their season. On August 3, second-string catcher Willard Hershberger, who was filling in for the injured Ernie Lombardi, committed suicide in his Boston hotel room while despondent over his role in a loss to the Braves. In September, the ball took yet another downward spin for Bill McKechnie's Reds when Lombardi was injured a second time, leaving third-stringer Bill Baker as Cincinnati's only able catcher. On the eve of the World Series, McKechnie pulled Jimmie Wilson off the coaching lines and activated him with the Tigers' permission as an emergency backup for Baker. To the Detroit brass, the move seemed no more than a goodwill gesture. Wilson, who was 40 years old and hadn't caught a full game in three years, hardly constituted a menace to Detroit's chances in the Series.

In Game 1, Wilson was no factor as Bobo Newsom, second only to Feller among AL pitchers in 1940, tucked a 7-2 win under his belt to get Detroit off the mark first. The following day, Bucky Walters evened the Series with a three-hit victory, and the action then moved to Detroit for the next three contests. By Game 3, Wilson had become McKechnie's number one backstopper and was on track to hit .353 and execute the only successful stolen base attempt in the Series. Another sub, Jimmy Ripple,

who was filling in for weak-hitting incumbent Harry Craft in center field, also was giving the Reds surprising zip. Nevertheless, the Tigers were leading the Series 3-2 when the contest returned to Cincinnati.

Needing victories in both games, McKechnie tapped his twin aces, Walters and Paul Derringer, for the job. Walters blanked Detroit in Game 6, 4-0, and aided his own cause with the Reds' second homer of the Series. Ripple, who had hit the other four-bagger in Game 2, emerged as the hero in the Series finale. With the Reds trailing 1-0 in the seventh to Newsom, Frank McCormick sliced a leadoff double. Ripple then doubled him home and later in the frame scored the go-ahead run on a sacrifice fly. When Derringer made the 2-1 lead stand up, the Reds had their first untainted world championship.

SEASON'S BEST

•Frank McCormick is NL MVP—the third different Red in as many years to win the award. McCormick ties an NL record when he leads the loop in hits (191) for the third consecutive season.

•Detroit's Hank Greenberg is voted AL MVP. Greenberg tops the AL in homers (41) and tops the majors in RBI (150), doubles (50), runs produced (238), SA (.670), and total bases (384). After the season, Greenberg becomes the first MLer to enlist in the armed services in preparation for WWII.

•Cleveland's Bob Feller pitches the only AL Opening Day no-hitter on April 16 versus Chicago. Feller's 27 wins top the majors. He also tops the AL in innings (320), CGs (31), and ERA (2.61). His 261 Ks are the most by any pitcher in the majors since 1924.

•Yankee Joe DiMaggio takes his second consecutive AL bat crown (.352).

•Johnny Mize of the Cardinals tops the NL in RBI (137), homers (43), SA (.636), and total bases (368).

•The Indians are nicknamed "The Crybabies" when they go to club owner Alva Bradley and demand he fire manager Ossie Vitt.

•Pittsburgh's Debs Garms wins the NL bat title (.355).

•The Reds win 41 one-run games to set an ML record.

•Willis Hudlin is the first player since 1904 to play with four different teams in the same year.

Johnny Mize

•The sacrifice fly rule is again abolished.

•Boston's Ted Williams leads the AL in runs (134) and OBP (.442) and is third in batting (.344).

•Cincy's Bucky Walters leads the NL in CGs (29), innings (305), and ERA (2.48).

•Detroit's Rudy York, second in the AL in RBI with 134, combines with teammate Greenberg for 284 runs batted in.

•Cleveland shortstop Lou Boudreau has 101 RBI and tops AL shortstops in assists, DPs, and FA.

•Forty-year-old Reds catcher Jimmie Wilson, playing for injured Ernie Lombardi, is the unlikely World Series hero, hitting .353.

BOB FELLER

Rapid Robert tosses Opening Day no-no, wins 27

Long before Kevin Costner ever met Joe Jackson on his *Field of Dreams,* a real-life Iowa farmer had cleared away part of his wheat crop to make a baseball diamond. The reason? He wanted to be able to help his young son develop his game. Given a start such as that, it's no surprise that Robert Feller was striking out big leaguers at a record clip by age 17 and was the top winner in the majors with a 27-11 record just four years later.

He burst on the big-league scene quickly in 1936, striking out 15 St. Louis Browns in his first AL start. From that point on, "Rapid Robert" was considered the league's fastest hurler and biggest drawing card on the mound. Two years later, Bob set an ML record by collecting 18 strikeouts against the Tigers in that season's final game. The AL's top winner (going 24-9) by 1939, he was not only the league's strikeout king two years running but also its leader in walks—including a record 208 allowed in '38. Conquering his lapses in control seemed to be all that was keeping Feller from even greater heights. From his start in 1940, the maturing 21-year-old showed the brilliance that could come with better placement.

Pitching a 1-0 no-hitter against the White Sox on Opening Day (the only time the feat has been accomplished in big-league history), Feller cut down on his walks considerably and went on to collect

baseball's three most coveted pitching titles for the only time in his career. In addition to his 27 wins (a career high), he led all AL pitchers in strikeouts (261) and ERA (2.61) while also setting the pace in shutouts (four), innings (320⅓), and complete games (31). The only tarnish on the year came late, when Feller lost a three-hitter to Detroit in the season's climatic game to help the Tigers secure the pennant.

Feller followed with another outstanding season (a league-best 25 wins and 260 strikeouts) in '41, but then he was off to the Navy for nearly four years. It's estimated he lost anywhere from 75-100 wins and probably around 1,000 strikeouts over the stretch. In 1946, his first full year back, he went 26-15 (again leading the league in wins). He also struck out 348 batters, a major-league record that stood for 27 years until it was broken by Sandy Koufax. Feller never reached such heights again, but he did win over 120 more games and helped the Indians to a pair of pennants. Upon his retirement in '55, he owned a 266-162 record, 46 shutouts, and 2,581 strikeouts. The author of three no-hitters and 12 one-hitters, his career numbers would have been much higher were it not for the war—a fact sportswriters acknowledged by making him the first pitcher since Walter Johnson voted into the Hall of Fame in his first year (1962) of eligibility.

YANKS WIN AFTER OWEN DROPS THE BALL

W hen the 1941 season is recounted, the exploits of two men command almost all the space allotted to the tale. What attention is not lavished on New York Yankees outfielder Joe DiMaggio and his 56-game hitting streak is devoted to Ted Williams, who hit .406 and vaulted the Boston Red Sox, otherwise a mediocre team offensively in 1941, to the ML lead in runs, batting average, and slugging average.

With the Yankees once again occupying the penthouse after a one-sided pennant race that left second-place Boston 17 games in the distance, it was only natural the media should focus on individual achievements, especially two as noteworthy as DiMaggio's and Williams's. The exploits of another player in 1941—even though they had a much larger impact on a pennant race—are nearly forgotten now.

It was different a half a century ago, though, when the name of Pete Reiser was as well-known as any. After a solid but unspectacular rookie season at age 21, Reiser bloomed in 1941 into the youngest batting title winner in NL history. That year he hit .343 and led the senior loop in runs, slugging average, doubles, and triples. Reiser's performance rocketed the Brooklyn Dodgers to their first flag since 1920 after a tight three-way struggle with the Cincinnati Reds and the St. Louis Cardinals. The Reds caved eventually and finished 12 games back, but the Cards hung in with the Dodgers until the last weekend of the season before slipping 2½ games behind.

Reiser exemplified the Dodgers not only in spirit but also in the manner by which he came to wear their uniform. In point of fact, not a single one of the Dodgers' important cogs—from General Man-

Dodgers catcher Mickey Owen chases the most famous passed ball in history as Yankees batter Tommy Henrich heads to first.

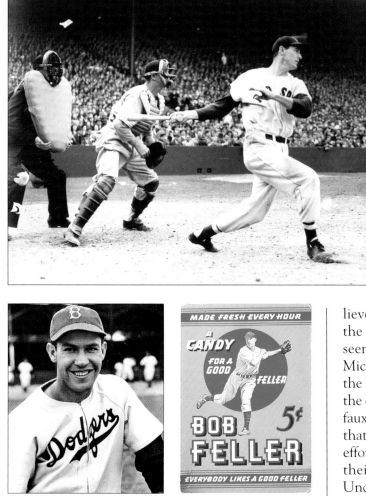

dinals' farm system, and rookie shortstop Pee Wee Reese was purchased from the Red Sox' Louisville affiliate. All of the other key actors in the Dodgers' dramatic production were acquired in trades or after another club had given up on them. The only homegrown product who played more than a bit role in Brooklyn's sudden ascension was 37-year-old Luke Hamlin. He was once a Brooklyn mound mainstay, but in 1941, he went just 8-8 and was destined not to appear at all in the first Subway Series that embraced the borough of Brooklyn.

The most memorable moment from that Series occurred in Game 4 at Ebbets Field. The Dodgers were up 4-3 with two out in the top of the ninth. Brooklyn reliever Hugh Casey fanned Tommy Henrich to end the game—seemingly—but suddenly Henrich was seen sprinting to first base and Dodgers catcher Mickey Owen back toward the screen in pursuit of the ball. Owen's dropped third strike, which opened the door to a 7-4 Yankees victory, is the most famous faux pas in Series history. With the passage of time, that moment has come to characterize the Dodgers' effort in the 1941 Series and to set the tone for all their future fall appearances while in Brooklyn. Under pressure, especially when compared to the Yankees whom they always seemed to find themselves matched against, the Dodgers simply did not quite have what it took; they self-destructed.

In truth, however, the Dodgers gave the Yankees all they could handle in 1941. Every one of the five

Boston's Ted Williams (top) *hit .406, but Joe DiMaggio was AL MVP. Brooklyn's Pete Reiser* (bottom left) *hit .343, making him the youngest player to win an NL batting title. Cleveland's Bob Feller* (bottom right) *led the majors with 260 strikeouts.*

ager Larry MacPhail and field boss Leo Durocher down to their eight regulars and four top moundsmen—had been with the franchise before 1937. Emanating from MacPhail, who signed on with Brooklyn after his unconventional approach to running a ballclub began to wear on Cincinnati's owners, the Dodgers had in four short years changed their image from that of the game's most casually operated franchise to one of the shrewdest. Trades, something Brooklyn avoided in the past, had now become the organization's forte. Third sacker Cookie Lavagetto, who had been garnered from Pittsburgh in 1937, was the oldest member of the 1941 Dodgers regulars in terms of service with the club. Reiser had originally apprenticed in the Car-

Babe Ruth pays his respects to former Yankee teammate Lou Gehrig, who was just 37 years old at the time of his death.

games was tense and up for grabs until the last pitch, and, with a break or two at the right moment, Brooklyn could have swept the Series in four straight. Game 3, on the afternoon prior to Owen's gaffe, was typical of the Dodgers' luck—or lack of it. Freddie Fitzsimmons, after holding the Yankees scoreless through seven innings, was forced to the sidelines when his kneecap was broken by a line drive hit from his mound opponent, Marius Russo.

Minus Fitzsimmons, the Dodgers surrendered two runs in the top of the eighth and lost, 2-1. Yet they fought back the next day, only to see it slip away on Owen's passed ball, and then again in the finale before succumbing 3-1 to Tiny Bonham.

SEASON'S BEST

•Brooklyn's Dolph Camilli is the NL MVP. Camilli leads the NL in homers (34) and RBI (120).

•New York's Joe DiMaggio wins the AL MVP Award. DiMaggio strings together an ML-record 56-game hitting streak. He leads the majors in RBI (125) and total bases (348).

•Boston's Ted Williams is batting .39955 on the last day of the season, but he closes with a 6-for-8 performance in a doubleheader to finish at .406. With this effort, he becomes the last ML player to hit .400 or more. He leads the AL in runs (135), homers (37), OBP (.551), runs produced (218), walks (145), and SA (.735). In the All-Star Game, he hits a three-run homer with two out in the bottom of the ninth to give the AL a 7-5 win at Detroit.

Dolph Camilli

•Brooklyn's Pete Reiser, age 22, becomes the youngest in history to win the NL bat crown (.343). Reiser paces the NL in runs (117), doubles (39), triples (17), runs produced (179), SA (.558), and total bases (299).

•Lou Gehrig dies on June 2 at age 37.

•The Phils lose a franchise-record 111 games.

•The Tigers give $52,000 to Dick Wakefield, who becomes the first of what will soon become a flurry of big-bucks bonus babies.

•On March 8, Hugh Mulcahy of the Phils becomes the first MLer to be drafted in WWII.

•Cleveland's Bob Feller tops the majors in wins with 25. Feller's 343 innings pitched are the most in ML since 1923. He tops the majors again with 260 Ks and also leads the AL in shutouts with six. At the end of the season, Feller enlists in the Navy.

•The Dodgers become the first team to wear plastic batting helmets after Reiser and Pee Wee Reese are beaned.

•Wes Ferrell leaves the game with an ML-record 38 homers by a pitcher.

•White Sox Taffy Wright collects at least one RBI in an all-time AL-record 13 straight games.

•Cincinnati's Elmer Riddle tops the NL in both winning percentage (.826) and ERA (2.24).

•Lefty Grove wins his 300th game, becoming the last to accomplish the feat until 1963.

JOE DIMAGGIO

Joltin' Joe hits safely in 56 straight games

To those who saw him play, Joe DiMaggio had a mystical grace that transcended his statistics, great as they were. It is perhaps fitting, then, that he had a predilection for streaks. Most who know about DiMaggio's major league-record 56-game hitting streak in 1941 don't know that, immediately afterward, he started in on a 16-game streak; even fewer are aware that when he was 18 and playing in the Pacific Coast League, he put together a 61-game streak.

It wasn't news when Joe started his streak with a scratch single off the White Sox' Edgar Smith on May 15. Things got interesting around game 30, when the newspapers began to dust off old hitting

streak marks, like George McQuinn's 34-game streak, which DiMaggio equaled on June 21. By the time he surpassed Ty Cobb's 1911 40-game streak and George Sisler's 1922 AL-record 41, the "Yankee Clipper" was a national sensation. Pressure was building not only on Joe but on official scorers, opposing fielders, and especially pitchers, who wanted to end the streak but not to cheat posterity by pitching around him. On July 2, DiMaggio homered off Boston's Dick Newsome to move past the major-league record of 44 games set by Baltimore's Wee Willie Keeler back in 1897 (before foul balls counted as strikes).

Two weeks later, 67,468 Cleveland fans saw the streak come to an end. Twice, third baseman Ken Keltner made sparkling plays on DiMaggio drives down the line. In the eighth inning, DiMaggio hit a hard grounder up the middle that appeared to take a sudden hop toward the glove of shortstop Lou Boudreau, who started a 6-4-3 double play.

Looking at the statistical summary, DiMaggio's streak becomes even more miraculous. Overall, he batted .408 (relatively low considering that he had to distribute only 91 hits over the 56 games). He made four hits in a game only four times and 34 times kept the streak alive with a single hit. On several occasions the streak hung by the slimmest of threads—many of them, curiously, coming against the White Sox. Facing his great pitching nemesis, Sox righty Johnny Rigney, four times during the streak, DiMaggio barely managed to squeak by, going 1-for-3, 1-for-5, 1-for-4, and 1-for-3 for a .267 batting average.

DiMaggio's streak carried the Yankees from a .500 record to first place by a good margin. Far from shortening his swing for the sake of a record, Joe produced runs in abundance; in 223 at bats, he scored 56 runs, drove in 55, and hit half of his season total of 30 homers. This, and not the streak, is why DiMaggio was voted MVP over the .406-hitting Ted Williams.

NY TEAMS BOW TO RED-HOT CARDS

In this first wartime season, most teams had already begun to lose key players either to the draft or enlistment. The Cleveland Indians were missing 25-game winner Bob Feller; the Washington Senators were without shortstop Cecil Travis, runner-up to Ted Williams for the 1941 AL bat title with a .352 BA; the Detroit Tigers lost slugger Hank Greenberg early in the 1941 campaign; and the last-place Philadelphia A's, who had little to lose, were sheared of second sacker Benny McCoy, the recipient only a few months earlier of a huge $45,000 signing bonus after he was declared a free agent by Commissioner Kenesaw Mountain Landis. Meanwhile the New York Yankees, the team with the most to lose to military call-ups, began the 1942 season missing only first baseman Johnny Sturm, a .239 hitter as a rookie and no sure thing to keep his job anyway.

Replacing Sturm with veteran NL first sacker Buddy Hassett, Yankees skipper Joe McCarthy proceeded to garner his sixth pennant in the past seven seasons with only slightly more stress than usual. Owing to Marius Russo's sore arm and Joe DiMaggio's slip from his .357 BA and .643 SA in 1941 to the more mortal figures of .305 and .498, respectively, the Yankees posted only a nine-game bulge at season's end over the second-place Boston Red Sox.

The Brooklyn Dodgers, also bidding to be a repeat pennant-winner in 1942, looked for most of the summer as if they would have a much easier time of it than the Yankees. As late as mid-August, the Dodgers held what seemed to be a prohibitive 10½-game lead. On August 4, though, the St. Louis Cardinals swept a doubleheader from Brooklyn and suddenly caught fire. When defending batting champ Pete Reiser was felled by a severe head injury and then was only partially himself after he returned to action, Leo Durocher's Dodgers grew increasingly vulnerable.

Whitey Kurowski grabs a pop foul by Yankee hitter Joe Gordon. Kurowski's ninth-inning homer in Game 5 broke a 2-2 tie and clinched the World Series for the Cards.

The hotter the weather grew, the hotter the Cardinals got. From 10½ games the Brooklyn lead shrank to a mere 5 games and then below 3. Piloted by Billy Southworth, the Cardinals fielded the youngest team in the majors with an average age of only 26. In fact, they had only one regular who was 30 years old when the season began—swingman Jimmy Brown, who was equally comfortable at second, third, or short. At the other end of the continuum were Howie Pollet and Stan Musial, two 21-year-old rookies who a year earlier had been left-handed mound candidates. Now only Pollet

was still a pitcher, while Musial had taken over in left field after Johnny Hopp was moved to first base to fill the vacancy created by Johnny Mize's sale to the New York Giants.

Mize, who held the Cards' single-season home run record until 1998, had been put on the market because he was nearing his 30th birthday, as it was by careful design that the Cards were so young. General Manager Branch Rickey subscribed wholeheartedly to youth. Rickey's supporters said it was because he believed young players were hungrier and more dedicated, but detractors contended his consideration was not so much philosophical as economic. The younger a player was, generally the less he had to be paid.

In any case, Rickey's youth movement worked to perfection in 1942 as Musial and Pollet combined with 26-year-old Enos Slaughter, the NL leader in hits, and 29-year-old Mort Cooper, the loop's top winner, to spearhead the Cardinals to 43 wins in their last 51 games. It was not as much that the Dodgers collapsed as that the Cardinals passed them like a wildfire.

The Yankees thought they had doused the conflagration when they grabbed a 7-0 lead in Game 1 of the World Series but then had to hang on for dear life. The Cardinals banged out four runs in the bottom of the ninth before being subdued by Spud Chandler, working in relief of Red Ruffing. Game 2 belonged to the Cardinals' Johnny Beazley, the only

Yankee Joe Gordon, AL MVP with a .322 average and 103 RBI, crosses the plate after another homer (top). Cardinal Mort Cooper (bottom left) was NL MVP with 22 wins, a 1.77 ERA, and 10 shutouts. Boston's Tex Hughson (bottom right) led the AL in complete games (22), strikeouts (113), and innings (281).

rookie in 1942 who was superlative to Musial. A 21-game winner during the regular season, Beazley appeared to be unawed by the Yankees. He cruised to a 3-0 lead and then refused to crumple when Charlie Keller rifled a two-run homer in the eighth to tie the game. After Musial singled Slaughter home in the bottom of the frame to put the Cards ahead again, 4-3, Beazley worked a scoreless ninth to knot matters at 1-all.

With the next three games slated to be played at Yankee Stadium, many expected the Series would not return to St. Louis. Few could have imagined that it would be the Yankees who were facing their last at bat of the season in the ninth inning of Game 5. New York threatened, putting its first two men on against Beazley, but catcher Walker Cooper picked a runner off second, and Beazley then retired the next two hitters to notch his second fall win as the Yankees dropped their first World Series since 1926.

SEASON'S BEST

- Mort Cooper of the Cards is NL MVP. He tops the NL in wins (22), ERA (1.77), and shutouts (10).

- Joe Gordon of the Yanks is AL MVP. Gordon leads the league in errors, strikeouts, and double plays grounded into, though he hits .322 with 103 RBI.

- Boston's Ted Williams wins the Triple Crown (.356 BA, 36 homers, 137 RBI) but once again loses out on the MVP vote. Williams also leads the AL in runs (141), walks (145), runs produced (242), total bases (338), OBP (.499), and SA (.648).

- The Phils finish last for the fifth consecutive year, setting an NL record.

Lou Boudreau

- Cleveland's Lou Boudreau, age 24, is the youngest ML manager to begin the season at the helm of a team.

- The Cardinals' Johnny Beazley wins 21 games as a rookie, enters the armed services, and is never again an effective pitcher.

- Boston's Tex Hughson tops the AL in wins (22) and innings (281) and ties for the lead in Ks (113) and CGs (22).

- The Dodgers' 104 wins tie an ML record for the most wins by an also-ran.

- New York's Mel Ott wins his last NL home run crown (30).

- Red Sox rookie Johnny Pesky hits .331, tops majors with 205 hits.

- White Sox Ted Lyons goes 14-6 as he makes just 20 mound appearances, all of them complete games.

- The Braves' Paul Waner collects his 3,000th hit.

- The average player's salary is down to $6,400.

- Phillie outfielder Danny Litwhiler is the first ML regular to play a whole season without an error.

- On August 14, the Yankees set an ML record with seven DPs versus the A's.

- On May 13, Brave Jim Tobin becomes the only pitcher in this century to hit three homers in a game.

- Gordon and shortstop Phil Rizzuto set an AL keystone record (since broken) when they combine for 235 DPs.

- St. Louis's Enos Slaughter leads the NL in hits (188), triples (17), total bases (292), and runs produced (185).

TED WILLIAMS

The Splendid Splinter leads the league in everything

Asked once his life's ambition, Ted Williams said he hoped one day to be able to walk down the street and have people say, "There goes the greatest hitter who ever lived." Six batting titles, four home run crowns, and nine slugging championships gave Williams ample cause to feel his wish was granted. Some might argue the exploits of Ty Cobb or Babe Ruth, but the record shows that when it came to combining power and average no player dominated his era like Teddy Ballgame—the 1942 Triple Crown winner.

Born August 30, 1918, to indifferent parents, he was soon gaining acceptance on the ballfields of San Diego with an obsession for hitting that would stay with him through parts of four decades in the majors. Carrying his bat to class at Herbert Hoover High, the 6'3", 145-pounder (hence his nickname, "The Splendid Splinter") joined the minor-league San Diego Padres of the Pacific Coast League before graduation. In 1937—on what may have been the greatest scouting trip in history—he and San Diego teammate and fellow Hall of Famer Bobby Doerr were signed up by Red Sox general manager Eddie Collins. By 1939, the 20-year-old Williams was starting in right field for the Red Sox. The left-handed hitter's exceptional rookie season (a .327 batting average with 31 homers and a league-best 145 RBI) prompted Boston owner Tom Yawkey to move in Fenway's right-field fence to provide an easier target. Although Williams (now in left field) "slumped" to .344, 23, 113 totals in 1940, he would more than make up for it the following two years.

Beginning on May 15, 1941, Williams hit in 23 straight games (the longest streak of his career) with a .488 batting average. Joe DiMaggio was in the midst of a record 56-game hitting streak at the same time; however, Williams out-hit Joe over the 56 contests and wound up with a .406 mark for the season (making him the last major leaguer ever to bat .400) along with 120 RBI and a league-best 37 homers, 135 runs, and an astounding .551 on-base percentage. DiMaggio, however, was named MVP with a .357 average for the world champion Yankees.

It was more of the same in '42, as Williams was again MVP runner-up to a pennant-winning Yankee with lesser stats (this time Joe Gordon) despite a Triple Crown season in which he hit .356 with 36 homers and 137 RBI and paced the majors in runs (141), walks (145), slugging (.648), total bases (338), and on-base percentage (.499). His abrasiveness with sportswriters may have helped deny the cocky, headstrong Williams some postseason honors, but as he headed off to the Navy in 1943 there was no denying Ted's place as baseball's greatest hitter.

WAR RAGES ON; YANKS RIP CARDS

With war raging throughout Europe and the Pacific, baseball found itself struggling to keep afloat. Before the onset of the 1942 season, there was considerable doubt the game would be allowed to continue in view of the massive war effort. Finally, in response to a written request from Commissioner Kenesaw Mountain Landis on how baseball could best serve the nation, President Roosevelt issued his famous "green light" letter, proclaiming that he felt it would be best for the country to keep baseball going.

By 1943, professional teams were forced to operate with both older and younger players, as well as those who had been deemed 4-F on their service physicals. Some clubs were made to pack away their uniforms for the duration. The Texas League, the training ground for such great St. Louis Cardinals stars as Ducky Medwick and Dizzy Dean, shut down entirely in 1943 and did not resume operation until 1946. The Redbirds, however, could claim to have the most wide-flung network of farm clubs in the game. They simply beckoned in other directions to procure replacements for stalwarts from their '42 championship squad, including the likes of Enos Slaughter, Creepy Crespi, Terry Moore, Howie Pollet, and Johnny Beazley after they marched off to war. Harry Brecheen and Alpha Brazle were re-cruited to bolster the pitching. Lou Klein joined the Cards to replace Crespi at second base, and Danny Litwhiler was acquired in a trade with the Philadelphia Phillies to patch up a hole in the outfield.

When the Cardinals rambled to their second straight flag by an 18-game spread over the second-place Cincinnati Reds, they seemed not only to have circumvented the manpower shortage that beset their rivals but also the loss of longtime general manager Branch Rickey, who startled St. Louis fans by fleeing to Brooklyn after the 1942 season. Rickey replaced Larry MacPhail, who had now become a lieutenant colonel in the Army. Rickey's new Brooklyn club trudged past the wire in third place, 23½ games behind his old club and 21½ games slower than the Dodgers' pace in 1942. The

Yankees catcher Bill Dickey tags Cardinal Danny Litwhiler out at the plate. Dickey was the hitting hero with a two-run homer in New York's Series-clinching 2-0 victory in Game 5.

Pitcher Mort Cooper, left, and catcher Walker Cooper (top left) are the only sibling teammates to finish among the top five in MVP voting. Manager Joe McCarthy (top center) *won the last of his record seven World Series. The Cubs' Bill Nicholson (top right)* led the NL with 29 homers and 128 RBI. Joe DiMaggio served his country (bottom) *while the Yanks won another title.*

biggest performance drop in the NL, however, occurred in the borough of Manhattan, where the tenants of the Polo Grounds, a solid third in 1942, experienced their first basement finish in 28 years. Now under the guidance of right fielder Mel Ott, the New York Giants both were harder hit than most clubs by service inductions and had less draft-deferred new blood in their farm system.

The New York Yankees, in contrast, not only still had an abundance of spare parts, but they had Joe McCarthy as manager. During the war, McCarthy had to do some of his best work just to pre-serve his record of never finishing out of the first division, but in 1943, his target was still the pennant. To surmount his service losses, he and General Manager Ed Barrow engineered the purchase of first baseman Nick Etten from the Phillies, and called up rookies like Snuffy Stirnweiss and Billy Johnson. They also converted Johnny Lindell, primarily a relief pitcher in 1942, to a center field wartime stand-in for Joe DiMaggio. The result of these changes was another easy pennant for McCarthy, although the Washington Senators put up an astonishingly strong fight in the first half before the Yankees pulled away to a 13½-length triumph.

The Cards, two years younger on average than the Yankees and winners during the regular season of 105 games, embarked on defending their world title as firm favorites. Even McCarthy publicly conceded that his team was no longer the impregnable machine it had once seemed. Asked the previous year to explain the Yankees' stunning Series loss to the Cardinals, he had said, "What's there to explain? Haven't you noticed this team's won eight World Series in a row? What did you think, that we were going to win every one forever?" Privately, though, he let his players know that he expected them to gain revenge.

In the Series opener, when McCarthy led boldly with his ace, Spud Chandler, Cards manager Billy Southworth backed away from a confrontation between Chandler and his own hurling ace, Mort Cooper (21-8), and called for Max Lanier. The jockeying for position seemed a standoff for the moment as Chandler won the lidlifter, 4-2, and Cooper

topped Tiny Bonham the following day, 4-3. How-ever, after the Yankees took the next two games be-hind Hank Borowy and Marius Russo and McCarthy named Chandler his Game 5 starter, Southworth had no alternative but to counter with Cooper. Even though the Cards knocked Chandler for 10 hits,

they were all singles and spaced so carefully that St. Louis never scored. When catcher Bill Dickey ripped a two-run homer in the sixth off Cooper, it was all Chandler needed to complete the Yankees' 180-degree reversal from their five-game Series de-feat in 1942.

S E A S O N ' S   B E S T

- •Yankee pitcher Spud Chandler is AL MVP. He leads the league in ERA (1.64) and winning percent-age (.833) and ties in wins (20), CGs (20), and shutouts (five).

- •Stan Musial is NL MVP, beating out Cardinal teammate Walker Cooper. Musial wins his first NL bat crown (.357). He also leads the NL in OBP (.425), SA (.562), hits (220), doubles (48), triples (20), and total bases (347).

- •Chicago's Luke Appling becomes the lone AL shortstop to win two bat crowns (.328).

- •Detroit's Rudy York tops the AL in homers (34), RBI (118), runs produced (174), SA (.527), and total bases (301).

- •Chicago's Bill Nicholson leads the NL in homers (29) and RBI (128).

- •ML teams conduct spring training in northern sectors due to WWII travel restrictions.

- •The Browns add to their ongoing ML record when they complete their 42nd season without having won a pennant.

- •Washington's George Case wins his fifth consecutive AL theft crown (61).

- •To save on rubber, a new balata baseball is introduced. There are no homers in the first 11 games of the season, and the new ball is shelved.

Rudy York

- •New York's Mel Ott is second in the NL with 18 homers—all 18 are hit in his home park.

- •The White Sox play an ML-record 44 doubleheaders.

- •The bankrupt Phils franchise is sold to the NL. William Cox becomes owner. Later, Commissioner Kenesaw Mountain Landis bans Cox for life for betting on his own team.

- •The A's lose an AL-record (since broken) 20 straight games.

- •In September, Philly's Carl Scheib, age 16, becomes the youngest player ever to appear in an AL game.

- •The AL wins the first All-Star Game played at night, 5-3 at Shibe Park.

- •Detroit rookie Dick Wakefield tops the AL in hits (200) and doubles (38) and is second in batting (.316) and total bases (275).

- •The Giants' Ace Adams sets a new modern ML record with 70 mound appearances.

STAN MUSIAL

Stan the Man wears his first of seven bat crowns

He never won a Triple Crown, hit .400, or slugged 40 home runs. He went the last 17 seasons of his career without playing on a pennant winner, and offered fans neither the flamboyancy of a Babe Ruth nor the brash confidence of a Ted Williams. All Stan Musial did was play baseball, and he did so with such consistency and excellence over 22 superb seasons that when he was done he had put together more records than any hitter in National League history. Among these accomplishments was a 1943 batting title that helped the St. Louis Cardinals to the world championship and earned Stan Musial MVP recognition.

His modest approach to the game was born out of a hardened but happy upbringing. Born in 1920 to immigrant parents who worked in a Donora, Pennsylvania, nail mill, he grew up with few material items but a deep love and respect for family and sacrifice. From the time he began hitting balls made by his mother from scraps found around the house, Stan dreamed of being a big leaguer. His teenage pitching success for local semi-pro clubs earned him a contract from the Cards in 1938. He went 18-5 at minor-league Daytona Beach in 1940, and his .311 batting average assured him of outfield assignments when he wasn't pitching. While making a diving catch on one such occasion, Musial hurt his left shoulder so badly he could barely pitch the following spring.

The prospects for the lame-armed left-hander didn't look good, but there was one thing that saved him— he still had his bat!

Hitting well over .350 combined for two minor-league clubs in 1941, Musial was called up to St. Louis and hit .426 (20-for-47) in the thick of a pennant race. (The Cards eventually lost to Brooklyn by just 2½ games.) Despite the fact that he was often platooned early on during the following season, the 6', 175-pounder hit .315 with 10 homers and 72 RBI as the Cardinals came back from a 10-game deficit to win 43 out of their final 51 games en route to the pennant. Stan batted a disappointing .222 in a five-game World Series victory over the Yankees, but no one would remember the following year anyway.

In addition to winning his first of seven batting crowns in '43 with a major league-best .357 mark, Musial paced the majors in slugging (.562), hits (220), doubles (48), triples (20), total bases (347), and on-base percentage (.425). The Cards took another pennant—this time losing to the Yanks in a five-game Series—and Musial won the first of his three NL MVP Awards. Adding in his 108 runs (second in the NL) and 81 RBI (fifth), the 22-year-old with the corkscrew batting stance and unlimited hustle had compiled quite a season—and there would be 20 more much like it to come.

SAD-SACK BROWNIES MAKE IT TO WS

The Detroit Tigers have a lifelong tradition of making the most of their opportunities. In 1907, the first time they were seriously embroiled in an AL pennant race, they beat out the Philadelphia A's in the closing days of the season. A year later they won out over the Cleveland Indians and the Chicago White Sox on the final day of the campaign. Again in 1940 they managed to stifle a late challenge from Cleveland in the only down-to-the-wire race in the AL between 1922 and 1943.

In 1944, the Tigers were once more poised to snatch a pennant, as they found themselves in the first junior circuit race since 1908 to enter the last day of the season still awaiting a resolution. What's more, the Bengals not only had tradition on their side, they also had 27-game winner Dizzy Trout, one half of the top-winning mound tandem since the close of the dead-ball era, primed to pitch the finale. They also were slated to play at home against the cellar-dwelling Washington Senators. There was, however, one more factor in their favor, and this one, in some ways, was the most important of all. The Tigers began the last morning of the season tied for first place with the St. Louis Browns, a team that had never won a pennant in its lengthy 42-year history. The Browns, on the other hand, were matched that afternoon against the defending world champion Yankees.

Under normal circumstances, a St. Louis win over the Yankees coupled with a Detroit loss to the Senators would have warranted Commissioner Kenesaw Mountain Landis to consider calling for an investigation, but 1944 was not a normal season. The Browns, accustomed to long losing skeins, had opened the campaign by winning their first nine games, but since that jump start they had gone only 79-65 to match the Tigers' mark of 88-65. This meant that the AL flag-bearer in 1944 would triumph with, at best, a .578 winning percentage (89-65), the lowest in history to that point. To further

The Browns were unlikely winners of the AL pennant, but couldn't pull off a victory over their St. Louis brethren, the Cardinals, in the World Series. The Cards won in six games.

The Browns trailed 2-0 in the fourth and were still looking for their first hit off Queen when Mike Kreevich broke the ice with a single. Chet Laabs then followed with a two-run homer, and the following inning fans experienced a thrilling few moments of deja vu as Kreevich again singled with two out and Laabs, who had begun the day with just three dingers and 19 RBI, pumped his second two-run shot into the bleachers. After the Browns added a run in the eighth to go ahead 5-2, everyone in the park suddenly began to study the scoreboard, which showed the Senators leading the Tigers, 4-1.

When the Detroit score was posted as final, the Browns found themselves headed for their first post-season encounter. They had only to go back to their homes and wait until that Wednesday, though, as the opponents they drew were their fellow tenants of Sportsman's Park, the St. Louis Cardinals, which meant that the entire World Series would be played at the same site.

The Cards had notched their third straight flag after an NL race that was as dull as the AL chase was exciting. Redbirds skipper Billy Southworth had almost the same lineup intact that had gone 105-49 in 1943 and it produced an identical result—105 wins in 154 tries and a double-digit lead over the Pittsburgh Pirates at the finish line.

Shortstop Vernon Stephens (top) knocked in 109 runs for the Browns. Detroit's Dizzy Trout (bottom) tallied 33 complete games, a 2.12 ERA, seven shutouts, and 352 innings pitched.

Cardinals second baseman Red Schoendienst, left, spent '44 in the service, while infield mate Marty Marion had an NL MVP season. Marion, the Cardinals' shortstop, edged Bill Nicholson of the Chicago Cubs by one vote.

underscore the parity that the war had wrought, last-place Washington stood only 25 games out of first place on farewell day.

Browns fans, starved for a pennant of any kind, could not have cared less that analysts had already prepared a half-dozen excuses if they somehow miraculously won. Those fortunate enough to turn up at St. Louis's Sportsman's Park on that October 1 afternoon saw a sequence of events unfold that have never been matched before or since. Yankees manager Joe McCarthy handed the game ball to Mel Queen, a hard-throwing rookie who was 6-2 in his nine previous ML starts, while Browns manager Luke Sewell went with 35-year-old Sig Jakucki, plucked earlier that year from the semi-pro ranks. Never more than a marginal prospect, Jakucki had exited from the majors way back in 1936, winless in seven appearances.

Though the Browns were everyone's sentimental choice in the World Series, the Cards were where people put their money. Led by the hitting of first sacker George McQuinn and two complete-game wins from Denny Galehouse and Jack Kramer, the Browns held a 2-1 edge after the first three games. Then, their bats went dead, and the combo of Harry Brecheen, Mort Cooper, and Ted Wilks checked them with just 19 hits and two runs over the next 27 innings to bring the Cards a 4-2 Series win.

S E A S O N ' S   B E S T

•Cardinal shortstop Marty Marion is NL MVP.

•Detroit's Hal Newhouser wins the AL MVP Award. Newhouser wins 29 games for the second-place Tigers, most since 1931 by an ML lefty.

Dixie Walker

•Dizzy Trout wins 27 for the Tigers to give the club a post-dead-ball tandem record of 56 wins from two pitchers. Trout is second in the AL MVP vote—first time two pitchers from the same team have finished one-two.

•Brooklyn's Dixie Walker tops the NL in batting at .357.

•Cleveland's Lou Boudreau wins the AL bat title at .327. Boudreau is involved in 134 DPs, an all-time major-league record for shortstops in a 154-game season.

•Cub Bill Nicholson tops the majors in homers with 33 and RBI with 122. Nicholson leads the NL in runs (116), runs produced (205), and total bases (317).

•AL homer leader Nick Etten of the Yankees belts just 22.

•Giant rookie Bill Voiselle wins 21. He's the last rookie in ML history to pitch 300 or more innings, as he works 313.

•Yankee Snuffy Stirnweiss, a .219 hitter in 1943, tops the majors with 205 hits. Stirnweiss tops the AL in runs (125) and steals (55) and ties for the lead in triples (16).

•Elmer Gedeon becomes the first former major leaguer to be killed in action in WWII.

•On June 10, the Reds use 15-year-old pitcher Joe Nuxhall, the youngest player in this century.

•Cincinnati's Ray Mueller sets an NL record when he participates in 217 consecutive games as a catcher.

•At the end of August, the Cards have a 91-30 mark, but they're only 14-19 the rest of the way. The Redbirds lead the majors in batting (.275), runs (772), homers (100), fielding (.982), and ERA (2.67).

•On April 27 versus the Dodgers, Jim Tobin of the Braves becomes the first pitcher to hit a homer while tossing a no-hitter.

•On August 10, Red Barrett of the Braves throws just 58 pitches in a CG shutout of the Reds.

•St. Louis's Stan Musial tops the NL in doubles (51) and SA (.549) and ties for the lead in hits (197).

HAL NEWHOUSER

Wartime replacements no match for Prince Hal

Between 1942 and '45, major-league baseball began to increasingly take on an image as more of a patriotic necessity than a locale for the game's top talent. Those left behind on rosters by '45 were for the most part considered second-rate players who would be gone at war's end, and their accomplishments have been watered down in the 50 years since by comments like, "Remember, that was a war year." Even truly outstanding performances have not escaped the wrath, and Detroit lefty Hal Newhouser's back-to-back MVP seasons of 1944 and '45 are still viewed by some detractors as an anomaly rather than the peak of a Hall of Fame career.

Those who argue against the worthiness of "Prince Hal's" achievements point to his 34-52 record through 1943, but Newhouser was then a young hurler still refining his craft. An American Legion star in Detroit, he signed with his hometown Tigers for $400 in 1938 and was a starter for the 1940 AL champions as a 19-year-old. Struggling with wildness on the mound (he walked 442 over 690⅔ innings his first five seasons), he earned a reputation off it as an overly intense troublemaker with a violent temper. When he learned to quell his emotions while controlling his fastball and overhand curve, the results were extraordinary.

Still just 22 when the 1944 season began, Newhouser turned in a devastating 29-9 year to become the AL leader in wins and strikeouts (187). He and teammate Dizzy Trout (27-14) nearly pitched the Tigers to the pennant, with Detroit finishing just one game behind the Browns. That season, Hal edged Trout in the MVP balloting. Newhouser then followed up with an even more spectacular year in '45, pacing the AL in wins (with a 25-9 mark), ERA (1.81), strikeouts (212), shutouts (eight), innings (313⅓), and complete games (29). This time the Tigers won the pennant on the very last day of the season. Newhouser went on to pitch two complete-game victories—one of which proved to be the clincher—in a seven-game World Series triumph over the Cubs. Once again named MVP, Hal became the first and only pitcher to win the award two years in a row.

The anti-Hal contingent predicted his demise when baseball's best returned from war the following year. Contrary to the naysayers, Newhouser almost took his third straight MVP honor by going 26-9 and again topping the AL in wins and ERA (1.94). In fact, he finished second in voting for the award to Ted Williams. Four more solid seasons followed (including another 20-win campaign in '48), but Newhouser's shoulder troubles reduced him to a spot starter by 1951. Moving to the bullpen, he helped the Indians to the '54 pennant with a 7-2 mark and seven saves to close out his career with a tidy 207-150 record. After leading the majors in victories (170) and strikeouts (1,579) while compiling a 2.84 ERA during the '40s, he could hardly be called a wartime wonder. Hal eventually won Hall of Fame distinction in 1992.

MEDIOCRE TIGERS TAKE THE TITLE

Many observers thought that parity was not really the right word to describe the AL race in 1944. A more accurate term was mediocrity. As one writer put it: "The game being played on the field in 1944 was recognizable, but many of the players were not."

Even fewer recognizable performers checkered the major-league scene in 1945, and there were unfamiliar faces off the field as well. Kenesaw Mountain Landis, the only commissioner the game had known since his appointment to the newly created job in 1920, died on November 25, 1944, and the

owners named as his replacement Albert B. "Happy" Chandler, a U.S. senator from Kentucky. In 1945, Chandler had to oversee a sport that was forced by wartime travel restrictions to cancel its All-Star Game and that employed a one-legged pitcher for a single game and a one-armed outfielder for the entire season.

Pete Gray, the outfielder with a missing limb, belonged to the St. Louis Browns and ostensibly was signed only as a gate attraction. Gray had been the MVP choice, however, the previous year in the Southern Association and was certainly no less qual-

The 1945 World Series wasn't pretty, except for Hank Greenberg's swing. Greenberg returned from the Army that season and hit .304 with two home runs and seven runs batted in as the Tigers beat the Cubs in seven games.

ified for major-league duty than
many other career minor leaguers
who filled empty ML slots during
the war. Bert Shepard, the one-
legged hurler, was a disabled veteran the Washington Senators used
for five innings on one occasion in
a mop-up role. Last in 1944, the
Senators began the 1945 season
with little more in mind than to get
through the summer as quickly and
as economically as possible while
they waited for the war to end.
Owner Clark Griffith was therefore
amenable to juggling the schedule
in order to end the Senators' season
a few days early so that the Washington Redskins of the National Football League
could use his park on what normally would have
been the final week of the baseball campaign.

To Griffith's dismay, he fielded a contender in
1945. Deep into September, the Senators were en-
tangled in a three-way dogfight with the Detroit
Tigers and the St. Louis Browns, while the fourth-
place New York Yankees lagged only a few percentage points behind. The Browns eventually tired,
leaving the chase between Washington and Detroit
as to who would meet the NL champion Chicago
Cubs in the World Series. On their closing date, the
Senators dropped a heartbreaker to the last-place
Philadelphia A's when center fielder Bingo Binks
left his sunglasses behind in the dugout and the A's
scored the winning run on a lazy fly ball that he lost
in the sun. Even though their season was over, the
Senators retained a shot at a meeting with the NL
champion Cubs, for the Tigers still had to play a season-closing series with the Browns. With two games
to play, Detroit had a one-game lead on Washington and needed just one more victory to clinch.
Rain in St. Louis forced a doubleheader to be scheduled for the final day. On the afternoon of September 30, it began to rain again. Finally, the first game
of the twinbill began under still threatening skies.
Virgil Trucks started for Detroit but gave way to Hal
Newhouser when he loaded the bases in the sixth.
Newhouser smothered the rally to keep the Tigers
ahead 2-1 but then surrendered a run in the seventh
and another in the eighth. With the Browns up 3-2
in the top of the ninth, all in Washington who were
glued to their radios listening to reports from St.

Snuffy Stirnweiss (top left) *hit only .309, but won the AL
batting title. Senators pitcher Bert Shepard* (top right) *is the
only one-legged player in major-league history. Happy
Chandler* (bottom left) *became commissioner in '45. The
Cubs' Phil Cavaretta* (bottom right) *won MVP honors
with a .355 batting average.*

Louis sat with bated breath. They tensed when Detroit loaded the bases with one out. Up stepped
Hank Greenberg, back from a four-year military
stint. Greenberg took a 1-1 pitch deep for a grand
slam to put the Tigers up a game and a half and ren-
der the second contest unnecessary.

Detroit's winning percentage of .575 (88-65)
broke the Browns' year-old record for the lowest
mark by a flag-winner and gave critics of the wartime game all the more ammunition. On the eve of
the World Series, Warren Brown, a Chicago sports
editor, was asked whether he fancied Detroit or the
Cubs. Brown replied that he didn't think either club

was capable of winning. The Cubs, who had set a record in 1945 by sweeping 20 doubleheaders en route to dethroning three-time National League champion St. Louis, promptly set out to prove Brown wrong by bombing Newhouser, 9-0, in the opener. Detroit then won three of the next four before losing an 8-7 melee in 12 innings that has been called "the worst game of baseball ever played in this country."

Game 7 pitted Newhouser against Hank Borowy for the third time in the Series. Borowy, who had won Game 6 in relief, wound up a 9-3 loser in the decider, causing him to be remembered as the last Cubs hurler to both win and lose a Series clash.

SEASON'S BEST

•Chicago's Phil Cavarretta is named NL MVP.

•Detroit's Hal Newhouser wins his second straight AL MVP Award. Newhouser tops the majors with 25 wins, a .735 winning percentage, a 1.81 ERA, 212 Ks, eight shutouts, and 29 CGs.

•Boston's Tommy Holmes hits in 37 consecutive games—new modern NL record. Holmes is the only player ever to lead the league in homers (28) and fewest batter Ks (nine). He tops the NL in hits (224), doubles (47), total bases (367), and SA (.577).

•Yankee Snuffy Stirnweiss tops the AL in BA at just .309. Stirnweiss leads the AL in runs (107), SA (.476), steals (33), hits (195), triples (22), and total bases (301).

•One-armed outfielder Pete Gray plays the full season for the Browns, hitting .218.

•Brooklyn's Dixie Walker tops the majors with 124 RBI and 218 runs produced.

•Brooklyn's Branch Rickey signs Jackie Robinson to a contract.

•Happy Chandler is named the new commissioner of baseball.

•The All-Star Game is not held due to the war—only cancellation in history.

Tommy Holmes

•On August 20, Dodgers shortstop Tommy Brown, age 17, becomes the youngest player in ML history to homer.

•Brooklyn's Eddie Stanky sets a new NL record for walks with 148.

•Bert Shepard, a one-legged pitcher, appears in a game for Washington.

•The Senators hit only one home run in their home park—and that's an inside-the-park homer by Joe Kuhel.

•Philly's Andy Karl pitches 167 innings in relief to set an NL record that will last until 1974.

•On July 21, the Tigers and A's play to a 1-1 tie in 24 innings. Les Mueller pitches 19⅔ innings for the Tigers.

•The Cubs sweep an all-time ML-record 20 doubleheaders to break their own year-old mark.

•The Cards lose Stan Musial and Walker Cooper to the armed services prior to the season and finish three games back of the Cubs without them.

PETE GRAY

One-armed outfielder smacks .218 in 234 at bats

Of all the ballplayers who were able to reach the majors or sustain their big-league careers during World War II, perhaps no one better symbolized the state of baseball during the period than Pete Gray of the St. Louis Browns. Teenagers, career minor leaguers, and grizzled veterans whose best years were long behind them all became common sights on major-league rosters from 1942 to '45, but only the Brownies could claim a one-armed outfielder.

Gray was born in the town of Nanticoke, Pennsylvania, in 1915. He was six when he mangled his right arm in the spokes of a farmer's provision wagon. His arm had to be amputated above the elbow, but the natural right-hander taught himself to bat lefty and catch one-handed. Pete developed an excellent batting eye. He rarely ever struck out and became a strong line-drive hitter and expert bunter. As an outfielder, he devised a method where he would catch the ball, toss it in the air as he tucked his glove under the stump of his right arm, then recatch and throw the ball with his left hand. He achieved all of this with one fluid motion. Special gloves with almost no padding and worn on just one finger made the job easier, and hitters soon learned not to challenge Gray's supposed handicap.

Major-league teams were initially reluctant to sign him, but after he won Southern Association MVP honors in 1944 by batting .333 with a league record-tying 63 stolen bases for the Class-A Memphis Chicks, he was purchased by the defending American League champion Browns for $20,000. Batting second in the lineup on Opening Day in 1945, he singled in three trips against Detroit's Hal Newhouser in his major-league debut. It didn't take long, however, for the hits to become far less frequent. Pitchers learned Gray had more difficulty with curves than fastballs, and he was soon seeing a steady diet of off-speed pitches. Unable to compensate, his batting average dipped near .200 despite his ability to make contact (he struck out just 11 times in his 234 at bats). Infielders and outfielders played him shallow both to cut off his bunts and exploit his lack of power. Unlike his time in the minors, major-league opponents routinely took successful chances on his outfield arm.

Gray became a fan favorite, but several Browns players privately and publicly blamed his outfield play for costing the team a half-dozen or more games en route to a third-place finish, six games behind the Tigers. By year's end, his batting average was down to .218 with six doubles, two triples, and five steals. The Browns optioned him to Toledo the following season. By 1949, at age 32, he was out of baseball. He went back to Nanticoke a bitter man who would live out his years fending off reporters and fans still moved by his story nearly a half-century after his time in St. Louis.

CARDS SLAUGHTER THE BOSOX IN WS

Those fans who had shunned ballparks during the war bought their tickets prior to the 1946 season with the expectation that the game they remembered and loved would immediately reappear. It never quite happened. Many leading stars had been away too long to resume their careers or else, like Cecil Travis, had sustained combat-related injuries and ailments that blunted their skills. Travis hit just .252 for Washington in 1946, down 107 points from his .359 mark five years earlier in his last pre-war season. Conversely, though, another Senators performer, first baseman Mickey Vernon, smoked pitchers for a .353 BA, up 85 points from his previous look at American League hurlers in '43.

While Vernon's torrid bat just wouldn't quit, it prevented Ted Williams from resuming where he had left off 1942. Indeed, Williams wound up as the runner-up in each of the three Triple Crown departments. Nevertheless, he had little trouble propelling the Red Sox to their first pennant in 28 years. Between Williams and pitchers Boo Ferriss and Tex Hughson, who had managed to compile a combined record of 45 wins against 17 losses, the Red Sox blazed out of the starting gate and were so far ahead by the middle of May, the season was virtually over for the other seven AL clubs.

The NL race, expected to be between the St. Louis Cardinals (victors from 1942 through '44) and the Chicago Cubs (winners in 1945), had an interloper—namely Leo Durocher and his Brooklyn Dodgers. Dormant during the war, Brooklyn melded a corps of returning servicemen with holdover Dixie Walker and an influx of talented rookies like Carl Furillo, Bruce Edwards, and southpaw Joe Hatten to post a reminder that the last NL pennant before the war had flown in Flatbush.

Hobbled by injuries to Andy Pafko, Stan Hack, Mickey Livingston, and Don Johnson, the Cubs were never able to mount a sustained charge and fin-

Despite playing with a broken elbow, Cardinal Enos Slaughter managed to slide home with the winning run from first base in the eighth inning of Game 7.

Cardinal hitter Marty Marion and Dodger catcher Bruce Edwards follow a fly ball during the '46 playoff for the NL pennant (top). A ninth-inning Dodgers rally in the playoff series stalled when Eddie Stanky (bottom) struck out.

They received a momentary thrill as the Dodgers tallied three runs and had the tying run at the plate with just one out. But Harry Brecheen, summoned in relief, struck out Eddie Stanky and pinch hitter Howie Schultz to make the Cardinals the first-ever pennant-playoff victors.

In Game 1 of the World Series, Rudy York's solo 10th inning homer off Pollet won it for the Red Sox, and the teams then took turns winning the next five contests. Cards manager Eddie Dyer had set up his mound rotation so that he would have Pollet, the NL's top winner, rested and ready if a seventh game was necessary. When Pollet pulled up lame in his second Series start, Dyer had to go with Dickson. Sox skipper Joe Cronin selected Ferriss for the all-important assignment.

By the bottom of the eighth, neither starter was still around. Brecheen, already a winner twice as a starter, had replaced Dickson in the top of the frame when the Sox pushed across two runs to tie the game, 3-3. Hurler Bob Klinger was working for Boston. Enos Slaughter, playing with a broken elbow since early in Game 5, singled but was still on first with two out. Harry Walker then hit a looping liner over shortstop Johnny Pesky's head. Leon Culberson

ished a poor third. St. Louis and Brooklyn, meanwhile, entered the final day of the season tied with 96-57 records and were to face the Cubs and the Boston Braves, respectively. Since the game in the East started first, the Cards learned that their former teammate, Mort Cooper, had shut out the Dodgers, 4-0, while their own contest was still in progress. They were, however, still unable to avert an 8-3 loss to Chicago. With both combatants bowing to defeat, for the first time in history a pennant race ended in a dead heat, requiring a playoff.

The NL constitution called for a best-of-three format, and after losing the coin flip, the Dodgers journeyed to St. Louis for the first game. Minus Pete Reiser, who broke an ankle three weeks earlier, Brooklyn lost, 4-2, to Howie Pollet. When the Cards came to Ebbets Field two days later, 31,437 watched Murry Dickson give up a first inning run and then hold their Dodgers scoreless for the next seven innings. Since the score by then was 8-1, only diehards lingered until the bottom of the ninth.

Hal Newhouser was in top form again in '46, leading the majors in ERA (1.94) and finishing second in the AL MVP voting.

was in center field due to a sprained ankle that sent Dom DiMaggio limping off just minutes earlier. Culberson's arm was not the strongest, but even so, none of the Red Sox imagined Slaughter, running at the crack of the bat, would not pull up at third. Instead Slaughter kept motoring and Pesky, unable to hear the cries of his teammates over the roar of the crowd, held Culberson's relay throw a fraction of a second before firing it home. Slaughter slid in ahead of the ball with the run that won the championship.

SEASON'S BEST

•Boston's Ted Williams is selected AL MVP. Williams tops the AL in SA (.667), total bases (343), runs (142), runs produced (227), OBP (.497), and walks (156).

•St. Louis's Stan Musial is named NL MVP. Musial tops the majors in batting (.365), total bases (366), hits (228), and triples (20). He tops the NL in runs (124), doubles (50), and SA (.587).

•The AL wins the most one-sided All-Star Game of all time, 12-0 at Fenway, as Williams belts two four-baggers.

•Cleveland's Bob Feller fans 348 in first full year back from the Navy.

•Feller and Detroit's Hal Newhouser tie for the ML lead with 26 wins. Newhouser tops the majors in ERA (1.94) and is second in the AL MVP vote.

•Washington's Mickey Vernon leads the AL in batting at .353.

•Pittsburgh's Ralph Kiner is the first rookie to lead the NL in homers (23).

Bob Feller

•Detroit's Hank Greenberg leads the majors with 44 homers and the AL with 127 RBI.

•The Yankees become the first team in ML history to draw more than 2,000,000 at home.

•The Mexican League lures several ML stars by offering them more money than the majors are paying.

•Jackie Robinson becomes the first African-American to play a full season in organized baseball in this century.

•A four-man group, including John Galbreath and Bing Crosby, buy the Pirates.

•The players form the American Baseball Guild in their fourth attempt to unionize. The Guild helps raise the minimum ML salary to $5,000.

•Bill Kennedy of Rocky Mount in the Coastal Plains League fans 456 hitters and posts a 28-3 record with a 1.03 ERA.

•Brooklyn's Pete Reiser steals home seven times, setting an ML record.

•Joe Cronin of the Red Sox is the first to manage two different AL teams to flags.

•Cardinal Howie Pollet is the NL ERA king (2.10) and also tops the NL in wins (21).

•Harry Brecheen wins three World Series games for the Cards.

TED WILLIAMS

Fenway favorite crushes the eephus, powers the Sox

Every major-league team lost large portions of its roster to the armed forces during World War II, but perhaps no club was more affected than Boston's. The Red Sox appeared finally ready to challenge the New York Yankees for the American League pennant in 1942, with such stars as Bobby Doerr, Johnny Pesky, and Dom DiMaggio just reaching their prime. Soon, however, all would be taken into the military. The biggest name on the Red Sox' list of missing talent was Ted Williams, who followed his Triple Crown season of '42 by leaving for a three-year stint as a Navy pilot. When the war ended, fans wondered if The Splendid Splinter would ever be able to regain his stroke.

They would not have to wonder long. Williams went 3-for-3 with two homers and seven RBI in a March 3, 1946, spring training contest with the Braves. When the regular season got underway, it quickly became apparent that Ted and the Red Sox would be impossible to stop in the AL. Ted hit .346 in April, adding 19 homers and 53 RBI during May and June. Boston put together a 15-game winning streak and a 32-9 start. That effectively ended the pennant race; the Red Sox' lead never went under 10 games after mid-July, and they clinched the AL title with a 1-0 win at Cleveland on September 13—the run fittingly scoring on the only inside-the-park homer of Williams's career.

There were plenty of other dramatic moments for Ted during the season. He hit a 430-foot homer on June 9 that crushed the straw hat of a man seated in the right field bleachers at Fenway Park (a red chair still marks the spot), and he thrilled a hometown crowd at Fenway during the All-Star Game by going 4-for-4 with five RBI, four runs scored, and two homers—the second coming off the infamous slow, blooping "eephus" pitch of Pittsburgh's Rip Sewell. Williams hit .400 in September, and by year's end, Ted ranked second in the American League in batting (.342), homers (38), and RBI (123) while finishing first in runs (142), slugging (.667), total bases (343), and on-base percentage (.497). Showing pitchers had lost none of their respect for him in his absence, Williams also coaxed a league-high 156 walks.

Ted's heroics helped the Red Sox into the World Series with the St. Louis Cardinals, but after he was beaned in the elbow during a game that preceded it, the magic ended. Williams hit .200 with just five singles (including a bunt!) and one RBI in a seven-game Series loss. He tearfully gave his Series share to Boston's clubhouse boy in disgust. When Ted finally got an MVP Award to make up for second-place finishes in '41 and '42, he was already thinking about redeeming himself the next season.

HEROES EMERGE AS YANKS NIP DODGERS

As had happened in 1909 when Ty Cobb and Honus Wagner opposed each other in the World Series, the eagerly awaited confrontation between Stan Musial and Ted Williams in the 1946 fall classic became a moot point when neither played a significant role in the result; the heroes instead were Enos Slaughter, Harry Walker, and Harry Brecheen. However, the three Cardinals who produced the most memorable moments in the 1946 World Series at least were all significant contributors during the decade of the 1940s. In contrast, the three performers who fashioned the most vivid memories in the 1947 postseason fray dropped from view almost as soon as the last pitch was thrown.

The contenders for the 1947 world title were the New York Yankees and the Brooklyn Dodgers. Each triumphed after a pennant race that was not nearly as interesting as its subplots. Brooklyn skipped home five games ahead of the St. Louis Cardinals and eight up on the surprising Boston Braves, who scaled their highest height in 31 years. In one way, though, the fourth-place New York Giants were *the* team that year. Not only did they blast 221 homers to shatter all then-existing team records, but they unveiled Clint Hartung, the most vaunted rookie to come along in years; Larry Jansen, the first post-war rookie to win 20 games; and Bobby Thomson, the top frosh slugger in all of baseball.

The Giants did not own the Rookie of the Year, however; in the first season this prize was formally awarded, the honor went to Brooklyn's Jackie Robinson, the first African-American to play on the major-league level since 1884. Robinson was joined later in the season by Dan Bankhead, the first African-American hurler to reach the majors. When Robinson led the NL in stolen bases while hitting a solid .297 and Bankhead homered in his first big-league at bat, the Dodgers had two more of the necessary ingredients to help them shatter a team record

of their own. In 1889, their ancestors, the Brooklyn Bridegrooms, set the 19th-century single-season attendance record. By the close of the 1947 season, the Dodgers owned the 20th-century NL mark for attendance despite playing in Ebbets Field, one of the smallest parks in the majors.

The Yankees, who had established a new AL attendance record the previous year, continued to keep the turnstiles clicking in '47 with the sort of team that would confound the rest of the AL for the

Catcher Yogi Berra argues a non-call with the ump, saying Dodger hitter Hugh Casey interfered on a foul pop. Berra lost the argument, but the Yanks won the Series.

next 17 years. Although they lacked a 20-game winner, a 100-RBI man, or a player who finished among the top five in batting, the Bombers rattled off an AL record-tying 19 consecutive wins in July and paced the junior loop in virtually every important team hitting and pitching department. In his first season at the Yankees helm, Bucky Harris made winning the pennant look so easy that many other AL moguls feared that a new dynasty might be developing in the Bronx.

The World Series began as had so many others over the past 25 years that involved the Yankees. Rookie Spec Shea, with relief help from Joe Page, gave Harris's men a routine 5-3 win in the opener. Then Allie Reynolds, backed by 15 hits and 10 runs, put the Yankees up 2-0 the following day.

On October 2, the action moved to Ebbets Field, and the Dodgers won a 9-8 donnybrook, surviving the first pinch homer in Series history, struck by rookie catcher Yogi Berra. Forced to use five pitchers in the slugfest, Harris had little left for Game 4 except 30-year-old Bill Bevens. Hurler Bevens's 7-13 record was one of the poorest ever for a starting pitcher on a pennant winner.

Though he averaged a walk an inning, Bevens allowed the Dodgers no hits through eight frames and entered the bottom of the ninth ahead 2-1. One out away from the first no-hitter in Series competition, Bevens had pinch-runner Al Gionfriddo on second when Dodgers skipper Burt Shotton sent Pete Reiser up to pinch-hit. Harris ordered Bevens to surrender his 10th free pass of the game and walk

Boston's Ted Williams (top left) won the Triple Crown, but New York's Joe DiMaggio (bottom left) won the AL MVP Award by one vote. Top right: Pirate Ralph Kiner, left, and Giant Johnny Mize staged another slugfest, tying for the NL home run crown for the second consecutive season with 51. The Braves' Bob Elliott (bottom right) was the first third baseman to be named MVP.

Reiser intentionally. In doing so, Harris violated the first cardinal rule of baseball by deliberately putting the potential winning run on base. For his manager's crime, Bevens paid dearly. Shotton called Eddie Stanky, the next scheduled hitter, back to the bench in favor of Cookie Lavagetto.

Lavagetto delivered one of the most famous postseason pinch hits, a two-run double off the right field wall that cost Bevens both his no-hitter and the game. After an easy 2-1 Yankee win the next day, both teams returned to the Bronx. In Game 6, Gionfriddo robbed Joe DiMaggio of a homer with the most famous Series catch to that point and

helped send the postseason skirmish to a seventh game for the third year in a row.

The deciding contest resulted in perhaps the Series's least eventful game, a 5-2 Yankees win, but it marked Bevens's last ML appearance—a short stint in middle relief. As for Gionfriddo and Lavagetto, that day also marked the last time they were on display in big-league uniforms. All three of the most remembered figures in the Series were released during the off-season.

SEASON'S BEST

•New York's Joe DiMaggio wins the American League MVP Award by one vote over Boston's Ted Williams, 202 to 201.

•Williams again wins the Triple Crown, batting .343 with 32 homers and 114 RBI. He leads the AL in runs (125), total bases (335), runs produced (207), walks (162), OBP (.499), and slugging (.634).

•Detroit's Hank Greenberg, the reigning AL homer and RBI king, is sold prior to the 1947 season to Pittsburgh for $75,000.

Larry Doby

•Bob Elliott wins the NL MVP Award—the first Brave to do so since 1914.

•The Yanks tie an AL record by winning 19 straight games.

•Brooklyn's Jackie Robinson wins the Baseball Writers Association of America's first Rookie of the Year Award.

•Harry Walker of the Phils, sent to them by the Cards, becomes the first player traded in midseason to win the NL bat crown (.363).

•Cincinnati's Ewell Blackwell no-hits the Braves on June 18 and pitches eight hitless innings in his next start. Blackwell wins 16 straight games, a Cincinnati club record. He leads the NL in wins (22), CGs (23), and Ks (193).

•New York's Johnny Mize and Pittsburgh's Ralph Kiner again tie for the NL homer crown (51).

•The Giants hit 221 homers, a new ML record.

•Brooklyn manager Leo Durocher is suspended for the season by Commissioner Happy Chandler for associating with gamblers.

•Larry Doby debuts with Cleveland on July 5 to break the color line in the AL.

•Attendance everywhere is at an all-time high as the post-war baseball boom is in full swing.

•Spud Chandler retires holding the record for the highest career winning percentage (.717) of any ML pitcher with at least 100 career wins.

•Dan Bankhead of the Dodgers is the first African-American to pitch in the majors.

•Mize tops the NL in RBI (138), runs (137), and runs produced (224).

•Boston's Warren Spahn tops the NL in ERA (2.33), innings (290), and shutouts (seven) and posts 21 wins.

JACKIE ROBINSON

Courageous Dodger smashes the color barrier

There are two ways of looking at Jackie Robinson's breaking of the major league's color line in 1947. One view is that World War II probably spelled the beginning of the end for many forms of institutionalized racism in America. Another perspective is that baseball's integration came about primarily through Dodger executive Branch Rickey's clever manipulation of events and Robinson's personal courage. Either way, the integration experiment succeeded for one reason: Jackie Robinson was a winning ballplayer.

Baseball's color line began in 1884, when brothers Moses and Welday Walker of the old American Association became the last African-Americans allowed to play in the majors for 61 years. In 1945, Rickey decided the time was right for the next African-American major leaguer. He wanted a man who was comfortable in the white world, educated, and self-disciplined enough not to respond to the hostility that he would inevitably encounter—in short, someone acceptable to mainstream whites. As a 27-year-old former Army officer and UCLA football star with a bland California accent, Jackie Robinson fit the bill and Rickey signed him to a Triple-A contract with the Montreal Royals for the 1946 season.

Even Robinson's former Negro League teammates were surprised at how well he played in Montreal. Robinson hit .349 with a league-leading 113 runs scored and was the International League Rookie of the Year. It was Rickey's turn to be surprised when the Dodgers players nevertheless refused to accept him in spring training of 1947. Things came to a head when a group of Dodgers—not, contrary to popular belief, exclusively Southerners—circulated an anti-Robinson petition. After Rickey threatened to trade the petitioners and Dodger manager Leo Durocher personally confronted them, most backed down. Robinson then opened the season as the Dodgers' first baseman. Although the feelings of his teammates mellowed to

mere indifference and the Brooklyn fans welcomed him, opposing teams and their fans tortured Robinson in the opening weeks of the '47 season with the vilest possible insults as well as knockdown pitches and intentional spikings. Robinson stoically played his hardest, and by the end of the year he had a league-leading 29 stolen bases, 125 runs scored, the NL Rookie of the Year Award—and an ulcer. The Dodgers had a pennant.

By 1949, Robinson had moved to second base, his natural position. Now a team leader on and off the field, he helped Brooklyn to his second of six pennants with an MVP season that included a batting title, 122 runs scored, 124 RBI, 37 stolen bases, and 16 home runs. He left behind a legacy of excellence in nearly every area of the game and courage on and off the field.

BOUDREAU'S BOYS BOP THE BRAVES

In 1948, two teams—Cleveland and Boston— won pennants for the first time in 28 and 34 years, respectively. These two teams also became the seventh and eighth different winners in the past four seasons, and the AL had its first pennant playoff game ever. This impressive string of accomplishments can largely be credited to two men. One, Billy Southworth, the manager of the Boston Braves, is the only 20th-century manager to win as many as four pennants and not make the Hall of Fame. The other, Bill Veeck Jr., the daring and innovative owner of the Cleveland Indians, was not enshrined in the Hall until 1991, long after many of the players who were pivotal in the events that summer were inducted.

One of those players, shortstop Lou Boudreau of the Indians, made it almost entirely on the basis of his superlative achievements in 1948. The last player-manager to win a world championship, the last player to amass over 100 RBI with fewer than 10 strikeouts, the *only* shortstop to post the best fielding average in his league nine years in a row— those were only his tangible contributions. In the past 50 years, no other player (except Carl Yastrzemski in 1967) has ever had a season under pressure anywhere near as remarkable as Boudreau's in 1948. When the Indians looked up on Labor Day evening and saw themselves in first place after doubleheader action everywhere in the majors that afternoon, parallels were instantly made to the Tribe's 1920 march to the flag under another player-manager who led by example, Tris Speaker.

Yet, there was a second eerie parallel that was less publicized nationally for obvious reasons. It was, however, taken notice of by those in Cleveland. In 1920, when Ray Chapman died after being hit by a pitch, the Indians won the flag despite suffering the only player loss in history to an on-field incident. In '48, the Tribe nearly suffered a second such casualty as pitcher Don Black, after authoring the AL's first no-hitter under the lights the previous year, sustained

Cleveland players, left to right, Joe Gordon, Bob Lemon, Lou Boudreau, and Gene Bearden celebrate the Indians' World Series victory over the Braves.

Yankee great Babe Ruth (top left) died of throat cancer at the age of 53. Warren Spahn, left, and Johnny Sain (top center) pitched the Braves to the NL flag. The Cards' Harry Brecheen (top right) led the NL with a 2.24 ERA and 149 Ks. Ted Williams, left, and Bobby Doerr (bottom) powered the BoSox lineup.

a cerebral hemorrhage while batting in a game. Though Black survived, he never played again, and his near-fatal episode was very much on his teammates' minds as the season drew to a close.

Meanwhile, the climate in Boston was one of utter ecstasy as fans there envisioned an MTA Series and Beantown's first world championship since 1918. The Braves did their part, capturing the NL flag by 6½ games over the St. Louis Cardinals. The Red Sox still had one final hurdle to clear. On the last day of the season, Joe McCarthy's club trailed Cleveland by a game, and the Indians' Bob Feller needed only to beat Hal Newhouser of the Detroit Tigers to clinch the flag for the Tribe. However,

when Newhouser stopped Cleveland and the Red Sox rebuffed the Yankees in their own closer, it set up a one-game playoff for the AL crown.

After a coin flip determined the game would be played in Boston, an all-Beantown Series seemed nearly certain, especially when Boudreau named rookie left-hander Gene Bearden to pitch for Cleveland at Fenway Park, the most difficult place in baseball for a visiting southpaw to gain a victory. McCarthy vacillated on his pitching choice, hoping one of his hurlers would step forward and demand the critical assignment, but when none did, the honor fell, almost by default, to veteran Denny Galehouse.

Like Floyd Giebell in 1940, who beat Feller to ace Cleveland out of the AL flag that year, Galehouse was destined to never win another game after the 1948 season, but the Red Sox would not have minded if he could just win the playoff. The two teams traded first-inning runs, but then Cleveland broke the game open with four runs in the top of the fourth, allowing Bearden to sail to an 8-3 triumph.

Behind Johnny Sain, the Braves trimmed Feller 1-0 in the Series opener. The lone run was scored by Boston catcher Phil Masi after he was apparently picked off second base by Boudreau, an incident that seemed certain to become a *cause celebre* if the Braves won the Series. Tribe ace Bob Lemon topped Warren Spahn in Game 2, however, and the scene then shifted to Cleveland. The Tribe had all the momentum after winning Game 3, 2-0, behind Bearden and then receiving another fine bit of pitching from Steve Gromek the following day in a 2-1

squeaker. Trailing 3-1, the Braves then blasted Feller and four relievers, 11-5, in Game 5 to send the action back to Boston.

In Game 6, Lemon took a 4-1 lead into the bottom of the eighth but then lost steam and allowed the Braves to push home two runs. Bearden came on in relief and engineered a rally-stifling double play on a misfired sacrifice bunt to get the save that earned the Cleveland Indians their second postseason championship.

SEASON'S BEST

• Cleveland's Lou Boudreau is the AL MVP. He's the last player-manager to win the award and the last to win a World Series. Boudreau tops AL shortstops in FA for the eighth time to tie an ML record. He is the first shortstop in AL history to hit over .350 and drive in more than 100 runs in the same season.

• St. Louis's Stan Musial is named NL MVP. Musial's 429 total bases are the most by any ML player from 1933 through 1994. He misses the Triple Crown by a margin of just one home run.

• Al Dark of the Braves is named Rookie of the Year and is third in the NL MVP vote.

• Pittsburgh's Ralph Kiner and New York's Johnny Mize again tie for the NL homer crown (40).

Satchel Paige

• Johnny Sain of the Braves tops the majors with 24 wins.

• Boston's Ted Williams tops the AL in BA (.369), SA (.615), and OBP (.497).

• Rookie Gene Bearden wins 20 games for Cleveland, tops the AL in ERA (2.43), and wins the pennant playoff game vs. the Red Sox.

• The Negro National League disbands, as most of its top players have jumped to the majors.

• Cleveland owner Bill Veeck signs Satchel Paige. Paige is the first African-American to pitch in the AL and the first to pitch in a World Series game.

• Babe Ruth dies of throat cancer on August 16.

• Casey Stengel, manager of the pennant-winning Oakland Oaks of the PCL, is hired to manage the Yankees for the '49 season.

• Pat Seerey of the White Sox hits four homers in an 11-inning game on July 18.

• The A's win 84 games; it's their best season from 1933 through 1968.

• Cardinal Harry Brecheen tops the NL in winning percentage (.741), ERA (2.24), Ks (149), and shutouts (seven).

• Cleveland's Bob Lemon leads the AL in innings (294), CGs (20), and shutouts (10).

• New York's Joe DiMaggio tops the AL in RBI (155), homers (39), and total bases (355).

• Cleveland tops the AL in BA (.282), homers (155), ERA (3.22), and FA (.982) but barely wins the flag.

STAN MUSIAL

Cards star turns it up a notch, slugs .702

As a pure hitter, Stan Musial had never needed work. In his three seasons leading to 1947, he had won two MVP Awards while leading the National League each year in hits, doubles, and slugging percentage, twice setting the pace in batting and triples. He averaged an incredible 215 hits, 50 doubles, and 18 triples per year over the stretch.

What distinguished him from other power hitters, however, was his lack of home run proficiency. Despite a slugging percentage that had peaked at .587 in '46, the Redbird outfielder had never hit more than 19 homers in a season going into 1948. The addition of more pop to his game that season resulted in a third MVP trophy and the greatest year of his career.

Emerging from a compressed, corkscrew batting stance in which Stan would hunch his back and coil up like a spring, Musial could hit equally well to all fields—making it over the fences was another matter. Were it only for glory he might not have minded, but when Stan (then making $31,000) saw 40-homer guys like Ted Williams and Hank Greenberg commanding close to six-figure salaries, he had all the incentive he needed to drop his hands down on the bat and let loose. By year's end, he was one rained-out homer away from leading the NL in every significant offensive category, and had gathered five hits in a contest four times, a feat previously achieved only by Ty Cobb. His 39 homers (a career high) placed him one behind Ralph Kiner and Johnny Mize, but Musial topped the NL in batting (.376), RBI (131), runs (135), hits (230), doubles (46), triples (18), slugging (.702), total bases (429), and on-base percentage (.450). His batting, slugging, and total base marks—all also career highs—were not matched in the NL for over 40 years. Despite his added aggressiveness at the plate, Stan the Man struck out just 34 times.

His newfound power eventually led to 10 consecutive years with 20 or more home runs, but when Musial retired in '63, his 475 homers were only the tip of his statistical iceberg. His 3,630 hits (fourth on the all-time list), 725 doubles (third), 1,951 RBI (fifth), 1,949 runs (seventh), .559 slugging percentage (17th), seven batting titles, and .331 career batting average speak for themselves. Perhaps just as astounding was the consistency with which he compiled exactly 1,815 hits both home and away while averaging 92 RBI and 92 runs over 21 full seasons. He finished second in MVP voting four times in addition to the three years he won the honor. In spite of all these grand accomplishments, those who view the bronze statue of Musial outside Busch Stadium in St. Louis probably remember most the modest, professional manner with which this Hall of Famer approached every game he played.

YANKS EDGE SOX, OUTCLASS DODGERS

On July 8, 1949, Ebbets Field denizens saw an event that had never before occurred in a big-league game when New York Giants third sacker Hank Thompson prepared to bat against Brooklyn Dodgers rookie whiz Don Newcombe. It was the first time two African-Americans—hitter and pitcher—had opposed each other. It seemed only fitting that it came in Brooklyn, where the color barrier in existence ever since 1885 had finally been broken.

Three months and one day later, Ebbets Field habitués experienced another moment that had begun to seem only fitting. They witnessed their beloved Dodgers bow to the New York Yankees for the third time in the 1940s. To rub still more salt into their wounds, the Yankees' triumph was engineered by the clown who had been more responsible than anyone for the Dodgers' image of zany futility barely a decade earlier.

That same clown had already stung seven AL teams that season. His return to the majors in 1949 caused eyebrows to lift everywhere. What were the Yankees thinking? Here was Casey Stengel, who only once in his nine previous seasons as a big-league manager had finished above .500, now at the helm of a team that had not finished below .500 since 1925. Had George Weiss, the Yankees' new general manager, snapped?

The Boston Red Sox were the first to discover that Weiss had concocted a plan even more invidious than the one his predecessor, Ed Barrow, had formulated in 1930 when the Yankees snatched Joe McCarthy the moment the Cubs freed him. On the final weekend of the 1949 season, the Red Sox rolled into Yankee Stadium with a one-game lead, needing only to win either of their last two games to snag the pennant. How could they fail? They had swept a crucial three-game series with the Yankees only the weekend before. Moreover, unlike the previous year, when Joe McCarthy had been forced to go with Denny Galehouse in the season-deciding game, he had Mel Parnell and Ellis Kinder—with 48 wins between them—ready for the Yankees. McCarthy also had four .300-hitting regulars and the last two men in the AL to knock home over 150 runs in a season (Ted Williams and Vern Stephens). Poor Stengel, in contrast, did not have

Many doubted Casey Stengel was the right choice to lead the mighty Yankees, but soon New York was celebrating another world championship over Brooklyn.

Yankees pitcher Joe Page was a success coming out of the bullpen (top), *setting a major-league record with 27 saves. Boston's Vern Stephens* (bottom) *tied teammate Ted Williams for the RBI lead with 159. Stephens's total set a major-league mark for RBI by a shortstop.*

season's final day, skipper Burt Shotton got it when his Dodgers took a 9-7, 10-inning cliff-hanger from Eddie Sawyer's resurgent Philadelphia Phillies.

Even with the loss, the Phils finished with 81 victories for their best showing since 1917. The Boston Braves, the NL's Cinderella team in 1948, had dropped below .500 when first sacker Earl Torgeson was sidelined by a shoulder injury, Johnny Sain had a poor year, and Jeff Heath was unable to rebound from the broken leg that had ended his 1948 season on the eve of the World Series.

Brooklyn, with a pitching staff that averaged only 25 years of age and lacked a bellwether, was accorded little chance in the 1949 Series unless its five-man brigade of Gil Hodges, Jackie Robinson, Duke Snider, Roy Campanella, and Carl Furillo all had a big week offensively. As it turned out, yearling Don Newcombe battled Allie Reynolds in the

Brooklyn's Jackie Robinson (top) *slides into third ahead of the ball against the Braves. Robinson, Rookie of the Year in '47, won MVP honors in '49. Cardinal Stan Musial* (bottom) *was consistent as usual, but his .338 average wasn't enough to lift St. Louis over Brooklyn in the NL. The Dodgers edged the Cardinals by one game to take the National League pennant.*

a single .300 hitter or 100-RBI man and, indeed, had only one regular (Phil Rizzuto) who had been healthy enough to play more than 128 games.

It ought to have been no contest, and in a sense it wasn't. The Red Sox never had a chance. The Yankees knotted the race with a gritty 5-4 win on Saturday and then stifled a Boston rally the following day to end the 1940s—as they had not only the 1920s but also the 1930s—with their fifth pennant in the decade.

The Dodgers likewise had to go down to the wire to nail the NL pennant. Boasting a solid corps of veteran regulars built around Stan Musial and Marty Marion, plus the best and the deepest pitching staff in the NL, Eddie Dyer's St. Louis Cardinals seemed poised as the season began its final week to match the Yankees by claiming their fifth pennant of the '40s. The Cards, however, proceeded to lose four straight games and allow Brooklyn a chance to climb into the driver's seat. Needing a win on the

opener on even terms until the bottom of the ninth when he surrendered a leadoff homer to Tommy Henrich. Newcombe ended up losing a 1-0 heart-breaker. The following day, Brooklyn's Preacher Roe made prognosticators who had derided the Dodgers' pitching look foolish when he made a second-inning run hold up and blanked the high-scoring Yankees, 1-0. With the Series evened up, the teams moved to Ebbets Field for the next three games.

Those who had tickets for the final two contests at Yankee Stadium never got to use them. After winning a 4-3 squeaker in Game 3 despite making just five hits, the Yankees permitted the many who had predicted the Dodgers' weak pitching would decide the issue to breathe a sigh of relief. In Games 4 and 5, Stengel's men got their offense on track, tallying a total of 16 runs and 21 hits to win all three frays in Brooklyn.

SEASON'S BEST

• Brooklyn's Jackie Robinson is selected NL MVP. Robinson tops the NL in hitting (.342) and stolen bases (37).

• Boston's Ted Williams is AL MVP. Williams tops the AL in homers (43) and ties for the lead in RBI (159). He loses the Triple Crown when he finishes a fraction behind Detroit's George Kell in batting, as both hit .343. He also tops the AL in runs (150), doubles (39), total bases (368), SA (.650), OBP (.490), and walks (162). Williams is the last player in ML history to produce 250 or more runs in a season.

• Mel Parnell of the Red Sox tops the majors with 25 wins.

• Pittsburgh's Ralph Kiner wins his fourth consecutive NL homer crown with 54, threatening the NL record. Kiner hits 25 homers on the road—a new NL record. He also paces the NL in RBI (127), walks (117), and SA (.658).

• Boston's Vern Stephens ties Williams for the AL RBI lead with 159, an ML record for shortstops.

• Yankee Joe Page sets a new ML record with 27 saves.

• The AL wins a wild All-Star Game, 11-7 at Brooklyn. This marks the first appearance of African-American players in an All-Star Game.

Ralph Kiner

• Joe DiMaggio signs the first $100,000 contract in ML history.

• The A's perform an all-time ML-record 217 double plays.

• New York's Dave Koslo tops the NL in ERA (2.50) and is the first leader without a shutout.

• The Cards have only 17 stolen bases—an all-time record low for an NL team.

• Boston's Dom DiMaggio has a 34-game hitting streak.

• The Red Sox collect an ML-record 835 walks.

• St. Louis's Stan Musial tops the NL in hits (207), doubles (41), total bases (382), and OBP (.438) and ties in triples (13).

• Boston's Warren Spahn tops the NL in wins (21), innings (302), CGs (25), and Ks (151).

TED WILLIAMS

Sox star falls just short of Triple Crown, AL flag

Despite great expectations following Boston's 104-50 record and seven-game World Series loss to the Cardinals in 1946, the Red Sox were never able to fulfill the lofty goals set for them. A third-place finish in '47 was followed up by two consecutive seasons in which the Red Sox wound up just one game behind the American League pennant winner. Perhaps no player better symbolized their heroic but futile efforts than their moody, misunderstood slugger—1949 MVP Ted Williams.

Williams was indisputably baseball's best hitter, but after hitting .200 in the '46 Series he was never quite good enough for Boston's tough sportswriters and fans. He hit .343 with 32 homers and 114 RBI in 1947 to become only the second player ever to win two Triple Crowns, but for the third time in four active seasons (not counting the war), he was second to a pennant-winning Yankee in the MVP voting. Joe DiMaggio hit just .315 with 20 homers and 97 RBI, but finished one point over Williams when a Midwestern writer left Ted off his ballot entirely. Rumors that the snub had come from Boston journalist Mel Webb came as no surprise to New Englanders, especially since Williams's feuds with the local scribes were already legendary.

More disappointment came Ted's way in 1948. He hit .369 with 25 homers and 127 RBI in a thrilling three-way pennant race (winning his fourth

batting title), but wound up frustrated again after collecting one single in four at bats as the Red Sox ended their season with a one-game playoff loss to the Cleveland Indians. The shell-shocked Sox began 1949 slow, but soon gained steam behind 11 homers from Williams during May. Boston fans were hoping this would finally be the year Ted and the team put it all together. After going 43-13 in August and September, the Red Sox entered the final two days of the season in New York leading the Yankees by one game.

Again Williams was looked to for leadership, and again he failed to meet expectations. He could not put together anything at the plate and misplayed a crucial fly ball as Boston lost both games and the pennant. His performance also cost him a third Triple Crown, as Detroit's George Kell singled twice on the final afternoon to edge him by .0002 in the AL batting race. Both rounded off to .343, but Ted was alone atop the league in homers (43), runs (150), doubles (39), slugging (.650), total bases (368), on-base percentage (.490), and walks (162) while tying teammate Vern Stephens with a career-high 159 RBI. Williams earned a second MVP Award for his efforts, but he accepted again with a hollow heart while thinking of next year and another crack at the World Series.

Unfortunately for Ted, that chance would never come in his remaining 11 pro seasons.

THE 1950s

B aseball attendance sagged in the 1950s as more and more Americans moved to the suburbs and watched games on TV. Most of the excitement occurred in the Big Apple, as New York teams hoisted 14 pennants.

The American popular imagination now sees the 1950s as a time of tranquility, as a time when there was little social strife, drug concern, or economic depression. And during the decade, baseball was the national game. College football was still for the few who went to college, professional basketball was still a secondary sport, and pro football was still scarcely noticed until the Colts-Giants "sudden death" championship game in 1958. It is remembered as a time of peace and prosperity, and baseball dominated.

There were problems with baseball in the 1950s, of course, and most were ignored. Though nobody wanted to admit it, baseball was in big trouble. Television was supposed to create vast new crowds, but instead it had the same effect on baseball that it had on boxing: fewer people turned out to see a show they could get for free at home. In the AL, attendance dropped from a post-World War II peak of 11 million in 1948 to just under seven million by 1953 (it wouldn't hit over 10 million again until the 1961 expansion year). The NL reached a record-high 10.4 million in 1947 and then dropped each year until '52, not surpassing the 10-million mark until 1958.

Of course, there was another reason why fans didn't come out as often: After millions of them returned home at the end of World War II, they moved to the suburbs, far away from the inner city where most ballparks were located. Most suburbanites had automobiles and the stadiums simply couldn't accommodate the new means of transportation. The ballparks themselves were crumbling; most had been built before 1920 and renovation in declining areas was expensive and not a very good investment for team owners.

The Dodgers' rotation included left-handers (top) Preacher Roe, left, and Johnny Podres. Bottom: Joe DiMaggio, left, had a few laughs with Abbott and Costello. Television, which helped popularize baseball in the 1940s, hampered the sport in the '50s.

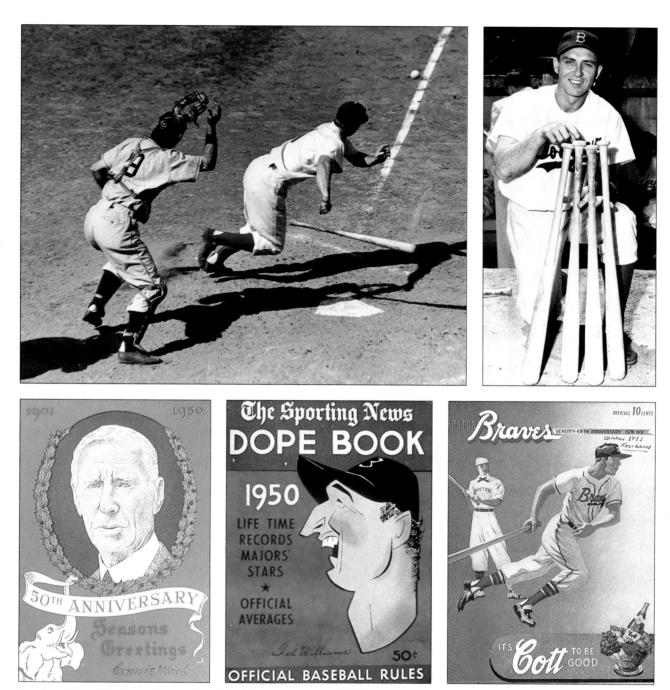

Brooklyn's Pee Wee Reese (top left) led the NL when he swiped 30 bases in 1952. Gil Hodges (top right) *anchored the Dodgers with 100-plus RBI for seven straight years, from 1949 to 1955. Connie Mack, featured on a 1950 Christmas card* (bottom left), *moved his A's to Kansas City following the 1954 season. A caricature of Ted Williams graced the cover of* The Sporting News Dope Book *in 1950 (bottom center).* The Boston Braves celebrated their 75th anniversary in 1951 (bottom right), *then moved to Milwaukee two years later.*

Television was an immediate source of new revenue, but it also cut down on attendance.

Worse, television had a terrible side effect that became apparent a couple of years into the decade: It began to kill off attendance in minor-league cities. There were many areas of the country where fans had no easy access to major-league games, and the teams from the minor leagues were their only source of organized, professional baseball. Televised big-league games didn't destroy interest in the minor leagues overnight, but it was cut back enough to put a lot of teams and players out of business. The major-

league farm system helped some teams survive financially, but minor-league franchises could not count on their major-league organizations as their only revenue source. Not until the 1980s would minor-league baseball face up to the ever-present threat of expanded big-league TV coverage and find new ways to promote itself.

Stung with these problems, the people who ran baseball didn't always try to find solutions by working with their cities and communities. The owners took the easy way out: They moved south and, finally, west.

The first teams to move were those that were in competition with other teams in their cities. In the case of the Boston Braves, the move was probably long overdue; the Braves were a forgotten commodity in Boston, a town that was not even showing attendance support for the Red Sox. The Braves drew about 280,000 fans in 1952, their last year in Boston, and it can't be said that many were sad to see them go. A similar case could

Bobby Thomson, batting, attempts to get out of the way as Monte Irvin slides in while stealing home against the Yankees in the first game of the 1951 Series (top). Thomson's pennant-clinching "Shot Heard 'Round the World" (bottom).

Duke Snider, who hit four home runs in both the 1952 and 1954 World Series, is greeted at the plate after his only round-tripper in the '53 fall classic (top). Knuckleball reliever Hoyt Wilhelm (bottom) hit the only homer of his career in his first at bat, in 1952.

because the A's were so steeped in history, no one noticed how wretched their recent performance had been, and how attendance had declined in Philadelphia's increasingly shabby inner-city area.

Precisely the same problems were bothering the National League's two most famous teams, the Brooklyn Dodgers and the New York Giants, but their plans to remedy the situation were even more sensational. The improvement in air travel, or more specifically, the jet airliner, now made it possible for teams to travel to and from California, allowing baseball to cash in on the most booming economic region in the United States. Dodgers owner Walter O'Malley picked the richest plum for himself, Los Angeles, and he convinced Giants owner Horace Stoneham to join him and transplant the old Dodgers-Giants rivalry to new ground by moving his team to San Francisco. It sounds cynical, and it was, but the truth is that both O'Malley and Stoneham had legitimate gripes with the city of New York and that their grievances concerning parking, security, and declining attendance fell on deaf bureaucratic ears. The move of the Dodgers to LA and the Giants to the Bay Area can't just be blamed entirely on the greed of the owners.

Beyond the off-field problems, baseball in the 1950s just wasn't as multidimensional as it would become in the 1960s. For one thing, few players stole bases in large numbers. It wasn't for lack of speed; it

be made for the departure of the St. Louis Browns. A city the size of St. Louis was hard-pressed to support both the Cardinals and the Browns. So the Brownies—who were sort of to the American League what the Braves were to the National League—relocated from St. Louis to Baltimore, a town that richly deserved a major-league franchise.

With the move of the Athletics from Philadelphia to Kansas City after the 1954 season, however, many longtime fans were jolted. The A's were one of baseball's oldest and most history-laden teams. It was the club that Connie Mack had managed for half a century, the team of Lefty Grove, Jimmie Foxx, Eddie Collins, Mickey Cochrane, and Al Simmons, more great players than the Braves and Browns had ever seen put together. Even though Philadelphia had the National League's Phillies, there were many Athletics fans in Philly. Probably

His career was winding down in the 1950s, but Jackie Robinson was still money in the bank to Dodgers fans.

just wasn't the style to run. This rendered baseball a much more limited game as skills such as running, pitchers holding runners on base, and catchers throwing them out were seldom displayed. The offensive strategy was simple: Play for the big inning and wait for one of the big hitters to belt one out—which they frequently did in an era when so many parks, particularly Boston's Fenway, Brooklyn's Ebbets Field, and the Giants' Polo Grounds, were designed for home run hitters.

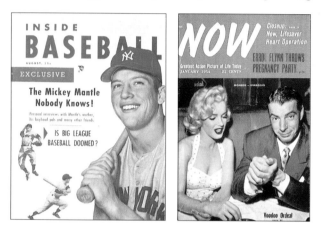

Comparing the home run and stolen base team averages from the 1950s to the 1970s helps to relate the evolution of offensive strategy. National League teams averaged 139 home runs in 1954, 158 homers in '55, and 152 homers in '56. NL teams averaged 107 home runs in 1974, 103 homers in '75, and 93 homers in '76. In 1954, NL teams averaged 42 stolen bases; in '55, 47 steals; in '56, 46 steals. In 1974, NL teams averaged 105 steals; in '75, 98 steals; in '76, 114 steals. The change in strategy is evident in the American League even though from 1974 to '76, the AL had an additional batter (and basestealer) with the designated hitter. AL teams in 1954 averaged

Mickey Mantle (top left) *was the new man in New York, but Joe DiMaggio's marriage to Marilyn Monroe kept the retired Yankee Clipper in the spotlight* (top right). *Catcher Joe Garagiola, left, and slugger Ralph Kiner were shipped from the Pirates to the Cubs in a blockbuster deal in 1953* (bottom). *Pittsburgh received five players and $150,000 in the trade.*

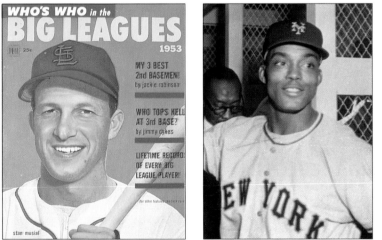

The Boston Braves started the exodus as ballclubs packed up and headed elsewhere. The Braves received a warm welcome when they arrived in Milwaukee in 1953 (top). Stan Musial, still going strong for the Cardinals, was a Who's Who in the Big Leagues in '53 (bottom left). Monte Irvin (bottom center) led the NL with 121 RBI in 1951, but broke his ankle in spring training prior to the '52 season. Right-hander Robin Roberts (bottom right) won 20 games a season from 1950 to 1955 and became the Phillies' first 20-game winner since Grover Alexander in 1917.

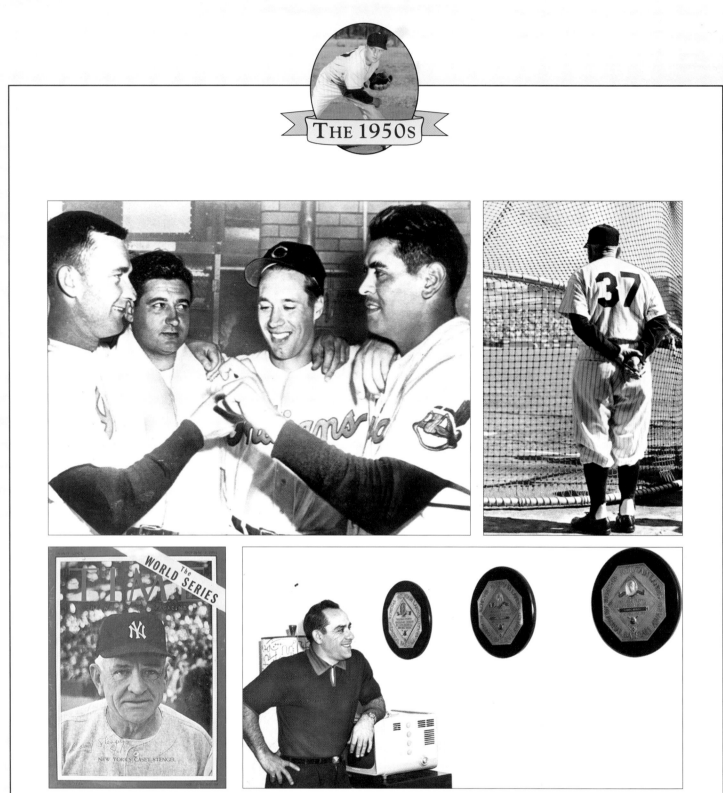

The 1954 Indians boasted one of baseball's best rotations, left to right: Bob Lemon, Early Wynn, Bob Feller, and Mike Garcia (top left). Casey Stengel (top right) didn't have the most talented team, but he made the most of what he had with his Yankees. Stengel (bottom left) was featured on Time magazine in '55, the year his squad lost a seven-game World Series to crosstown rival Brooklyn. Yankee catcher Yogi Berra brought home three MVP Awards (bottom right), in 1951, 1954, and 1955.

103 home runs; in '55, 120 home runs; in '56, 134 homers. American League teams averaged 114 home runs in 1974; 122 homers in 1975; and 94 homers in '76. American League teams averaged 45, 40, and 44 stolen bases in 1954, '55, and '56. AL teams averaged 103, 112, and 141 stolen bases in 1974, '75, and

'76. Getting on base and waiting for the big hit was more important in this era than in the 1970s.

It was also an era pretty much dominated by a couple of teams, most notably the New York Yankees. The Yanks won four of the 1950s' first five World Series. Though they won only two in the last five years of the decade, their shadow seemed to hang over every season no matter who won. The Yankees' winning percentage for the 1950s was .621. In retrospect, the Yankees look just as good as they must have looked to their opponents: Mickey Mantle was the league's (and possibly the majors') best player over the 10-year span, Yogi Berra was the best catcher, and Whitey Ford might have been the best pitcher.

But in reviewing the pennant races year-by-year, it is not at all clear that the Yanks had a top-to-bottom edge over the AL's best teams (particularly Cleveland in the first half of the decade) in overall talent. Certainly not in front-line talent: The Yanks never possessed anything like the starting rotation of the Indians' Bob Lemon (perhaps the most underrated pitcher of the decade), Early Wynn, Mike Garcia, and Bob Feller. And the Yanks never fielded a starting lineup as solid top to bottom as the Dodger teams they beat in three of four World Series; Brook-

As suggested by their 1955 Yearbook (top), the New York Giants had the world in their hands after winning the '54 World Series. Dodger catcher Roy Campanella chases a foul pop-up into the seats near the commissioner's box in the 1955 World Series (bottom). *Campanella hit 32 homers that season and two more in the World Series.*

The 1956 Series between the Yanks and the Dodgers (top) was hardly a sellout. The Cubs' Ernie Banks (bottom left) became the first shortstop to hit 40-plus HRs in 1955. Cy Young winner Warren Spahn (bottom right) led the Braves to the title in 1957.

lyn's lineup included Gil Hodges, Jackie Robinson, Pee Wee Reese, Carl Furillo, Duke Snider, and Roy Campanella. Looking back on those pennant races and World Series, it became more apparent that Casey Stengel was the first modern manager. He wrote the book now in use on the art of platooning, relief pitching, and pinch-hitting. The Yankees had three Hall of Fame stars in the 1950s, but the team's spectacular success was primarily due to Casey Stengel's remarkable talent for making use of what he had available.

Of course, the one enduring argument that fans, even those who are too young to remember the 1950s, still love to engage in is: Who was the greater ballplayer, Mickey Mantle or Willie Mays? The argument will probably endure as long as baseball, long after all those who watched them play are gone. Bill James's remarkable statistical analysis in his *Historical Baseball Abstract* reaches the conclusion that at his peak, Mantle was the better ballplayer. He hit with more power, reached base more often, and used up fewer outs. James's analysis is almost certainly correct; the real question is whether or not the evidence which shows Mantle a greater ballplayer *at his peak* justifies the conclusion that "Mickey Mantle

The best center fielder in New York? The debate rages on over Yankee Mickey Mantle, left, and Giant Willie Mays (top). *The Giants said good-bye to the Polo Grounds in 1957* (bottom) *and headed to San Francisco.*

was the greatest player of the 1950s." By James's own methods it's clear that Mays had the better seasons in 1954 and 1955, Mantle was better in 1956 and 1957, and that the choice is about even for 1958 and 1959. Both had good rookie years in 1951. In terms of year-in, year-out value it appears pretty much a jump ball, though there's no disputing that Mantle's 1956 and '57 seasons were the best of any player in the decade. What's often overlooked is that Mays lost two peak years to the Army; he hit 20 home runs as a rookie before he went in, and 41 the year he came out. If he had hit just 30 each for 1952 and '53, he would have broken Babe Ruth's lifetime home run record before Henry Aaron.

Willie Mays was a hero in the comics, (top left). Growing up near Ebbets Field prompted Roger Kahn's The Boys of Summer *(top center). Harvey Kuenn (top right) was the AL's Rookie of the Year in 1953 and won the AL batting title in '59 when he hit .353. Minnie Minoso, left, and Luis Aparicio, right, (bottom) helped the ChiSox to second place in 1957.*

The Braves got the early jump on the Yanks in the 1958 World Series (top), *but saw their early success fade. Whitey Ford (top right) was a model of consistency and finished his career with a .690 winning percentage, tops among modern-day pitchers with 200 or more victories. Detroit's Al Kaline (bottom right) joined the big leagues directly from the sandlots of Baltimore in 1953, never playing an inning in the minors. NL President Warren Giles presented the Cardinals' Stan Musial with his seventh—and last— batting title in 1957 (bottom left).*

YANKS TEACH WHIZ KIDS A LESSON

On the final day of the 1950 season, for the second straight year, the NL race came down to a clash between the Brooklyn Dodgers and the Philadelphia Phillies. The difference, though, was that in 1949 the Dodgers had stood to clinch the pennant with a victory while the Phils had little but pride at stake. On this occasion, though, the Phils had everything at stake, for if they won the finale, they would earn their first postseason date since 1915. The Dodgers, on the other hand, could gain at most a first-place tie with a victory.

Virtually everyone believed that Brooklyn would win the resultant playoff series if the race ended in a deadlock, for the Phils were on the skids. Holding a seven-length lead with less than two weeks to go, they had allowed all but one game of their edge to dissipate in just nine days. Furthermore, Eddie Sawyer's Phils were crippled and tired. All season the Phillies had had youth on their side. So youthful, in fact, the Phils had been dubbed the "Whiz Kids" when they seemed certain to be the NL's fall representative. Now, however, things were looking less than hopeful. Catcher Andy Seminick was playing on an injured ankle; Sawyer's number two hurler, Curt Simmons, had been called to active military service on September 10; and his third and fourth starters, Bob Miller and Bubba Church, were both ailing. Sawyer had no alternative but to call on team ace Robin Roberts, making his third start in five days. Dodgers manager Burt Shotton had an iron man of his own in Don Newcombe. Just a few weeks earlier, Newcombe had nearly become the only

hurler in the last 68 years to notch two complete-game wins in a doubleheader when he toppled the Phils 2-0 in the opener and then worked seven innings of the nightcap before departing for a pinch hitter.

So it was Roberts and Newcombe in the most important game of the 1950 season on October 1 at Ebbets Field. Each was shooting for his 20th victory

Yogi Berra is greeted at home plate by Joe DiMaggio after hitting a home run in Game 4 as the Yankees swept the Phillies in the '50 Series.

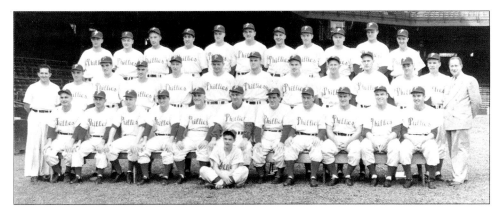

The NL champion Phillies (top left) *featured starter Robin Roberts and Jim Konstanty, the first reliever named MVP. Brooklyn's Duke Snider* (top right) *led the NL in hits (199) and total bases (343). Left to right: Ted Williams, Bobby Doerr, and Walt Dropo after the Red Sox drubbed the Browns 29-4 on June 8* (bottom left). *Phil Rizzuto, left, was the 1950 AL MVP, while Yankee teammate Joe DiMaggio put up MVP-like numbers* (bottom right).

of the season. If Roberts had an advantage, it could only be that in the Phils' bullpen was Jim Konstanty, who already had 22 saves and 16 wins in relief. When the game went into the bottom of the ninth tied 1-1, Roberts faltered. Cal Abrams, the potential first place-tying run, was now on second with no one out. All heads swiveled to the Phils bullpen, expecting to see Konstanty.

Instead Sawyer let Roberts work out of the jam. Helped by center fielder Richie Ashburn, who threw Abrams out at the plate in a bid to score on Duke Snider's single, Roberts then retired Carl Furillo and Gil Hodges with the bases loaded, thrusting the game into extra innings. When Dick Sisler sliced an opposite-field three-run homer in the top of the 10th, Sawyer's men were champs, 4-1, and Roberts

was the Phils' first 20-game winner since 1917.

In the AL, the Cleveland Indians won 92 games, one more than the Phillies, but whereas the Phils' 91st victory brought them the flag, the Indians' 62nd defeat consigned them to being the best fourth-place team in history. Ahead of the Tribe in third place were the Red Sox, and one length in front of Boston were the Tigers. Three games ahead of Detroit sat a team whose triumph in 1949 had seemed the last gasp of an aging warrior. With center fielder Joe DiMaggio (now 35), first sacker Johnny Mize (37), and all of Casey Stengel's main pitchers on the wrong side of 30, the Yankees looked in the spring of 1950 as if even a first-division finish would be a stretch. By June, though, Stengel summoned a 21-year-old southpaw named Whitey Ford from the minors and a few weeks later GM George Weiss orchestrated another of the intricate interleague waiver deals for which the Yankees would become infamous during the 1950s; he relieved the Pirates of Johnny Hopp, at the time the second-leading hitter in the NL with a .340 BA. In addition, a mid-season trade with the Browns brought Tom Ferrick to bolster the bullpen, a weakness when former relief ace Joe Page skidded to a 5.04 ERA.

The Yankees entered the 1950 World Series geared to win while the Phils seemingly were just happy to be there. In the opener, though, Sawyer unleashed the biggest autumn surprise since Connie Mack had started Howard Ehmke against the Cubs

in the first game of the 1929 classic. Sawyer's choice was relief ace Jim Konstanty. Though he hadn't started a game in four years, Konstanty gave up just one run and went the route. Unfortunately for Konstanty, though, that one run was enough for Vic Raschi to triumph 1-0. The Yankees then won two more one-run nailbiters before taking the finale 5-2, completing what seemed at a glance to be a rout but was actually the most closely contested Series sweep ever.

SEASON'S BEST

- Yankee shortstop Phil Rizzuto is selected AL MVP.

- Phillie Jim Konstanty is NL MVP, becoming the first reliever to win the award.

- St. Louis's Stan Musial tops the NL in hitting (.346) and slugging (.596). Musial hits in 30 consecutive games.

- Red Sox Billy Goodman wins the AL bat crown (.354)—the only player ever to win the hit title without having a regular position.

- Cleveland's Bob Lemon tops the majors with 23 wins.

- Brooklyn's Gil Hodges hits four homers in a game on August 31.

- Cleveland's Early Wynn tops the AL with a 3.20 ERA—highest ERA in ML history by a leader.

- NL wins All-Star Game 4-3 at Comiskey Park, as St. Louis's Red Schoendienst homers in the 14th to win it.

- A's manager Connie Mack retires after 50 years at the helm. His 3,731 wins and 3,948 losses are all-time records.

Bob Lemon

- All Mexican League jumpers are reinstated by organized baseball for the 1950 season after a suit by Danny Gardella vs. Happy Chandler. Sal Maglie, one of the jumpers, wins 18 games for the Giants and tops the NL in winning percentage (.818).

- On May 18 vs. Brooklyn, Cardinal third sacker Tommy Glaviano makes errors on three straight plays, blowing the game.

- On September 10, New York's Joe DiMaggio becomes the first to hit three homers in a game in Washington's Griffith Stadium.

- On June 8, the Browns are beaten 29-4 by the Red Sox at Fenway Park—the most lopsided game this century.

- On April 18 at St. Louis, the Cards and Pirates play the first "Opening Night" game in ML history.

- TV provides baseball with an extra $2.3 million in new revenues in 1950.

- Yankee Vic Raschi sets an ML record (since broken) when he retires 32 batters in a row.

- Brooklyn's Duke Snider tops the NL in hits (199) and total bases (343).

JIM KONSTANTY

Palm ball specialist wins 16, saves 22, named MVP

There were two things Philadelphia baseball fans could usually count on for most of the 20 years leading up to 1950: poor finishes from both their major-league teams. Connie Mack's once-powerful Athletics were regular tenants in the AL's second division, and the Phillies were consistent NL cellar dwellers without even a rich past to look back on. Only once in their dismal 67-year history had the Phillies won a pennant, and even after the club improved 15 games to an 81-73, third-place finish in 1949, hardened followers didn't get their hopes up. What they didn't know was a bespectacled 33-year-old reliever was about to explode with an MVP season the likes of which the NL had never seen.

Like the Phillies themselves, Jim Konstanty had emerged from a humble past to reach stardom. He had kicked around the Cincinnati minor-league system for several seasons before making the majors at age 27. After going 6-4 in a brief trial with the Reds in 1944, he was off to the Navy for a year. A lackluster effort for the Braves in '46 prompted his return to the minors, but Konstanty taught himself a palm ball that winter and caught the eye of minor-league manager Eddie Sawyer. Sawyer took Konstanty along as a reliever when he got the Phillies managerial post in '48, and Jim's version of the slider soon had NL batters lunging and cursing on a regular basis.

Posting a solid 9-5 mark with seven saves and a 3.25 ERA in 1949, Konstanty had his career year the following season. In 1950, he went 16-7 with a major league-best 22 saves and a 2.66 ERA over a then-record 74 appearances. The emergence of Joe Page on the world champion Yankees a few years before had shown the importance of relief pitching to a team's success, but Konstanty was the first National League player to star in the closer role. The Phillies got strong years from starters Robin Roberts (20-11) and Curt Simmons (17-8), but it was the man in the bullpen who enabled the "Whiz Kids" to beat out a much stronger Dodger team for the pennant on the season's final day.

Sawyer surprised everybody by starting Konstanty in the first game of the World Series against the Yankees (his only start of the season), and Jim responded with a five-hitter in a 1-0 loss. The Yankees wound up with a Series sweep, but Konstanty still earned distinction as the first relief pitcher ever to win an MVP Award. While his invincibility ended the following year as hitters learned to lay off his palm ball until it fell out of the strike zone, Jim would be remembered long after his departure from the majors in '56 as a prototype for the modern relief specialist.

THOMSON'S SHOT SHOCKS BROOKLYN

The Brooklyn Dodgers had been there before. Indeed, it was the third year in a row that their season rested on how well they fared against the Philadelphia Phillies in an extra-inning battle on the final day of the campaign. Two years earlier Jackie Robinson had been the hero, and he was once again a hero in 1951. By virtue of both his bat and glove, the Dodgers staved off the most improbable comeback in baseball history, at least temporarily, by downing the Phils in 14 innings to create the necessity for the third pennant playoff in the past six seasons.

The Dodgers' playoff opponents were the Giants. Managed by former Dodgers pilot Leo Durocher, the Giants had won on Opening Day in 1951 but then failed to capture another win until their 13th game of the season. After that rocky start, the Giants had only themselves to fault on August 12 when they looked up and saw the Dodgers were 13½ games ahead of them. Just a few days later, however, the Giants launched what would turn out to be a 16-game winning streak and gradually climbed back into the race. As in 1942 when the Dodgers lost a seemingly insurmountable lead, it was not so much that they collapsed but rather were victimized by a super-hot team. Down the stretch, Durocher whipped the Giants to 39 wins in their last 47 games, creating a 96-58 deadlock at the wire.

After losing to the St. Louis Cardinals in the first-ever pennant playoff series in 1946, many of the Dodgers got a sinking feeling that history was against them when they dropped the opener of the best-of-three set, 3-1, at Ebbets Field on October 2. It meant that the remaining two frays would be played at the Polo Grounds in front of the Giants' rabid rooters—the remaining two games, if that many were necessary. A third game looked highly unlikely from a Brooklyn standpoint when first-year Dodgers skipper Chuck Dressen had no one ready to toe the rubber in the second contest but Clem Labine, a rookie who was best suited for relief work. However, when Labine, backed by 13 hits, spun a nifty 10-0 shutout, it set up probably the most famous game in history.

New York's Bobby Thomson is mobbed by Giant teammates at home plate after his home run beat the Dodgers in a playoff for the 1951 NL pennant.

In his only major-league at bat, the Browns' Eddie Gaedel (top) drew a walk on four pitches against the Tigers. Gaedel, just 3'7", was used by owner Bill Veeck as novelty to draw fans. Bottom: Dodger catcher Roy Campanella copped the '51 NL MVP Award.

On October 3, Don Newcombe was pitching against Dodgers nemesis Sal Maglie. Brooklyn shattered a 1-1 tie with three runs in the eighth and hung onto their 4-1 lead with one out in the last of the ninth. Newcombe, though, was on the ropes, and he surrendered a double to Whitey Lockman. That double narrowed the score to 4-2, put Giant runners on second and third, and made Dressen look to his bullpen. His choice might have been Labine if Labine had not worked a complete game the previous day, but with his options limited, Dressen elected to bring in Ralph Branca. Normally a starter, Branca had already lost the playoff opener in a starting role and now had the unenviable task of getting two outs with the tying run perched right behind him on second base. Confronting him was Bobby Thomson, the Giants' leading slugger with 31 homers already in his tank.

Wearing a uniform bearing the number 13, Branca took the mound. His first pitch was a called strike. His second pitch was a waist-high fastball that Thomson rode into the short left field stands

for a three-run homer. This feat spelled a pennant for the Giants that was labeled "The Miracle of Coogan's Bluff" (the name of the hill above the Polo Grounds) and earned Thomson everlasting fame for "the shot heard 'round the world."

Captured on television, radio, and film, Thomson's four-bagger prepped the entire nation for the Giants' meeting the following day with the New York Yankees in the World Series opener. After the Giants won, 5-1, with Dave Koslo, and then triumphed again in Game 3 to go up 2-1, they appeared to have luck, momentum, and destiny all on their side.

Suddenly, the Yankees caught a break. Reeling from the Game 3 loss which saw Phil Rizzuto and Yogi Berra—two of the most reliable Yankees under pressure—make key errors to open the floodgates for five Giants runs in the fifth inning, the Bombers were down to their number four starter in Game 4. The trouble was that Casey Stengel did not have a fourth starter. He had somehow managed to get along all season with a three-man rotation of Eddie Lopat, Vic Raschi, and Allie Reynolds after 1950 rookie whiz Whitey Ford was inducted into the Army. Now Ford's absence looked likely to cost the Yankees the Series.

Pittsburgh's Ralph Kiner (top) hit 42 home runs to capture his sixth consecutive HR crown. Boston's Ted Williams (bottom) led the AL in total bases, walks, and runs produced.

As fate would have it, it rained in New York on Sunday, October 7, and Stengel was given a reprieve. The following afternoon he was able to recall Allie Reynolds, his Game 1 starter. With that, the Giants lost their luck, their momentum, and, in short order, the Series. Reynolds won Game 4, 6-2; in Game 5 the Yankees routed five Giants twirlers in a 13-1 laugher; and a day later Raschi, with relief help from Johnny Sain and Bob Kuzava, won game, set, and match for the Yankees.

SEASON'S BEST

Bob Feller

• Yankee catcher Yogi Berra is AL MVP.

• Dodger catcher Roy Campanella is named NL MVP.

• Giant teammates Sal Maglie and Larry Jansen tie for the ML lead in wins (23).

• St. Louis's Stan Musial tops the NL in batting (.355), runs (124), triples (12), total bases (355), and runs produced (200).

• Pittsburgh's Ralph Kiner wins his sixth consecutive NL homer crown (42). Kiner also leads the NL in walks (137), SA (.627), and OBP (.452).

• Bill Veeck buys the Browns after selling the Indians. Veeck signs midget Eddie Gaedel, who appears in a game on August 19 as a pinch hitter and draws a walk.

• Ford Frick is named new commissioner after Happy Chandler's contract is not renewed by ML owners.

• On July 1, Bob Feller becomes the first to throw three career no-hitters in the 20th century, as he blanks Detroit.

• Dodger Preacher Roe's .880 winning percentage is the highest in history by an NL 20-game winner.

• Boston's Warren Spahn leads the NL in CGs (26) and shutouts (seven) and ties in Ks (164).

• On September 14, Bob Nieman of the Browns becomes the only player in ML history to homer in his first two ML at bats.

• Paul Lehner ties the AL record when he plays for four teams in the same year.

• On September 13, owing to rainouts, the Cards play the Giants at home in the afternoon and the Braves at home at night.

• Cleveland has three 20-game winners—Feller (22), Early Wynn (20), and Mike Garcia (20).

• Philly's Gus Zernial tops the AL in homers with 33.

• The Giants' Willie Mays is NL Rookie of the Year after beginning the season in the minors.

• Brave rookie Chet Nichols tops the NL in ERA (2.88).

• Ferris Fain of the A's wins the AL batting title (.344).

• Yankee Ed Lopat is the World Series pitching star with two CG wins and an 0.50 ERA.

• Giant Monte Irvin leads all hitters in the World Series with 11 hits and a .458 batting average.

1951

YOGI BERRA

Silly-talking catcher speaks best with his bat

They earned a reputation as the most regal of ballclubs, but many of the New York Yankees who played between 1947 and '64 will insist that the most important member of their team was the homely, roly-poly catcher with a knack for saying things nobody quite understood. A squat 5'8" by the time he finished growing, Lawrence Peter Berra earned the nickname "Yogi" because a childhood friend eyeing him on the bench felt he more closely resembled someone contemplating yoga than a future major leaguer. There wasn't anything complacent about the way this universally loved character led the Yankees to an incredible 14 pennants and 10 World Series titles—including a third consecutive championship during his first of three MVP seasons in 1951.

Growing up in the Italian section of St. Louis with buddy and fellow future major-league catcher Joe Garagiola, Berra was signed by the Yankees for $500 and, after a hitch in the Navy, was catching for the world champion New Yorkers in 1947. A .280 hitter from the start, Yogi was quick but unpolished defensively until some tips from Hall of Famer Bill Dickey helped him become the AL's most consistent defensive receiver. "Bill is learning me his experiences," Yogi said of the tutoring. He proved an apt pupil. In fact, he eventually led the league in games caught and chances accepted eight times and double plays six

times. Yogi also went for a 148-game stretch from 1957 to 1959 without making an error.

His excellent handling of pitchers and keen insights prompted Yankee manager Casey Stengel to refer to Berra as "my assistant," but Yogi was just as deadly at the plate as behind it. Known as one of baseball's best bad-ball hitters and clutch performers, he slugged at least 20 homers and drove in 82 or more runs for 10 seasons in a row between 1949 and '58. The '51 campaign was actually one of his worst years offensively (a .294 BA with 27 homers, 88 RBI, and a horrible September slump), but Yogi was the league leader in putouts, assists, and double plays as the Yankees won the pennant and took a six-game World Series from the Giants. These games would mark just a few of the eventual-record 75 Series contests Berra would play in.

Yogi eventually hit 329 of his 358 lifetime homers while catching, setting a record since broken. Despite his stellar playing and managerial career (Yogi led the Yankees and Mets to pennants, becoming only the second man to manage champions in both major leagues), he is still best known for the things he said or allegedly said. The most famous Yogi-ism— "It ain't over 'till it's over"—has become a baseball standard. While some have mocked him, it would appear this Hall of Famer has had the last laugh.

STENGEL'S YANKS WIN ANOTHER ONE

After replacing Lou Boudreau as Cleveland manager in 1951, Al Lopez steered the Tribe to 93 wins and a close second-place finish behind the New York Yankees. In 1952, Lopez sculpted a pitching staff that had three 20-game winners and an attack that produced both the AL's home run and RBI kings. By Labor Day, he had the Tribe in first place, 2½ games ahead of the Yankees and in control of their own destiny. In the season's final month, the Indians were slated to play 20 of their last 22 games at home while the Yankees took to the road for 18 of their final 21 contests.

Lopez seemed to have all of his ducks perfectly aligned in '52, yet on closing day his crew stood right where it had the previous autumn. For all their league-leading performers and favors from the schedule-maker, the Indians once again won 93 games

and were the Yankees' bridesmaids. Cleveland's failure was largely attributed to Bob Feller, who fell from a 22-8 mark in 1951 to 9-13, but their real downfall was the bullpen. Whereas the Yankees had in Allie Reynolds and Johnny Sain two starters who were also stellar relievers and collected 13 saves between them, Cleveland's two top firemen—Lou Brissie and Mickey Harris—combined for just three saves.

There was, however, no manager in '52 who had a bullpen as prolific as Charlie Dressen's. The Brooklyn Dodgers skipper received a record 38 wins from his relief corps, including 14 from rookie star Joe Black, six from Clem Labine, and five from Billy Loes. In addition, the Dodgers bullpen totaled 24 saves, again led by Black with 15. The heavy contribution from his relievers was not something that

Dressen sought. It was rather that his starters all were either brittle or erratic. In 1952, the Dodgers set another odd mound record when they had 16 pitchers who hurled more than 10 innings in the course of the season yet won the NL pennant.

Second to Brooklyn, standing at 4½ games back, were the New York Giants. They had figured to win the flag, especially after they got off to a 16-2 start. As the season progressed, however, two glaring shortcomings caught up to

Manager Casey Stengel and the Yankees won their fourth straight World Series championship, a feat even defeated Dodgers manager Chuck Dressen couldn't help smiling about.

them. In spring training, left fielder Monte Irvin, the 1951 NL RBI leader, was shelved until late summer after he broke an ankle sliding. Then, a few weeks after the season began, Willie Mays was inducted into the Army, leaving the team without a center fielder. Leo Durocher was forced to shuttle Bobby Thomson and Hank Thompson between third base and center field and platoon aging Bob Elliott and several second-line outfielders in left. Still, the Giants remained in contention until the last lap of the season and might have won if they had been as ruthless as the Dodgers when they played the Cincinnati Reds, the Boston Braves, and the Pittsburgh Pirates. Against the NL's three weak sisters, Brooklyn compiled an astounding 54-11 record while the Giants were only 44-22.

The World Series shaped up to be a reprise of the 1949 fall affair: a question of whether the Dodgers' superior hitting could prevail over the Yankees' superior pitching. For the opener, Dressen borrowed a page from Eddie Sawyer's 1950 book and started reliever Joe Black against Allie Reynolds. Black then accomplished something that no other Dodgers hurler had ever done. He got his team ahead of the Yankees in the Series with a route-going 4-2 victory.

Following Vic Raschi's 7-1 triumph in the second game to even the conflict, 37-year-old Preacher Roe dumbfounded the experts by producing Brooklyn's second complete-game win on the third day of the fray. The surprising turn of events continued in Game 4 as Black, in his second matchup with Reynolds, improved on his initial outing by limiting the Yankees to just three hits and one run in seven

Cardinals manager Ed Stanky, left, and Stan Musial check out Real *magazine, which named Musial the game's greatest player (top left). Bobby Shantz (top center), just 5'6" and 139 pounds, was AL MVP after going 24-7. Brooklyn's Jackie Robinson (top right) hit .308 with 19 homers and 24 stolen bases. Cleveland's Larry Doby (bottom)* led the AL with 32 HRs and 104 runs.

innings of work. But Reynolds was even better, holding the Dodgers scoreless on four hits to win 2-0.

After Brooklyn won Game 5 in 11 innings, Reynolds was needed in relief when the Dodgers threatened to overcome Raschi's 3-1 lead in the eighth inning of Game 6. Consequently, Yankees skipper Casey Stengel was unable to counter with his ace again when Dressen started Black for the third time in the decisive seventh game. However, Reynolds came on in the fourth inning and got his

second Series win when Mickey Mantle stroked a solo homer in the sixth off Black for the run that put the Yankees ahead to stay in their 4-2 triumph.

While Reynolds was the main villain from Brooklyn's perspective—with two wins and a save—nearly as much damage was done to the Dodgers by 39-year-old Johnny Mize. After collecting only four homers in 78 games during the regular season, the ancient slugger pounded Dodger hurlers for three four-baggers and six RBI in just 15 Series at bats.

SEASON'S BEST

- Cub Hank Sauer is NL MVP. He leads the NL in RBI (121) and ties in homers (37).

- Robin Roberts wins 28 games for the Phils, most in the NL since 1935, but doesn't win MVP honors.

- Philly's Bobby Shantz wins the AL MVP. Shantz tops the AL with 24 wins.

- St. Louis's Stan Musial tops the majors with a .336 BA. Musial leads the NL in hits (194), slugging (.538), total bases (311), and doubles (42) and ties for the lead in runs (105).

Hank Sauer

- Philly's Ferris Fain wins his second consecutive AL bat crown (.327).

- Pittsburgh's Ralph Kiner ties Sauer for the NL homer crown to give Kiner his seventh consecutive NL title.

- Ted Williams leaves Boston to fight in the Korean War; the Red Sox tumble to sixth place.

- On April 23, Giant Hoyt Wilhelm homers in his first ML at bat; he'll never homer again.

- The Pirates lose 112 games under new GM Branch Rickey, who was ousted by Dodgers owner Walter O'Malley the previous year.

- Virgil Trucks of Detroit no-hits Washington 1-0 on May 15. Trucks then no-hits the Yankees 1-0 on August 25. In another game against Washington, he allows a single to the first batter, then no-hits the Senators the rest of the way.

- Tiger pitcher Fred Hutchinson is named team manager; he's the last pitcher to serve as player-manager.

- On May 21 in the first inning, 19 straight Dodgers reach base safely against the Reds.

- Detroit's Walt Dropo ties an ML record with 12 hits in 12 consecutive at bats.

- On August 6, the Browns' Satchel Paige, at age 47, shuts out Detroit 1-0 in 12 innings.

- Cleveland's Larry Doby tops the AL in runs (104), homers (32), and SA (.541).

- Cleveland's Al Rosen leads the AL in RBI (105) and runs produced (178).

- Yankee Allie Reynolds paces the AL in ERA (2.06) and Ks (160).

- Brooklyn's Joe Black is the first African-American pitcher to win a World Series contest (Game 1). Black is the NL Rookie of the Year.

ROBIN ROBERTS

Rubber-armed Phillies hurler wins 28 games

Reliever Jim Konstanty claimed the National League MVP Award when the Phils emerged from a 35-year postseason hiatus to win the 1950 NL pennant, but another member of Philadelphia's starting staff quietly put together an outstanding 20-11 season of his own to help the cause. Although the fortunes of Konstanty and the team quickly slid the following year, dependable right-hander Robin Roberts won 20 games during each of the next five years as well—including an outstanding 28-7 mark in 1952 that nearly earned him a Most Valuable Player Award of his own.

A baseball and basketball star at Michigan State University before signing with the Phillies, Roberts' record was 15-15 his first full major-league season in 1949 before leaping to the next level just when the team needed him. His 20-11 slate in '50 included a 10-inning, pennant-clinching victory on the final day of the season. After he be-

came the team's first 20-game winner since Grover Cleveland Alexander in 1917, Roberts followed up with a 21-15 mark for a fifth-place Phillies club in 1951.

The pattern was set. While the team was annually mediocre at best, Roberts continued to shine. He was most brilliant in '52. Winning the most games of any NL pitcher since Dizzy Dean 18 years earlier (and a total unmatched since), Roberts also led the league in innings (330) and complete games (30) while finishing third with a 2.59 ERA and 148 strikeouts. His performance was so dominating—no other NL pitcher won more than 18 games—that an MVP Award seemed a lock. In the end, Roberts lost a close vote to Cubs slugger Hank Sauer. The slow-footed, poor-fielding Sauer did lead the league with 37 homers and 121 RBI, but the snub was probably due at least partly to the fact Roberts did not possess the charisma and speed of someone like Bob Feller. Instead, he finessed hitters with craftiness and control (never walking more than 77 batters in a season), and earned a reputation as a thinking-man's pitcher able to get the job done despite a lack of fanfare.

Even if accolades didn't come his way, the rubber-armed Roberts continued to have success. He led the NL with 23 victories the next three seasons (going 69-45 while the Phillies languished around .500), and each time he topped the senior circuit in innings, starts, and complete games. All told, he averaged 323 innings and 27 complete games a year between 1950 and '55, and despite dropping to 73-87 the next five seasons, he remained among baseball's most durable hurlers. Roberts allowed plenty of home runs (including a then-record 46 in 1956), but usually made his mistakes with nobody on base. After resurrecting his career in his late 30s, the Hall of Famer wound up just short of 300 wins with a solid 286-245 record. His popularity and good sense served him well as a leader in the early days of the Major League Baseball Players Association.

FIVE IN A ROW!
NY BOMBS BROOKLYN

In 1952, Casey Stengel tied Joe McCarthy's record by winning his fourth successive world championship. In 1953, Stengel toppled all existing records after Whitey Ford returned from two years in the service and led the New York Yankees to their fifth Series victory in a row.

No statistical examination of the Yankees' five-year run can explain how they did it. Stengel didn't have a hitter among the top five batters in the AL until '52. After Joe Page lost his effectiveness in 1950, the bullpen was never the same. Even more so than McCarthy, Stengel was adroit at assembling teams that were better than the sum of their parts. But no member of the Yankees—not even Mickey Mantle or Yogi Berra—played a more pivotal role during the Bombers' five-year run than pitcher Allie Reynolds. While he had celebrated his 27th birthday before reaching the majors, Reynolds won 182 games and saved 49 others. Moreover, Reynolds was 7-2 with four saves in Series action.

In 1953, a low railroad trestle ripped the roof off the Yankees' team bus after a night game against the Philadelphia A's. Reynolds, injured in the incident, was never again the same pitcher. That fall, however, he managed to collect both a win and a save in the Series as the Yankees once again found their stairway to the penthouse blocked by the Brooklyn Dodgers.

Chuck Dressen's Bums relied on the same formula that had worked the previous year—only in 1953 it worked even more effectively. Mounted behind the NL's most awesome offensive force since World War II was a nondescript crew of starting pitchers backed by a huge cast of relievers. In '53, the Dodgers shattered their own year-old mark when they notched 40 relief wins, spread among eight different hurlers. Two of the eight—Billy Loes and Carl Erskine—were customarily starters, but the others were all bona fide firemen as Brooklyn had no fewer than five pitchers who made at least 27 relief appearances.

Supported by an attack that yielded 208 homers and 955 runs, Dressen's pitchers streaked to a club-record 105 wins and a 13-length bulge over the sec-

Yogi Berra, left, is the first to greet Yankee teammate Mickey Mantle, center, after Mantle hit a home run in the '53 Series.

ond-place Milwaukee Braves. In their first season in the Dairyland, the transplanted Braves showed a remarkable 27½-game improvement over their 1952 performance. Sophomore third sacker Eddie Mathews broke Ralph Kiner's seven-year reign as the NL's home run king while establishing new four-bagger and RBI records for a hot corner operative.

Mathews's AL counterpart in 1953 was Al Rosen. The Cleveland Indians' third sacker likewise set loop slugging marks for his position and narrowly missed winning the Triple Crown when he lost the batting title to Washington's Mickey Vernon by a single point. Rosen's team missed out by a wide margin, however, as compared to the previous two seasons. Though they still finished second to the Yankees in '53, the Tribe settled 8½ games behind at the curtain and looked to be on the wane.

Boasting a regular lineup that had five .300 hitters, the Dodgers for the first time embarked on a postseason collision as favorites. However, they ran into one of the most prominent examples of Stengel's strength: wringing the maximum out of an otherwise mediocre player. A second baseman with only average skills, Billy Martin had a knack for rising above his ability under pressure—and especially in Series action.

In 1952, Martin beat the Dodgers with his glove. In the seventh inning of Game 7, Brooklyn trailed 4-2 but had the bases loaded with two out. When Jackie Robinson hit a pop fly between the mound and first base, Yogi Berra called for first sacker Joe Collins to handle it. Collins, blinded by the sun, lost the ball. Martin managed to make a last-second charge that carried him halfway to home plate, where he grabbed the ball two feet from the ground. Had Robinson's pop fly fallen safely, the game would have been tied and the Yankees' record championship string in jeopardy, for Dodgers outfielder Carl Furillo had already crossed the plate and Billy Cox was only a few feet from it when the catch was made.

Martin marked his 1953 fall appearance by killing the Dodgers with his bat. In the six-game Series he collected a record 12 hits, including a dou-

Four of the six Dodgers to score more than 100 runs in 1953 (top, left to right): Junior Gilliam (125), Pee Wee Reese (108), Duke Snider (132), and Jackie Robinson (109). AL MVP Al Rosen (center left) just missed the Triple Crown. Warren Spahn (center right) led the NL with a 2.10 ERA. President Eisenhower presented a silver bat to AL batting champ Mickey Vernon (bottom).

ble, two triples, and two home runs. His 23 total bases in 24 at bats produced a .958 slugging average and eight RBI to lead all postseason participants. To top it off, it was Martin who came to the plate with the score tied 3-3 in the bottom of the ninth in Game 6. The potential Series-winning run was on second base. Facing Martin was Brooklyn's best reliever, Clem Labine. In a flash, Billy lashed a single to cement the Yankees' unparalleled skein of five straight world titles.

SEASON'S BEST

•Cleveland's Al Rosen is named AL MVP. Rosen misses the Triple Crown when he loses the bat title by failing to beat out a ground ball in his final at bat of the season. He hits .336 with 43 homers and 145 RBI. Rosen tops the AL in SA (.613), runs (115), total bases (367), and runs produced (217).

•Brooklyn's Roy Campanella wins his second NL MVP Award. Campanella's 41 homers set an ML record for catchers.

•Brooklyn's Carl Furillo takes the NL bat crown at .344.

•The Braves move prior to the season to Milwaukee, creating the first ML franchise shift since 1903.

•The Dodgers tie an ML record with six men scoring 100 runs or more. The team homers in an NL-record 24 straight games (since broken).

•Vic Janowicz of the Pirates becomes the first Heisman Trophy winner to play in the majors.

•Phillie Robin Roberts tops the majors in CGs (33), Ks (198), and innings (347) and ties for the ML lead in wins (23).

Eddie Mathews

•Milwaukee's Eddie Mathews leads the major leagues in home runs (47).

•Detroit rookie Harvey Kuenn tops the majors in hits (209). Kuenn is named AL Rookie of the Year.

•On May 6, the Browns' Bobo Holloman becomes the only pitcher this century to toss a no-hitter in his first ML start, as he blanks Philly.

•Washington's Mickey Vernon wins his second AL bat title (.337).

•On June 18 in the seventh inning, the Red Sox score a 20th-century ML-record 17 runs. In that game, Red Sox Gene Stephens becomes the only player in modern ML history to get three hits in an inning.

•On May 25, Max Surkont of the Braves becomes the first in this century to fan eight batters in a row in a game.

•Pittsburgh's O'Brien twins, Johnny and Eddie, each play 89 games for the Pirates.

•On April 17 in Washington, Mickey Mantle hits the longest measured home run in history—565 feet.

•Yankee Ed Lopat paces the AL in winning percentage (.800) and ERA (2.42).

•Milwaukee's Warren Spahn tops the NL in ERA (2.10) and ties Roberts for the lead in wins (23).

ROY CAMPANELLA

Squatty catcher cranks out 41 homers, 142 RBI

Once he had re-integrated baseball after more than 60 years by bringing up Jackie Robinson in 1947, Brooklyn Dodgers president Branch Rickey set out to surround the National League's first Rookie of the Year with other top African-American players who could ease Jackie's burden, further the cause, and help the Dodgers win a World Series. The third African-American brought up by the team—gregarious and easygoing catcher Roy Campanella—was the perfect complement to the stern, intense Robinson and was one heck of a ballplayer himself. Campy helped Brooklyn in its quest for five pennants and a world championship, was named MVP three times from 1951 to '55, and in 1953 turned in what was to that point the greatest offensive season ever by an NL catcher.

Unlike Robinson, a college graduate who had just one year of pro ball under his belt when signed by the Dodgers, Campanella was a year-round veteran of nine Negro League, Winter League, and Mexican League seasons before Rickey came calling. Born in Philadelphia to an African-American mother and Italian father in 1921, he quit school at 16 to play full-time for the Negro League's Baltimore Elite Giants. He was already nearing age 28 when he finally got his shot in the majors. An outstanding defensive player with a rocket arm, the squat, 5'9", 190-pound perpetual smiler was also a slugger, the

likes of which had never been seen behind the plate. After hitting .287 with 22 homers for the 1949 pennant winners, he cranked out 31 homers in 1950 as the Dodgers lost out on a return trip to the World Series on the season's last day. Another heartbreaking final-day defeat followed in '51, but Campy earned his first MVP prize with a .325 average, 33 homers, and 108 RBI.

Down a bit the following season (.269 with 22 homers), Roy rebounded with a vengeance in '53 as the Dodgers went 105-49 and came within one game of their elusive world title. Back over .300 with a .312 batting mark, Campy compiled his best-ever power numbers with 41 homers (third in the NL), 142 RBI (first), and a .611 slugging percentage (third). They were the highest homer and RBI totals by a catcher until another great receiver—Johnny Bench—was able to top them in 1970. They earned Campy, who added a homer and six runs scored in the World Series, his second MVP Award. A third came in '55 when with only slightly lower totals (.318, 32, 107) he got the Dodgers back into the Series, then scored the winning run in Game 7. Campy's career ended tragically in 1958 when an off-season car crash left him a paraplegic and confined to a wheelchair. Regardless, the Hall of Famer still became a longtime Dodger coach and goodwill ambassador, always maintaining his youthful enthusiasm for the game.

MAYS AND RHODES AMAZE THE TRIBE

Shooting for his sixth straight world title, Casey Stengel assembled his best team ever in 1954. Everything his previous New York Yankees championship clubs had lacked was present that season. Johnny Sain led all AL relievers with 22 saves, rookie Bob Grim won 20 games, Yogi Berra's 125 RBI were just one short of the loop lead, and when third baseman Andy Carey in his first full season hit .302 and Mickey Mantle finally began to realize his

This historic catch by Giants center fielder Willie Mays put an end to a Cleveland threat in the opening game of the Series.

potential, Stengel savored the rare taste of four .300-hitting regulars.

With every part finally in place, Stengel had his career year in the dugout as the Yankees won 103 games and finished 34 lengths ahead of the fourth-place Boston Red Sox. There was only one problem. In 1954, the AL had a team that came home 42 games in front of the Red Sox and in the process scored 111 wins to break the 1927 Yankees' old loop record of 110.

That team was Cleveland, and like every other season when the Indians won the pennant, the 1954 campaign abounded with ironic developments. For one, a number of the Tribe's regulars, rather than having career years—as normally happens when a team breaks through—had miserable seasons. Right fielder Dave Philley hit .226, shortstop George Strickland bottomed out at .213, and even the team's spark plug, Al Rosen, broke a finger in May and did little in the last four months of the season. There was more. Rudy Regalado, probably the Indians' most highly touted rookie ever, proved to be a bust, and Dave Hoskins, a standout frosh hurler in 1953, was a total washout as a soph. Still worse, slugging first sacker Luke Easter, who had missed most of the 1953 season after breaking his foot, was cut when the injury cost him most of what little speed he had.

The Indians had something in 1954, though, that more than made up for all the subpar years, rookie flops, and injury-riddled sluggers. What they had, in a word, was pitching. Manager Al Lopez owned four marquee names in Early Wynn, Bob Lemon, Bob Feller, and Hal Newhouser who each won between 207 and 300 games in their careers. If that weren't enough, he also had a fifth, Mike Garcia, who collected 19 wins in 1954 and led the AL in ERA. On top of that, Lopez unearthed two rookie relievers—Don Mossi and Ray Narleski—who com-

Between their superior bullpen and the hitting of Mays and Don Mueller (.342), the Giants turned back the Brooklyn Dodgers by five games. The result was a disappointment to most NL enthusiasts who felt the Dodgers would give Cleveland a stiffer postseason challenge with their more balanced attack. The consensus was that all the Indians pitchers had to do was stop Mays and the rest of the Giants would go in the dumpster.

Like the 1906 Chicago Cubs, the NL record holders for wins, the Indians began the World Series favored in every quarter. While the Cubs had fallen prey to lightly regarded utility man George Rohe, the Indians were done in by an incredible catch from Mays and a furious four-game hitting binge from sub outfielder Dusty Rhodes.

The immortal grab by Mays came in the eighth inning of the opener with the score knotted 2-2 and two Tribe runners on base with none out. As Vic Wertz strolled to the plate, Durocher yanked Sal Maglie, who had already surrendered three hits to Wertz, in favor of Don Liddle. Liddle was immediately tagged for a 425-foot rocket that Mays caught with his back to the plate. Footage of the play has

Bob Lemon of the Indians (top) *tied for the AL lead in wins, 23, with teammate Early Wynn. Mike Garcia, Lemon, and Wynn also ranked one-three-four in ERA. Yankee catcher Yogi Berra, known for comical sayings, had his story told in a comic book* (bottom).

bined for 20 saves and just 115 hits allowed in 182 innings.

Yet even with all that hill strength, Cleveland's wondrous 1954 campaign was beset by one final irony. After winning 111 of their first 153 games, the Tribe ended the season with a five-game losing streak.

Largely responsible for the Indians' late skid were the New York Giants, back on top in the NL after a two-year sabbatical. In the interim, manager Leo Durocher had groomed only one new regular (second baseman Davey Williams) and two new starting pitchers (Johnny Antonelli and Ruben Gomez). Durocher had made significant changes, though, in his bullpen, where two senior firemen, Marv Grissom and Hoyt Wilhelm, teamed for 22 wins and 26 saves in 113 appearances. Also helpful was having center fielder Willie Mays on hand for his first full big-league season.

Johnny Antonelli (top) *won 21 games with a 2.29 ERA for the Giants. Ted Williams* (bottom) *lost the batting title by walking 136 times.*

probably been rerun more often than any other incident in the game's history, but, in any case, it doomed Cleveland to a scoreless eighth. Three frames later, Rhodes looped a pinch-hit fly ball to right that would have been a routine out in any other park but the Polo Grounds, where it fell for a three-run homer that won Game 1. Unable to recover from the fantastic catch and cheap home run, the Indians were swept in four, and a case can be made that they still haven't recovered.

SEASON'S BEST

• Prior to the season, the Browns are sold and move to Baltimore, becoming the first AL franchise to be moved since 1903.

• New York's Willie Mays is named NL MVP. Mays tops the NL in batting (.345) and slugging (.667) after spending the previous two years in the armed services.

• Yankee catcher Yogi Berra is AL MVP.

• Cleveland pitchers Mike Garcia, Bob Lemon, and Early Wynn rank one-three-four in ERA, Garcia leading at 2.64. Wynn and Lemon tie for the ML lead in wins with 23.

• On August 1 vs. the Dodgers, Milwaukee's Joe Adcock hits four homers and sets an ML record with 18 total bases.

• Players are no longer allowed to leave their gloves on the playing field while their team is batting.

• Boston's Ted Williams returns from Korean War duty and hits .345 for the season.

• Cleveland's Bobby Avila is awarded the AL batting title (.341) because Williams has fewer than 400 at bats.

• Cleveland's Larry Doby tops the AL in homers (32) and RBI (126).

Ted Kluszewski

• The Giants' Johnny Antonelli tops the NL in winning percentage (.750) and ERA (2.30).

• On August 8 in the eighth inning, the Dodgers score 12 runs with two out and the bases empty.

• Cards rookie Rip Repulski collects an ML-record two or more hits in 10 consecutive games.

• The sacrifice fly rule is reinstated once again.

• Cincy's Ted Kluszewski sets a 20th-century NL record when he scores at least one run in 17 consecutive games. Kluszewski tops the NL in homers (49) and RBI (141).

• The AL wins the All-Star Game 11-9 in Cleveland, as hometown star Al Rosen hits two homers and knocks in five runs.

• After the season, the Yankees and Orioles make a record 18-player swap.

• On May 2, Stan Musial becomes the first to hit five homers in a doubleheader. Musial leads the NL in doubles (41) and runs produced (211) and ties in runs (120).

WILLIE MAYS

Dynamic outfielder hits 'em deep, makes "The Catch"

It is a largely forgotten piece of baseball lore, lost amidst recordings of announcer Russ Hodges screaming and poignant photographs that have captured the moment for all time. When Bobby Thomson hit his "shot heard 'round the world"—a ninth-inning homer that gave the New York Giants the 1951 National League pennant in a three-game playoff win over the Brooklyn Dodgers—there was a rookie center fielder who had perhaps the best view in the Polo Grounds to the drama unfolding. Twenty-year-old Willie Mays was on deck when Brooklyn's Ralph Branca delivered the fatal pitch to Thomson, but within a few years the spotlight would be on Mays as he developed into one of the most exciting performers in major-league history and the 1954 NL Most Valuable Player.

One of the first great African-American players to reach the majors while still very young, Mays was a living example of baseball's changing times. A native of Westfield, Alabama, 16-year-old Willie began playing for the Negro League Birmingham Black Barons in 1947 just as Jackie Robinson was breaking into the majors. By the time Mays himself was signed by the Giants three years later, teams like the Black Barons were no longer needed. Former Negro Leaguers were infusing the majors with a refreshing blend of speed and power, and few combined the elements as well as Willie. Rookie of the Year in '51 when he hit .274 with 20 homers, he was an instant hit with Giants fans for his graceful outfield play and style on the basepaths.

After missing most of the '52 season and all of '53 serving in the Army, Mays returned to another strong Giants team in 1954 and promptly tore apart the National League. Winning his only batting title with a .345 average, Willie also topped the senior circuit in slugging (a career-high .667 mark) and triples (13) while finishing second in total bases (377, just one behind leader Duke Snider), third in homers (41) and runs (120), and sixth in RBI (110). Mays got hotter as the year progressed, and the Giants won the pennant by five games over an excellent Dodger club.

Winners of an American League-record 111 games during the regular season, the Cleveland Indians were heavy favorites in that year's World Series. The score was 2-2 in the opening game at the Polo Grounds when Cleveland's Vic Wertz hit a deep fly ball to center with two men on that appeared headed to the distant wall. Running with his back to the plate, Mays caught the ball over his shoulder—425 feet from home plate—to snuff the rally. New York went on to win the game and sweep the Series. Mays had shown a national television audience what Giants fans already knew, namely that he was the best fielder in the business. Even now, the catch is still being called the best ever.

BROOKLYN BREAKS THE YANKEE CURSE

The Cleveland Indians returned to their old ways in 1955, winning 93 games for the third time in the past five seasons. The AL standings also reverted, as the Indians' return to earth allowed the Yankees to reclaim their throne by a 3-game spread over the Tribe. An additional two lengths back were the Chicago White Sox, who were beginning to seem as if they would never be more than perennial hopefuls after they had staked four third-place finishes in a row.

Fourth for the second consecutive year were the Boston Red Sox piloted by rookie skipper Pinky Higgins. The Crimson Hose, after winning a first-division record low 69 games for Lou Boudreau in 1954, showed an enormous improvement of 15 games. It wasn't, however, reflected in the standings because the AL had a semblance of balance again now that both the Indians and the Yankees had come back to the pack a bit.

The New York Giants also descended from the top of the mountain in 1955, plopping into third place after snaring what would prove to be the last world championship for the franchise to date in 1954. Poor performances from their four main starting pitchers accounted for

Dodger Johnny Podres had reason to smile after two complete-game wins, including a Game 7 shutout, over the Yankees.

the Giants' tumble. Johnny Antonelli, Sal Maglie, Jim Hearn, and Ruben Gomez, who were an aggregate 60-30 in New York's championship season, fell to 46-47. For the first time in the '50s, the Brooklyn Dodgers had come upon a starter who packaged durability, steadiness, and a decent ERA all in the same arm. The pitcher—Don Newcombe, in his second year back from a two-season military interruption—went 20-5 with a 3.20 ERA and 17 complete games. Newcombe's outstanding season, together with the superlative relief work of Clem Labine, compensated for mediocre 9-10 and 8-6 outputs from Johnny Podres and Karl Spooner, the Dodgers' twin southpaw sensations in 1954. With Gil Hodges, Duke Snider, Roy Campanella, Carl Furillo, and Pee Wee Reese enjoying their usual fine years, Walter Alston became the fifth Dodgers pilot since the inception of World Series play in 1903 to make a fall classic appearance.

In only his second season at the Brooklyn helm, Alston had a relatively easy journey to the flag after his charges won 22 of their first 24 games and opened up a 12½-length lead over the pack by July 4. A Sep-

tember slump by the Dodgers came too late for the second-place Milwaukee Braves to draw closer than 13½ games at season's end, but it boded ill for the thousands in Brooklyn who had dreamed only a few weeks earlier that Alston might succeed where his four predecessors had failed. All of that seemed but an idle fantasy now, especially when the Yankees once again awaited their Bums. When a World Series share was in the offing, the Yankees simply did not know how to lose.

It was that almost-automatic World Series share that Yankees general manager George Weiss used for leverage in salary negotiations. Weiss would open discussion by telling each player that his World Series check figured as part of his salary.

"He'd give you this line that you'd make six or eight thousand in Series money," Ed Lopat said, "so he could keep your salary down. Once I said, 'What if we don't win? Will you make up the difference?' He said, 'We'll win.' That was the end of it."

In 1955, though, Lopat and his cohorts faltered in a fall classic, thereupon ending the two longest postseason streaks extant. The Yankees' stumble not only interrupted their skein of seven straight Series wins but terminated the Dodgers' streak of seven consecutive Series losses.

What made the event all the sweeter was that the Yankees won the first two games, making it appear dead certain that Brooklyners would once again have to resurrect their rallying cry of "Wait 'til next year." Game 3 was a different story, though. Podres, Alston's desperation choice for the third matchup,

Al Kaline (top left) *won the batting crown at age 20, the youngest ever to do so.* Willie Mays *(top center)* hit 51 homers to lead the majors. Herb Score *(top right)* set a rookie record with 245 Ks. Mickey Mantle *(bottom)* topped the AL with 37 homers.

posted an 8-3 win. Then the Dodgers bagged the next two games at Ebbets Field. When it was time for the Series to travel north again to Yankee Stadium on October 3, Brooklyn was up 3-2.

Whitey Ford slowed the Dodgers with a four-hit 5-1 win in Game 6. The following afternoon, all the marbles were put in the hands of Podres and Yankees southpaw Tommy Byrne. Podres clung to a 2-0 lead in the bottom of the sixth but proceeded to give up a walk and an infield hit to Gil McDougald. Yogi Berra then sliced a fly ball toward the left field cor-

ner. Sandy Amoros, shading Berra toward center, sprinted for the looper, speared it with an awkward last-second lunge, and then spun and threw to Reese, who relayed the ball to Hodges at first to dou-ble up McDougald. Given that boost, Podres sailed through the final three innings to blank the Yankees 2-0 and present Brooklyn with its first 20th-century world title.

SEASON'S BEST

- New York's Yogi Berra is named AL MVP for the third time in five years.

- Roy Campanella is NL MVP for the second time in three years.

- Detroit's Al Kaline wins the AL bat title (.340) at age 20—youngest bat crown winner in ML history. Kaline leads the AL in hits (200), total bases (321), and runs produced (196).

- Cleveland rookie Herb Score tops the AL in Ks with 245, setting an ML rookie record for Ks. Score is named AL Rookie of the Year.

Richie Ashburn

- Dodger pitcher Don Newcombe cracks 42 hits and bats .359. Newcombe wins 20 games and tops the NL in winning percentage (.800).

- Cub rookie pitcher Toothpick Sam Jones sets a modern NL record with 185 walks. Jones no-hits the Pirates on May 12 after walking the bases full in the ninth and then fanning the side.

- Phillie Richie Ashburn leads the NL in batting (.338).

- Philly's Robin Roberts again tops the NL in wins, as he earns 23.

- Yankee Mickey Mantle wins his first AL homer crown (37). Mantle also leads the AL in OBP (.433), walks (113), and SA (.611) and ties in triples (11).

- The Giants' Willie Mays leads the NL in homers (51), SA (.659), and total bases (382) and ties in triples (13).

- Brooklyn's Duke Snider leads the majors in runs (126), RBI (136), and runs produced (220).

- Elston Howard is the first African-American to play for the Yankees, one of the last teams to break the color line.

- Down 5-0 at one point, the NL rallies to win the All-Star Game 6-5 in 12 innings at Milwaukee.

- Cincinnati's Ted Kluszewski slams 47 home runs, giving him 136 homers and only 109 strikeouts from 1953-55.

- Pirate Bob Friend leads the NL in ERA (2.84).

- Calvin Griffith, adopted son of Clark, takes over as Senators president upon his father's death.

- Washington's Harmon Killebrew hits his first ML home run on June 24 at age 18.

- Ernie Banks of the Cubs hits five grand slams.

DUKE SNIDER

The Duke of Flatbush outshines Willie and The Mick

The battle among New York City baseball fans raged throughout most of the 1950s. Blessed by the presence of three of the game's all-time greatest center fielders during the same decade, New Yorkers argued the virtues of Willie, Mickey, and the Duke on a constant basis as the trio and their respective clubs—the Giants, Yankees, and Dodgers—routinely contended for championships. Brooklyn's Duke Snider usually came up short to flashier Willie Mays and Mickey Mantle in such comparisons, but in 1955 he was the indisputable king of New York and the leader of the only World Series winner in Brooklyn history.

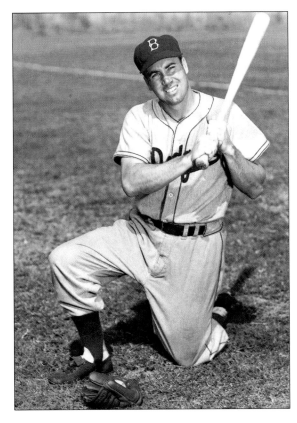

Snider signed with the Dodgers in 1944 following a stellar high school career in California, and by 1947, the 20-year-old was on Brooklyn's Opening Day roster. Demoted after batting just .241 with 24 strikeouts in his first 83 at bats, he was back with the parent club for good two years later and en route to stardom. Some tips from Hall of Famer George Sisler on "establishing an acquaintance with the strike zone" helped Duke to hit .292 with 23 homers for the National League champs in '49. The Duke followed it up with three comparable seasons before beginning a string of five outstanding campaigns in 1953.

Perfectly suited to the cozy confines of his home park, the left-handed Snider hit 40 or more homers all five years and averaged 117 RBI and 116 runs during the stretch while pairing with Carl Furillo and Andy Pafko in the majors' best defensive outfield. A complete player who hit as high as .341, the classy but moody slugger was adored by Brooklyn fans. The player they dubbed "The Duke of Flatbush" would wind up leading all major leaguers with 326 home runs during the '50s, out-homering even Mantle and Mays during their four full seasons together in New York. The Dodgers won six pennants between 1947 and '55, each time meeting the mighty Yankees in a subway World Series. They lost the first four such battles, but in '55 there would be no denying Snider and Brooklyn from finally getting their due. Putting together one of his finest all-around seasons with a .309 batting average, 42 homers, and league highs of 126 runs and 136 RBI, Duke was also second in the NL in slugging (.628) and on-base percentage (.421) while playing his usual excellent center field. The NL MVP followed the year up with a fantastic World Series against the hated pinstripers—batting .320 with four homers and seven RBI—and Brooklyn prevailed in seven games.

Another Series loss to the Yankees followed in '56, and two years later the Dodgers were off to Los Angeles. Snider remained a steady performer for seven more seasons (eventually collecting 407 homers to go with a .295 career batting average and .540 slugging mark), but the Hall of Famer will forever be associated with the borough where he did his best work.

LARSEN'S PERFECTO SPARKS THE YANKS

It is numbing to think that if the Brooklyn Dodgers had merely concluded the seasons of 1946, 1950, and 1951 with victories rather than losses, they would have won nine pennants in the 11 years between 1946 and 1956, including five in a row at one point. As it was, the Dodgers won six flags in that span, and much as they might have liked to encounter a little variety in the postseason, it was not to be, for the New York Yankees snatched eight pennants during that same period.

In 1956, the Yankees claimed their easiest pennant during the Casey Stengel regime. They seized the AL lead early and then gradually lengthened their margin until it closed at 9 games over the second-place Cleveland Indians. In their last year with

Al Lopez at the reins, the Tribe continued to display the finest corps of starters in the game, but the quality had begun to thin. While Early Wynn, Bob Lemon, and soph strikeout king Herb Score all won 20 and were a combined 60-32, the rest of Cleveland's hurlers posted just 28 wins to go with 34 losses.

Three games back of Cleveland and anchored for the fifth straight season in third place were the Chicago White Sox. They were in their second full season with former Cardinals shortstop Marty Marion at the controls. Marion had replaced the innovative-yet-unsuccessful Paul Richards, who had since taken over the Baltimore Orioles. In only their third season in Maryland, the Orioles had yet to rise above sixth place. The A's, after rising to sixth the year before in their initial season in Kansas City, tumbled into the basement. Nearly as bad a club in 1956 were the Washington Senators. Among them, the Senators, A's, and Orioles franchises had not achieved a first-division finish since 1952 when the A's, then still in Philadelphia, had snuck into fourth.

The situation in the National League was just as bleak for the Chicago Cubs and the Pittsburgh Pirates. In 1956, after four cellar finishes in a row, the Pirates ascended to sev-

Yogi Berra, left, and Don Larsen check out a replica of Berra's glove used to catch Larsen's perfect game in the World Series. Larsen struck out Dale Mitchell for the final out.

enth, leaving the bottom rung to the Cubs, who had not seen first-division light since 1946.

However, the Cincinnati Reds broke out of a strange sort of slumber during the '56 campaign. The Reds languished in the second division, yet somehow magically escaped ever finishing in last place for 11 consecutive years between 1945 and '55 before Birdie Tebbetts suddenly put a fire under them. In '56, Tebbetts actually had the Reds in the running for the entire season on the strength of a record-tying 221 home runs and not much else. Even at that, Cincinnati finished just 2 games shy of the Dodgers.

If the Reds were a pleasant surprise to southern Ohioans, the Braves, who finished just a game out of first, were a source of despair for Wisconsiners. Following a slow start that put them barely over .500 with the season nearly a third over, the Braves came to life after Charlie Grimm got axed and his spot in the dugout was handed to Fred Haney. Heading into the final weekend of the season, Milwaukee led Brooklyn by one game with three left to play. While the Dodgers closed in a rush, sweeping three straight from Pittsburgh, the Braves dropped two of their last three to the St. Louis Cardinals.

Don Newcombe, whose 27 wins netted him both Cy Young and MVP honors, got most of the credit for the Dodgers' last-gasp triumph, but to manager Walter Alston the real savior was Sal Maglie, 13-5 after he was garnered on waivers from Cleveland. It was Maglie whom Alston picked to open the Series against Whitey Ford. When the Barber coasted to a 6-3 win and the Dodgers rallied from a six-run deficit the following day and triumphed 13-8, the hex the Yankees had held for so many years seemed to be broken for good.

Cincinnati's Frank Robinson (top left) tied an NL rookie record with 38 home runs. Early Wynn (top right), one of three Cleveland 20-game winners. NL MVP Don Newcombe (bottom left) was the first Cy Young winner. Milwaukee's Hank Aaron (bottom right) won the NL batting title with a .328 average.

New York, however, took the next two clashes at Yankee Stadium to even the battle at 2-all pending Maglie's second Series appearance in Game 5. For his opponent, Maglie drew Don Larsen. Nine years and five days after Bill Bevens lost his bid for immortality to a Brooklyn pinch hitter, Larsen used his newly developed no-windup delivery to fan Brooklyn pinch hitter Dale Mitchell and nail the first and only perfect game in postseason play.

The Dodgers then received nearly as brilliant an effort from Clem Labine in Game 6. Hurler Labine turned in a 10-inning effort that yielded a 1-0 shutout which evened up the match again. Game 7, though, was a climactic flop as the Yankees sent Newcombe and four other Dodgers hurlers to early showers by hammering four home runs, two by Yogi Berra, in a 9-0 wipeout.

SEASON'S BEST

- Brooklyn's Don Newcombe wins the NL MVP Award. Newcombe also wins the first-ever Cy Young Award. (Only one is awarded each year until 1967.) Newcombe leads the majors in wins (27) and winning percentage (.794).

- Yankee Mickey Mantle is AL MVP. Mantle wins the Triple Crown, hitting .353 with 52 homers and 130 RBI. Mantle is the first switch-hitter to lead a major league in batting since 1889. Mantle leads the AL in runs (132), runs produced (210), SA (.705), and total bases (376).

- The Reds hit 221 homers to tie the ML record.

- In May, Dale Long of the Pirates hits home runs in an ML-record eight consecutive games.

- The Reds' Frank Robinson clubs 38 homers to tie the NL rookie record (also an ML record at the time). Robinson tops the NL in runs (122) and is named NL Rookie of the Year.

- Milwaukee's Hank Aaron wins the NL batting crown (.328). Aaron tops the NL in hits (200), total bases (340), doubles (34), and runs produced (172).

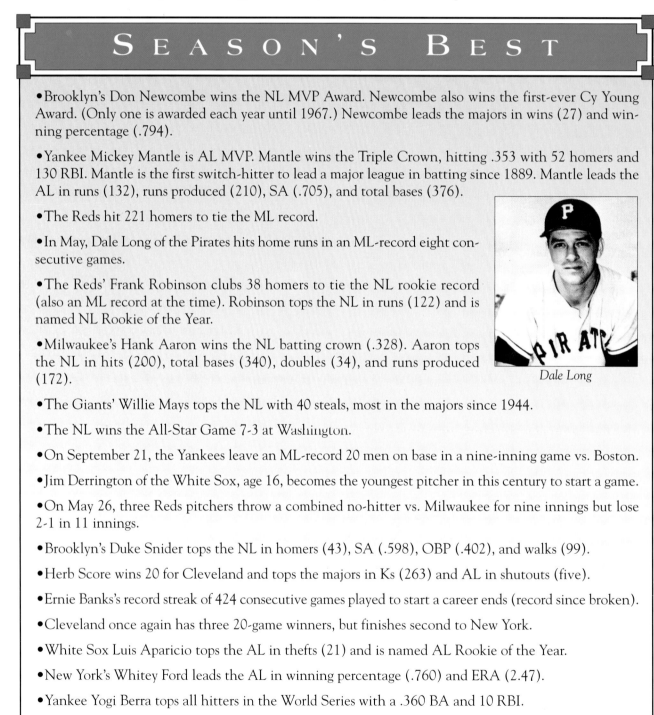

Dale Long

- The Giants' Willie Mays tops the NL with 40 steals, most in the majors since 1944.

- The NL wins the All-Star Game 7-3 at Washington.

- On September 21, the Yankees leave an ML-record 20 men on base in a nine-inning game vs. Boston.

- Jim Derrington of the White Sox, age 16, becomes the youngest pitcher in this century to start a game.

- On May 26, three Reds pitchers throw a combined no-hitter vs. Milwaukee for nine innings but lose 2-1 in 11 innings.

- Brooklyn's Duke Snider tops the NL in homers (43), SA (.598), OBP (.402), and walks (99).

- Herb Score wins 20 for Cleveland and tops the majors in Ks (263) and AL in shutouts (five).

- Ernie Banks's record streak of 424 consecutive games played to start a career ends (record since broken).

- Cleveland once again has three 20-game winners, but finishes second to New York.

- White Sox Luis Aparicio tops the AL in thefts (21) and is named AL Rookie of the Year.

- New York's Whitey Ford leads the AL in winning percentage (.760) and ERA (2.47).

- Yankee Yogi Berra tops all hitters in the World Series with a .360 BA and 10 RBI.

MICKEY MANTLE

The Mick mashes 52 homers, dons the Triple Crown

He hit 536 home runs and compiled a lifetime .557 slugging percentage, but baseball fans and historians will forever view Mickey Mantle as much for the things he might have done as the feats he accomplished. The switch-hitting New York Yankee center fielder was routinely hampered by a long list of leg and other injuries that eventually ended his career, but while he was relatively healthy, Mantle was as great a player as the game has ever seen—especially in the summer of 1956.

Although a football ankle injury suffered at age 15 resulted in a bone disease that would regularly ravage his legs thereafter, Mantle defied doctors who said he would never play again by reaching the Yankees as a 19-year-old outfielder in 1951. The numbers that this rookie from Oklahoma posted were not spectacular (a .267 batting average and 13 homers in 96 games), but the 5′11″, muscle-bound youngster had fans abuzz with his blazing speed down the line and tape-measure homers. Joe DiMaggio's retirement the following year put the pressure on Mantle to step in as the next great Yankee superstar. While he excelled on three pennant winners from 1952 to '55, it wasn't until 1956 that Mickey finally reached the expectations New York fans and manager Casey Stengel had set for him.

Capturing the American League Triple Crown with a .353 batting average, 52 homers—including a record 20 by the end of May—and 130 RBI, Mickey was also tops in runs (132), slugging (.705), and total bases (376) while reaching everything hit his way in center. A unanimous choice for MVP, he added three homers in the World Series as the Yankees beat the Dodgers for one of the seven world championships they would win during his career. Another MVP season followed in '57, but fans wanting more Triple Crowns were soon booing the 16-time All-Star despite brilliant play in the wake of almost yearly leg operations. It took an injury-marred run at Babe Ruth's season record of 60 home runs in 1961 (he finished with 54) to finally turn the crowds around, and from that point on Mantle was viewed as a valiant hero overcoming adversity to lead his team.

With his legs wrapped in bandages before every game, and his legendary speed all but gone, Mantle still managed to limp his way to a third MVP Award in 1962. He also took the Yankees to five consecutive pennants through 1964. Mickey broke Ruth's Series record of 15 homers that fall, but when the Yankee dynasty toppled into the second division the following year, he began fading with it. Moved to first base to help his legs, he hobbled through four more years before quitting in dismay when his .237 BA in '68 dropped his career mark below .300. The Hall of Famer is remembered as baseball's greatest warrior but, when questioned, admitted he too wondered what might have been.

BRAVES, BURDETTE BEST THE BOMBERS

At the close of the 1955 season, Fred Haney had managed some five and a half seasons in the majors. During that time, his teams had lost 526 out of 814 games for an abominable .354 winning percentage. Furthermore, he had piloted the Pittsburgh Pirates to three straight cellar finishes. Haney had little ammunition with which to argue when he was informed by Pirates general manager Branch Rickey that his contract would not be renewed.

Two years later, Haney found himself living proof of the axiom that a manager is only as good as his players. In 1957, Haney sat at the helm of the pennant-winning Milwaukee Braves, clearly the best team in the NL at that moment. Clever trades had brought the Braves Red Schoendienst, Joe Adcock, Andy Pafko, and Lew Burdette, but the rest of the club had been built from the franchise's farm system. Beginning with Warren Spahn in the early 1940s, the Braves' minor-league affiliates had supplied Del Crandall, Eddie Mathews, Johnny Logan, Frank Torre, Bob Buhl, and Gene Conley—good, solid players one and all, but they were only part of the club's talent pool. The Braves front office had observed early on the way the New York Giants and Brooklyn Dodgers began dominating the NL during the 1950s and recognized one of the prime reasons for it was that both clubs vigorously pursued African-American players. The other five NL clubs made the same observation, but only the Braves opted to act on it quickly and decisively. By the mid-1950s the Braves had nearly as many promising young African-American players in their farm system as did the Giants and the Dodgers. Among the Braves' youthful talent were Hank Aaron, Billy Bruton, and Wes Covington.

In 1957, Aaron, Bruton, and Covington were highly instrumental in breaking the Giants' and Dodgers' six-year monopoly on the NL pennant. Second to the Braves were the St. Louis Cardinals, managed by Fred Hutchinson who was rapidly establishing himself as one of the best young pilots in the postwar era. The Dodgers fell to third, their lowest placing since 1948, owing to encroaching age

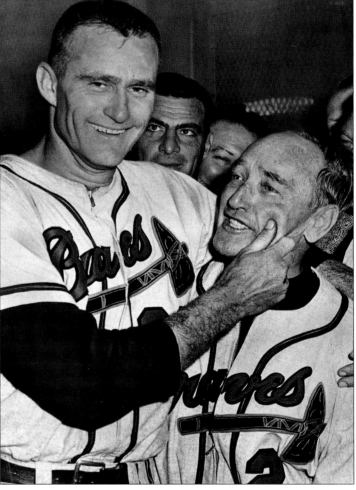

Braves pitcher Lew Burdette, left, who had three complete-game Series wins (two shutouts), clowns around with manager Fred Haney.

and a poor year by Don Newcombe, and the Cincinnati Reds finished fourth after keeping pace with the Cardinals for first place during most of the spring and early summer.

Much of the Reds' improvement in recent years lay in the fact that they also had begun courting talented African-American players, starting with Frank Robinson. The Reds, however, still remained a long step behind the Braves, the Dodgers, and the Giants. Also in the hunt for talent from this pool were the Pirates and the Cubs, but they too had some catching up to do. As a result, the Braves, Dodgers, and Giants would win every NL pennant between 1951 and 1959. Meanwhile the Philadelphia Phillies, the most dilatory senior loop team in recruiting African-American players, would be the weakest club in the circuit by the end of the decade after beginning it as the strongest.

In the AL, the Cleveland Indians—second only to the Dodgers at wooing African-American players while Bill Veeck owned the team—had regressed badly since he had sold the club. When their star southpaw Herb Score was nearly killed by a line drive early in the season, the Indians dropped like lead all the way to sixth place. Their descent at last freed the second-place slot for the Chicago White Sox. No longer an also-ran in the AL, the Pale Hose featured strong pitching, aggressive baserunning, and a shrewd new manager in Al Lopez. They still could not, however, beat the Yankees. By losing 14 of the 22 games between the two clubs, Chicago

The White Sox double-play combo of (top left) *Luis Aparicio, left, and Nellie Fox. Yankee Mickey Mantle* (top right) *beat Boston's Ted Williams* (bottom left) *by one vote in the AL MVP race. Williams led the AL with a .388 batting average, highest since his own .406 in 1941. Herb Score of Cleveland* (bottom right) *was hit in the eye by a line drive and nearly killed early in the season.*

wasted a fast start and finished eight lengths off New York's pace.

Since both pennant races were decided well before the season ended, baseball buffs searched for an auxiliary story to occupy their interest in the waning weeks. They got it when both the Dodgers and the Giants announced they would desert the New York area for the West Coast in 1958. The news left the Big Apple in shock, and the Yankees only added to it in the World Series. After splitting the first two

games at Yankee Stadium, Casey Stengel's crew pulverized the Braves, 12-3, in the first Series game ever played in Milwaukee. The next two contests at County Stadium, however, belonged to Spahn and Burdette.

Upon returning to New York, Bob Turley staved off the Braves with a four-hit 3-2 victory in Game 6.

Haney opted to go with Burdette on just two days of rest in Game 7 rather than a fresher Spahn, and it could not have worked out better for him. The millions of fans who were revved to second-guess Haney were stilled when Burdette whitewashed the Bombers for his third Series win and the Braves' first championship in Milwaukee.

SEASON'S BEST

• The Braves' Hank Aaron is named NL MVP and wins his first NL homer crown (44). He also tops the NL in runs (118), RBI (132), total bases (369), and runs produced (206).

• Yankee Mickey Mantle repeats as AL MVP. He leads the AL in runs (121) and walks (146).

• Boston's Ted Williams, at age 39, tops the AL with a .388 BA, highest in the majors since his own .406 in 1941. He also leads the AL in SA (.731) and OBP (.528). Williams reaches base in 16 consecutive plate appearances to set an all-time ML record.

Roy Sievers

• Milwaukee's Warren Spahn leads the majors with 21 wins and wins the Cy Young Award.

• St. Louis's Stan Musial wins his last NL bat crown (.351).

• The Senators steal 13 bases, fewest ever by an ML team.

• Cleveland's Herb Score is nearly killed when hit in the eye by a line drive; he'll never regain his overpowering fastball.

• The Giants and Dodgers both play their final games as New York-based teams.

• Gold Glove Awards are originated, but only one is given at each position in 1957.

• The Giants' Willie Mays, Detroit's Al Kaline, and Minnie Minoso of the White Sox win the first three Gold Gloves for outfielders. Other Gold Gloves go to White Sox Nellie Fox (second base), Red Sox Frank Malzone (third), and Cincy's Roy McMillan (short). Remaining Gold Gloves go to Dodger Gil Hodges (first base), White Sox Sherm Lollar (catcher), and Yankee Bobby Shantz (pitcher).

• Mays tops the NL in triples (20) and steals (38).

• Washington's Roy Sievers leads the AL in homers (42), RBI (114), and total bases (331).

• Cincinnati fans stuff ballot boxes; most of the Reds regulars are voted All-Star starters. Commissioner Ford Frick disallows the vote and replaces some of the Reds with what he deems more deserving players.

• Brave Lew Burdette wins three complete games in the World Series, including two shutouts.

HENRY AARON

Braves star savors his only MVP, sole world title

Long before he ever became synonymous with Babe Ruth and the all-time home run record, Henry Aaron was a talented but unassuming young outfielder for an excellent Milwaukee Braves team that had finished second or third in the National League pennant race four years running. His talent was not given much attention outside Wisconsin, but when the Braves finally went all the way to the world championship in '57, Aaron was suddenly in the headlines. He was putting together an MVP season that took him out of the shadows and gave most baseball fans their first real glimpse of the eventual home run king.

Aaron's father had once climbed a tree in Mobile, Alabama, to watch Babe Ruth play in spring training. Henry grew up in Mobile poor but happy as long as there was a ballgame. Originally playing the position of shortstop with the Negro League Indianapolis Clowns, he was quickly signed by the Boston Braves soon after turning 18 in 1952. The Braves had already moved to Milwaukee in 1954 when a broken leg suffered by left fielder Bobby Thomson got Aaron into the Opening Day lineup. Henry quickly became a favorite of the frenzied, record-breaking crowds that packed County Stadium.

Runner-up in the Rookie of the Year balloting in '54 with a .280 batting average and 13 home runs, Aaron moved to right field and blossomed into a .314 hitter as a sophomore while slugging 27 homers and a league-high 37 doubles. The slim (6', 180 pounds) right-hander won his first batting title the following year with a .328 mark. He also topped the NL with 200 hits and 34 doubles, but despite 27 more homers, he was still considered a line-drive hitter entering 1957. He wasn't even the biggest home run threat on his own team. Eddie Mathews routinely hit over 40 homers, so when Aaron began the '57 season with a homer on Opening Day and followed with several quickly thereafter, many thought it was just a temporary hot streak.

Seven home runs in an eight-day June spree convinced everybody that Aaron's power was for real. Despite a sprained ankle suffered in July he claims cost him the Triple Crown, he had a league-best 44 homers by year's end. One of these shots was an 11th-inning homer on September 23 that clinched the pennant for the Braves. Hank's 132 RBI, 118 runs, and 369 total bases also topped the senior circuit, and he placed second with 198 hits and third with a .322 batting average and .600 slugging average. The Braves were decided underdogs in the World Series against the Yankees, but with Lew Burdette winning three times and Henry hitting .393 with three homers, Milwaukee prevailed in seven games.

Many more great seasons were to come, but even after passing Ruth's records nearly 20 years later, Aaron would always claim his only MVP year was his sweetest in baseball.

NEW YORK'S TURLEY SAVES THE DAY

Opening Day for the Dodgers and Giants in 1958 came on Friday, April 18, at the 94,000-seat Los Angeles Coliseum. The Dodgers' temporary new West Coast home—while they waited for their park in Chavez Ravine to be constructed—brought a record 78,672 to watch the Giants knock off the home club in the first installment of the newly transplanted geographical rivalry that reached all the way back to 1889. Thanks to the spacious Coliseum, the Dodgers set a new franchise attendance record of 1,845,556. While owner Walter O'Malley's contention that the Dodgers could make more money in Los Angeles than in Brooklyn was immediately vindicated, many of the Dodgers players yearned for Ebbets Field. Duke Snider, for one, slumped from 40 homers to 15 when he was faced with the vast right field in the Coliseum, ranging to 440 feet in the power alley. Don Drysdale, also suffering with the specter of a 251-foot left field fence behind him, faded from a 17-9 mark in 1957 to a lowly 12-13.

The Dodgers consequently finished seventh, their worst showing since the 1944 war year. The Giants, though, seemed to revel in their new home, Seals Stadium, tiny at a 22,000 capacity. Its cozy uniformity, however, enabled rookie Orlando Cepeda to bang 25 homers and hit .312 and the club as a whole to pace the NL in runs. Only mediocre pitching prevented the new San Francisco contingent from making a run at Fred Haney's defending champion Milwaukee Braves, but then none of the other senior loop clubs did, either. The bridesmaid spot, in fact, was claimed by the Pittsburgh Pirates. Closing fast in their first full season under manager Danny Murtaugh, the Pirates not only gained second place but their first look at the first division since 1948.

Though his Braves were eight full games ahead of the Pirates on farewell day, Haney's quest for a second consecutive flag had not been altogether without worry. Second baseman Red Schoendienst learned during the season that he was battling tu-

The Dodgers and Giants headed west, leaving the Yankees alone in New York in 1958. The Yanks made the most of it, winning their fourth straight AL flag and then beating the Braves in the World Series.

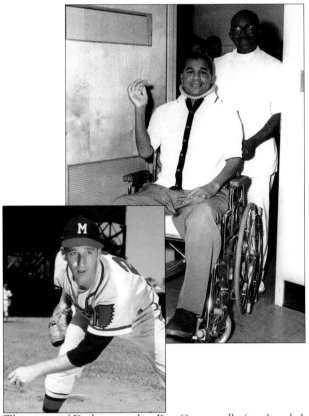

The career of Dodgers catcher Roy Campanella (top) ended when a car accident in January 1958 left him paralyzed below the waist. The Braves' Warren Spahn (bottom) won 22 games, tying for the major-league lead, and two of his three Series starts.

berculosis; super sub Bob Hazle, who swatted .403 in 1957, was waived when his BA disappeared below .200; and a wing ailment kept Gene Conley winless all season. The Braves made do, though, by acquiring veteran hurler Bob Rush from the Chicago Cubs and hurrying the development of Juan Pizzaro and Joey Jay, two promising young pitchers.

The New York Yankees also had a few holes to patch up in 1958, and it was no mystery to fans in the other seven AL cities where General Manager George Weiss would look for solutions. Long before that season, the Yankees had begun fending off accusations that Kansas City, a New York farm team before the Philadelphia A's moved there in 1955, functioned as if it were still a New York minor-league club. During the 1958 season, as usual, a flock of players swapped KC uniforms for Yankee pinstripes and vice versa. Already in possession of just about every decent A's pitcher—including Bobby Shantz, Art Ditmar, and Ryne Duren—by that Sep-

tember the Yankees had also annexed Virgil Trucks, Murry Dickson, and Duke Maas.

It wasn't so much that Yankee skipper Casey Stengel was fortifying his team for the stretch drive (much in the way Weiss had helped him to do earlier in the decade via interleague waiver deals); there was no need for that these days. In 1958, even though they won just 92 games—their lowest pennant-winning total ever under Stengel—the Yanks nevertheless gamboled to the AL flag by 10 lengths. The rest of the loop seemed content just to give up the chase and play for second place. That rather hollow honor went to the White Sox after a six-team fight that even embraced the seventh-place A's well into September.

While the struggle for second place went on far below them, the Yankees busied themselves in maintenance, in keeping in shape, and, above all, in helping their new teammates from the lowly A's learn what life in baseball was meant to be. Life in baseball was meant to include a World Series share every year, and preferably a winning one—especially if there had only been a losing share the year before.

In 1958, the Yankees were determined they would not again go home for the winter with only a loser's share. Even when they trailed the Braves three games to one, they only had to listen to Yogi

Top: *Rookie of the Year Orlando Cepeda, left, and Willie Mays gave the Giants a potent attack. Richie Ashburn (bottom), the second player on a last-place team to win the batting title.*

Berra tell them, "It ain't over 'til it's over." Then they rallied behind Bob Turley (Stengel's choice in Game 5), even though the Cy Young winner had been bombed out by the Braves in the first inning of Game 2.

Turley proceeded to perform incredibly. He won Game 5 with a route-going shutout, saved Game 6, and won Game 7 in relief to make the Yankees the first team since the 1925 Pirates to come back from a 3-1 Series deficit.

SEASON'S BEST

- The Dodgers and Giants move to Los Angeles and San Francisco, respectively.

- Chicago's Ernie Banks is NL MVP. Banks tops the NL in homers (47), RBI (129), total bases (379), runs produced (201), and SA (.614).

- Boston's Jackie Jensen is AL MVP.

- Yankee Bob Turley wins the Cy Young and is second in the AL MVP vote. He leads the AL in wins (21) and winning percentage (.750) and ties in CGs (19).

- San Francisco's Orlando Cepeda is the unanimous choice as the NL's top rookie. He tops the NL in doubles (38) and hits .312 with 25 homers.

- St. Louis's Stan Musial becomes the first player since Paul Waner to collect 3,000 hits.

Jackie Jensen

- Roy Campanella's career ends when he's left paralyzed by an auto accident.

- Richie Ashburn of the last-place Phillies tops the majors in BA (.350), hits (215), and triples (13) and leads the NL in walks (97) and OBP (.441). Ashburn also ties an NL record by leading outfielders in chances for the ninth time.

- Milwaukee's Warren Spahn and Pittsburgh's Bob Friend tie for the ML lead with 22 wins. Spahn tops the NL in CGs (23) and innings (290) and ties for the lead in winning percentage (.667)

- Boston's Ted Williams wins the AL bat crown (.328) at age 40.

- Gold Glove selections are made for the first time in both leagues.

- On September 20, Oriole Hoyt Wilhelm wins his first game as a starting pitcher when he no-hits the Yankees.

- Willie Mays leads the NL in runs (121) and steals (31).

- Giant Stu Miller leads the NL in ERA (2.47).

- New York's Mickey Mantle leads the AL in homers (42), runs (127), runs produced (182), total bases (307), and walks (129).

- The Reds make just 100 errors to set a new ML record.

- Yankee Ryne Duren tops the AL with 20 saves and fans 87 in just 75⅔ innings.

ERNIE BANKS

Happy-go-lucky shortstop puts up serious numbers

For those who never saw him early in his career, the current image of Ernie Banks as an ever-smiling gentleman of baseball has blurred somewhat his prowess as a shortstop with the lackluster Chicago Cubs of the 1950s. Long before he became known as the ageless first baseman on Chicago's near-miss teams of the late '60s and a goodwill ambassador famous for his credo, "Let's play two," Banks was the most devastating power hitter ever seen at short. As a testament to his greatness, he became the first National Leaguer in 1958 and '59 to win the MVP Award two years in succession.

Discovered at age 17 by a semipro scout while playing in a church-sponsored softball league, Banks went directly from the Negro Leagues to the Cubs

in September 1953. He was the team's starting shortstop the following season. Banks played 424 consecutive games to start his career before a hand injury sidelined him during the '56 season. After just a few weeks off, he promptly played another 717 in a row. Slim (6'1", 180 pounds) but strong with powerful wrists and legs, he had 19 homers and 79 RBI as a rookie before switching to a lighter bat in '55. The result was a leap to 44 homers (a record for shortstops) and 117 RBI. From that year through 1960, Ernie would hit more home runs (248) than any player in the majors.

The 1958 campaign was perhaps his finest, as Banks hit a career-high .313 and led the league with 47 homers, 129 RBI, a .614 slugging percentage, and 379 total bases. His 119 runs and 11 triples both ranked second in the NL, and although he made a career-high 32 errors at short, his fielding was vastly improved from earlier in his career. The Cubs were a fifth-place, 72-82 team, but Banks so impressed voters that he became the first player from a losing club ever to be named MVP. Ernie repeated the feat the next year, hitting .304 with 45 homers and 143 RBI (tops in the majors) for a 74-80 team. He also reduced his errors (12) and set a major-league record for fielding percentage (.985).

Forty-one more homers (tops in the majors) and a Gold Glove followed in 1960, but while the Cubs improved over the second half of Ernie's career, Banks was never as dominating a player again due in part to an ailing knee. He moved to first base in 1962 to ease the pain and lasted there until 1971. He collected 512 homers and 1,636 RBI to go with his neat .500 slugging percentage, but missed his only chance at postseason play when the Cubs blew a 9½-game lead to the Miracle Mets in 1969. Not the sort to hold grudges, the man known affectionately as Mr. Cub still donned the Chicago uniform for old-timer's games.

GO-GO SOX RUN OUT OF GAS IN LA

On the morning of May 20, 1959, the country awoke to a stunning realization. There might actually be an AL pennant race that season that did not involve the New York Yankees. Nothing so remarkable as that had happened since 1925. What made it even more surreal was the fact that the Yankees occupied last place. Now *that* hadn't happened since ... well, probably since before anyone on the Yankees had been born—including Casey Stengel.

Eventually the Yankees managed to climb back into contention but never close enough to seriously threaten the Cleveland Indians or the Chicago White Sox. The Sox were making their first legitimate pennant bid since 1919, and, as it would develop, the Indians were in the last sustained pennant bid they would make for almost 35 years. At the time, all anyone knew for sure was that the World Series, for the first time since 1945, would not have an entry from a city east of the Ohio River.

It began to seem likely that for the first time in history, there would be an entry from west of the Rockies. Out in San Francisco, Giants officials began debating as early as August whether to play the World Series in Seals Stadium or to open their planned new home, Candlestick Park, even though it was still not finished. By mid-September the need for a decision grew urgent. With just eight games left, the Giants led both the Milwaukee Braves and the Los Angeles Dodgers by two lengths.

While the Giants brass was still dithering over whether it would be Seals Stadium or Candlestick, the Dodgers flew to San Francisco for a three-game series on the weekend of September 19-20. When the Dodgers left town 48 hours later following a three-game sweep, they were in first place and the Giants had fallen to third.

A Series entry from west of the Rockies still remained a real possibility. First, however, the Braves would put in their two cents' worth. During the final week of the season, Fred Haney's two-time NL

Dodger Wally Moon slides in ahead of the throw as White Sox catcher Sherm Lollar awaits the ball. The Dodgers won in six games to bring the first World Series title to the West Coast.

champions kept pace with the Dodgers while the Giants dropped four out of five to the St. Louis Cardinals and Chicago Cubs, making for seven losses in the final eight games. On closing day, Sunday, September 27, Roger Craig won his 11th game for Los Angeles and Bob Buhl won his 15th for Milwaukee to end the race in a deadlock and create the NL's third pennant playoff series since 1946.

Awaiting the winner were the White Sox, triumphant by 5 games over the Indians. Al Lopez's Go-Go Sox, with their high-speed running game, had taken over first place July 28 and seemed to have it locked up when they swept a four-game series in Cleveland on the weekend of August 28-30. The Indians, though, refused to quit, forcing the Sox to go down to the last week before clinching. After that, all of the Sox turned their attention to the NL race. Most Chicago players rooted for Milwaukee so they could commute from their Windy City homes during the Series, but the front office, eyeing the mammoth LA Coliseum, pulled for the Dodgers.

Already losers twice in pennant-playoff competition, the Dodgers continued to feel jinxed when Milwaukee won the toss to determine who would host the first game. The crowd that turned up for the contest was so sparse, however, it erased part of the Braves' home-field advantage. Then it rained, delaying the start of the game for nearly an hour. LA jumped on top with a run in the first, but the Braves scored twice in the second to knock out Danny McDevitt. In came rookie Larry Sherry to twirl 7⅔

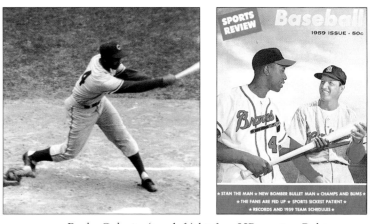

Rocky Colavito (top left) *hit four HRs against Baltimore.* *Roy Face* (top center) *won 17 straight in relief. Luis Aparicio* (top right) *swiped 56 bases for the Sox. Ernie Banks* (bottom left) *was again MVP. Hank Aaron and Stan Musial* (bottom right) *on a* Sports Review *cover.*

scoreless innings in relief and give the Dodgers a 3-2 verdict.

Firemen played a crucial role in the second game as well. Up 5-2 in the ninth, Haney had to twist on the bench in agony as four of his hurlers could not hold the lead. With Sherry unavailable after his long stint the previous day, Dodgers manager Walter Alston had to dip into his starting corps when the game went into overtime. The victory went to Stan Williams in 12 frames, with Gil Hodges scoring the pennant-winning run on a throwing error by Felix Mantilla.

Two days later, the Dodgers—still recovering from the strain of the past week—were blown out of the water, 11-0, in the Series opener at Chicago's Comiskey Park. White Sox first baseman Ted

Kluszewski supplied most of the damage with two homers.

Kluszewski continued to hammer most of the Dodgers pitchers throughout the Series, hitting .391 with 10 RBI, but not even he could do much with Sherry. Following up on his sterling relief job in the first pennant playoff game, Sherry either saved or won every one of the four LA victories that brought California a championship in only its second season as part of the major-league fabric.

SEASON'S BEST

• Cub Ernie Banks repeats as NL MVP. He tops the ML in RBI (143) but loses the NL homer crown to Milwaukee's Eddie Mathews (46-45). Banks sets NL shortstop marks with 143 RBI and .985 FA.

• White Sox second baseman Nellie Fox is AL MVP.

• The Braves' Hank Aaron tops the majors in BA at .355 and leads the NL in hits (223), total bases (400), SA (.636), and runs produced (200).

• Detroit's Harvey Kuenn hits .353 to lead the AL. He also leads the AL in hits (198) and doubles (42).

• White Sox Early Wynn leads the majors with 22 wins and takes the Cy Young Award.

• Pumpsie Green is the first African-American player to join the Red Sox, the last ML team to break the color line.

• On August 31, Dodger Sandy Koufax becomes the first NL hurler in this century to fan 18 in a game.

• Pirate Harvey Haddix pitches a record 12 perfect innings vs. Milwaukee on May 26, but loses 1-0 in 13 innings.

• Boston's Jackie Jensen repeats as AL RBI champ (112) but hits no triples for the second year in a row.

• For the first time, there are two All-Star Games; the NL wins the first 5-4 at Pittsburgh, and the AL takes the second 5-3 at LA.

Harvey Haddix

• Joe Cronin is named AL president—first ex-player to reach that pinnacle.

• Bill Veeck buys the White Sox.

• Cleveland's Rocky Colavito hits four homers on June 10.

• Elroy Face wins a season-record 17 straight games in relief (22 games over a two-year period). He finishes 18-1 with a .947 winning percentage.

• Baltimore's Dave Philley collects a record nine consecutive pinch hits.

• Detroit's Eddie Yost tops the AL in runs (115), walks (135), and OBP (.437).

• Washington's Harmon Killebrew ties Colavito for the AL lead in homers (42).

• Larry Sherry of the Dodgers is Series MVP, winning two games and saving two others.

1959

NELLIE FOX

ChiSox second sacker does lots of little things

From the time that Babe Ruth began crushing baseballs over fences at an unheard-of rate in 1920, the quickest route to fame and fortune in the major leagues had been through the home run. No team was better suited to that trend than the mighty New York Yankees. But when the Bronx Bombers were dethroned after four straight American League pennants in 1959, their fall came at the hands of a Chicago White Sox club whose leader was a 5'10", 160-pound second baseman who had hit just two homers all year: AL MVP Nellie Fox.

The son of a semipro second baseman, Fox debuted at the position with the Athletics in 1948. After hitting .255 with no homers in 1949, he was traded that November to the White Sox for long-forgotten catcher Joe Tipton. It would prove to be one of the few times Connie Mack showed poor judgement assessing talent, as Fox became the heart and soul of a team that bucked the long-ball trend by building itself on speed, defense, and pitching. Chicago Manager Paul Richards took a special interest in Nellie, and after the two put in long hours of infield and batting practice, Fox led the AL in chances per game and tweaked his batting average to .313 with 189 hits, 32 doubles, 93 runs, and only 11 strikeouts in 1951. This was to be a fairly typical season for the left-hander with the compact, lurching swing. Fox routinely finished with 180 or more hits (finishing first or second in the AL eight times during the decade) and close to 100 runs scored while never striking out more than 18 times.

Teaming with a pair of excellent shortstops in Chicago (Chico Carrasquel, then Luis Aparicio), the 12-time All-Star placed among the leaders in putouts, assists, double plays, and chances on a yearly basis while winning four Gold Gloves. He also excelled at the strategic parts of the game—bunting, sacrificing, and always taking the extra base when he could—and set a major-league record with 798 consecutive games at second between 1956 and '60. The White Sox steadily improved around him, and after Nellie belted a 14th-inning homer (his first in two years) to win the 1959 opener, they were on their way to their first pennant in 40 years. Fox was hitting .330 that July before finishing at .306 (fourth in the league). He also won a Gold Glove for his AL-best fielding average (.988) and claimed top putout and assist totals.

The White Sox hit just 97 homers as a team, but until the Dodgers knocked them off in the World Series (Fox hitting .375 with three doubles), they showed that sometimes less is more. In what became a Hall of Fame career—only 35 dingers but 2,663 hits, a lifetime fielding average of .984, and just 216 strikeouts in 9,232 at bats (the third-best ratio in major-league history)—nobody proved that axiom better than Nellie.

THE 1960s

Baseball expanded its scope in the 1960s, adding eight more teams and eight more games to the schedule. Though home runs continued to fly, ERAs shrank as the decade progressed.

Baseball finally expanded in the 1960s. First, both the AL and NL grew from eight to 10 teams, and then to 12 teams in each league. The schedule increased from 154 to 162 games.

These changes led to a wider audience for baseball and for the network and local television that covered it, and revenues for most franchises increased appreciably. For example, local television brought the 16 major-league clubs to a total net income of $2.3 million in 1950. By 1969, big-league baseball had grown to 24 teams and the net local TV revenues had leaped to $20.7 million.

Individuals and groups who wanted to start up teams in their cities had been petitioning the baseball owners for years seeking permission to join them. But the owners turned down every request for expansion, until Branch Rickey and Bill Shea scared them with the announcement in 1959 that they were starting a Continental League to compete with the major leagues in two years. The new league was to have clubs in New York—which the Dodgers and Giants had left after the 1957 season—Houston, Denver, Toronto, Minneapolis-St. Paul, Buffalo, Atlanta, and Dallas.

The major-league owners did not want to compete with a new league for talent or television rights, so they agreed to allow expansion by adding two new teams in each league. New York was the plumb market, with a huge potential audience of former Dodgers and Giants fans. As the American League already had a New York team in the Yankees, the

Pittsburgh's Hal Smith crosses the plate after his three-run homer in Game 7 of the 1960 World Series. His shot set the stage for Bill Mazeroski.

Dodger speedster Maury Wills (top left) shattered Ty Cobb's single-season stolen base record of 96 by swiping 104 in 1962. Orlando Cepeda (top right) gained popularity with Giants fans when he hit 46 homers and knocked in 146 runs in '61. Vada Pinson (bottom left), signed by the Reds out of Oakland's McClymonds High School, hit .343 and scored 101 runs in 1961. Giants outfielder "Say Hey" Willie Mays had a board game named for him (bottom right).

National League got the franchise as the Mets were born in 1962, along with the Houston Colt .45s.

The AL insisted on putting a team in Los Angeles, the nation's fastest-growing market, and the Angels were born in 1961. That year, Calvin Griffith pulled his Senators out of Washington, because he had lost many fans to the Baltimore Orioles, and moved to Bloomington, Minnesota. The team, drawing from the Twin Cities of Minneapolis-St. Paul, was named the Twins. Meanwhile, an expansion team, the new Senators, was installed in the nation's capital and played its games in the new D.C. Stadium. This club fared no better than the former Senators, as the Orioles with their "Baby Birds" pitching staff continued to attract fans from the Washington area. In earlier years, the saying was that Washington "was first in war, first in peace, and last in the American League." Washington finished last in the AL from 1961 to '63.

Expansion teams fared poorly in their early years, because they were stocked by the most expendable players from the established teams. Fifteen players from each team's 40-man roster were made available to the new clubs for purchase at a fixed rate of $75,000 per man. The established teams not only picked up a nice chunk of money, they rid themselves of veterans who were on their way out and youngsters who tended to lack real skills or for whom they could find no place on the roster.

While the Senators and Twins played in new stadiums in 1961, the Los Angeles Angels played their maiden season in a ramshackle minor-league ballpark. But its short outfield fences resulted in the

competence that led newspaper columnist Jimmy Breslin to write the book *Can't Anyone Here Play This Game?* as their won-lost record read 40-120. Yet the Mets truly were amazing when they moved into Shea Stadium—named for Bill Shea, the man who had fought hard to bring another ballclub into New York—for they outdrew the Yankees.

The Houston Colt .45s played their first few years in a minor-league park, then, in 1965, changed their name to the Astros—in keeping with the space program headquartered in Houston—and moved into the Astrodome, baseball's first stadium with a roof over its head. It featured luxurious suites set up just under the roof and the facility was the so-called "eighth wonder of the world," and millions of people paid just to tour the place. Unfortunately, though, the grass that had been planted in the Astrodome's playing field could not survive. That produced one of the greatest curses ever perpetrated on sports (according to many athletes who have played on it): Astroturf, and all of the other artificial playing surfaces that have followed. Initially the surfaces consisted of a layer of macadam covered by a plastic carpet, which made it as hard as concrete. Batted balls caromed off it like missiles, picking up topspin as they bounced. Infielders had to play deeper and

Giants first baseman Willie McCovey (top), Rookie of the Year in 1959, belted 44 homers in 1963 and 45 in 1969. Another first baseman, Detroit's Norm Cash (bottom), won the American League batting title with a .361 average in 1961.

Angels having five hitters—Steve Bilko, Ken Hunt, Leon Wagner, Earl Averill, and Lee Thomas—who had 20 or more home runs for the season. The Angels surprised by winning 70 games and finishing eighth, only a half game behind the Twins, who were led by Harmon Killebrew and his 46 home runs. In 1962, the Angels became tenants of Walter O'Malley in brand-new Dodger Stadium. Their home run production decreased by some 50, but they won 86 games to become a startlingly successful expansion team.

That was the year NL expansion gave America the "Amazin' Mets," who played in the decrepit Polo Grounds that had been the site of the former New York Giants' heroics. Managed by the irrepressible Casey Stengel, the Mets set a record for in-

Casey Stengel, never at a loss for words, was the focus of a 1963 recording.

outfielders could not charge too hard any ball hit in front of them that they couldn't catch on the fly since the ball might bounce 20 feet over their heads.

In addition to the Senators' shift to Minnesota, two other teams moved to new locales in the 1960s. The Braves had been in Milwaukee only 13 years, after decades in Boston, when they accepted an offer they couldn't refuse to move to Atlanta in 1966. They were provided with a new stadium, a long-term low rental arrangement, and a generous television contract. Milwaukee promptly sued the league for approving the move.

Charlie Finley, who owned the Kansas City Athletics, was also angry because he had been planning to move his team to Atlanta. The A's, of course, had played for decades in Philadelphia, until 1955 when they scurried to Kansas City. They would join the Braves in becoming baseball's ping-pong ball franchises, as Finley began negotiating with Oakland, which was building a new stadium and offering a sweet deal to entice the A's to go West. The AL owners refused to permit the move until Finley threatened to sue his fellow owners for the right to take his team wherever he wished. Finley almost had to move anyway, after he alienated fans in Kansas City, and when the AL granted him permission, he opened for business in Oakland in 1968.

Fearing an anti-trust action might be on the horizon from the jilted cities, baseball promised that expansion teams would be placed in Milwaukee and

The 1963 New York Mets (top) *improved upon their 120-loss initial season by losing "only" 111 games. Elston Howard* (bottom), *who broke the color barrier for the Yankees in 1955, received the MVP Award from Joe Cronin in 1963.*

Kansas City. In 1969, Kansas City got another team, and Seattle got one in the AL, too. The senior circuit fielded new teams in San Diego and Montreal. Both leagues split into six-team divisions, the win-

Roberto Clemente (top left) hit .312 or better for eight straight seasons. Two of the decade's best at third (top center): Brooks Robinson, left, and Clete Boyer. Jim Kaat (top right) won 25 for the Twins in 1966; Whitey Ford (bottom left) won 24 for the Yanks in '63. St. Louis's Carl Warwick had three pinch hits in four at bats in the '64 Series (bottom right).

ners of which would meet in a three-out-of-five postseason playoff to determine the pennant winner.

While the folks in Kansas City were overjoyed to have a ballclub again, Milwaukeeans were disappointed. But the Seattle franchise went bankrupt and the AL had to take over the Pilots before the '69 season's end. The next year the team shifted to Milwaukee, which naturally precipitated a lawsuit from Seattle, so the AL promised that in its next expansion, *that* city would again have a baseball team.

Expansion and the shifting of franchises brought with it the building of eight new ballparks in the 1960s, five in the National League and three in the American. All of the new ballparks had virtually the same outfield dimensions, as the owners had agreed upon in 1958. Likewise, they all tended to remain similiar in appearance. Dodger Stadium in Chavez Ravine was the lone new stadium that could be called beautiful.

In 1964, Ford Frick retired as commissioner and for months there was speculation as to who would replace him. When the new commissioner was finally announced in 1965, it was someone whose name had not been mentioned, a man of whom seemingly no one in baseball had ever heard. He was William "Spike" Eckert, a former Army general. "My God," said New York writer Larry Fox when the general was introduced at a press conference, "they've named the Unknown Soldier." Eckert lasted only three years in the job and was replaced in 1969 by Wall Street lawyer Bowie Kuhn, who would become a stronger voice of the owners.

It wasn't until 1966 that the players hired a full-time executive director of the Major League Baseball Players Association. Marvin Miller had spent most of his 48 years working as a labor economist for the United States Steel Workers of America, but he proved himself to be a labor genius the next year when he negotiated a basic agreement between the owners and the Association. His key victories were getting the owners to agree to contribute $4.5 million a year to the player pension fund and to increase the minimum salary—which for a decade had held between $7,000 to $10,000. When this agreement expired two years later, Miller's negotiations raised the minimum salary to $13,500 and got the owners to permit players to be represented in contract talks by agents, who would push salaries much higher in the coming years. Another key concession in this agreement was the introduction of outside arbitrators to settle salary disputes between players and owners. Arbitration would become the means by which players scored some of their biggest salary increases.

It seems unbelievable but the average salary of a major-league player in 1964 was reportedly only $14,800 and in 1967 was only $21,000. In 1966 there were only four players who earned $100,000 salaries: Mickey Mantle, Willie Mays, Sandy Koufax, and Don Drysdale. Teammates Drysdale and Koufax staged a joint holdout to get salary increases. In '65, Koufax had earned $70,000 while posting a 26-8 record that included eight shutouts and an astonishing 382 strikeouts. Drysdale posted seven shutouts among his 23 victories. They held out in the spring asking for salaries of $175,000 apiece and had lawyer J. William Hayes negotiate for them. When Dodger general manager Buzzie Bavasi mentioned the reserve clause, Hayes said that if he in-

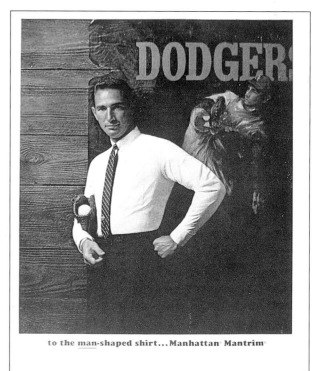

to the man-shaped shirt...Manhattan Mantrim

Jim Bunning (top left), *who won more than 100 and struck out more than 1,000 in each league, threw a perfect game against the Mets in 1964. Minnesota's Tony Oliva* (top right) *became the only player in history to win batting titles in his first two seasons (1964 and '65). Sandy Koufax, the Dodgers' model pitcher, was also a model pitchman* (bottom).

voked it there would be a lawsuit in federal court. Koufax reportedly signed for $130,000 and Drysdale for $110,000. Owners feared the courts would find the reserve clause—which said that teams owned players forever—was illegal.

On the field in the 1960s there were some truly remarkable performances, most notably Roger Maris's 61 home runs in 1961—which broke the record set by Babe Ruth in 1927—Denny McLain's 31 victories in 1968—which made him the first pitcher to win 30 games or more in the majors since Dizzy Dean did so back in 1934—and the tremendous contributions made by African-American and Hispanic players as more and more of them arrived in the majors during this decade.

From 1947 to 1970, African-American and Hispanic players led the league in batting 17 times, won the home run crown 15 times, won the MVP Award 19 times, won a Triple Crown, were 20-game winners 22 times, and set an all-time stolen-base record

Houston's Astrodome (top), *featuring AstroTurf, opened in 1965. Robert F. Kennedy took part in Mickey Mantle Day in 1965* (bottom left), *while "Charlie O," a three-year-old mule, was a publicity stunt by A's owner Charles O. Finley (bottom right).*

Hank Aaron (top) *lost the 1963 Triple Crown when he finished third in the race for the batting title. The Reds traded* Frank Robinson (bottom), *who won the AL Triple Crown in 1966.*

when Maury Wills of the Dodgers filched 104 in 1962. In 1969, African-American and Hispanic batters so dominated that there were 13 of them among the 18 players who hit for an average of .300 or better.

Going into the 1961 season, Roger Maris did not seem the likely candidate to approach Ruth's home run record—Mickey Mantle did. After all, Mantle had hit 52 home runs in '56. Maris's left-handed stroke, in which he pulled most pitches down the line, was ideally suited to Yankee Stadium's nearby right field stands. But in his first year in New York (1960), Maris had won the MVP Award by driving in a league-leading 112 runs while hitting 39 home runs to Mantle's 40. The 39 homers were then a career high for Maris.

Both Mantle and Maris figured to have a shot at increasing their home run totals because expansion had diluted the pitching in the AL and the schedule had been increased by eight games. They both

got off to a fine start and by the end of May, Mantle had hit 14 home runs and Maris 12. During the next two months the pair really got hot, as Mantle banged out 25 home runs and Maris topped him, hitting 28.

As both Maris and Mantle were on a pace to break Babe Ruth's record of 60 homers hit 34 years earlier, the media began to swarm over them for interviews. Commissioner Ford Frick announced that if the record were broken beyond the 154-game schedule that Ruth had played, there would be an asterisk next to it.

Mantle was used to the pressures in New York generated by the media and fans. But Maris had never felt such pressure as he moved into September with 51 home runs to Mantle's 48, and it seemed like Maris could never be left alone at the ballpark. Maris grew surly with the press and uncommunicative, and his crewcut hair began to fall out in tufts under the nervous tension.

Mantle was knocked out of the home run race with his friend by troubling leg injuries and an in-

Boog Powell (top) *was Comeback Player of the Year in 1966 with 34 homers and 109 RBI. Marvin Miller* (bottom) *was elected president of the Major League Players Association in 1966.*

fection. But Mantle still hit a career-high 54 home runs in '61. In the schedule's 154th game, Maris hit homer number 59, but he didn't connect with number 60 until five days later, tying Ruth's total with an asterisk. Maris went into the last game of the season looking for number 61, and he hit it into the right field stands at Yankee Stadium, happy with his accomplishment, asterisk and all. For the first time in months, Roger Maris could smile.

Meanwhile the Yankees, who had won the pennant in 1960, were winning another one. They would extend their streak to five pennants in a row through 1964. Then the Yankees, who had dynasties that won a number of pennants from the 1920s to the 1960s, would fall on hard times. In fact, the Yankees would not win another pennant for 12 years, until 1976. During

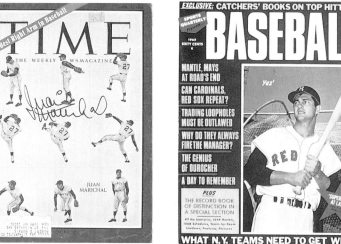

After a 23-12 record in 1965, Dodger pitcher Don Drysdale (top) went 13-16 the next two seasons. The famous leg kick of Juan Marichal was featured on the cover of Time magazine (bottom left). Baseball coverboy Carl Yastrzemski (bottom right) was already a star in Boston in 1965.

many of those years the once-proud Yankees were relegated to the second division.

No American League team managed to follow the Yankees by winning back-to-back pennants through the 1960s. But the Baltimore Orioles had been threatening for several years, building a ball-club with potential, and when they traded for Frank Robinson in 1966, they had the man who would lead them to pennants that season, in 1969, and in the first two years of the 1970s. Robinson was a true superstar, the only man to win the MVP Award in both the NL and the AL. Reds general manager Bill DeWitt said Robinson was "an old 30" when he traded him from Cincinnati in '66. So all old Frank did was win the Triple Crown and earn MVP honors in the Orioles' World Series victory over the Dodgers.

In the National League, the Los Angeles Dodgers had a dynasty led by Sandy Koufax and Don Drysdale, and a manager in Walter Alston who knew how to juggle his troops and eke out runs on generally weak-hitting teams. The Dodgers won pennants in 1963, '65, and '66. The St. Louis Car-

Top: *Owner Walter O'Malley, left, opened Dodger Stadium in 1962. The 1969 Miracle Mets outfield* (bottom, left to right): *Cleon Jones, Tommie Agee, and Ron Swoboda. Jones hit .340 and scored 92 runs while Agee led the team with 26 home runs and 74 RBI. Swoboda actually platooned with Art Shamsky during the season, but hit .400 in the World Series.*

dinals were the other power of the 1960s. With a pitching staff anchored by hard-throwing right-hander Bob Gibson and an offense led by Lou Brock, the Cardinals won pennants in 1964, '67, and '68.

Pitchers tended to dominate hitters after the strike zone was expanded in 1963, because the authorities felt that baseball was being overwhelmed by offense. Maris and Mantle's combining for 115 home runs in '61—which passed the 107 hit by Ruth and Lou Gehrig in '27—was no small factor in the owners' decision. The strike zone had been defined from the armpits to the knees, with the top of the knees being generally the lowest point where strikes were called. The new rule defined the strike zone from the shoulders to the bottom of the knees,

St. Louis hurler Bob Gibson (top) dominated in 1968 with a 1.12 ERA and 35 strikeouts in the World Series, including 17 in Game 1. Billy Williams of the Cubs (bottom) once held the NL record for consecutive games played (1,117) from 1963 to 1970.

Pete Rose (top left), *the NL's top rookie in 1963, won consecutive batting titles in 1968 and 1969. Leo Durocher* (top center), *who left the dugout to become a TV commentator, returned to manage the Cubs from 1966 to 1972. Detroit's Denny McLain* (top right) *won 31 games in 1968. Don Drysdale* (bottom left) *and Brooks Robinson* (bottom right) *had records of a different kind.*

giving the pitchers much more room, high and low, to operate on batters.

But what was supposed to be a blow against home runs—which decreased by 10 percent in '63— also reduced batting averages by 12 points. In 1968, known as "The Year of the Pitcher," Carl Yastrzemski won the AL batting title with the lowest average ever at .301, Denny McLain won 31 games, Bob Gibson posted a 1.12 ERA, and Don Drysdale threw 58 consecutive innings of scoreless ball. So the own-

ers decided in 1969 to bring the strike zone back to the area over the plate between the armpits and the knees. Another rule in '69 lowered the height of the pitcher's mound, which was also designed to give hitters a break. It's interesting that during the years when the pitchers were supposed to have an advantage, Robinson won the Triple Crown in '66 and Yastrzemski won it the following year. No player in major-league baseball has won the Triple Crown since 1967.

MAZ WINS WS WITH DRAMATIC BLAST

Ever so slowly during the 1950s, the Pittsburgh Pirates rebuilt from ground zero. Beginning the decade with a cast of players that for the most part would soon disappear from the majors, the Pirates went through several more unsatisfactory cast changes before finishing the decade with a team that seemed only a pitcher or two short of being a genuine contender.

In 1960, Pittsburgh got its two pitchers. One, Bob Friend, had actually been with the club in 1959 but pitched as if his head had been elsewhere. From an 8-19 mark in 1959, one of the worst ever for an above .500 team, Friend sprang to 18-12 in 1960. Then the Pirates landed Vinegar Bend Mizell in late May from the St. Louis Cardinals for two minor leaguers. With Mizell going 13-5, the Bucs began to gather steam. Already slightly ahead in the NL race, Danny Murtaugh's men pulled away to a final margin of 7 games over second-place Milwaukee.

So easily had the Pirates won, all considered that their feat was reminiscent of the New York Yankees' way of tending to business. Meanwhile, the real Yankees—for the second year in a row—were behaving very un-Yankee-like. To manager Casey Stengel's consternation, his charges stumbled through May and into June behind the Chicago White Sox and the Baltimore Orioles. Guided by Paul Richards, the Orioles were the fashionable choice for the flag if only because of their extraordinary team composition. Left fielder Gene Woodling, at 37, was the only regular position player over 30. Of the six primary contributors on the O's pitching staff, four were barely old enough to vote and the other two, Skinny Brown and Hoyt Wilhelm, were past 35.

By September, though, it was the "Baby Birds" and the "Go-Go White Sox" who began to wear down rather than the jejune Yankees. In the final two weeks of the season, New York turned a tight three-team race into a runaway by winning its last 15 contests to take the flag by an 8-game margin. Many wanted to trace Casey Stengel's 10th pennant in only his 12th year at the Yankees' wheel to yet another trade with New York's Kansas City "farm team." This one brought Roger Maris to the Bronx,

Bill Mazeroski caused a mob scene when he led off the bottom of the ninth with a home run to win the 1960 World Series.

Top left: *Four of the five top home run hitters of 1960 were, left to right: Harmon Killebrew (31), Mickey Mantle (40), Jim Lemon (38), and Roger Maris (39). Ernie Banks (top right),* the only shortstop to lead the league in homers and win a Gold Glove. NL MVP Dick Groat of Pittsburgh *(bottom left). Milwaukee's Eddie Mathews (bottom right) led the NL in runs produced with 193.*

where he quickly blossomed into the best young slugger in the game. The triumph, though, was just as much a tribute to Stengel's careful handling of a patchwork hill staff. The crew nearly became the first in history to hoist a pennant without a single pitcher who worked at least 200 innings. Only Art Ditmar, who labored exactly 200 frames, kept the Yankees from achieving this eerie distinction.

To Ditmar, as the staff "ace," fell the honor of opening the World Series at Forbes Field. A win, however, was to elude him. In fact, he didn't even get out of the first inning as the Pirates racked up three quick runs and then stemmed a late Yankees'

rally to win 6-4. It rang an ominous bell in Pittsburgh skipper Danny Murtaugh's head, though, when New York collected 13 hits even in losing. Over the next three days, every head in Pittsburgh began ringing. In Game 2, the Yankees crushed 19 hits and then added 16 more two days later when the festivities adjourned to New York.

Down 2-1 after being trashed 16-3 and 10-0, the Pirates somehow recovered to take the next two contests in New York and return home with a 3-2 advantage. In Game 6, however, the roof fell in on Pittsburgh again. Whitey Ford, the beneficiary of 10 runs and 16 hits in his last outing, was given an even dozen markers on 17 hits this time. The latest Yankees' blowout evened the Series at 3-all—but in name only. Through the first six contests, the Yankees had accumulated 78 hits and outscored the Pirates 46-17.

Only Cy Young winner Vernon Law had escaped total destruction at the Yankees' hands thus far, twice winning with relief help from Roy Face. Since Law was due to pitch Game 7, the Pirates had one last breath of hope left in them.

Some of those in attendance at the Series finale in 1960 had also been present at Forbes Field in 1925, the only other time it had hosted a seventh Series game. None of them, though, could have dreamt they were in for a denouement even more bizarre and exciting than the one they had witnessed 35 years earlier. Ahead 4-0 going into the fifth inning, the Pirates found themselves trailing 7-4 by the bottom of the eighth. A rally, capped by a dramatic three-run homer by Hal Smith, put Pittsburgh

back in front, 9-7, but the Yankees tied the game at 9-all in the top of the ninth. Still swallowing their disappointment, Pirates fans had barely settled back in their seats when Bill Mazeroski stepped to the plate, leading off the bottom of the ninth.

On Yankee right-hander Ralph Terry's second pitch, Mazeroski jerked a drive over the left field wall for the most historic home run in Series play and the only four-bagger ever to end a seven-game postseason conflict.

SEASON'S BEST

•Yankee Roger Maris is AL MVP. Maris tops the AL in RBI (112) and SA (.581).

•Pirate Dick Groat is named NL MVP.

•On April 17, Cleveland swaps Rocky Colavito to Detroit for Harvey Kuenn.

•Branch Rickey's proposed rival major league, the Continental League, forces majors to expand for the first time since 1901. The AL grants expansion franchises for the 1961 season to Washington and Los Angeles. The AL also approves the transfer of the existing Washington franchise to Minneapolis-St. Paul.

•Lindy McDaniel of the Cards records 26 saves, a new NL record.

•Pittsburgh's Vern Law goes 20-9 and wins the Cy Young Award.

•White Sox owner Bill Veeck is the first to put player names on the backs of his team's uniforms. Veeck also unveils the first exploding scoreboard.

•Boston's Ted Williams hits his 500th homer on June 17. Williams homers in his last ML at bat on September 28.

•San Francisco's Juan Marichal debuts on July 19 with a one-hit shutout of the Phils.

Vern Law

•On August 10, Detroit trades manager Jimmy Dykes for Cleveland manager Joe Gordon.

•Orioles manager Paul Richards devises an oversized catcher's mitt to handle Hoyt Wilhelm's knucklers.

•The Cubs' Ernie Banks leads the majors with 41 homers.

•New York's Mickey Mantle leads the AL in homers (40), runs (119), and total bases (294).

•Milwaukee's Warren Spahn and Cardinal Ernie Broglio top the majors with 21 wins.

•For the first time in ML history, both batting leaders hit under .330.

•Detroit's Frank Lary tops the AL with 15 CGs—lowest total to this juncture to lead a league.

•Annual income from TV tops $12 million for the first time in ML history.

•Manager Casey Stengel is fired after his World Series loss despite winning nine World Series in 12 seasons at the Yankee helm.

TED WILLIAMS

Baseball's greatest hitter goes out with a bang

After winning his sixth and seventh batting titles the previous two seasons (including a .388 batting average with 38 home runs in 1957), Ted Williams had struggled to a career-low .254 mark with just 10 homers during the 1959 campaign. A pinched nerve in his neck had hampered his effectiveness. Teammates and even Red Sox owner Tom Yawkey urged the 41-year-old veteran to retire. Proud and stubborn to the end, Williams demanded instead that Yawkey give him a nearly 30-percent pay cut to $90,000 before setting out to prove his worth with a final season.

The 1960 Red Sox were a second-division ballclub playing before mostly tiny crowds at Fenway Park, but Williams spent the summer putting on a show for folks who made the trip there and to any other AL venue. His neck still gave him trouble, and, after homering in each of his first two games, he pulled a muscle trotting around the bases and was sidelined for a month. He returned in late May, hit his 500th homer on June 17 in Cleveland (becoming the fourth major leaguer to reach the mark), and by July 4 had 12 homers in his last 80 at bats—the best such streak of his career.

Ted was in the running for his seventh batting title by August, but injuries kept him from getting enough plate appearances to qualify. (He wound up with 29 homers, 72 RBI, and a .316 batting average in just 310 at bats.) His 512th homer on August 10 in Cleveland put him past Mel Ott and into third-place on the all-time list behind Babe Ruth and Jimmie Foxx. One week later, *The Sporting News* named Williams its "Player of the Decade" over such competition as Mickey Mantle, Willie Mays, and Jackie Robinson.

The official word this was Ted's final season came on September 26, and just 10,454 showed up at drizzly Fenway for his final home game two days later. Williams made them glad they did. After a walk and two deep fly-ball outs into the stiff wind, Ted came up in the eighth inning against Baltimore's Jack Fisher and belted a 1-1 pitch toward right field. When the hit ball bounced in the Red Sox bullpen, it mark his 521st and last major-league home run. Williams had already privately decided not to accompany the team to New York for a meaningless season-ending series. As he rounded the bases following his final at bat, he just might have been thinking that coming back for one final year was worth it after all.

His .344 lifetime batting average (ninth all-time), 521 homers (tied for 12th), 1,839 RBI (12th), and .634 slugging percentage (second) were strong support to Ted's wish that he be remembered as the greatest hitter who ever lived.

LUMBER-LOADED YANKS POUND REDS

Now that television had replaced radio as America's most influential medium and jet travel had shrunk the distance between the country's two coastlines, major-league expansion was inevitable. The move of the Dodgers and the Giants to California had not appeased the cravings of the growth-hungry baseball people like Branch Rickey; in fact, it only served to whet their appetites for more. As a result, the AL found itself with 10 teams and a 162-game schedule when the 1961 season got underway. The new additions were the Los Angeles Angels and the Washington Senators, a replacement for the old Washington Senators who had fled to the Minneapolis-St. Paul area over the winter and changed their identity to the Minnesota Twins.

Even though the schedule structure and team names and locations were altered in 1961, the end product was still much the same. The New York Yankees threatened to assemble still another dynasty as they won their second straight pennant. Yet there was a significant difference about this one. Now managing the club was former Yankees catcher Ralph Houk, hired when Casey Stengel was jettisoned after the Bombers' stunning loss in the 1960 World Series. Yankees brass had tried to soft-pedal the transition by claiming Stengel was retiring because of age, but when the press asked Stengel to tell it like it really was, he said, "Resigned, fired, quit, discharged, use whatever you please. I don't care. You don't see me crying about it." Later, though, he would elaborate, "I'll never make the mistake of being 70 again."

Presented with an ML-record 240 home runs from his offensive corps and a glittering 25-4 season from Whitey Ford, Houk rode the Yankees' talent-laden van to 109 victories and an eight-game spread over the Detroit Tigers. Under Bob Scheffing, probably the most unremembered man to pilot a team

The Yankees' lineup was loaded again in 1961, with left to right: Roger Maris, Yogi Berra, Mickey Mantle, Elston Howard, Bill Skoworn, and Johnny Blanchard. New York won 109 games and swept the Reds in the World Series.

The fabulous season of Detroit's Norm Cash, in which he hit .361 with 41 homers and 132 RBI, was overshadowed by the exploits of Roger Maris.

that won 100 games, the Tigers outdid even the Yankees in the scoring column, plating 840 runs, as both Rocky Colavito and Norm Cash knocked home over 130 RBI.

The generally high hitting totals across the board helped conceal that offense had been on the decline for several years prior to expansion. Even the NL, though still at eight teams for the moment, profited from the dilution in pitching talent that was a natural outgrowth of stocking two completely new franchises. The senior loop batting average jumped seven points to .262 in 1961 with the Cincinnati Reds showing the largest gain at .270 after hitting .250 the previous year. Unlike the other seven NL clubs, however, which had a corresponding jump in team ERA, the Reds staff actually showed a marked dip, dropping from 4.00 to 3.78.

With such a large improvement on both offense and defense, Cincinnati set a new 20th-century standard for the largest gain by a pennant winner over the previous season's showing. Sixth in the NL in 1960 with a 67-87 mark, the Reds vaulted straight to the top of the standings at 93-61, a leap of 26 games. Most of the credit belonged to manager Fred Hutchinson, for the team was not nearly as strong as its record. Indeed, the Reds lacked a solid catcher until rookie Johnny Edwards arrived late in the sea-

son and had two middle infielders—Eddie Kasko and Don Blasingame—who produced just 48 RBI between them. Luckily, Hutchinson himself had been a former pitcher and was especially adept at bringing along young arms that had yet to bloom. His 1961 Reds had plenty to challenge him.

Foremost was Joey Jay, a onetime Milwaukee Braves bonus baby who was 24-24 after his first seven seasons in the majors. Acquired in a winter trade with the Braves, Jay immediately matured into a 21-game winner under Hutchinson's tutelage. Joining him in the Reds' starting rotation were Bob Purkey, Jim O'Toole, and rookie Ken Hunt. All but Hunt won big in 1961. With Jim Brosnan and Bill Henry—the top righty-lefty relief duo in the game at the time—there to back them up, Hutchinson not only produced a huge upset pennant winner, but he got the Reds home first in an astonishingly easy fashion. Throughout May, rookie pilot Alvin Dark kept the San Francisco Giants in front, but in June, the Reds went on a tear, winning 21 of 28 games and opening up a five-game bulge. In August, Cincinnati faced a brief challenge from the Los Angeles Dodgers, but when the Dodgers lost 10 straight in mid-month, the race was effectively over.

The Reds began the World Series as if they meant to give a good account of themselves. After bowing to Ford, 2-0, in the opener, they mustered behind Jay to take the second clash at Yankee Stadium, 6-2. Then, Hutchinson's bubble burst. The Yankees outscored his Reds 23-7 in the next three games and exited, victorious again, after five.

Yankee pitcher Whitey Ford (left) *posted an amazing 25-4 mark in 1961. Right:* Vada Pinson, *left, and* Frank Robinson *sparked the Reds to the NL flag.*

SEASON'S BEST

•AL now has 10 teams as the Minnesota Twins and Los Angeles Angels are added. The AL's season is expanded to 162 games.

•New York's Roger Maris is AL MVP. Maris breaks Babe Ruth's ML season record by hitting 61 homers. Maris leads the AL in RBI (142) and total bases (366) and ties fellow Yankee Mickey Mantle for the lead in runs (132).

•Mantle hits 54 homers, giving him and Maris a teammate record of 115 four-baggers. The Yankees hit 240 homers to set a new ML record. The team has six players who hit 20 or more homers, which also sets an ML record.

Orlando Cepeda

•The Reds' Frank Robinson is named NL MVP.

•Cubs owner William Wrigley, tired of second-division finishes, has four coaches manage the team at various times of the year. They finish 64-90.

•The Giants' Willie Mays hits four homers on April 30 vs. the Braves.

•Detroit's Norm Cash tops the expanded AL in batting with a .361 BA.

•Yankee Whitey Ford tops the majors with 25 victories and wins the Cy Young Award.

•The Phillies lose an ML-record 23 straight games.

•Pittsburgh's Roberto Clemente wins his first NL bat crown (.351).

•Giant Orlando Cepeda tops the NL with 46 homers and 142 RBI.

•Milwaukee's Warren Spahn tops the NL in wins for the eighth time, as he and the Reds' Joey Jay win 21. Spahn wins his 300th game—first NL southpaw to do so.

•NL wins the first All-Star Game of the year, 5-4 in 10 innings at San Francisco. The second All-Star Game ends in a 1-1 tie at Boston, as rain stops play after nine innings.

•Ty Cobb dies on July 17.

•On May 9, Jim Gentile hits grand slams in two consecutive innings for Baltimore.

•The Braves hit four consecutive homers on June 8 vs. the Reds to set an ML record.

•NL opts to expand to 10 teams in 1962, placing franchises in New York and Houston.

•Baltimore's Dave Philley sets a new ML record when he collects 24 pinch hits.

•Luis Arroyo of the Yankees sets a new ML record when he notches 29 saves.

•Detroit rookie Jake Wood fans 141 times to set a new ML record.

•Milwaukee's Eddie Mathews hits 30 or more homers for the ninth consecutive year to set an NL record.

•The Giants' Willie Mays leads the NL in runs (129) and runs produced (212).

ROGER MARIS

Yankees slugger one-ups the Babe, cracks 61 HRs

When Roger Maris began to close in on Babe Ruth's record for the number of home runs in a single season in 1961, he was fighting more than history. In the 34 years since Ruth had hit his 60 homers in 1927, the Babe had come to be regarded as a baseball god. Most fans were horrified at the idea of a mere mortal challenging the Babe's holiest record. By season's end, Commissioner Ford Frick had decided that an asterisk would be placed next to Maris's record if it took him more than 154 games—the length of a season in Ruth's time—to reach 60.

The years that have passed since 1961 haven't helped Maris's reputation; if anything, it has dropped a notch or two. For one thing, Maris may have been

an excellent right fielder, good enough to win two MVP Awards on Yankee teams that featured Whitey Ford, Yogi Berra, and Mickey Mantle—but any comparison of Maris to Ruth is inappropriate. Ruth batted .356 in 1927, 87 points higher than Maris's 1961 average. Maris's career high in batting was .283; Ruth didn't hit as low as the .280s until his last full season, when he was 39. The colorless Maris also failed to measure up to the Bambino in the area of press relations. While Ruth was outrageous, charming, and an endless source of good newspaper copy, Maris was brusque and testy, or worse. As the march toward the record progressed, his relationship with the press deteriorated.

Maris had another problem, namely the popular Mickey Mantle, who also made a run at Ruth's record in '61. The Yankee fans added to the mounting pressure on Maris by rooting vigorously for Mantle. In mid-July, Maris narrowly led Mantle, who batted behind him in the cleanup position, 35 homers to 33. By September 13, Maris was up 56 to 53. Mantle then fell off the pace because of an injury and ended the season with 54. With game number 154 only a week away, Maris was still four homers short of tying Ruth. Unable to escape from an oppressive barrage of media and public attention and even with his hair falling out from nerves, Maris nevertheless continued to hit home runs and inch closer to the record. In game 154, he came within one long foul ball off Orioles pitcher Dick Hall of tying Ruth in the Babe's hometown of Baltimore.

Six days later, Maris hit his 60th and, after taking a day off to regroup emotionally, hit number 61 into the right field seats at Yankee Stadium off Boston's Tracy Stallard on the last day of the season. Finally showing joy, Maris danced and celebrated his way around the bases and, for once, the crowd at the Stadium cheered him.

Today, Frick's asterisk has long been forgotten. Maris's career may be underrated, but his achievement no longer is.

YANKEES SURVIVE A GIANT SCARE

The Philadelphia Phillies, the NL's doormat in 1961 with 107 losses, made a magnificent turnaround the following season, winning 81 games and finishing above .500. But who noticed? In 1962, the only thing that the Phils' return to respectability brought them was seventh place, as the senior loop had swelled to 10 teams. The two additions were the Houston Colt .45s and a new Gotham entry, the New York Mets.

Catcher Elston Howard (32) grabs winning pitcher Ralph Terry, as the rest of the Yankees converge after beating the Giants 1-0 in Game 7.

The Mets were so ghastly that not even Casey Stengel at the controls could spare them from losing a record 120 games. Houston, on the other hand, embarrassed the Chicago Cubs by ending up ahead of them in eighth place. Still, the bottom three clubs in the NL were so weak in 1962 that the other seven teams all finished above .500 and four won over 90 games. The Cincinnati Reds even accomplished something that no senior circuit team had done since the 1934-35 St. Louis Cardinals. After winning the NL flag the previous year, the Reds failed to repeat in 1962 despite posting a better overall record.

Actually, the Reds dipped to third when the race in the NL distilled into a battle between Northern and Southern California. The southern entry showcased new Dodger Stadium and an electrifying attack built around the legs of shortstop Maury Wills and the bat of left fielder Tommy Davis. (Davis, in fact, produced 153 RBI, the most by an NL player since 1930.) The pair joined with mound duo Don Drysdale and Sandy Koufax to lure a record 2,755,184 fans into the new park and point the Dodgers toward an almost certain pennant. Even after Koufax was lost for a long stretch with a circulatory ailment in his pitching hand, Los Angeles was 98-51 with 13 games left and stood a chance of tying the 1954 Cleveland Indians for the second-highest victory total ever at 111. Instead, the Dodgers lost 10 of their last 13 while their northern rivals, the San Francisco Giants, won seven to tie them on the final day of the season.

Embroiled in a pennant playoff series for the fourth time in the franchise's exis-

Willie Mays (left) hit 49 homers, but was edged out for MVP honors by Maury Wills. Minnesota's Harmon Killebrew (center) hit 48 home runs, but struck out a record 142 times. Cy Young winner Don Drysdale (right) went 25-9 for the Dodgers.

tence, the Dodgers got Koufax back in time to start the first game at San Francisco's Candlestick Park. Koufax failed to survive the second inning, though, and the Giants piled it on to win 8-0. Game 2 also shaped up as a Giants' rout when they led 5-0 with just 12 outs to go. Starter Jack Sanford tired in the sixth, however, and Giants manager Alvin Dark brought in Stu Miller after a leadoff walk to Jim Gilliam. By the time the dust settled, Dark had used 23 players in a futile attempt to stem a flood of Dodger runs, and Los Angeles won 8-7.

The following afternoon it was Walter Alston's turn to cover his eyes while the Dodgers squandered a 4-2 lead with just three outs to go. When reliever Stan Williams lost the plate, sandwiching two walks around a wild pitch, the Giants went up 6-4. Billy Pierce then came on in the bottom of the ninth to nail the lid on the Dodgers' coffin.

For a few pixillating days early in the summer, it looked as if there might be an all-Los Angeles World Series. The expansion Los Angeles Angels swept a doubleheader on July 4 from the Washington Senators and moved up near the top of the standings. Though their rise was thwarted, the Angels nevertheless held on to finish third and become the first expansion team to achieve a first-division finish. Second in the junior circuit in 1962 were the Minnesota Twins with 91 wins and the AL's home run and RBI king, Harmon Killebrew. When Killebrew

hit just .243, though, it was the first time a slugging average leader had batted under .250.

Killebrew's questionable feat, though, was virtually the only novelty in the AL by the time the season closed. Once again the New York Yankees were on top, five games ahead of the Twins.

On October 4, when the World Series began at Candlestick Park, it signified the seventh fall meeting between the Yankees and the Giants. The Yankees took the opener, although the Giants ended Whitey Ford's Series-record scoreless skein in the second inning. Six days later, the Series caravan headed westward again with New York up 3-2 and both teams hurting for a starting pitcher in Game 6. However, a three-day rain delay allowed Ralph Houk to bring back Ford. Dark countered with Billy Pierce.

When the Giants won 5-2, it made for a seventh-game match between each team's ace. Jack Sanford (24-7) represented the Giants and Ralph Terry (23-12) the Yankees. The two locked horns in perhaps the most tense Series finale ever. A fifth-inning run sent Terry into the bottom of the ninth with a 1-0 lead. The Giants got runners to second and third with two out and Willie McCovey up. McCovey laced a rocket off his bat, destined to win the Series for the Giants if it got past the infield, but second baseman Bobby Richardson speared the line shot to win it for the Yankees.

SEASON'S BEST

•Dodger Maury Wills is NL MVP, edging out San Francisco's Willie Mays. Wills sets an ML record with 104 stolen bases.

•Yankee Mickey Mantle is named AL MVP. Mantle tops the AL in OBP (.488) and walks (122).

•Dodger Don Drysdale tops the majors with 25 wins and earns the Cy Young prize.

•Tommy Davis of LA wins the NL bat crown (.346) and knocks home 153 runs, most by anyone in the majors since 1949. Davis leads the majors with 230 hits and 246 runs produced.

•Mays leads the majors with 49 homers and 382 total bases.

•The expansion New York Mets amass 120 losses, a 20th-century ML record.

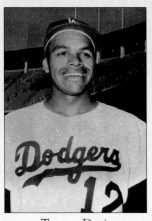

Tommy Davis

•Jackie Robinson becomes the first African-American player inducted into the Hall of Fame.

•Jack Sanford wins 16 straight games for the Giants.

•Harmon Killebrew tops the AL in homers (48), RBI (126), and SA (.545). Killebrew sets an ML record when he fans 142 times.

•The expansion Angels finish third in the AL, leading the loop as late as July 4.

•Minnesota pitcher Jim Kaat wins his first of a record 14 consecutive Gold Gloves.

•On September 12 vs. Baltimore, Washington's Tom Cheney fans an ML-record 21 batters in a 16-inning game, winning 2-1.

•Five no-hitters are tossed during the year. The Angels' Bo Belinsky, Boston's Earl Wilson and Bill Monbouquette, the Dodgers' Sandy Koufax, and Minnesota's Jack Kralick blank their foes.

•The three Sadowskis—Ted, Ed, and Bob—are the last trio of brothers to all be active in the AL in the same year.

•Dodger Stadium opens on April 10, LA vs. Cincinnati.

•Pirate reliever Diomedes Olivo, age 43, is probably the oldest rookie in ML history.

•Cub pitcher Bob Buhl is hitless for the full season in 70 at bats to set the ML record for futility.

•On October 2, the Dodgers and Giants play for four hours and 18 minutes, setting the NL record for longest nine-inning game.

•The Reds' Frank Robinson tops the majors in runs (134), doubles (51), and SA (.624), and he leads the NL in OBP (.424).

•Pirate Elroy Face sets a new NL save record with 28.

MAURY WILLS

LA speedster runs wild, pilfers 104 bases

One year after Roger Maris topped Babe Ruth's single-season home run record, another venerable baseball record came crashing down: Ty Cobb's single-season milestone of 96 stolen bases. Set in 1915, Cobb's mark had stood for 47 years, 13 years longer than Ruth's, before Dodger shortstop Maury Wills stole 104 bases in 1962.

Originally a pitcher, Wills was rejected by a Giants scout who said, "There's no such thing as a 155-pound pitcher." Signed by the Dodgers as a shortstop, Wills lacked consistent hitting ability. Major-league teams had little use for his speed, because of the static offensive philosophy of the 1950s. Wills spent eight years in the minors before playing his first full season with the Dodgers in 1960 at age 27. Two years later, the baseball world began to notice that Wills, who had stolen 50 bases in his 100 games, was a serious threat to Cobb's record.

On August 26, Wills stole his 72nd; suddenly, much like Maris the previous year, Wills came under tremendous mental and physical strain. He played through foot injuries, hitting slumps, and a bad right hamstring to reach 95 steals in 154 games. Commissioner Ford Frick chose that moment to revive his ridiculous asterisk idea (putting an asterisk next to a record to show that there was a different number of games played), which posterity has fortunately ignored. Wills passed Cobb in game 156—actually the number of games Cobb played in 1915 because of two replayed ties. Wills added numbers 101 to 104 in the three-game pennant playoff against the Giants. Even though the Dodgers lost the pennant, Wills was voted MVP over Willie Mays (who hit 49 homers) and Dodger teammate Tommy Davis (who had 153 RBI).

In a historical sense, Wills's record was a more significant achievement than that of Maris, who was a power hitter in a power-hitting era. By helping to revive the art of basestealing, Wills changed the face of the game. Use of the stolen base as an offensive tactic had remained dormant since 1920, when Ruth showed how to score runs in bunches with one swing of the bat.

Wills led the NL in stolen bases three more times after 1961, and stole 94 in 1965. He retired in 1972 with 586 career stolen bases, then good for fifth on the all-time list, behind dead-ball stars Cobb, Eddie Collins, Max Carey, and Honus Wagner. In the succeeding two decades, however, Wills has been pushed down on the list by his followers: Lou Brock (who broke Wills's season record with 118 steals in 1974), Rickey Henderson (who broke Brock's record with 130 in 1982), Joe Morgan, and Tim Raines, among others.

DODGERS PITCHERS HUMILIATE YANKS

Two years after they had produced a teammate-record 115 home runs, Roger Maris and Mickey Mantle collected only 38 circuit clouts between them. Both had an excuse, though, for their markedly decreased power stats in 1963. After breaking his foot, Mantle played in just 65 games, and a bad back limited Maris to 90 contests. With the M&M Boys not even able to participate in a full quota of 162 games between them, if ever the Yankees' latest dynasty was going to be terminated, 1963 seemed the year.

However, rather than end, this new Yankees dynasty emerged with the third four-year pennant skein in the club's history. To combat Mantle's absence, skipper Ralph Houk moved 1962 rookie flash Tom Tresh from shortstop to center field. When Maris's back required a rest, Johnny Blanchard, by trade a catcher, went to right field. Tresh slipped from .286 to .269 and Blanchard hit just .225, but figures like that were the norm by 1963. Tresh even had the third highest batting average among Yankees regulars as the Bombers hit a mere .252, the sort of mark for a dead-ball era pennant winner.

The 1963 season, though, was in no other way reminiscent of the dead-ball era. The stolen base, seemingly a revived weapon only a year earlier, had once again become relatively infrequent as Maury Wills, after swiping 104 sacks in 1962, led the NL with a modest 40 thefts and AL leader Luis Aparicio had the same number. Meanwhile, balls flew out of the yard in every major-league city at a record rate. The Minnesota Twins hit 225 home runs all by themselves, the second highest team total ever, yet finished in third place. One rung above them were the Chicago White Sox, who hit only 114 homers but led the AL in ERA and fewest runs surrendered.

Sandy Koufax is in the middle of the mob as the Dodgers captured the 1963 World Series with a surprising sweep of the Yankees. Koufax won Games 1 and 4 as the Los Angeles pitching staff posted an ERA of 1.00.

Bobby Allison (top) was part of a Twins outfield in which each player hit 30 or more homers. He swatted 35, Harmon Killebrew 45, and Jimmie Hall 33. Yankee Whitey Ford (bottom) won 24 games in 1963.

Of course, the Yankees held control of first place, leaders in no important team departments except one—victories.

While there was no question by the All-Star break what team would head the AL, the NL leader remained in doubt until the third week in September. On Labor Day, the Los Angeles Dodgers had looked like a runaway winner, but suddenly the St. Louis Cardinals began to burn up the league. The biggest spark came from 42-year-old Stan Musial, who announced that this would be his last season. Wanting Musial to go out a winner, his teammates won 19 of 20 games to pull within one game of the top on September 16 when the Dodgers arrived in St. Louis for a three-game series.

Johnny Podres cooled off the Cards, 3-1, in the opener and then Sandy Koufax really put a chill into the Redbirds' bats, blanking them 4-0. Suddenly finding themselves three games back, the Cards desperately tried to salvage the finale and led 5-1 after seven innings. The Dodgers got to Bob Gibson for three runs in the eighth, and in the ninth rookie Dick Nen rocked a solo homer, his only hit of the season, to tie the game. The Dodgers subsequently

won in 13 innings to sweep the series and avert a second straight embarrassing late-season fold.

For the eighth time in their history, though, the Dodgers found themselves pitted against the Yankees in the World Series, a situation that always had a high potential for embarrassment. Many managers would have played it safe and refused to slot their pitching ace against the Yankees top hurler in the opener, but Walter Alston felt that if anyone ought to back off, it should be Yankees skipper Ralph Houk. After all, Sandy Koufax had won the NL pitching triple crown while Whitey Ford had led the AL only in wins.

Alston also had a gut feeling that former Yankees first baseman Moose Skowron, just a .203 hitter during the regular season, might cause his old teammates some havoc. Few shared his optimism, though, until Koufax blew the Yankees away in the opener with 15 strikeouts and Skowron knocked home two runs. In Game 2, Podres continued to suppress the Yankees with Ron Perranoski's relief help and a homer from Skowron.

Game 3 marked the inaugural Series contest in Dodger Stadium and the first time since 1921 that the Yankees had ever fallen behind 3-0 in a postsea-

Giants pitcher Juan Marichal (top) tied LA's Sandy Koufax in wins with 25. Braves slugger Hank Aaron (bottom) tied Willie McCovey for the league lead with 44 homers.

317

son conflict as Don Drysdale edged Jim Bouton, 1-0. Held to just three runs thus far, the Yankees were realistic enough to realize they were unlikely to do better when they discovered Koufax would again be their fare in Game 4, and such was the case. A homer by Frank Howard and an error by Yankees first sacker Joe Pepitone gave Koufax the only two runs he needed to hand the Yankees the same sort of embarrassing fall defeat they had so often administered.

SEASON'S BEST

•Yankee Elston Howard is the first African-American player to win AL MVP honors.

•Dodger Sandy Koufax is NL MVP. Koufax is also the first unanimous choice for the Cy Young Award. He sets a new modern NL record with 306 Ks and a modern ML record for southpaws with 11 shutouts.

•Milwaukee's Hank Aaron leads the majors in runs (121), RBI (130), total bases (370), SA (.586), and runs produced (207). Aaron ties the Giants' Willie McCovey for the NL homer crown (44).

Carl Yastrzemski

•Boston's Carl Yastrzemski wins his first AL bat crown (.321). Yaz also leads the AL in hits (183), doubles (40), walks (95), and OBP (.419).

•LA's Tommy Davis repeats as NL bat crown winner (.326).

•Minnesota's Harmon Killebrew leads the AL in homers (45) and SA (.555).

•Roger Craig of the Mets ties an NL single-season record when he loses 18 consecutive games. Craig finishes with a 5-22 record and suffers nine shutout losses, most by any NL hurler since 1908. The Mets lose 22 straight games on the road to set a modern ML record.

•Milwaukee's Warren Spahn breaks Eddie Plank's record for most career wins by a southpaw when he collects his 328th victory. Spahn, at age 42, becomes the oldest 20-game winner in history when he goes 23-7 for the Braves.

•White Sox Dave Nicholson fans 175 times, breaking the ML record by 33.

•The Twins crush 225 home runs—second most in ML history.

•Boston reliever Dick Radatz has 25 saves, a 15-6 record, and 162 Ks in 132⅓ innings for a seventh-place team.

•Cincinnati's Pete Rose wins the NL Rookie of the Year prize.

•On September 13, the three Alou brothers briefly play together in the outfield for the Giants in the same game.

•On July 31, Cleveland becomes the first AL team to hit four consecutive homers—all are off Angel Paul Foytack.

•Stan Musial retires as the holder of NL records for games (3,026), at bats (10,972), hits (3,630), RBI (1,951), runs (1,949), and doubles (725) (all since broken).

•Early Wynn wins his 300th game on July 13.

SANDY KOUFAX

NL batters, Yankees hitters can't touch hurler's heat

It was a stretch of outstanding pitching unmatched in big-league history, and it came without warning. Los Angeles Dodger left-hander Sandy Koufax had a 36-40 career record entering the 1961 season, and six years after signing as a bonus baby, had shown only flashes of the brilliance that had been predicted for him. Then, following some simple tinkering with his delivery in spring training, that all changed; Koufax was suddenly the most overpowering pitcher in the majors—and by 1963 he was the Most Valuable Player in the National League.

Born Sanford Braun before taking his stepfather's name, the Brooklyn-bred Koufax was attending the University of Cincinnati on a basketball scholarship when he joined the school's baseball team on a whim and notched 51 strikeouts in 32 innings. The Dodgers signed the 18-year-old for a $14,000 bonus and $6,000 salary in 1954, but despite showing occasional signs of his potential—including a record-tying 18 strikeouts against San Francisco in 1959—he looked to be headed nowhere after an 8-13 record in 1960.

Then, during a spring training session the following year, Dodger backup catcher Norm Sherry suggested that Sandy "have some fun" by not pitching so hard and throwing more curves and change-ups. Koufax found the adjustment gave him fantastic control, and after an 18-13 mark and league-high 269 strikeouts in '61 he began his remarkable five-year stretch: a 111-34 record, 33 shutouts, and 1,444 strikeouts in 1,377 innings while carrying the Dodgers to three pennants and two world championships. The NL ERA leader every season from 1962 through 1966 (three times under 2.00), Sandy also pitched a no-hitter four years in a row—capped by a perfect game against the Cubs in 1965. His MVP and Cy Young Award season of '63 (the Cy Young went to only one major-league pitcher until 1967) included ML highs in victories (on a 25-5 record), ERA (1.88), strikeouts (306), and shutouts (11), and for good measure he polished off the Yankees twice in a World Series sweep—including a then-record 15-strikeout performance in the first game.

Koufax was 19-5 in August of '64 when an elbow injury revealed traumatic arthritis. While cortisone shots would help, Sandy pitched in pain the remainder of his career. He went without throwing between starts in 1965 to lessen the discomfort, and the result was a 26-8 mark with a 2.04 ERA, a record 382 strikeouts, and another Series win and Cy Young trophy. It was more of the same in '66, as he went 27-9 with a 1.73 ERA, 317 strikeouts, and still another pennant and Cy Young. By this time, however, the shots and pain had increased to the point Koufax no longer felt like jeopardizing his future health. He retired just shy of his 31st birthday. When he was inducted into the Hall of Fame five years later, the youngest player ever so honored was still standing by his decision.

PHILS FOLD; CARDS HOLD WINNING HAND

After chasing the Los Angeles Dodgers to the finish line in 1963, the St. Louis Cardinals were rated a good bet in 1964 to run up their first flag since 1946—especially when the Dodgers lost Johnny Podres for most of the season to an elbow injury and also got limited duty from Sandy Koufax's left arm. On June 15 the Cards were optimistic after acquiring Lou Brock from the Chicago Cubs. Two months later, with his club in fifth place, Cards owner Gussie Busch fired General Manager Bing Devine and intimated that the axe was also likely to fall soon on manager Johnny Keane.

The Cincinnati Reds, also expected to contend, experienced a different and even more demoralizing inner test when it was revealed in August that popular manager Fred Hutchinson was suffering from lung cancer and had to step down. Replacing Hutchinson was Dick Sisler, whose three-run homer on the final day of the 1950 season had brought the Philadelphia Phillies the NL pennant.

Meanwhile, the climate in the camp of the 1964 Philadelphia Phillies was all sunshine and light as manager Gene Mauch had his version of the "Whiz Kids" in the driver's seat. Built around rookie sensation Richie (later Dick) Allen and 25-year-old right fielder Johnny Callison, Mauch's team was actually younger on the average than the 1950 Phils. If there was a negative feature, it was that few team members had ever been in a pennant race. With just two weeks to go in the season, there was only the semblance of a race in the NL. The Phils led by 6½ games and had already received authorization to print World Series tickets.

The tickets, however, would never be used, as the Phils went into a complete tailspin and dropped 10 games in a row. Suddenly not only the Cardinals and the Reds but also the San Francisco Giants were in a four-way battle with the Phils for the flag.

By the final day, the Giants had dropped out and the Phils had all but eliminated themselves with their long losing skid. The Cardinals had not exactly done themselves proud either, losing twice to the last-place Mets on the season's closing weekend to

Ken Boyer won the 1964 MVP Award, driving in 119 runs and leading the Cardinals to a seven-game win over the Yankees in the World Series.

Hoyt Wilhelm (top left) *was 41 when he saved 27 games for the White Sox. Dean Chance* (top center) *of the Angels won the Cy Young with a 1.65 ERA. Philadelphia's Dick Allen* (top right) *was Rookie of the Year. Willie Mays* (bottom) *clubbed 47 home runs to lead the NL.*

set up a must-win situation for both themselves and the Reds on the final day of the campaign. Philadelphia faced the Reds, and when both the Phils and Cards won, Johnny Keane, on the verge of being fired barely a month earlier, instead was in line to be named Manager of the Year.

The wild finish in the NL diminished interest in the AL race, which had looked to be the more exciting only a few days earlier. The New York Yankees, after getting off to a sluggish start, were riddled with dissension by the All-Star break. Many of the

veteran Yankees lacked respect for Yogi Berra, who had been appointed manager when Ralph Houk was kicked upstairs to the General Manager's post after losing the 1963 World Series. The final straw appeared to come in mid-August when Berra and utility infielder Phil Linz got into a shouting match on the team bus over whether Linz should be allowed to play his harmonica. Oddly enough, the ludicrous incident, rather than further dividing the team, seemed to pull it together. When Mickey Mantle returned to the lineup from a leg injury and Mel Stottlemyre was summoned from the minors in time to collect nine late-season victories, the Yankees went 22-6 in September to catch and then pass both the Baltimore Orioles and the Chicago White Sox. On the next-to-last day of the season, the Bronx Bombers tied their own record when for the second time they clinched a fifth straight pennant.

In the World Series, Bobby Richardson collected 13 hits for the Yankees and Tim McCarver 11 for the Cardinals to lead their respective teams to three victories apiece after six games had been played. The real story, though, was on the mound, where Stottlemyre and Bob Gibson were slated to battle in the decisive seventh game. Remarkably, neither had started the Series opener for his team, and, as a result, both were making their third starts in a seven-day period.

Stottlemyre lasted only until the fifth inning when the Cards took a 6-0 lead, but Keane was determined to let a battered and weary Gibson go the route. In an outing that recalled Walter Johnson's

game effort in the 1925 Series final, albeit with a different result, Gibson survived three late-inning Yankees home runs and brought the championship back to St. Louis after an 18-year drought.

The following day, Keane resigned as Cardinals manager, and the Yankees fired Berra. The Yanks turned around and gave Keane the job of leading the team to a sixth straight pennant.

SEASON'S BEST

- St. Louis's Ken Boyer is named NL MVP.

- Brooks Robinson of Baltimore is AL MVP.

- Tony Oliva of the Twins is named AL Rookie of the Year, as he wins the bat title (.323). Oliva leads the majors and sets an AL rookie record for hits (217). He also tops the majors in total bases (374) and the AL in runs (109) and doubles (43).

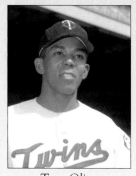

Tony Oliva

- Philly's Dick Allen is named NL Rookie of the Year, as he tops the NL in total bases (352)—an NL rookie record—and runs (125) and ties in triples (13).

- Boston's Dick Radatz has 16 wins and an ML-high 29 saves for a team that wins only 72 games.

- On May 31, the Mets and Giants play a twinbill that lasts nine hours, 52 minutes—an all-time ML record.

- Wally Bunker, age 19, wins 19 games for the Orioles—most in this century by a teenage pitcher.

- New York's Shea Stadium opens on April 17—the Mets vs. Pittsburgh. The Mets finish last for the third consecutive year under Casey Stengel, losing an ML-record 340 games over a three-year period.

- Jim Bunning pitches a perfect game vs. the Mets on June 21—first perfect game in the NL this century.

- Houston's Ken Johnson becomes the first ML hurler to lose a CG no-hitter in nine innings, as the Reds beat him 1-0 on April 23.

- LA's Sandy Koufax no-hits the Phils on June 4. It's his third no-no in three years. Koufax Ks 18 Cubs on April 24. Koufax is held to 223 innings by arm trouble, but he still leads the NL in shutouts (seven), winning percentage (.792), and ERA (1.74).

- Boston's Tony Conigliaro, age 19, hits 24 homers and has a .530 SA—both records for a teenage player.

- Baitimore's Luis Aparicio leads the AL in steals (57) for the ninth consecutive year.

- Johnny Wyatt of KC is the first pitcher in ML history to appear in at least half of his team's games (81 of 162).

- The Giants' Willie Mays tops the NL in homers (47) and SA (.607).

- LA's Dean Chance tops the AL in ERA (1.65), shutouts (11), innings (278), and CGs (15).

BROOKS ROBINSON

Orioles' "Hoover" vacuums 'em up at third base

He is remembered for his glove, and with good reason. Brooks Robinson was the greatest fielding third baseman in major-league history, and won a record 16 consecutive Gold Gloves while manning the hot corner for the Baltimore Orioles. His diving and throwing feats during the 1970 World Series seem more impossible each time they appear on the highlight films, but in viewing these and other acrobatic acts it's easy to forget Brooksie was also a first-class hitter much of his career—especially during his MVP season of 1964.

Robinson didn't play high school ball when he was growing up in Little Rock, Arkansas. Instead, it was while performing at second base in a church league that he was discovered by the Orioles and snatched up for a $4,000 bonus. He first appeared in Baltimore as an 18-year-old in 1955, but a weak bat and George Kell's presence at third kept him shuttling back and forth to the minors most of his first five seasons. Moving his hands down and elongating his swing in 1960, Robinson suddenly became a deadly clutch hitter with solid 20-home run power. His fielding was never in doubt, and once the package was complete the mild-mannered and immensely popular "human vacuum cleaner" began a string that summer of 15 straight All-Star Game starts for the American League—each one complimented by a Gold Glove at season's end.

The Orioles were one of several strong AL teams chasing the Yankees in the early 1960s, and with Robinson leading the way in 1964 they held first much of the year. When the bubble burst and the Yanks overtook them in September, it certainly wasn't Robinson's doing. He had hit .464 the final month with 24 RBI in the last 17 games. All told, Brooksie lead the league with his career-high 118 RBI, while also setting personal bests with a .317 batting average (second in the league), 194 hits (second), 28 homers, and a .521 slugging percentage. Of course, he led the AL in fielding percentage for the fifth straight year.

Robinson would not put up such offensive numbers again, but he remained a dangerous clutch hitter for close to another decade. Frank Robinson arrived from the Reds in 1966 to share the slugging load. The pair proceeded to lead the Orioles to four pennants and two world championships through 1971. When Brooks batted .429 with two homers in a World Series victory over Cincinnati in '70, it seemed only appropriate that a half dozen of the greatest fielding plays anybody had ever seen overshadowed his offense. Reds players nicknamed him "Hoover," and despite eventually collecting 2,848 hits, 482 doubles, and 268 homers, it was his 11 seasons leading the AL in fielding and record 2,697 putouts, 6,205 assists, and 618 double plays over 23 years that got Brooksie into the Hall of Fame.

KOUFAX QUIETS THE UPSTART TWINS

Johnny Keane took the wheel of the New York Yankees' steamroller in 1965, feeling as if Lady Luck had smiled on him. Customarily, the manager of a championship team cannot in good conscience resign for a more lucrative job, but Keane had been bad-mouthed all during the 1964 season by Cardinals owner Gussie Busch. So even though the Cards won the 1964 World Series, Keane felt licensed to tell Busch to take his job and shove it when the most coveted manager's post in the game was offered to him.

Keane arrived in New York expecting to mastermind the Yankees' march to a sixth straight pennant and who knew how many more after that. Instead he found himself presiding over a team that was coming apart at the seams, and he lacked even a clue how to stop its destruction. A deeply religious man and an adamant disciplinarian, Keane was out of his element among free spirits like Mickey Mantle, Joe Pepitone, and Whitey Ford. In 1965, the Yankees finished sixth for their worst showing in 40 years.

The Yankees' sudden collapse left no clear-cut heir to their empire. For the first two months of the season, the Cleveland Indians, the Baltimore Orioles, the Chicago White Sox, and the Detroit Tigers took turns giving the appearance of being pennant worthy, but by July the Minnesota Twins had begun to assert their authority.

Dismissed by experts after mound ace Camilo Pascual was lost for six weeks with a torn back muscle, the Twins found a new stopper in Mudcat Grant. The AL's win leader with 21, Grant had come to

the Twins from Cleveland the previous year in a one-sided deal for Lee Stange. Two years earlier, the Twins had also fleeced the Indians of Jim Perry in return for a much lesser pitcher. As just one indication of how significant these deals were to the fortunes of both teams, Perry would later win a Cy Young Award with the Twins, and had there been a pitching trophy given in both leagues in 1965, Grant would have been the likely AL winner.

Sandy Koufax had two complete-game shutouts against the Twins in the World Series, including a 2-0 win in Game 7.

Grant and Perry were supported in 1965 by 18-game winner Jim Kaat and Al Worthington, who won 10 games in relief and saved 21 others. For middle relief, manager Sam Mele had Johnny Klippstein, a former starter who moved to the bullpen in 1957 and became one of the most unsung firemen of his time.

As a matter of fact, the Twins pitching staff on the whole was unsung in 1965. Power was expected to be their forte. Mele's crew had bombarded AL pitchers for 221 homers in 1964 and topped the loop with 737 runs. Even more damage was anticipated in 1965, but in a sense the Twins disappointed when they slumped to just 150 four-baggers. Amazingly, though, they hiked their run total by 37 while clubbing 71 fewer homers. The principal reason for this incongruous achievement was shortstop Zoilo Versalles. In 1965, Versalles accomplished a rare feat when he paced the AL in both runs and strikeouts. He also led the loop in doubles, triples, and total bases, and in December, quite properly, he found himself the loop leader in MVP votes.

Aided by batting titlist Tony Oliva and center fielder Jimmie Hall, Versalles enabled Mele to survive off years from Harmon Killebrew and Bob Allison. At the season's end, the Twins accomplished something the franchise never did while it was in Washington. They broke 100 wins and bagged the AL flag by seven games over second-place Chicago.

The NL race boiled down in mid-September to a tug-of-war between the two California entries. The Los Angeles Dodgers had the NL's best mound tandem since World War II in Sandy Koufax and Don Drysdale but a pop-gun attack that was paced in both homers and RBI by second baseman Jim Lefebvre with just 12 and 69, respectively. Their northern rivals, the San Francisco Giants, in contrast, cannonaded opponents with Willie Mays, Willie McCovey, and Jim Ray Hart, but had a thin hill crew. When Giants ace Juan Marichal was suspended for nine days after a bat-swinging incident

Jim Kaat (top left) won 18 games to lead the Twins to the AL flag, but lost a 2-0 heartbreaker in the final game of the Series. Willie McCovey (top right) hit a "quiet" 39 homers for the Giants. Don Drysdale (bottom left) teamed with Sandy Koufax to win 49 games for the Dodgers. Pittsburgh's Roberto Clemente (bottom right) won his second straight batting title.

involving Dodgers catcher Johnny Roseboro, his absence during San Francisco's final trip to Los Angeles proved crucial. Without Marichal, the Giants ceded the flag to the Dodgers by a slim two-game margin.

The Twins stunned the Dodgers by beating Koufax and Drysdale in the first two games of the World Series but then instituted a postseason pat-

tern that continues to this day. They dropped all three road matches at Los Angeles. When Grant won Game 6 after the teams returned to the Twins' Bloomington home, Koufax and Kaat got the call in the deciding contest. Kaat allowed just two runs, but the Twins never got close to denting Koufax. His second straight shutout handed the Dodgers the crown.

SEASON'S BEST

• The Giants' Willie Mays is named NL MVP. Mays leads the majors in homers (52), total bases (360), SA (.645), and OBP (.399). He also smacks an NL-record 17 homers in a month.

• Minnesota's Zoilo Versalles is chosen AL MVP over teammate Tony Oliva. Versalles tops the AL in runs (126) and total bases (308) and ties for the lead in doubles (45) and triples (19).

• For the second time, Dodger Sandy Koufax is a unanimous choice for the Cy Young Award, as he Ks 382 to set a new ML record. Koufax tops the majors with 26 wins, .765 winning percentage, 336 innings, 27 CGs, and a 2.04 ERA. He pitches a perfect game and the fourth no-hitter in four years, beating Chicago 1-0 on September 9.

• Majors adopt an annual free-agent (rookie) draft.

• Jim Maloney of the Reds pitches a no-hitter for 10 innings over the Mets on June 14 but loses in 11 innings. Maloney has to go 10 hitless innings to win a no-hitter, 1-0 over Chicago on August 19.

• At 65, Satchel Paige is the oldest to play in an ML game when he hurls three scoreless innings for KC vs. Boston on September 25.

• The first indoor stadium, the Astrodome, opens on April 9—Houston vs. Yankees in an exhibition game.

• The Mets lose 112 games for a four-year ML record of 452 losses.

Sam McDowell

• Bert Campaneris plays all nine positions for the A's on September 8.

• Spike Eckert replaces Ford Frick as baseball's commissioner.

• Ted Abernathy's 31 saves for the Cubs set a new ML record.

• Oliva again leads the AL in batting (.321) and also leads in hits (185) and runs produced (189).

• Boston's Carl Yastrzemski tops the AL in OBP (.398) and SA (.536) and ties for the lead in doubles (45).

• Boston's Tony Conigliaro leads the AL with 32 homers, and at 20 is the youngest ever to win a league homer crown.

• Cleveland's Sam McDowell leads the AL in ERA (2.18) and sets a new AL southpaw record for Ks (325).

• LA manager Walter Alston wins an NL-record fourth World Series.

WILLIE MAYS

Giants superstar launches 52 homers—17 in August

In the 10 years following his MVP season of 1954, Willie Mays had solidified himself as one of baseball's most exciting and devastating performers. The swift, elegant center fielder won eight consecutive Gold Gloves with the Giants after the award was established in 1957, and he averaged a .315 batting mark with 39 home runs, 109 RBI, and 118 runs a season over the decade—topping the National League in homers once, slugging three times, and in stolen bases four seasons in a row. He led the Giants to within one run of the '62 world championship four years after moving with the club from New York to San Francisco, but it wasn't until 1965 (his last dominating season) that Mays was able to capture his second MVP trophy.

Perhaps the most complete offensive player the game has ever seen—his 1957 season included 26 doubles, 20 triples, 35 homers, and 38 steals—the charismatic Mays was so outstanding his achievements were often taken for granted. He would eventually hit 20 or more homers for 15 straight seasons, score 100 or more runs 12 years in a row, and win a dozen consecutive Gold Gloves. These things came to be expected of him. Beloved by the New York fans who had watched him develop into a superstar, Mays was never accorded the same warmth from the fans in San Francisco who favored their own home-grown talent such as Orlando Cepeda and Willie McCovey.

Still, it was hard not to like what Mays did for the ballclub. After belting 47 homers to top the NL in 1964, he came back with a career-high 52 the following year as the Giants chased the Dodgers all summer for the pennant. He had a home run and great backhanded catch in the All-Star Game, then stroked a then-record 17 homers in August and keyed a 14-game winning streak during the September championship drive. The Giants finished two games short in the end, but Mays topped the majors in homers, slugging (.645), total bases (360), and on-base percentage (.399) while finishing among the NL leaders with 118 runs (second), 112 RBI (third), and a .317 batting average (third).

The season increased speculation that the 34-year-old Mays would break Babe Ruth's all-time record of 714 home runs—he had 505 following the year—but after he hit 37 more homers in '66, Willie began to wear down. He never hit 30 homers or drove in 100 runs again and was passed in the Ruth chase by eventual champion Henry Aaron. Mays wound up safely in third place with 660 dingers alongside his 3,283 hits (10th), 1,903 RBI (eighth), and 2,062 runs (sixth). The Hall of Famer ended his career where it began, in New York with the Mets. While millions of fans remember watching an old and out-of-shape performer stumble his way through the 1973 World Series, few recall his last major-league hit—a 12th-inning single that won the second game.

BALTIMORE ACES SMEAR THE DODGERS

Interleague trades were still rare in the early 1960s, as most teams proceeded cautiously before utilizing a recently legislated rule that permitted them. Even more rare were deals that involved former MVP winners who were still in their prime.

The Cincinnati Reds flaunted both traditions when they swapped Frank Robinson to the Baltimore Orioles after the 1965 season, and their departure from custom made Hank Bauer's Orioles an immediate pennant winner and Reds general manager Bill DeWitt a target of Cincinnati fans for years afterward.

The Orioles' ascension to their first pennant since moving from St. Louis to Baltimore—only the second in the franchise's 66-year history—coincided with the New York Yankees' descent to last place. How, in the short space of two years, the club had managed to sink from the penthouse to the basement was a question that perplexed observers at the time. How, with basically the same lineup the Yankees had fielded in 1964 save for shortstop Tony Kubek, could it have happened? Manager Johnny Keane, who was fired when the team got off to a dismal start in 1966, shouldered most of the blame, but after Ralph Houk stepped down from his general manager's post and took the reins again, the team only continued its downward spiral.

For where the real blame should be placed, one has to go back to the late 1950s when the Yankees brass stubbornly refused to recruit African-American and Latino players long after most of the other teams had realized it was essential in order to remain competitive. By 1966, the Yankees had several African-American and Latino players, but only Roy White and Horace Clarke were still on the uphill side of their careers. It was too little, too late.

The Boston Red Sox, in some ways even more reactionary than the Yankees in their recruitment of African-American and Latino talent, escaped the cellar by only half a game in 1966, a feat that in the long view would be nearly as significant as the Yankees' first basement finish in 54 years. Yet both teams came in only 26 and 26½ games, respectively, behind the first-place Orioles, creating one of the most closely balanced AL seasons in recent years.

Baltimore manager Hank Bauer, left, wraps his arms around Game 4 winner Dave McNally, who shut out the Dodgers to complete the Orioles' sweep of the 1966 Series.

The high leg kick was a trademark of San Francisco hurler Juan Marichal (left), who won 25 games in 1966. Cub Ron Santo (right) hit .312 with 30 homers and 94 RBI in '66 but saw his streak of 364 consecutive games played at third come to an end.

Unfortunately, though, the balance did not extend to the top, where Baltimore stood 9 games up on second-place Minnesota. With first baseman Boog Powell and the Robinsons—Frank and Brooks—supplying the fireworks, the Orioles paced the AL in most of the important offensive departments and by so substantial an amount that it shielded the team's shaky mound corps. Between arm and shoulder ailments and general inconsistency, Bauer was unable to establish a regular pitching rotation. The Orioles had as their fulcrum 20-year-old Jim Palmer with just 15 wins. From their other hurlers, only Dave McNally worked enough innings to qualify for the ERA crown.

The exact opposite of the Orioles were the NL repeat champion Los Angeles Dodgers. Beginning with Triple Crown winner Sandy Koufax—27 wins, 317 strikeouts, and a 1.73 ERA—manager Walter Alston's club had four hurlers who worked over 200 innings, plus Phil "The Vulture" Regan and Ron Perranoski anchoring the bullpen. Both the San Francisco Giants and the Pittsburgh Pirates had far better everyday lineups than the Dodgers, but neither could approach Alston's pitching. Accordingly, the Giants finished in the runner-up slot for the second year in a row.

A length and a half back of San Francisco was Pittsburgh, with arguably the best all-around offensive club in the 1960s. Leading skipper Harry Walker's blistering attack was an all-.300-hitting outfield of Roberto Clemente, Matty Alou, and Willie Stargell. Not far behind Walker's wrecking crew in 1966 were the Braves, who smoked an ML-best 207 homers and 782 runs in their first season in Atlanta. The Braves were seen as the closest NL team to the Orioles—stocked with an outstanding first baseman (Felipe Alou), right fielder (Hank Aaron), and third baseman (Eddie Mathews) but questionable pitchers.

Since a suspect pitching staff matched against a formidable pitching staff is a virtual guarantee of a short World Series, many came out to the first two games at Dodger Stadium thinking it would be their only chance to see the combatants. They were right. Once the action moved to Baltimore it never returned to Los Angeles.

However, everyone in the country had been wrong about which team had the edge in pitching.

Despite a 27-win, 317-strikeout year, Dodger ace Sandy Koufax (right) retired after the season because of elbow problems. Atlanta's Felipe Alou (left) was second in the NL with a .327 batting average, topped by his brother Matty of Pittsburgh (.342).

In a fashion even more spectacular than that of the 1905 Giants, a quartet of Orioles hurlers buried the Dodgers hitters. Held to a .142 BA, Los Angeles scored just two runs in the four-game Baltimore sweep and none after the third inning of Game 1. After tabulating just one shutout among them all season, Palmer, McNally, and Wally Bunker posted three in a row in the Series.

SEASON'S BEST

- Baltimore's Frank Robinson is named AL MVP after winning the Triple Crown (.316, 49, 122). Robinson also leads the AL in runs (122), total bases (367), runs produced (195), OBP (.415), and SA (.637).

- Pittsburgh's Roberto Clemente is NL MVP.

- An arthritic elbow forces Sandy Koufax to retire after the season. In his final season, Koufax tops the majors with 27 wins, 27 CGs, 317 Ks, and 323 innings. He also tops the NL in ERA an all-time record fifth consecutive time with a 1.73 mark. Koufax wins his third unanimous Cy Young Award in the last four years.

- Prior to the season, Koufax and Don Drysdale stage the first dual holdout by teammates in ML history.

- The Yankees tumble into the cellar for the first time since 1912.

- Marvin Miller is elected president of the Major League Baseball Players Association.

- Pitcher Tony Cloninger of the Braves hits two grand slams in a game on July 3.

- The Braves move to Atlanta. The first game in Dixie is on April 12 at Fulton County Stadium, Pirates vs. Braves.

- Pittsburgh's Matty Alou leads the NL in BA (.342); brother Felipe Alou of Atlanta is second (.327). Felipe leads the NL in runs (122) and total bases (355) and tops the majors in hits (218).

Hank Aaron

- Minnesota's Tony Oliva tops the AL in hits in each of his first three seasons in majors, as he collects 191 in '66.

- Cards rookie Larry Jaster ties for the NL lead in shutouts with five, all against the Dodgers.

- First game in Anaheim Stadium is on April 19, White Sox vs. Angels.

- First game in Busch Stadium is on May 12, Braves vs. Cards.

- Jack Aker's 32 saves for KC set a new ML record.

- The Braves' Hank Aaron paces the NL in homers (44) and majors in RBI (127) and runs produced (200).

- The Giants' Juan Marichal wins 25 and tops the majors in winning percentage (.806).

- The AL has only two hitters above .288—Robinson (.316) and Oliva (.307).

- Jim Kaat leads the AL with 25 wins, 305 innings, and 19 CGs.

FRANK ROBINSON

Reds castoff wins Triple Crown, stars in Series

The Baltimore Orioles were on the verge of overtaking the Yankees in the American League during the early 1960s, but although the youthful Birds had several All-Star performers such as Brooks Robinson and Luis Aparicio, they lacked a hitter who could strike fear into opposing teams each time he came to bat. The Cincinnati Reds had such a player in right fielder Frank Robinson. When Cincinnati general manager Bill DeWitt decided his superstar was "an old 30" and traded him to Baltimore, he gave the Orioles just what they needed to go over the top in '66—an MVP and Triple Crown winner.

The roots of one of the worst trades in baseball history began far before Robinson was shipped to Baltimore for pitcher Milt Pappas and two throw-ins on December 9, 1965. Robinson signed with the Reds as an 18-year-old in 1953, and after two solid minor-league campaigns, burst on the National League with a vengeance in '56. His Rookie-of-the-Year season included 38 homers (then a record for first-year players) and a league-leading 122 runs, and he followed it up with four similar seasons through 1960 while becoming a Gold Glove outfielder.

Beginning in 1961 the quiet, hard-sliding plate-crowder took his game to another level, leading the Reds to the NL pennant with an MVP year that included 37 homers, a .323 batting average, 22 stolen bases, and a league-high .611 slugging percentage. He showed no signs of slowing down through 1965 (when he hit .296 with 33 homers and 113 RBI), but DeWitt felt he was on the downslide. Attendance in Cincinnati tumbled following the trade, and "Old Man" Robinson immediately stepped in as leader of his new club.

Homering in the season opener at Baltimore's Memorial Stadium, he became the first player to hit a ball completely out of the park nine games later and went on to the best offensive season in Orioles history. In addition to his Triple Crown numbers— a .316 batting average, 49 homers, and 122 RBI— Robinson paced the league in runs (122), total bases (367), slugging (.637), and on-base percentage (.415) while finishing second in hits (182) and third in doubles (34). He added a triple and two homers in a World Series sweep of the Dodgers, and for his efforts was unanimously named the AL MVP, making him the first player to win the award in both leagues.

Despite nagging injuries, Robinson hit an additional 130 homers for the Orioles the next five years, helping them to three more pennants and a second world championship from 1969 through '71. He then wound down his career with the Dodgers and Angels. When he was named player-manager of the Indians in 1975, Frank became the first African-American ever to get a managerial post. His 586 homers and 1,829 runs still rank fourth and 11th, respectively, on the all-time lists.

GIBSON, BROCK STUFF THE SOX

Never in its 67-year history had the AL seen a team vault from the basement to a pennant the following season, but the 1966-67 Boston Red Sox came within a hairsbreadth of being the first to do it. After avoiding the AL cellar by a mere half game in 1966, the Red Sox snatched their first flag since 1946 on the last day of the 1967 campaign. Their remarkable climb from oblivion was superseded, though, by the even more remarkable manner in which they won.

In 1967, the AL staged the greatest pennant race in big-league history. Entering the final week, no fewer than four teams still were vying for the right to face the runaway NL champion St. Louis Cardinals. Cast in the mold of their manager, Eddie Stanky, the Chicago White Sox had a .225 team BA, but stayed in the fight on pitching, defense, and tenacity. The Detroit Tigers were a veteran team and had a history of winning when they hung close into the homestretch. The youngest team in the majors, the Red Sox, and their rookie pilot Dick Williams were the nation's darlings. However, Tony Conigliaro, their top slugger, had gone down for the year after being beaned, and their catching was in the hands of 38-year-old Elston Howard, who was only hitting .147. Besides, Boston faced a season-closing series with Minnesota, the team with the best balance of hitting and pitching among the four contenders.

Chicago bowed out of the race by losing a doubleheader to last-place Kansas City on September 27. Detroit got a bad break when rain forced the Tigers to play back-to-back doubleheaders with the California Angels on the last two days of the season. Meanwhile, Minnesota came to Boston's Fenway Park on the final weekend with a one-game lead on both the Red Sox and the Tigers.

On Saturday, on the verge of elimination, the Red Sox rallied against Twin relievers after Jim Kaat was forced to leave with an injury and won, 6-4. The Tigers, with a chance to take the lead on percentage points, instead ended the day half a game back of the Red Sox and the Twins when they split a pair with the Angels. On Sunday, Jim Lonborg, shooting for his 22nd win of the season, topped Dean

Series heroes, from left: Lou Brock, with a Series-record seven stolen bases; Julian Javier, with a three-run HR in Game 7; and Bob Gibson, who won three games.

Pittsburgh's Roberto Clemente (top left) *led NL outfielders in assists for the fifth straight year. Minnesota's Harmon Killebrew* (top center) *tied for the AL lead with 44 HRs. Detroit's Al Kaline* (top right) *won his 10th, and last, Gold Glove. Atlanta's Hank Aaron* (bottom) *won his last NL HR title with 39.*

Chance, who was trying for his 21st, to put Boston in first place and eliminate Minnesota. Detroit, though, was still very much alive. When the Tigers won the first game of their Sunday twinbill with the Angels, they remained only half a length back of Boston.

Knowing a Detroit victory in the second game would end the season in a tie, fans in most parts of the country thanked their local TV stations for bringing the contest to them on the small screen. Hours after their Red Sox had beaten the Twins that afternoon, Bostoners began the celebration in earnest when the Angels beat the Tigers, 8-5.

With it a foregone conclusion that Carl Yastrzemski would win the AL MVP Award and Or-lando Cepeda nearly as certain to win the NL's top honor, the World Series promised to match the game's two finest players in 1967. While Yastrzemski did his part in the fall affair, batting .400 and leading all participants with three home runs and 21 total bases, Cepeda had a dismal nine days and hit just .103. More than picking up the slack for the Cardinals, though, was Lou Brock.

Although one of the Cards' leaders during the regular season as Red Schoendienst's club rollicked home 10½ games ahead of second-place San Francisco, Brock had achieved little national recognition prior to the 1967 Series. After he led all participants with a .414 BA on 12 hits and collected a record seven stolen bases, he was known to fans everywhere.

Notwithstanding his dazzling offensive show, Brock still had to take a backseat to teammate Bob Gibson and Red Sox right-hander Lonborg. With Gibson and Lonborg both winning twice, the Cardinals and the Red Sox split the first six games of the Series. Game 7 then offered the most delectable mound matchup in a Series finale since the 1925 clash between Washington's Walter Johnson and Pittsburgh's Vic Aldridge. Just as Johnson and Aldridge, Gibson and Lonborg were both 2-0 thus far and vying to enter the elite circle of hurlers who had won three games in a Series. The winner would certainly have much to celebrate.

Lonborg was working on just two days rest while Gibson had enjoyed three. The difference helped Gibson to prevail when the Cards tagged Lonborg for seven runs by the sixth inning. After exiting for a reliever, Lonborg could only watch in frustration as Gibson held the Red Sox to just three hits and blazed to his third Series win, 7-2.

SEASON'S BEST

•Boston's Carl Yastrzemski is the near-unanimous AL MVP after winning the Triple Crown (.326, 44, 121). Yaz also leads the AL in runs (112), hits (189), total bases (360), runs produced (189), OBP (.421), and SA (.622).

•St. Louis's Orlando Cepeda wins the NL MVP Award.

•Tom Seaver wins a club-record 16 games for the Mets and is NL Rookie of the Year.

•Boston's Tony Conigliaro is beaned by Angel Jack Hamilton; his vision is impaired and he's out of the game until 1969.

•The Red Sox jump from ninth place in 1966 to first in '67—the first team to do so in this century.

•Two Cy Young Awards are given for the first time. Boston's Jim Lonborg is an easy winner in the AL. San Francisco's Mike McCormick wins the NL Cy Young and leads the loop with 22 wins.

•The NL wins the longest game in All-Star history, 2-1 in 15 innings at Anaheim, as Red Tony Perez homers to win it.

•Al Kaline wins the last of his 10 Gold Gloves as an AL outfielder.

•Yankee Mickey Mantle hits his 500th homer on May 13.

•The Mets trade Bill Denehy and $100,000 to Washington in order to obtain Gil Hodges as their manager.

•On April 30, Orioles Steve Barber and Stu Miller lose a combined no-hitter to Detroit, 2-1 in nine innings.

•Whitey Ford retires with a .690 career winning percentage, best this century among 200-game winners.

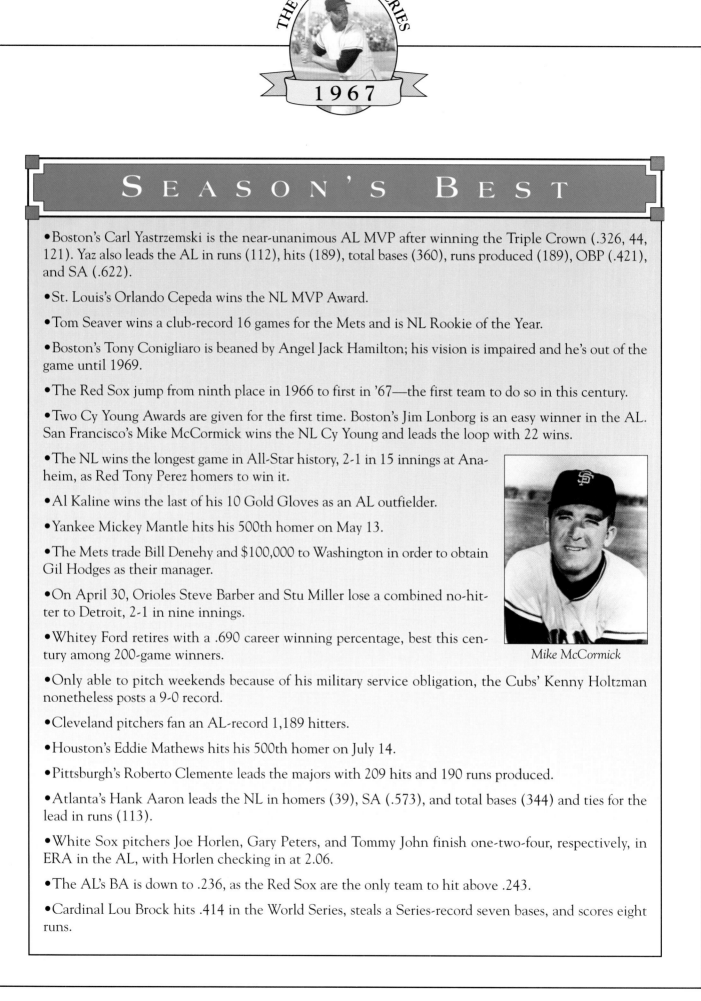

Mike McCormick

•Only able to pitch weekends because of his military service obligation, the Cubs' Kenny Holtzman nonetheless posts a 9-0 record.

•Cleveland pitchers fan an AL-record 1,189 hitters.

•Houston's Eddie Mathews hits his 500th homer on July 14.

•Pittsburgh's Roberto Clemente leads the majors with 209 hits and 190 runs produced.

•Atlanta's Hank Aaron leads the NL in homers (39), SA (.573), and total bases (344) and ties for the lead in runs (113).

•White Sox pitchers Joe Horlen, Gary Peters, and Tommy John finish one-two-four, respectively, in ERA in the AL, with Horlen checking in at 2.06.

•The AL's BA is down to .236, as the Red Sox are the only team to hit above .243.

•Cardinal Lou Brock hits .414 in the World Series, steals a Series-record seven bases, and scores eight runs.

CARL YASTRZEMSKI

Triple Crown winner bats .523 down the stretch

His manager called him "the perfect player," and anybody who saw the Red Sox perform during the '67 season would have a hard time disagreeing. American League MVP and Triple Crown winner Carl Yastrzemski helped the Crimson Hose win ballgames so often and in so many different ways that summer, he was able not only to finally shed the burden of replacing Ted Williams in the Boston outfield, but also to take a long shot that had finished ninth the previous year to within one game of the world championship.

His coming of age was more astounding than anybody had imagined, but big things had always been expected of Yastrzemski. The 21-year-old son of a Long Island potato farmer came to Boston in 1961 as a rookie left fielder—a spot occupied most of the previous two decades by just-retired Ted Williams. The comparisons between the two left-handed batters began. Yaz was the American League batting (.321) champ by '63 and had several fine seasons, but a six-year high of 20 homers wasn't enough for fans expecting another Ted. A weak supporting cast kept Yastrzemski's teams in the second division, and the young star was blamed as the prima donna force behind several managerial changes.

When Dick Williams was brought in as manager following a 72-90 season in 1966, few gave much hope beyond the long 100-1 Vegas odds of Boston coming out on top. A seemingly confident Williams predicted "we'll win more than we lose" in spring training, and with Yaz leading the way the Red Sox soon found themselves in the midst of the wildest pennant race in AL history. Four teams spent the summer often separated by two or three games, and through it all, Carl was forever making the clutch hit, catch, or baserunning play to key Boston victories. As the games grew in importance, he just got better. For the last 12 games of the season, he batted .523 with five home runs and 14 RBI. He also went 7-for-8 with five runs knocked in the final two days against Minnesota—when the Red Sox had to win twice to claim the pennant.

When it was all over, Yaz had claimed a Gold Glove and led the league with career highs in nearly every statistical category—including batting (.326), homers (44—tied with Harmon Killebrew), RBI (121), runs (112), hits (189), total bases (360), slugging (.622), and on-base percentage (.421). He added a .400 mark and three homers as the "Impossible Dream" ended with a seven-game World Series loss to St. Louis, and was one vote shy of being a unanimous MVP.

Although Carl never came close to duplicating his '67 heroics, 16 solid seasons highlighted by another batting title and pennant followed. Seven Gold Gloves, 3,419 hits (seventh all-time), 1,844 RBI (11th), and 452 home runs in a 23-year career earned him a spot in the Hall of Fame, but as the first ALer with 3,000 hits and 400 homers, the lefty from Long Island would always be remembered by New Englanders for "The Year of the Yaz."

LOLICH, TIGERS FLOOD ST. LOUIS

Most managers who have a third baseman hit .200 and a pair of shortstops hit a combined .145 find themselves unemployed at the end of the season. Detroit Tigers skipper Mayo Smith found himself headed for the World Series in 1968 with Don Wert (.200) at third base and Ray Oyler (.135) and Dick Tracewski (.156) platooning at shortstop. So skewed were things that year in both major leagues that the Tigers' triumph despite such anemic production from the left side of their infield did not even arouse much comment.

In 1968, the once-mighty but now very ordinary New York Yankees hit .214—yet finished in the first division. The Chicago White Sox carved a 2.75 staff ERA and allowed just 3.25 runs a game but finished 28 games below .500 because their hitters could only produce 2.86 runs a game. Though their hurlers fanned an AL-record 1,157 and were second in the majors with a 2.66 ERA, the Cleveland Indians finished only 11 games above .500 when Tony Horton (with a .249 BA) was the team's top batting title qualifier, leading the club with 14 homers and 59 RBI. In the AL basement were the Washington Senators, featuring slugger Frank Howard who socked 44 homers, the most in the majors, but tallied a mere 79 runs.

In the NL, conditions were somewhat more normal. They were so normal that Bob Gibson, while pitching on a pennant winner and allowing only slightly more than one earned run in every full game he hurled, nevertheless managed somehow to lose nine games. Ray Sadecki went 12-18 for a second-place team despite notching a 2.91 ERA.

That second-place team was the San Francisco Giants, who may have been alone in having a normal season that year. In 1968, the Giants finished second in the NL for the fourth straight time. If it seemed to Giants fans that their team was in a rut, New York Mets fans had no sympathy for them. For the Mets, 1969 marked their seventh year of existence—and they had never finished higher than ninth. The single positive omen for them was that lefty Jerry Koosman had nearly become the club's first 20-game winner in his frosh season before settling for 19. Between them, Koosman

Denny McLain was the ace, but Mickey Lolich was Detroit's Series hero. Lolich, third from left, is congratulated after a Series win by catcher Bill Freehan, far right.

Year of the Pitcher. For nearly a decade it had been in the making. Roger Maris's record-breaking 61 homers had been the final hinge on the door that restrained batters from ignoring everything they had learned about hitting in order to swing for the fences. In 1958, Harry Anderson had led the NL with 95 strikeouts. Never again would a major-league leader have fewer than 100 strikeouts, and by 1968 there were few teams that did not have at least one player who fanned in triple digits.

The Cards and the Tigers were not among the teams that escaped the strikeout deluge in 1968. Lou Brock, while leading the NL again in steals, whiffed 124 times and third sacker Mike Shannon K'd on 114 occasions. For the Tigers, Willie Horton racked up 110 Ks and Dick McAuliffe, with 99, just missed the 100 club. With Gibson matched against Detroit's 31-game winner Denny McLain, the Series shaped up as a reprise of the 1966 affair. It was just a question of which team would hold the other scoreless while managing an occasional solo homer.

When Gibson drubbed McLain in the opener, 4-0, with a record 17 whiffs, the question seemed answered. Things were not to be so clear-cut, though. In Game 2, the Tigers unleashed a 13-hit assault to win 8-1, and in the next contest it was the Cardinals' day to mount 13 hits in a 7-3 victory.

Another 13-hit St. Louis barrage in Game 4 brought Gibson his fifth Series win in two years and put the Tigers down 3-1 in games. Even though Mickey Lolich won the finale in the Motor City, Detroit gained little in confidence because McLain, who had been badly mauled twice by the Cards, was slated to go in Game 6.

McLain, however, joined Gibson and Lolich as the only hurlers in the Series who seemed to remember it was the Year of the Pitcher when he won, 13-1. McLain's victory knotted the count at 3-all and for the second year in a row orchestrated a Series confrontation between two pitchers—Gibson and Lolich—who were both 2-0. Gibson started

With a 22-9 record and 1.12 ERA, St. Louis's Bob Gibson (top left) claimed both the NL MVP and Cy Young honors. Baltimore's Dave McNally (top right) had 18 complete games on his way to a 22-win season. Cardinal Lou Brock (bottom left) swiped 62 bases. Cleveland's Luis Tiant (bottom right), who later played for Boston, struck out 19 batters in a 10-inning game.

and Tom Seaver, the 1967 NL Rookie of the Year, clicked for 35 wins and just 24 losses, not bad on a team that finished just one game out of the cellar.

It was that kind of season from top to bottom. As 1930 was the Year of the Hitter, 1968 was the

Game 7 as if he would be untouchable, but Lolich looked equally unbeatable through the first six innings. In the seventh with two Tigers on base, Jim Northrup ripped a ball to deep center that Curt Flood misjudged and played into a two-run triple. It was all Lolich needed to lift the Tigers to the title and become the first AL southpaw to win three games in a Series.

SEASON'S BEST

•St. Louis's Bob Gibson posts a 1.12 ERA, lowest in the ML since 1914, and is named the NL's MVP and Cy Young winner. He also has 13 shutouts, most in ML since 1916. Gibson sets a World Series record on October 2 when he fans 17 Tigers.

•Detroit's Denny McLain, first 30-game winner in ML since 1934, cops both the AL MVP and Cy Young honors by racking up 31 wins.

•The A's move to Oakland and top the AL with a .240 BA, lowest in ML history by a loop leader.

•Houston beats the Mets 1-0 in 24 innings on April 15—longest 1-0 game in ML history.

•LA's Don Drysdale sets a new ML record when he pitches 58 consecutive scoreless innings.

•Boston's Carl Yastrzemski wins the AL bat crown with a .301 BA, lowest in ML history to lead a league.

•The Yankees set a post-dead-ball era record for lowest team batting average when they hit just .214.

•NL wins the first indoor All-Star Game 1-0 at Houston, as the winning run scores on a double-play grounder. The Giants' Willie Mays becomes the first player to win two All-Star MVP Awards.

•Luis Tiant Ks 19 batters for Cleveland in a 10-inning game on July 3.

•The Player Relations Committee and the Players Association hammer out their first "Basic Agreement."

•Cesar Tovar plays all nine positions for the Twins on September 22.

•Giant Jim Davenport's ML-record streak of 97 consecutive errorless games at third base ends.

•Atlanta's Hank Aaron hits his 500th homer on July 14.

•On July 29, Washington's Ron Hansen performs an unassisted triple play vs. Cleveland.

Frank Howard

•On May 8, Catfish Hunter of the A's pitches a perfect game vs. the Twins and collects three hits and four RBI in his own cause.

•Washington's Frank Howard tops the majors with 44 homers, 330 total bases, and a .552 SA.

•San Francisco's Willie McCovey leads the NL in homers (36), RBI (105), and SA (.545).

•The Giants' Juan Marichal tops the NL in wins (26), CGs (30), and innings (326).

•Lou Brock of St. Louis tops all World Series batters with a .464 BA and a record-tying seven steals.

DENNY MCLAIN

Tigers ace is the first since Dizzy to win 30

The 1968 season will always be known as "The Year of the Pitcher." It was a year in which one hurler (Bob Gibson) produced a microscopic earned run average of 1.12, another (Don Drysdale) set a record with 58 consecutive scoreless innings, and a third won 30 games for the first time in 34 years (Denny McLain). It was also a season in which an American League batting title was won with an average just over .300 (.301 by Carl Yastrzemski).

When the confident and colorful Dizzy Dean won 30 games for the St. Louis Cardinals in 1934, four of those were in relief (as were four of the 31 Lefty Grove won three years earlier). When the confident and colorful 24-year-old McLain won 31 in leading the Detroit Tigers to a pennant, all the victories came as a starter.

Ironically, the Tigers tried to trade him when he went 17-16 in 1967, after posting a 20-win season in '66. It was one of those proverbial "the best trades are the ones not made" scenarios. Although McLain went 0-2 in his first two starts, he had won his 15th game by July 3. Pitching every fourth day, McLain notched his 20th victory on July 27, becoming the first pitcher to win 20 by August 1 since Grove. Overall, the hard-throwing right-hander won 23 of his next 26 decisions.

McLain's unusual success in 1968 was twofold. He added a slider to his sidearm fastball and curve, making him especially tough on right-handed hitters. He also had terrific offensive support. With a lineup of such hitters as Al Kaline, Norm Cash, Willie Horton, and Bill Freehan, the Tigers led the league in runs, totaling 57 more than any other team.

McLain went for win 30 in the September 14 game against Oakland. Although Dizzy Dean was in the stands and the game was nationally televised, McLain didn't seem up to the task. Going into the bottom of the ninth, two Reggie Jackson homers had put the A's up 4-3. The Tigers, however, were not surrendering. Kaline, pinch-hitting for McLain, walked. Next, Mickey Stanley singled, putting the winning run on. An infield error tied the game, and Horton won it with a blast to left field.

McLain won his next start for number 31, staking his claim in the process for the Cy Young and MVP Awards. He ended the season by leading the AL with 28 complete games, 336 innings pitched, and a .838 winning percentage. He was in the top five in the league with a 1.96 ERA and 280 strikeouts.

Denny followed that sterling season with a 24-9 year and another Cy Young honor. Unfortunately, he lost 21 games in 1971 and was out of baseball at age 28 in 1972.

MIRACLE METS SHOCK THE WORLD

By 1969, the Chicago Cubs, the game's winningest team prior to 1920, had gone 24 years without a pennant. For some time now the franchise and its owner, P.K. Wrigley, had become almost a joke. Wrigley's refusal to put lights in his park made his club seem anachronistic, and his experiment with rotating managers or "coaches" in the early 1960s had given it a carnival atmosphere when a different ringmaster appeared every other week to lead the team. Even Leo Durocher, named manager in 1966, seemed overwhelmed by the task when he brought the Cubs home last in his first season despite having the services of such stars as Ernie Banks, Billy Williams, Ron Santo, Fergie Jenkins, and Ken Holtzman.

The addition of two new expansion teams in each league in 1969 forced both circuits to split into two divisions. The split would put the Los Angeles Dodgers, San Francisco Giants, and Cincinnati Reds in the NL West. This move seemingly left the Cubs alone to challenge the St. Louis Cardinals for supremacy in the NL East.

When Red Schoendienst's Cards experienced a collective batting slump, Durocher shot his Cubs into first place by 9½ games in early August. Suddenly, the New York Mets, after being the game's laughingstock for eight years, caught fire and rocketed to within two games of the Cubs on September 8 when Chicago came to Shea Stadium for a two-game series. A sweep of the series moved the Mets into first place on September 10, and they continued to win until they had left the Cubs eight games behind them at the season's end.

Mets manager Gil Hodges was called a miracle worker, but there was a logical explanation for his club's triumph. The expansion draft to stock the four new teams had saddled the other contenders with at least one glaring weakness while leaving the Mets relatively unscathed. A ninth-place team in 1968 with few position players the expansion Montreal Expos and San Diego Padres wanted, the Mets consequently were able to focus their concentration on protecting their corps of fine young pitchers from the draft. During the summer of 1969, while the older hill staffs in the NL were tiring, the youthful Mets grew stronger. Yet the deciding issue was not pitching but center field play. A rejuvenated Tommy

The Mets, who won 38 of their last 49 to win the NL East, completed their amazing season by stunning the heavily favored Orioles in five Series games.

Paul Blair's suicide squeeze in the 12th inning (top left) *won the AL flag for the Orioles. Hank Aaron* (top center) *slugged 44 homers while Reggie Jackson* (top right) *of the A's had a career-high 47. The Twins' Harmon Killebrew* (bottom left) *was AL MVP; Giant Willie McCovey* (bottom right) *won the NL award.*

Agee gave the Mets their first quality center fielder, while the Cubs entered the homestretch with no one better than Don Young, a .239 hitter whose erratic fielding cost them a game against the Mets that Durocher claimed was his club's ruin.

The Atlanta Braves team that faced the Mets in the first best-of-five NL championship series had only Hank Aaron remaining from the club that had ended the last decade with a pennant playoff loss to the Dodgers. In their second season under Lum Harris, the Braves had slipped home ahead of the Giants and the Reds by wringing one last good season out of aging veterans like Orlando Cepeda and Tony Gonzalez after acquiring them in trades. Cepeda, Aaron, and Gonzalez hit a combined .385 against Mets pitching in the LCS, but the Braves got such dismal pitching that the Mets tallied 27 runs in a three-game sweep.

The air was expected to go out of the Mets' balloon quickly in the World Series. Confronting them were the Baltimore Orioles, who had won 109 games to tie the 1961 Yankees' major-league record for the most victories since expansion. Piloted by Earl Weaver, a former minor-league second sacker, the Orioles had needed only three games in the AL Championship Series to wipe out the Minnesota Twins, led by former major-league second sacker Billy Martin. A brilliant but volatile manager, Mar-

tin injured Twins' 20-game winner Dave Boswell in a scuffle and was subsequently fired by owner Calvin Griffith.

Hodges and his Mets were expected to depart less bellicosely but just as rapidly as the Twins. In the Series opener, 23-game winner Mike Cuellar had little difficulty putting away the Mets' 25-game winner Tom Seaver, 4-1. The following day, however, Jerry Koosman carried a no-hitter into the seventh inning and ultimately beat Dave McNally, 2-1, when the Mets put together three singles to score the go-ahead run in the top of the ninth.

After the Series moved to New York, Hodges was made to look like a magician when every one of his moves worked. An ardent believer in platooning, Hodges played Donn Clendenon at first base against lefties and Ed Kranepool against right-handers. Since both Cuellar and McNally were southpaws and opened for the Orioles in four of the five Series games, Clendenon got four starts, and he made the most of them, leading all hitters in homers and RBI. As for Kranepool, he homered in his only start, and another platoon player, Al Weis, was the Series' top batter at .455 after hitting just .215 during the season.

With everything Hodges touched turning to gold, the Mets needed only five games to crown the most improbable championship season ever.

THE RACES/THE SERIES
1969

SEASON'S BEST

•The AL and NL both expand to 12 teams and divide into two divisions, with division winners to play best-of-five playoffs. The four new teams are the San Diego Padres and Montreal Expos (NL) and Kansas City Royals and Seattle Pilots (AL).

•On April 14 in the first ML game played outside of the United States, Montreal beats the Cards 8-7 at Jarry Park.

•Bowie Kuhn is the new commissioner, replacing Spike Eckert.

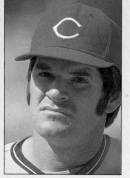

Pete Rose

•To add more offense, rules are made to reduce the height of the pitcher's mound and the size of the strike zone. The NL's BA jumps seven points; the AL's 16.

•The Twins' Harmon Killebrew leads the majors with 49 homers and 140 RBI and is AL MVP.

•The Giants' Willie McCovey is named NL MVP after leading the league in homers (45), RBI (126), SA (.656), and OBP (.458). McCovey receives an ML-record 45 intentional walks.

•By bunting his way on base in his last at bat of the season, Pete Rose of the Reds breaks a tie with Roberto Clemente and wins the NL batting title.

•The Mets' Tom Seaver tops the majors with 25 wins and cops the Cy Young Award.

•Detroit's Denny McLain leads the AL with nine shutouts and 24 wins. McLain and Baltimore's Mike Cuellar share the AL's Cy Young Award.

•Minnesota's Rod Carew steals home seven times to tie the ML season record.

•Baltimore's Dave McNally sets a franchise record by winning 15 games in a row.

•Ted Williams is hired as Washington's manager; the team finishes over .500 for the first time in its nine-year history.

•The Curt Flood case begins vs. organized baseball after Flood is traded to the Phils by the Cards and refuses to report to his new team.

•Twins manager Billy Martin beats up one of his own pitchers, Dave Boswell.

•LA's Willie Davis hits in 31 consecutive games.

•Houston hurlers fan an ML-record 1,221 hitters.

•Wayne Granger of the Reds is the first pitcher to appear in 90 games.

•Bobby Bonds of the Giants fans 187 times, setting an ML record.

•Jim Maloney of Cincinnati no-hits Houston on April 30; the next day, Houston's Don Wilson no-hits Cincinnati.

•On September 15 vs. the Mets, St. Louis's Steve Carlton strikes out an ML-record 19 batters.

TOM SEAVER

Tom Terrific terrifies foes, fires up Mets

It was the year of the first moon landing and Woodstock, so baseball fans should have known the 1969 season would be a little different. Laughingstocks of the National League since their inception seven years before, the New York Mets were suddenly in a pennant race one year after barely escaping the cellar. By the time October rolled around and the folks at Shea Stadium were through pinching themselves, there was a World Series champion in Flushing Meadow, thanks largely to a 24-year-old right-hander who earned a Cy Young Award for his part in the miracle.

A star immediately upon joining New York after one season in the minors, the handsome 6'1" flamethrower was named 1967 NL Rookie of the Year after going 16-13 with a 2.76 ERA—unheard-of statistics for Mets fans whose team had averaged 109 losses and finished last four of its first five years. The club went 61-101 even with their young phenom. In '68, Seaver went 16-12 to help boost the Mets to an improved 73-89 finish, and the laughing was beginning to stop. The Mets had quietly assembled a hodgepodge of talented players around Seaver (including young pitchers Jerry Koosman and Nolan Ryan), and in '69 they were finally able to achieve the lofty regions of .500 baseball and beyond.

Two victories in three July games with the first-place Cubs at Shea got fans fired up, especially with Seaver sparking one of the wins by finishing two

outs shy of a perfect game and settling for a one-hitter. An August slump dropped New York 9½ games behind Chicago, but then the Mets caught fire. They went 38-10 down the stretch to finish in first at 100-62. The record marked a 27-game improvement from the previous season, and nobody was more responsible than "Tom Terrific." Winning his last 10 games to pace the majors in victories at 25-7, Tom was also tops in the NL in winning percentage (.781), lowest opponent batting average (.207), and fewest hits allowed per nine innings (6.65). His 2.21 ERA (fourth), five shutouts (tied for sixth), 18 complete games (tied for seventh), and 208 strikeouts (10th) also ranked high. He went on to add victories in the NL playoffs and World Series as the Mets completed their miracle. One vote shy of being a unanimous Cy Young choice, he finished a close second to Giants slugger Willie McCovey for MVP honors.

Great seasons and two more Cy Young trophies were to come for Seaver, including another pennant with the Mets in '73 and a third with the Boston Red Sox in his final (1986) year. Four 20-win seasons, nine consecutive years with 200 or more strikeouts and three ERA titles in a four-year span speak of his sustained dominance, and 311 lifetime victories of his longevity. For the millions of Mets fans who watched a miracle unfold, however, none of it compared to '69 when "The Franchise" came of age.

THE 1970s

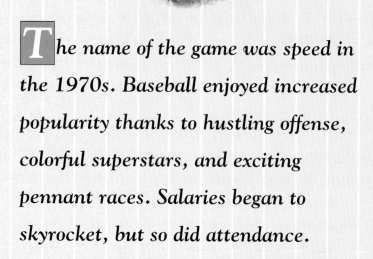

The name of the game was speed in the 1970s. Baseball enjoyed increased popularity thanks to hustling offense, colorful superstars, and exciting pennant races. Salaries began to skyrocket, but so did attendance.

The one consistent factor in baseball during the 1970s was change. New stadiums, new teams, new rules, new uniforms, new attitudes, and new legal decisions—all were making an impact and would have long-lasting repercussions on America's favorite pastime.

Stadium architecture dramatically affected the way the game was played. The new parks built between the years 1965 and 1977 had relatively the same dimensions—330 feet down the foul lines—as opposed to the old stadiums which had varied distances and their own individual personalities. All had artificial turf.

The new stadiums included: Three Rivers Stadium in Pittsburgh (1970), Riverfront Stadium in Cincinnati (1970), Veterans Stadium in Philadelphia (1971), Royals Stadium in Kansas City (1973), Olympic Stadium in Montreal (1977), and the Kingdome in Seattle (1977). Even Yankee Stadium was renovated (1976) and its deep left-center and center field was brought in by about 30 feet. By 1980, only four old parks remained: Tiger Stadium in Detroit, Fenway Park in Boston, and Chicago's Comiskey Park in the American League and Wrigley Field in the National League.

Scores of fans mourned the transformation. They insisted that baseball was meant to be played on grass and complained that going to the park was like being in a shopping mall. While purists did not like artificial turf, fans liked the new game that artificial turf created.

Speed, speed, and more speed was the name of the game on the new synthetic surface. Since balls hit on the "carpet" would pick up speed as they traveled and would bounce extremely high, teams placed a premium on fleet-footed infielders and outfielders who could get a quick jump on the ball. Such skilled singles hitters as Pete Rose, Rod Carew, and Mickey Rivers punched, chopped, and sliced the ball past infielders. Roadrunners Lou Brock, Rickey Henderson, and Willie Wilson changed the way pitchers pitched and the way defenses aligned themselves. Indeed, A's owner Charles O. Finley was so taken with the running game that in 1974 he signed Herb Washington, a world-class sprinter with no baseball experience, as a designated runner.

Oakland's Bert Campaneris (top) was a key contributor in the '70s, and helped give rise to Latin-American players. Bowie Kuhn's reign as commissioner (bottom) was filled with controversy.

Curt Flood (top left) went to court to challenge the reserve clause, opening the door for eventual free agency. *Boston's Carl Yastrzemski (top center)* in 1979 became the first AL player to hit 400 home runs and collect 3,000 hits. *Don Sutton (top right)* kept alive the tradition of Dodger pitching greats. *Manager Danny Murtaugh (bottom)* saw his Pirates beat the Orioles in the first night game in World Series history in 1971.

Baseball in the 1970s aligned itself with changes in the population. In 1972, the Washington Senators left the nation's capital, moved to Dallas-Ft. Worth, and became the Texas Rangers. The granting of American League expansion franchises to Seattle and Toronto in 1977 gave fans in the Northwest and Canada new teams to follow. It also, by in-creasing the number of teams in each division, reduced the number of times intradivision rivals, such as the Yankees and Red Sox, played each other.

From 1969 to 1979 major-league baseball enjoyed a 64-percent rise in attendance. There were several reasons for the dramatic growth in fan interest. The improved accessibility of the new stadiums made it easier for fans to get to the game. The split into two divisions in 1969 increased the number of teams that had a chance to win the pennant. Although the Reds, Pirates, and Phillies dominated the National League during the decade and the A's, Orioles, and Yanks became mini-dynasties in the American League, there were many competitive pennant races. The 1975 World Series, one of the greatest Series in baseball history, showed fans (62 million watched Game 6) how exciting good baseball could still be, wiping out the sentiment shared by many that the game had seen its better days. The decline of the Yankee empire in 1964 made the race for the American League title a legitimate challenge instead of a fight for second place.

Ticket prices were cheap compared to those of rival sports. Baseball had largely become a nighttime event, dished up to the customer in comfy surroundings. Before the game and between innings fans were serenaded by Top-40 tunes and on-field entertainment. (Mascots like San Diego's Chicken began strutting around the field and in the stands.)

Yankee catcher Thurman Munson, the 1970 Rookie of the Year and 1976 AL MVP, was well on his way to a Hall of Fame career when he died in a crash of his private jet in Canton, Ohio, on August 2, 1979.

Electronic scoreboards flashed messages, led cheers and sometimes offered replays of the game. It was almost like watching the game on the tube in your own living room.

But baseball also owes its boom in the 1970s to increased offense and colorful superstars. For the first time in years there were .350 hitters (Rico Carty, Rod Carew, and Joe Torre) and 40-home run men (Hank Aaron and George Foster) challenging Cy Young Award winners (Tom Seaver, Jim Palmer, Steve Carlton, Catfish Hunter, and Vida Blue). Fans were also treated to the newest superstar in baseball: the relief pitcher. The most effective and best paid were Sparky Lyle, Goose Gossage, and Rollie Fingers. The new emphasis on running saw such speedsters as Davey Lopes, Billy North, and Lou Brock challenge excellent catchers Johnny Bench, Carlton Fisk, and Thurman Munson.

Longtime stars Hank Aaron, Willie Mays, Pete Rose, Roberto Clemente, Al Kaline, Lou Brock, and Carl Yastrzemski joined the 3,000 hit club, pushing its ranks to 15 members. In 1979, Manny Mota rang up a record number of career pinch hits (147), and

that same season Brock became baseball's all-time leader in steals with 938. (The 40-year-old star retired the same season and capped the year by batting .304 and joining the 3,000 hit club.)

This offensive explosion was due in part to some of the rules changes that were instituted in 1969 to help the hitters. One made the strike zone smaller. The other reduced the height of the pitcher's mound. A third and even more radical change, adopted by the American League in 1973, was the introduction of the designated hitter (DH) rule. DHs would bat in place of the pitcher, but would not play the field. The rule extended the careers of great aging hitters—Orlando "The Baby Bull" Cepeda, Jim Ray Hart, Tony Oliva, and Tommy Davis are examples. In 1973, Davis helped boost the Orioles to the East title by batting .306 with 89 RBI. Not only did batting averages rise, but DHs became among the highest paid players in the league.

Traditionalists, however, insisted that the rule would turn managers into puppets, since strategy would be reduced. The number of sacrifice bunts

Overshadowed by Roberto Clemente early in his career, Willie Stargell (right) brought the Pirates a World Series title in 1979. Jim Bouton's Ball Four *(left) caused quite a stir.*

Mets Tug McGraw and Jerry Koosman (above, left to right), *who keyed the 1969 miracle, did it again in the '73 pennant drive. The last hit of Roberto Clemente* (top right) *was his 3,000th. Marvin Miller, head of the Players Association, and St. Louis player Joe Torre announce the end of the '72 strike* (bottom right).

would drop and use of pinch hitters would decline. Pitchers would throw too many innings because they wouldn't have to be removed for pinch hitters. Those in favor of the rule said that the game would be more exciting having one less "automatic out" at the plate, and that a manager would still have to think on his feet. The DH rule is in effect at every level from high school on through the minor leagues, though the National League has yet to adopt it.

The ballplayer of the 1970s looked stylish both on the field and on color television. Gone from all but a few clubs were the familiar baggy flannel uniforms. Bright colors marched into the game and styles swung from wide stripes to thin stripes. Shirts went from button-down to pullovers. The Chicago White Sox even tried shorts. In 1971, the new-look Pirates wore sexy, skin-tight threads that caught on. Charlie Finley, the most controversial owner of the era, outfitted his A's in vivid white, green, and gold uniforms of imported material that they would wear in different color schemes every game (and teams like the Pirates, with their black and gold, soon followed suit). Finley even encouraged his players to grow long hair, sideburns, and mustaches; he paid

$300 per face in an attempt to evoke a "Gay '90s" look.

By the late 1970s most catchers wore fiberglass helmets, better masks, and neck flaps that were invented by Dodger Steve Yeager, who was seriously injured when a shattered bat struck him in the throat. They also donned lighter chest protectors, made possible by the advent of high-impact plastic that preserved safety and increased mobility. Baseball mitts grew even larger, which enabled players to make flashy one-handed grabs. In addition, life improved for reckless outfielders when clubs installed padded barriers.

Athletes of the era were faster, bigger, stronger, more numerous (due to expansion), and better educated than they had been for decades; they also possessed a different attitude toward the game, which was hard for some of the old-timers to swallow. The Spartan code of "playing with the small hurts" changed in the 1970s; more players admitted to injuries, refused to play hurt, demanded specialized treatment, and used their newly won rights to a guaranteed year's pay if disabled. (In July of 1979, there were 127 disabled players, a figure three times higher than the entire year of 1970.)

Players of the 1970s possessed a more casual attitude toward the game, and many flaunted their personalities like never before. The volatile political climate of the 1960s that dominated the rest of the country cast a shadow over baseball. Players—such as Reggie "I'm the straw that stirs the drink" Jackson, Ken "The Hawk" Harrelson, and Tug "You Gotta Believe" McGraw—looked more like rock stars than role models; the players mirrored, in part, America's fascination with flamboyant, outspoken

figures. They wore long hair, jewelry, batting gloves, sweatbands, and white shoes. They were also quotable, contentious, and most of all, entertaining.

In 1972, the average salary was estimated at $34,000, and 23 players earned $100,000 or more. Hank Aaron reportedly earned the most, followed by Carl Yastrzemski, Willie Mays, Bob Gibson, and Roberto Clemente, each topping the $150,000 mark. A year later, 30 players broke the $100,000 barrier, with slugger Dick Allen topping the list with an annual income of $225,000. By 1978, players drew salaries that averaged more than $100,000. People compared them to Broadway entertainers, and the public's appreciation showed in better attendance at games and even higher television ratings, which produced additional revenue that the Players Association demanded and received after the strike in 1972.

While jealousy and resentment surrounded some of these I've-just-got-to-be-me characters, it only helped baseball at the box office. Tug McGraw explained how he planned to spend his hefty con-

Mets pitcher Tom Seaver (top left) *was the first non-20-game winner to take the Cy Young, accomplishing the feat in 1973. Charlie Finley's A's were colorful winners* (top right). *Roberto Clemente's death brought donations from around the country* (bottom left). *Artificial turf was a fixture in new parks like Cincinnati's Riverfront Stadium* (bottom right).

tract by saying, "Ninety percent I'll spend on good times, women, and Irish whiskey. The other 10 percent I'll probably waste." Another wacky southpaw, Bill "Spaceman" Lee, openly mocked the baseball establishment by paying a fine imposed by Commissioner Bowie Kuhn for his use of marijuana and then turning around and filing a grievance petition. When asked if he preferred natural grass or artificial turf, McGraw uttered another classic line, "I dunno. I never smoked Astroturf."

A younger, less awestruck breed of sportswriters made sure that the age of "The Ballplayer Can Do No Wrong" ended as quickly as the hula hoop. Players were exposed, dissected, and analyzed in print and on television like never before. Carl Yastrzemski, the venerable Boston Red Sox slugger, was accused by some teammates of masterminding the dismissal of those scribes he disliked. Dodger Steve Garvey, the clean-cut conservative slugger, was labeled "Goody Two-shoes" and sarcastically called "The All-American Boy." Some players, such as Reggie Jackson and Dick Allen, enjoyed their newfound bad-boy celebrity—it did after all mean more cash and glory. Others, such as Steve Carlton, Dave Kingman, and Amos Otis, treated baseball writers as social outcasts.

The 1974 A's and the 1978 Yankees had many documented arguments. Fistfights broke out among the Oakland players, who also denounced owner Charles Finley as a raving lunatic and their manager Alvin Dark as a religious fanatic. Raging conflicts between Yankee superstar Reggie Jackson, his man-

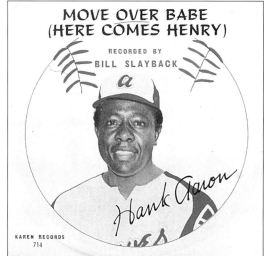

Yankee pitcher Fritz Peterson (top left) *and teammate Mike Kekich made headlines when they traded wives and families in 1973, a year before Kekich was dealt to the Indians. Ron Blomberg of the Yankees* (top right) *made his own news as the first designated hitter. Hank Aaron's pursuit of Babe Ruth's home run record earned him a record of a different sort* (bottom).

ager Billy Martin, and owner George Steinbrenner made Liz Taylor and Richard Burton's liaison seem tranquil. Nevertheless, these two rocky clubs stayed together long enough to win half the decade's World Series titles—three for Oakland in 1972, '73, and '74, and two for the Yankees in 1977 and '78.

In addition, former Yankee pitcher Jim Bouton's *Ball Four*, published in 1970, probably did more to demystify America's heroes than any behind-the-

scenes work before or since. Bowie Kuhn's attempt to suppress the book led to a humorous sequel. Other bawdy activities were reported in 1973 when Yankee pitchers Fritz Peterson and Mike Kekich engaged in a much publicized wife and family swapping experiment that made great copy but, to say the least, shocked baseball's brass. At times, this "tell it like it is" style of journalism was in questionable taste.

In 1970, a record 20 African-Americans played in the All-Star Game. The impact of the African-American athlete on the game moved toward its zenith in the mid-1970s, when 26 percent of the active major leaguers were African-American. Some shortsighted owners (and fans) worried that African-Americans were taking over the game and the numbers lessened after that (from one in four to one in five), but during the decade African-Americans continued their awesome offensive display, adding 15 more batting titles, 10 home run titles and usually leading in stolen bases, RBI, runs scored, and total hits.

Former Oakland star Jim "Catfish" Hunter (left) found himself in a Yankee uniform after being declared a free agent in 1975. Dodger second baseman Davey Lopes (right) *tied a major-league record with five stolen bases in one game in 1974.*

The rhetoric that had reigned years earlier on the streets of Mobile, Alabama, and Washington, D.C., began infiltrating major-league clubhouses. In 1974, Hank Aaron, who accused owners of treating African-Americans as "trained monkeys," broke perhaps the most cherished record in baseball history when he belted his 715th career homer off Al Downing at Atlanta Stadium. That same year Lou Brock stole 118 bases to break Ty Cobb's old mark. (Maury Wills had previously broken it in 1962.) When he was passed over for MVP honors, Brock accused the voters of racism at worst and ignorance at best. Pittsburgh's Dock Ellis labeled Pirate officials as cheapskates and bigots.

In 1974, Frank Robinson, a superstar of the 1960s, became player-manager of the Cleveland Indians, making him the first African-American ever to manage a major-league team. (After two seasons he also became the first African-American manager to be fired.) Nevertheless, in 1979, there was only

Baltimore manager Earl Weaver (left) had his share of run-ins with the men in blue as well as his share of AL championships. *The basestealing capabilities of Lou Brock garnered the Cardinal speedster a record (right).*

one African-American umpire among 60, few African-American coaches, and very few African-Americans in administrative posts.

Another minority, Latin Americans, continued to produce some of baseball's top stars, such as Orlando Cepeda, Tony Perez, Bert Campaneris, Luis Tiant, Dave Concepcion, Juan Marichal, Rico Carty, and Rod Carew. Some claimed they were underpaid. Willie Montanez spoke for many when he said, "When it comes down to an American and a Latin fighting for the same spot...the Latin has gotta be twice as good. Else he don't get past April."

After the Pirates downed Baltimore in a dramatic seventh game in the 1971 World Series (the Series also featured the first World Series night game), Roberto Clemente, a native of Puerto Rico, complained to reporters of discrimination while manager Danny Murtaugh spoke to President Richard Nixon, who called to offer congratulations. At the close of the 1970s, officials at Yankee Stadium staged the first Latin American night in baseball history to honor past Latino greats.

But more than anything else, the 1970s will be known as the decade of intense legal battles in the players' fight for freedom from owners, who could control their rights for their entire playing career. Spearheaded by a shrewd economist named Marvin Miller, the Major League Baseball Players Association grew from a passive organization into an effective, powerful tool that earned the players increased average salaries and the right to arbitration to settle disputes between players and owners.

Philadelphia third baseman Mike Schmidt (top) led the NL in home runs from 1974 to '76 and hit four in one game at Wrigley Field in 1976. Royals Stadium in Kansas City (bottom) opened to rave reviews in 1973.

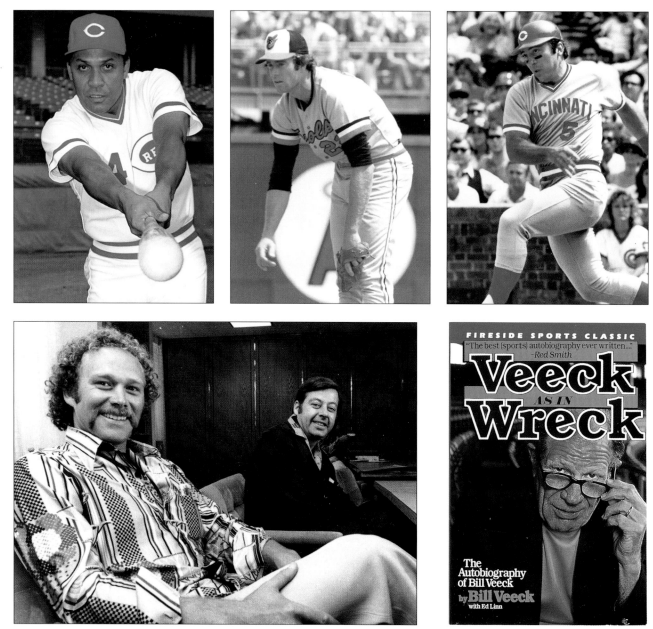

Tony Perez (top left) *and Johnny Bench* (top right) *led "The Big Red Machine." Jim Palmer* (top center) *won his third Cy Young in 1976. Andy Messersmith* (bottom left) *challenged the reserve clause and won. The autobiography of Bill Veeck* (bottom right).

The players-owners war really began in 1970, when outfielder Curt Flood was traded from the St. Louis Cardinals to the Philadelphia Phillies. He likened the transaction to plantation owners trading slaves, refused to report, and filed a suit against baseball's "reserve clause," which bound a player forever to the team that held his contract. Flood in-

sisted that he should have the right to sign with the team of his choice. In protest, he sat out the entire season, a move that hurt his career but helped pave the way for several significant cases that followed.

In 1972, Miller organized a players strike that wiped out spring training as well as some of the early games. The net result, however, gave players with four years of service a monthly pension check starting at age 50. After the 1972 strike, the owners traded 16 player reps and intimidated even more into resigning. Owners waged a propaganda war against Miller, citing inflated salary figures and exaggerated losses to turn the public sentiment against the players. Ironically, the players' cause was helped when owners like Oakland's Charles Finley, St. Louis's August Busch Jr., and San Diego's Ray Kroc acted like tyrants. Kroc, the owner of McDonald's hamburger chain, did little to help his brethren by calling his players "dummies" and then declared, "I won't subsidize idiots."

The Players Association was able to get some new concessions for the players in a negotiated agreement with the owners at the start of the 1973 season. A system was established for arbitration of salary disputes. If a player and his team could not agree to terms, each would submit their final figures to an impartial arbitrator. The decision of the arbitrator was binding, and some players—Reggie

Jackson, Sal Bando, and Rollie Fingers among them—were awarded contracts that owner Charlie Finley had zealously refused to offer.

Another result of the 1973 agreement was the "10 and five" rule, which stated that a player who had 10 years of major-league experience, the last five with the same club, could veto a trade involving him (a ruling which would have allowed Curt Flood to stop the 1970 trade which led to his lawsuit).

Such provisions set the stage for Jim "Catfish" Hunter's battle with Finley after the 1974 season. Hunter (25-12 on the year) claimed that Charlie O. had failed to make certain payments under his contract and that this failure dissolved that contract and made him a free agent. The arbitration ruling then allowed Hunter to sell his services to the highest bidder, which turned out to be George Steinbrenner's New York Yankees.

Perhaps the most significant legal ruling occurred in 1975 in what is now known as "The Messersmith Case." Andy Messersmith of the Los

Manager Billy Martin, center, and George Steinbrenner, holding son Hal, had their share of squabbles through the years, but were all smiles after the Yankees defeated the Dodgers in the 1977 World Series.

An advertisement instructed parents to have their kids learn hitting from the best, Rod Carew (top left). Carew won seven batting titles in his career with the Twins and Angels. Billy Martin (top right) got along with umpires about as well as he did with owners, but did manage to pick up four Manager of the Year Awards. Cincinnati's Pete Rose (bottom), nicknamed "Charlie Hustle" by former Yankee great Whitey Ford, was named Player of the Decade by The Sporting News. Rose won his third batting title in 1973, the year he was named NL MVP.

Angeles Dodgers and Dave McNally of the Montreal Expos had decided to play the 1975 season without signing contracts. As a result, they argued that they had become "free agents," free to sign with any team that they chose to negotiate with. The owners understandably screamed foul, because it effectively did away with the reserve clause. The issue went to arbitration, and arbitrator Peter Seitz ruled that a player's contract cannot be renewed indefinitely by the original owner until the player is traded, sold, released, or retired. (The owners fired Seitz and appealed his decision to the courts, which refused to change the ruling.) Although McNally retired, Messersmith signed a three-year deal with the Atlanta Braves for $1 million, a figure well above the Dodgers offer. Within two years after the decision, an annual free-agent draft sent salaries skyrocketing.

After the frenzied bidding of the first draft in 1976, 24 players (led by Reggie Jackson's five-year Yankee pact worth $2.93 million) had won a total of $25 million in contracts. Once again, fans read of newly minted millionaires and responded by pushing attendance and television ratings sky-high.

The biggest winner of the decade was Pittsburgh's Dave Parker, who in 1978 signed a five-year contract worth $900,000 a season. Jim Rice's seven-year pact with Boston averaged $700,000 a year. Vida Blue, Pete Rose, and Rod Carew also netted huge multiyear deals. As the dust settled from the latest salary explosion, 1979 (when pitcher Nolan Ryan snared the first million dollar annual salary) saw top baseball stars earning more than their counterparts in football and basketball.

This surplus of cash and glory cast players of the 1970s as a breed apart from their predecessors. In a sport as tradition bound as baseball, this transformation was terribly disturbing to the embittered owners, who viewed Marvin Miller and the Players Association as self-serving marauders out to destroy baseball.

As the decade closed, it seemed apparent that this bitter struggle would continue on into the 1980s, with dramatic changes in the game still to come.

Arm surgery nearly forced Cub Bruce Sutter (top) out of the game, but his career as a reliever took off with the development of the split-fingered fastball. The San Diego Chicken (bottom) was one of many attractions used to lure fans.

ORIOLES WIN 108, THEN RIP THE REDS

Bill Rigney is arguably the best manager of his time who never won a pennant. After several years as the Giants skipper, he was fired just when the club was finally ready for flagdom in the early 1960s. Rigney then took over the expansion Los Angeles Angels and swiftly made them into an astonishingly competitive team and the envy of every other expansion franchise.

In 1970, Rigney at last got his chance to contend for a World Series. Replacing Billy Martin as the Minnesota Twins' skipper, he seemingly had the best four-man rotation in the game in Jim Perry, Jim Kaat, Dave Boswell, and Luis Tiant (who had come from Cleveland in a trade). However, Boswell would never recover from the back injury he sustained the previous fall in a scrape with Martin, and Tiant was decked by a broken shoulder. Rigney's solution was to ease 19-year-old Bert Blyleven and 23-year-old Bill Zepp into the rotation, backed by plenty of relief help from Stan Williams and Ron Perranoski, two former Los Angeles Dodgers relievers, and 22-year-old Tom "The Blade" Hall, a combination starter-reliever who fanned 184 batters in just 155⅓ innings.

The concoction brought the Twins one more win than they achieved in 1969 and a return date with the Baltimore Orioles in the AL Championship Series. Unfortunately for Rigney, the Orioles, after winning a post-1961 record 109 games in 1969, won only one game less in 1970. Given the privilege of starting three 20-game winners—Mike Cuellar, Dave McNally, and Jim Palmer—in the LCS, Baltimore

skipper Earl Weaver obtained the same result he had the previous year: a three-game sweep and a Series engagement.

Unlike 1969, though, the Orioles were not thrown up against a team that had seemingly won with smoke and mirrors. Their opponents were the Cincinnati Reds, winners of 102 games for rookie pilot Sparky Anderson. In 1970, Anderson already had several ingredients of what would soon be labeled "The Big Red Machine." Foremost among them were Pete Rose, Tony Perez, Dave Concepcion, and Johnny Bench. Bench, in 1970, had become the youngest MVP winner in history to that point. Anderson, a weak-hitting second baseman in his playing days, utilized an attack that led the NL in

While Oriole teammate Brooks Robinson was the Series MVP, Frank Robinson (above) managed to hit two home runs, in Games 3 and 5.

Jim Palmer (right) was one of three 20-game winners for the Orioles, joining Mike Cuellar and Dave McNally. Willie *Stargell (left)* had 31 homers as the Pirates captured the NL East.

lenges raised by Denny McLain's gambling, Curt Flood's antitrust suit against baseball, Jim Bouton's publication of *Ball Four,* and the bankrupt Seattle Pilots franchise, which had to be transferred to Milwaukee just four days before the season opened.

For the second year in a row the new LCS format was less than an aesthetic success, as not only the Orioles, but also the Reds, took just three games to dispose of their foes. However, while the Twins were badly overmatched, the Pirates at least gave Cincinnati a stiff tussle in each fray before bowing to the Reds' superior pitching. By not hesitating to call for relief help every time one of his starters was pressed, Anderson saw his club hold Pittsburgh to just three runs in the sweep.

In the Series, Anderson tried the same formula, but with the notable exception of Clay Carroll, his bullpen failed him. With a perfect 0.00 ERA in four relief appearances and nine innings, Carroll might have been the Series MVP if the result had been different. It just so happened that Brooks Robinson picked the 1970 fall classic to put on the most extraordinary week of third-base play ever witnessed, and he hit .429 to boot. Since center fielder Paul Blair had a week that was not far behind Robinson's, the Orioles waltzed in five games.

homers and slugging average to vanquish the second-place Los Angeles Dodgers by 14½ games.

The Reds, though, with 20-game winner Jim Merritt and Gary Nolan (18-7), also had the best mound staff in the NL West to go along with their offense. In contrast, the Pittsburgh Pirates, their opponents for the NL title, lacked a true hill leader and revolved around Roberto Clemente, Willie Stargell, and Bob Robertson, who had all missed significant time during the season with nagging injuries.

As a result, the Pirates notched only 89 victories and a .549 winning percentage, the lowest yet of any team to qualify for postseason play. Just as the last Steel City champion in 1960, Pittsburgh had as its guiding spirit Danny Murtaugh, back at the wheel after a lengthy absence due to a heart condition. Murtaugh's return made for a perfect postseason square in 1970. All four corners were occupied by clubs managed by scrappy former second sackers with good gloves and unimpressive bats.

The four clubs had another common feature. They were among the few teams free of scandal or tumult in perhaps the game's most difficult summer since 1920. In his second season as commissioner, Bowie Kuhn never knew a dull moment. On the legal front alone he had to cope with thorny chal-

Minnesota's Jim Perry (right) led the AL with 23 wins and grabbed the Cy Young Award. Boston's Carl Yastrzemski *(left)* was the All-Star MVP.

SEASON'S BEST

•The Seattle franchise is moved to Milwaukee just prior to the season; the team name is changed from Pilots to Brewers.

•Boog Powell of Baltimore is the AL MVP.

•The Reds' Johnny Bench is named NL MVP. Bench tops the majors in homers (45) and RBI (148).

•St. Louis's Bob Gibson wins his second NL Cy Young Award, as he ties the Giants' Gaylord Perry for the NL lead in wins (23).

•Minnesota's Jim Perry is the AL Cy Young winner, as he ties two others for the AL lead in wins (24). The Perrys are the first brothers to top their respective leagues in wins.

•The Orioles win 108 games, giving them 217 victories over the last two years.

•Atlanta's Rico Carty leads the ML with a .366 BA. He hits in 31 straight games.

•Angel Alex Johnson wins the AL batting title (.329) by a fraction of a point over Boston's Carl Yastrzemski.

Billy Williams

•On April 22, Tom Seaver sets an ML record when he fans 10 Padres in a row and ties the ML record by fanning 19 total.

•Cub Billy Williams sets a new NL record when he plays in his 1,117th consecutive game. Williams tops ML in runs (137), total bases (373), and runs produced (224) and ties for ML lead in hits (205).

•The Giants' Willie Mays collects his 3,000th hit.

•The NL wins its eighth straight All-Star Game, 5-4 in 12 innings at Cincinnati.

•Cincinnati's Wayne Granger sets a new ML record with 35 saves.

•Giant Bobby Bonds fans 189 times to set the all-time ML record.

•Three Rivers Stadium opens on July 16, the Reds vs. Pirates.

•Riverfront Stadium opens on June 30, the Braves vs. Reds.

•The Conigliaro brothers, Tony and Billy, hit 54 homers for the Red Sox.

•Atlanta's Hank Aaron gets his 3,000th hit.

•Cardinal Vic Davalillo ties the ML record with 24 pinch hits.

•Detroit's Cesar Gutierrez is the first in this century to go 7-for-7 when he accomplishes it on June 21 in a 12-inning game.

•Washington's Frank Howard leads the AL in homers (44), RBI (126), and walks (132).

JOHNNY BENCH

Gold Glove catcher explodes for 45 HRs, 148 RBI

Johnny Bench was beginning his first full season in the majors when he met hitting great Ted Williams during spring training of 1968. He awkwardly asked the seven-time batting champ for his autograph, and Williams responded by signing the 20-year-old catcher's ball with the following inscription: "To Johnny Bench, a Hall of Famer for sure." Ted was never one for being blunt, but within two years—when Bench was named 1970 National League MVP following perhaps the greatest season by a catcher in big-league history—his prediction was already being realized.

A fan of fellow Oklahoman Mickey Mantle as a kid, Bench was drafted by the Reds in 1965. Following a one-month apprenticeship late in 1967, he was named Cincinnati's starting catcher for the '68 campaign. Mature beyond his 20 years, the muscle-bound, 6'1" receiver promptly led all NL catchers in putouts and assists to earn Gold Glove and Rookie of the Year selections at season's

end. His smooth one-hand catching style, rocket arm, and take-charge attitude won the praise of Reds pitchers, and his .275 batting average, 15 homers, and 82 RBI made for a devastating total package. By the time he added 26 homers, 90 RBI, a .293 batting mark, and another Gold Glove his second season, Bench was recognized as the best all-around catcher in the majors.

Despite steady progress to this point, Bench surprised everyone with his fantastic 1970 campaign.

The Reds were expected to challenge for the pennant, and after Johnny exploded for a record 36 homers through July 31, they cruised to the NL West title by 14½ games. Bench finished with league-leading totals of 45 homers and 148 RBI (both still records for catchers), and his 355 total bases and .587 slugging percentage ranked second and third, respectively. The numbers overshadowed a third straight Gold Glove year defensively, and even after a disappointing World Series loss to Baltimore (in which Johnny hit .211) more success seemed assured for Johnny and the Reds.

After a down season in '71, Bench responded with another MVP campaign in '72 (with a league-best 40 homers and 125 RBI) and a third RBI crown two years later. Bench's leadership on both sides of the plate was a main factor as Cincinnati's "Big Red Machine" won five West division, four National League, and two World Series championships through 1976. Johnny eventually earned 10 consecutive Gold Gloves and 13 All-Star appearances in a row. The wear and tear of catching over 100 games his first 13 years caused his production to drop dramatically after age 30, but Bench remained a popular and consistent performer in stints at third and first base before retiring in 1983 with 389 homers (329 as a catcher, a record at the time), 1,376 RBI, and the nod from most as baseball's greatest all-time receiver. Six years later, Ted Williams's prediction came true on the first ballot.

WHAT A BLASS! BUCS BEST THE O'S

In 1971, the Baltimore Orioles became the only pennant winner ever to be blessed with four 20-game winners. From Dave McNally, Mike Cuellar, Pat Dobson, and Jim Palmer, Earl Weaver got 81 wins and 70 of the O's AL-leading 71 complete games. Nevertheless, Weaver saw his club continue on a downward slide from its peak of 109 wins in 1969. After winning 108 games the previous year, Weaver's 1971 crew could achieve a mere 101 victories. A drop of seven wins, though, still didn't create anything that could be construed as a pennant race in the AL East. At curtain call, the Orioles stood alone at center stage, 12 games ahead of the second-place Detroit Tigers.

The AL West offered an even less competitive product in 1971. Gradually improving every year since their move from Kansas City to Oakland in 1968, the A's made a quantum leap in 1971, their first season under Dick Williams. By winning 24 games and notching 301 Ks and a 1.82 ERA in his first full season, 21-year-old Vida Blue assured himself of being the youngest MVP recipient to date and spurred the A's to the AL West championship by an enormous 16-game spread over their replacement club in Kansas City, the expansion Royals.

Achieving the franchise's first title of any kind in 40 years would have to be good enough for the A's for the moment, as the Ori-oles continued to be impenetrable in LCS play. Oakland was ahead 3-1 as late as the seventh inning of the opener but then never led again at any juncture in the O's three-game sweep.

The NL, on the other hand, staged the first mildly competitive LCS when the Pittsburgh Pirates needed four games to shed the San Francisco Giants after losing the opener to Gaylord Perry. Even more so than the A's, the Giants ought to have been grateful just to participate in postseason action. After jumping to a 10½-game advantage in the NL West as early as May, the Giants still led the second-place Los Angeles Dodgers by 8½ games on September 5. Followers of the two bitter rivals—who could never forget the events of 20 years earlier that

The Pirates celebrated a World Series title as Pittsburgh's Steve Blass won two games, outdueling Baltimore's Mike Cuellar 2-1 in Game 7.

culminated in Bobby Thomson's famed last-ditch home run—saw what looked to be a replay of the 1951 season. Only this time it would be the Dodgers' turn to catch the Giants. After Willie Mc-Covey was felled by a knee injury, Manager Charlie Fox helplessly watched his Giants lose 16 of their last 24 tilts. By September 14, the 8½-game lead of nine days earlier had melted to a single game. The elder Perry brother and Juan Marichal then took charge down the stretch. Between them, the two San Francisco hill aces protected the Giants' slim edge so that on closing day it still stood at one game.

Chicago Cub Ferguson Jenkins (top left) had his best season in '71, winning 24 games and the Cy Young. Oakland's Vida Blue (top center) was the AL MVP and Cy Young winner, posting 24 victories and 301 strikeouts. Baltimore sent Frank Robinson (top right) to the Dodgers. A .363 average and 137 RBI brought the NL MVP to the Cardinals' Joe Torre (bottom).

Short of reliable starting pitchers a year earlier, the Pirates were bolstered by an injury-free season from Steve Blass and Dock Ellis's emergence as a 19-game winner. Danny Murtaugh's crew got an added lift from its outstanding bullpen. Although Dave Giusti, the NL's top fireman in 1971, was its hub, two 35-year-old converted starters—Mudcat Grant and Bob Veale—also contributed heavily, as did Bob Miller after he was picked up from San Diego in mid-August.

The NL's surprise team in 1971 was the St. Louis Cardinals, who rebounded to 90 wins and second place in the NL East after enduring two poor seasons following their back-to-back flags in 1967 and '68. The biggest senior loop disappointment was the Cincinnati Reds. Consistently the best hitting team in the majors for the past five seasons, the Reds un-derwent a dreadful slump that saw 29 points evaporate from the team BA and a resultant drop in runs of nearly 200.

In the first World Series to be played in part under the lights, the Bucs left Baltimore trailing 2-0. A route-going 5-1 victory by Blass in Game 3 got Pittsburgh off the starting block. The next evening, in the initial Series night game, the Pirates rallied from a 3-0 deficit to win 4-3, and Nelson Briles then blanked the Birds, 4-0, in Game 5.

Returning to Baltimore down 3-2, the Orioles survived a Roberto Clemente homer to win Game 6, 3-2. The next day, though, Clemente bombed another four-bagger, providing the game's only run until the eighth inning. When the Bucs got another tally in the top of the frame, Blass had the cushion he needed. After giving up a single marker in the bottom of the eighth, he put down the Orioles in order in the ninth and the Pirates had their second championship in two Series tries under Murtaugh.

SEASON'S BEST

- Cardinal Joe Torre is NL MVP, as he leads the league in BA (.363), hits (230), RBI (137), and total bases (352).

- Oakland's Vida Blue wins both the MVP and Cy Young Awards in the AL. Blue fans 301 in his first full ML season. He goes 24-8 and leads the AL in ERA (1.82) and shutouts (eight).

- Chicago's Ferguson Jenkins cops the NL Cy Young, as he leads the loop in wins (24), CGs (30), and innings (325).

- Tiger Mickey Lolich leads the AL in wins (25), innings (376), CGs (29), and Ks (308). Lolich's 45 starts and 376 innings are the most by any hurler since the dead-ball era.

- Pittsburgh's Willie Stargell leads the majors with 48 homers.

- Chicago's Bill Melton tops the AL in homers with 33.

- The Orioles become the only flag winner in ML history to have four 20-game winners.

- Expo Ron Hunt sets the modern ML record when he's hit by pitches 50 times.

Tom Seaver

- The Astros play an all-time ML-record 75 one-run games.

- Veterans Stadium opens on April 10, the Expos vs. Phils.

- Phillie Larry Bowa's .987 FA is a new ML record for shortstops.

- Cleveland third baseman Graig Nettles compiles an ML-record 412 assists.

- The Twins' Tony Oliva wins his third AL bat crown (.337).

- Atlanta's Earl Williams, a catcher-third baseman, hits 33 homers, an NL rookie record for both catchers and infielders.

- Phillie rookie Willie Montanez cracks 30 homers.

- On June 23, Rick Wise of the Phils no-hits Cincinnati and hits two homers.

- St. Louis's Lou Brock tops the majors in runs (126) and steals (64).

- Minnesota's Harmon Killebrew leads the AL in RBI (119) and walks (114).

- The Mets' Tom Seaver tops the NL in Ks (289) and ERA (1.76), winning 20 games.

- Game 4 at Pittsburgh is the first night game in World Series history.

- Pittsburgh's Roberto Clemente is the overall Series star, hitting .414 with 12 hits and two homers.

ROBERTO CLEMENTE

Aging Pirate finally earns the respect he deserves

For 17 seasons, he had dazzled Pittsburgh Pirate fans with his unparalleled outfield play and clutch hitting. It wasn't until the 1971 World Series, however, that over 60 million television viewers were able to fully appreciate the graceful style of Roberto Clemente. His MVP performance in Pittsburgh's seven-game victory over the Baltimore Orioles prompted writer Roger Angell to suggest the 37-year-old right fielder played "a kind of baseball that none of us had ever seen before—throwing and running and hitting at something close to the level of perfection." The proud Clemente, however, wondered what had taken everyone so long to notice.

Playing in a small-market city at the same time fellow outfielders Willie Mays and Mickey Mantle were rising to stardom in New York, Clemente had long been miffed by his lack of exposure. One of the first great Puerto Rican players to make the majors, the handsome, dark-skinned competitor claimed much of the reason was prejudice—but his failure to hit many home runs most of his career was probably as big a factor. His 1960 performance (a .314 batting average with 94 RBI) helped the Pirates to the world championship, but despite nagging back injuries, Roberto had far better seasons ahead of him. In the next seven years, he would hit as high as .357 and win four batting titles.

Clemente's overall batting average of .328 during the 1960s was the best in the majors. When he added power (a career-high 29 homers and 119 RBI) to his arsenal in 1966, he finally won an MVP Award. Still, it was as a right fielder that he stood without peer. Forever diving or leaping to make impossible catches, Roberto played the tricky right field corner of Pittsburgh's Forbes Field flawlessly and nailed runners with long, accurate throws. He led the league in assists five times (reaching a high of 27 before runners learned to stop taking chances), and won a Gold Glove each of his last 12 seasons.

His numbers in '71 included a .341 batting average (fourth in the National League), a .502 slugging mark, and 86 RBI in just 132 injury-marred games, followed by his virtuoso Series performance in which he hit .414 with two homers and 12 hits, and played stellar defense. His double in his final game of the 1972 regular season made him the 11th player in big-league history with 3,000 hits, and he looked forward to increasing his career totals of 240 homers, 440 doubles, and 166 triples with at least one more season. That opportunity would never come, as he was killed in a cargo plane crash December 31, 1972, while carrying emergency relief supplies to earthquake-ravaged Nicaragua. Mourned as a national hero in Puerto Rico, he was taken into the Hall of Fame with a waived waiting period the following year—images of his great October still on everyone's mind.

TIGERS, REDS PUSH A'S TO THE LIMIT

The season began with the death of New York Mets manager Gil Hodges during spring training. Following that was the first strike in the game's history, resulting in 13 days and 86 games being scratched from the schedule. Then, on the final day of 1972, Pittsburgh star Roberto Clemente perished in a plane crash while on a mercy mission to aid victims of an earthquake in Nicaragua.

Accordingly, the action on the field was somewhat muted, especially in Baltimore where the Orioles were bidding for their fourth consecutive pennant. Instead, Earl Weaver's club plummeted to just 80 wins. Only one of the four 20-game winners from the previous year—Jim Palmer—was able to repeat; the quartet as a whole was just 68-57. Replacing Baltimore as AL East champs were the Detroit Tigers. Continuing their tradition of prevailing in tight races or when scheduling vagaries are influential, the Tigers became the only team in either major league since 1908 to win a title by less than a full game. By dint of having one less contest wiped out by the strike than the Boston Red Sox, Detroit finished at 86-70, three percentage points ahead of Boston's 85-70.

Joe Rudi went to the wall to grab this shot and prevent an extra-base hit against the Reds in the '72 World Series.

The last team to win in a like manner was, no surprise, the 1908 Tigers under feisty Hughie Jennings.

Jennings, however, was a pussycat compared to Detroit's skipper in 1972, Billy Martin. When he took over the club the previous season, Martin quickly realized he had only two dependable starting pitchers, Mickey Lolich and Joe Coleman. Martin went deep into the 1972 season before he admitted that he still had developed no other trustworthy starters. On August 2, he secured Woody Fryman's purchase from the Philadelphia Phillies. Fryman went 10-3 in the final two months, thereby earning himself two starts in the LCS.

The latter outing came on the day that made the 1972 championship series the first AL affair ever to go the five-game limit. Fryman's opponent was Oakland right-hander Blue Moon Odom, who had beaten him 5-0 in Game 2. By rights, the A's, repeating as AL West champs by 5½ lengths over the runner-up Chicago White Sox, ought to have long since put the Tigers out of their misery. Oakland had three quality starters in Catfish Hunter, Ken Holtzman, and Odom, plus a fourth if and when

Willie Stargell (top left) *hit 33 homers and drove in 112 runs, but slumped in the NLCS, hitting just .063. Johnny Bench and Tony Perez* (top center) *helped engineer the drive of "The Big Red Machine." Gaylord Perry* (top right) *copped the AL Cy Young with his 24-16 record and 1.92 ERA. Backed by 22 wins from Mickey Lolich* (bottom), *the Tigers captured the AL East by a half game over the Red Sox.*

Vida Blue rounded into shape after a long holdout battle with owner Charlie Finley. In addition, manager Dick Williams had a formidable trio of relievers in Rollie Fingers, Bob Locker, and Darold Knowles. Yet the Tigers took the A's to the limit before succumbing 2-1 in the finale when Blue, who relieved in four of the five contests, came on in the sixth inning and nailed the save.

For all its drama, the AL championship series was overshadowed in 1972 by the NLCS, which had been resolved the previous day in Cincinnati. Heavily favored after repeating with ease as NL East winners, the Pittsburgh Pirates had taken a 2-1 LCS lead by copping the opening contest at the Queen City two days earlier. Reds lefty Ross Grimsley knotted matters in the fourth clash, but Pittsburgh still seemed in control when Sparky Anderson had only Don Gullett (9-10) available to start the deciding match. Like so many talented young Reds pitchers in recent years, Gullett had stumbled after a stellar rookie season. A complete recovery by the many Reds hitters who had swooned in 1971 brought a routine division title nonetheless.

In Game 5 of the NLCS, Gullett paired off against Steve Blass (19-8). Holding a 3-2 lead, Blass was replaced in the eighth by Ramon Hernandez. Down to their final three outs, the Reds glumly watched rookie Bucs skipper Bill Virdon summon re-lief ace Dave Giusti. In short order, Virdon was forced to signal for starter Bob Moose when Giusti ran into trouble and the Reds tied the game, 3-3. Now everyone back in Pittsburgh sat paralyzed in front of their televisions as the Reds rudely yanked the pennant from the Corsairs' grasp when Moose wild-pitched home the pennant-winning run from third base.

The down-to-the-wire pattern persisted in the World Series. Although it is seldom cited by historians, the 1972 fall classic ranks among the best for excitement. All but one of the first six contests were one-run battles, and three were determined by ninth-inning tallies.

Gene Tenace, a second-string catcher during the season who went 1-for-17 in the ALCS, carried the A's through Game 6 with a Series-record four homers, and the Reds hero to that point was pitcher Jack Billingham. In the seventh game, however, Billingham tired and left in the sixth inning. The A's quickly racked up two runs to lead 3-1 as Tenace doubled in the go-ahead marker. Two A's starters turned firemen, Hunter and Holtzman, then held the Reds until the eighth when Fingers was beckoned with Cincinnati threatening. After giving up a sacrifice fly, Fingers clamped down the lid, and the A's bagged their fourth one-run victory and the crown.

S E A S O N ' S   B E S T

•The Washington franchise moves to Texas and is renamed the Rangers.

•Cincinnati's Johnny Bench wins his second NL MVP Award. Bench leads the majors in homers (40) and RBI (125).

•Chicago's Dick Allen is AL MVP. Allen leads the AL in homers (37), RBI (113), runs produced (166), OBP (.422), and SA (.603).

•Steve Carlton wins 27 of Philly's 59 victories and cops Cy Young honors. Carlton leads the majors in wins and CGs (30) and tops the NL in Ks (310), innings (346), and ERA (1.97).

•Cleveland's Gaylord Perry wins the AL Cy Young after tying for the loop lead in wins (24) and leading in CGs (29).

•The first players strike in ML history ends on April 10; missed games are not made up, and Boston loses to the Tigers by a half-game.

•Pittsburgh's Roberto Clemente produces his 3,000th hit on September 30, and then dies in a December plane crash.

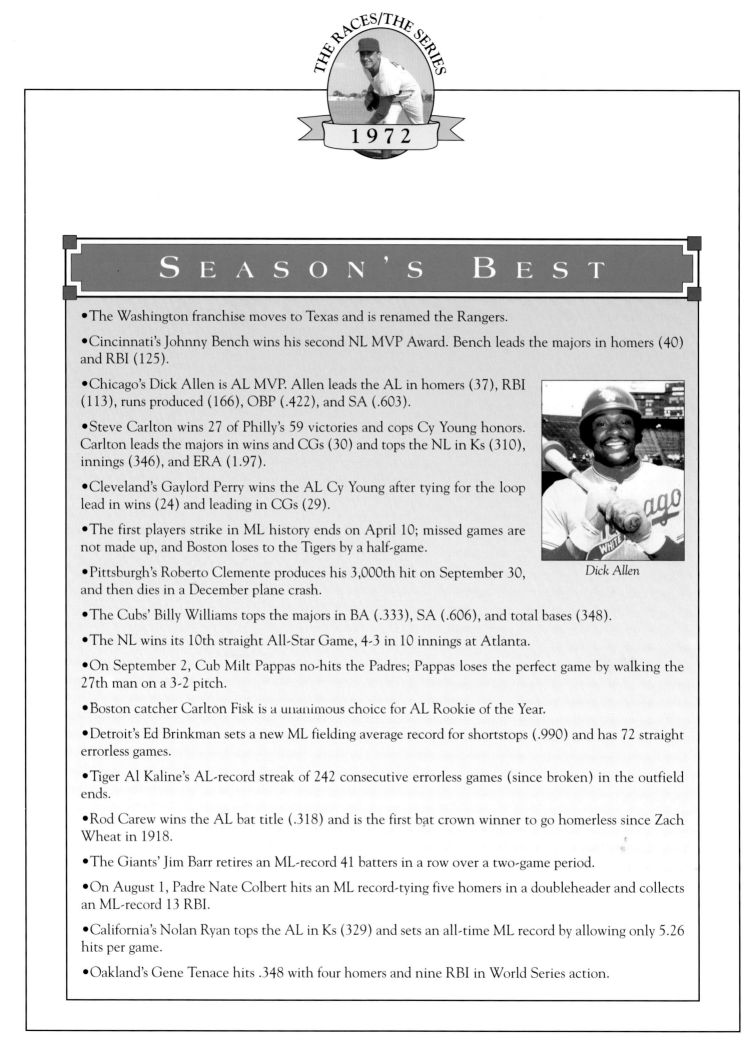

Dick Allen

•The Cubs' Billy Williams tops the majors in BA (.333), SA (.606), and total bases (348).

•The NL wins its 10th straight All-Star Game, 4-3 in 10 innings at Atlanta.

•On September 2, Cub Milt Pappas no-hits the Padres; Pappas loses the perfect game by walking the 27th man on a 3-2 pitch.

•Boston catcher Carlton Fisk is a unanimous choice for AL Rookie of the Year.

•Detroit's Ed Brinkman sets a new ML fielding average record for shortstops (.990) and has 72 straight errorless games.

•Tiger Al Kaline's AL-record streak of 242 consecutive errorless games (since broken) in the outfield ends.

•Rod Carew wins the AL bat title (.318) and is the first bat crown winner to go homerless since Zach Wheat in 1918.

•The Giants' Jim Barr retires an ML-record 41 batters in a row over a two-game period.

•On August 1, Padre Nate Colbert hits an ML record-tying five homers in a doubleheader and collects an ML-record 13 RBI.

•California's Nolan Ryan tops the AL in Ks (329) and sets an all-time ML record by allowing only 5.26 hits per game.

•Oakland's Gene Tenace hits .348 with four homers and nine RBI in World Series action.

1972

STEVE CARLTON

Phillies lefty finishes 27-10; mound mates go 32-87

For four years, the St. Louis Cardinals had waited for Steve Carlton to develop into the dominant left-handed pitcher they thought he'd be when he came up for good in 1967. He'd constantly tease the Cardinals management with games like a 19-strikeout classic he threw against the New York Mets in 1969. The Cards also knew they had to be patient, considering the baseball axiom that says left-handers take longer to develop than right-handers. Finally, in 1971, after a disappointing 10-19 season, Carlton blossomed and went 20-9.

When Carlton hassled with Cardinal owner Gussie Busch over his contract, however, the beer baron traded Carlton to the Philadelphia Phillies for their ace right-hander Rick Wise. Nobody had to wait three to five years to see who would get the better of this deal. After just one year, it was called one of the worst trades ever made.

The 1972 Phillies were a terrible team. They won just 59 games and lost 97; only the four-year-old expansion San Diego Padres were as bad. Just imagine how really bad the Phillies would have been without him and his 27 victories. On the days Carlton pitched, Philadelphia played almost like pennant contenders. His victories represented 46 percent of the team's total wins.

"It was really hard to explain," shortstop Larry Bowa, who played behind Carlton that year, once recalled, "but when 'Lefty' was on the mound, we always felt confident we would win. We felt like a different team because he always kept us in the game. I guess we were trying to live up to his excellence."

In winning his first of a record four Cy Young Awards in 1972, Carlton also won pitching's triple crown, adding NL leads in ERA (1.97) and strikeouts (310) to his league-best 27 victories, becoming just the 23rd pitcher since 1900 to accomplish the feat. It was one of the greatest pitching seasons in history. He also tallied league leads for innings pitched (346) and complete games (30), and he threw eight shutouts, and had a .730 winning percentage—second in the league in those categories. He also had a 15-game winning streak. In 1972, and for most of his career, Carlton possessed an excellent fastball and curve. His out pitch was a devastating slider that was especially tough on righty hitters.

The media couldn't get much from Carlton to explain his phenomenal success in '72. Notoriously inaccessible to the press, Carlton eventually stopped talking to reporters altogether by 1978 and was nicknamed "Silent Steve." He preferred to let his work on the mound do his talking. He continued being unhittable for the next 16 years, accumulating 329 lifetime victories and 4,136 strikeouts.

A's Oust the O's, Douse the Mets

In the top of the 13th inning of a tie game at Shea Stadium on September 20, 1973, between Pittsburgh and the New York Mets, Pirates outfielder Richie Zisk edged off first base as the pitch was delivered to his rookie teammate Dave Augustine. Suddenly Zisk was running full tilt as Augustine connected and the ball rocketed toward deep left field.

What happened next will be fodder for eternal debate. Augustine swears to this day that his shot hit the top of the fence for what should have been a two-run homer, and everyone in Pittsburgh agrees. Mets rooters insist that the blast bounced off the facing of the fence, allowing Mets left fielder Cleon Jones to retrieve the ball and relay it to third baseman Wayne Garrett, who fired it home to Jerry Grote in time to nail Zisk, representing the potential winning run. The four umpires working the game, after consulting among themselves and listening to vehement protests from the Pirates, sided with the Mets rooters and ruled Zisk out.

The Mets then won the game with a run in the bottom of the 13th and went on to bag the NL East crown. Had the Pirates instead won this disputed game, the two clubs would have finished the season half a game apart, requiring the Mets to make up a postponed game. A loss in the makeup game would have left the Mets, Pirates, and St. Louis Cardinals all tied at 81-81, forcing a three-way playoff for the division crown. So, perhaps the umpires' ruling was for the best.

As it was, the Mets' 82-79 record was the poorest ever to qualify for postseason action, and their mediocre .509 winning percentage was a fair indicator of the kind of team they had. That year, the Mets had no .300 hitters. They also had no 20-game winners. They were 11th in the NL in runs scored, and they occupied last place in their division as late as August 26. So uneven, though, were the NL's two divisions in 1973, that the Mets lost only one less game than the fourth-place Houston Astros in the Western sector, and were the lone Eastern team to finish above .500.

Despite all of this, the Mets succeeded in

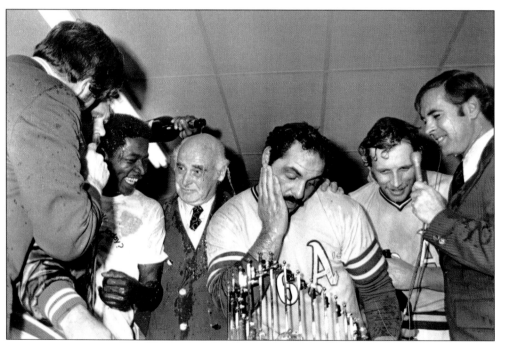

Owner Charlie Finley, flanked by players John "Blue Moon" Odom, left, Sal Bando, center, and Joe Rudi, right, received a champagne bath after the A's won the Series.

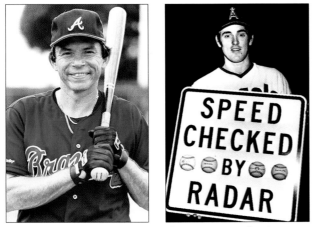

Darrell Evans (left) was one of three Braves with 40 or more home runs in '73, joining Dave Johnson and Hank Aaron. California's Nolan Ryan (right) fired two no-hitters, against the Royals on May 15 and two months later against the Tigers.

making Yogi Berra only the second manager to win pennants in both leagues when they rocked the Cincinnati Reds in the NLCS. After grabbing the West title with 99 wins and the best record in the majors in 1973, Cincinnati figured to use the Mets as a tune-up for their third Series date in the past four seasons. The Mets, however, stubbornly refused to roll over and play dead even after a heartrending 2-1 12-inning loss in Game 4. The following day Tom Seaver logged a 7-2 triumph that set him and his teammates up for what seemed a certain slaughter in the World Series.

The Mets' expected executioners were the Oakland A's, back for a return fall engagement after vanquishing the Baltimore Orioles. It had taken the A's five full rounds, though, as for the second year in a row both the ALCS and NLCS went the limit. Expected to be a high-scoring affair since both clubs had led their respective divisions in runs, the ALCS match evolved instead into a succession of pitching duels. The classic was Game 3, an 11-inning battle between Baltimore's Mike Cuellar and Oakland's Ken Holtzman, won by Holtzman, 2-1.

Prior to the World Series, prognosticators gave Berra the edge over A's skipper Dick Williams in only one area. Mets pitchers had taken their cuts all year whereas A's hurlers had remained on the bench when it came their turn in favor of a designated hitter. However, even that advantage was promptly negated when Holtzman doubled in the third inning of the opener for Oakland's first hit and then

notched the Series' initial tally on a New York error. By the time the inning ended, Oakland had a second run, which was all Holtzman needed to beat Jon Matlack, 2-1.

The Mets then regained the improbable resiliency that had overcome Cincinnati in the NLCS. They won Game 2 in 12 innings and shrugged off a demoralizing 3-2, 11-inning loss two nights later by taking the next two weeknight games in New York.

When the Series returned to Oakland, the A's needed both of the two final contests to retain their crown. In the first, Catfish Hunter and two Oakland relievers made a pair of RBI doubles by Reggie Jackson stand up for a 3-1 win over Seaver. Then, Game 7 brought Matlack and Holtzman together for a rubber Series match after each had previously beaten and lost to the other once. Benefiting from a pair of two-run homers in the third inning by Bert Campaneris and Jackson, Holtzman left in the sixth with a four-run lead. The Mets could only carve it to three before Darold Knowles retired the last batter, placing the A's back in the winner's circle.

Switch-hitting Pete Rose of Cincinnati (right) won his lone NL MVP Award in 1973, hitting .338 with 230 hits. Jim Palmer (left) won the first of his three AL Cy Young Awards. Palmer went 22-9 with a 2.40 ERA.

SEASON'S BEST

•Oakland's Reggie Jackson is AL MVP, leading the loop in homers (32), RBI (117), runs (99), SA (.531), and runs produced (184).

•The Reds' Pete Rose cops NL MVP honors. Rose wins the NL bat crown (.338) and leads the majors in hits (230).

•The Mets' Tom Seaver is voted the Cy Young winner in the NL even though he wins just 19 games, five less than Ron Bryant of the Giants. Seaver leads the NL in ERA (2.08) and Ks (251) and ties for the lead in CGs (18).

•Baltimore's Jim Palmer wins his first Cy Young Award in the AL.

•The AL adopts the designated hitter rule—pitchers no longer have to bat for themselves. On April 6, Yankee Ron Blomberg becomes the first DH to bat in an ML game.

•The Pirates' Willie Stargell tops ML in homers (44), doubles (43), RBI (119), and SA (.646).

•George Steinbrenner buys the Yankees.

Wilbur Wood

•The third "Basic Agreement" gives players the right to salary arbitration and to the "five and 10" rule with respect to trades.

•White Sox Wilbur Wood is the first pitcher in 57 years to both win and lose 20 games in a season, as he goes 24-20 and ties Bryant for ML lead in wins. On July 20, Wood becomes the last ML hurler to start both games of a doubleheader; he loses both.

•Oriole Bobby Grich's .995 fielding average sets an ML record for second basemen.

•Detroit's John Hiller sets a new ML record with 38 saves.

•California's Nolan Ryan fans an ML-record 383. Ryan no-hits KC on May 15 and Detroit on July 15.

•The Braves have three men with at least 40 homers—Dave Johnson (43), Darrell Evans (41), and Hank Aaron (40).

•Yankee pitchers Mike Kekich and Fritz Peterson swap wives, families, houses, and pets.

•The NL wins the All-Star Game 7-1 at Kansas City, as a record 54 players participate.

•The Twins' Rod Carew leads the AL in BA (.350) and hits (203) and ties for the lead in triples (11).

•Giant Bobby Bonds just misses becoming the first "40-40" player in ML history, as he hits 39 homers and steals 43 bases.

•Met Rusty Staub tops all batters in the World Series with 11 hits, a .423 BA, and six RBI.

REGGIE JACKSON

Brash basher talks the talk, walks the walk

He was the driving force on two great teams and the first player reporters wanted to talk to in the locker room. His erudite self-promotion often bordered on obsessive, but like fellow world-class boaster Muhammad Ali, he could usually back up his claims while providing plenty of entertainment. Reggie Jackson ruffled plenty of feathers and made his share of enemies during a tumultuous 21 major-league seasons, but with 11 playoff appearances—including a World Series title in his MVP year of 1973—nobody could challenge him when it came to winning.

Confident to the point of cockiness, the free-swinging left-hander signed with the Athletics for a $90,000 bonus in '66 and gave a hint of what was to come with 21 home runs and 71 strikeouts in 56 games for minor league Modesto that summer. His 29 homers—many of the tape-measure variety—made him a hit with Oakland fans as a 1968 rookie,

but his .250 batting average and 171 strikeouts (just four shy of a major-league record) showed a lack of discipline that would rankle managers throughout his career. Leading the league in whiffs his first four years, Reggie still showed flashes of brilliance. He hit a record 40 home runs through July 29, 1969, and despite a horrific second-half slump, finished with 47 homers, 118 RBI, and a league-high 123 runs. Unable to approach these totals over his next three seasons, he added improved right field defense and speed (26 steals in 1970) to his arsenal.

His titanic homer over the right field roof at Tiger Stadium in the '71 All-Star Game drew headlines, but although Jackson was a key contributor to Oakland's 1972 world championship, it wasn't until the following year he put it all together. Leading the AL in homers (32), RBI (117), slugging (.531), and runs (99), he was also fourth in total bases (286) and on-base percentage (.387) while registering 22 steals and a then-career high .293 batting average. The A's won their second straight AL pennant, then defeated the upstart Mets in a thrilling seven-game World Series—Jackson leading the way with a .310 batting average, six RBI, and a clutch homer in the final game. Two more great seasons in Oakland followed (a third consecutive world championship in '74, a league-high 36 homers in '75), but Reggie eventually fled tightwad owner Charlie Finley for greener pastures. He joined the Yankees in 1977 for $3 million over five seasons, and while he infuriated teammates by declaring himself "the straw that stirs the drink," no one complained when he hit a record five homers in the World Series that fall. He eventually helped the Yankees to two more pennants, and Hall of Fame voters agreed his 563 lifetime homers (eighth all-time) and World Series-record .755 slugging percentage made up for his big mouth and record 2,597 strikeouts.

A's Slap Dodgers For Title No. 3

Upon winning his second successive world championship in 1973, Dick Williams resigned as manager of the Oakland A's. He reportedly was fed up with having to deal with owner Charlie Finley. Williams cited Finley's attempt during the 1973 Series to have second baseman Mike Andrews improperly put on the disabled list after Andrews made two costly errors as the catalytic event. Finley was hardly shattered by his manager's defection. He gave Williams's job to Alvin Dark, and in his second dugout stint with the A's, Dark guided them effortlessly to their fourth straight division crown.

The only significant difference from the A's three previous wins was that in 1974 their closest pursuer was the Texas Rangers. Transplanted from Washington to the Arlington area the previous year, the Rangers had commemorated the move by losing 105 games for the worst record in the majors. Late in the 1973 season, however, owner Bob Short hired Billy Martin to manage the club almost the moment Martin was fired by the Detroit Tigers.

The game of musical chairs among managers extended to the AL East in 1974 as Ralph Houk left the New York Yankees for the Tigers' dugout slot. Replacing Houk was Bill Virdon, who had been let go by Pittsburgh late in the 1973 campaign. The Boston Red Sox also had a new pilot in Darrell Johnson. Virdon and Johnson kept their clubs in the thick of the AL East chase well past Labor Day; even the Cleveland Indians had a remote flag hope until the late going. In the end it was longtime incumbent Earl Weaver and his Baltimore Orioles who triumphed. The Orioles won 28 of their last 34 games—including a three-game series with the Yankees in mid-September—to beat Virdon's vastly improved club by 2 games and the Red Sox by 7.

So evenly balanced was the AL in 1974, that the Orioles topped the loop with just 91 wins. The California Angels, with 94 defeats, were the lone team to collect more than 90 losses. Unhappily, the same sort of parity did not exist in the NL, where the hapless San Diego Padres for the second year in a row lost 102 games. The Chicago Cubs and New York Mets also were beaten more than 90 times. At

Oakland catcher Ray Fosse and outfielder Billy North celebrate Fosse's second-inning home run in the Series-clinching Game 5.

least the two division races were competitive. The Los Angeles Dodgers, largely on the strength of reliever Mike Marshall's rubber arm and Steve Garvey's MVP bat, captured the West, finishing with an ML-best 102 wins and a four-game bulge on the second biggest winner in the majors in 1974, the Cincinnati Reds.

Indeed, even the NL West third-place Atlanta Braves, with their 88 wins, matched the victory total posted by the top team in the East as the two NL divisions once again were badly imbalanced. Danny Murtaugh, his health permitting him to return for a fourth and final stint at the Pittsburgh helm, coaxed the Pirates home 1½ games ahead of Red Schoendienst's St. Louis Cardinals. Spirited by Lou Brock's 118 steals and sturdy bullpen work from Al Hrabosky, the Cards nearly overcame poor seasons from all of their starters (except Lynn McGlothen) before faltering on the last lap.

The A's and the Dodgers both needed just four games to capture their respective LCSs. Baltimore gave Oakland a scare, though, by winning the opener. However, the O's were then held scoreless for an LCS-record 30 consecutive innings by Ken Holtzman, Vida Blue, and Catfish Hunter before breaking through for a solo run off Rollie Fingers in the last frame of the finale.

The same four Oakland hurlers, plus Blue Moon Odom, united to give Walter Alston a painful postseason sendoff by beating his Dodgers in five games.

While the 1974 Series was Alston's last taste of fall play, the A's would be back again in 1975 for their fifth consecutive appearance in the ALCS. Only in retrospect is it apparent how remarkable a team the A's were in the early 1970s. Not only were

Pittsburgh's Al Oliver (top left) hit .321. Baltimore's Mike Cuellar (top center) won 20 games for the last time. Dodger Steve Garvey (top right) was the NL's MVP while teammate Mike Marshall (bottom) was the first reliever to win the Cy Young.

they the first non-Yankee team to win three successive world titles, but they were the last to accomplish the feat in the 20th century. Now that an extra playoff tier has been added to the postseason format, it makes the climb to the top all the more arduous. Even by the 1970s, the A's had an obstacle that the 1936 to '39 and the 1949 to '53 Yankees never had to face while stringing together four and five straight world titles, respectively. Neither Yankees dynasty had to triumph year after year in LCS action to earn the right to play in the World Series.

In a sense, then, the 1972 to '74 Oakland A's are the most impressive dynasty of all. No other team, after all, has ever won six straight postseason matches.

SEASON'S BEST

•Dodger Steve Garvey is NL MVP.

•Ranger Jeff Burroughs wins the AL MVP Award, topping the loop in RBI (118) and runs produced (177).

•Oakland's Catfish Hunter wins the AL Cy Young in a close vote over Ranger Ferguson Jenkins, as both tie for the ML lead in wins with 25.

•LA's Mike Marshall appears in an all-time ML-record 106 games and is the first reliever to cop the Cy Young Award.

•Atlanta's Hank Aaron hits his 715th career homer on April 8 off Al Downing of the Dodgers to set the all-time ML record. Aaron defeats Japanese slugger Sadaharu Oh 10-9 in a specially arranged home run contest in Tokyo.

•Phillie Mike Schmidt tops the majors with 36 homers.

•St. Louis's Lou Brock shatters the ML record by stealing 118 bases.

•Minnesota's Rod Carew takes the AL bat crown (.364) and leads in hits (218).

•White Sox Dick Allen tops the AL in homers (32) and SA (.563).

•The Reds' Pete Rose makes an all-time ML-record 771 plate appearances. Rose tops the ML with 110 runs and 45 doubles.

Lou Brock

•Ron LeFlore debuts with the Tigers a year after being released from prison.

•On June 4 in Cleveland, 10-cent beer night results in a near riot and forfeit of a game to Texas.

•Brewer Don Money's .989 fielding average sets a new ML season record for a third baseman.

•The Orioles set an AL record when they win five straight games by shutouts.

•Cincinnati's Johnny Bench leads the NL with 129 RBI and 315 total bases.

•Atlanta's Ralph Garr tops the NL with a .353 BA, 214 hits, and 17 triples.

•The NL wins the All-Star Game 7-2 at Pittsburgh for its 11th win in the last 12 games.

•Pittsburgh's Richie Zisk has 21 RBI in a 10-game span.

•Ray Kroc, founder of McDonald's, buys the Padres.

•George Steinbrenner is suspended by Commissioner Bowie Kuhn for a year because of his part in the Watergate scandal.

•Detroit's Al Kaline gets his 3,000th hit, then retires after the season.

•The Cards beat the Mets 4-3 on September 11 in a 25-inning night game.

•Buzz Capra of the Braves tops ML in ERA (2.28).

HANK AARON

Ruth's record falls; Hammerin' Hank nails No. 715

During a career that spanned from 1954 through 1976, Hank Aaron was never known as just a home run hitter. He could hit homers, to be sure, leading the NL four times and belting at least 44 homers in four different seasons. Aaron never hit more than 47 in any season, but the silent superstar was methodical and consistent. "Hammerin' Hank" had a quick, efficient swing, which derived its power from strong, sinewy wrists.

Aaron walked away with the MVP crown in 1957 (he hit a late September home run to give Milwaukee the pennant), batting titles in 1956 and 1959, and a .364 batting average in 14 World Series games. It was not until June 10, 1972, however—when Aaron hit his 649th homer to pass Willie Mays and take second place on the all-time list—that his power exploits drew national attention.

Suddenly, there was great interest in the 38-year-old Aaron and in the possibility of him hitting another 66 homers—the number needed to break the lifetime record of 714 round-trippers set by Babe Ruth. "Even if I'm lucky enough to hit 715 home runs," Aaron said modestly, "Babe Ruth will still be regarded as the greatest home run hitter who ever lived."

Going into the 1973 season needing only 42 homers to pass Ruth, Aaron was bombarded by pressure from all sides. "It should have been an enjoyable time," he later remembered, "but instead, everywhere I went people were talking about home runs. And I had no privacy."

Aaron hit number 713 on the next to the last day of the 1973 season. When the Braves' 1974 season began on the road, the team's owners tried to bench Aaron. They wanted him to break the record at home. Commissioner Bowie Kuhn ruled that the club would have to play him during its first three games. On April 4, Aaron tied Ruth on his first swing of the season with a shot off Cincinnati Reds pitcher Jack Billingham into left-center field. It had taken Aaron 2,498 more at bats than the Babe to hit 714 homers.

Four days later, the Braves played a nationally televised game against the Los Angeles Dodgers. There were 53,000 people in the stands at Atlanta Stadium and another 35 million viewers, all hoping to witness history. Hammerin' Hank did not disappoint. Al Downing walked Aaron on five pitches in the second inning. Then, on his first official at bat of the game in the fourth inning, he knocked a fastball over the fence in left field for the monumental homer. Aaron had conquered what he called "the Cadillac of baseball records."

Aaron traveled around the bases a few more times before he was through, accumulating 755 homers upon his retirement two years later (as a member of the Milwaukee Brewers).

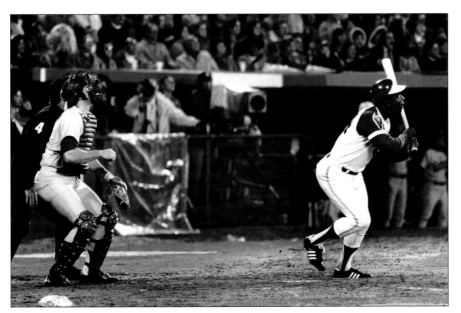

REDS WIN DESPITE FISK'S HISTORIC HR

Many vote the sixth game of the 1975 World Series as the greatest in the history of baseball. Likewise, a number of authorities consider '75 a linchpin season. In their view, the events of that year and the fervor they aroused restored baseball as our national pastime.

Spiraling attendance figures, TV contracts, and player salaries in the years following the 1975 campaign support the argument that baseball experienced an enormous renaissance, but there is a persuasive counterargument. Among the points it makes are that the 1975 regular season was actually quite dull and that, with the exception of Game 6, the World Series was no more exciting than several other fall affairs in the recent past.

There is even merit to the claim that Game 6 was far from a classic demonstration of baseball at its best, but the game did have several vital ingredients. An underdog, on the brink of elimination, won in overtime after coming from behind in the late innings. The winning hit was a home run. Still more, the victorious team was the Boston Red Sox, who had not won a championship in 56 years. Of course, perhaps most important of all, the Red Sox nevertheless lost the Series and continued to tease the millions who wallow in the postseason curse that has hovered over the franchise ever since it sold Babe Ruth to the New York Yankees.

In truth, the Red Sox were underdogs in 1975 long before the World Series. After helping the Oakland A's to win three straight world championships, pitcher Catfish Hunter was made a free agent because owner Charlie Finley neglected to abide by a clause in Hunter's contract. When the New York Yankees signed Hunter for a package in upwards of $3 million, they instantly were favored to win the AL East.

While Hunter met expectations with a 23-14 mark, the Yankees' other three main starters were an aggregate 41-42, leading owner George Steinbrenner to dump manager Bill Virdon in August for Billy Martin. The former Yankees second sacker and disciple of Casey Stengel had long seemed bound for the Yankee Stadium dugout. It was only after the Yankees floundered under Virdon, however, and Martin had worn out his welcome with the Texas Rangers—his third AL dugout stop since 1969—that the timing felt right to Steinbrenner.

To Boston skipper Darrell Johnson the timing felt right in April to bench Juan Beniquez and Bernie Carbo, two outfield regulars in 1974, and give their jobs to a pair of heralded rookies, Jim Rice

Carlton Fisk was mobbed at home after his 12th-inning homer beat the Reds in Game 6, keeping the Red Sox alive.

Minnesota's Rod Carew (right) hit .359, the third straight season he batted .350 or better. Dave Parker of the Pirates (left) emerged, batting .308 with 25 homers and 101 RBI.

and Fred Lynn. Rice responded with 22 homers, 102 RBI, and a .309 BA. Even though this was one of the best frosh seasons ever, he failed to be named the best yearling on his team, let alone in the AL, when Lynn produced several loop-record rookie marks.

With Rice and Lynn providing such a dynamite one-two punch, not even a subpar year from Carl Yastrzemski could halt Boston's bid to represent the East in the ALCS against five-time West champion Oakland. The match only highlighted A's manager Alvin Dark's inability to replace Hunter. After the Red Sox bested Ken Holtzman and Vida Blue in the first two clashes, Dark had no one better than Holtzman to throw in Game 3. Working on only two days' rest, the A's southpaw gave it his all until the fifth inning. By the end of that frame, though, the Red Sox were up 4-0, and 12 outs later the A's three-year reign at the top had been ended by a surprisingly simple Boston sweep.

The Cincinnati Reds had an even easier road to the World Series. A postexpansion loop-record 108 wins gave the Reds the NL West crown by a gigantic 20-game spread over the Los Angeles Dodgers. Pittsburgh, meanwhile, presented manager Danny Murtaugh with one last postseason opportunity by capturing its fifth division title in six years. In the NLCS, though, Reds pilot Sparky Anderson efficiently used his deep pitching staff to end the match in three games.

Cincinnati's hill depth was on display for the entire nation in Game 6 of the World Series. Up 3-2 in games and ahead 6-3 in the bottom of the eighth, the Reds needed only six outs to close it out. When Carbo tied the count with a three-run homer, however, a desperate Anderson went through a record eight hurlers. The eighth, Pat Darcy, was on the rubber in the bottom of the 12th with the score still tied 6-6. That's when Carlton Fisk stepped up and tagged a drive that hugged the left field foul line at Fenway Park. With Fisk giving it body English to keep it fair, the ball hit the foul pole above the Green Monster, and the Red Sox were still alive.

The following night Boston led 3-0, but then the Reds proved they too could mount a clutch comeback. Tony Perez's two-run homer in the sixth narrowed the gap to 3-2, and in the top of the ninth, Joe Morgan's bloop single plated Pete Rose to give Cincinnati a 4-3 lead. When reliever Will McEnaney induced Yastrzemski to loft a lazy fly for the last Series out, the Reds nailed their first championship in 35 years.

After signing with the Yanks as a free agent, Catfish Hunter (top) won 23 games and the Cy Young Award. NL MVP Joe Morgan of Cincinnati (bottom) had the World Series-clinching hit in Game 7, scoring Ken Griffey Sr.

SEASON'S BEST

• Boston's Fred Lynn becomes the only player in ML history to be named Rookie of the Year and MVP in the same season. Lynn tops the AL in runs (103), doubles (47), runs produced (187), and SA (.566). He drives in 105 runs, while rookie teammate Jim Rice knocks in 102.

• Cincinnati's Joe Morgan wins the NL MVP Award.

• The Mets' Tom Seaver leads the NL with 22 wins and cops the Cy Young Award.

• Baltimore's Jim Palmer wins his second AL Cy Young, as he leads the loop in ERA (2.09) and shutouts (10) and ties for the lead in wins (23).

• Chicago's Bill Madlock takes his first NL bat crown (.354).

• In a historic decision, arbitrator Peter Seitz grants pitchers Dave McNally and Andy Messersmith free agency.

• Frank Robinson is named manager of Cleveland to become the first African-American manager in major-league history.

• Nolan Ryan throws his fourth no-hitter in three years on June 1 vs. Baltimore.

• The Tigers lose 19 games in a row.

Mike Schmidt

• Yankee Catfish Hunter becomes the last ML pitcher to toss 30 CGs.

• Davey Lopes of LA sets a new ML record when he steals 38 consecutive bases without being caught.

• The Pirates beat the Cubs 22-0 on September 16—most one-sided shutout in ML since 1883. In the game, Rennie Stennett of the Pirates becomes the lone player in the 20th century to go 7-for-7 in a nine-inning game.

• Four A's pitchers combine to no-hit California on September 28.

• Bob Watson of the Astros scores the millionth run in ML history.

• Harmon Killebrew retires with 8,147 at bats, 573 home runs, no sacrifice bunts, and no bunt hits.

• Dave Cash of the Phils sets a new ML record (since broken) when he has 699 at bats.

• Cincinnati's Pete Rose leads the NL in runs (112) and doubles (47).

• Phillie Mike Schmidt leads the majors with 38 homers.

• Brewer George Scott leads the AL in RBI (109) and total bases (318) and ties Oakland's Reggie Jackson for the lead in homers (36).

• Billy Martin is fired as Texas manager in midseason, then hired by the Yankees to replace Bill Virdon.

FRED LYNN

Red Sox rookie outslugs everyone, named AL MVP

The Boston Red Sox blew a seven-game lead in the AL East during the final five weeks of the 1974 season, but amidst the gloom of eight straight losses and a 14-24 stretch run, one player just up from the minors offered some hope for the future. His .419 batting average and 10 RBI in 15 games wasn't enough to stave off disaster then, but in '75 Fred Lynn would see to it that the Red Sox didn't wilt when it counted. Lynn put together an incredible season and became the first rookie to ever win an MVP Award.

A member of three championship teams at the University of Southern California, the tall 185-pounder was chosen by the Red Sox in the second round of the 1973 draft and debuted in Boston just one year later. Bursting with confidence and a beautiful, compact swing, the left-handed Lynn quickly won over Fenway Park fans anxious for a new outfield hero to complement aging Carl Yastrzemski. Going above .300 for good in the fourth game of the season, he got the attention of the baseball world June 18 with three home runs, a triple, and a single good for 10 RBI and a record-tying 16 total bases at Detroit.

When he wasn't making the crucial hit, the Gold Glove winner was saving games in center. In fact, he made diving, somersaulting catches and leaps against Fenway's famed Green Monster so often it had to be padded the following season. By year's end, the Sox had won the East by 4½ games over the Orioles, and Lynn was among the leaders in almost every statistical category. He was the first rookie ever to be tops in slugging (.566). Lynn was also first in runs (103) and doubles (47), second in hitting (.331), third in runs batted in (105), and fourth in total bases (299) while hitting 21 homers. After hitting .364 in the playoffs against Oakland and .280 with five RBI and several great fielding plays in a seven-game World Series loss to Cincinnati, Lynn was handed nearly every major award the sports community could dish out—including AL Rookie of the Year and MVP honors.

"Fragile Freddy" was an All-Star each of his first nine full seasons, but with the exception of an outstanding performance in '79 (.333 batting average, 39 homers, 122 RBI) was injury-plagued and unable to match his rookie numbers. He would have been fine were he able to play all his games in cozy Fenway (where he hit .350 versus .270 on the road). After his trade to California in 1981, his .308 lifetime batting average plummeted. He remained a 20-plus homer threat with four teams until his 1990 retirement (hitting .283 lifetime), but injuries mounted and may have endangered his possible Cooperstown induction.

REDS SWEEP PHILS, ROUT THE YANKS

Because of a ruling by arbitrator Peter Seitz in December 1975, pitchers Dave McNally and Andy Messersmith were declared "free agents" after they opted to play out the 1975 season without signing contracts with their respective teams, the Montreal Expos and the Los Angeles Dodgers. When McNally, who only wanted to prove a point, then retired and Messersmith accepted an offer from the Atlanta Braves, players on every club found themselves locked out of spring training by the angry owners of all 24 franchises.

Commissioner Bowie Kuhn intervened to get major-league baseball's centennial season started on time, but by then a deep schism had appeared in the game's fabric. Following the 1976 season, the free-agent era would begin in earnest as star performers in both leagues—using the Seitz decision as leverage—chose to play without contracts and then sell their services to the highest bidder.

Initially, the chief beneficiaries of the new method to build a team were the New York Yankees and their deep-pocket owner George Steinbrenner. Before the 1977 season, Steinbrenner would sign Reggie Jackson, one of the main cogs for the Oakland A's dynasty in the early 1970s. Unwilling to meet Jackson's financial demands, A's owner Charlie Finley traded him prior to the 1976 season to the Baltimore Orioles along with pitcher Ken Holtzman, who had also begun clamoring for more money.

In June 1976, Holtzman went to the Yankees as part of a phenomenal 10-player deal that in the long run helped both clubs but at first did more for the Yankees. Holtzman gave manager Billy Martin a dependable fourth starter; Doyle Alexander, another piece of the deal, became the Yankees' fifth starter; and reliever Grant Jackson, also part of the trade, was a perfect 6-0 with a 1.68 ERA as a setup man for closer Sparky Lyle.

"The Big Red Machine" continued to roll, thanks to, left to right: Tony Perez, Johnny Bench, Joe Morgan, and Pete Rose. The Reds scored 857 runs in 1976, 232 more than any other NL team.

Phillie Mike Schmidt (top left) *led the NL with 38 HRs. The Yankees' Thurman Munson* (top center) *was AL MVP. Chris Chambliss was mobbed after his homer sent the Yanks to the Series* (top right). *KC's George Brett* (bottom) *won the AL batting title* (.333).

Jackson, meanwhile, could not help the Orioles to get closer than 10½ games to the Yankees on farewell day. The margin represented Earl Weaver's longest distance from the top spot since his full-time tenure with Baltimore began in 1969 and was largely traceable to a thin hill corps and poor seasons from several regulars. The Boston Red Sox, hoping to repeat as AL champs, faded to third when only Luis Tiant of their starting pitchers could approach his previous year's output.

Having already lost Reggie Jackson and all of their pitching stars except Vida Blue and Rollie Fingers, the Oakland A's also lost Alvin Dark when he became owner Charlie Finley's latest managerial casualty. Dark's replacement was Chuck Tanner. Tanner somehow kept the A's in the hunt until the waning days of the season despite an attempt by Finley to unload Blue to the Yankees and Fingers and outfielder Joe Rudi to the Red Sox for $3.5 million. Even though Kuhn stopped the fire sale, calling it detrimental to the game, Finley's way of combating spiraling player salaries destroyed most of what little harmony was left in the A's clubhouse and simplified the Kansas City Royals' task in ending Oakland's five-year domination of the AL West.

The Pittsburgh Pirates, similarly dominant in the NL East during the same period, won 92 games, enough to win the division crown in every year since 1970. In 1976, though, that total left them 9 games back of the Philadelphia Phillies. Mike Schmidt's power production and .300 seasons from all three outfielders—Greg Luzinski, Jay Johnstone, and Garry Maddox—lifted the Phils over the century mark in wins for the first time in their history.

Awaiting the Phils in the NLCS were the powerhouse Cincinnati Reds, who had also won more than 100 games. Reds skipper Sparky Anderson, seeing no reason to change the mix that made his club world champs in 1975, again spread the hill work among a wide assortment of pitchers. No fewer than six of Anderson's hurlers made at least 20 starts, and all six won between 11 and 15 games. Backing them was the best crew of firemen in the game, led by Rawley Eastwick with 11 wins and 26 saves. Though his team was dubbed "The Big Red Machine" because of its hitting, Anderson let it remain a well-kept secret that his pitching staff was his real forte.

The Phils were overmatched against the Reds, bowing out of the NLCS in just three games, but the Yankees were expected to provide more competition

after a gritty win over the Royals in the ALCS, culminating in Chris Chambliss's solo homer that won the deciding fifth game, 7-6, in the bottom of the ninth. Instead, the Yankees were a party to the least competitive World Series in recent memory and a gala Cincinnati achievement. By sweeping four straight games, the Reds succeeded in doing something no other NL club since the 1921 and '22 New York Giants had done: win back-to-back world championships.

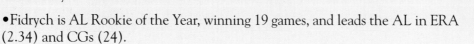

SEASON'S BEST

- Cincinnati's Joe Morgan is again NL MVP, after stealing 60 bases and leading in SA (.576).

- Thurman Munson is AL MVP and tops Yankee hitters in the World Series with a .529 BA.

- San Diego's Randy Jones takes the NL Cy Young, topping the NL with 22 wins.

- Baltimore's Jim Palmer claims his third AL Cy Young in four years, as he leads the AL with 22 wins.

- In June, A's owner Charlie Finley tries to sell Joe Rudi, Rollie Fingers, and Vida Blue, but Commissioner Bowie Kuhn vetoes the deals.

- The Royals' George Brett wins a controversial bat crown over teammate Hal McRae, .333 to .332. Brett wins the title on his last at bat of the season, as Twins outfielder Steve Braun seems to deliberately misplay the ball. Brett leads the AL in hits (215), total bases (298), and triples (14).

- Philly's Mike Schmidt leads the majors in homers (38) and total bases (306). Schmidt hits four homers in a 10-inning game on April 17.

- The NL wins the All-Star Game 7-1 at Philadelphia, as Detroit rookie Mark Fidrych starts for the AL and takes the loss.

Bill Madlock

- Fidrych is AL Rookie of the Year, winning 19 games, and leads the AL in ERA (2.34) and CGs (24).

- Ted Turner buys the Braves.

- Hank Aaron retires with all-time ML records for homers (755), RBI (2,297), and total bases (6,856).

- The only "rainout" in Astrodome history occurs on June 15 when heavy rains prevent fans and umps from getting to the dome.

- On September 12, at age 54, Minnie Minoso of the White Sox becomes the oldest player to get a hit in an ML game.

- The Reds' Pete Rose tops the NL in hits (215), doubles (42), and runs (130).

- Chicago's Bill Madlock wins the NL bat crown (.339).

- The Reds' Johnny Bench leads all World Series hitters with a .533 BA, two homers, and six RBI.

- Free-agency bidding begins in earnest after the 1976 season; the Yankees sign Reggie Jackson for $3.5 million.

MARK FIDRYCH

Flaky Tiger talks to the ball, mows down hitters

He was a breath of fresh air at a time when the game was changing, a wonderful reminder of what baseball was all about just as free agency, salary arbitration, and million-dollar contracts were taking hold. Mark Fidrych joined the starting rotation of the Detroit Tigers in May 1976, and by the time the gangly 22-year-old with the curly blond locks was through talking to the ball five months later he had earned 19 victories, the American League Rookie of the Year Award, and the hearts of everyone who saw him shake and smile his way to victory.

The Messersmith decision granting all six-year players the right to sell themselves to the highest bidder became baseball law in 1976, and salaries would soon escalate to dizzying heights. It was the last summer to see youngsters struggling to make the grade at under $20,000 a year. One of these final hopefuls was Fidrych—a lanky 175-pound bundle of energy from Worcester, Massachusetts, who had spent most of the previous season in Class-A ball. Not even on the Detroit roster during spring training, he made just two relief appearances the first six weeks as the Tigers slid toward the AL East cellar.

Fidrych was beginning to get edgy about the situation when Manager Ralph Houk finally gave him a chance May 15 in Cleveland. Mark completed a 2-1, two-hit victory and allowed only one walk. He managed this accomplishment in under two hours. Houk liked what he saw (the Tigers didn't have much else), and Fidrych became a regular member of the rotation. By June 28, the eccentric young right-hander with the strong slider and excellent control was 7-1 with six complete games in eight starts. When he defeated first-place New York 5-1 on a June night before 47,855 in attendance and a nationwide television audience, a star was born.

Less than two months after the Cleveland game, Mark started for the American League in the All-Star contest at Philadelphia. An expected Fidrych appearance was now the hottest ticket in the American League. Fans were very anxious to see the screwball who sprinted to the mound before each inning, shook hands with his infielders following great plays, and seemed to talk to the ball before pitching it. Nicknamed "The Bird" partly because of his curly blond hair, Fidrych wound up 19-9 with a league-best 2.34 ERA and 24 complete games (five of 10 innings or more) in just 29 starts. Tiger attendance increased by 408,000 despite a fifth-place finish, as Mark appeared poised for continued stardom.

Then, all too quickly, it was over. Fidrych hurt his knee and arm in the spring of 1977, and despite several comeback attempts, went just 10-10 before calling it quits in spring training of 1981. Although 10-game winners would soon be making millions of dollars, it almost seemed appropriate that the guy making folks laugh just as the game was becoming big business missed out on the big dough.

YANKEE DEALS PAY HUGE DIVIDENDS

Seemingly only a string of arm ailments contracted by several key pitchers prevented George Steinbrenner's liberal use of his checkbook from making the New York Yankees unstoppable in 1977. During the off-season, Steinbrenner plunged headlong into the new free-agency pool by signing not only Reggie Jackson but also Cincinnati Reds southpaw star Don Gullett.

Just as important, though, to the Yankees' return to power after a 12-year absence were the behind-the-scenes contributions of Steinbrenner's general manager, Gabe Paul. In 1972, while still acting GM for the Cleveland Indians, Paul dealt Graig Nettles to New York for a packet of lesser players. Two years later, the Yankees snared Chris Chambliss and Dick Tidrow from the Tribe in an equally one-sided deal. Following the 1975 season, Paul—by then the Yankees' front office chieftain—engineered two remarkable trades on the same day. In the first, he garnered pitcher Ed Figueroa and center fielder Mickey Rivers from the California Angels for Bobby Bonds. Before the stroke of midnight, he swung a deal with the Pittsburgh Pirates that had an even farther-reaching influence on the Yankees' fortunes. In exchange for pitcher Doc Medich, New York received hurler Dock Ellis and a young minor-league prospect named Willie Randolph who, as fate would have it, would become the best all-around second baseman in the AL during the decade ahead.

Yet, even with all their high-price free agents and trade plums, the Yankees were pushed hard until the last week of the 1977 season by both the Boston Red Sox and the Baltimore Orioles. Only a great stretch drive brought New York its second AL East crown in a row and saved Billy Martin from being fired from his fourth dugout assignment. Martin had jeopardized his job by nearly engaging in a fistfight with Jackson in the Yankees dugout under the harsh eye of a national TV camera.

In comparison, Kansas City skipper Whitey Herzog had an uneventful time steering the Royals to their second consecutive AL West title. The runner-up Texas Rangers' managerial climate, how-

Yankee Reggie Jackson was deserving of his "Mr. October" tag with three homers on three successive pitches in Game 6 and five homers in the Series.

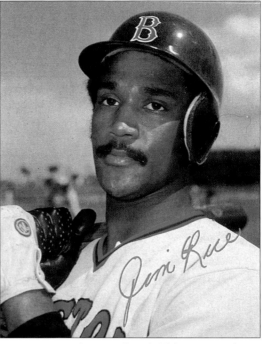

Minnesota's Rod Carew (top left) hit .388 and captured AL MVP honors. After coming to the Dodgers the year before, Dusty Baker (top center) hit 30 homers in '77. Philadelphia's Greg Luzinski (bottom) was a bull at the plate, with 39 homers and 130 RBI. Jim Rice of Boston (top right) hit .320 and led the AL with 39 home runs.

ever, made even Martin's situation seem laidback. In the spring, infielder Lenny Randle flattened incumbent pilot Frank Lucchesi and was promptly suspended by the team. Lucchesi himself was dumped halfway into the season for Eddie Stanky. However, after only one game in the Rangers dugout, Stanky quit when he discovered his competitive fires had cooled. A few days later Billy Hunter was hired and stoked the Rangers to a torrid 60-33 finishing kick. The Royals, though, enjoyed such a huge lead that they still came home 8 games in front.

Managerial reshuffling also impacted on the NL race. Danny Murtaugh's off-season death impelled the Pittsburgh Pirates to pluck Chuck Tanner from the Oakland A's dugout. Though Tanner drove the Bucs to 96 wins, they were never really in the NL East race as Danny Ozark got 101 victories from his Phillies. Even less competitive, though, was the NL West, where rookie helmsman Tom Lasorda assumed the burden of replacing popular longtime Los Angeles Dodgers mentor Walter Alston. In his first three weeks at the wheel, Lasorda got LA off to a 17-3

start. Though the Cincinnati Reds nibbled away, they were unable to cut into the Dodgers' huge early lead and wound up finishing 10 games out.

Despite winning over 100 games for the second year in a row, Ozark suffered the same result in the NLCS. The Phils took an early lead by snaring the opener in Los Angeles behind Steve Carlton but self-destructed in the ninth inning of Game 3, turning a 5-3 advantage into a 6-5 deficit. Tommy John then beat Carlton to give the Dodgers the pennant in four games. This early decision also allowed the Dodgers the luxury of watching on TV the following night while the Yankees and the Royals settled who the AL Series representative would be.

Five superlative relief innings by Cy Young winner Sparky Lyle had won Game 4 for the Yankees to knot the ALCS at 2-all but appeared to leave Martin without his bullpen ace in the finale. When New York scored in the top of the eighth, though, to trim Kansas City's lead to 3-2, Lyle got the call and held the fort in the bottom half. Three outs from the first pennant by an AL expansion team, a trio of Royals

hurlers instead served up three runs in the ninth. When Royals hitters surrendered meekly to Lyle in their final turn at bat, the Yankees had their 31st pennant.

Nine days later, the Yankees celebrated their 21st world championship after Jackson's slugging and the pitching of Mike Torrez and Ron Guidry subdued the Dodgers in six rounds.

SEASON'S BEST

- The AL swells to 14 teams, taking on two new franchises—Toronto and Seattle.

- Cincinnati's George Foster is NL MVP, as he leads ML with 52 homers and 149 RBI. Foster also leads the NL in runs (124), SA (.631), total bases (388), and runs produced (221).

Steve Carlton

- Minnesota's Rod Carew wins the AL MVP Award after hitting .388, top BA in majors since expansion. Carew leads the ML with 239 hits, 128 runs, and a .452 OBP and the AL in triples (16) and runs produced (214).

- Philadelphia's Steve Carlton wins the Cy Young in the NL, as he leads the majors with 23 wins.

- Yankee Sparky Lyle becomes the first reliever to win the AL Cy Young.

- California's Nolan Ryan fans an ML-high 341 batters in 299 innings.

- Boston's Jim Rice leads the AL in homers (39), SA (.593), and total bases (382).

- The Dodgers become the first team in history with four 30-homer men—Ron Cey, Steve Garvey, Dusty Baker, and Reggie Smith.

- The Mets, frustrated by salary disputes with Tom Seaver, trade him to the Reds for four players of no particular consequence.

- Chicago's Chet Lemon sets the AL record for outfielders with 512 putouts.

- The Royals put together a 16-game win streak.

- On April 10, Cleveland and Boston combine to score an ML-record 19 runs in one inning.

- On July 4, the Red Sox beat Toronto 9-6 on the strength of eight homers.

- KC's Hal McRae leads the ML with 54 doubles.

- Pittsburgh's Dave Parker tops the NL in BA (.338), hits (215), and doubles (44).

- Pirate John Candelaria tops ML with a 2.34 ERA and .800 winning percentage.

- The Royals are the first expansion team this century to top the majors in wins, as they net 102.

- Reggie Jackson, "Mr. October," leads World Series hitters with a .450 BA and five homers, including three in Game 6.

- The Yankees' Billy Martin wins his only world championship as a manager.

GEORGE FOSTER

Reds slugger cracks the 50-homer barrier

George Foster was a study in perseverance. Considered a top prospect by two big-league organizations, he nonetheless spent seven seasons being shifted back and forth between the majors and minors before sticking with the Cincinnati Reds in 1975. Then, as if to show that the waiting was worth it, the quiet and deeply religious Foster took just two years before putting together the greatest slugging season the National League had seen in over a decade during 1977.

The scowl he appears to be giving the camera on his 1971 baseball card said it all about Foster's early career. The third pick of the San Francisco Giants in 1968 out of tiny El Camino College in California, Foster had only brief major-league trials before being traded to Cincinnati for shortstop Frank Duffy and pitcher Vern Geishert in May '71. It didn't look like such a bad move when George hit .234 in 101 games for the Reds, but it wound up one of the worst transactions in Giants history.

Batting just .200 with two homers in 145 at bats for the Reds during 1972, Foster was a part-timer and minor leaguer before finally being inserted into the big club's starting lineup for the '75 campaign at the insistence of Cincinnati manager Sparky Anderson. Sparky's hunch that Foster would produce if given an everyday shot was dead-on, as George hit .300 with 23 homers for the 1975 world champions

before upping the numbers to .306 and 29 (along with a National League-leading 121 RBI) as the Reds repeated the following season.

After a slow start in 1977 (four home runs through mid-May), Foster had a stretch of seven homers in six games that catapulted him to the top of the NL power charts. The 6'1", 180-pound left fielder added 12 dingers in both July and August—highlighted by three in one game against the Braves July 14—and wound up with the most homers (52) of any big leaguer since Willie Mays reached the same figure in 1965. Batting .320 (third in the league) with a record 31 of his homers on the road, the league MVP was just the seventh NL player to hit 50 or more—and his huge numbers also included an NL-best 149 RBI, 124 runs, 388 total bases, and a .631 slugging percentage.

Foster had an NL-leading 40 homers and 120 ribbies in '78 (pacing the majors in RBI for a record-tying third straight year) and remained a 30-homer threat his last three years in Cincinnati. He then signed for over $10 million with the Mets, but pitchers discovered his appetite for curveballs in the dirt. By 1986, he was struggling to hit .225 before throwing in the towel. His career totals of 348 homers, 1,239 RBI, and 13 grand slams are not quite up to Hall of Fame standards, but for a few years at least, Foster's patience had paid off.

YANKS DENT BOSOX,
BUST THE DODGERS

Kansas City Royals executives were both lucky and astute during the 1970s. Placed by chance in the weakest of the four major-league divisions in 1969, the Royals were the lone expansion team never to finish in last place during its formative years. Meanwhile, a combination of shrewd trades and wise selections in the amateur draft poised the Royals to replace Oakland as the dominant team in the AL West when free-agent losses and a series of economically motivated trades sheared the A's of most of their talent.

By 1977, only Vida Blue remained of the major contributors during Oakland's dynasty years, and the A's consequently dropped to last in the AL West. Even Blue was gone the following year. Although the A's began to rebuild with young blood, they still only finished ahead of the Mariners in the West and were 23 games back of the first-place Royals.

Kansas City's third straight division crown was matched by the New York Yankees, but only after the wildest race since the start of division play. On July 17, after a defeat put the Yankees 14 games behind the Boston Red Sox, manager Billy Martin suspended Reggie Jackson for bunting against orders. A week later Martin remarked to the press that Jackson was a born liar and owner George Steinbrenner was a convicted liar, a reference to Steinbrenner's illegal contributions to Richard Nixon's 1972 presidential campaign. Under pressure, Martin then quit and was replaced by Bob Lemon who had been fired as manager of the Chicago White Sox just three weeks earlier.

Lemon took over a friction-ridden team that trailed the Red Sox by 10½ games. Within days, his task was further complicated when Steinbrenner announced that regardless of how Lemon did, Martin would return to manage the team in 1980. Because of Ron Guidry's efforts, however, Lemon did better than anyone could possibly have expected.

In the fall of 1976, Guidry—after bouncing around the Yankees organization for years without distinguishing himself— had nearly been left unprotected in the expansion

Davey Lopes managed to slide under Thurman Munson to score from first on Bill Russell's double, but it was the Yankees who walked off with the Series.

by a 20-game winner in 1978. Every one of Guidry's 25 victories was needed as the Yankees overtook the wilting Red Sox in early September only to begin floundering themselves. Though Boston left New York in mid-month trailing by 2½ games after the final regular-season meeting between the two teams, skipper Don Zimmer then rallied Boston to a strong finish.

On the final day of the season, New York needed only to beat sixth-place Cleveland to clinch the division title. When the Tribe upset the Yankees and Boston also won, it forced the first division play-off game in history. On October 2 at Boston's Fenway Park, the Red Sox led 2-0 in the seventh. The Yankee bats then came to life for two singles off Mike Torrez, bringing shortstop Bucky Dent to the plate with two out. Torrez went right at Dent, who had just four homers and 37 RBI on the year to that point, and pinned two quick strikes on him. On the 0-2 pitch, Dent lofted a fly ball to left that settled into the screen above the top of the Green Monster.

Even though the Yankees now led 3-2, the game was far from over. It came down to relief ace Goose Gossage against Carl Yastrzemski in the bottom of the ninth with the tying run on second. When Yaz fouled out, the Yankees had the first leg on their march to another Series date.

For the third year in a row in the ALCS, the Royals came up short against the Yankees. The Phils had the same experience in the NLCS, falling in four games to the Los Angeles Dodgers. Wins from Tommy John and Burt Hooton at Dodger Stadium

Dodger Steve Garvey (top left) *hit four homers to help beat the Phillies in the NLCS. The Royals' George Brett* (top right) *dipped to .294, but led the AL with 45 doubles. Jim Rice of Boston* (bottom) *grabbed the AL MVP by hitting .315 with 46 homers and 139 RBI.*

draft to stock the new Seattle and Toronto franchises. The following spring Martin grew so exasperated with Guidry that he told him, "Show me somebody you can get out and I'll let you pitch to him." Guidry then saw no action until Martin needed a lefty reliever one night when the score was tied, there was a runner on second, and Kansas City's George Brett was up to bat. Brett promptly singled to center, but the runner hesitated just long enough for Mickey Rivers to throw him out at the plate. After the Yankees later scored, Guidry held off the Royals to record his first major-league win. "If it hadn't been for Mickey's throw," Guidry later said, "that might have been the end of me right there."

Instead, Guidry went on to win 16 games in 1977 and then logged one of the best seasons ever

Roy White (6) and Chris Chambliss greet Bucky Dent after his homer beat the Red Sox for the AL East title.

got Tom Lasorda's men off to a 2-0 advantage in the Series, but the complexion changed as soon as the action moved to New York. After Guidry took Game 3, the Yankees benefitted from a controver- sial non-interference call involving Jackson to win Game 4, 4-3. The Dodgers then died on the vine, losing the remaining two contests by a combined score of 19-4.

SEASON'S BEST

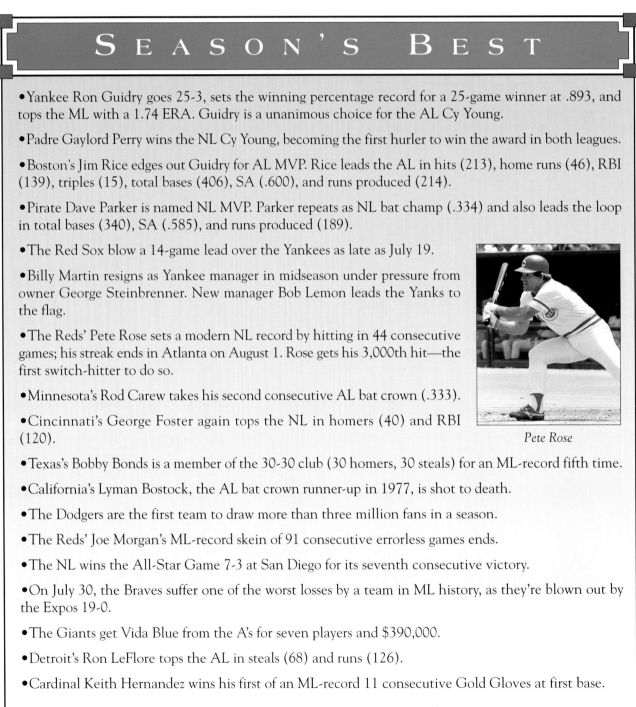

- Yankee Ron Guidry goes 25-3, sets the winning percentage record for a 25-game winner at .893, and tops the ML with a 1.74 ERA. Guidry is a unanimous choice for the AL Cy Young.

- Padre Gaylord Perry wins the NL Cy Young, becoming the first hurler to win the award in both leagues.

- Boston's Jim Rice edges out Guidry for AL MVP. Rice leads the AL in hits (213), home runs (46), RBI (139), triples (15), total bases (406), SA (.600), and runs produced (214).

- Pirate Dave Parker is named NL MVP. Parker repeats as NL bat champ (.334) and also leads the loop in total bases (340), SA (.585), and runs produced (189).

- The Red Sox blow a 14-game lead over the Yankees as late as July 19.

- Billy Martin resigns as Yankee manager in midseason under pressure from owner George Steinbrenner. New manager Bob Lemon leads the Yanks to the flag.

- The Reds' Pete Rose sets a modern NL record by hitting in 44 consecutive games; his streak ends in Atlanta on August 1. Rose gets his 3,000th hit—the first switch-hitter to do so.

- Minnesota's Rod Carew takes his second consecutive AL bat crown (.333).

- Cincinnati's George Foster again tops the NL in homers (40) and RBI (120).

Pete Rose

- Texas's Bobby Bonds is a member of the 30-30 club (30 homers, 30 steals) for an ML-record fifth time.

- California's Lyman Bostock, the AL bat crown runner-up in 1977, is shot to death.

- The Dodgers are the first team to draw more than three million fans in a season.

- The Reds' Joe Morgan's ML-record skein of 91 consecutive errorless games ends.

- The NL wins the All-Star Game 7-3 at San Diego for its seventh consecutive victory.

- On July 30, the Braves suffer one of the worst losses by a team in ML history, as they're blown out by the Expos 19-0.

- The Giants get Vida Blue from the A's for seven players and $390,000.

- Detroit's Ron LeFlore tops the AL in steals (68) and runs (126).

- Cardinal Keith Hernandez wins his first of an ML-record 11 consecutive Gold Gloves at first base.

RON GUIDRY

Louisiana lefty catches lightning in a bottle

Skinny, bowlegged, and weighing 160 pounds following Thanksgiving dinner, young left-hander Ron Guidry seemed an unlikely hero alongside the brawny sluggers and grizzled veterans on his '78 Yankees ballclub. Yet by the time the Yanks had completed the greatest comeback in AL annals, the Cy Young winner was at center stage following one of the greatest individual pitching performances in major-league history.

Unimpressive in stature at just 5'11", the Louisiana-bred Guidry had waited patiently in the Yankee farm system for six years. Given brief major-league trials as a reliever, Guidry finally joined the Yanks to stay in 1977 and compiled a 16-7 record (10-2 following the All-Star break) plus two wins in the postseason as the Yanks claimed their first World Series title in 15 years. Despite the performance by the swift-working hurler with the smooth motion, strong slider, and devastating fastball, no one anticipated what would come the following year.

Guidry was overpowering from the start in '78, and by the time he struck out 18 California Angels to improve to 11-0, "Louisiana Lightning" was the talk of New York. He eventually reached 13-0 before losing July 7, but with team-wide injuries and ineffectiveness plaguing other Yankee starters, the club fell 14 games behind the sizzling Boston Red Sox by July 19. Then the injury bug hit the Red Sox, and when the Yanks came back to force a one-game playoff in Boston, Guidry got the 5-4 win in what many call the greatest game ever played.

Adding two more postseason victories as the Yanks claimed their second straight World Series, Guidry won the AL Cy Young Award unanimously while finishing second to Boston slugger Jim Rice for MVP. His incredible final record of 25-3 (tops in the majors), gave him the highest winning percentage ever for a 20-game winner (.893), and his majors-best ERA of 1.74 placed him behind only Sandy Koufax for the lowest by a left-hander since Carl Hubbell's 1.66 in 1933. His nine shutouts (also tops in the majors) were the most in the American League since Dean Chance's 11 in 1964, and his 248 strikeouts (second in the league) set a Yankee record. Opponents hit just .193 against him.

He was never again nearly as dominating, but Guidry did manage to go 18-8, win 11 straight after the All-Star break and lead the AL with a 2.78 ERA in '79. He eventually paced the majors with 168 victories (including two more 20-win seasons) from 1977 through '87, but the Yankees made just one more World Series appearance—a loss to the Dodgers in '81—before he retired following 1988 elbow surgery. His career may have been too short for Hall of Fame distinction, but his scintillating .651 lifetime winning percentage (on a 170-91 record) and 1978 heroics ensure Guidry will be remembered.

TIGHT-KNIT BUCS CHOKE THE BIRDS

By winning two successive world championships in convincing fashion, the New York Yankees appeared to be on the threshold of establishing yet another dynasty when the 1979 season opened. A series of disasters derailed the club, however, and made the AL East race a wide-open affair.

The first was a clubhouse fracas that shelved Goose Gossage with torn thumb ligaments. Starter Ron Guidry unselfishly volunteered to go to the bullpen until Gossage recovered. Manager Bob Lemon eventually was able to restore Guidry to the rotation once rookie Ron Davis matured and set off on a splendid 14-2 season. Then, tragedy befell the club. Between team leader Thurman Munson's death in a private plane crash and the loss Lemon himself suffered when his son was killed in an auto accident, not even Billy Martin's return to pinstripes less than a year after he'd apparently burned his bridges behind him could lift the Yankees above fourth place in the AL East.

Third belonged to the equally disappointing Boston Red Sox, while the Milwaukee Brewers achieved the highest finish in the franchise's 11-year history by gaining the second spot. Eight games up on the Brewers were the Baltimore Orioles. Missing from postseason play for five years, Earl Weaver had only Jim Palmer and Al Bumbry left from his last division winner in 1974.

In 1979, the California Angels, piloted by Jim Fregosi, garnered their first-ever postseason date when they slipped home three games ahead of the Kansas City Royals and the rest of an uninspiring AL West field. The Angels' 88 wins would have bought them only a fifth-place finish had they been in the East division as the disparity between the two AL sectors grew even more pronounced at the end of the decade than it had been at the beginning.

Still, even an ALCS appearance was a nice reward for Nolan Ryan after toiling for years with drab Angels teams. In 1974, Ryan had set an AL record when he won 22 games for last-place California. Accustomed to making do with little offensive support, Ryan ought to have thrived in 1979 when the Angels floored even their most optimistic followers by topping the AL in runs. Unfortunately, he was a lackluster 16-14 and lost his status as staff workhorse to Dave Frost.

Bill Madlock, left, and Grant Jackson celebrate in the locker room after the Pirates "Family" captured the World Series over the Orioles.

Boston's Fred Lynn, AL bat title winner, was mobbed after a homer (top left). Baltimore's Mike Flanagan (top right) took the AL Cy Young, while Angel Don Baylor (bottom left) was MVP. Tom Seaver (bottom right) had a terrific 16-6 season with the Reds.

In the ALCS, Baltimore's superior pitching stifled Don Baylor, the eventual loop MVP winner, holding him to a .188 BA and just two RBI. Rod Carew and Dan Ford picked up some of the slack, but the O's still needed only one round more than the minimum to win.

The NLCS went the absolute minimum in games, as the losing Cincinnati Reds sent only 33 batters to the plate, six above the minimum, in the third and final contest. Both the Reds and their conquerors, the Pittsburgh Pirates, underwent exhausting ordeals before winning their divisions. The Reds were able to shake the Houston Astros by only a game and a half while the Pirates had to overtake the Montreal Expos on the last lap.

Until the last week of the season, it had looked as though only Baltimore's prohibitive lead over Milwaukee would keep the postseason from being entirely an expansion-team affair. Then, manager Chuck Tanner and the all-around leadership of Willie Stargell ignited the Pirates in the homestretch, and the youthful Astros, most of whom had never been exposed to pennant-race pressure, gave way to the veteran Reds.

Cincinnati, despite still retaining many members of "The Big Red Machine," got precious little hitting in the NLCS. In the opener, the Reds bowed in 11 innings after collecting just two runs and seven hits. The following day, they got only two scores again while losing in 10 frames. The finale in Pittsburgh was a vintage 7-1 win by Bert Blyleven.

Blyleven also won Game 2 of the World Series, but the Orioles riddled the rest of the Pirates mound staff to take a commanding 3-1 lead in games. It was time for "Pops" Stargell to rally "The Family," as the tight-knit Pirates were known, and remind them that the challenge ahead, while formidable, was not impossible. Even though only one other NL team had ever overcome a 3-1 Series deficit, it had been, after all, the 1925 Pirates, so the precedent did exist.

In Game 5, the Bucs trailed 1-0 going into the bottom of the sixth and seemed ready for their last rites. Suddenly their bats erupted for seven runs to force a sixth game. Two days later in Baltimore, a seventh match was made necessary when Kent Tekulve preserved John Candelaria's 4-0 shutout and earned his second Series save.

Twenty-four hours later—after Stargell put them ahead to stay with a two-run homer in the sixth, and Tekulve came in two frames later to save the day once again—the Pirates were champions.

SEASON'S BEST

•Pirate Willie Stargell, age 39, becomes the oldest MVP in history, as he and Cardinal Keith Hernandez finish in a tie for the NL award.

•Hernandez tops the NL in batting (.344), doubles (48), runs (116), runs produced (210), and OBP (.421).

•Angel Don Baylor wins the AL MVP Award after leading the ML in runs (120), RBI (139), and runs produced (223).

•Boston's Fred Lynn wins the AL bat crown (.333) and also leads in SA (.637).

•Baltimore's Mike Flanagan leads the ML in wins with 23 and cops the AL Cy Young.

•Cub reliever Bruce Sutter wins the NL Cy Young, as he tops the majors with 37 saves.

•Cub Dave Kingman tops the ML in homers (48) and NL in SA (.613).

•San Diego's Dave Winfield tops the NL in RBI (118) and total bases (333).

•Major-league attendance soars to a record 34 million.

•The average player's salary shoots up to $113,500.

•Yankee star Thurman Munson dies in a plane crash on August 2.

Dave Kingman

•Phillie Larry Bowa sets an ML record for shortstops with a .991 fielding average.

•Toronto loses 109 games.

•Philly's Pete Rose gets 200 or more hits for an all-time ML-record 10th time.

•Billy Martin takes over for Bob Lemon as Yankee skipper 65 games into the season, only to be fired again after the season.

•Cardinal Lou Brock gets his 3,000th hit. Brock retires with the ML record for career stolen bases (938).

•Boston's Carl Yastrzemski gets his 3,000th hit.

•Cardinal Garry Templeton is the first switch-hitter to get at least 100 hits from each side of the plate in a season.

•On May 31, Detroit's Pat Underwood makes his ML debut against brother Tom of Toronto; Pat beats Tom 1-0.

•Phil Niekro of Atlanta and his brother Joe Niekro of Houston tie for the NL lead in wins (21).

•Milwaukee's Gorman Thomas leads the AL with 45 homers; he also has 123 RBI.

•Houston's J.R. Richard leads the ML in Ks (313) and ERA (2.71).

•After the 1979 season, the Astros sign free agent Nolan Ryan for an estimated $1 million a year.

WILLIE STARGELL

Pittsburgh's Pops leads team to the promised land

The numbers were far from overwhelming; in fact, he had topped them himself many times in his long career. Willie Stargell's 1979 season was not one of statistical excellence—at least not until the postseason—but rather one of leadership by example. The classy Stargell was already on the downside of a Hall of Fame career when the Pittsburgh Pirates won the '79 world championship, but when players on that team were asked the main reason they had gotten there, they were quick to point to "Pops," the National League's oldest MVP ever.

Stargell had been claiming friends and crushing baseballs on a professional level for nearly 20 years before all the fuss began. A 1959 signee of the Pirates, the big (6'2", 225-pound), lumbering right-handed batter was the club's starting left fielder by 1963. The following year he began a string of 13 consecutive 20-homer seasons, including many shots of the tape-measure variety. Developing a reputation as a great teammate and a genuinely wonderful guy, Stargell put together his best offensive years from 1971 to '73 (averaging 42 homers and 119 RBI) while finishing in the top three in MVP balloting each year. Taking over as leader of the Pirates following the 1972 death of Roberto Clemente, he continued to toil admirably as leg, ear, and elbow ailments beat him down. Despite never playing more than 126 games in a season after 1974, he still lead all major leaguers with 296 homers during the 1970s.

An NL force throughout that same decade (including a '71 World Series win), the Pirates were in contention for another championship in 1979. Giving out "Stargell Stars" for great plays that his teammates would stick on their caps, the 39-year-old first baseman was the ever-smiling motivator. He and the close-knit club adopted the disco hit "We Are Family" as its team song and danced their way to the NL East title. His .281 batting average, 32 homers,

and 82 RBI in 126 games were also of great help, but it was when the playoffs began that Pops provided his greatest numbers and leadership.

After batting .455 with six RBI and two homers—including an 11th inning shot to win the opener—Stargell was named NLCS MVP as the Pirates swept the Reds in three games. The World Series was even finer, as Willie hit .400 with four doubles, three dingers, and seven ribbies, setting Series records for extra-base hits and total bases (25) in the process. He also went 4-for-5 with two doubles and a game-winning homer in the seventh game. Named Series MVP, he shared the National League's regular season MVP honor with Keith Hernandez in the only tie in the award's history. Although the weak-kneed hero could muster just 14 more of his 475 career homers before hanging up his cleats in '82, he had hit enough clutch shots in two weeks of October to make for a happy retirement.

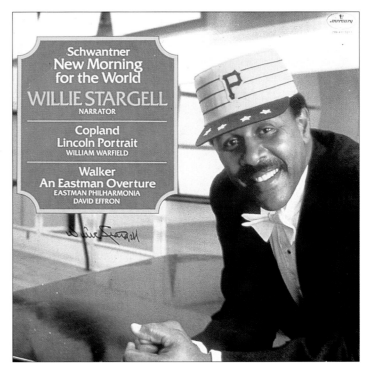

THE 1980s

The focus of the game shifted from balls and strikes to bucks and strife during the 1980s. Players and owners played billion-dollar tug-of-war, with the players gaining the upper hand.

In the 1980s, such words as free agent, arbitration, collusion, drugs, and palimony became as much a part of the baseball lexicon as hits, runs, and errors; the word "strike" took on a whole new meaning. Still, even with baseball's imperfections glaring, the game's popularity was never greater.

Red Smith, the Pulitzer Prize-winning sportswriter for *The New York Times*, called 1981 "baseball's dishonest season." A players' strike forced the cancellation of 713 games in the middle of the regular season and resulted in an estimated $146 million in lost player salaries, ticket sales, broadcast revenues, and concession revenues. Not since the "Black Sox" scandal of 1919 had baseball been so traumatized.

Although the strike, which began on June 12, was called by the players, many sportswriters and fans placed the blame on the owners. The club owners desperately wanted to win back the prerogatives over the players that they had already lost at the bargaining table and in the courts on the issue of the free-agency draft. *Sports Illustrated* magazine stated its opinion loud and clear with the cover headline that read "STRIKE! The Walkout The Owners Provoked."

So bitter were the negotiations that when the strike was finally settled after seven weeks, the players' representative, Marvin Miller, and the owners' negotiator, Ray Grebey, refused to pose with each other for the traditional "peace ceremony" picture. At issue during the negotiations was the owners demanding compensation for losing a free-agent player to another team; the compensation would be a player selected from the signing team's roster (not including 15 "protected" players). The players maintained that any form of compensation would undermine the value of the free agent.

The stalemate ended, coincidentally, when the insurance policy that the owners had taken out with Lloyds of London expired. On July 31, a compromise was reached. The settlement gave the owners a limited victory on the compensation issue. Teams that lost a "premium" free agent could be compensated by drawing

Montreal's Tim Raines (top) *was one of the premier leadoff hitters of the decade, averaging 60 steals per year. Dodger pitcher Fernando Valenzuela (bottom) was the Rookie of the Year and Cy Young winner in the strike-shortened 1981 season.*

Kansas City's George Brett (top left) *hit .390 in his MVP season of 1980. Dave Winfield* (top center) *was a big winner in free agency, signing a 10-year pact with the Yankees worth at least $13 million and up to $20 million. Detroit's Jack Morris* (top right) *became the winningest pitcher of the decade. Players Association representative Marvin Miller* (bottom) *was a household name in 1981.*

one from a pool of players left unprotected from the rosters of all the clubs, not just the signing club.

When the dust finally settled, the players had lost $4 million a week in salaries, and the owners suffered a total loss of $72 million. The schedule had been cut by one-third. Management came up with a split-season arrangement (with a playoff at the end) that was not popular. Despite the close second-half races in all four divisions, attendance dropped in 17 of 26 cities and television ratings slumped sharply.

There were some bright spots: Philadelphia's Pete Rose broke Stan Musial's NL hit record on the day the "second season" resumed; Nolan Ryan of the Houston Astros pitched a record-breaking fifth no-hitter; and Fernando Valenzuela, a 20-year-old rookie for the Los Angeles Dodgers, became Mexico's answer to Sandy Koufax.

These performances, however, were obscured by the constant complaining over the playoff format, the hostility that lingered between the players and owners, and the boos that the fans showered on the players. In one incident, St. Louis Cardinals short-stop Garry Templeton answered an obscene fan with a finger gesture of his own, earning a fine and a suspension. Cesar Cedeno of the Houston Astros took matters into his own hands and attacked a fan in the stands, and a Yankee fan assaulted an umpire.

Surprisingly enough, fans ushered in the 1982 season with renewed enthusiasm. Ticket sales matched those of baseball's best years and it almost seemed as if the events of '81 had never occurred. In fact, the strike and its resulting agreement escalated a trend that was already taking place from 1978 to '81, when 43 players negotiated contracts worth over $1 million each. (The highest going to Dave Winfield, who in November 1980 signed a 10-year contract worth at least $13 million with the New

York Yankees and a cost-of-living clause that made it worth as much as $20 million.)

Such stars as Gary Carter, George Foster, Ken Griffey Sr., Bill Madlock, and Mike Schmidt joined the million-plus-per-year club. By 1982, the *average* salary was almost $250,000 (compared to $50,000 in 1976). One of the reasons the owners doled out such hefty contracts was that they were afraid of losing disgruntled stars in the free-agent reentry draft and paid them the new going rate to keep them at home. The Cincinnati Reds traded Griffey and Foster to the Yankees and Mets, respectively, where owners willingly paid the higher price tags. Cincinnati management figured they would lose both players to free agency anyway.

In 1988, the major-league minimum salary was $62,000 and the average salary was $449,862. Ozzie Smith, the defensive magician for the St. Louis Cardinals, was the highest-paid player, earning $2.34 million. Nine other players made $2 million or more. Some sportswriters speculated that if Ted Williams, Joe DiMaggio, or Stan Musial were free agents in this era, owners would have to assign them half the franchise.

Fans could read about the game in Bill James's Baseball Abstract (top left), while moviegoers saw the fictitious Roy Hobbs, portrayed by Robert Redford in The Natural (top right). Bottom: While they feuded often, Billy Martin, left, and George Steinbrenner staged an argument at a news conference in which Martin was hired for the third time as Yankee manager.

Versatile Paul Molitor of the Brewers (right) *set a Series record with five hits in one game in 1982. Detroit's Alan Trammell* (left), *batting cleanup despite being a shortstop, hit .343 with 28 homers and 105 RBI in 1987.*

Some justification for these huge salaries came about in 1983, when NBC and ABC television networks signed a deal that guaranteed the teams $1.1 billion over six years, which amounted to $6 million per team each season even if no fans showed up. The last contract, signed in January 1989 with CBS, was worth $1.1 billion for four years. ESPN, a national cable-sports network, paid another $400 million for a three-year package. One reason why George Steinbrenner has been tossing huge salaries to free agents is because the New York Yankees signed a $500 million deal with a local cable station in December 1988.

Free agency not only meant more money for players, but more player movement. As a result, baseball had a streak of 10 different World Series champions in 10 years (1978-87). The only team to win two world titles during the 1980s was the Los Angeles Dodgers (1981 and '88). In '87, Los Angeles lost 89 games. The next year, the Dodgers won 94 and the World Series.

The 1986 world champion Mets went on a 488-320 tear from 1984 to '88 after manager Davey Johnson took over. Outside of the Cardinals and Royals combining for five World Series appearances, the Mets franchise was probably the closest thing baseball had to a dynasty during the decade. In fact, Johnson became the first NL manager to win 90 or more games each of his first five seasons.

These developments did not hurt the game's image as much as the hottest topic of the decade: substance abuse. In '83, four players from the Kansas City Royals—Willie Wilson, Jerry Martin, Willie Mays Aikens, and Vida Blue—were found guilty of cocaine use. In fact, it seemed like almost every other day a different player was checking into a rehabilitation center. Such established stars as Ferguson Jenkins, Keith Hernandez, Dave Parker, and Dale Berra admitted to having problems with drugs.

Commissioner Bowie Kuhn was both praised and attacked for the firm stand (including heavy fines and suspensions) that he levied against offending players. In 1982, some of the owners organized a move to push Kuhn out of office. In '83, Kuhn and his supporters made a last-ditch effort to renew his contract. They failed, but he was retained until 1984 when a successor could be found.

Kuhn's replacement was Peter Ueberroth, who had made the 1984 Summer Olympics a success as the president of the Los Angeles Olympic Organiz-

Carlton Fisk left Boston and his No. 27 behind and headed to Chicago. Sporting No. 72, the White Sox catcher hit 37 home runs at the age of 36 in 1985.

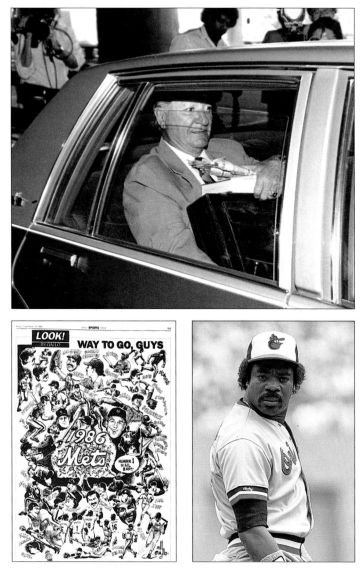

Dodger vice president Al Campanis (top left) *found himself out of a job after making disparaging remarks about African-Americans in 1987. Pete Rose wept in the arms of first base coach Tommy Helms after breaking Ty Cobb's career hits record* (top right). *The 1986 Mets had their share of characters, but also won a world title* (bottom left). *Eddie Murray* (bottom right) *didn't win many fans with his attitude that baseball was "just a job," but he remains the Orioles' all-time home run leader.*

ing Committee. Ueberroth promised to improve the financial health of baseball and he delivered on that promise. He marketed baseball furiously, negotiated the record television deals, and urged the owners to

run their teams like they ran their other businesses: more prudently. The owners responded by drastically cutting back on signing other teams' free agents in 1986 and '87 and holding the line on multiyear deals. Ueberroth took an even stronger stance on drugs, calling for what seemed a drastic measure: mandatory urine tests for all players during the season. The commissioner failed, because mandatory testing was not allowed under the Players Association contract. During the winter of 1986-87, Ueberroth said that the game was free of drugs, but as the 1987 season was about to open, Dwight Gooden of the New York Mets failed a drug test, checked into a rehab clinic and did not return to the rotation until mid-May. As the year ended, another promising pitcher, Floyd Youmans of the Montreal Expos, became another victim of substance abuse.

The 40th anniversary of Jackie Robinson breaking the color barrier in major-league baseball was celebrated in 1987. Dodgers vice president Al Campanis appeared on ABC-TV's late-night network news show *Nightline* in what was supposed to be a tribute to the legendary Robinson. Instead, Campanis stated that African-Americans "lack the necessities" to become successful major-league managers and executives. *Nightline* host Ted Koppel gave Campanis several opportunities to clarify his statements, but Campanis unwittingly buried himself even deeper when he began comparing innate attributes of Caucasians and African-Americans.

During the ensuing uproar, Campanis was fired by the Dodgers, ending a 40-year association. Ueberroth responded by saying that he planned to de-

velop an "affirmative action" plan for baseball. No African-Americans, however, were hired as managers or general managers during the season. In fact, by the end of the 1980s, only a few African-Americans had ever managed in the big leagues. These pioneers included Frank Robinson (Cleveland, San Francisco, Baltimore), Larry Doby (Chicago White Sox), Maury Wills (Seattle), and Cito Gaston (Toronto). In '87, there were 879 administrative positions in baseball, but only 17 of them were held by African-Americans. According to Ueberroth, more African-Americans were being hired for coaching, front-office, and minor-league jobs. Robinson, base-

Mets Dwight Gooden and Darryl Strawberry (above, left to right) were back-to-back Rookies of the Year. Peter Ueberroth (top right) was hired to restore order to the game. Umpire Pam Postema (bottom right) made headlines, but not the big leagues.

ball's first African-American manager in 1975, became manager of the Baltimore Orioles, the worst team in baseball during the '88 season (54-107). Bill White, a former player and broadcaster, was named as the National League's president after the 1988 season, becoming the first African-American to head either league.

Some other stories made headlines in '88. Pam Postema almost became the first woman to call balls and strikes in the major leagues. During spring training, Postema, age 33, was one of seven umpires invited by the NL to try out for two openings in the umpire ranks. She received much publicity when she worked several major-league exhibition games. When the season began, though, she was back in the minors for the 12th straight year.

The tradition-bound Chicago Cubs made front page headlines across the country when the Tribune Company, which owns the team, installed lights at Wrigley Field during the 1988 season. A horde of journalists descended on the Windy City for the Cubs' first home night game ever. On August 8, the game against the Phillies was rained out after 3½ in-

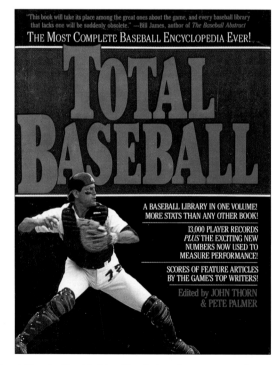

Total Baseball *prided itself as being the most complete encyclopedia on the game.*

nings of play. The clash against the Mets the following night became the first official night game at Wrigley Field.

The most compelling story of the summer of '88 occurred when a team of U.S. college all-stars returned from Seoul, South Korea, with America's first-ever baseball gold medal. A 5-3 win over Japan, the defending gold medalist in '84, made winning pitcher Jim Abbott from the University of Michigan the best-known amateur baseball player ever. Abbott, who was born without a right hand, won the Sullivan Award as the top amateur athlete in any sport.

Slow afoot but dangerous in every other phase of the game, Yankee first baseman Don Mattingly became the AL's premier fielding first baseman (four Gold Gloves). Using 10 offensive categories, a statistical study determined that for the last half of the '80s Mattingly had been the best player in major-league baseball. Mattingly batted .332, while averaging 205 hits, 27 home runs, 115 RBI, and 100 runs scored in five full seasons. Eddie Murray, Los Angeles's new first baseman in '89, finished a distant second and Boston's Wade Boggs placed third.

The new emphasis on speed which came about in the late 1970s gave birth to some of the best lead-off men in the history of the game. The two best of the '80s were Rickey Henderson and Tim Raines. Henderson holds the ML career and single-season records for steals. Like Henderson, Raines hit for average and power (he led the NL in batting with a .334 average in 1986), averaged 60 steals a year, and posted an amazing 87.5-percent success rate on theft attempts. Willie Wilson, Kansas City's center fielder, was always among the stolen base leaders. Wilson hit as high as .332 and stole as many as 83 bases in a season. In St. Louis, Cardinals outfielder Vince Coleman became the first player in history to steal 100 bases three years in a row. He had an "off year" in 1988 and still stole 81. Coleman passed 400 career steals faster than any other player in history.

It used to be that scouts sought out fleet-footed jitterbug types to play shortstop like Baltimore's Mark Belanger and Bud Harrelson of the New York Mets. In the AL, a new breed of "big" shortstops redefined the way the position is played. Cal Ripken

Dodger ace Orel Hershiser (top left), the NL Cy Young winner
in 1988, had reason to smile after signing a three-year, $7.9-
million contract in 1989, making him the highest-paid player in
the game. The Ripken clan (top right) ruled the Orioles in
1987, with left to right: Billy at second, Cal Sr. as manager,
and Cal Jr. at shortstop. The 1987 world champion Twins were
fueled by (center, left to right) Tom Brunansky, Kirby
Puckett, and Kent Hrbek. A week after banning Pete Rose for
life because of gambling, Commissioner A. Bartlett Giamatti
(center right) died of a massive heart attack. Actor Kevin
Costner (bottom left) helped bring Shoeless Joe Jackson and
other stars of the past back to life in the 1989 flick Field of
Dreams.

Jr. led American League shortstops in assists four times and currently ranks as the greatest home run-hitting shortstop in history. The 6'4" Ripken broke Lou Gehrig's consecutive-game record in 1995 and has won Rookie of the Year (1982) and Most Valuable Player honors (1983 and 1991). Alan Trammell of Detroit transformed himself from a slick-fielding shortstop with a decent bat to a cleanup hitter with power. In 1987, Trammell hit .343 with 28 homers and 105 runs batted in. He batted .300 seven times in his career. Robin Yount played shortstop for the Milwaukee Brewers for 11 seasons before switching to the outfield. In 1982, Yount had the greatest season in many years by a shortstop. That season he hit .331, with 29 home runs and 114 runs batted in.

In 1988, Oakland A's outfielder Jose Canseco (42 home runs, 40 steals) became the charter member of the 40-40 club. The year before, Cincinnati Reds center fielder Eric Davis (37 homers, 50 steals)

just missed this distinction. Also in '87, New York Mets Darryl Strawberry (39 home runs, 36 steals) and Howard Johnson (36 home runs, 32 steals) became the first two teammates in history to join the 30-30 club, and Pittsburgh's Barry Bonds hit 25

Top: *First basemen Don Mattingly, left, and Jack Clark both saw action for the Yankees in 1988. Mattingly played first and hit .311, while Clark, the DH, slugged 27 homers. Lights came to Wrigley for the first time in 1988 (bottom).*

The 1980s saw the emergence of baseball in Japan (top left). Reliever Jeff Reardon of the Twins (top center) saved a career-high 42 games in 1988. Oakland's Jose Canseco (top right) bashed his way into the 40-40 club, becoming the first player to hit more than 40 home runs and steal more than 40 bases in a season. A deadly earthquake in San Francisco was seen live by millions of viewers tuning in to watch Game 3 of the 1989 World Series (bottom left). Cincinnati manager Pete Rose was grilled daily by the press (bottom right) as the National League investigated allegations of his gambling.

home runs and stole 32 bases. (Barry's father, Bobby Bonds, was a member of the 30-30 club five times between 1969 and '79.)

Improved conditioning has been responsible for some of the success of this "new breed" of power-and-speed players and seems to be one of the major reasons why so many players are able to play (and perform well) at an advanced age. Of course, there is the added incentive to stay in shape when pulling in a six-figure salary.

Steve Carlton, who won the Cy Young Award when he was 37 years old, strengthened his body by doing martial arts exercises. He was one of the best conditioned athletes in professional sports. Hall of Famer Carl Yastrzemski, who played 23 years for the Boston Red Sox, exercised religiously in the off-season. Chicago White Sox catcher Carlton Fisk hit a career-high 37 homers at the age of 36 and credited his late-career power to the weight work he did throughout the season. Pitchers Jerry Koosman, Jim Kaat, Phil Niekro, Gaylord Perry, Tom Seaver, Don Sutton, and Nolan Ryan were able to pitch effectively beyond their 40th birthdays.

In addition, the advent of laser surgery has helped prolong the careers of many players. Arthroscopic surgery has enabled players to come back

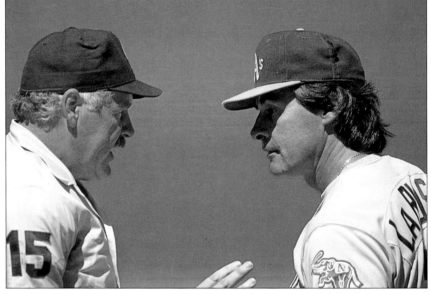

Ranger Nolan Ryan acknowledged the applause after fanning the A's Rickey Henderson in 1989, the 5,000th strikeout in Ryan's career (top left). Manager Tony LaRussa (top right), with a law degree from Florida State, knew how to win oral arguments in 1989 when he guided his A's to the world title. Bottom: San Francisco's Will Clark, left, succeeded Keith Hernandez, right, as the NL's best at first base. Clark thrilled Giants fans with a .333 average, 23 homers, and 111 RBI in 1989.

from knee injuries in weeks where they used to miss whole seasons.

The 1988 World Series between the Los Angeles Dodgers and the Oakland Athletics highlighted another trend in baseball: the middle-inning "set-up" reliever. While both staffs had true late-inning closers in Jay Howell (Dodgers) and Dennis Eckersley (A's), they also possessed a corps of relievers that were called upon to keep games close until the closer could come on to save the day in the eighth or ninth inning. Almost every team in baseball now has at least one pitcher who fills this increasingly important role.

When Peter Ueberroth became commissioner in 1984, he pledged to improve the financial health of baseball, and he did just that. Major-league attendance shattered records in each of the seasons between 1984 and 1988. Many franchises are now estimated to be worth over $100 million. For instance, in 1980 the cellar-dwelling New York Mets were sold for $40 million, but by 1989, a last-place club like the Atlanta Braves was worth more than $80 million. Because revenues increased, the number of clubs thinking about relocating decreased.

Despite the financial boom, Ueberroth left the commissioner's office on April 1, 1989. Though his successor, A. Bartlett Giamatti, the former president of the NL, inherited an immensely popular game, he

nesota Twins and New York Yankees. They declined and Morris had no other choice but to re-sign with Detroit. Tim Raines, Montreal's superstar outfielder, didn't receive an offer, either. Raines had to wait until May 1 to re-sign with the Expos. Bob Horner (Braves), Rich Gedman (Red Sox), Ron Guidry (Yankees), Bob Boone (Angels), and Doyle Alexander (Braves) were also forced to re-sign with their clubs. (Horner instead went to Japan to play.) In fact, only two big-name free agents were signed, Andre Dawson (Chicago Cubs) and Lance Parrish (Philadelphia), both for less than their former clubs were offering. After the '87 season, with Jack Clark moving from St. Louis to the Yankees and Bob Horner returning from Japan to sign with the Cardinals, the Players Association arbitrators again agreed with the players' charge of collusion. The players freed from their contracts after the arbitrator's decision were called "new look" free agents. These developments led to major problems in the 1990s.

Cincinnati's Eric Davis (top) hit 37 home runs and stole 50 bases in 1988. Minnesota's Bert Blyleven (bottom) gave up a major-league record 50 homers in 1986, but found himself in California in 1988, registering his 3,500th strikeout.

faced difficult times. Unfortunately, he had only a relatively short time to fill the post as he passed away later that summer.

The Basic Agreement between players and owners ended at the conclusion of the 1989 season. Fierce negotiations followed, and relations between Major League Baseball and the Players Association dramatically deteriorated, which planted the seed for the bitter labor dispute that cancelled the 1994 postseason. In 1986, the Players Association argued that Ueberroth and the owners were conspiring to prevent the movement of free agents. The most prominent member of the group was Tiger Kirk Gibson, who, after offering his services to the other major-league teams, was forced to return to the Tigers when no other team tried to sign him. In '87, Gibson's teammate, Jack Morris, the winningest pitcher of the 1980s, offered his services to the Min-

California's Wally Joyner, left, and Oakland's Mark McGwire, right, represented the power-hitting first basemen of the late '80s. Joyner, who transformed Anaheim into "Wally World," hit 34 homers in 1987, the same year McGwire slammed 49.

PHILS WIN FIRST TITLE IN 98 YEARS

The Houston Astros are the NL equivalent to the Cleveland Indians. A much better team at the outset than their sister expansion team (the New York Mets), the Astros nevertheless had no postseason history entering their 19th season of play whereas the Mets, with a much poorer composite record, already possessed two pennants and a world championship. Even more distressing was the ill fortune that hounded the franchise, especially its pitchers. Ranging from career-ending arm ailments to terminal illnesses and suicides, Astros hurlers always seemed to be suffering one blow or another.

In 1980, J.R. Richard became the club's latest casualty when he had a stroke and was never able to pitch again. Coming off a 313-strikeout season, Richard was 10-4 at the time he was found to have a life-threatening blood clot in his neck. Yet even without Richard, the Astros continued to hold a commanding lead in the NL West.

On the final weekend of the season, Houston invaded Los Angeles needing to win only one game of a three-game series with the Dodgers to take their first division crown. Bill Virdon fortunately had his ace Joe Niekro available in case the unthinkable happened and the Dodgers swept the series to tie the race, and it proved to be the Astros' salvation. After his teammates dropped all three

weekend clashes, Niekro chilled the Dodgers, 7-1, on the Monday after the regular season ended to notch his 20th win and guarantee the Astros a spot in the NLCS against the Phillies.

The Phils themselves had little time to relish their fourth NL East triumph in five seasons. Only 48 hours before, on the next-to-last day of the season, a home run by Mike Schmidt had turned out to be the blow that mathematically eliminated the Montreal Expos. Still, the Phils were the better situated of the two clubs since skipper Dallas Green

With their victory over the Royals, the Phillies celebrated their first world title. Prior to 1980, Philadelphia was one of six teams never to have won a World Series.

weary combatants went into overtime. A run in the top of the 10th off reliever Frank LaCorte won it for the Phils when the Astros couldn't dent Dick Ruthven in the bottom half for the equalizer.

Limp from probably the most physically and emotionally taxing postseason match ever played, the Phils had only two days to recuperate before the World Series started. Their opponents, the Kansas City Royals, had four days of rest after sweeping the Yankees in the ALCS. The Royals' crushing triumph not only helped avenge three successive postseason defeats to the Yankees between 1976 and '78 but also removed the team with the best record from further tournament action. So tormented was George Steinbrenner by the loss that he pushed rookie skipper Dick Howser into resigning despite the Yankees' 103 wins in 1980, their highest total since 1963.

Kansas City, which had a rookie pilot of its own in Jim Frey, had the further satisfaction of beating former Yankees manager Billy Martin out of the division title. Relations between Steinbrenner and Martin seemed severed irreparably after an off-season altercation with a marshmallow salesman precipitated Martin's second fall from grace. True to form, however, Martin bobbed up again quickly, grabbing the Oakland managerial job and bringing the A's home second, albeit a distant 14 games from the Royals.

The World Series promised to be a duel between Mike Schmidt and George Brett, perhaps the two greatest third basemen in history, as well as one between a team that had reached the championship round in just its 12th season and one that was still searching for its first World Series title in its 98th season.

Brett and Schmidt each enjoyed a fine Series, though Schmidt had a sizable edge in run production and collected the MVP Award, but where the Phils really lorded over the Royals was in pitching. Carlton netted wins in both of his starts and Tug McGraw logged a win and two saves. The pair combined in Game 6 to stop the Royals, 4-1, ending the Phils' painful distinction as the only one of the 16 franchises in existence when the first modern World Series was played in 1903 that had never won an interleague championship.

Montreal's Gary Carter (top) *was tough behind the plate and with the bat, hitting 25 homers and driving in 101 runs. Baltimore's Steve Stone* (bottom left) *captured the AL Cy Young with a 25-7 mark, and then retired a year later. Reliever Goose Gossage of the Yankees* (bottom right) *tied for the AL lead with 33 saves.*

had his top pitcher, Steve Carlton, fresh for the opener of the NLCS while Niekro could not go again for Houston until Game 3.

By Game 3, however, the match had already given hints of being a classic, and Niekro only added to it when he blanked the Phils for 10 innings. Because his teammates couldn't score either, Niekro was out of the game when Houston finally pushed across a run in the bottom of the 11th to win 1-0. Having bagged Game 2 in 10 innings, the Astros were only one victory shy of the pennant. It never came. Game 4 went to the Phils in 10 frames, and the following day for the fourth time in a row the

SEASON'S BEST

•KC's George Brett is named AL MVP, as he hits .390 after flirting with .400 for much of the season.

•Phillie Mike Schmidt sets an ML record for third basemen with 48 home runs. He leads the ML in homers, RBI (121), SA (.624), and total bases (342) and grabs NL MVP honors.

•Oriole Steve Stone wins the AL Cy Young, as he leads the ML with 25 wins.

•Philly's Steve Carlton cops the NL Cy Young, as he wins 24 games.

•On October 5, LA's Manny Mota collects his ML-record 150th career pinch hit.

Cecil Cooper

•Mike Parrott of Seattle loses 16 straight games.

•Houston pitching star J.R. Richard's career is ended by a stroke.

•Cub relief ace Bruce Sutter is awarded a staggering salary of $700,000 when he takes the club to arbitration.

•After losing to the Royals in the ALCS, Yankee manager Dick Howser is fired despite leading the club to 103 wins during the regular season.

•Padre Ozzie Smith sets an ML record for shortstops with 621 assists.

•The NL wins the All-Star Game 4-2 at LA. It's the league's ninth straight victory and 17th triumph in its last 18 games.

•Willie Wilson of the Royals sets the new ML-record with 705 at bats. Wilson leads the AL in hits (230) and runs (133) and ties for the lead in triples (15).

•Income from TV accounts for a record 30 percent of the game's $500 million in revenues.

•The average player now makes about $185,000.

•KC is the first AL expansion team to win a pennant.

•In their first year under Billy Martin, the A's rise to second in the AL West and post 94 complete games, most in the majors since 1946.

•Cub Bill Buckner leads the NL in batting at .324.

•Cardinal Keith Hernandez tops the NL in runs (111), runs produced (194), and OBP (.410).

•Brewer Cecil Cooper leads the AL in RBI (122) and total bases (335).

•New York's Reggie Jackson and Milwaukee's Ben Oglivie tie for the AL homer lead (41).

•Oakland's Rickey Henderson becomes the first AL player to steal 100 bases (100).

GEORGE BRETT

Achy third baseman falls 10 points short of .400

It began with a bruised heel and .247 batting average through mid-May, included torn right ankle ligaments and tendinitis that sidelined him for 35 games in midseason, and ended with a painful case of hemorrhoids. George Brett's 1980 season wouldn't appear memorable given such hardships, but despite the obstacles, the Kansas City Royals third baseman and American League MVP managed to capture the attention of the nation by launching a valiant run at the most coveted and elusive of all batting achievements—a .400 average.

Born into a great baseball family (three older brothers played pro ball, including major-league pitcher Ken), George offered little hint of what was to come early in his career. An error-prone infielder and .281 hitter in the minors, he batted .282 with just two homers as a 21-year-old Royals rookie in 1974. The rugged, left-handed pull hitter longed for big home run totals, but it wasn't until famed Kansas City batting instructor Charlie Lau convinced him to ease his swing and hit to all fields that George flourished. He won his first batting title with a .333 mark in 1976, and became the fifth major leaguer to notch 20 doubles, triples, and homers in the same season three years later.

By now an excellent fielding third baseman as well, Brett began the 1980 campaign hurt. This did not stop him from hitting at a .337 clip by the All-Star break. The Royals set a dizzying pace that had them all but clinching the division by Labor Day,

and George kept up his torrid attack. On August 17, he got four hits against Toronto and reached .400. No batter had attained the mark since Ted Williams hit .406 in 1941, and the media now descended on the usually quiet Kansas City clubhouse.

Reporters and photographers were with him in clubhouses, planes, and restaurants over the next month—something Williams never had to deal with in his .400 chase—and Brett later admitted the pressure affected him. A 3-for-19 slide with two weeks left dropped him out of the .400 hunt (he finished at .390), but considering his assorted injuries, his numbers were outstanding: 118 RBI (tied for second in the league) in just 117 games, 24 homers, 33 doubles, nine triples, and a league-best .664 slugging average. He slugged two homers in a three-game playoff sweep of the Yankees, then despite his much-ballyhooed hemorrhoid flare-up hit .375 during a six-game World Series loss to Philadelphia.

Brett never did hit .400, but only in 1994, when Tony Gwynn hit .394, has anybody come closer. George's sustained excellence over the next 14 seasons and his ability to age beautifully (his third batting crown in 1990 made him the first man ever to win the championship in three different decades) made him one of baseball's most popular stars, and when he retired in 1993 with 3,154 hits, 665 doubles, 317 homers, and a .305 lifetime average, his place in Cooperstown was assured.

LA WINS A WATERED-DOWN TITLE

In 1981, for the first time since the NL was founded in the Centennial year of 1876, not a single American citizen attended a major-league baseball game on Independence Day. More than that, the entire month of July elapsed without so much as an inning of baseball being played in a major-league park. In fact, every one of the 26 big-league facilities sat idle during the longest strike to that point in sports history. So mammoth was the shutdown that 713 games were cancelled and an estimated $146 million in revenue was lost.

When the strike began on June 12, observers initially expected it would be brief. After it extended to July 31, though, the four teams that had been leading their respective divisions when the shutdown began were declared the winners of the first half-season and automatically slated for the opening playoff round. The fortunates were the New York Yankees in the AL East, the Oakland A's in the AL West, the Philadelphia Phillies in the NL East, and the Los Angeles Dodgers in the NL West.

According to the revised postseason format, the first-half champions would meet the second-half champs in a best-of-five division playoff, with the four survivors then moving on to the two best-

Fernando Valenzuela of the Dodgers was a bright spot in an otherwise dark season.

of-five league championship series. The proposal seemed an equitable solution under the circumstances but proved to be full of pitfalls. Since a proviso was added that if a team won its division in both halves of the season it would still face a playoff round against the second-place club in the second half, all the first-half winners, lacking incentive to repeat, dawdled through the second half of the season and finished with a composite second-half record that was only three games above .500. Even more annoying to purists, the Cincinnati Reds, who had the best full-season record in the game, failed to make the playoffs, and the Kansas City Royals, despite owning just the fourth-best full-season record in their division, nevertheless qualified for postseason action.

What saved the Royals was going 20-13 after Dick Howser supplanted Jim Frey as manager. The Reds fell out due to finishing a half a game behind the Dodgers in the first half-season and then trailing the Houston Astros by 1½ games when the second half expired.

Joining the Royals and the Astros as second-half winners were two new postseason entries— the Montreal Expos and the Milwaukee Brewers. The Expos proceeded to

move on to round two when Steve Rogers allowed the Phils just one run in two starts and 17⅔ innings.

Rogers's second outing, a masterful 3-0 shutout in the decisive fifth game, made the Expos the first big-league titlists from outside the United States. Milwaukee, seeking the first AL title for the state of Wisconsin, had come up a hair short of beating the Yankees. Though the Brewers mauled New York's two top starters, Ron Guidry and Tommy John, they were handcuffed by reliever Ron Davis and rookie Dave Righetti, who won Game 2 as a starter and the crucial fifth game in a bullpen role.

The A's, in their second season under Billy Martin's care, showcased "Billy Ball" to sweep the Royals in the division playoff but then were swept in turn by New York. By capturing the flag, the Yankees awarded Bob Lemon with a return Series engagement against Tom Lasorda. Lemon had replaced Gene Michael in September even though Michael's 48 wins were the most of any manager in the AL at the time.

Lasorda's Dodgers had 63 wins, the most of any NL postseason qualifier, but still had to overcome two stiff postseason challenges to reach the Series. In the division playoff, Bill Virdon's Astros snatched the first two games at the Astrodome but departed when they could score only two runs in the next three contests at Dodger Stadium. The Dodgers then rebounded after being down 2-1 to Montreal in the NLCS when a rainout gave Fernando Valenzuela an extra day of rest. The reprieve helped

Expo Andre Dawson (top left) *had 24 homers to go with his .302 average. When Billy Martin took his A's to the ALCS* (top right), *he became the first manager in history to win division titles with four different teams. Oriole Mark Belanger heard from the fans* (bottom) *as strike negotiations broke down.*

Valenzuela to win Game 5, 2-1, on Rick Monday's ninth-inning homer.

Lasorda had to gather his forces for yet a third postseason comeback after the Dodgers dropped the first two Series games at New York. The Yankees abetted him when they came totally unglued, both on and off the field, and lost four straight. Owner George Steinbrenner issued a graceless public apology for his team's poor showing. It only heightened the Yankees' embarrassment when he sported a cast on his hand after breaking it in what he claimed was a fight with a Dodgers fan.

SEASON'S BEST

•Players strike cancels eight weeks of the season. The settlement results in the first split-season campaign in the majors since 1892. Owing to the split-season format, the team with baseball's best record, Cincinnati, doesn't qualify for postseason play.

•LA's Fernando Valenzuela wins NL Rookie of the Year and Cy Young honors, as he tops the NL in innings (192), CGs (11), shutouts (eight), and Ks (180).

•Milwaukee's Rollie Fingers is named MVP and Cy Young winner in the AL. He leads the majors with 28 saves.

•Phillie Mike Schmidt is NL MVP. Schmidt leads the ML in homers (31), RBI (91), total bases (228), SA (.644), runs produced (138), and OBP (.439). He also leads the NL in walks (73) and runs (78).

•Philly's Pete Rose tops the ML in hits (140) to become the only 40-year-old player ever to accomplish the feat. Rose collects his 3,631st hit, breaking Stan Musial's NL record.

•Phillie Steve Carlton becomes the first ML left-hander to collect 3,000 career strikeouts.

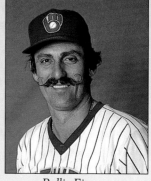

Rollie Fingers

•On August 24, Kent Hrbek of the Twins homers in his first major-league game. That September 20, two other Minnesota rookies, Gary Gaetti and Tim Laudner, also connect for four-baggers in their first major-league contest.

•The NL wins its 10th straight All-Star Game, 5-4 in Cleveland.

•Charlie Finley sells the A's to Levi's jeans magnates.

•Bill Veeck sells the White Sox for the second time in his life.

•The Cubs are sold to the Chicago Tribune Company.

•Len Barker of Cleveland pitches a perfect game against Toronto on May 15.

•Houston's Nolan Ryan throws an ML-record fifth no-hitter on September 26 vs. LA. Ryan has the best ERA in majors (1.69).

•Rochester and Pawtucket of the International League play a 33-inning game—longest in organized baseball history—over a two-day period.

•Expo Tim Raines sets an ML rookie record with 71 steals despite an abbreviated season (record since broken).

•Boston's Carney Lansford wins the AL bat crown at .336.

•Pirate Bill Madlock barely qualifies for the NL BA title but wins at .341.

•Oakland's Rickey Henderson leads the AL in runs (89) and steals (56).

MIKE SCHMIDT

Phillies slugger clubs 31 HRs in summerless season

It was a year that left a bad taste in everybody's mouth and sent reporters scurrying to their calculators. The 1981 major-league baseball strike wiped out 713 games from June 12 to August 9. While most people agree the biggest losers were the fans, the layoff also derailed what could have been fantastic statistical seasons for several players. Dodgers rookie pitching phenom Fernando Valenzuela was likely cost a shot at 20 wins and 10 shutouts, Expos outfielder Tim Raines was denied a crack at Lou Brock's stolen base record, and despite winning his second straight National League MVP Award, Mike Schmidt of the Phillies missed out on a chance at the one offensive honor that eluded him in his great career—an NL batting championship.

Schmidt was no stranger to success before the abbreviated '81 campaign. A .196 hitter.with 136 strikeouts in 132 games his rookie season of 1973, he rebounded to lead the NL in homers each of the next three years and eight times overall. He eventually learned to hit to all fields and became one of baseball's most complete players: a consistent hitter (between .260 and .270) with speed (15-20 steals a year) and the finest fielding third baseman in the NL. The Phillies were a consistently strong team through the '70s, but in 1980 both the club and Schmidt reached new levels. Setting career highs with a .286 batting average, 48 homers, and 121 RBI while winning his first NL MVP Award and fifth straight Gold Glove, he was then named World

Series MVP after batting .381 with two homers and seven RBI in a six-game victory over Kansas City— the first world championship for the Phillies in their 97-year history.

There would be no repeat championship in '81, but the 31-year-old Schmidt became just the third National Leaguer to repeat as MVP. Slugging nine home runs in May alone, he went into the strike with 14 homers, 41 RBI, and a .284 batting mark. He then picked things up considerably in the "second half," belting 17 homers, driving in 50, and batting .356 in 52 post-strike contests. His final batting average of .316 (fourth in the NL) was by far the highest of his career, and in August, he had perhaps his finest month in the majors—batting .380 with nine homers and an .817 slugging percentage. He finished first in the league with 78 runs, and his 31 homers, 91 RBI, .664 slugging average, 228 total bases, and .439 on-base percentage all topped the majors. There was also, of course, another Gold Glove.

Schmidt continued as a top performer for the Phillies until his 1989 retirement, winning a third MVP Award in.'86 and hitting over 30 homers a season each year through 1987. This gave him nine straight years of 30-plus homers and 13 overall. His final totals of 548 homers (ninth all-time), 1,595 RBI, and 10 Gold Gloves make him a logical pick as the greatest third baseman in history. He was enshrined in Cooperstown in 1995.

CARDINALS QUIET THE WALLBANGERS

For years, the Cincinnati Reds had prospered while refusing to participate in the free-agent market, but their success had been contingent on keeping their many stars financially happy. Beginning in 1977, the Reds lost Don Gullett first, then Pete Rose, and finally back-to-back MVP winner Joe Morgan to the lure of free agency. Still, the club remained competitive and even had the top regular-season record in the majors in 1981. During the off-season, though, skipper John McNamara saw his entire starting outfield of Dave Collins, George Foster, and Ken Griffey Sr. vanish either to free agency or a trade forced by the threat of free agency, and in 1982 his Reds sank like a stone to the bottom of the NL while suffering the first 100-loss season in franchise history.

Cincinnati's demise appeared to make the war for the NL West title exclusively between the Los Angeles Dodgers and the Houston Astros, but an intruder surfaced when new manager Joe Torre got the Atlanta Braves off to a 13-0 start. A hideous 10-day stretch in early August, during which they lost eight games to the Dodgers, seemed to pop the Braves' balloon. However, with Dale Murphy's slugging and an amazing 17-4 season from 43-year-old Phil Niekro, Atlanta came to the final Saturday morning of the season with a one-game lead on LA and two on the San Francisco Giants.

The Dodgers eliminated the Giants that day while the Braves topped San Diego. The following afternoon the Giants turned the tables on the Dodgers, dumping them 5-3, with Joe Morgan's homer delivering the killer blow. San Francisco's favor made the Braves champs even though they lost their own finale to the Padres. Unhappily for the Braves, they then performed much as they had in their only previous NLCS experience in 1969. None of Torre's starters—except Niekro—were even nominally effective, and his hitters produced only 16

total bases. Atlanta was unceremoniously swept under the rug by the St. Louis Cardinals.

Fueled by the NL's top baserunning crew and Bruce Sutter, the best fireman in the game, the Cards rewarded Whitey Herzog with his first taste of World Series action in his second full season at the helm. Choosing to build over the winter via the trade route rather than with free agents, the Cards had acquired shortstop Ozzie Smith and left fielder Lonnie Smith. Their addition to an otherwise solid lineup enabled St. Louis to finish three games ahead

After being traded by the Padres, shortstop Ozzie Smith brought his wizardry to St. Louis.

Reggie Jackson (right) became an Angel and led California to the AL West title with 39 homers and 101 RBI. An MVP season from Dale Murphy (left) helped bring the NL West title to Atlanta.

the sell-out Baltimore throng while MVP Robin Yount thrilled Brewers fans by ripping two home runs to lead Milwaukee to a 10-2 win.

The Brewers then threatened to end manager Harvey Kuenn's inspirational season with only a division crown by losing the first two ALCS games in Anaheim. In June, with Milwaukee lagging in fifth place, Kuenn, a longtime coach, had replaced Buck Rodgers in the dugout. After grappling with cancer, heart trouble, and a leg amputation, Kuenn was hardly about to submit just because his team was down 2-0. Under their skipper's relaxed leadership, "Harvey's Wallbangers" recovered to snag all three ALCS games at Milwaukee and capture their first pennant.

While Kuenn had gotten away with using Pete Ladd as his closer against the Angels, his luck wouldn't hold out much longer. The season-ending elbow injury Brewers relief ace Rollie Fingers sustained a few weeks earlier proved insurmountable for the World Series battle. Up 3-2 after five games, Milwaukee journeyed to St. Louis one win short of the top prize in baseball. The win never came. In Game 6, Cardinals rookie John Stuper breezed to a 13-1 triumph. The next day the Brewers bullpen, minus not only Fingers but Ladd as well, saw a 3-1 lead slip to a 6-3 deficit, and Sutter shut the door on the Wallbangers to save Joaquin Andujar's second Series win.

of the Philadelphia Phillies and sew up the NL East title on September 27, the earliest clinching date of the four division winners.

By mid-September in the AL West, the Kansas City Royals seemed bent on being the earliest titlist to clinch. Thanks to a late sag that saw them lose 10 of 11 games, the door was opened for the California Angels. The Angels barged through and proceeded to wrap up their second division crown on the final Saturday of the season.

That same afternoon found the Milwaukee Brewers in Baltimore, still in need of just one more win to bag their first title. The previous night, Earl Weaver's Orioles had swept a twinbill from the Brewers to shrink a three-game Milwaukee lead on the season's final weekend to a single game. When the Orioles won on Saturday, it created a do-or-die situation for both teams the following day. Fittingly the mound opponents were the Brewers' Don Sutton and Baltimore's Jim Palmer, two great veterans now in the twilight of their careers. It was not to be a glorious day for Palmer, who had already nursed 15 wins that year out of his aging arm. He disappointed

AL MVP Robin Yount (right) had a career year in Milwaukee, hitting .331 with 29 HRs and 114 RBI. Al Oliver (bottom) won the batting title in his first season with Montreal, hitting .331.

SEASON'S BEST

•Milwaukee's Robin Yount is AL MVP. Yount leads the AL in hits (210), total bases (367), runs produced (214), and SA (.578) and ties for the lead in doubles (46).

•Atlanta's Dale Murphy wins the NL MVP Award.

Steve Carlton

•Phillie Steve Carlton wins a record fourth Cy Young. Carlton tops ML in wins (23), innings (296), complete games (19), Ks (286), and shutouts (six).

•Milwaukee's Pete Vuckovich wins a controversial Cy Young vote in the AL.

•The Braves open the season with 13 consecutive wins, an NL record.

•Oakland's Rickey Henderson steals an ML-record 130 bases.

•Carl Yastrzemski retires after 23 years with the Red Sox, tying Brooks Robinson's record for most seasons with the same team.

•Milwaukee's Rollie Fingers becomes the first in history to collect 300 saves.

•NL wins its 11th straight All-Star Game, 4-1 at Montreal.

•Phillie Garry Maddox wins his last of eight consecutive Gold Gloves as an NL outfielder.

•Joel Youngblood gets hits for two different teams in two different cities in the same day when he's traded from the Mets to the Expos.

•The Metrodome opens on April 6, the Mariners vs. Twins.

•Royal Hal McRae tops the majors with 133 RBI, a new record for a DH.

•Seattle's Gaylord Perry wins his 300th game on May 6.

•Royal John Wathan sets an ML record for catchers with 36 stolen bases.

•Montreal's Al Oliver leads the NL in BA (.331), hits (204), doubles (43), and total bases (317) and ties for the lead in RBI (109).

•Philadelphia's Mike Schmidt leads the NL in walks (107), OBP (.407), and SA (.547).

•New York's Dave Kingman leads the NL with 37 homers; his .204 BA is the lowest ever for a homer leader.

•KC's Willie Wilson tops the AL in batting (.332) and triples (15).

•Angel Reggie Jackson and Brewer Gorman Thomas tie for the AL homer lead with 39.

•Boston's Bob Stanley sets an AL record by pitching 168 innings in relief.

•Terry Felton leaves baseball with an 0-16 lifetime record—worst mark ever.

•Brewer Paul Molitor gets a World Series-record five hits in the opener.

RICKEY HENDERSON

Speed demon commits grand larcency: 130 thefts

There was a time when stolen base records could be neatly divided into pre-Maury Wills and post-Maury Wills records. Before Wills, the National League record-holder for stolen bases in a season was Cincinnati's Bob Bescher, who swiped 81 in 1911. Bescher was still the NL leader 51 years later when Wills stole 104. It was the same story in the AL, where the pre-Wills major-league record of 96 was set by Ty Cobb in 1915. New ML marks were set in 1974 by Lou Brock and in 1982 by Rickey Henderson. The list of 100-stolen base seasons grew to Wills, Brock, Henderson, and Vince Coleman.

Henderson's career as a basestealer began when Billy Martin introduced "Billy Ball" in order to stimulate a powerless Oakland offense. As Martin put it: "I managed around him. If Rickey got on base, we scored runs." Henderson's stolen base total jumped from 33 to 100 in 1980, and the A's moved from last place to second. Billy Ball took the A's to the strike-year playoffs in 1981, but they lapsed to 94 losses in 1982.

It was the lost '82 season that enabled Martin to turn Henderson completely loose on the basepaths. With the team going nowhere, he stole second and third with abandon, regardless of game situations. Although his success rate fell to 75 percent (excel-lent, but more than five points below his career percentage) and he set a new major-league record by being caught stealing 42 times, Henderson's 130 steals smashed Brock's ML-record by a dozen.

Henderson stole his 100th base early in August. When he went against Brewer pitcher Mike Caldwell on August 26, Henderson had 117 steals (and Brock was in attendance). He opened the game with a single. Caldwell attempted to keep Henderson close to the bag, but on the fourth pitch he took off and was safe at second, tying Brock's record. Henderson was unable to break Brock's record that night. The next night, off of Doc Medich, Henderson walked his first time up. After Medich threw several times to first to lessen Henderson's lead, the pitcher finally tossed one over home. Henderson flew toward second and got his 119th steal. The game was stopped for a short ceremony. When the contest continued, the new record-holder went on to steal three more bases.

Actually, basestealing is not the strongest part of Henderson's game. The main thing he does is score runs—around 100 a year. He also delivers about a .290 batting average, a .400 on-base average, and power (he holds the major-league record for most home runs leading off a game). Henderson will be remembered as one of the top leadoff men in the game's history.

WEAVER-LESS O'S WHIP WHEEZE KIDS

Late in the 1982 season, Earl Weaver had announced that it would be his last year as the Baltimore skipper. His retirement proclamation had spurred the Orioles to catch fire and nearly erase the Milwaukee Brewers' seemingly invincible lead down the homestretch. In 1983, the Orioles continued to play as if they were ablaze for their new manager, Joe Altobelli. The former San Francisco Giants skipper brought his troops home an uneventful six games ahead of Sparky Anderson's Detroit Tigers, but the race for the AL East crown seemed fraught with tension compared to the chase in the West. After years of peering in the window at the trophy room without ever showing near enough fiber to set foot in it, the Chicago White Sox suddenly smashed the window and stormed inside.

In the most lopsided race since the inception of division play, Tony LaRussa steered the Sox to 99 wins, 20 more than the second-place Kansas City Royals. Furthermore, the White Sox were the only AL West team to break .500, but even a lack of competition could not detract from their awesome performance. Scoring an AL-leading 800 runs, the White Sox made huge winners of LaMarr Hoyt and Rich Dotson, who were a combined 46-17, and masked LaRussa's one grave weakness: a mediocre bullpen. In the ALCS, the Orioles had no need to exploit the Sox bullpen flaw because Chicago could never get a lead for its relief corps to hold. After Hoyt won the opener 2-1, the heavy-hitting Sox applauded themselves for triumphing despite plating just two runs. Over the next three games, their bats succeeded in producing a grand total of one marker as Greg Luzinski, Ron Kittle, Harold Baines,

and Carlton Fisk—after slugging 111 homers among them during the regular season—combined to dent Baltimore pitchers for no dingers and just 12 total bases.

The Orioles' triumph in four LCS clashes was matched by the Philadelphia Phillies in the NL Championship Series. So top-heavy with aging stars

Scott McGregor and catcher Rick Dempsey celebrate the Orioles' World Series title after McGregor tossed a shutout in the decisive Game 5.

George Brett was ready to tar and feather the umpire after his two-run homer in the ninth against the Yankees was disallowed because the pine tar on Brett's bat exceeded 18 inches.

like Pete Rose, Joe Morgan, and Steve Carlton that they were called the "Wheeze Kids," the Phils trudged along in the early going at a .500 clip. However, the NL East was so weak that season that Philadelphia held a share of first place on July 18 with just a 43-42 mark. At that point, General Manager Paul Owens decided that Manager Pat Corrales should be doing better with the talent he had. To prove it, Owens took over the field post himself and shepherded the Phils to a 47-30 finish, holding a six-game lead over the second-place Pittsburgh Pirates.

Owens was made to match wits in the NLCS with Tom Lasorda, a pilot who already had seven years of big-league experience and three World Series appearances under his belt. It was a very uneven match. Presented with two excellent starting stints by Steve Carlton and a combined .448 BA and 10 RBI by Mike Schmidt and Gary Matthews, Owens offered a new demonstration of the old baseball axiom that players make a manager.

Meanwhile, another old axiom that championship teams customarily show their class again the fol-

lowing year continued to be defied in 1983. Favored in the preseason to become the first back-to-back pennant winner since the 1977 and '78 Yankees, the St. Louis Cardinals instead finished four games below .500. When the Milwaukee Brewers, the California Angels, and the Atlanta Braves also failed to repeat as division champions, baseball pundits for the first time began to comment on the wild fluctuations in team performances from one year to the next in recent seasons.

One popular explanation for the phenomenon was that long-term guaranteed contracts and multi-million-dollar salaries were robbing many players of the necessary intensity to repeat once they tasted victory. In any event, the 1983 season probably signaled the change from a time when it was possible to predict the postseason combatants with a reasonable degree of accuracy to an era in which a team's past performance was a nearly useless barometer to a prognosticator.

The 1983 World Series was also one of the last occasions when form held true. The Orioles, with a pitching staff that had reduced the White Sox bats to rubble in the ALCS, won in five games. The victories were spread among three starters—Mike Boddicker, Storm Davis, and Scott McGregor—and the fourth went to Jim Palmer in one of his rare relief appearances.

Only Philadelphia's Cy Young winner John Denny, with bullpen help from Al Holland, averted a sweep by curbing Baltimore, 2-1, in the opener.

Pedro Guerrero (left) *brought power to the hot corner for the Dodgers with 32 homers and 103 RBI. Phillie Mike Schmidt* (right) *slugged an NL-best 40 HRs.*

SEASON'S BEST

•Atlanta's Dale Murphy wins his second consecutive NL MVP Award. Murphy leads the NL in RBI (121) and SA (.540).

•Baltimore's Cal Ripken is AL MVP. Ripken tops the ML in hits (211) and doubles (47) and leads the AL in runs (121).

•Philadelphia's John Denny is awarded the NL Cy Young after topping the loop with 19 wins.

•LaMarr Hoyt of Chicago wins the AL Cy Young and leads the ML in wins (24).

•Padre Steve Garvey's NL-record streak of 1,207 consecutive games ends when he breaks his thumb.

•KC's Dan Quisenberry sets a new ML record with 45 saves.

•Houston's Nolan Ryan and Philly's Steve Carlton both surpass Walter Johnson's career K record of 3,508.

•Boston's Jim Rice leads the AL in homers (39) and total bases (344) and ties for the lead in RBI (126).

•Boston's Wade Boggs wins his first AL bat crown (.361).

•Pittsburgh's Bill Madlock wins his fourth and final bat crown in the NL (.323).

Jim Rice

•With 108 steals, Oakland's Rickey Henderson becomes the first to swipe at least 100 bases in consecutive years.

•The Louisville Red Birds become the first team in minor-league history to draw one million fans in a season.

•KC's George Brett hits his famous "Pine Tar" homer versus the Yankees on July 24.

•The AL breaks its skein of 11 consecutive losses in the All-Star Game by beating the NL 13-3 at Comiskey Park. California's Fred Lynn hits a grand slam.

•On July 3, Texas beats the A's with 12 runs in the 15th inning—an ML record for most runs scored in an overtime frame.

•Seattle is the first ML team this century to go through a season without playing a doubleheader.

•Dodger Steve Howe and Royal Willie Aikens are the first players to be suspended for a full year for drug abuse.

•Expo Tim Raines sets an NL record when he scores 19.6 percent of his team's runs, as he leads the ML with 133 runs.

•Phillie Mike Schmidt tops the NL in homers (40), walks (128), and OBP (.402).

•Atlee Hammaker of the Giants paces the majors with a 2.25 ERA.

CAL RIPKEN

Shortstop leads in doubles, double plays, durability

When infielder Cal Ripken Jr. joined his hometown Baltimore Orioles in 1981, the first base coach and future manager of the team was none other than his father, Cal Sr. The elder Ripken heard the snickers about nepotism the next year when his son began the season 7-for-60. Displaying the courage and excellence that have marked his extraordinary career, he recovered to become the American League's MVP within two years while leading Baltimore to the 1983 world championship.

Ripken had wanted to wear an Orioles uniform since following Baltimore's championship clubs as a kid, but felt some trepidation when drafted by the team his father had been employed by as a player,

manager, and coach for over 20 years. "Junior's" fears appeared resolved his rookie year of '82 when he went 3-for-5 with a home run on Opening Day in Baltimore, but a 4-for-55 slump followed to drop his average to .117 on May 1. A beaning came a few days later, but Cal hit .281 the rest of the way to finish with a .264 batting average, 28 homers, and 93 RBI—figures that earned him Rookie of the Year honors. The last game he missed during the season—the second game of a May 29 doubleheader—would also be the last he would miss for over 16 years. On May 30 he began a string of playing 2,632 consecutive games, breaking Lou Gehrig's 2,130 in 1995.

Baltimore lost the '82 AL East title to Milwaukee on the final day of the season, but there would be no stopping the Orioles or Cal in 1983. After a decent start that saw him batting .282 through June, Ripken caught fire the rest of the way—hitting .347 to finish with a career-high .318 mark (good for fifth in the league). He wound up leading the AL with 211 hits, 47 doubles, and 121 runs; he also finished second with 343 total bases and notched 27 homers and 102 RBI as Baltimore won the pennant and World Series. Playing every game at shortstop, he also led the league in assists and double plays.

Ripken's career since 1983 has been one of incredible consistency and astounding durability. In addition to his consecutive games streak, he played 8,243 straight innings over 904 games before finally taking a rest September 14, 1987. He had at least 20 homers and 80 RBI for 10 years in a row until 1992. Cal's 345 career homers as a shortstop are a major-league record, and the Gold Glove winner has lead the league in assists at the position a record seven times. He won a second MVP Award in 1991 and has been an All-Star starter the past 16 seasons. When he played alongside brother and second baseman Billy from 1987 through '92, nobody said a word about nepotism—even when Cal Sr. was the manager.

TIGERS CRUISE AFTER 35-5 START

In Willie (Guillermo) Hernandez and Aurelio Lopez, Detroit Tigers manager Sparky Anderson possessed an unparalleled bullpen tandem in 1984. The lefty Hernandez and the righty Lopez coupled for a 19-4 record with 46 saves while surrendering just 205 hits in 278 innings. Not surprisingly the Tigers bagged the AL East title, but the manner in which they won defied credibility.

The Motor City crew launched the 1984 season by winning 10 of their first 11 games, including a no-hitter thrown by Jack Morris. Already off to a sizable early lead in their division race, the Tigers then really turned on the juice. By late May they had steamrolled to a 35-5 mark and were so far ahead of the other six AL East entrants that they could have played .500 ball from then on and still won out over the second-place Toronto Blue Jays by 7 games.

As it was, the Tigers played at just a .566 clip the rest of the way, but even that pace was far swifter than any of the seven AL West contestants could maintain for any length of time. Figured to repeat as division champs, the Chicago White Sox struggled all year to break .500 and finally finished 14 games below the waterline of mediocrity. The California Angels and the Minnesota Twins then took a turn at flirting with first place before winding up exactly at the .500 mark in a tie for second. When no one else seemed to want to face the Tigers, eventually Dick Howser decided his Kansas City Royals would bear the burden of being the West representative in the 1984 ALCS. First, though, Howser had to wait out George Brett's knee injury and Willie Wilson's suspension for a drug conviction. In the interim, Howser patiently worked two young rookie right-handers, Bret Saberhagen and Mark Gubicza, into his starting rotation and slipped Darryl Motley into the outfield vacancy left by the departure of the team's elder statesman, Amos Otis. By late September, Howser's team at least had an appearance of respectability, and in a short series anything could happen.

What did happen was that the Tigers made the 1984 ALCS very short. Detroit held the Royals to just four runs and a .170 BA in a sweep so quick that it left Anderson fearful his club would lose its edge while it waited for the NLCS to end.

Kirk Gibson's two home runs in the decisive Game 5 against the Padres had all of Motown roaring as Detroit completed its amazing season.

Detroit reliever Willie Hernandez (top left, center) *captured both Cy Young and MVP honors, earning 32 saves in his first 32 opportunities. The trio of* (top right, left to right), *Carmelo Martinez, Tony Gwynn, and Kevin McReynolds helped bring the NL flag to the Padres. Cy Young winner Rick Sutcliffe* (bottom left) *found new life in Chicago, going 16-1 for the Cubs after starting the season with a 4-5 record in Cleveland. Dan Quisenberry* (bottom right) *saved a league-high 44 games for the AL West champion Royals.*

The two senior loop combatants were both a surprise. One, the San Diego Padres, had emerged at the head of a weak NL West field after finishing above the .500 mark for only the second time in the franchise's 16-year history. The other was the Chicago Cubs, making their first postseason appearance in 39 years. Jim Frey's Cubs were both the popular and the logical choice in the NLCS.

Chicago had survived a tough division race while San Diego trotted a dozen games ahead of the 80-82 Atlanta Braves and Houston Astros, who had tied for second in the West. As late as July 28, the Cubs trailed the equally surprising New York Mets by 4½ games. In 1983, the Mets and the Cubs had finished last and next-to-last, respectively, in the NL East, but a few key personnel changes had enabled the two to turn the division standings upside down. New York enrolled rookie manager Davey Johnson and 19-year-old Dwight Gooden, the most dominant frosh hurler since Herb Score. To basically the same regular lineup they employed in 1983, the Cubs made three critical pitching additions via midseason, interleague trades. From the Boston Red Sox, Chicago garnered Dennis Eckersley, and Cleveland supplied Frey with reliever George Frazier and starter Rick Sutcliffe.

A phenomenal 16-1 in 20 starts, Sutcliffe arrived in time to help the Cubs beat the Mets seven out of eight times in head-to-head battles and turn a 4½-game deficit into an eventual 6½-game division triumph.

Sutcliffe and Steve Trout then handily dispatched the Padres in the first two NLCS games at Chicago. The seemingly prohibitive Cubs' advantage fanned the flames of controversy in the commissioner's office. Having just assumed the job on October 1 after Bowie Kuhn stepped down, Peter Ueberroth mounted a case that TV commitments demanded that lights be installed in Wrigley Field for the World Series. The debate became moot for the time being, however, when the Padres stunned the Cubs and their millions of sympathizers by snatching the final three NLCS games in Jack Murphy Stadium.

Manager Dick Williams, Steve Garvey, Tony Gwynn, and the other Padres had barely been introduced to the home fans when the Tigers got on the board in the first inning of the World Series opener. It was an accurate harbinger of how the rest of the fall affair would go as Detroit took only five games to send the Padres the way of the 13 AL also-rans in 1984.

S E A S O N ' S B E S T

•Tiger reliever Willie Hernandez claims Cy Young and MVP honors, as he earns 32 saves in his first 32 save opportunities.

•Chicago's Ryne Sandberg takes the NL MVP Award. Sandberg leads the NL in runs (114) and ties for the lead in runs produced (179) and triples (19).

•Cub Rick Sutcliffe is the only Cy Young winner who began the year with another team. He goes 4-5 with Cleveland, is traded, and then goes 16-1 with the Cubs.

•Met Dwight Gooden is NL Rookie of the Year, as he sets an ML rookie K record with 276.

•Tony Armas of Boston leads the ML in homers (43), RBI (123), and total bases (339).

•The Tigers win 26 of their first 30 games, and 35 of their first 40—best starts for any ML team this century. They also win an AL-record 17 straight games on the road.

Dwight Gooden

•Montreal's Pete Rose gets his 4,000th hit on April 21. Rose achieves 100 or more hits for the 22nd consecutive year, an ML record. He also sets a new ML record when he plays in his 3,309th game.

•California's Reggie Jackson hits his 500th homer on September 17.

•Cardinal Bruce Sutter ties the ML record with 45 saves.

•Atlanta's Dale Murphy leads the NL in total bases (332) and SA (.547).

•Boston's Dwight Evans tops the ML in runs (121) and runs produced (193).

•Yankee Don Mattingly leads the AL in BA (.343), hits (207), and doubles (44).

•Detroit's Sparky Anderson becomes the first manager to win world championships in both leagues.

•Phillie Steve Carlton wins his 300th game.

•Mike Witt of the Angels pitches a perfect game against Texas on September 30, the final day of the season.

•After the regular season, Peter Ueberroth replaces Bowie Kuhn as commissioner.

•Padre Tony Gwynn wins his first NL bat crown with a .351 average, and he tops the ML with 213 hits.

•Philly's Mike Schmidt ties Murphy for the NL homer crown (36) and Montreal's Gary Carter for the RBI crown (106).

RYNE SANDBERG

Gold Glover racks up doubles, triples, homers, steals

When Philadelphia Phillies infielder Ryne Sandberg singled for his first major-league hit at Chicago's Wrigley Field on September 27, 1981, the host Cubs were a last-place club that hadn't won a championship of any kind since 1945. Few, if anybody, knew then that Sandberg would be wearing a Cubs uniform the following season. If fans at Wrigley had been told the slap-hitting speedster would be slugging Chicago to the verge of the National League pennant with an MVP year in 1984, they would have known better than to believe it. After all, these were the *Cubs*.

Named after flaky New York Yankees reliever Ryne Duren, Sandberg was somehow destined to

have an impact on the dubious history of Chicago's National League team. A .286 hitter with little power in the minors, he was considered a throw-in when Philadelphia traded Larry Bowa to the Cubs for Ivan DeJesus in an exchange of shortstops prior to the '82 season. Moved to third from his natural position of short, Sandberg started off his rookie season 1-for-32. He surprised everyone by finishing that season hitting .271 with 103 runs, 32 steals, and just 12 errors. The right-handed batter dropped to .261 when moved again to second the following year, but won his first Gold Glove for the fifth-place Cubs.

Finally settled into a position, Sandberg appeared to be part of a slow rebuilding process in Chicago. The plan skipped a few beats in '84, however, as the Cubs won the NL East and Ryne finished the year with a .314 batting average (fourth in the NL) and a league-leading 19 triples and 114 runs. He wound up just shy of becoming the first player in major-league history with 200 hits, 20 doubles, 20 triples, 20 homers, and 20 stolen bases (he had 200 hits, 36 doubles, 19 homers, and 32 steals). He did win another Gold Glove after pacing major-league second basemen in total chances (870) and assists (550) while making only six errors. He then batted .368 in the NL Championship Series against San Diego, but after winning the first two games, the Cubs returned to form and lost three straight and the series.

The fortunes of the team varied following the turnaround of '84 (a second division title and playoff loss would come in 1989), but Sandberg remained a consistent superstar. By the time he retired following the 1997 season, the Pride of Chicago had slugged 282 homers (including a league-leading 40 in 1990), rapped 2,386 hits, and stolen 344 bases while batting .285. He had won seven Silver Slugger Awards and nine Gold Golves. A hard-nosed competitor who always played with class, he appears a lock for the Hall of Fame. Not bad for a throw-in.

KC Pulls Off Royal Comeback

If any defending champion deserved to be an odds-on choice to win a second pennant in a row, it was the 1984 Detroit Tigers. However, baseball oracles, after watching the violent nosedive that virtually every winner since the late 1970s had taken, were cautious about the Bengals' chances. Nor, for the same reason, were they ready to bet the house on the Chicago Cubs or the San Diego Padres, the two easy NL division winners in 1984.

In truth, though, the 1985 season proved to be an anomaly in that all four division winners were clubs that were expected to be contenders, and one, rather remarkably, was a repeat titlist.

The crystal-ball gazers saved some face when the return champ was the Kansas City Royals, by far the weakest of the four 1984 postseason entrants. In an event similar to the previous season, the Royals were squeezed by the California Angels with a last-minute lunge at the wire that left Gene Mauch's club a game back.

In the AL East, Bobby Cox's Toronto Blue Jays got off ahead of the pack while the New York Yankees struggled to a 6-10 start. Annoyed, owner George Steinbrenner bounced Yogi Berra and returned the club's reins to Billy Martin. In 145 games under Martin, the Yankees played the best ball in the majors, but the Blue Jays nevertheless continued to nurse a narrow lead. Come September, while everyone looked for his young Jays to unravel, Cox held them steady. At the finish, it was the Jays by two games.

They managed this even though they had no regulars who hit .300 or tallied 100 RBI, and Cox's staff ace, Dave Stieb, posted just a 14-13 record despite pacing the AL in ERA.

Back on top in the NL West after a year away were the Los Angeles Dodgers with a veteran team that had only one key contributor, pitcher Orel Hershiser, who had not been a vital cog on Tommy Lasorda's 1983 division champion club. Hershiser's marvelous 19-3 season played a large hand in the Dodgers' serene ride across the finish line 5½ games ahead of the Cincinnati Reds.

The defending West titlist, San Diego, meanwhile finished tied for third with a credible .512 winning percentage, but the Cubs, the 1984 NL East champ, came home at .478 (77-84). Davey Johnson was hopeful at first that the Cubs' demise would leave his Mets uncontested heirs to the division

Given new life by an umpire's call in Game 6, the Royals formed a mob at the mound after completing the comeback by trouncing the Cards in Game 7 of the "I-70" Series.

Toronto's Dave Stieb (right) led the AL with a 2.48 earned run average. Cardinal Willie McGee (left) had the highest average ever for a switch-hitter, batting .353.

throne. By June, though, Johnson realized he was in a hard fight with the St. Louis Cardinals. As in 1983, Whitey Herzog's club had refurbished via the trade route. An off-season deal with San Francisco brought first baseman Jack Clark, and pitcher John Tudor came from Pittsburgh. When Tudor won 21 games, Clark led the Cards with 22 homers, and Johnson also found himself forced to counteract sensational rookie speedster Vince Coleman, his Mets ended the race 3 games short of the Cardinals.

In the NLCS, Tudor lost the opener to Fernando Valenzuela, and Joaquin Andujar, the Cards' other 21-win pillar in 1985, was blasted in the second contest. The new best-of-seven format gave Herzog a cushion, though, to absorb the shock. Refusing to panic, he used his extensive bullpen to shut the Dodgers off like a switch and take the next four games.

Their fourth victory on the afternoon of October 16 allowed the Cardinals to watch the ALCS finale that evening on TV. Like the Cards, the Royals had dropped the first two LCS games on the road, but they had then also lost Game 4 at Kansas City to trail 3-1. Dick Howser had since marshalled the Royals to win the next two contests and now had Cy

Young winner Bret Saberhagen ready to go against Stieb in Game 7.

When the Royals knocked Stieb out with a four-run sixth to take a 6-1 lead, Cox had an accurate premonition that his club, seemingly on a certain path to the World Series just three days earlier, was now only nine outs away from being on theme for the winter.

Eleven nights later, Herzog knew the same feeling. He had seen a 3-1 Series lead melt into a devastating loss after a tawdry 11-0 finale that left his Cardinals in utter disarray and shouting that they had been robbed. Up to a point, St. Louis had a good case. In Game 6, behind 2-1 and just three outs away from elimination, the Royals had wrenched out a 3-2 victory with the help of probably the most litigious umpiring decision in postseason history. While Herzog and the Cards could blame Don Denkinger for ruling Royals pinch hitter Jorge Orta safe at first on what the TV cameras clearly showed was an out, they could still have won the Series if Jack Clark had caught a pop foul later in the inning. Clark's miscue opened the door, however, to a total team disintegration.

In Game 7, Herzog threw seven pitchers in a vain attempt to stop the debacle, while Saberhagen blanked the Cards on just seven hits to win the "I-70 Series."

Mets pitcher Dwight "Doc" Gooden (right) had an NL-best 24 wins, 1.53 ERA, and 268 strikeouts. Yankee Don Mattingly (left) captured AL MVP honors on the strength of 35 homers and 145 RBI.

433

SEASON'S BEST

•Willie McGee of the Cards is voted NL MVP, as he leads the league in BA (.353), hits (216), and triples (18).

•New York's Don Mattingly is AL MVP. His 145 RBI lead the ML by 20. Mattingly also leads the AL in runs produced (217), total bases (370), and doubles (48).

•The Mets' Dwight Gooden wins the NL Cy Young Award, as he leads the NL in wins (24), ERA (1.53), Ks (268), CGs (16), and innings (277).

•Kansas City's Bret Saberhagen cops AL Cy Young honors.

•On September 11, Pete Rose cracks his 4,192nd career hit, breaking Ty Cobb's ML record.

•Vince Coleman of the Cards steals 110 bases, setting an ML rookie record.

•Boston's Wade Boggs leads the ML with 240 hits, most in the majors since 1930. Boggs also leads the ML in BA (.368) and OBP (.452).

•Yankee Rickey Henderson scores 146 runs, most in the majors since 1949.

•Baltimore's Cal Ripken breaks Buck Freeman's record for consecutive innings played, as he reaches 5,342 innings without respite.

•Don Sutton becomes the first pitcher in ML history to fan 100 or more hitters in 20 consecutive seasons.

Wade Boggs

•Padre Steve Garvey's ML-record streak of 193 consecutive errorless games at first base ends.

•Angel Bobby Grich's .997 fielding average sets a new ML record for second basemen.

•Larry Bowa retires with the record for highest career fielding average by a shortstop (.980).

•Houston's Nolan Ryan fans his 4,000th batter on July 11.

•The Angels' Rod Carew collects his 3,000th hit.

•Yankee Phil Niekro picks up his 300th win.

•Tom Seaver of the White Sox collects win number 300.

•Darrell Evans is the first to notch 40 or more homers in a season in each league, as he cracks an ML-leading 40 for Detroit.

•The players strike on August 6 for two days.

•Atlanta's Dale Murphy leads the NL in homers (37), runs (118), and walks (90).

•Dave Parker, now with the Reds, tops the NL in RBI (125), total bases (350), and doubles (42).

•LA's Pedro Guerrero paces the NL in SA (.577) and OBP (.425).

•Bert Blyleven, traded by Cleveland to Minnesota in midseason, tops the AL in complete games (24), innings (294), shutouts (five), and Ks (206).

PETE ROSE

Reds hero catches Cobb, spanks hit No. 4,192

When he got his first hit for the Cincinnati Reds in April of 1963, John Kennedy was in the White House and America was hoping its space program could get a man to the moon within the decade. Some 22 years later, John Kennedy Jr. was prepping for a law career, space shuttles were routinely making week-long forays high above the earth, and with a single off Eric Show on a September night in Cincinnati, Reds first baseman Pete Rose was doing what he had done 4,191 times since that long-ago day and more than anybody in history—hitting safely in a major-league game.

Pete Rose would be the first to admit that he did not possess the hitting ability of a Ty Cobb, the man he passed as baseball's all-time hits leader. However, from the time the 140-pound, crew-cutted 19-year-old signed with his hometown Reds in 1960, he was determined to get as much out of his talent as possible. When the switch-hitter batted .273 with 101 runs scored to be named National League Rookie of the Year in '63, what folks noticed most were his sprints to first base—even after being given a free pass. The guy seemed to play the game for the sheer enjoyment of it. While his style rankled some opponents, it was hard not to respect such aggressiveness.

He could also play a little. By 1965, he was a .312 hitter whose 209 safeties (his first of 10

times over 200) topped the NL. In 1968 and '69, he won consecutive batting crowns with averages of .335 and .348. He averaged 107 runs, 38 doubles, and 204 hits a season from 1965 to '78 (leading the league in hits six times over the span), added a third batting crown in '73—when he was named NL MVP—and in his initial swan song with the Reds in '78 recorded an NL record 44-game hitting streak. He had helped the Reds to four pennants and two world championships when he signed with the Phillies as a 38-year-old free agent in 1979, and within two years they were World Series winners for the first time in their history.

Pete was a lumbering singles hitter when he returned to the Reds as player-manager in the summer of '84, but he got the remaining hits needed to pass Cobb along with a few more. When his playing days ended the following year, Rose stood first all-time with 4,256 hits and 3,562 games, second with 746 doubles, and fourth with 2,165 runs. His lifetime .303 batting average was considerably lower than Cobb's untouchable .367, but even after banishment from baseball for allegedly betting on games and a jail term for tax evasion, the only man to be an All-Star at five different positions can still proudly call himself the Hit King—which he does quite often on his nationally-syndicated radio show.

METS WIN AS SOX, ANGELS AGONIZE

The 1986 season marked a return to the new normalcy in baseball. All four of the 1985 division winners not only failed to repeat, but three finished below .500 and the fourth, the Toronto Blue Jays, came home fourth in the AL East.

Nine and a half games up on the Jays and 5½ ahead of the New York Yankees, who headed the rest of field, was a team nowhere to be found in the previous year's race, the Boston Red Sox. In his first full injury-free season, Roger Clemens went 24-4 for the Sox and was the savior Manager John McNamara needed to make his club the sixth different AL East division winner in six years. The only team left out in the cold for the moment were the Cleveland Indians, but when the Tribe topped the majors in both runs and batting in 1986, many looked for them to make it seven different teams in seven years in 1987.

The closest thing thus far to a dynasty in the 1980s ended sadly in Kansas City when Dick Howser, after spurring the Royals to two straight AL West titles and a world championship, was diagnosed with a brain tumor. After his health forced Howser to step down in late July, the Royals finished tied with the Oakland A's for third in the AL West, 16 games back of first-place California. Four years after sustaining a disastrous defeat in the ALCS, Gene Mauch finally got his Angels back for another try at their first pennant when he added rookie Wally Joyner to an aging team. Joyner's club-leading 100 RBI assisted veterans like Brian Downing, Bob Boone, Don Sutton, Doug DeCinces, Bobby Grich, and Reggie Jackson in holding the Texas Rangers at bay and winning the West by 5 games.

The two NL races were even more one-sided, making the 1986 regular season one of the most uneventful since the onset of division play. Blessed with a wealth of pitching talent, Davey Johnson's Mets streaked to an NL post-expansion record-tying 108 wins and a huge 21½-length lead over second-place Philadelphia. With four starters in Dwight Gooden, Bob Ojeda, Sid Fernandez, and Ron Dar-

It was a miracle finish for the Mets, who escaped defeat in Game 6 on a slow roller between Bill Buckner's legs, and won the title with a victory in Game 7.

ling who were an aggregate 66-23, the Mets far out-stripped the Houston Astros, winners in the NL West by 10 games over the Cincinnati Reds. In the NLCS opener, though, Astros Cy Young winner Mike Scott outdueled Gooden, 1-0, and it set the tone for what was perhaps the most aesthetically pleasing League Championship Series yet seen. The Mets subdued the Astros in six games, but it could as easily have been Houston winning in five. Three of New York's wins were by one run and the last two were both extra-inning classics. The finale lasted a postseason-record 16 innings before the Mets pushed home three runs in their turn and then fought to suppress a furious Houston rally that ended with the tying and winning runs on base.

For sheer drama, Game 6 of the NLCS was more than matched by the fifth game of the ALCS three days earlier. Trailing the Angels 3-1 in games, the Red Sox entered the top of the ninth in Game 5 behind 5-2. Two outs later they were still down 5-4 and Angels reliever Donnie Moore had two strikes on substitute Boston outfielder Dave Henderson. Henderson managed to stay alive by fouling off the next pitch and then drilled a two-run homer—his only hit in nine ALCS at bats—to put Boston up 6-5. California tied the game in the bottom of the ninth, only to lose 7-6 in the 11th on a sacrifice fly by none other than Henderson. Even though his Angels still led in games, 3-2, Mauch had already seen too many seemingly certain pennants slip from his grasp not to feel doomed. Sure enough, the Red Sox became the second AL team in two years to win an LCS after falling behind 3-1 in games.

A no-hitter by Mike Scott (top left) clinched the AL West for the Astros. A homer by Dave Henderson (top center) had Boston on its way to winning the ALCS. Wally Joyner (top right) had 22 HRs and 100 RBI his rookie year. The toast of New York (bottom): Yankee Don Mattingly, left, and Met Darryl Strawberry.

Bostonians really began to believe that this was the year their Red Sox would garner their first world championship since 1918 when the Crimson Hose took the first two Series games at Shea Stadium. Even after the Sox dropped two of the three matches at Fenway Park, things looked safe again when Dave Henderson resumed his postseason heroics by leading off the top of the 10th inning of Game 6 with a home run. The Sox added another run to lead 5-3 and reliever Calvin Schiraldi then got the first two outs in the bottom of the 10th routinely.

The last out, however, never came. Instead the Mets began a hunt-and-peck rally that culminated

when Ray Knight scored the winning run as Mookie Wilson's roller trickled through Sox first baseman Bill Buckner's legs. Although Game 7 remained to be played, few in Boston still believed the Red Sox could win it. They were right. Reminiscent of what had happened in the seventh game of the 1975 Series, Boston led 3-0 as late as the sixth inning before succumbing, 8-5.

SEASON'S BEST

• Boston's Roger Clemens wins the AL Cy Young and MVP Awards, as he leads the ML in wins (24) and winning percentage (.857). Clemens fans an all-time ML-record 20 Mariners on April 29.

• Philadelphia's Mike Schmidt is named NL MVP and sets an NL record by leading his league in homers for the eighth time, as he clubs 37. Schmidt leads the NL in SA (.547) and RBI (119) and also wins the last of his 10 Gold Gloves, an NL record for third basemen.

Dave Righetti

• Houston's Mike Scott wins the NL Cy Young. He no-hits the Giants on September 25—the only no-hitter in NL history to clinch a pennant or division crown.

• Oakland's Jose Canseco is named AL Rookie of the Year, as he hammers 33 homers and totals 117 RBI.

• For the first time in history, every club in the majors exceeds one million in attendance.

• Don Mattingly hits .352 and sets Yankees franchise records with 238 hits and 53 doubles. Mattingly tops the ML in hits, doubles, SA (.573), and total bases (388).

• Boston's Wade Boggs leads the ML in BA (.357), walks (105), and OBP (.455).

• Pete Rose retires holding ML career records for hits (4,256), games (3,562), and at bats (14,053).

• Cardinal Todd Worrell is NL Rookie of the Year, as he sets an ML rookie record with 36 saves.

• KC's Bo Jackson becomes the second Heisman Trophy winner to play in the majors.

• On July 6, Atlanta's Bob Horner becomes the only player in this century to hit four homers in a game lost by his team.

• Yankee Dave Righetti sets a new ML record with 46 saves.

• Phillie Steve Carlton becomes the first lefty to collect 4,000 career Ks.

• California's Don Sutton wins his 300th game.

• The Mariners set the AL team record when they fan 1,148 times.

• The average player's salary reaches $412,000; the minimum salary is now $62,500.

• Minnesota's Bert Blyleven gives up 50 home runs, setting an ML record.

• Toronto's Jesse Barfield leads the majors with 40 homers.

ROGER CLEMENS

Rocket Roger starts out 14-0, punches out 20 M's

There had been times in his two previous injury-prone seasons when Roger Clemens had shown the awesome potential he possessed as a major-league pitcher, but it was in the span of a few hours on the night of April 29, 1986 that 13,414 shivering fans at Fenway Park saw the 23-year-old right-hander pass from prospect to legend. Clemens struck out 20 Seattle Mariners (while walking none) that evening to set a major-league record for a nine-inning game, and the performance provided the springboard to a spectacular season in which the AL Cy Young and MVP winner would pitch Boston to the brink of its first World Series title in 68 years.

Drafted by Boston in 1983, the 6'4", 220-pounder with the strong curve and consistent 95-mph fastball joined the Red Sox the following year and went 16-9 over parts of two seasons while beset with arm and shoulder woes. His injuries had experts doubting the right-hander would ever be a big winner entering the '86 season, but the skeptics disap-peared after his 20-strikeout effort and the ensuing media blitz that followed. Clemens sent his shirt from the game on to the Hall of Fame, then won his next 11 decisions to run his record to 14-0 (the fifth-best start in history) before finally losing to Toronto July 2.

The Red Sox had an eight-game lead in the AL East by this point, and after a second loss and perfect three-inning MVP stint in the All-Star Game, Clemens went 12-2 the rest of the way as the club overcame an August slump to win their first division title in 11 years. "Rocket Roger" wound up leading the AL in victories and winning percentage with his 24-4 mark, compiled the league's lowest ERA (2.48), and had an excellent ratio of 238 strikeouts (second in the league) and just 67 walks over 254 innings. Adding a victory in the ALCS as the Red Sox defeated California, he left Game 6 of the World Series with a 3-2 lead in the eighth inning—Boston needed just six outs to beat the Mets and become world champions. The Sox

never got the necessary outs and lost the Series, but Clemens was still named AL MVP and the unanimous Cy Young winner.

From 1986 through '92, Roger won two Cy Youngs and three ERA crowns while winning more games than anyone else (136-63). After battling injury problems for several years, he returned with a vengeance as a Toronto Blue Jay in 1997. He copped another Cy that year while leading the league in wins (21-7), ERA (2.05), and whiffs (292). In 1998, he captured his record fifth Cy Young while repeating the Triple Crown feat (20-6/2.65/271). Along the way, he has acheived 3,000 strikeouts and, amazingly, another 20-K masterpiece (September 18, 1996).

TWINS TOPPLE THE CARDS IN SEVEN

The onset of the 1987 season marked 33 years that the Cleveland Indians had wandered in the wilderness since being swept in the 1954 World Series by the New York Giants. Now, however, the Indians' brutal history for the past three and a half decades seemed about to change. Claiming the top rung in slugging and scoring in the majors in 1986, the Tribe was featured in the annual *Sports Illustrated* baseball issue and designated the magazine's choice to win the AL East.

Season ticket sales swelled, as even the most skeptical Clevelanders crossed their fingers that the unbearable jinx which seemed to hang over the Indians' franchise might at last be at an end. They were only to be disappointed again, although for once it was not fate that leveled the Indians. It was unwise judgement. Possessing a suspect pitching corps, Cleveland foolishly opted to stand pat rather than trade any of its hitters for pitching help. The Tribe's reward in 1987 was not its first pennant in 33 years but the worst record in the majors. At 61-101, the Indians lost only one less game than in 1985 when they had also posted the worst mark in the majors before what seemed to be a turnaround.

Cleveland's nemesis in the 1954 World Series, the Giants, likewise had bottomed out in 1985, sustaining 100 losses in their worst season since moving to San Francisco. Unlike the Indians, though, the Giants' leap in 1986 to 83 wins and a third-place finish in the NL West truly did mark the beginning of a turnaround. By gaining another seven wins in 1987, San Francisco nabbed its first division crown since 1971.

Long plagued by an inept front office, Giants owner Bob Lurie made his first wise de-

cision in years when he hired Al Rosen as general manager. Rosen quickly appointed Roger Craig to the field post and then began to despoil the Giants' image as everyone's patsies in the trading market. Deals netted Kevin Mitchell, Dave Dravecky, and Candy Maldonado at little cost. When these acquisitions were added to Will Clark and Robby Thompson, two impact rookies in 1986 who continued to blossom, the Giants found themselves suddenly on the threshold of a World Series match that seemed almost too good to be true. Their only remaining

St. Louis won at home, but Gary Gaetti & Co. had Ozzie Smith and the Cards stumbling in the Metrodome.

First baseman Will Clark (right) thrilled 'em in San Francisco by hitting .308 with 35 home runs. Toronto's George Bell won the award, but Tiger shortstop Alan Trammell (left) put up MVP-like numbers.

On the final Sunday, still having a chance to tie Detroit, Toronto was blanked by soft-tossing Tigers southpaw Frank Tanana. In the ALCS, it was a different story as Tanana and the Tigers' other three starters—Jack Morris, Doyle Alexander, and Walt Terrell—all pitched as if their tanks were on empty. Pasted to the tune of 34 runs and a 6.70 ERA, Detroit lasted only five rounds.

As had the ALCS, the World Series opened in Minnesota, which did not bode well for the Cardinals. Herzog was confident, though, that his club would roll once the action moved to St. Louis. He was right.

After dropping the first two contests at the Metrodome, the Cards' relief pitching came to the fore in the Mound City. All year long, Todd Worrell and Ken Dayley had rescued a patchy starting corps that had no one who won more than 11 games and hurled 200 innings. Herzog worked the same tack to put the Cards up 3-2.

Unhappily for Herzog, though, the Twins didn't need to win in St. Louis since the Series called for four games in the park of the AL flag winner. Back in the deafening Metrodome, Minnesota defused Herzog's bullpen weapon by feasting on the Cards starters. Running up 33 runs in the four contests at Minnesota, the Twins exploited the home-court advantage to bring the franchise its first world championship since 1924.

hurdle was that they needed one more win in the NLCS and the last two games were slated to be played in St. Louis. Very much in their favor, though, was that Jack Clark, the Cards' spiritual and slugging leader, was idled by an injury, and without him the Cards would probably not score much.

As it turned out, St. Louis didn't need to score much because in the last two NLCS games the Giants were unable to score at all. A harrowing 1-0 victory followed by a 6-0 laugher put the Cards instead of the Giants in the World Series against the team everyone wanted to play. In 1987, each of the four division winners was severely flawed, but the Minnesota Twins were the most flawed. The Twins were baseball's version of Jekyll and Hyde. Although very tough to beat in their home park, the Metrodome, Tom Kelly's Twins were a nightmare on the road. In 1987, the Twins won just 29 away games—a record low for a division winner, let alone a pennant winner—and only 85 games total.

Minnesota's opponent in the ALCS was the Detroit Tigers. This mix of ancients and unhappy veterans, like Darrell Evans and Kirk Gibson, had won the AL East by waiting like vultures for the more talented Toronto Blue Jays to self-destruct and squander a huge lead in the last week of the season.

George Bell (right) did it all, hitting .308 with 47 home runs and an AL-high 134 runs batted in. Andre Dawson (left) belted 49 homers and had 137 RBI, becoming the first player on a last-place team to be named NL MVP.

SEASON'S BEST

- The Cubs' Andre Dawson is named NL MVP.

- George Bell of Toronto is AL MVP.

- Roger Clemens repeats as AL Cy Young winner.

- Steve Bedrosian wins the Cy Young in the NL, as he saves an ML-leading 40 games.

- Mark McGwire of the A's is AL Rookie of the Year, as he hits an ML rookie-record 49 homers and ties Dawson for most homers in the majors.

Tony Gwynn

- Padre Benito Santiago is NL Rookie of the Year after setting a new frosh record by hitting safely in 34 straight games.

- San Diego's Tony Gwynn takes the NL bat crown with a .370 BA, highest in the NL since 1948.

- Boston's Wade Boggs wins his fourth AL bat crown in the 1980s (.363).

- Cardinal Vince Coleman steals 100 or more bases for an ML-record third straight season.

- Brewer Paul Molitor hits in 39 consecutive games, most in the AL since Joe DiMaggio's 56 in 1941.

- Arbiter Thomas Roberts rules owners guilty of collusion after they fail to sign free agents.

- The NL wins the All-Star Game 2-0 in Oakland, as Tim Raines wins it with a two-run triple in the top of the 13th.

- Yankee Don Mattingly hits six grand slams on the season (setting an ML record) and also hits at least one homer in eight consecutive games (tying an ML record).

- The Brewers tie an ML record by opening the season with 13 consecutive wins.

- Angel Bob Boone sets a new career record for catchers when he catches in his 1,919th game.

- Reggie Jackson retires with an ML career-record 2,597 Ks.

- Cal Ripken Sr. of the Orioles is the first man to manage two sons in the ML—Cal Jr. and Billy. The Ripken sons are the first brothers to form a keystone combo in the majors since Pittsburgh's Johnny and Eddie O'Brien in 1956.

- Toronto hits an ML single-game record 10 homers.

- Cal Ripken's record skein for the most consecutive innings played (8,243) comes to an end.

- Attendance tops 52 million, as the Cardinals and Mets each draw more than three million.

- A record 4,458 homers and 19,883 runs are produced in the majors during the regular season.

MARK MCGWIRE

Freshman first baseman sends 49 into orbit

The 1987 season was a bonanza year for offense in general and the home run in particular. Among the many hitting milestones from that year was a new major-league record for total home runs with 4,458; 20 or more homers hit by a record 51 AL players; three teams (Detroit, Toronto, and Baltimore) hit over 200; Toronto hit a record 10 homers in one game.

Amid all this excitement, it's not hard to see how the Oakland Athletics Mark McGwire's total obliteration of the rookie home run record got somewhat lost in the shuffle. McGwire actually broke a number of rookie home run records, many of which had stood for a long time. Cleveland's Al Rosen set the AL mark in 1950 with 37. The NL record had been set by Wally Berger, who hit 38 in 1930, and matched by Frank Robinson in 1956.

Great things were not predicted for McGwire in 1987. In fact, he came into spring training as a long shot to unseat Carney Lansford at third; the A's plan was to give first base to Rob Nelson, who had swatted 52 home runs over the previous two minor-league seasons. Despite McGwire's meager .167 batting average in spring training, the powers that be saw something more. In fact, he seemed to hold so much promise that he was given Nelson's job within the first week of the regular season. Teammate Jose Canseco predicted that "(McGwire is) going to hit 30 homers and drive in more than 100 runs."

McGwire made half a prophet out of Canseco by hitting 33 homers before the All-Star break. Inevitably, speculation started about the rookie's chances of breaking Roger Maris's record. Of course, there are reasons why many more than 100 men have hit 40-plus home runs in a season and only 17 have reached 50, and McGwire was much too level-headed to put that kind of pressure on himself. Things were tough enough already with American League pitchers being a little more careful with him in the second half; he hit only three home runs (with only 12 RBI) in August. He had the flu so severely during that time that he lost 10 pounds. McGwire, though, came back healthy, laid off bad pitches, and rebounded with a nine-homer September to break the rookie home run record with 49, shattering the old mark by a margin of almost 30 percent.

McGwire ended the season with the rookie-season record not only for home runs but also for slugging percentage (.618). He tied the team RBI mark of 118. Against Cleveland in June, he hit five home runs in two games, and he scored nine runs in nine consecutive plate appearances, tying another AL record. For the season, 17 of McGwire's home runs came on first pitches, while 20 homers came when he was leading off the inning.

McGwire became the first unanimous Rookie of the Year selection since Carlton Fisk in 1972.

GIBSON'S HEROIC HR FIRES UP LA

With their improbable triumph in the 1987 postseason tournament, Tom Kelly's Minnesota Twins became the 10th different team in 10 seasons to land a world championship. However, no one, not even in Minneapolis-St. Paul, could realistically imagine they would repeat. Not only had the Twins scored the top prize with the lowest winning percentage (.525) of any flag winner in AL history, but they were unlikely even to prevail in their own division race come 1988. Suddenly the Oakland A's looked ready to return to power.

In their first full season under Tony LaRussa, the A's owned Dave Stewart, one of only two 20-game winners in 1987, and their second consecutive Rookie of the Year in Mark McGwire. Stewart's emergence was particularly disturbing to Oakland rivals. He had been picked off the scrap heap by the A's midway through the 1986 season and almost immediately revealed a talented arm that would produce annual 20-win seasons for the rest of the decade.

Another underrated performer who became an important cog on the revitalized A's was Dave Henderson, the Red Sox 1986 postseason hero. After drifting from team to team for several years without ever quite securing a regular spot, Henderson seized the A's center field slot in 1988 and had his career year with 24 homers, 94 RBI, and a .304 BA. Next to him in right field was Jose Canseco, the AL leader in every major slugging department. The pair worked with McGwire, Stewart, third sacker Carney Lansford, newly emergent relief ace Dennis Eckersley, and two key pitching acquisitions, Bob Welch and Storm Davis, to stampede through the competition for 104 wins in the regular season.

A bonus for LaRussa was frosh shortstop Walt Weiss, whose quick maturation made him the club's third straight Rookie of the Year recipient. Among Weiss's rivals for the award was Jody Reed. Likewise a shortstop, Reed was a linchpin for the Boston Red Sox in 1988, but even more so was longtime coach Joe Morgan, who took control of the club when John McNamara was axed in mid-July.

Slogging along in the middle of the AL East under McNamara, the Red Sox instantly came alive for Morgan, winning 19 of the first 20 games he managed. The burst provided Boston with just

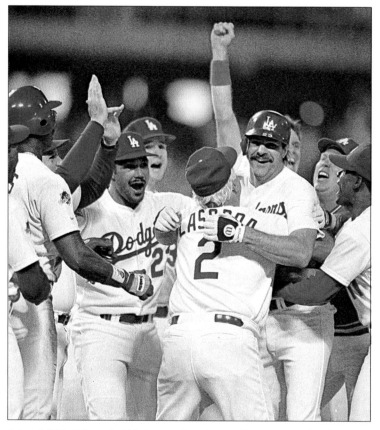

Injured Kirk Gibson hobbled up to the plate in the opener and drilled the game-winning homer to spark the Dodgers on their way to the title.

Met Darryl Strawberry (top left) *led the NL with 39 home runs. Minnesota's Kirby Puckett* (top center) *hit .356 with an ML-best 234 hits. Dave Stewart struck out Wade Boggs with the bases loaded in the ALCS opener* (top right) *as the A's swept Boston. Oakland had three straight Rookies of the Year in* (bottom, left to right) *Jose Canseco, Mark McGwire, and Walt Weiss.*

enough momentum to win 89 games and snatch the AL East title by one length over the Detroit Tigers.

After being the junior circuit's superior division for years, the East fell to its nadir in 1988. Baltimore lost 107 games, the most in the majors, and every club except the Orioles and Cleveland took a feeble stab at the division lead in the last month of the season before allowing the Red Sox to win almost by default.

The NL East was another matter as the New York Mets bagged an even 100 victories, 15 more than runner-up Pittsburgh. The previous year, the Mets had been a disappointment when the crown jewel of their pitching staff, Dwight Gooden, spent considerable time on the disabled list because of injuries and a drug problem. Due to these circumstances, manager Davey Johnson had been driven to rush several inexperienced young hurlers into the breach. By 1988, the Mets looked ready to reassert the authority they had shown two years earlier. Mounted behind senior circuit home run leader Darryl Strawberry were Gooden, David Cone, and Ron Darling, the best trio of starters in the game. A combined 55-21, the three surpassed the NL West champion Los Angeles Dodgers' top threesome, who had an aggregate 52-25 record.

Orel Hershiser owned 23 of those 52 wins for the Dodgers, though, and in 1988 there was no one else even close to him. After propelling the Dodgers past the finish line 7 games ahead of the Cincinnati Reds, Hershiser put on an awesome show in the NLCS. Nicked for just three earned runs in 24⅔ innings, the Dodgers Cy Young winner capped the event by dunking the Mets, 6-0, in the deciding seventh game.

The upset victory gave Tom Lasorda his fourth pennant since taking command of LA, but a world championship in 1988 seemed out of reach when Kirk Gibson finished the NLCS too lame to play in the World Series. At best Gibson had one pinch-hit appearance left in his legs, and Lasorda opted to use it in the bottom of the ninth in Game 1.

Down 4-3, the Dodgers had the tying run on with two out when Gibson hobbled to the plate to face Eckersley. Working Gibson inside, the A's relief kingpin got two strikes on him, but then served up a slider that caught too much of the plate.

Gibson promptly drilled a two-run homer to win the opener, 5-4, and launch the Dodgers on an upset course. The next four days belonged to Hershiser and Dodgers utility man Mickey Hatcher, who hit .368 as Gibson's sub. Canseco and McGwire, Oakland's "Bash Brothers," meanwhile had just two hits between them, and only a ninth-inning homer by McGwire in Game 3 prevented a Dodgers sweep.

SEASON'S BEST

•LA's Orel Hershiser wins the NL Cy Young. Hershiser sets a new ML record with 59 consecutive scoreless innings pitched. He also wins two complete games in the World Series and bats a perfect 1.000.

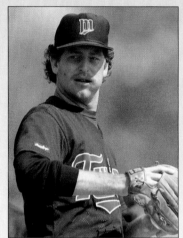

Frank Viola

•Minnesota's Frank Viola wins the AL Cy Young. Viola leads the ML with 24 wins and the AL with a .774 winning percentage.

•Dodger Kirk Gibson is named NL MVP.

•Oakland's Jose Canseco is named AL MVP, as he becomes the first MLer to steal 40 bases and hit 40 homers in the same season. Canseco tops the majors with 42 homers, 124 RBI, and .569 SA.

•Walt Weiss is the third consecutive A's player to win AL Rookie of the Year honors.

•The first official night game at Wrigley Field is played on August 9, the Mets vs. Cubs.

•Billy Martin is fired as Yankee manager a record fifth time.

•The Orioles open the season by losing 21 consecutive games to set an ML record.

•Padre Tony Gwynn leads the NL with a .313 BA, the lowest in history by an NL leader.

•Don Baylor retires with the modern career record for being hit the most times by pitches (267).

•Toronto's George Bell is the first player in ML history to hit three home runs on Opening Day.

•Tom Browning of Cincinnati hurls a perfect game vs. LA on September 16.

•Toronto's Dave Stieb is denied a no-hitter in two consecutive games by two-out, two-strike base hits in the ninth inning.

•David Cone has a 20-3 record for the Mets and tops the NL with an .870 winning percentage.

•New York's Darryl Strawberry leads the NL with 39 homers and a .545 SA.

•Expo Andres Galarraga tops the NL in hits (184), doubles (42), and total bases (329).

•Wade Boggs paces the AL with a .480 OBP, highest in the majors since Mickey Mantle's .488 in 1962. Boggs also leads the ML in batting (.366), doubles (45), walks (125), and runs (128).

•Minnesota's Kirby Puckett tops the ML in hits (234), runs produced (206), and total bases (358) and has a .356 BA.

•The Cubs have now gone 43 years without a pennant to break the old ML record of 42 years held by the St. Louis Browns.

1988

OREL HERSHISER

Dodgers pitcher cranks out 67 0's in a row

It is referred to as "a career year," that one amazing season when a baseball player puts it all together and plays better than anyone, including himself, ever dreamed he could. Orel Leonard Hershiser IV had one of those career years in 1988, the season in which he shattered one of the game's most unbreakable of records—Don Drysdale's streak of 58 consecutive scoreless innings.

The long and lean 29-year-old Los Angeles Dodgers right-hander had been one of the National League's best pitchers since coming up in 1984. Nicknamed "Bulldog" by Dodgers manager Tommy Lasorda, Hershiser featured an above-average fastball, an outstanding curve, a tremendous sinker—and the control to throw them anywhere in the strike zone. After four years in the league, he had become an intelligent hurler, studying hitters and pitching to their weaknesses.

Hershiser was in the midst of dissecting the NL's batters when the streak originated on August 30.

Going 17-8 and pitching the Dodgers to the NL West pennant, he just then seemed to shift into high gear. One team after another fell victim to his shutout spell—Atlanta (3-0), Cincinnati (5-0), Atlanta again (1-0), Houston (1-0), and San Francisco (3-0)—until September 28, when Hershiser was just nine shutout innings shy from tying the benchmark set by Drysdale, another great Dodgers right-hander. Hershiser matched the 20-year-old record during that game, putting up nine goose eggs against the San Diego Padres. The Dodger offense, however, also failed to score, giving Hershiser a chance to pitch another inning and break the record. "It was the best I'd ever seen (Hershiser) pitch," said Padre Tony Gwynn, one of the game's best hitters. "I grounded out four times on a sinker and he set me up differently each time."

The only question that remained was whether or not the pitching sensation would make it through a 10th inning. Lasorda and pitching coach Ron Perranowski persuaded Hershiser, who said he would be satisfied sharing the record with Drysdale, to go for the break. "If he hadn't," said Drysdale at a press conference after the game, "I would have gone out there and kicked him in the rear." Hershiser took the mound and retired the Padres in order, pitching 59 consecutive scoreless innings.

Hershiser extended his career year into postseason play, claiming both the NLCS and World Series MVP Awards in leading the Dodgers to a world championship. By opening the NLCS against the Mets with eight shutout innings, Hershiser racked up 67 straight innings in which he was not scored upon; he then closed the series with a shutout in the deciding seventh game. He went on to keep the Oakland A's scoreless in one of the World Series games. The Cy Young Award winner finished the season with a 23-8 record and a 2.26 ERA.

SERIES SHAKEN BY GIANT QUAKE

Though the Oakland A's had looked during the 1988 World Series as if Kirk Gibson's game-winning pinch homer in the opener had stunned them into submission, they rebounded brilliantly over the winter. Free-agent pitcher Mike Moore was signed, the catching job was given to Terry Steinbach, and halfway into the 1989 season Rickey Henderson was reacquired in a trade with the Yankees. Those key moves enabled Tony LaRussa to withstand potentially devastating injuries to shortstop Walt Weiss and slugger Jose Canseco.

At the end of September, LaRussa again had Oakland high above the rest of the AL crews with 99 wins. Closest to the A's were their own division rivals, the Kansas City Royals, winners in 92 games, as the East remained much the weaker sector. Such was the lack of quality in the East that the Baltimore Orioles, last in 1988, led the race much of the summer and hung in until the final weekend before bowing to the Toronto Blue Jays.

Replacing the Orioles as the worst team in the majors were the Detroit Tigers, a division winner only two years earlier. The rapid rise and fall elsewhere made Toronto seem a model of consistency. Though the Blue Jays were still seeking their first pennant, the 1989 season marked the seventh consecutive year they had finished above .500. No other AL team could make that claim. Nor, for that matter, could any of the 12 clubs in the NL.

Even the Los Angeles Dodgers, something of a marvel in the current era, were suddenly quite ordinary. Previously able to avoid the violent performance swings that haunted every other club, the Dodgers suffered the ignominy of tumbling six games

The World Series of '89 will be forever remembered by the deadly San Francisco earthquake prior to Game 3. As Al Michaels told television viewers, "We're having an earthquake," players came onto the field to search for their families.

below .500 while trying to defend their world championship.

With the Dodgers out of the hunt, the San Francisco Giants, who had barely broken .500 in 1988 after winning the division the year before, resurfaced as the best in the NL West. Skilled at wringing the last drop of juice from an aging pitching arm, skipper Roger Craig pulled 17 wins from 40-year-old Rick Reuschel and got 37 saves from his lefty-righty relief·tandem of Craig Lefferts and Steve Bedrosian. Kevin Mitchell, the majors' top slugger in 1989, and Will Clark supplied 70 homers and 236 RBI between them and aided center fielder Brett Butler in tallying 100 runs. The three were the only batting title qualifiers for the Giants, however, to top .241 as San Francisco hit just .250 in a generally down year offensively.

Leading the NL in both batting and runs were the Chicago Cubs. In their second season under Don Zimmer and their first full season playing under the lights in their home park, the Cubs converted their .261 BA and 702 tallies into a division crown that was nearly as unexpected as their triumph in 1984. Their road was made easier when the New York Mets, much the better team on paper, never performed up to capacity.

The outstanding baserunning and hitting by Rickey Henderson and Dave Stewart's two wins highlighted the A's victory over the Blue Jays in the ALCS. Although they lasted only five rounds with the powerful A's, the Blue Jays put up a much stronger effort than anticipated. Each of the final two games of the match was a one-run cliff-hanger that fell the A's way primarily because they had Eckersley on hand to close it out.

The Giants also needed only five games to extend the Cubs' pennantless skein for another year. The media made it seem that the NLCS was a duel between the two rival first basemen, Will Clark and Mark Grace, with Clark the slight winner with a .650 BA and eight RBI to Grace's .647 BA and eight RBI. As it turned out, the decisive factor was really Steve Bedrosian, who saved each of the Giants' last three victories.

The first Bay Area World Series began in Oakland with two one-sided A's wins. At 5:04 P.M. on October 17, half an hour before Game 3 was slated to begin in San Francisco's Candlestick Park, the Bay Area was suddenly hit by a giant earthquake. Measuring 7.1 on the Richter Scale, it forced Com-

Rickey Henderson (top left) *sparked Oakland with a league-leading 77 steals. Royal Bret Saberhagen* (top right) *took the Cy Young with 23 wins and a 2.16 ERA. NL MVP Kevin Mitchell* (bottom left) *was a giant at the plate with 47 HRs and 125 RBI. Ryne Sandberg* (bottom right) *powered the Cubs with 30 homers.*

missioner Fay Vincent to postpone the Series indefinitely.

When the action finally resumed 10 days later, Oakland scored 22 runs in the next 18 innings and completed its sweep of the Giants. The domination by the A's was so thorough, that for the first time in Series history the losing team not only never had the lead in any of the four games but never once had the tying run at the plate in its final turn at bat.

The earthquake was the darkest shadow on a year that was heavily blighted by tragedy. Vincent's predecessor as commissioner, Bart Giamatti, died of a heart attack on September 1 shortly after he banned Cincinnati manager Pete Rose for life for betting on baseball games. On Christmas night, Billy Martin, another pilot who had taxed Giamatti, was killed in a truck crash.

SEASON'S BEST

•The Giants' Kevin Mitchell is named NL MVP, as he tops the majors in homers (47), RBI (125), SA (.635), and total bases (345).

•Milwaukee's Robin Yount wins his second AL MVP Award and is the first player to win the honor while playing two different positions.

•KC's Bret Saberhagen wins his second AL Cy Young. Saberhagen leads the majors with 23 wins and has the ML's top winning percentage (.793).

•San Diego reliever Mark Davis wins the Cy Young in the NL. He leads the majors with 44 saves.

•Minnesota's Kirby Puckett tops the ML with a .339 BA and 215 hits.

Nolan Ryan

•Ranger Ruben Sierra tops the AL in SA (.543), RBI (119), triples (14), and total bases (344).

•Texas's Nolan Ryan Ks his 5,000th victim, Rickey Henderson.

•Cardinal Vince Coleman steals an ML-record 50 consecutive bases without being caught.

•Pete Rose is banned from baseball for gambling activities. Commissioner Bart Giamatti dies of a heart attack shortly after banning Rose.

•Boston's Wade Boggs collects 200 hits for a 20th century-record seventh consecutive year. Boggs tops the majors with 51 doubles.

•Baltimore's Gregg Olson is AL Rookie of the Year after he sets a new loop rookie saves record with 27.

•Toronto's Tony Fernandez makes just six errors and sets an ML fielding average record for shortstops (.992).

•Angel Jim Abbott, the first one-handed pitcher since the 1880s, wins 12 games and fans 115.

•Houston's Terry Puhl ends the season with the best career fielding average of any outfielder in ML history (.993).

•Ken Griffey Sr. and Ken Jr. are the first father-and-son tandem in ML history to both be active in the majors at the same time.

•The SkyDome opens on June 5, Milwaukee vs. Toronto. Thanks in part to their new home, the Blue Jays set a new AL attendance record.

•Billy Martin dies in a truck crash on Christmas Day.

•San Diego's Tony Gwynn wins the NL bat crown (.336).

•St. Louis's Ozzie Smith sets an ML record for shortstops when he cops his 10th Gold Glove.

JIM ABBOTT

Valiant hurler humbles big-league hitters

In the years after Jim Abbott debuted as a pitcher with the California Angels in 1989, there was a subtle change in the way the press and general public came to view the young left-hander's ability. It was an omission of only a few words in the way folks described him, but it showed perhaps more than anything else just how remarkable a competitor Abbott proved to be on the mound. He was still known as one of the few players to go straight from college to the major leagues, his slider was still one of the best in the business, but very rarely was he referred to any longer as the "one-handed pitcher."

As far as Abbott is concerned, being born with a right arm that ended just above the wrist was never really a handicap to making the major leagues. The Flint, Michigan, native taught himself to transfer his glove from his left to right arm by throwing against a brick wall as a youngster, and by the time he reached high school, teams had long since given up trying to bunt on the excellent fielder. Turning down an offer from the Blue Jays to pitch for the University of Michigan, Jim earned a spot on the 1988 U.S. Olympic Team and won the Gold Medal game against Japan.

After receiving the 1988 Sullivan Award as the best amateur athlete in America, Abbott was California's No. 1 pick in that year's major-league draft. The media descended on Jim in spring training of '89, but the 21-year-old handled each request and repetitious question with a smile and kind word. When the Angels decided to keep him on the big-league roster with no prior professional experience, some speculated owner Gene Autry was trying to boost attendance by exploiting Abbott—accusations similar to those the St. Louis Browns had faced in bringing one-armed outfielder Pete Gray to the majors in 1945.

The critics grew louder as Abbott began the year 2-3 with a 4.50 ERA, but he rebounded to finish at 12-12 with a solid 3.92 ERA. He allowed three or fewer runs in 21 of 29 starts, shut out the Boston Red Sox twice, and may have fared even better had the Angels scored more than 23 runs in his 12 losses. No longer did anyone question whether he belonged in the majors, and by the time he went 18-11 with a 2.89 ERA and finished third in the Cy Young voting in 1991, he was considered one of the league's best pitchers. His charitable endeavors have also become legendary, but when he thrust his arms over his head following his September 1993 no-hitter for the Yankees he probably did more for kids with disabilities—and everybody watching—than he could ever hope to off the field.

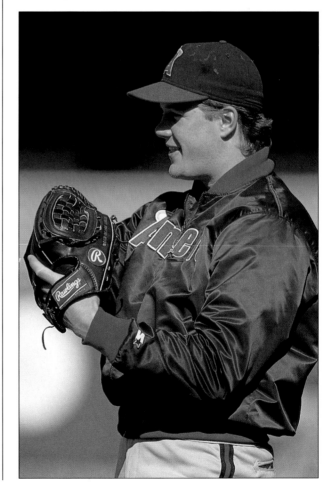

THE 1990s

The money war between the players and owners resulted in a 1994 strike that wiped out that season's World Series. By 1998, however, the slugging exploits of Mark McGwire and Sammy Sosa rejuvenated the game.

Starting explosively with a spring-training lockout by major-league owners, the 1990s offered baseball fans a little of everything: scandal and strife, growth and greed, adversity and achievement. The game underwent perhaps its darkest period since the Black Sox scandal during the eight-month strike by players against ownership in 1994-95. But less than five years later, the heroics of home run kings Mark McGwire and Sammy Sosa put America's pastime back on the front pages as the nation's most popular spectator sport.

Four new teams joined the growing big-league circuit, and moves to a six-division format (including wild-card playoff teams) and interleague play survived early skepticism to become immensely successful. Player-owner squabbles initially left fans disheartened and caused an alarming drop in attendance. But the decade closed with folks packing sparkling new "retro" stadiums in record numbers to see the greatest collection of young talent to emerge at one time in half a century.

By 1999, in fact, it was safe to say that the game was in better shape than anybody could have imagined just a few years before. The triumphant assault in '98 by McGwire and Sosa on Roger Maris's 37-year-old mark of 61 home runs (the duo finished with 70 and 66, respectively) helped bridge a gap between young and old fans that had been widening for years. The classy way in which the record-breakers treated both the fans and each other while enduring the biggest media crush in sports history all but erased ill feelings left over from the strike years. Fans the world over embraced the pair as much for their charitable deeds as for their mighty bats. All of a sudden, thanks to a couple of sweet-hearted sluggers, baseball was "in" again.

Other individual achievements of historic proportions were also positively impacting the game. Sagging attendance at the National Baseball Hall of Fame, already helped tremendously by the arrival of artifacts from the "Great Chase," received another boost early in 1999. Word came that, for the first time since the Hall opened 63 summers earlier, three players had all been voted into Cooperstown during their first year of eligibility—Nolan Ryan, George Brett, and Robin Yount.

"Iron Man" Cal Ripken briefly turned the spotlight toward Baltimore during the final week of the '98 season when he voluntarily ended his incredible record streak of 2,632 consecutive games played. And both Yankee oddball David Wells (perfect game) and Cubs rookie Kerry Wood (20 strikeouts in one contest) offered memorable moments on the mound.

In addition, several players were nearing major statistical milestones as the decade drew to a close. Ripken, Tony Gwynn, and Wade Boggs all entered 1999 within striking distance of the 3,000-hit plateau reached by just 21 players in history—nearly all of whom are now in the Hall of Fame. Fresh from toppling Maris's record, McGwire bashed 65 homers in '99, surpassing 500 big flys for his career. Barry Bonds set his sights on becoming the first player with 500 homers and 500 steals

Before retina damage forced him to hang up his cleats in 1996, Kirby Puckett spent 12 years with Minnesota.

Hall of Famer Nolan Ryan struck out 5,714 batters and threw seven no-hitters in his extraordinary 27-year career.

Wood—all superstars well before the age of 25—further hastened baseball's comeback. In an age when many top athletes in other sports were making headlines for sex scandals, drug offenses, and just plain selfishness, this quartet and more like them possessed images so squeaky-clean by comparison that they almost seemed too good to be true. While the NBA struggled through its own work stoppage and the retirement of marquee player Michael Jordan during 1998-99, and the NFL endured the wrath of its fans for woeful officiating and escalating ticket prices, MLB leadership could look toward the 21st century with confidence. Baseball was back.

What a difference a decade makes. Heading into the 1990s, the game was enduring a downward spiral of bad luck. The August 1989 banishment of all-time hit leader Pete Rose in a gambling scandal and the death of Commissioner Bart Giamatti (who had ordered the ousting) one week later rocked the sport. Then, an earthquake measuring 7.1 on the Richter scale struck the Bay Area just before the third game of the World Series at San Francisco's Candlestick Park and forced a 10-day postponement of the "All-Bay" championship between the Giants and Athletics.

(only he has achieved 400/400), while ageless Rickey Henderson loosened up his 40-year-old legs in pursuit of a 13th stolen base title and Ty Cobb's record of 2,246 runs scored. Among pitchers, Roger Clemens and Greg Maddux continued their climb to 300 victories, Randy Johnson crept toward 3,000 strikeouts, and reliever Jesse Orosco neared retiree Dennis Eckersley's newly minted record of 1,071 pitching appearances.

Team accomplishments were also in the spotlight. The "Murderer's Row" Yankees of 1927 were long considered a team of incomparable greatness, but the multifaceted 1998 Bronx Bombers gave fans 114 reasons (with a 114-48 record) why they should be considered in the same breath as Babe Ruth's wrecking crew. Thanks in large part to the reemergence of the Yankees as a force—manager Joe Torre's charges won World Series titles in 1996 and '98—as well as the staying power of perennial contenders such as Atlanta and Cleveland, baseball was bouncing back big-time from its strike-infested doldrums.

The meteoric rise of young major-leaguers such as Nomar Garciaparra, Alex Rodriguez, Scott Rolen, and

Commissioner Fay Vincent (left) resigned in 1992, while Donald Fehr (right) had his hands full during the strike as head of the players' union.

455

Baltimore's Oriole Park at Camden Yards opened its doors in 1992, paving the way for future ballparks to cater only to baseball teams, such as Jacobs Field in Cleveland and The Ballpark in Arlington, Texas.

New Commissioner Fay Vincent was applauded for his deft decision-making in the wake of the disaster and its aftermath, but his mettle was being tested again before the next season got under way. The five-year Basic Agreement between players and owners was due to expire on December 31, 1989, and the two sides spent the months trying to iron out long-standing disagreements over free agency and arbitration. Salaries for top players were already nearing the $3-million-a-year level, and owners desperate to stop the salary hike proposed an economic partnership in which revenue sharing would play a major role.

The owners set forth a plan in which 48 percent of gate receipts and all revenue from local and network broadcasting would go toward paying player salaries. These salaries would be based on a pay-for-performance scale, in which players with less than six years experience would be compensated based on a ranking against their peers. Finally—and most importantly—a salary cap would be placed on each club, with a stipulation that teams reaching the cap could make no more free-agent signings or salary increases.

Owners claimed average player salaries would rise over 20 percent to $770,000 by 1993 under the plan, citing rising attendance figures and solid television contracts with CBS and ESPN. Revenue sharing of this type had worked well in the NBA. Major League Baseball Players Association (MLBPA) Executive Director Donald Fehr, however, feared that a salary cap would restrict the number of choices free agents could make and that a pay-for-performance scale would eliminate multiyear contracts. The two sides remained at an impasse, and in February 1990 owners announced that spring training would not be starting as scheduled. The lockout—the seventh work stoppage in baseball since 1972—lasted 32 days and wiped out all of spring training. Vincent worked feverishly with both sides, and on March 19 a new Basic Agreement was finally reached. The minimum major-league salary was raised from $68,000 to $100,000, and a six-man study committee on revenue sharing was established. Opening Day was moved back a week to April 9, and the season was extended three days to accommodate the normal 162-game schedule.

The problems were just beginning. Television ratings fell further over the next two years, and upwardly spiraling salaries remained the trend until owners, still angry over Vincent's intervention during the 1990 lockout, forced him from office in September 1992. Governing authority was passed to an Executive Council comprised of the two league presidents and eight owners, and Milwaukee Brewers President Bud Selig stepped in as the council's chairman. The council grappled with such issues as a proposed National League realignment for 1993 (when two expansion franchises would join

Barry Bonds (below) *became the first player to win three MVP Awards (1990, '92, and '93) in a four-season period. Toronto's Joe Carter* (right) *celebrates his title-winning blast in the 1993 World Series.*

the circuit) and the possible sale and relocation of the Giants from San Francisco to St. Petersburg, Florida. Neither panned out initially, and Selig and others wondered if another lockout might be necessary when discussions of a collective-bargaining agreement with the MLBPA continued to lead nowhere.

A new commissioner had still not been found by the spring of 1993, but ownership claims remained the same. Unless teams agreed to share local broadcasting revenue and enact a salary cap, small-market clubs would fall by the wayside. Realignment into six divisions and the addition of a third playoff round for each league was approved for 1994.

When the TV contract with CBS—which lost $500 million over four years—expired that year, a new joint venture between Major League Baseball,

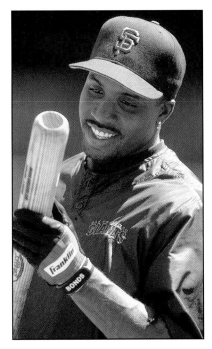

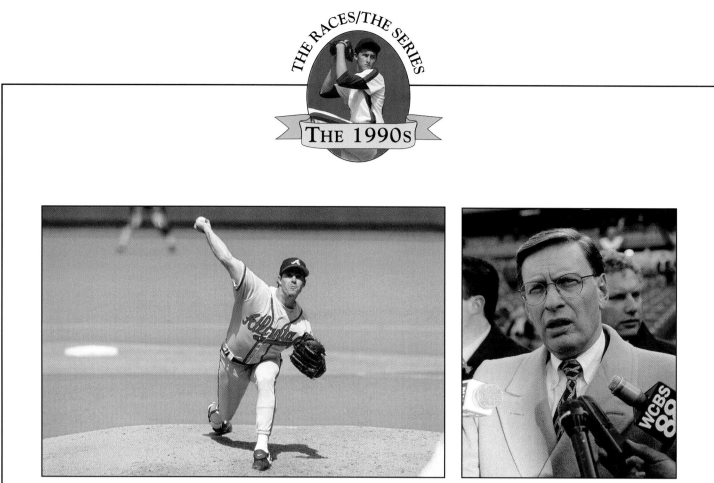

Atlanta's Greg Maddux (left) became the first pitcher to win the Cy Young Award four consecutive years (1992-95). The owners named Bud Selig (right) chairman of the game's Executive Council in 1992.

CBS, and NBC was formed. Instead of rights fees being paid by the networks, Major League Baseball would get 87.5 percent of all net revenues up to $160 million—with the two networks splitting the rest. The networks also promised not to begin any World Series weekend broadcasts after 7:20 P.M.

Eastern Standard Time; postseason games had routinely aired on the East Coast at 9 P.M. or later in the 1990s. Joe Carter's World Series-winning homer in 1993 was struck after midnight in the East. Baseball and television network executives noticed that young fans were no longer enraptured by baseball.

Despite the promise of the NBC-CBS contract and a six-year, $255-million deal with ESPN to televise three games a week, player-owner relations reached rock bottom in 1994. The main hurdle for both sides was the salary cap: The owners wanted it, the players did not, and neither side appeared willing to budge. When owner representative Richard Ravitch officially unveiled the ownership proposal on June 14, it called for a cap that would guarantee players a record $1 billion in salary and benefits. But it would force clubs to fit their payrolls into a more evenly based structure. Salary arbitra-

Ken Griffey Jr. of Seattle (left) crushed 334 homers from 1990 to 1998. Big Frank Thomas (right) won back-to-back MVP Awards in 1993-94.

tion would be eliminated, and while free agency would begin after four years rather than six, owners would retain the right to keep a four- or five-year player by matching his best offer. Owners claimed the proposal would raise average salaries from $1.2 million in 1994 to $2.6 million by 2001.

MLBPA leader Donald Fehr quickly rejected the offer. Believing a salary cap was simply a way for owners to clean up their own disparity problems with no benefit to players, he said the MLBPA would never go for it—and set a strike date of August 12, 1994. Bargaining by both sides was unsuccessful, and after Seattle defeated Oakland behind a grand slam from Ken Griffey Jr. on August 11, ballparks around the majors went silent—as they would remain well into the following spring. Most teams had played 115 or fewer games of their 162-game schedule. All told, 669 contests were eventually wiped out—and the World Series was canceled for the first time since 1904.

While disenchanted fans began filling minor-league parks (the minors were unaffected by the strike), the MLBPA offered a counterproposal to ownership on September 8 calling for a two-percent tax on the 16 teams with the highest payrolls to be divided among the other 12 clubs. Teams in both

Houston's Jeff Bagwell was a unanimous selection as NL MVP in 1994, hitting .368 with 39 homers and 116 RBI.

Jacobs Field, home of the Cleveland Indians, opened in 1994. The stadium has the largest free-standing scoreboard in the United States.

Atlanta fans show their discontent with the possibility of a strike looming. On August 12, 1994, the season came to a halt.

leagues would share 25 percent of all gate receipts under the new plan. Owners, however, claimed the measures would not meet costs. On September 12, Selig officially canceled the rest of the 1994 season and the playoffs, a move that meant the loss of $580 million in ownership revenue and $230 million in player salaries. Teams drastically cut front-office staffs to keep afloat. The most serious consequence of the strike was baseball's blue-collar brigade of ticket takers, vendors, and other support staff facing a long, hard winter without a huge chunk of their yearly income.

The most frustrating aspect from the point of view of players and fans was the outstanding individual and team performances forced to a sudden halt. The Yankees had been leading the AL East in pursuit of their first Eastern title since 1981, while the long-woeful Cleveland Indians were in position for a wild-card berth and their first postseason play since 1954. The Expos had the best record in the majors (74-40) despite one of the big league's lowest payrolls, and the Dodgers were back on top after several years of rebuilding. All these clubs had hopes

of ending Toronto's two-year hold on the world-championship trophy, but by September such aspirations had dissolved into thoughts of what might have been.

The same was true for individual goals. Griffey Jr. began the year on a torrid pace that had him ahead of Maris's then-record 61 homers much of the summer (he finished with an AL-best 40 in 111 games), and Griffey was soon joined in his pursuit by the likes of Matt Williams, Jeff Bagwell, Albert Belle, and Frank Thomas. Williams eventually blasted 43 (best in the majors and a 62-homer pace) for San Francisco before the strike hit. The best testimony to the incredible years turned in by Williams and other sluggers was that they would have led their leagues in various categories over many complete seasons. The strike cost San Diego's Tony Gwynn (who hit .394 in winning his fifth batting title) a full shot at the first .400 average since Ted Williams achieved the feat in 1941. Atlanta's Greg Maddux (16-6 with a 1.56 ERA) and the Yankees' Jimmy Key (17-3) were likely denied 20-win campaigns. Griffey summed it up best when he said, "We picked a bad season to have a good year."

The strike went on through the winter, and with the mid-February opening of spring training upon them owners came up with an idea: replacement players. Guaranteed $5,000 for reporting and another $5,000 if they made the Opening Day roster, veterans of the minor leagues, industrial leagues, and

Owners threatened to start replacement players (pictured) on Opening Day in 1995, but the strike ended two days prior.

softball leagues began popping up on rosters. Former Red Sox pitcher Oil Can Boyd was one big-name signee, but most legitimate players didn't want to take a chance on alienating themselves with big-leaguers who might someday be teammates. As a result, most clubs were fielding the likes of Yankee hopeful Frankie Eufemia, who last pitched in the majors with the '85 Twins and spent 1994 hurling in a New Jersey beer league.

Frankie almost got his chance. Just two days before the scheduled season opener between the expansion Colorado Rockies and Florida Marlins, on Sunday, April 2, 1995, players ended their 232-day strike. U.S. District Judge Sonia Sotomayor issued an injunction restoring baseball's old work rules despite the lack of a collective-bargaining agreement. The owners consented, and a revised 144-game season and 21-day spring training were set up—along with a special camp for the 200 unsigned free agents left over from the previous season. When the final numbers were tallied, owners had lost approximately $800 million in revenue during the strike, players $350 million in salary. Issues still unresolved were the luxury tax, free agency, and service time.

The conclusion of the 50-day major-league strike in 1981 had brought euphoria and an attendance record the following season, but this time around fans were less forgiving. Three men wearing T-shirts emblazoned with the simple credo "Greed" leaped onto the field at Shea Stadium on Opening Day and tossed more than $150 in $1 bills at players. In Cincinnati, a fan paid for a plane to fly over Riverfront Stadium dragging the sign "Players and Owners—To Hell With You."

Attendance at openers and ensuing games was way down from the previous year in virtually every major-league ballpark. The lackluster crowds often booed their way through rusty fundamentals, shoddy defense, and high-scoring contests (meaning hitters were way ahead of pitchers) usually reserved for the exhibition season. Eventually the level of play and crowds improved, the latter helped by Cal Ripken, who broke Lou Gehrig's storied streak of 2,130 straight games in September 1995.

While Cal was chasing and passing the "unreachable" mark, the offensive explosion begun in 1994 continued. Fans were witnessing an era of power unlike anything seen before. Even with the '95 campaign shortened to 144 games, the Rockies crushed 200 homers as a team and Albert Belle had 50 (along with 52 doubles) all by himself. Excitement generated by these feats also helped turn boos to cheers, as did the league realignment from two divisions into three—a move that increased the number of playoff participants from two to four teams (each division winner plus the remaining club with the best record) in both the AL and NL. Some mourned the loss of "traditional" pennant races, but

San Diego outfielder Tony Gwynn (left) came within six points of hitting .400 in 1994, but the strike ended his attempt. Juan Gonzalez (middle) earned AL MVP Awards in 1996 and 1998. Cleveland's Albert Belle (right) in 1995 became the first player to accumulate 50 homers and 50 doubles in a single season.

Alex Rodriguez (left) *hit .356 in 1996, the highest by a righty since Joe DiMaggio in 1939. Cleveland's Eddie Murray* (right) *collected his 3,000th hit in 1995.*

'98, Ken Griffey averaged 54 homers and 144 RBI for the Mariners with a Gold Glove each year, yet only once in the span was he named AL MVP.

Remarkably, there were still pitchers able to shine amidst the slugging. Greg Maddux won 176 games and four Cy Young Awards from 1990-99, and his ERA of 2.14 during 1992-98 was the lowest over a seven-year span since World War II. Fellow Braves Tom Glavine (two Cy Youngs, 164-85 record) and John Smoltz (one Cy, 143 wins) also excelled in the '90s, as did fellow Cy honorees Kevin Brown (143-98) and Pedro Martinez (a 2.83 ERA, 1,534 strikeouts).

far more teams had a shot at the postseason in September, and this meant more meaningful games down the stretch.

The bats kept blasting in '96, as 4,962 home runs were hit in the majors to break the 1987 record. The Orioles set a one-team mark with 257—led by surprising slugger Brady Anderson's 50—and all told 10 of 28 teams set new highs in the department. Mark McGwire topped Anderson by slamming 52 for the A's, and it was the first time since 1961 that two players had crushed 50 in one year. In addition, there were an incredible 43 more players with at least 30 homers. The RBI also piled up. The 100-ribbie mark, once reserved for only the best of run producers, also became commonplace.

Among the new power elite were pure hitters such as Frank Thomas, Belle, Mo Vaughn, and Mike Piazza. But as the decade neared an end, a growing number of five-tool players emerged who gracefully combined speed, defense, and offense. Nomar Garciaparra, Alex Rodriguez, Andruw Jones, and Craig Biggio were capable any season of belting 25 homers, knocking in 100 runs, batting .300, stealing 30 bases, and winning a Gold Glove. Whereas 30/30 was once the private domain of Barry Bonds, there were now players joining the club each year. How competitive had things become? From 1996 through

Six-foot-10 Randy Johnson replaced Nolan Ryan as the game's most intimidating hurler by going 111-40 and fanning 1,869 in just $1,431^{2/3}$ innings from 1993-99. Roger Clemens recovered from

Cal Ripken salutes the Baltimore faithful after he appeared in his record 2,131st consecutive game in 1995.

Mo Vaughn (above) signed a six-year, $80 million contract with Anaheim. Texas's Ivan "Pudge" Rodriquez (right) picked up his seventh consecutive Gold Glove in 1998.

a three-year slump to add his fourth and record fifth Cy Young trophies in 1997-98. Top relievers through '99 included John Wetteland (296 saves and a 2.53 ERA over eight years) and Trevor Hoffman (228 and 2.53 over seven seasons).

As these energizing performers took center stage, several future Hall of Famers called it quits during the decade. Dave Winfield and Eddie Murray became just the fifth and sixth players to total both 3,000 hits and 400 home runs before retiring in 1995 and '97, respectively, with Eddie eventually reaching No. 15 on the all-time homer list with 504. Ryan pitched no-hitters (his record sixth and seventh) in 1990 and 1991, and he finished his career two years later with 324 victories. When he finally hung up his fastball at age 46, the "Ryan Express" had a record 5,714 strikeouts—nearly 1,600 more than No. 2 man Steve Carlton.

Carlton Fisk bowed out in 1993 after hitting more homers (355) and playing more games (2,226)

as a catcher than any major-leaguer in history. The ever-hustling Paul Molitor, who garnered 3,319 hits, 1,782 runs scored, and 504 stolen bases despite numerous injuries, kept on ticking until 1998. Andre Dawson spent half of his career playing on bad knees, yet he left in 1996 as just the second man (after Willie Mays) to record both 400 homers and 300 steals. Dennis Eckersley, a starter turned ace reliever, set a new record for most games pitched (1,071) in his final regular-season appearance in 1998 and amassed the incredible combination of 197 wins and 390 saves.

With free agency continuing to turn even great players like these into well-seasoned travelers, fans likely saw the last one-team superstars pass from the scene. George Brett singled in his final at-bat in 1993 to conclude a 21-year stay with the Royals, during which he collected 3,154 hits and three batting titles—each in a different decade. Shortstop and center fielder Robin Yount of the Brewers called it quits in spring training of '94 with 3,142 hits and two MVP Awards to show for 20 years in Milwaukee. Ryne Sandberg retired once, sat out a year, came back, and then left a final time in 1997 after 15 stellar seasons with the Cubs. Ryno's 277 home runs at second base set a new major-league mark. And Lou Whitaker of the Tigers said goodbye in '95 after spending a record 18 seasons alongside the same double-play partner—fellow Detroit hero Alan Trammell. After one lonely summer on his own, Trammell retired.

These greats were walking away from a nice living. The average yearly salary had gone from $597,000 in 1990 to over $1 million two years later. By the '94 strike, the annual wage was up to $1.2 million, making it hard for fans to feel much pity when their heroes went a while between paychecks. Each year it seemed the dollars doled out to top stars couldn't go higher, and each year they did. In January 1990, Will Clark was baseball's highest-paid player at $3,750,000 per season. By 1992, Barry Bonds was No. 1 at $7,291,666 per annum. And following the '98 campaign, free agent Mo Vaughn took over the top spot by signing a six-year deal with Anaheim slated to make him $13,333,333 each year.

Money or no money, there was still great baseball being played in the 1990s—including some of the most exciting World Series action in history. The 1991 "worst-to-first" Series between the Braves and Twins (each had finished last in their respective divisions the year before) went down to the 10th inning of the seventh game before Minnesota finally prevailed 1-0 on a complete-game shutout by hometown hero Jack Morris. The 1992 battle between Toronto and Atlanta featured four games decided by one run—including an 11-inning battle in the sixth and final contest won by the Blue Jays. In 1995, the pitching-rich Braves finally got over the hump with a six-game win (including five one-run contests) over another perennial loser turned superteam—the 100-44 Indians. The '97 Series was a battle between one of baseball's oldest franchises (Cleveland) and one of its newest (the expansion Florida Marlins, then in their fifth year of existence), won by the Marlins on an 11th-inning single by Edgar Renteria in Game 7.

All these fall classics, however, took a back seat to the wild Series staged in 1993. The Blue Jays overcame a five-run deficit in the eighth inning to win the fourth game over Philadelphia 15-14, then trailed 6-5 heading into the bottom of the ninth in Game 6. Closer Mitch Williams (the Game 4 loser) came in for the Phillies. And with one out and two runners on, Joe Carter became just the second player in World Series history (following Bill Mazeroski in

1960) to end a Series with a home run. His shot deep into the left-field seats gave the Jays an 8-6 victory and their second straight world championship.

Even when teams didn't win it all, giving people what they wanted paid big dividends. The expansion Colorado Rockies and Marlins proved immensely popular in their inaugural season of 1993, fielding competitive clubs and drawing huge crowds (Colorado's season total of 4,483,350 set a major-league record) to baseball-starved regions. A similar pilgrimage took place when the Arizona Diamondbacks and Tampa Bay Devil Rays debuted five years later, even though their on-field success was not immediate. Interleague play, introduced in 1997, also boosted attendance, as regional rivalries such as Yankees-Mets and Cubs-White Sox popped up. Fans in both AL and NL cities lined up to see stars from the "other" league.

Further proving that change can be a good thing, crowds rushed to beautiful new ballparks in Chicago (new Comiskey Park), Baltimore (Camden Yards), Cleveland (Jacobs Field), Texas (Ballpark at Arlington), and Denver (Coors Field). Architects moved away from the cookie-cutter format of all-purpose stadiums to build baseball-only parks that blended modern conveniences with the splendor and tradition of the game's past. When financial woes and lagging attendance prompted owners in Seattle, San Francisco, Milwaukee, and Houston to consider moving their clubs, promises from private

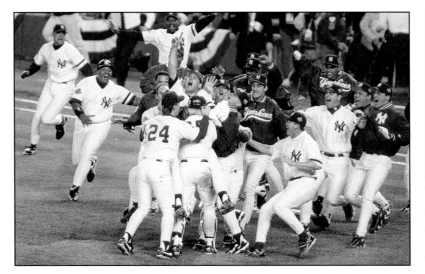

The Yankees (left) celebrate their 1996 championship. Jeff Maier (above) earned his spot in Yankee history when he reached over the fence and snagged a fly ball, giving New York a home run during the 1996 ALCS.

St. Louis's Mark McGwire, left, and Chicago Cubs outfielder Sammy Sosa led the resurgence of baseball in 1998.

The families of Cleveland Indians pitchers Tim Crews, Steve Olin, and Bob Ojeda were having an off-day picnic together at Crews's lake-side house near Orlando on March 22 when the three hurlers decided to go for a boat ride. Driving the trio back to shore just after dark, Crews slammed his boat into the side of a long dock at high speed. Olin was killed instantly. Crews died the next morning of a brain injury, and Ojeda underwent surgery for severe damage to his scalp and was unable to pitch again until August 6. Another devastating loss came on Opening Day of 1997, when veteran umpire John McSherry collapsed and died of a massive heart attack while working an Expos-Reds game.

Even as baseball was basking in the success of its extraordinary 1998 season, Bud Selig faced huge challenges when he was finally named commissioner in July '98 after nearly six years filling the post on an interim basis. Escalating player salaries and the widening profitability gap between big-market and small-market teams threatened to disrupt the game's competitive balance. The current labor agreement between owners and players, which runs only through 2001, needed to be expanded before another breakdown similar to 1994 happened. And there was talk of more expansion, with even a "World Cup" series against international teams a topic of discussion.

Whatever the future holds for Selig and the game, however, it will be tough to top the recent past in terms of excitement—and change.

investors and city officials to help build new stadiums encouraged them to reconsider. In 1999, even grand old Tiger Stadium (circa 1912) played its swan song, and another 87-year-old house of worship—Fenway Park—was expected to soon follow.

As in any era, some people managed to find trouble for themselves during the '90s. Owner George Steinbrenner of the Yankees was forced by Fay Vincent out of his role as the team's operating president in 1990 due to his relationship with Howard Spira—a noted gambler whom Steinbrenner allegedly paid to supply damaging information on Yankee star outfielder Dave Winfield. Steinbrenner was reinstated in 1992, in time to build another great Yankee team. Cincinnati owner Marge Schott was not so lucky. She received a one-year suspension and a $25,000 fine in 1993 for making racial and antisemitic remarks, then was asked to sell the Reds after similar incidents later in the decade.

When Albert Belle wasn't crushing home runs, he was being fined or suspended for such incidents as verbally abusing a female reporter and chasing young trick-or-treaters off his property with his car. Baltimore's Roberto Alomar was vilified for spitting in the face of umpire John Hirschbeck during the 1996 AL playoffs, and umps nearly went on strike when it was ruled that Alomar didn't have to serve his five-game suspension until the following spring.

Far more tragic than any strike or suspension was what happened during spring training of 1993.

Pitcher Kevin Brown, right, signed a seven-year, $105 million contract following the '98 campaign.

REDS TURN NASTY, BLOW AWAY THE A'S

A long lockout abbreviated spring training in 1990 and delayed the start of the regular season. Several teams were still not in peak form when the gates finally opened, and they stumbled badly at the start. The Chicago White Sox, on the other hand, came out of the chute like a rocket. Last in the AL West in 1989, Chicago won 94 games in 1990 for second-year pilot Jeff Torborg.

The 1988 NL Rookie of the Year, Chris Sabo batted .563 during the Reds' sweep of the A's in the 1990 fall classic.

Indeed, the White Sox had the third best record in the majors that season. Yet they missed out on postseason play because they had the ill luck to be in the same division with the Oakland A's. The defending champions continued to be so strong that the White Sox were never seriously in contention. Chicagoans were thus forced to take solace in the fact that for the third year in a row the second-place team in the AL West had a better record than the East winner, a sharp reversal of the situation for most of the preceding 17 seasons.

The A's went on to sweep the Boston Red Sox in the ALCS to capture their third pennant in a row. It began to appear that only the enormous upset loss to the Los Angeles Dodgers in the 1988 World Series would prevent Tony LaRussa's club from matching the 1972 through '74 Oakland A's post-expansion record of three consecutive world championships.

Certainly the Red Sox were as good as anything the NL had to offer. In the East, the Pittsburgh Pirates, after a long climb back into contention, finally made the big jump all the way to the top. Only once in their previous four seasons under Jim Leyland had the Pirates broken .500. By 1990, however, Leyland had the best outfield in the game with Andy Van Slyke in center flanked by Barry Bonds and Bobby Bonilla. However, not even Doug Drabek's startling emergence as the top winner in the NL could conceal the fact that the Bucs did not have wonderful pitching. Apart from Drabek, no Pittsburgh hurler put in enough innings to qualify for the ERA crown, and the bullpen had no true closer.

In contrast, Cincinnati—the West titlist—had a fine relief corps. Randy Myers was the main closer with 31 saves, but Rob Dibble also collected 11 saves with a magnificent 1.74 ERA in 68 appearances. With the addition of spot starter-middleman Norm Charlton, the bullpen trio garnered the nickname of

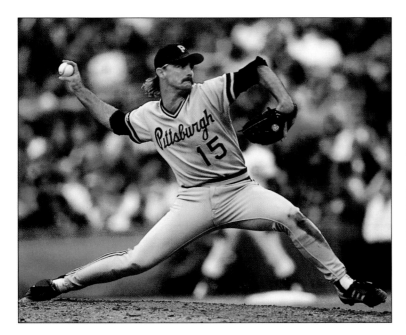

Pirate Doug Drabek (top left) *led the NL with 22 wins. Randy Myers* (top right) *of Cincinnati notched 31 saves. Myers's cohort, Rob Dibble* (bottom left), *brought 99-mph heat as a set-up man. Bob Welch of the Athletics* (bottom right) *won 27 games and the Cy Young Award.*

Nasty Boys. In their first season in Lou Piniella's charge, the Reds had no starters of Drabek's caliber. Nevertheless, Cincinnati had led the NL West from wire to wire if only because all of the other clubs in the division had even more severe pitching problems. The Los Angeles Dodgers, after losing Cy Young winner Orel Hershiser for the season, hovered around the .500 mark most of the summer before organizing a last-ditch rush that got them into second place but left them still five games short of the top. San Francisco Giants ace Rick Reuschel, finally feeling his age, toppled to just three wins. Houston's Mike Scott slumped from 20 wins to nine.

San Diego's highly touted rookie hurler Andy Benes, expected to be the staff bulwark, was just 10-11. Then there were the Atlanta Braves, who were overflowing with promising young pitchers like John Smoltz, Tom Glavine, and Steve Avery, but were unable to shake the malaise that had stolen over the franchise in the mid-1980s and finished with the worst record in the NL for the third year in a row.

In the NLCS, Leyland's three-star outfield hit under .200 as a unit and produced just five RBI. When the rest of the Bucs' bats also failed time and again to deliver with runners on base, the Reds triumphed in six games.

Noting that Myers and Dibble saved all four of Cincinnati's NLCS victories, LaRussa strove to come up with an A's batting order that would negate the Nasty Boys by scoring early and often. Accordingly, he looked for ways to utilize two veteran acquisitions, Willie Randolph and Willie McGee, along with Rickey Henderson, the greatest leadoff hitter in history, as table-setters for Jose Canseco and Mark McGwire.

Playing in their third consecutive World Series together, the Bash Brothers finally seemed primed to showcase their full prowess to a nationwide audience. After they belted 76 home runs between them in the 1990 regular season, Canseco and McGwire were the focus of LaRussa's thoughts when he plotted his batting order for the Series.

Somehow, though, the A's hitters that LaRussa chose, rather than scoring early and often, scored

not at all in Game 1. Jose Rijo, with late relief help, got Cincinnati off the launching pad with a 7-0 shutout. The next three games saw more scoring by the A's but the same result. Rijo and two hot hitters, Billy Hatcher and Chris Sabo, led the Reds to arguably the most stunning sweep in Series history.

SEASON'S BEST

•Pittsburgh's Barry Bonds is the NL MVP. He becomes the first player in ML history to hit .300 with 30 homers, 100 RBI, and 50 stolen bases.

•Oakland's Rickey Henderson is the AL MVP. He leads the league in runs (119), stolen bases (65), and OBP (.441). Henderson steals his 893rd base, breaking Ty Cobb's AL record.

•Oakland's Bob Welch grabs the AL Cy Young Award after leading the ML in wins (27) and winning percentage (.818). Welch's 27 wins are the most in the ML since 1972.

•Pittsburgh's Doug Drabek wins the NL Cy Young Award. He leads the league in wins (22) and winning percentage (.786).

•The Royals' George Brett leads the AL in batting (.329), becoming the first player in ML history to win BA titles in three different decades.

•Detroit's Cecil Fielder leads the AL in homers (51), RBI (132), slugging (.592), total bases (339), and strikeouts (182).

•On August 17, Carlton Fisk hits his 328th homer as a catcher—a new ML record.

•Roger Clemens goes 21-6 for Boston and leads the AL in ERA (1.93).

George Brett

•Texas's Nolan Ryan, at age 43, leads his loop in Ks (232) for the 11th time. Ryan also wins his 300th game and fires an ML-record sixth no-hitter vs. the A's on June 11.

•White Sox Bobby Thigpen breaks the ML save record by 11, as he slams the door 57 times.

•Oakland's Dennis Eckersley saves 48 games, posts a 0.61 ERA, and walks four batters in 73⅓ innings.

•Chicago's Ryne Sandberg leads the NL in home runs (40), runs (116), and total bases (344).

•Willie McGee, traded from St. Louis to Oakland in August, still wins the NL BA title (.335).

•Seattle's Ken Griffey Sr. and Ken Griffey Jr. become the first father-son duo to play on the same team.

•Pete Rose is sent to prison for cheating on his taxes.

•On July 17, the Minnesota Twins become the first ML team to make two triple plays in one game.

•Nine no-hitters are thrown during the season—a new ML record. On July 1, Yankee Andy Hawkins no-hits Chicago in a regulation nine-inning game but loses 4-0.

•Cincinnati's Billy Hatcher hits an all-time World Series-record .750 (9-for-12), as he collects seven hits in his first seven at bats.

CECIL FIELDER

Detroiters like the looks of new Japanese import

Since the 1950s, major leaguers with careers on the decline have sought new life and extended income in baseball by filling roster spots on Japanese professional teams. While big-league flops such as John Sipin, Clarence Jones, and Randy Bass have gone on to stardom across the ocean, there was little precedent for anyone returning from their stay abroad to resume their career a better major leaguer than before—until 1990 home run and RBI king Cecil Fielder came along.

The beefy (6′3″, 250-pound) first baseman had four successful seasons in the minors before joining the Toronto Blue Jays in 1985 and hitting .311 over 30 games. He was sent back to Triple-A after starting the next year at .157 however, and Fielder's up-and-down career continued until he convinced Toronto to sell him to the Hanshin Tigers following the 1988 campaign so he could prove his worth as a full-time player. After 31 homers in just 506 major-league at bats, he felt he deserved full-time work.

Quickly adjusting to his new surroundings, Fielder became one of the most powerful sluggers in the Japanese Central League. Playing in 106 games, he finished first in slugging (.628); third in homers (38), on-base percentage (.403), and RBI (81); and ninth in batting (.302). He also learned patience in walking 67 times (far above the pace he had set in his brief career in the majors). When the year was over, another pennant-starved Tiger team—this one in Detroit—signed the huge right-handed Califor-

nian to a two-year, $3-million contract. They were hoping for a comeback. Little did they know what was in store.

Beginning with seven homers and 19 RBI in April, the affable Fielder went on to one of the most devastating offensive seasons of the last quarter century. He hit three homers in a game twice, was named to the American League All-Star team, and when he hit his 40th homer in Detroit's 127th game, it marked the earliest any AL player had reached the mark since Reggie Jackson's incredible 97-game explosion to start 1969. Needing a homer on the season's final day to reach 50 dingers, he responded by stroking two at Yankee Stadium to finish at 51—making him just the 11th player to reach the magical 50 mark.

All told, Fielder led the majors in homers, RBI (132), and slugging (.592) while finishing first in the AL with 339 total bases and second (to Rickey Henderson) with 104 runs. He also finished second to Henderson in the MVP voting, a decision that angered many fans even though the Tigers finished at 79-83 while Henderson's Oakland team went to the World Series. Fielder still hadn't won the honor entering 1995—despite tying a record with three straight years (1990 to '92) atop the majors in RBI. Cecil remained one of the game's top producers with a five-year average (including the strike season) of 38 homers and 119 RBI since returning from Japan. Not bad for an import.

TWINS FLIP BRAVES IN WS THRILLER

Around Labor Day in 1991, sportswriters began hearkening back to the 1890 season. In that tumultuous, long-ago year, a war between players and owners over a proposed salary cap resulted in the formation of a player-controlled circuit called the Players' League. Owing to the many defections to the rebel loop, the war also caused massive changes in the composition of existing teams. The upheaval helped the Louisville Colonels of the American Association to become the only club ever to win a pennant after finishing in the basement the previous year.

In 1991, there was no overt warfare between players and owners, nor even any particular tumult, but the 1889 and '90 Louisville Colonels nevertheless lost their unique status. The Atlanta Braves, possessors of the worst record in the majors in 1990, leapfrogged to the NL pennant, and the Minnesota Twins rose from the AL West cellar to grab the junior circuit flag.

The Braves' improvement was not a complete surprise to many observers. After Bobby Cox had forsaken the front office the previous year to take field command of the team, Atlanta's horde of talented young players soon began to play as a unit and grow in confidence. There were, however, no observers prescient enough to imagine the Braves' improvement would be so enormous.

Making Atlanta's sudden ascension even more incredible was the fact that in midsummer the young Braves had trailed the seasoned Los Angeles Dodgers by 9½ games. By then, though, Cox had assembled the best starting rotation in the majors. Headed by Cy Young claimant Tom Glavine, the lone 20-game winner in the NL, and 18-game winner Steve Avery, Cox's four-man rotation bagged 67 victories and got the Braves home first in the NL West one length ahead of the Dodgers.

The Twins were not the AL's worst club in 1990, but they were close, finishing in a tie with the Milwaukee Brewers for 12th in the loop's aggregate standings. In a way, though, to go from worst to first in their division, the Twins had faced an even stiffer challenge than the Braves. While Atlanta had finished 26 games out of first in the NL West in 1990, Minnesota had trailed the Oakland A's by 29 games in the AL West. Moreover, in 1991 the A's were coming off three consecutive pennant wins.

Atlanta's Greg Olson is head over heels; the Twins' Dan Gladden is out.

Howard Johnson of the Mets (left) led the NL with 38 home runs and 117 RBI. Montreal's Dennis Martinez (right) twirled a perfect game against the Dodgers on July 28.

Minnesota's task was considerably eased when Carney Lansford, the A's spark plug, was sidelined nearly all season by a knee injury, and Dave Stewart and Bob Welch, after combining for 49 wins the previous year, collected just 23 victories between them in 1991. Additional help came the way of skipper Tom Kelly when the Twins, never before particularly successful in the free-agent market, garnered Chili Davis and Minnesota native Jack Morris. Functioning as a DH, Davis led the Twins in homers and RBI, and Morris supplied 18 wins. When the Chicago White Sox, Oakland's only real competition in 1990, got subpar years from all their starting pitchers except Jack McDowell, the Twins had only daylight ahead of them after they reeled off 16 straight wins early in the season.

In the ALCS, Toronto, likewise an easy winner in the East, once again fizzled. Between the two wins from Morris and Kirby Puckett's nine hits and six RBI, the Blue Jays were eliminated in just five rounds.

The Twins then had a four-day wait before they learned the identity of their World Series opponent. On October 14, Pittsburgh seemed the probable foe after Zane Smith and Roger Mason combined to ice the Braves, 1-0, and put the Pirates up 3-2 in games. Just two nights later, Avery and Alejandro Pena

teamed to beat Doug Drabek by a 1-0 score. The following evening the Bucs, who had led the NL in both hitting and scoring, were zeroed for the third time in the NLCS when Smoltz set them down, 4-0, to solve the mystery of whom the Twins would meet.

After three one-sided fall classics in a row, baseball people could only pray that the Twins and the Braves would continue to play like Cinderella teams. Their prayers were answered. The 1991 World Series ranks among the best. Not only did it go the seven-game limit, but five of the contests were decided by one run and the last two went into extra innings

Like the St. Louis Cardinals in 1987, it was the Braves' fate, though, to oppose a Minnesota team in an odd year. Had it been an even year, the Braves, as the NL representative, would have hosted four games, including the decisive finale.

Instead, Minnesota drew the home-field advantage and once again made the most of it. The Twins snared Game 6 at the Metrodome, 4-3, on Puckett's solo homer in the bottom of the 11th. Twenty-four hours later, after Jack Morris had held the Braves runless for 10 frames, Gene Larkin resolved the only scoreless overtime Game 7 in Series history by singling home Dan Gladden.

Larkin's hit gave the Twins their second world championship even though, after their third fall classic appearance, they still had never won a Series game on the road.

Second base was strong in the AL. Left: Julio Franco of Texas led the AL with a .341 average. Robby Alomar (right) came into his own and helped the Jays into the ALCS.

471

SEASON'S BEST

•Cal Ripken of the Orioles wins his second MVP Award, as he extends his consecutive-games-played streak to 1,573. He leads the AL in total bases with 368. Ripken also becomes the first shortstop in AL history to hit .300 with 30 or more homers and 100 or more RBI.

•Third baseman Terry Pendleton of Atlanta wins the NL MVP Award. He cops the hitting crown (.319), tops the loop in hits (187), and ties in total bases (303).

Cal Ripken

•Boston's Roger Clemens paces the AL in ERA (2.62), strikeouts (241), innings (271), and shutouts (four) and wins his third Cy Young Award.

•Atlanta's Tom Glavine wins 20 games for the Braves and bags the NL Cy Young Award.

•Howard Johnson of the Mets paces the NL in home runs (38) and RBI (117).

•The Mets' David Cone ties the NL record when he fans 19 Phillies on the last day of the season.

•Dennis Martinez of the Expos pitches a perfect game against the Dodgers on July 28, winning 2-0. Martinez leads the NL with a 2.39 ERA and five shutouts and also ties in complete games with nine.

•Two days before Martinez's gem, Mark Gardner of the Expos loses a no-hitter to the Dodgers, 1-0 in 10 innings.

•Reliever Lee Smith of the Cards sets a new NL record when he nets 47 saves.

•Cecil Fielder of Detroit repeats his 1990 slugging feat when he paces the AL in both homers (44) and RBI (133).

•Milwaukee's Paul Molitor paces the ML in both runs (133) and hits (216).

•Texas's Julio Franco wins the AL bat crown (.341).

•Rickey Henderson tops Lou Brock's ML record for career thefts and finishes the season with 994 stolen bases. Henderson also cops his ML-record 11th stolen base crown (58).

•The Expos have only 68 home dates and are forced to finish their season on the road after a section of Olympic Stadium collapses and cannot be repaired.

•The Blue Jays set a new AL attendance record when they draw more than four million fans.

•The Angels (81-81) become the first team in ML history to finish in the basement without a losing record.

•Rob Deer of Detroit hits just .179, the lowest BA in 105 years by a regular outfielder.

•Nolan Ryan throws his ML-record seventh no-hitter on May 1 against the Blue Jays.

NOLAN RYAN

Forty-five-year-old K King still brings the heat

Comparing the career of Nolan Ryan to that of any other major-league pitcher is an impossible task. Others have won more games, compiled lower earned run averages, and hurled for multiple championship clubs, but none was ever as overpowering or durable as the quiet man from Texas. His total of 5,714 career strikeouts over a record 27 seasons is so far ahead of nearest competitor Steve Carlton that it compares to a slugger belting nearly 1,000 homers to top Hank Aaron's 755. When Ryan struck out 203 batters with the 1991 Rangers, it marked his 15th time above the 200 mark—not bad for a 45-year-old.

Drafted out of high school by the then-lowly Mets, Ryan had always possessed a blazing fastball but had trouble controlling it early in his career. The right-hander was 6-3 with a 3.53 ERA as a spot starter and reliever on the 1969 world champions, but wildness and a disappointing 10-14 mark in '71 prompted the Mets to trade the 25-year-old to the California Angels before the following season. No longer stuck behind the likes of Tom Seaver and Jerry Koosman, Nolan suddenly blossomed in 1971 with a 19-16 record, 2.28 ERA, and an incredible 329 strikeouts (then the third-highest total of the modern era) in 284 innings.

So began the second stage of Ryan's career. Setting a modern record in '73 with 383 strikeouts (topping Sandy Koufax by one), the 6'2", 195-pound fitness maniac with the 100-mph fastball averaged

302 strikeouts and 163 walks in eight seasons for the Angels through 1979 while earning recognition as baseball's most dominant and unique hurler. California was usually a mediocre team, however, and despite 40 shutouts and four no-hitters "The Ryan Express" could muster just a 138-121 record over the span while earning a reputation as a ".500 pitcher."

The label didn't seem to bother the Houston Astros, who made the free agent baseball's first $1 million-a-year player in '80. Helped by vastly improved control, the ageless competitor added a record fifth no-hitter and went 106-94 with 207 strikeouts a year before moving on to the Texas Rangers in 1988 to finish his career.

Expected to be winding down at age 42, Ryan wound it up instead in '89 and went 16-10 with 301 strikeouts and a sixth no-hitter in just 239 innings. His 300th victory followed the next year (along with 232 more strikeouts), and in 1991 Ryan was still going strong despite constant shoulder irritation. That season, he finished 12-6, fanning 203 and ranking fifth in the AL with a 2.91 ERA. Opponents hit just .172 against him (the best mark in the league), and on May 1 he threw his seventh and final no-hitter—striking out 16. The future Hall of Famer retired two years later with a 324-292 record and 61 shutouts. Over the course of 5,387 innings and seven presidential administrations, he had allowed fewer hits per game (under 6.7) than any pitcher in history.

CANADA'S JAYS SLIP PAST BRAVES

Many of the events that happened in 1992 were predictable. For one, the Boston Red Sox landed in the AL East basement just two years after winning the division title. Similarly, the Los Angeles Dodgers, after finishing the 1991 campaign just one game back in the NL West, had the bottom fall out completely. In 1992, the Dodgers' proud 85-year skein without a cellar finish ended when they came in dead last in the National League for the first time since 1907.

In several important respects, though, the 1992 season fooled prognosticators. After watching the wild rollercoaster rides teams had taken from one year to the next during the past decade, no reasonable mind could have predicted that three of the four defending division champions would repeat. Only the Minnesota Twins faltered—and even at

that, they didn't falter too badly. In 1992, Minnesota finished a solid second in the AL West, six games back of the Oakland A's.

Oakland's return to the top after only a year's absence was also, of course, something that could not have been predicted. Tony LaRussa again got only 23 combined wins from Dave Stewart and Bob Welch, his expected Big Two. Then, Jose Canseco—between his erratic off-field behavior and his lackadaisical on-field behavior—put himself so deeply into the A's doghouse that he was dealt to the Texas Rangers. More than compensating for these debits, though, were Carney Lansford's return from a year on the shelf and Dennis Eckersley's 51 saves and 1.91 ERA.

In the 1992 ALCS, however, the A's drew a different Toronto team than they had dispatched in postseason play three years earlier. Cito Gaston still sat at the helm, but only third baseman Kelly Gruber, shortstop Manny Lee, catcher Pat Borders, southpaw Jimmy Key, middle relievers David Wells and Duane Ward, and closer Tom Henke from the 1989 cast were still lead performers. In the interim the Blue Jays minor-league system had furnished pitchers Todd Stottlemyre and Juan Guzman and first baseman John Olerud; trades and free agency had brought Joe Carter, Dave Winfield, Roberto Alomar, Devon White, Jack Morris, and Candy Maldonado.

Despite all their cast changes, they could not erase the Jays' long-standing reputation for failure in postseason action. The low esteem in which Toronto was held by pundits seemed likely to continue when the A's won Game 1 of the ALCS behind Stewart. The Jays took the next two contests, though, and then put a large hole in their

Toronto catcher Pat Borders (left) congratulates closer Tom Henke after a save in the ALCS. Borders went on to be the World Series MVP.

Dave Stewart of the A's (top left) *celebrates after Game 5 of the ALCS. Philadelphia catcher Darren Daulton* (top center) *led the NL with 109 RBI. Dennis Eckersley of the Athletics* (top right) *was the AL MVP.* Bottom: *Sid Bream scores the series-winning run in the NLCS.*

image as losers under pressure by rallying from a five-run deficit to win Game 4, 7-6, in 11 innings.

Stewart kept the A's alive by winning Game 5, but two afternoons later, upon returning to Sky-Dome, the Jays blasted out a 9-2 triumph to become the first Canadian World Series entrant.

That same evening the Pittsburgh Pirates and the Atlanta Braves—for the second year in a row—prepared to play Game 7 in the NLCS. Though they had lost the crucial seventh contest the previous year and had also dropped the ball in the NLCS in 1990, in another way the Pirates had history on their side. Twice before a Pittsburgh team had come back from a 3-1 deficit in games to win a postseason match, and manager Jim Leyland and his 25-man crew looked for October 14, 1992, to mark the third such occasion.

As the fray entered the bottom of the ninth, TV cameras showed the Atlanta fans looking grim and the Braves dugout a mass of heads wearing their caps backwards to evoke a rally. On the mound stood Pirates ace Doug Drabek, sitting on a 2-0 lead.

Three batters later Drabek was gone, having loaded the bases while getting no one out. In came Stan Belinda.

Belinda managed to get two outs, including Ron Gant's sacrifice fly that narrowed the score to 2-1. With the tying run on third and Sid Bream, the pennant-winning run, on second, third-string catcher Francisco Cabrera slashed a pinch single to left. Bream lumbered around third and slid home safely when Barry Bonds's throw was off-line. Atlanta had its second straight pennant and Pittsburgh its third straight NLCS defeat.

Three nights later, Tom Glavine needed only Damon Berryhill's three-run homer to rebuff Morris in the Series opener, 3-1. Until the ninth inning of Game 2, Atlanta was poised to take a 2-0 lead, but then pinch hitter Ed Sprague tagged Jeff Reardon for a two-run homer that gave the Jays a 5-4 win.

Borders, who led all hitters with 15 total bases in the Series, took charge in the next three games as the Blue Jays moved to a 3-2 advantage. In Game 6, verging on extinction, Atlanta scored a ninth-inning run to tie the count 2-2. Two frames later, when the Braves could only counter with one run in their last at bat, Winfield cracked a two-run double that made Toronto the first world champion from outside the United States.

SEASON'S BEST

•Barry Bonds of the Pirates wins the NL MVP Award. Bonds leads the NL with a .624 SA, 127 walks, .461 OBP, and 109 runs. He signs a $43 million contract with San Francisco after the season.

•Dennis Eckersley of the A's sweeps both the AL Cy Young and MVP Awards. Eck leads the majors with 51 saves.

Gary Sheffield

•The Cubs' Greg Maddux bags the NL Cy Young Award after winning 20 games and posting a 2.18 ERA.

•San Diego's Gary Sheffield rebounds from a miserable .194 season with Milwaukee to lead the league in batting (.330) and total bases (323).

•Fred McGriff of San Diego tops the NL with 35 homers.

•Phillies catcher Darren Daulton leads the NL in RBI with 109.

•Seattle's Edgar Martinez leads the major leagues in batting (.343) and ties in doubles (46).

•Minnesota's Kirby Puckett tops the AL with 210 hits and 313 total bases.

•Cecil Fielder of the Tigers becomes the second player in history to top the ML in RBI three years in a row (124).

•Texas's Juan Gonzalez wins the AL homer title with 43 dingers.

•Boston's Roger Clemens tops the AL with five shutouts and a 2.41 ERA.

•Bill Swift of the Giants paces the majors with a 2.08 ERA.

•Lee Smith of the Cards leads the NL with 43 saves.

•Fay Vincent, under unrelenting pressure from club owners, steps down as commissioner, leaving the game without a titular leader.

•Baltimore draws 3,567,819 fans to its new stadium, Oriole Park at Camden Yards.

•George Brett of the Royals and Robin Yount of the Brewers both collect their 3,000th hit.

•Shortstop Ozzie Smith of the Cardinals wins his 13th straight Gold Glove.

•Boston's Jeff Reardon breaks Rollie Fingers's record of 341 career saves.

•Oakland's Rickey Henderson becomes the first player in the ML history to accumulate 1,000 career stolen bases.

•Seattle's Bret Boone joins father Bob and grandfather Ray as the majors' first three-generation family.

•Deion Sanders of the Braves plays in a World Series game and an NFL game in the same week.

•On September 20, second sacker Mickey Morandini of the Phils performs the first unassisted triple play in an NL game since 1927.

BARRY BONDS

Bobby's kid cracks homers, steals bases, wins MVP

In the days before their numbers were routinely splashed across television screens and cited in salary arbitration drives, major leaguers were concerned only with their most vital statistics. Even players with both the power to sock 30 homers and the speed to steal 30 bases didn't worry about making the "30-30 club," so nobody really noticed when outfielder Bobby Bonds tackled the feat a record five times. This being the case, it only seemed appropriate that when the world went stat crazy nearly 20 years later, the next great 30-30 man to come along was the guy who had watched Bobby closer than anybody else over the years—1992 National League MVP Barry Bonds.

Young Barry grew up in the game, palling around and playing catch with godfather Willie Mays and Willie McCovey while they were his father's San Francisco Giant teammates. Drafted by the Pirates in 1985 and called up a year later, Barry was a .283 hitter within two years. In 1989, he was down to .248, and even with 19 homers and 32 steals, this was viewed as a disappointment. Only in 1990 did the left-handed batter finally catch up with his potential. Hitting .301 with 114 RBI, he became only the second player in major-league history with over 30 homers (33) and 50 stolen bases (52)—a feat even his father hadn't accomplished in a 332-homer, 461-steal career. He was named the league's MVP for his efforts, and followed it up with a nearly identical campaign in '91 with a .292 batting average, 25 homers, 116 RBI, and 43 steals, but he could only muster a .148 batting mark as the Pirates lost in the NLCS for the second straight year.

Denied a second straight MVP Award (he finished second), an emotionally driven Bonds set out to win a championship and regain his honor in 1992. He accomplished half the task, taking the MVP back by hitting a career-high .311 with 109 runs, 127 walks, a .624 slugging average, and a .461 on-base percentage (all first in the NL), 34 homers (second), and 103 RBI (fourth). He also won his third Gold Glove in a row as the best left fielder in the majors. Despite his improved .261 average in the playoffs, the Pirates lost again.

Feeling he was not being fairly compensated for his work, the 28-year-old signed a six-year contract worth $43.75 million following the '92 season and headed for the familiar confines of Candlestick Park (just 20 miles from his boyhood home) to play for the Giants and batting coach Bobby Bonds. Taking his father's uniform No. 25, he won his third MVP in 1993 with a .336 batting average, 46 homers, and 123 RBI—all career highs and near Triple Crown numbers. By the time a similar season (.312 with 37 homers) followed in strike-shortened '94, Barry had firmly established himself as one of the all-time greats—and he and his dad as the greatest father-son act in baseball annals.

CARTER'S CLOUT KILLS THE PHILS

Throughout the spring of 1992, the San Francisco Giants had performed as if they would give the Atlanta Braves a run for the NL West title. When the final standings were printed, though, they showed the Giants in fifth place, 26 games off the pennant pace.

The Giants' second-half collapse was probably directly linked to the apathy that pervaded the club when it seemed certain the franchise would be moved to the Tampa-St. Petersburg area prior to the 1993 season. A new group of owners, however, stepped in, pledged to keep the ballclub in San Francisco, and then signed on popular coach Dusty Baker to run it on the field. Candlestick Park no longer seemed like such a bad place to watch a ball game. Indeed, the 'Stick became one of the hottest tickets in the majors once the fledgling owners announced that Barry Bonds had signed on as a free agent.

With Bonds leading the charge, the Giants roared through April, May, and into June far ahead of the defending division champion Atlanta Braves. Meanwhile the three-time champion Pittsburgh Pirates, no longer having Bonds's heavy artillery, lagged even farther off the pace in the NL East. Long be-

fore June, it was clear the Bucs' three-year rein was over, and the Philadelphia Phillies gave every appearance of being the new rulers.

By late September, the Phils had solidified their claim after brushing back a furious closing rush by the Montreal Expos, but the situation in the NL West had changed drastically. The Giants, after leading the division all summer, were caught and passed by the Braves.

Just as the Braves were about to go into their victory lap, the Giants suddenly got hot again. On the last Friday of the season the two were in a dead heat at 101-58. While the Braves played a three-game set at home against the expansion Colorado Rockies, the Giants had to venture into Los Angeles for their final series.

It was the first time since 1934 that a Dodgers team faced a Giants team in a spoiler's role. San Francisco fans who knew their franchise's history craved a different result than the Dodgers' two-game sweep that had denied the New York Giants the 1934 flag.

As expected, the Braves won their first two contests with Colorado, and the Giants kept pace. If the same pattern held on the last Sunday of the season, the Giants stood

Joe Carter jumps for joy after pouncing on a Mitch Williams delivery for a World Series-ending home run in Game 6.

Toronto entered the ALCS favored nearly as strongly as the Braves were in the senior loop championship series. The Blue Jays fulfilled expectations, winning in six rounds, but the Braves found themselves in trouble. After taking a 2-1 lead in games, Atlanta skipper Bobby Cox sat by powerless while the meat of his batting order went into a deep coma. Spearheaded by center fielder Lenny Dykstra and pitcher Curt Schilling, the Phils put the Braves away in six games to earn their third Series trip in 14 seasons after making just two forays into the championship round in the previous 97 years.

The World Series also went just six games with Toronto emerging victorious. Joe Carter's three-run homer in the bottom of the ninth of the sixth contest lifted the Jays to a come-from-behind 8-6 win over Phils closer Mitch Williams. Williams also lost Game 4, a sloppy 15-14 melee that broke the modern record for the most runs in a postseason game.

Paul Molitor, who did little more than DH for the Jays during the regular season, was the Series MVP, but Dykstra could justifiably have won the award in a losing cause. It was perhaps only right, though, that the winner should come from the first team since the 1977 and '78 Yankees to win back-to-back world titles.

Paul Molitor (left) led the AL with 211 base hits. After signing with the Braves, *Greg Maddux (right)* led the NL with a 2.36 ERA and won his second Cy Young Award.

to regain the advantage, for the division playoff game would be played in San Francisco.

Such a game never came to be. The Braves picked over the Rockies again in their finale, 5-3, to sweep the season series 13-0 and set a new franchise record with 104 wins. Giants' players, learning the final result from Atlanta even before the first pitch was thrown in Dodger Stadium, knew they were in a must-win situation. It mattered little. Giants starter, 21-year-old rookie Salomon Torres, was in trouble by the third inning, and the San Francisco bullpen, exhausted by constant use in the stretch, had no help to offer. Featuring two home runs by Mike Piazza, the Dodgers shredded the Giants' dream, 12-1.

In the AL, the Toronto Blue Jays and the Chicago White Sox could afford to rest their regulars on the final weekend. Both had long since clinched their respective divisions. Chicago outran the Texas Rangers by 8 lengths, and Toronto gave Cito Gaston his third division crown by a 7-game margin over the New York Yankees.

Manager Dusty Baker (left) pushed the Giants to 103 victories in 1993. Right: *Jack McDowell of the White Sox had 22 wins—earning him the AL Cy Young Award.*

SEASON'S BEST

• The NL expands to 14 teams, adding the Colorado Rockies and Florida Marlins.

• The Giants' Barry Bonds wins his third NL MVP Award after leading the league in homers (46), RBI (123), slugging (.677), OBP (.458), and total bases (365).

• Chicago's Frank Thomas, with 41 homers and 128 RBI, is the AL MVP.

• Jack McDowell of the White Sox leads the AL in wins (22) and shutouts (four) and takes home the Cy Young Award.

• Atlanta's Greg Maddux wins the NL Cy Young Award after topping the circuit in ERA (2.36), innings (267), and complete games (eight).

• The Rangers' Juan Gonzalez cops his second straight home run crown (46).

• Albert Belle paces the AL in RBI (129).

Lenny Dykstra

• Seattle's 6'10" Randy Johnson fans an ML-high 308 batters.

• Toronto's John Olerud tops AL in batting (.363), doubles (54), and OBP (.473).

• Andres Galarraga of Colorado smacks .370 to lead the majors.

• Philly's Lenny Dykstra leads the NL in runs (143) and hits (194), then hits four homers in the World Series.

• Toronto's Paul Molitor leads the AL in hits (211) and collects 12 more in 24 at bats in the World Series.

• The Cubs' Randy Myers tops the majors in saves (53).

• The Rockies yield 927 runs (5.7 per game) but set an ML attendance record (4,483,350).

• Cleveland pitchers Steve Olin and Tim Crews are killed in a boating accident in spring training.

• The Mets' Vince Coleman is sentenced to three years probation after throwing a firecracker at a group of fans.

• The Tigers' 899 runs scored are the most in the majors since 1953.

• In February, Reds owner Marge Schott is suspended for one year for using ethnic slurs.

• Dodgers catcher Mike Piazza is the unanimous choice for NL ROY after hitting .318 with 35 homers.

• The major leagues go the entire season without a commissioner.

• Met pitcher Anthony Young loses his 27th consecutive game—an ML record.

• Montreal's Curtis Pride, born without hearing, doubles in his ML debut.

• Nolan Ryan retires as the ML leader in strikeouts with 5,714 (1,578 more than anyone else) and walks with 2,795.

• On September 7, St. Louis's Mark Whiten hits four homers with 12 RBI against the Reds.

FRANK THOMAS

It's unamimous: Big Hurt is AL's best bopper

Young Frank Thomas was a .400 hitter with power in high school, but was so bulky and strong even then that scouts who watched him his senior year figured him more for a tight end than a first baseman. Now that the 1993 MVP has become one of the best overall hitters in the American League, the folks whose job it is to know better would probably give anything to have another crack at the pride of Georgia's Columbus High School.

The 6'5" Thomas actually did play tight end on the Auburn University football team, but he quit after his freshman year to concentrate on baseball. A .403 hitter with 19 homers his senior year, Frank was drafted by the White Sox in 1989 only after their No. 1 choice was snatched up by another team. When the confident slugger started off 7-for-11 with a 425-foot homer off Nolan Ryan during his first major-league training camp the following spring, folks began looking at "The Big Hurt" more closely. Promoted from Double-A to Chicago August 2, he hit .330 the rest of the way to set the stage for the devastating seasons that followed.

In 1992, Thomas began a six-year stretch in which he combined power, average, and patience at the plate as no player since Ted Williams. Batting .318 with 32 homers, 109 RBI, and 138 walks in '91, Frank followed it up with near-identical numbers in 1992—leaving his poor fielding around first base as the only drawback to his game. Fans were willing to put up with a few errors in exchange for a divisional title and MVP season, and Thomas gave them both in 1993.

Leading Chicago into the ALCS against Toronto, he finished second in the AL with 128 RBI, third with 41 homers, and in the top 10 with a .317 batting average, 106 runs, a .607 slugging percentage, and 112 walks. He struck out just 54 times; became only the fifth player in major-league history to hit .300 with 20 homers and 100 RBI, runs, and walks for three consecutive years (the others are all in the Hall of Fame); and was a unanimous MVP selection. Although Chicago lost to the Blue Jays in the playoffs, Frank hit .353 with a home run.

It seemed impossible to top such a season, but even with the strike wiping out Chicago's final 49 games in '94 Thomas did just that. Batting a career-high .353, he had 38 homers, 101 RBI, 106 runs, and 109 walks this time while slugging an incredible .729. Named AL MVP for the second year in a row, he was well on the way to one of the greatest careers in major-league history. Folks no longer confuse him for a tight end.

BASEBALL STRIKES OUT; WS CANCELLED

Since the Giants beat the A's in the 1905 World Series, baseball always had an unequivocal champion to fete at the end of each season. That unbroken string came to an abrupt halt in 1994 after 89 years.

At midnight on August 12, action ceased at the major-league level when the players' union stubbornly refused to accept a salary cap proposed by an equally intransigent bloc of owners. Standing in the way of a compromise settlement was the absence of a commissioner ever since the owners had pushed Fay Vincent into resigning.

By the third day of the strike there was already evidence that play would not resume in 1994. Cleveland owner Richard Jacobs directed that all souvenirs being sold at the Indians' gift shop which carried the words "inaugural season at Jacobs Field" (Cleveland's new park in 1994) be sold at half price. Asked for his views on the strike, White Sox star Frank Thomas said, "I've had a career year, but I'm not going to finish it."

Thomas's assessment of his season was actually quite modest. Though the White Sox completed only 113 of their scheduled 162 games, Thomas already had 101 RBI, 106 runs, 38 home runs, and 34 doubles to go with his .353 batting average.

Other performers had mighty imposing stats as well. In just 113 games, Minnesota Twins second baseman Chuck Knoblauch amassed 45 doubles; with 47 games left to play, San Francisco Giants third sacker Matt Williams was just 18 home runs short of Roger Maris's record of 61 four-baggers.

Even more important, several teams that had been dormant for decades were flexing their muscles with a postseason goal in mind.

Prior to the 1994 season, both major leagues were split into three divisions and an extra playoff tier was added. The new structure called for five-team divisions in the East and the Central and a four-team division in the West. Since geography was the determining factor as to where a team was assigned, some apparent inequities occurred.

For one, the Atlanta Braves and the Philadelphia Phillies, the two NL division winners in 1993, were both placed in the East. When the Phils spun their wheels after first sacker John Kruk was sidelined while undergoing cancer treatment, the Braves appeared to have a smooth sail to their fourth straight division crown. A young Montreal team,

On August 11, fans pleaded with players and owners to resolve differences. As in the past, the fans' appeals fell on deaf ears.

however, outplayed Atlanta in every department each time the two clubs met. By July, Expos manager Felipe Alou not only had the satisfaction of looking over his shoulder at the Braves but also the pleasure of watching his son, Moises, blossom into one of the Expos' main components.

When action stopped on August 12, the Expos stood 6 games ahead of the Braves and boasted the best record in the majors at 74-40.

Second only to the Expos were the New York Yankees, who paced the AL East by 6½ games. Missing from postseason play for 13 years, their longest dry spell since the close of the dead-ball era, the Yankees were the antithesis of the home-grown Expos as owner George Steinbrenner continued to prowl the trade and free-agent markets in search of a winner.

Three of Steinbrenner's newer acquisitions— Wade Boggs, Jimmy Key, and Paul O'Neill—were particularly instrumental in the Yankees' return to contention. Cleveland also profited heavily in 1994 from the trade and free-agent route. The previous spring, the Tribe had suffered still another in a seemingly unending string of catastrophes when pitchers Tim Crews and Steve Olin were killed in a boating accident and a third hurler, Cliff Young, later died in an auto crash. A sixth-place finish resulted in 1993, but Cleveland decided to shoot the moon in conjunction with the opening of its new stadium.

During the winter the Indians gained possession of veterans Dennis Martinez, Eddie Murray, Jack Morris, and Omar Vizquel. The four melded with such earlier acquisitions as Sandy Alomar, Kenny Lofton, Carlos Baerga, and Mark Clark as well as four amateur draft prizes—Albert Belle, Manny Ramirez, Jim Thome, and Charles Nagy— to promise Clevelanders their most exciting team in eons.

Ken Griffey Jr. (top left) of Seattle had 40 homers in 111 games. The Twins' Chuck Knoblauch (top center) had 45 doubles in 109 games. Yankee Paul O'Neill (top right) led the AL with a .359 batting average. Matt Williams (bottom left) was on pace for 61 homers. Royal David Cone (bottom center) won the AL Cy Young Award. Bottom right: Michael Jordan flirted with baseball.

For the first time in 40 seasons, a promise in Cleveland seemed about to be fulfilled as the Indians trailed Chicago by only one game in the AL Central when the season shut down. They had also been first in line for the loop wild-card berth.

Texas Rangers fans were equally thrilled to find their club atop the AL West and possibly headed for the first postseason engagement in franchise history. Only two games back of the Rangers at stoppage time were the Seattle Mariners, who likewise had never played a postseason match.

At midnight on August 12, no fewer than 16 teams still had realistic playoff hopes. Their disappointment paled in comparison to the economic and emotional distress suffered by millions when Milwaukee owner/acting commissioner Bud Selig in September officially voiced what everyone already knew: that the 1994 season was dead.

SEASON'S BEST

- Each league breaks into three divisions. Six division winners plus two wild-card teams are scheduled to make the playoffs.

- The average ML salary is an estimated $1.2 million.

- Unable to reach a basic agreement, the major-league players strike on August 12. The owners want to impose a salary cap, but the players won't give in. On September 14, the season is officially cancelled.

- Chicago's Frank Thomas wins his second straight MVP Award. He leads the AL in slugging (.729), walks (109), and OBP (.487) and belts 38 homers.

- The NL MVP is Houston's Jeff Bagwell, who hits 39 homers and leads the loop in RBI (116), runs (104), and SA (.750—the highest mark since Babe Ruth).

- Atlanta's Greg Maddux wins his third straight Cy Young after leading the NL in ERA (1.56) and complete games (10) and tying in wins (16).

- Kansas City's David Cone cops the AL Cy Young Award.

- Jacobs Field in Cleveland and The Ballpark at Arlington open for play.

- Basketball star Michael Jordan, age 31, signs with the Chicago White Sox and is assigned to Double-A Birmingham, where he bats .202 over a full season.

- Cubs superstar Ryne Sandberg, age 34, abruptly retires in June.

- On July 9, Boston shortstop John Valentin performs an unassisted triple play.

- On July 28, Texas's Kenny Rogers tosses a perfect game against California.

- Matt Williams of the Giants leads the ML in homers (43).

- San Diego's Tony Gwynn wins his fifth BA title (.394) and also leads in OBP (.454).

- Yankee Paul O'Neill tops the AL in hitting (.359).

- Seattle's Ken Griffey Jr. tops the AL in homers (40).

- The Twins' Kirby Puckett leads the AL in RBI (112).

- Cleveland's Kenny Lofton leads the AL in hits (160) and stolen bases (60).

Tony Gwynn

- The Indians' Albert Belle hits .357 with 36 homers and 101 RBI.

- The Mets' Bret Saberhagen wins 14 games and walks just 13 batters.

- Cubs broadcaster Harry Caray celebrates his 50th year in the booth.

- The Rangers finish atop the AL West with a 52-62 record.

- Ken Burns's *Baseball*, a nine-part documentary that airs on PBS in September, helps fill the baseball void created by the strike.

JEFF BAGWELL

Red Sox reject puts up astronomical numbers

For Boston Red Sox fans, the sale of outfielder Babe Ruth to the hated New York Yankees in January 1920 was far more than the worst transaction in sports history. Red Sox teams have proven so unlucky since that people have begun believing there is still bad karma left over from the move, a "Curse of the Bambino" that has haunted the Olde Town Team through 75 subsequent years of near misses. Bad trades are a big part of the supposed curse, and when all is said and done the deal sending future (1994) National League MVP Jeff Bagwell to Houston for Larry Andersen may go down as the worst since the Big Guy himself left for the Bronx.

A Boston native drafted by his hometown team in 1989 after an outstanding career at the University of Hartford, Bagwell was named 1990 Eastern League MVP following a terrific .333 season at Double-A New Britain. The Red Sox were driving toward an AL Eastern League division title that fateful summer, and general manager Lou Gorman felt in need of a strong, experienced middle reliever. The hapless Houston Astros were making the right-handed Andersen available, and Gorman decided to go for broke and trade a 22-year-old prospect for a 37-year-old veteran.

Andersen compiled a 1.23 ERA as the Sox won the division, but they were then swept by Oakland in the ALCS. Andersen departed to San Diego as a free agent in 1991, while Bagwell went on to a Rookie of the Year season with the Astros by batting .294 with 15 homers and 82 RBI. The right-handed, baby-faced first baseman showed improvement in every area but average in '92 (.273 with 18 homers and 96 RBI), and in '93 was having his best year yet (.320, 20 homers, 88 ribbies) when he broke a bone in his left hand and missed the final 20 games.

He didn't get a whole year out of 1994 either because of the strike (ironically, he broke his hand again two days before it started), but what Bagwell accomplished in 110 games was more than any Houston player had previously managed in a full 162. Defying the diminishing effects of the Astrodome on power, Jeff set team records with 39 homers (second in the NL), a .368 batting average (second), 116 RBI (first), an incredible .750 slugging percentage (first and the highest in the majors since 1927), and 73 extra-base hits. The surprising Astros finished just one-half game out of first, and Bagwell was a unanimous MVP. Bagwell went on to post outstanding numbers well into the 2000s, becoming one of the game's greatest hitters.

BRAVES, GLAVINE FEND OFF THE TRIBE

When the Braves franchise moved from Milwaukee to Atlanta in 1966, nobody thought that it would take almost three decades for the Atlanta Braves to win a World Series. When the Cleveland Indians squared off against the Braves in the 1995 World Series, it capped that franchise's breakout season. Cleveland had not tasted postseason play since 1954 when the Tribe was humbled in four straight World Series games by the then New York Giants.

But for a slight reordering of events the Series combatants in 1995 could have been two teams that had never before qualified for postseason play. The Seattle Mariners, a perennial doormat since their inception in 1977, gave the Indians all they could handle in the American League Championship Series before bowing in six frames. The Colorado Rockies, in just their third year of existence, threw terror into the Braves in the division playoffs.

When the Braves had to use ace Greg Maddux to down the wild-card Rockies in Game 4, the Reds, after needing just three games to subdue the Western Division champion Dodgers, rated the favorite's role in the NLCS. Instead, the Reds exited meekly in four straight games when Reggie Sanders and Ron Gant, after spearheading the Reds all season, collected no RBI and scored just one run.

Seattle also was favored against Cleveland by many observers, if only because the Mariners appeared to have captured lightning in a bottle in 1995. In mid-August, the Mariners were a long shot to gain even the AL wild-card berth. But suddenly the Angels, holding an 11-game lead in the AL West as late as August 9, went into nosedive after shortstop Gary DiSarcina was idled by injury. Two separate nine-game losing streaks cost the Angels all of their seemingly insurmountable advantage. The M's and the Halos were tied after the final game of the season and needed a one-game playoff for the division crown. The Angels ran aground when they drew Mariners star pitcher Randy Johnson in the playoff. The Mariners were winners in 26 of Johnson's 29 starts during the regular season. In the one-game playoff they won for the 27th time behind Johnson to snatch their first division title in their 19-year history.

Facing the wild-card Yankees in the first round of postseason action, Seattle came home to the Kingdome down 2-0 in the best-of-five series. But Johnson staved off elimination in Game 3, and

Tom Glavine tamed baseball's most powerful attack in Game 6 of the World Series, pitching eight shutout frames to give Atlanta a title.

Cal Ripken (top left) *broke Lou Gehrig's consecutive-games record. Japanese sensation Hideo Nomo* (top center) *won the NL Rookie of the Year Award.* Top right: *Alan Trammell* (left) *and Lou Whitaker broke the loop record for teammates playing together. Jose Mesa* (bottom left) *gave the Tribe a dependable closer. Dodger catcher Mike Piazza* (bottom right) *had a .346 batting average.*

when the Mariners won again the following night, it came down to a pair of midseason free-agent acquisitions in Game 5. Yankee David Cone took the hill against the Mariners' Andy Benes. AL batting champ Edgar Martinez's two-run double in the bottom of the 11th inning plated Ken Griffey Jr. (who had slugged five home runs in the series) with the tally that boosted Seattle the next step up the ladder toward the AL pennant. Their thrillingly improbable climb to the ALCS gained them the hearts of many baseball fans.

In Game 1 of the ALCS, former Stanford star Bob Wolcott stopped Cleveland, 3-2. And the Mariners won Game 3 on a three-run 11th-inning homer by Jay Buhner to lead 2-1 in the series. But Tribe pitchers then reprised what they had done in the division playoffs to the AL Eastern Division titlist Boston Red Sox. The Tribe stopped the Mariners cold, allowing only two runs over the next three games and sweeping all three contests to advance.

The Indians' and the Braves' triumphs were an enormous relief to the "masterminds" who plotted the new three-tier playoff structure. Further criticism was leveled at the moguls who designed the new system when, first, the four division playoff games and, then, the two LCS battles were slated to begin at the same time to the minute. This ill-conceived plan justly triggered the wrath of fans everywhere when they discovered that only one game per night would be televised. Fortunately the two best teams in the game in 1995 overcame all the potential pitfalls to make the World Series.

The first two games of the fall classic in Atlanta went to the Braves. Greg Maddux survived two unearned runs to take the opener 3-2, and Tom Glavine and the Braves won another one-run squeaker the next night. In Cleveland, Eddie Murray's 11th-inning RBI single gave the Tribe a 7-6 nail-biter. When Atlanta cruised 5-2 a night later to go up 3-1, the Braves seemed a lock with Maddux and his four straight Cy Young Awards on tap for Game 5. But Orel Hershiser held the Braves to two runs in eight innings, and Cleveland survived Ryan Klesko's third home run in three nights in the ninth to win 5-4.

Back in Atlanta for Game 6, Glavine kept the Braves off-kilter with changeups on the outside corner, allowing only one bloop single in eight innings. The Braves took a 1-0 win to notch their first World Series victory in Atlanta and the franchise's first world championship since 1957. The thrilling Series was also a victory for baseball itself, as the wounds from the strike year of 1994 finally began to heal.

SEASON'S BEST

• Boston first baseman Mo Vaughn wins the AL MVP Award after tying for the AL lead in RBI (126) and leading Boston to an AL East flag.

• Barry Larkin of the Reds is selected as the NL MVP. He finishes fifth in batting (.319) and fifth in runs (98) and leads Cincinnati to an NL Central title.

• The Indians' Albert Belle becomes only the 12th player in history to collect 50 or more home runs in a season. He also is the first player since Stan Musial in 1948 to bag 100 or more extra-base hits. Belle led the AL with a .690 SA and 126 RBI (tied with Mo Vaughn).

Albert Belle

• Greg Maddux of the Braves is the first pitcher ever to win four straight Cy Young Awards. Because two of his crowns come in strike-shortened seasons, Maddux has the added distinction of being a four-time Cy Young recipient despite only twice being a 20-game winner.

• Los Angeles backstopper Mike Piazza notches a .346 batting average. It is the highest in history by an NL catcher in 400 or more at-bats. The old mark of .344 was set by Gabby Hartnett of the Cubs in 1935.

• Randy Johnson of Seattle leads the AL in strikeouts (294) for the fourth consecutive year. His 12.35 strikeouts per nine innings breaks Nolan Ryan's 1987 record of 11.48. Johnson also tops the loop with a 2.48 ERA.

• Seattle DH Edgar Martinez leads the AL with a .356 batting average and a .479 on-base average, and he ties Albert Belle for the loop lead with 126 runs scored and 52 doubles.

• Dante Bichette of the Rockies is tops in the NL with a .620 SA, 40 homers, and 128 RBI.

• Bichette (40), Larry Walker (36), Vinny Castilla (32), and Andres Galarraga (31) make the Rockies the only team except the 1977 Dodgers to have four players with 30 or more home runs.

• Cal Ripken of the Orioles breaks Lou Gehrig's record when he appears in his 2,131st straight game on September 6 against the Angels.

• Lou Whitaker and Alan Trammell of the Tigers set an AL record for the most games by a pair of teammates when they're both in the Detroit lineup for the 1,915th time on September 13 against Milwaukee.

• Tony Gwynn of the Padres is only the seventh player in ML history to capture six or more batting titles and is furthermore the first National Leaguer since Rogers Hornsby in 1929 to hit .350 or better three years in a row.

• Cleveland closer Jose Mesa notches an ML-best 46 saves.

• Los Angeles rookie hurler Hideo Nomo uses his whirling windup to confuse NL batters. He finishes second to Maddux in loop ERA (2.54) while leading the league in strikeouts (236) and Ks per nine innings (11.10).

GREG MADDUX

Atlanta ace garners his fourth straight Cy Young Award

Greg Maddux used precision and tenacity to become the most dominating right-hander since President Woodrow Wilson cheered on the legendary Walter Johnson at Washington's Griffith Stadium. When Maddux led the majors with a 19-2 record, 1.63 ERA, and 10 complete games for the Braves in strike-shortened '95, he earned a record fourth straight Cy Young Award for his efforts while continuing to stake his claim as the big league's top hurler.

Maddux went 75-29 for the Cubs (1992) and Braves over his streak, joining Hall of Famer Steve Carlton as a four-time Cy Young winner and becoming the first to cop the honor more than two consecutive years. His ERAs of 1.56 and 1.63 in 1994 and 1995 marked the first time anyone had been under the 1.80 mark in back-to-back campaigns since Johnson in 1918 and 1919. During The Big Train's era, home runs were a rarity and pitchers routinely hurled the same dirty, water-logged balls for nine innings. The league ERA had hovered around 3.00 when Johnson accomplished his feat. Maddux was an incredible 2.55 runs below the NL average of 4.18 in 1995. His 1.63 earned run average was nearly a full run better than AL leader Randy Johnson (2.48).

Historians cite that no player since 1920 has had such a brilliant four-year run of success, and the numbers back them up. Maddux finished 1995 with an 18-0, 0.99 mark in his last 20 road starts, and he allowed just 297 hits over his last 411 innings.

Dodger lefty Sandy Koufax had a remarkable 97-27 record and 1.86 ERA from 1963 to 1966, yet Maddux fared even better when the pair were viewed in their respective eras. The National League ERA during Sandy's scintillating stretch was 3.50; Greg has been below 2.37 each year (1.98 overall) since 1992, while the league average has risen as high as 4.21.

Tall, muscle-bound flamethrowers like Koufax and Johnson have compiled far more strikeouts than the seemingly unimposing 6-foot, 175-pound Maddux, but superb control (22 walks over $209\frac{2}{3}$ innings in '95) and devastating changeups compensate for 85-mph fastballs. Gold Glove fielding ability and a solid bat (he out-hit men he faced .222 to .197 in '94) haven't hurt his cause either. So while his physical gifts were not as impressive as those possessed by some others, Maddux's character and constancy enabled him to dominate like few others have.

YANKS PREVAIL IN YEAR OF THE HOMER

Fans disgruntled by strikes and salary squabbles needed a sock in the arm to be wooed back to baseball in 1996, and they saw plenty of socking during the first full ML season in three years.

A record 16 players slugged 40 or more homers during the regular season, and three clubs (the Orioles, Mariners, and A's) broke the old team record of 240 blasts set by the fabled 1961 Yankees. The 162 home runs hit by the '96 Yanks would have paced the majors as recently as 1989, but this year merely earned the eventual World Series champs a reputation as a "scrappy" offensive team. How devastating was the offense? The last club to score 900 runs prior to '96 was the 1953 Brooklyn Dodgers; this time around, six teams turned the trick.

Individually, Oakland's Mark McGwire led the bash parade with 52 homers despite missing 32 games, and may have had a shot at catching 60-shot men Babe Ruth and Roger Maris were he healthy the full campaign. Brady Anderson of the Orioles whacked 50 (topping his previous career best by 29), and perhaps no player better symbolized the craziness than Texas shortstop Kevin Elster, who slugged 24 after managing just 35 in nine previous seasons. This wasn't merely a free-swinging crowd, either: 24 regulars hit .320 or better, 46 had 100 or more RBI, and plenty did both.

Whether it was due to expansion, a rabbit ball, or just plain bad luck, pitchers were hit early and often in '96. The AL composite ERA was an unbelievable 5.00, despite an unofficial widening of the strike zone before the season that was expected to aid pitchers. Detroit's 6.38 mark was something out of a slow-pitch softball league.

While the NL recorded a bit more respectable 4.24 league figure, only six ERA title qualifiers finished below the 3.00 mark—including three (Atlanta's Tom Glavine, John Smoltz, and Greg Maddux) on the same staff.

The second year of the three-division, one-wild-card playoff format produced a number of entertaining pennant races, including an NL West battle that went down to the final weekend and produced a new twist: one team (San Diego) clinching a division over another (Los Angeles) that still made the postseason as a wild card. The Cardinals overtook Houston to win the NL Central, then

New York's Derek Jeter erases Atlanta's Andruw Jones in World Series action. Jones, age 19, slugged two homers in Game 1, but the Yankees won the Series in six.

Mark McGwire (top left) slugged 52 homers in 130 games, Ken Caminiti (top center) smashed 40 in 146, and Juan Gonzalez (top right) bashed 47 in 134. Bottom: Down 3-1 in games, Mark Lemke's Braves outscored John Mabry's Cardinals 32-1 in the final three games of the NLCS.

surprised the powerhouse Braves by going up 3-1 in the NLCS. St. Louis, though, promptly dropped three straight to the defending champs, including pastings of 15-0 and 14-0.

In the AL Central, surly Albert Belle and the Indians had a relatively easy time of things, while out West Seattle stayed close (despite the devastating loss of ace Randy Johnson most of the season) before slipping at the finish and giving the Rangers their first-ever playoff berth after 25 seasons. The Yankees took advantage of slow starts by the Orioles and Red Sox to build a 12-game lead in the East,

then saw it cut to 2½ as Baltimore's bats (eight players with 20-plus homers) rebounded and Boston regrouped. Tainting the race was a late-September incident in which Orioles star Roberto Alomar spat in the face of umpire John Hirschbeck while protesting a call—the latest black eye for a game still swelling from its recent past.

The Yankees held on, but Baltimore's rush earned it a wild-card spot. After doing away with Texas and Cleveland, respectively, the division rivals met in the ALCS. The Orioles hit another nine homers in the five-game battle but could manage just one win thanks to solid New York pitching and 12-year-old "hero" Jeff Maier. The youngster reached over the outfield fence of Yankee Stadium to slap a fly ball away from Orioles right fielder Tony Tarasco and into the bleachers, giving rookie Derek Jeter a home run and the Yanks a key Game 1 victory.

The Braves were heavy favorites in the World Series that followed. But after dropping the first two games at home, the Yankees roared back to take four straight—including a pivotal 8-6 victory in Game 4 at Atlanta during which they overcame a 6-0 deficit. New York's first title since 1978 made winners of a likable team seemingly devoid of big egos but filled with enigmatic personalities such as Darryl Strawberry, Dwight Gooden, David Cone, and Cecil Fielder. It also made a winner of classy manager Joe Torre, who had waited more than 4,200 games as a player and skipper to reach the fall classic. The world title came soon after his brother and former big-leaguer Frank Torre received a heart transplant. Joe's bittersweet triumph made thoughts of strikes and spit melt away—at least for the moment.

SEASON'S BEST

• Colorado's Ellis Burks leads the NL with a .639 slugging percentage, 142 runs, and 392 total bases—the NL's best since Henry Aaron had 400 for the 1959 Milwaukee Braves.

• Slick-fielding Ken Caminiti bats .326 with 40 homers and 130 RBI in leading the upstart Padres to the NL West title.

Ellis Burks

• Alex Rodriguez of Seattle paces the AL with a .358 average, 141 runs, 54 doubles, and 379 total bases.

• Oakland's Mark McGwire leads the majors in home runs (52) and slugging (.730).

• John Smoltz of the Braves goes 24-8 and leads the majors in victories and strikeouts (276).

• Andy Pettitte of the Yankees finishes 21-8 in his second ML season.

• John Wetteland notches an AL-best 43 saves during the regular season, then saves all four Yankee wins in being named World Series MVP.

• Tony Gwynn of San Diego hits .353 to win his seventh NL batting title.

• San Francisco's Barry Bonds becomes the fourth ML player to notch 300 career homers and 300 stolen bases, following his godfather Willie Mays, his father Bobby Bonds, and Andre Dawson. Barry also joins Jose Canseco's exclusive 40-40 club with 42 homers and 40 steals.

• Eddie Murray of Baltimore joins Hank Aaron and Willie Mays as the only ML players with 500 home runs and 3,000 hits.

• Minnesota's Paul Molitor becomes the 21st MLer with 3,000 hits, rapping an AL-best 225 to finish the season with 3,014.

• Frank Thomas of the White Sox has 20-plus homers and doubles and 100-plus runs, RBI, and walks for an ML-record sixth straight year.

• Lance Johnson of the Mets leads the majors with 227 hits and 21 triples.

• Brady Anderson of the Orioles hits an ML-record 12 of his 50 home runs leading off games.

• Roger Clemens of the Red Sox records 20 strikeouts at Detroit September 18 to tie his own 1986 record for Ks in a nine-inning game.

• Umpire John McSherry dies of a heart attack while working an Opening Day game at Cincinnati.

• The Rockies become the second team in ML history with three 40-homer men—Ellis Burks, Andres Galarraga, and Vinny Castilla.

• Andres Galarraga leads the NL with 47 homers and 150 RBI—the most in the ML since Tommy Davis's 153 for the '62 Dodgers.

• The Orioles, Mariners, and A's all break the ML home run record of 240.

ALEX RODRIGUEZ

Junior Jr. is the new king of the dome

In the summer of 1996, Cal Ripken singled out a 21-year-old shortstop as "a special player" who was "doing it like he has been in the league four or five years." With over 2,300 games of experience, the Iron Man probably knows a good thing when he sees it. In this instance, he happened to be looking at the best young player in the majors at his or any position.

Alex Rodriguez, who grew up with Ripken's poster on his bedroom wall, was the pick of fellow players as the American League's best all-around performer in 1996. The youngster's big-league average over parts of two previous seasons was .224, but he hiked it to a stratospheric .358 in '96 to top the majors in batting. Add to this 54 doubles, 379 total bases, and 141 runs (all AL highs); throw in 36 homers, 123 RBI, and a .631 slugging percentage; then sprinkle on some great instincts, range, and speed at short. Mix it all together into a 6'3" young man with green eyes and impeccable manners who lives with his mom and reads the motivational writings of Pat Riley and Anthony Robbins for inspiration and you have a player too good to be true—yet capable of getting better.

Rodriguez was the first AL shortstop since Lou Boudreau in 1944 to win a batting title and one of just five to hit 30 homers (he was the fifth-youngest player *period* to reach the figure). The guy Mariners followers affectionately call "A-Rod" already rivals Randy Johnson and even Ken Griffey Jr. atop Seattle popularity charts—and places first among the Kingdome's young female fans. In order to improve his already smooth PR skills, he has studied with a media consultant, a trick he may have learned from media darling Griffey. Rodriguez first met Junior shortly after becoming the first pick overall in the '93 draft, and he began a friendship that has grown ever since. Another nickname has since been tagged on Alex: "Junior Jr."

Playing for four teams in the Mariners' system

in 1994—including 17 games as just the third 18-year-old shortstop in the majors this century—Rodriguez split time the following year between Triple-A Tacoma (a .360 average) and the big club (.232) and was the youngest ML player to ever appear at short in the postseason. He came up to stay in the spring of '96 and promptly made the All-Star team and cover of *Sports Illustrated*. When July 27 rolled around, he became legally able to drink and signed a four-year, $10.5-million contract on the same day. Greater seasons and greater riches would soon follow.

INDIANS LET FLORIDA'S FISH WIGGLE FREE

In 1993, the expansion Florida Marlins made their debut in the NL East and finished 64-98. Within four years, they had improved to 80-82, but this still wasn't enough to save manager Rene Lachemann's job. General manager Dave Dombrowski brought in the much-respected Jim Leyland as skipper for '97, along with a boatload of high-priced new talent, including sluggers Bobby Bonilla and Moises Alou and pitchers Alex Fernandez and Dennis Cook. Free-agent signings alone cost owner Wayne Huizenga some $89 million that winter, but the Marlins—at least for one year—would prove to be the best team money could buy.

The road to the World Series wasn't an easy one for Florida. Alou and Bonilla had great years to pace the offense, ace Kevin Brown and Fernandez led the rotation, and Rob Nenn steadied the bullpen. But the Marlins still needed boosts from late-season arrivals Darren Daulton and Craig Counsell—along with 24 wins in their final at-bat—to finish 92-70 and make the NL playoffs as a wild card.

Their opponent in the Division Series was the San Francisco Giants, who had just emerged victorious in a grueling battle for the NL West title with the Los Angeles Dodgers. San Francisco's late-season surge (led by Barry Bonds, who hit seven homers in the final 11 games) actually helped Florida reach the postseason instead of the Dodgers, who finished just behind them for the wild-card spot at 88-74. It was a move the Giants probably regretted, however, when they were swept in three straight games by the Marlins, which included two ninth-inning rallies.

Next on the Marlin feeding list was a familiar NL East rival: the powerful Atlanta Braves, winners of more games (101) than any team in baseball during the regular season. The Braves rode the best starting staff in modern history (Cy Young winners Greg Maddux, John Smoltz, and Tom Glavine and 20-game winner Denny Neagle) and a solid batting order paced by Chipper Jones to their sixth straight division title not including the strike year of 1994.

The Braves finished nine games in front of Florida during the regular season, but in the playoffs it was a different story. After quickly doing in NL Central champ Houston in three games during the first round, Atlanta succumbed to Florida in six contests due to disastrous outings by Glavine and Smoltz and two dominating wins from Marlins right-hander Livan

Florida came from behind in eight of 11 postseason victories, including Game 7 of the World Series when Craig Counsell scored the winning run in the 11th against Cleveland.

"Rocket" Roger Clemens (top left) *landed in Toronto, winning his fourth Cy Young. L.A.'s Mike Piazza* (middle) *belted 201 hits, the most ever by a catcher. Seattle's Randy Johnson* (top right) *won 16 straight games, one short of an AL record. Nomar Garciaparra* (bottom left) *set an AL rookie record with a 30-game hitting streak.*

Hernandez, a Cuban defector. Hernandez struck out 16 in 10⅔ innings, and this plus two wins from Brown helped offset Florida's .199 team batting average to propel the five-year-old Marlins into the World Series.

Facing them in the fall classic was one of baseball's longest-suffering franchises, the Cleveland Indians. Just two years earlier, Cleveland had reached the postseason for the first time in 41 years, only to lose to the Braves in a tightly fought World Series. Still loaded with much of the same talent plus two key additions—30-homer men Matt Williams and David Justice—the Indians slugged 220 home runs as a team but often seemed to sleepwalk through a lackluster summer in the weak AL Central. The

Tribe finished just 86-75, but it turned up the juice in the playoffs, beating favored AL East titans New York and Baltimore.

Defending World Series champ New York won 96 games behind Tino Martinez's 44 homers and young pitching ace Andy Pettitte, but this was good for only second place in the division behind Baltimore's 98-64 mark. The Orioles had a balanced attack led by Rafael Palmeiro and hurlers Mike Mussina and Scott Erickson. It was two strong efforts from Mussina that held 56-homer man Ken Griffey Jr. of West champ Seattle to zero homers and a .133 average in Baltimore's four-game Division Series triumph. Cleveland knocked off the Yanks in a riveting five-game affair thanks to two wins from 21-year-old rookie Jaret Wright. Then the Indians sustained two more gems from Mussina (including 25 strikeouts and just four hits allowed over 15 innings) in the ALCS to beat Baltimore in six contests—the finale an 11-inning thriller won on Tony Fernandez's double.

After more than four decades of waiting, the Indians seemed destined to taste World Series success against the upstart Marlins. The series featured plenty of offense by both clubs. Florida captured 7-4, 14-11, and 8-7 victories in Games 1, 3, and 5 (two of them from Series MVP Hernandez), while Cleveland won Game 2 6-1 and Game 4 10-3. Florida returned home one win away from the title. The Indians rallied behind Chad Ogea for a 4-1 victory in the sixth game, and they entered the bottom of the ninth in Game 7 with a 2-1 lead and ace reliever Jose Mesa on the mound.

Then, as they had all season, the Marlins came back. They tied the score in the ninth on a sacrifice fly by Counsell, then won it all in the 11th when Fernandez bobbled a double-play grounder at second base and Edgar Renteria followed with the Series-clinching single off a Charles Nagy breaking ball. Capping off a year of Miami miracles, it only seemed fitting that the winning run for the millionaire Marlins was scored by Counsell—a rookie making the major-league minimum of $150,000.

SEASON'S BEST

• Mark McGwire belts 58 homers for Oakland and St. Louis—the most in the ML since Roger Maris's 61 in 1961.

• Interleague play debuts with a 4-3 win by host Texas over San Francisco on June 12.

• The Mariners' Ken Griffey Jr. is the unanimous AL MVP after leading the league with 56 homers (most in the AL since 1961) and 147 RBI.

Larry Walker

• The NL MVP goes to Colorado's Larry Walker, who hits .366 with 130 RBI and a league-high 49 homers. He also leads in slugging (.720) and on-base pct. (.452). His 409 total bases are the most in the majors since 1948.

• Toronto's Roger Clemens wins his record-tying fourth Cy Young Award and becomes the first pitcher since 1945 to lead the AL in wins (21), ERA (2.05), and strikeouts (292).

• Pedro Martinez of the Expos captures the NL Cy Young Award with 305 strikeouts and an ML-best 1.90 ERA.

• Boston's Nomar Garciaparra has an AL rookie-record 30-game hit streak. He tops the league with 209 hits and 11 triples and sets a record for leadoff men with 98 RBI.

• Rookie Scott Rolen has 21 homers, 92 RBI, and 35 doubles for last-place Philadelphia.

• Frank Thomas of the White Sox wins his first AL batting crown with a .347 average.

• San Diego's Tony Gwynn leads the NL with a .372 average and becomes the fifth player to win at least seven batting titles.

• Houston's Craig Biggio tops the majors with 146 runs.

• Dodgers catcher Mike Piazza raps .362 with 201 hits, 40 homers, and 124 RBI in what is considered the greatest offensive season ever for a backstop.

• Phillies pitcher Curt Schilling fans 319 batters, the most ever by an NL right-hander.

• The Mariners set an ML record with 264 home runs.

• The Orioles become the third team in AL history to hold first place each day of the season, joining the '27 Yankees and '84 Tigers.

KEN GRIFFEY JR.

Junior is the unanimous MVP after launching 56 homers

Like many young boys, Ken Griffey Jr. longed to grow up and be just like his father. This was a tough goal to strive for—Ken Sr. compiled a .296 average, 152 homers, and 852 RBI as a major-league baseball player—but "Junior" has more than matched it. The Seattle Mariners outfielder has gone on to carve out his own career in the majors, one so phenomenal that people routinely mention him in the same breath as Willie Mays and Hank Aaron.

Actually, Lou Gehrig might be a more appropriate comparison. While new home run king Mark McGwire grabbed the majority of headlines during the 1996-98 seasons, Griffey played Gehrig to Mac's Babe Ruth with a three-year stretch as good as any in history. He averaged 54 homers, 144 RBI, and 123 runs scored and won a Gold Glove each year. In 1997 alone, when McGwire bashed 58 homers during a season split between the AL (Oakland) and NL (St. Louis), Griffey led the AL with 56 homers, 147 RBI, and a .646 slugging percentage. This performance helped Seattle to the playoffs for only the second time in team history, and it earned the sweet-swinging lefty a unanimous selection as league MVP.

Griffey followed this up with a nearly identical season (56 home runs, 146 RBI) in 1998, but again he was overlooked as McGwire and Sammy Sosa shared the bulk of the spotlight for each topping Roger Maris's old record of 61 homers in one year. A check of the record books, however, shows that Junior reached some impressive marks of his own that year. Still just 28 years old at the end of the '98 season, he had become the youngest player to hit 350 homers and the fourth-youngest (behind Mel Ott, Jimmie Foxx, and Gehrig) to collect 1,000 RBI.

Junior's pedigree and performance growing up in Cincinnati drew him considerable hype, and the first pick in the 1987 draft didn't disappoint. Graceful and quick both in the field (where he's a perennial Gold Glover) and on the bases, he hit 16 homers as a 19-year-old rookie in '89. His love for the game, infectious grin, and habit of wearing his

cap backwards made him an immediate fan favorite. More stellar seasons followed, but it wasn't until 1993, when he cracked 45 four-baggers, that Griffey reached his full potential as a power hitter.

The balls have been flying out of ballparks ever since, and only a rained-out homer in 1996 (when he hit 49) kept Junior from joining McGwire as the first slugger to reach 50 three straight years. By the time he's done, Griffey may be second to none on the career power charts.

POWERHOUSE YANKS WIN 114—AND THE SERIES

In a season that many experts claimed was the greatest in major-league history, it made sense that one team was among the all-time best. The 1998 edition of the New York Yankees was two years and many players removed from the '96 World Series title, but after an 0-3 start the former champs won 22 of their next 25 games to leave no doubt that they were primed for another run at glory.

Manager Joe Torre's lineup was devoid of one true superstar, but veterans such as Bernie Williams, Paul O'Neill, and Derek Jeter jelled tremendously. The pitching staff, led by ace David Cone and stopper Mariano Rivera, was one of baseball's best. What put New York over the top, however, were the unexpected surprises. Third baseman Scott Brosius, who hit .203 for Oakland in '97, improved to .300 while driving in 98 runs. Lefty David Wells went 18-4 and tossed a perfect game. A recycled Darryl Strawberry hit 24 homers, and Cuban refugee Orlando Hernandez contributed a 12-4 mark and 3.13 ERA after coming aboard in late May.

By August 1, the Yankees were 77-27. Talk in New York turned to the record 116 victories turned in by the 1906 Chicago Cubs. Could the new Bronx Bombers challenge this mark? While folks waited for the answer, plenty of other intriguing playoff races heated up.

Cleveland enjoyed its annual cakewalk to a fourth straight title in the ever-feeble AL Central. In the West, the Angels and Rangers dueled all year

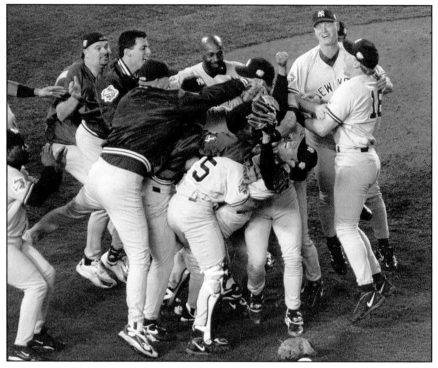

Reminiscent of the 1927 Yankees, the 1998 Bronx Bombers dominated the majors with a 125-50 overall record (.714) and captured their 24th championship.

before Texas clinched by winning five straight head-to-head meetings down the stretch. Boston's wild-card berth seemed a lock most of the summer, but the Red Sox had to overcome late surges by the Orioles and Blue Jays (led by former Sox ace Roger Clemens) before clinching in late September.

The NL featured no tight divisional battles but plenty of tension before the final playoff spot was filled. The Astros were challenged early on in the Central by Sammy Sosa and the Chicago Cubs, but a key trade for Randy Johnson (who went 10-1 with a 1.28 ERA in his 11 NL starts) helped Houston pull away. Pitching-rich Atlanta in the East and surprising San Diego in the West were the other champs, while the Cubs, Mets, and Giants all jockeyed for the wild-card berth. Chicago was the sentimental favorite in a season in which Sosa smashed 66 homers and legendary team broadcaster Harry Caray died, but it took an extra day for the Cubbies to finally get in. While the Mets fell apart during the final week, the Giants finished strong to force a one-game playoff at Chicago's Wrigley Field, which was won by the Cubs 5-3.

The Yankees didn't quite get their record, but they did surpass Cleveland's 111-win year of 1954 and set an AL mark with their 114-48 slate. Everybody feared facing New York in the playoffs, and the Rangers discovered why in the Division Series, as they scored just one run. Boston won Game 1 of the other AL Division Series thanks to Mo Vaughn's seven RBI. But the Indians came roaring back to win the next three straight to advance.

Next came New York's only real postseason challenge. After winning the first ALCS game over Cleveland 7-2 in Yankee Stadium, the Yanks dropped the second contest 4-1 in 12 innings. The shock continued when the Indians won Game 3 at home 6-1 behind Bartolo Colon's four-hitter. For the

David Wells of the Yankees (top) *blanked the Twins on May 17 with his perfect game. Houston's Craig Biggio* (left) *notched 50 doubles and 50 steals, a feat accomplished only once before him. Manny Ramirez* (right) *amassed 45 homers and 145 RBI for AL Central champ Cleveland.*

first time all year, Torre's troops seemed vulnerable. Yet the Yankees regrouped to win three straight.

Most folks figured the Yankees would meet the Braves, who quietly won 106 games themselves during the regular season. But after sweeping Sosa's Cubs convincingly in the Division Series, Atlanta met its match in San Diego—which was fresh off defeating Randy Johnson twice in a four-game playoff triumph over Houston. Seemingly on a mission of their own, the Padres won the NLCS in six games by keeping Atlanta's Cy Young trio winless.

The World Series was for the most part anticlimactic. The Yankees fell behind 5-2 in Game 1 at the Stadium, then rallied to score seven times in the seventh inning—four coming on a grand slam by Tino Martinez. New York followed up this 9-6 win

Behind Greg Vaughn's 50 home runs, San Diego advanced to the World Series for the first time in 14 years.

by crushing the Padres 9-3 in the second contest, then took two tighter battles in San Diego (5-4 and 3-0) to complete the sweep. The Yanks hit .309 as a team, led by Ricky Ledee's .600 average and MVP Brosius's six RBI and .471 mark. When New York sealed its 24th world championship with its record 125th win of the season, it was a fitting climax to a season filled with grand accomplishments.

SEASON'S BEST

• Mark McGwire of St. Louis hits 70 home runs, shattering Roger Maris's ML record of 61 set in 1961. McGwire beats out Cub Sammy Sosa, who also breaks the old record with 66 homers.

• Sammy Sosa is named NL MVP, leading Chicago to the playoffs with 158 RBI—most in the ML in 50 seasons. Sosa's 20 home runs in June set a new one-month homer record.

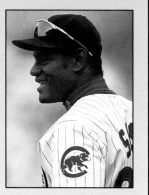

Sammy Sosa

• The world-champion Yankees set an ML record with 125 total victories and an AL mark with 114 regular-season wins.

• The Milwaukee Brewers become the first team since the inception of the AL in 1901 to switch leagues, moving from the AL Central to the NL Central.

• Expansion teams in Arizona (NL West) and Tampa Bay (AL East) boost ML membership to 30. Both clubs finish last.

• Oriole Cal Ripken voluntarily ends his record streak of 2,632 consecutive games played on September 20 in Baltimore.

• Juan Gonzalez of the Rangers tallies a record 35 RBI in April, drives in 157 runs overall, and wins his second MVP Award in three years.

• Tom Glavine of Atlanta wins his second Cy Young Award by going 20-6 with a 2.47 ERA.

• Blue Jay Roger Clemens earns his record fifth Cy Young, leading the AL in wins (20), ERA (2.65), and strikeouts (271) for the second straight year. Clemens goes 15-0 after May 29.

• Cubs 20-year-old rookie Kerry Wood ties Roger Clemens's ML record with 20 strikeouts in a nine-inning game vs. Houston on May 6. He finishes with 233 strikeouts in just 166⅔ innings.

• David Wells of the Yankees pitches the 13th perfect game in ML history, vs. the Twins on May 17.

• Seattle's Alex Rodriguez amasses 42 homers and 46 steals, becoming the third member of the "40-40" club.

• Bud Selig is officially named baseball's ninth commissioner after six interim years at the post.

• Craig Biggio of Houston is the second player this century with 50 steals and 50 doubles in one year.

• Tom Gordon of the Red Sox sets a new ML mark by converting 43 straight saves. Fellow Boston reliever Dennis Eckersley's last regular-season appearance is his 1,071st, also an ML record.

• Trevor Hoffman leads the ML with 53 saves for NL champion San Diego.

MARK McGWIRE

Big Mac outbashes Slammin' Sammy, belts out 70

How can an athlete in today's quote-conscious society get away with saying, "I'm in awe of myself"? How can he be so popular that thousands of fans arrive hours early just to watch him take batting practice? Who does this guy think he is, Babe Ruth?

No, just the next best thing. When McGwire demolished the old standards for home runs set by Ruth (60 in 1927) and Roger Maris (61 in '61) with his 70 homers during 1998, he did more than just set a new record; he made it look easy. As fans watched "Big Mac" stroke four home runs in his first four games, smash the record-breaking 62nd in front of Maris's children and a packed home crowd at Busch Stadium, and then punctuate it all with two homers on the season's final afternoon, it almost seemed as if he were hitting balls out of parks at will. His staggering final numbers for '98 also included 147 RBI, 130 runs, 162 walks (a National League record), and a .752 slugging percentage. But as it was with Babe and Roger, it's the homer total that folks will remember.

Part of the magic to Mac's '98 season was that he fit the mold of a mammoth "Ruthian" slugger. Fellow record-breaker Sammy Sosa of the Chicago Cubs (who hit 66 homers himself in '98 and was named NL MVP over McGwire) was an average-sized ballplayer who had never hit more than 40 homers previously. McGwire, in contrast, was a 6'5", 250-pound hunk of muscle who had been building his credentials as a threat to Ruth and Maris for more than a decade. Mac crushed a rookie-record 49 home runs for the Oakland A's in 1987, and he overcame severe back and heel injuries in mid-career to smash 52 and 58 long balls during 1996 and '97. Each year he crushed the ball farther and farther, and not since Ruth had anyone ever done so with more frequency.

Thus it was Mac who graced the covers of countless preseason publications in the spring of '98, and Mac who started getting the "Can you break the record?" questions the first day of spring training. He seemed stiff under the pressure at first, but the emergence of a friendly and high-spirited Sosa in the race took some of the weight off his shoulders, and McGwire eventually learned to bask modestly in the spotlight.

McGwire's strong focus on charity and his soft spot for kids further linked him to Ruth, who possessed both qualities. And so when Mac lifted his son into the air following homer No. 62 or expressed genuine awe over his own accomplishments, the gestures seemed just that—genuine.

YANKS ROLL TO ANOTHER SWEEP

One year after causing some analysts to declare they were the greatest of all time, the New York Yankees settled for being the best of 1999. It wasn't such a bad compromise.

By rolling to the World Series championship for the second straight season (and third in the last four), the Yanks proved themselves to be a rarity in present-day big-league sports: a true dynasty. In sweeping the Atlanta Braves, the Yanks won their 25th title of the century.

The triumph was made sweeter by the large dose of adversity the team had endured. During spring training, beloved manager Joe Torre announced that he had prostate cancer and would need to undergo immediate treatment. All of a sudden, the on-field talk about repeats and the excitement surrounding the off-season acquisition of five-time Cy Young Award winner Roger Clemens was replaced by the sadness of Torre's illness. Outfielder Darryl Straw-

berry added to the anxiety with his arrest on drug charges. And during the World Series, outfielder Paul O'Neill mixed the joy of winning with the grief of his father's death.

On the field, everything went right. Torre returned in the spring, retaking the team's reins from trusted lieutenant Don Zimmer, and led the Yanks to the AL East crown. To win the division, the Yanks had to fight off a surprising challenge by the Boston Red Sox, who behind Cy Young winner Pedro Martinez (23-4, 2.07 ERA, 313 strikeouts) and shortstop Nomar Garciaparra (.357, 27 homers, 104 RBI) battled their bitter rivals through the summer before fading in September.

The rest of the American League unfolded as expected. Cleveland quickly pulled away from the rest of the mediocre AL Central and won the division by a whopping 21½ games. Again, the Tribe offense, led by Manny Ramirez and his 44 homers and 165 RBI, was extremely potent, even if its pitching staff was shaky. In the West, Texas shrugged off a light challenge by young Oakland and won by eight games, riding the hot bat of Rafael Palmeiro (.324, 47 home runs, 148 RBI).

But the Rangers did their usual shrinking job in the playoffs, falling to the Yanks in three games while scoring just one run. The Red Sox, meanwhile, surprised the baseball world by taking out the Indians in a rousing five-game series. Despite losing Martinez to a back sprain in a Game 1 loss, the Sox climbed out of a 2-0 hole and blitzed the Tribe, winning 23-7 in Game 4.

Yankee outfielder Chad Curtis slammed two home runs in Game 3 of the World Series, including the winner in the 10th inning.

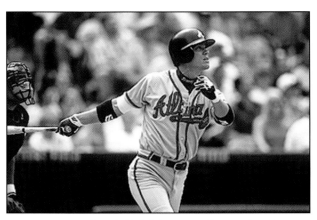

Manny Ramirez (top left) led the AL in slugging (.663). Randy Johnson's 364 strikeouts were second most in NL history (top center). Derek Jeter (top right) shined in the field and at the plate (219 hits). NL MVP Chipper Jones (bottom) sparked Atlanta's eighth straight Division title.

There was no such miracle in the ALCS. Although the Red Sox came close in the first two games, and rode Martinez to a 13-1 triumph in a raucous Game 3 at Fenway Park, the Yanks prevailed in five.

A little more drama unfolded in the National League, courtesy of the "other" New York team, the Mets, and Mark McGwire-Sammy Sosa II. The two sluggers again battled for the home run title, with Big Mac prevailing in the end, 65-63, in another thrilling long ball race.

The Mets, meanwhile, snuck into the playoffs by whipping Cincinnati in a one-game wild-card playoff. New York then tore through NL West champion Arizona, disregarding the Diamondbacks' 100-win regular season and Cy Young pitcher Randy Johnson (17-9, 2.48 ERA, 364 strikeouts). The Braves, meanwhile, dispatched Houston and its first-rate pitching staff in four games. Then came the showdown with the Mets, who were thought by many to be a mere speed bump. Indeed, those who were hoping for a Subway Series between the two New York teams were dealt a big blow when Atlanta raged to a 3-0 lead in the series, winning the games by a total of four runs.

But the Mets rallied, winning a pair of one-run games, including a thrilling, 15-inning affair in the fifth game. But that was all the Mets could do. In the sixth contest, the Braves held on for a 10-9 win that earned them another date with the Yankees.

For seven innings in Game 1, it looked like Atlanta might silence its critics and beat the Yankees. Braves ace Greg Maddux held down New York until the eighth, when the Yanks exploded for four runs and started their roll to a sweep. It was ironic that the triumph was accomplished primarily through great starting pitching, which had been thought to be the Braves' edge in the Series. Orlando "El Duque" Hernandez stifled Atlanta in the first game, while David Cone was the hero of Game 2. Chad Curtis's two home runs, including the game-winner in the 10th, gave New York a 3-0 Series lead.

Then Clemens took over, yielding just one run in 7⅔ innings to earn his first World Series ring and the Yankees' 25th title. Series MVP Mariano Rivera finished it off with his third strong outing, and the champagne flowed again.

The Yankees hadn't set any records, but they had laid a solid claim as the "Team of the 1990s." That was enough for anyone.

SEASON'S BEST

• Mark McGwire of the Cardinals again edges the Cubs' Sammy Sosa to win the ML home run title. McGwire finishes with 65 to Sosa's 63, as they become the only men in history to record back-to-back seasons of 60 or more. Mac also slugs his 500th home run.

• Ivan Rodriguez, Texas's Gold Glove catcher, raps .332-35-113 en route to AL MVP honors.

• Pedro Martinez of the Red Sox leads the AL in wins (23-4), strikeouts (313), and ERA (2.07)—all by huge margins. He wins the Cy Young Award.

• Atlanta's Chipper Jones belts 45 homers and takes the NL MVP Award.

• Randy Johnson of the Diamondbacks fans 364 batters and wins the NL Cy Young Award.

• Manny Ramirez of the Indians drives in 165 runs, most in the majors since Jimmie Foxx knocked home 175 in 1938.

Ivan Rodriguez

• Colorado's Larry Walker leads the NL with a .379 average.

• Nomar Garciaparra of the Red Sox paces the AL in batting at .357.

• Joe DiMaggio dies on March 8 at age 84.

• The Baltimore Orioles take baseball to Cuba, defeating that country's national team by a 3-2 score in a March exhibition. The Cubans later defeat the Orioles 12-6 in Baltimore.

• Baseball's opening pitch comes outside the U.S. or Canada for the first time ever, as Colorado defeats San Diego in Mexico on April 4.

• On April 23, Cardinal Fernando Tatis, who had never before hit a grand slam, becomes the first player in history to hit two in the same inning. Both come off of Dodger pitcher Chan Ho Park. His eight RBI in the inning also set a major-league record.

• Days apart, the Padres' Tony Gwynn and Devil Rays' Wade Boggs record their 3,000th career hits.

• In what is meant as a bargaining ploy, ML umpires make a June announcement that they plan to resign in September. The move fails mightily. Baseball accepts many resignations, promotes umps from the minors, and receives the fans' overwhelming support.

• David Cone fires the 14th perfect game in history, a 6-0 win over Montreal on Yogi Berra Day at Yankee Stadium.

• Roger Clemens, acquired by the Yankees from Toronto in a big trade before the season, sets an AL record by winning 19 consecutive decisions.

• McGwire's 70th home run ball from the 1998 season goes at an auction for $2.7 million, 23 times the record for any previous baseball item.

• Hideki Irabu and Mac Suzuki oppose one another in the first-ever ML matchup of Japanese starters.

PEDRO MARTINEZ

Boston ace goes 23-4, plays postseason hero

When the rowdy Fenway Park crowd had finally stopped its relentless cheering, and the Boston Red Sox had completed their 13-1 Game 3 ALCS win over the Yankees, New York manager Joe Torre couldn't disguise his feeling of awe. Sox ace Pedro Martinez had been brilliant in a seven-inning outing, allowing two measly hits, striking out 12, and erasing any doubts that he was baseball's dominant pitcher.

"He's an artist out there," Torre said. "He has a baseball instead of a paint brush."

The 1999 season was filled with masterpieces for Martinez, who dazzled AL rivals with a palette of pitches that left batters overpowered, fooled, and frustrated. En route to a second Cy Young Award (he captured the NL version in 1997 with Montreal), Martinez raged to a 23-4 record that could have been even more imposing had he not missed part of the season with a sore shoulder. After giving Boston fans a glimpse of his mastery by posting a 19-7 mark with 251 strikeouts a year earlier—his first in Boston—Martinez gave them the entire package in 1999.

His 313 strikeouts set a Boston record and made him just the second pitcher in major-league history (Randy Johnson is the other) to fan 300 batters in a season in both leagues. He led the AL with a 2.07 ERA, earned Pitcher of the Month honors a record four times, and made the Cy Young voting a mere formality. The Dominican native had been good, if not great, during his previous seven seasons, six of which were spent with the Expos and Dodgers, but 1999 was his finest.

Martinez began the season ablaze, finishing April with a 4-1 mark and 2.21 ERA. By the All-Star break, he was 15-3 and had earned the starting nod for the American League in front of the Fenway throng. He didn't disappoint. Martinez fanned the first four batters he faced, including Mark McGwire and Sammy Sosa, and finished his two-inning stint with five Ks, leading writers to vote him the game's MVP.

Once play resumed, talk turned to a bid for 30 wins. That was quickly quelled on July 24, when an aching right shoulder consigned Martinez to the disabled list. Though Martinez returned on August 3, he wasn't close to his previous form until later that month, when he began a season-closing 6-0 streak that propelled the Sox into the playoffs.

The injury bug hit Martinez again in the postseason. He suffered a muscle strain in his back during the first game of Boston's series with Cleveland and was unable to perform again until the Game 5 finale. Pitching with an altered motion because of the pain, he tossed six no-hit innings in relief to win the game. In the third game of the ALCS, he stifled New York and won a much-anticipated showdown with former Sox ace Roger Clemens. It was yet another museum-quality portrait created by a true artist.

THE 2000S

Despite staggering salaries and a national tragedy, baseball survived—and thrived—in the new century. As usual, the road to the world title led through New York City.

aseball's third century began with more financial woes, but between the headlines of salary caps and contraction was spectacular drama—some of the most majestic moments in baseball history.

The 2000 campaign saw a thrilling Yankees-Mets Subway Series, which ended with the Bronx Bombers' third straight Series win and their 26th overall. Each of the five games was decided by one or two runs. The following season's fall classic was even better, as the Diamondbacks and Yankees thrashed through a thrilling seven-game set that featured three amazing comeback victories—including Arizona's triumph in Game 7.

In September 2001, however, baseball came to a sudden halt. The September 11 terrorist attacks on New York City, Washington D.C., and rural Pennsylvania canceled games for a week—the first time that nonlabor-related events had shut down the game for that long since World War I.

When baseball geared up the 2001 pennant races again on September 17, patriotism was in full flower. Red, white, and blue bunting bedecked stadium fencing. "God Bless America" replaced "Take Me Out to the Ballgame" as seventh-inning stretch music. And a parade of firefighters and police officers threw out first pitches and received thunderous welcomes from crowds at the 30 homes of Major League Baseball.

The game couldn't fix all of America's problems, but it did seem to help Americans get their minds back on daily life. The presence of a New York team in the playoffs (and, eventually, the World Series) was a big part of that, but fans all over the country were treated to tight pennant races, exciting individual feats, and terrific postseason action.

Yet, leave it to baseball to shoot itself in the foot again. Following the 2001 World Series, Commissioner Bud Selig rained on the game's parade by announcing plans to eliminate two clubs for 2002, with the Twins, Devil Rays, Marlins, and Expos among those on the endangered list. Legal obstacles pushed back the commissioner's ill-timed and questionable strategy, but MLB still hopes to move Montreal to Washington, perhaps as soon as 2003.

While baseball certainly belongs in the nation's capital, moving a franchise because of a few seasons' worth of low attendance could be a mistake. Before the owner-provoked player strike of 1994, the Expos were one of baseball's best and fastest-rising teams. The failure of that club to win a crown in the strike season triggered a financial spiral in which ownership methodically dispatched high-salaried players. No wonder the fans stayed home. What if the Indians, Braves, or Mariners had been moved when they were spitting out losing records in the 1980s and early '90s?

In part, the problem affecting baseball remains a public perception that nobody is in charge. Having Selig—a former owner of the Brewers whose daughter now runs his old team—at the helm leaves the sport open to criticism from all angles. The secret of the

The lowlight of the 2000 Subway Series came when Yankee pitcher Roger Clemens (right) picked up part of Mike Piazza's broken bat and threw it toward him.

In San Francisco, fans and boaters arrived at new Pacific Bell Park to see if Barry Bonds would splash a homer into McCovey's Cove. Bonds launched 122 home runs in 2000-01.

success of the NFL and the NBA is a strong central office that makes decisions for the good of all teams, not just a few who happen to be in good graces with the current commissioner.

Moreover, as the country tries to overcome intolerance, so too does the grand old game. John Rocker of the Braves made disparaging comments during the 2000 season about homosexuals, women, and immigrants and became a pariah on his own team. He was finally traded to Cleveland, but he didn't make friends there, either. At different times during the 2001 season, there were nine African-American or Latino baseball managers, an all-time high. However, front-office positions remained scarce for minorities, and there were still no minority owners. Some thought it cynical that the men hired by Major League Baseball to run the 2002 Montreal Expos—a lame-duck franchise—were minorities.

Congress yet again considered repealing the game's antitrust exemption, and public funding of ballparks is still a hot-button issue. With communities scrambling for money to run essential social ser-

vices, funding millionaire owners' playpens no longer seems appropriate.

Despite claims of financial peril even from the wealthier clubs, contracts expanded into ridiculous figures in the new century. Shortstop Alex Rodriguez, formerly of the Mariners, inked a 10-year, $252 million contract with the Rangers in December 2000 to make him the highest-paid athlete ever. On the other side, the 2002 sale of the Red Sox brought the old owners more than $730 million.

This and other bank-breaking deals undermined the idea of baseball owners having to sell pencils to make their next payments. Yet some smaller-market clubs, such as the Pirates, Royals, and Reds, continued to work with shoestring budgets. Even the new parks that opened in Milwaukee, Detroit, and Pittsburgh during 2000 and 2001 were not the guaranteed bump in revenue of old days; fans wouldn't immediately flock to the yard to see bad teams.

Some feared that the difference between the haves and have-nots would widen to 1920s-1950s dimensions, with a permanent underclass of bad teams feeding talent to the good ones. But the suc-

cess stories of smaller-market teams in recent years should dispel the notion of inevitable failure based on past history. The Braves, Mariners, and Indians, moribund franchises in 1991, are three of the game's success stories. The Oakland Athletics, despite a small payroll, won 102 games in 2001 because of good decisions and an excellent minor-league system. Conversely, great gobs of ownership money in Los Angeles, Anaheim, Baltimore, and Texas didn't guarantee success.

Many complained that Yankees owner George Steinbrenner could simply buy a championship, but the pinstripers' dominance during the late 1990s and beyond was not solely due to their gargantuan budget. The Yanks knew when to say goodbye to past-prime players, refurbished their machine, and called up quality homegrown talent to augment their free agents.

At least one owner believed that pushing up the salary structure was the only way to win. Tom Hicks of the Rangers, owner of a hugely profitable group of radio stations, saw his costly A-Rod Squad end up last in the AL West in 2001. Rather than rethink his strategy, or wait for a long-dormant minor-league operation to begin producing players, he responded by signing more expensive free agents to complement Rodriguez.

As salaries soared, so too did home runs. Barry Bonds of the Giants had one of the greatest seasons of all time in 2001, breaking Mark McGwire's record for homers (with 73) and surpassing Babe Ruth's marks for slugging (at .863) and walks (with 177). Such sluggers as Sammy Sosa, Todd Helton, Jason Giambi, Luis Gonzalez, and Manny Ramirez made life miserable for pitchers in both leagues.

Oddly, the Mariners, who lost megastars Ken Griffey, A-Rod, and Randy Johnson in a period of two years, experienced one of the best regular seasons

ever in 2001, winning an ML record-tying 116 games with deep pitching and the bat of Ichiro Suzuki. However, the Mariners' inability to reach the World Series cost the club enough money that

Mike Piazza (top) *was one of many players to honor rescue workers after September 11; all players wore the flag. The Reds* (bottom) *saluted heroes and victims during a special ceremony.*

San Diego's Rickey Henderson scored his 2,246th run on October 4, 2001, to break Ty Cobb's ML record.

Yankee Scott Brosius tied Game 5 of the 2001 World Series with a two-out, ninth-inning homer.

they were in danger of losing critical players to free agency.

Money worries aside, baseball fans were also slammed by the retirements of three fabulously popular all-time greats. Tony Gwynn, Cal Ripken Jr., and McGwire all called it quits following the 2001 season. Gwynn ended up with 3,141 hits, the 18th highest total in history. Ripken left the majors with 3,184 hits of his own (rating 14th) and the all-time lead in consecutive games played. McGwire departed with 583 homers, fifth on the all-time list.

Other records fell in the first part of the decade. In 2001, Rickey Henderson busted Ty Cobb's record for career runs and Ruth's long-standing career walks record—and collected his 3,000th hit. Ageless lefty Jesse Orosco extended his appearances record to 1,131, while 39-year-old Roger Clemens of the Yankees vaulted into third place on the all-time strike-outs list (3,717) after a stunning 2001 performance (20-3).

Records will continue to fall, because the baseball now being played is the best ever. The players are stronger, the talent comes from a larger stream, the equipment has improved, and the facilities are better. Fans hope that the people in charge of protecting and administering the game are of the same caliber.

Buddies Randy Johnson (left) and Curt Schilling went a combined 43-12 with 665 strikeouts for Arizona in 2001.

YANKS OUST METS IN SUBWAY SERIES

Baseball, according to a consensus of historians, originated in New York City. And after more than 150 years of evolution and nurture in countless rural byways and suburban backyards, the game came full circle in the first year of the new millennium. It returned to its epicenter not only to resolve a "Subway Series" between the lines, but to kindle a national socio-political debate outside of them.

With both the Yankees and Mets trying to claw their way to the playoffs most of the summer, it was an Atlanta Braves relief pitcher who unwittingly galvanized the Big Apple. In a *Sports Illustrated* interview, John Rocker made crude remarks about people who ride the subway near the Mets' Shea Stadium. He demeaned homosexuals, young mothers, and foreigners who don't speak English, among others. Major League Baseball fined the brash lefty and suspended him briefly for what it called "a profound breach of the social contract" between the sport and its fans. The tumult over his remarks engulfed the country in controversy over the First Amendment and political correctness.

Crosstown from Shea Stadium, the Yankees aimed for a world championship "three-peat," a feat not achieved since the Oakland A's dynasty of the early 1970s. With most of its 1999 championship roster still glued together by owner George Steinbrenner's money, the Yanks stormed to 22 wins in their first 31 games. However, the Bombers played exactly .500 ball the rest of the way and blundered into the postseason on a seven-game losing streak.

New York won its division with an 87-74 record, but four AL teams did better—topped by the 95-67 Chicago White Sox, who snapped a string of four straight bridesmaids performances to win the Central. The highest drama was focused on the wild-card chase, as three teams were still drawing breaths for two playoff berths on the season's final day. Each won, leaving Oakland atop the West, Seattle with the wild-card, and Cleveland packing its bags.

Concurrently, New York's National League fans were captivated by their Mets, whose annual flirtation with the Braves approximated the futility of flagging a cab on Broadway during rush hour. While St. Louis and San Francisco had long since stashed away their divisional crowns, the NL East was a war zone.

In mid-May, the Mets were 20-20 and mudded into fourth place. In June, they split a four-gamer when Atlanta visited a supercharged Shea Stadium suffocated in Rocker-related security. In July, they surged. And in September, they actually stood alone in first for one day. Though the plucky, veteran Mets finished a game short of forestalling Atlanta's ninth

Derek Jeter and the Yankees won their third straight world title in 2000—and fourth in five years.

With 43 homers and 137 walks, AL MVP Jason Giambi led Oakland to the AL West title.

Frank Thomas's great comeback season (.328-43-143) led Chicago to the AL's best record (top). Anaheim's Darin Erstad (left) banged out 240 hits. Jeff Kent (right) plated 125 to earn NL MVP honors.

straight division title, they had come from behind in 45 of their 94 wins. In contrast to their Bronx counterparts, they started wild-card play having pocketed eight of their last nine.

As the playoffs opened, baseball fever was running rampant. Inflated by the christening of new stadiums in Houston, Detroit, and San Francisco, Major League Baseball had set an attendance record with 72.7 million fans. Teams had combined to hit 5,693 home runs, of which 176 were grand slams—also records. And the average of 10.28 runs per game was the highest in 64 years. So, of course, it was a shutout that turned the tide of the postseason.

After the Yankees lost Game 1 of their AL Division Series to the young A's, Andy Pettitte whitewashed Oakland for his club's fourth win in its past 20 contests. New York not only built upon his gem to close out that set in five, but it consolidated its momentum by eliminating Seattle, which had upset the White Sox.

The Mets, meanwhile, stayed on a roll. Neither the Giants nor the Cardinals (who had swept the Braves) posed a threat, as the Mets took three of four and four of five, respectively. The stage was set for the first Sinatra ("New York, New York") World Series since the Yankees defeated the Brooklyn Dodgers in 1956. It turned out to be worthy of all the hype the media could spew.

Game 1 was a 12-inning dance at Yankee Stadium that lasted a record 4 hours, 51 minutes. It ended when light-hitting Yankees infielder Jose Vizcaino singled home the winning run with two outs. The Mets showed no quit in Game 2 despite being down 6-0 in the ninth, but their rabid rally left them a run shy. The last three games, as well, were packed with tension: 4-2 Mets (ending the Bombers' 14-game Series winning streak), 3-2 Yanks, and, finally, 4-2 Yanks, as another offensively challenged utilityman, Luis Sojo, knocked in the game-winning run in the ninth.

For the Yankees, it was a methodical and professional performance, one that may not be bronzed but worth its weight in Steinbrenner's gold. "We may not have the best players," said manager Joe Torre, "but we have the best team." Start spreading the news.

SEASON'S BEST

• Oakland's Jason Giambi is named AL MVP. He swats 43 homers, drives in 137, and leads the league with 137 walks and a .476 on-base percentage.

• NL MVP Jeff Kent of San Francisco raps .334 with 33 homers and 125 RBI.

• Boston's Pedro Martinez is the first to win unanimous AL Cy Young Awards in consecutive seasons. His opponents' batting average of .167 is the lowest in modern history, and his ERA of 1.74 is less than half of the AL's second-place finisher.

Carlos Delgado

• Arizona's Randy Johnson (19-7, 2.84 ERA, 347 strikeouts) is the overwhelming choice for the NL Cy Young Award, becoming only the third to win it back-to-back.

• Colorado's Todd Helton tops the NL in batting (.372), hits (216), RBI (147), doubles (59), slugging (.698), and OBP (.463).

• Toronto slugger Carlos Delgado finishes fourth in the AL in batting (.344), home runs (41), and RBI (137) and leads with 57 doubles.

• Sammy Sosa finally wins his first NL home run crown, slugging 50 dingers for the Cubs.

• Anaheim's Troy Glaus leads the AL in homers with 47, a league record for a third baseman.

• Boston's Nomar Garciaparra wins his second straight AL bat title (.372).

• On March 29, the Cubs' Shane Andrews hits the first home run of the new millennium—in Tokyo against the Mets.

• On April 10, Cincinnati's Ken Griffey Jr. becomes the youngest player to hit his 400th home run (30 years, 248 days).

• The Angels' Darin Erstad cracks 240 hits and becomes the first leadoff hitter ever with 100 RBI.

• Jeff Bagwell of Houston becomes the first NL player to amass 45 homers, 100 RBI, and 150 runs.

• The errorless streak of the Mets' Rey Ordonez ends at 101 games (a record for an ML shortstop).

• Japanese import Kazuhiro Sasaki of the Mariners is named AL Rookie of the Year after setting an ML rookie record with 37 saves.

• The NL's Rookie of the Year is Atlanta shortstop Rafael Furcal, who bats .295 with 40 steals.

• Cal Ripken Jr. becomes the 24th player to rap 3,000 hits.

• Yankees closer Mariano Rivera breaks Whitey Ford's record by extending his consecutive postseason shutout streak to 33⅓ innings.

• Yankee Derek Jeter is the first to win All-Star Game and World Series MVP kudos in the same season.

2000

TODD HELTON

Humble Rockie makes a run at the Triple Crown

On August 20, 2000, Todd Helton stepped to the plate at Coors Field. The scoreboard illuminated his batting average—blink, squint; could that really say .399?—and, as if on cue, an adoring Colorado Rockies crowd intoned a chorus of "Happy Birthday" to their 27-years-old-today slugger.

They sang to one of baseball's premier hitters. Not a great hitter like tobacco-spitting Royal George Brett, who made a run at .400 in 1980; not a great hitter like the surgical, singles-spraying Padre Tony Gwynn, who fell a tad short in '94; not even a great hitter like the contemporary hulkoids who swat away home run records like Godzilla smacks airplanes. He's simply the kind of hard-working, unpretentious great hitter whose birthday party you might attend yourself.

In 2000, the birthday boy was connecting not only with his fans, but with virtually every pitch thrown his way. Helton had worked diligently—as is his habit—during the off-season to circumvent his usual slow start. The result was a .337 batting average in April followed by an unconscious .512 mark (with 11 home runs) in May.

Three at-bats into his August 21 game, the lefty-swinging first baseman actually reached .400—the latest any regular had claimed that number since the man to whom Bobby Cox compared him after the proceedings. "Todd Helton might be the best-looking hitter I've ever seen since George Brett," said the Braves manager. "Every swing is good. He is incredibly good."

What's more, his ever-burgeoning power, the buoyancy of the Denver air, and the alleged reconstitution of the horsehide also situated Helton within range of baseball's first Triple Crown since 1967.

It couldn't have happened to a nicer guy.

This was a man so respected that his teammates voted him their player rep immediately after his 1998 rookie season. He is so dedicated that he once hit for the cycle despite such severe wrist pain that he was sleepless the night before. He is so gosh-darned swell that Rockies GM Dan O'Dowd said of him: "We're really building our franchise around a guy like Todd. It's not the numbers. It's the rest of the package. It's the character and the preparation and attention to detail. It's what he stands for."

Ultimately, Helton fell short of .400 in 2000 and finished eight home runs short of the Triple Crown. Yet statistically, he still enjoyed one of the greatest seasons in history: league highs in batting (.372), on-base percentage (.463), and slugging (.698); the most doubles (59) in 64 years; the fourth-most extra-base hits (103) ever; and even a team-record 103 walks.

It was a performance of sufficient humble enormity to make prospective baseball dads everywhere close their eyes, blow out the candles on their own birthday cake, and make a wish for a son like Todd.

D'BACKS PREVAIL IN GAME 7 THRILLER

The 2001 baseball season began conventionally, proceeded into high drama, was interrupted by inconceivable tragedy, wound down amid historical consequence, and concluded with a big surprise. Just another year for the grand ol' game.

Virtually intact from '00, and having signed former Orioles ace Mike Mussina, the Yankees might well have ordered the lettering for their fourth straight championship banner in April. An immaculate amalgam of hitting and pitching, experience and youth, character and leadership, the club was never more than four games back all year, and on July 3 it assumed American League East leadership for good.

But in the distance, sabers were rattling. The senior circuit had spawned a slew of worthy contenders—three in each division, in fact. Atlanta was being pressured by the Phillies and Mets in the East; Houston, St. Louis, and Chicago were slugging it out in the Central; and the Giants, Dodgers, and a graying, heavily bankrolled Diamondbacks squad formed a tenacious triumvirate out west.

Back in their own league, the Yankees were most wary of the Seattle Mariners, the first team ever to win 20 games in April. Astonishingly, manager Lou Piniella's club never cooled off, taking at least 18 in every month through August. When the M's went to bed on September 10, they already were within a dozen victories of the all-time record. By the time they awoke, their achievements had been reduced to trivia.

The terrorist attacks of September 11 seemed to halt, for a moment, the very rotation of the earth. Games of that day were quickly canceled and, after a period of deliberation, so were those of the next five. As players slowly made their way home during the cessation of air transport, commissioner Bud Selig tacked a week of make-up action on to the back of the schedule.

On September 17, baseball began anew—shrouded in grief but awash in patriotic ceremony. A bleeding nation, unable even to bury its dead, prepared for war and looked for consolation in a game it was not sure it was even allowed to enjoy. Within days, it had no choice.

The captivating histrionics of the 2001 season rapidly unfolded on several stages simultaneously. With three weeks to go, four divisional races were undecided and 15 teams remained in the playoff hunt. Icons Cal Ripken Jr. and Tony Gwynn were taking their final bows and, though it wasn't known at the time, so was Mark McGwire. Rickey Henderson was chasing his 3,000th hit and Ty Cobb's record for runs scored. The Mariners had resumed pursuit of the 1906 Cubs' wins plateau. And Barry

Luis Gonzalez pumps his fist after plating the winning run in Game 7 of the World Series.

The Cubs' Sammy Sosa (left) *blasted 64 homers in 2001, giving him an average of 60 bombs since 1998. He also led the majors in runs (146) and RBI (160). With an AL-high 21 victories, Mark Mulder* (center) *helped Oakland close with a 58-17 record and finish with 102 wins. Ichiro* (right), *the AL MVP, cracked 242 hits to spark Seattle to 116 wins.*

Bonds breathed down the neck of McGwire's magical home run record of 70.

In one whirlwind, final week, the M's caught (but could not pass) the Cubs with their 116th win; Atlanta barely held off the Phillies and Mets; Houston clinched on the final day to relegate St. Louis to a wild-card; Arizona nudged San Francisco by two games in the NL West; Henderson reached both of his milestones; and Bonds—with the first of his two home runs on October 5—surpassed McGwire.

The Diamondbacks, in only their fourth year of operation, embarked upon postseason play with the sixth best record of the eight contestants. Rookie skipper Bob Brenly went to battle with three superstars—Randy Johnson (21-6, 372 strikeouts), Curt Schilling (22-6, 293 whiffs), and outfielder Luis Gonzalez (.325-57-142). On the strength of Schilling's 18 innings of one-run ball and shortstop Tony Womack's final-game, ninth-inning hit, Arizona brushed aside the Cards and awaited the Braves, who had swept the Astros.

Against Atlanta, the first team in professional sports to win a 10th straight division crown, the D'backs played near-perfect baseball. In five games it was over, as Schilling and Johnson combined to go 3-0 with a 0.72 ERA.

Their World Series opponents would be the Yankees. With 53 wins in their last 71 postseason games, the professional pinstripers systematically doused white-hot Oakland (the first team ever to win 100 games after being 10 under .500) and detoxed the victory-addicted Mariners.

The Bombers were expected to do the same to the Diamondbacks, but Arizona's two stud starters freeze-dried Yankee bats in Games 1 and 2 (9-1 and 4-0). After New York responded with a 2-1 nipper, surrealism rode in on a Trojan horse. The D'backs appeared to have Game 4 won on Halloween night, but Tino Martinez's two-out, two-run homer in the bottom of the ninth tied it, and Derek Jeter's shot in the 10th walked 'em off. Ditto Game 5: Scott Brosius hit the tying two-outer/two-runner in the ninth, and Alfonso Soriano finalized matters with a ribbie hit in the 12th.

How the Diamondbacks excised those daggers to romp, 15-2, in Game 6 defied logic, but the man-

Arizona's Byung-Hyun Kim (right) *coughed up game-tying, ninth-inning homers to Yankees Tino Martinez in Game 4* (pictured) *and Scott Brosius in Game 5.*

ner in which they won Game 7 mocked natural law. Forfeiting their 1-0 lead to a Yankee run in the seventh and another in the eighth, they were doomed to face closer Mariano Rivera—he of the 23 consecutive postseason saves—in the final frame. Yet Arizona weaved three hits, an error, a hit batter, a bunt, and finally a game-winning single by Gonzalez to win the World Series—and derail a dynasty. A baseball season of equal parts cheers and tears had ended, leaving a legacy no other ever will.

S E A S O N ' S   B E S T

- The Giants' Barry Bonds, as the first four-time MVP, hits 73 home runs to break Mark McGwire's single-season record of 70. He also sets ML records for walks (177) and slugging (.863).

- Mariners outfielder Ichiro Suzuki of Japan is both AL MVP and Rookie of the Year. He captures the batting title (.350), leads the league in steals (56), and sets an ML record for hits by a rookie (242).

- Roger Clemens of the Yankees fashions the first 20-1 start in history. He finishes 20-3 and wins his sixth Cy Young Award.

- Randy Johnson's fourth Cy Young effort includes the first-ever 20-strikeout game by a lefty, the third most whiffs (372) in history, and a record five postseason victories.

- Seattle's 116 wins set an AL record and tie the 1906 Cubs for the ML mark.

Albert Pujols

- San Diego's Rickey Henderson becomes the game's all-time leader in career walks and runs scored. On the final day of the season, he collects his 3,000th hit.

- Sammy Sosa of the Cubs slams 64 homers to become the first player to hit at least 60 in three seasons. His 160 RBI are third most in NL history.

- Alex Rodriguez debuts for Texas after signing a 10-year, $252 million contract. He leads the AL with an ML shortstop-record 52 home runs.

- Seattle's Bret Boone smashes AL records for homers (37) and RBI (141) by a second baseman.

- Colorado's Todd Helton hits .336-49-146 and becomes the first player ever to rip 100 extra-base hits in back-to-back seasons.

- Arizona's Luis Gonzalez crushes 57 home runs.

- Albert Pujols of the Cardinals is named NL Rookie of the Year after bashing .329 with 37 homers, 47 doubles, and 130 RBI.

- Arizona's Curt Schilling and the Cardinals' Matt Morris lead the majors with 22 wins.

- Yankees closer Mariano Rivera collects an ML-leading 50 saves.

- Oakland's Jason Giambi leads the AL in doubles (47), walks (129), OBP (.477), and slugging (.660).

- Lenny Harris of the Mets collects his 151st career pinch hit on October 6 to break Manny Mota's ML record.

- Legends Mark McGwire, Tony Gwynn, and Cal Ripken Jr. retire.

BARRY BONDS

Slugger fails to woo fans despite 73 bombs

America loves a hero and, following the terrorist attacks of September 11, desperately needed one. Barry Bonds, however, is a different kind of hero—if, in fact, he is a hero at all.

Inarguably smart and, at times, utterly charming, the Giants left fielder has an abrasive, aloof, boorish edge that makes him something of an anti-Sosa in the fans' eyes. Some days, Bonds accommodates all comers with thoughtful, graceful answers. On others, he shoos away even his teammates from his locker room subdivision as if they were mere flies on his picnic basket of life.

Traumatized fans *wanted* to like Bonds, to cheer for him during his pursuit of the home run record in 2001—just as they did for Mark McGwire and Sammy Sosa in '98. But in the end, they just could not find it in their broken hearts to do so.

In the beginning, nobody was linking Bonds and "70" in the same brain wave. After all, the 36-year-old had averaged barely half that number throughout his 15 seasons. On April 17, Bonds clubbed the 500th home run of his career. That, most assumed, would be his season highlight. What happened next defied prediction.

Bonds set an ML record with 17 home runs in May, and on June 4 he became the fastest ever to reach 30...as he was to 35, 40, and on up the ladder. When he launched his 60th big fly on September 6, he was a game ahead of McGwire's pace.

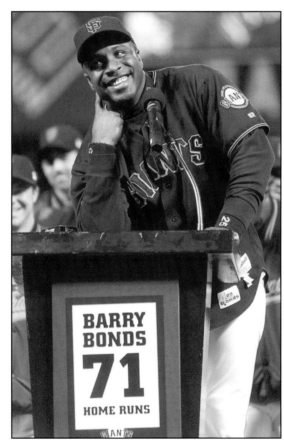

So loathe were managers to confront Bonds that he was purposely passed with first base occupied five times. In the final week, standing at 69, he was avoided so enthusiastically by the Astros that his two daughters raised a sign in the crowd that pleaded, "Pitch to Our Daddy."

Finally, on October 4, Houston rookie Wilfredo Rodriguez did—and Bonds slammed a mammoth shot into Enron Field's upper deck. The next day, back in San Francisco, he tagged a 1-0 fastball from the Dodgers' Chan Ho Park for No. 71, then added another two innings later.

In a postgame ceremony, Barry was a tearful teddy bear. "I love you very much," he told his teammates—some of whom were estranged from him. Turning to address the crowd, he added, "I love San Francisco and I love you fans...I'm proud to put on this uniform."

History will record that the enormity of Barry Bonds' 2001 season far transcended his home run total. He walked an all-time high 177 times, compiled the NL's highest on-base percentage (.515) since 1899, and slugged an unfathomable .863.

Shortly after he bombed No. 73 in the season finale, Lycos reported that "Barry Bonds" was not even among the top 10 athlete Internet searches that week. Bonds had changed the game but, apparently, not its fans' opinion of him.